# International Business

# International Business

*Economics, Environment, and Strategies*

## Parviz Asheghian
*St. Lawrence University*

## Bahman Ebrahimi
*University of North Texas*

**HarperCollins***Publishers*
Grand Rapids, Philadelphia, St. Louis, San Francisco,
London, Singapore, Sydney, Tokyo

*To members of our families:*
*Our parents, Dorothy, Daniel,*
*Laila, and Alex*

Color maps 1, 2, and 3 copyright © 1987 by Pluto Press, Limited.
Reprinted by permission of Simon & Schuster, Inc.
Color map 4 from THE WORLD DEVELOPMENT REPORT 1988 by the World Bank.
Reprinted by permission of Oxford University Press, Inc.

Sponsoring Editor:   Debra Riegert
Project Editor:   Lauren S. Bahr
Art Direction:   Lucy Krikorian
Cover Coordinator:   Mary Archondes
Cover Design:   Hudson River Studio
Production:   Paula Roppolo

**INTERNATIONAL BUSINESS**

**Library of Congress Cataloging-in-Publication Data**
Asheghian, Parviz, 1943–
   International business / Parviz Asheghian, Bahman Ebrahimi.
      p. cm.
   Includes bibliographical references.
   ISBN 0-06-040351-9
   1. International business enterprises—Management.
2. International trade.   3. International economic relations.
4. Strategic planning.   I. Ebrahimi, Bahman.   II. Title.
III. Title: International business.
HD62.4.A75   1990                                          89-26827
658′.049—dc20                                                CIP
90  91  92  93      9  8  7  6  5  4  3  2

# Contents

## Chapter 3    Theories of Foreign Direct Investment and the Multinational Corporation   49

## Chapter 4    National Policies Affecting International Trade   62

## Chapter 5    The International Monetary System  98

## Chapter 6    The Balance of Payments  117

## Chapter 7    The Foreign Exchange Market   139

# PART TWO    ENVIRONMENTAL ASPECTS OF INTERNATIONAL BUSINESS  199

## Chapter 8    Broad Environmental Factors Facing an MNC  201

# Chapter 11 Technological Forces and Technology Transfer 289

## Chapter 12    Patterns of International Involvement   315

# PART THREE    OPERATIONAL AND STRATEGIC ASPECTS OF INTERNATIONAL BUSINESS  391

## Chapter 13    A Framework for Global Strategic Management  393

## Chapter 14    Application of Global Strategic Management Process   427

## ∫ Chapter 15    Human Resource Management and Organizational Structure   464

## ✓Chapter 16    International Marketing Management and Strategy  496

## Chapter 17    International Financial Management and Strategy  527

## Chapter 18    International Operations Management and Strategy   558

# PART FOUR    SOCIAL RESPONSIBILITY AND THE FUTURE OF INTERNATIONAL BUSINESS   617

## Chapter 19    Social Responsibility and Ethical Issues Facing MNCs   619

## Chapter 20    Conflicts Between Home Countries and Host Countries   639

# Chapter 21    Looking into the Future   662

# Preface

The rapid and sustained growth of international business in recent years has contributed to the importance of this subject as a course of study. In recognition of this fact, the American Assembly of the Collegiate Schools of Business (AACSB), the accreditation body for schools and colleges of business, has called for the internationalization of business curricula. This has been achieved by mandating all of the AACSB accredited schools either to incorporate international topics into their curricula or to require students to complete one course in international business. Many schools have chosen the latter, and, therefore, require a comprehensive, yet easily accessible, textbook that will introduce students to all facets of international business, laying the foundation for further specialized study in the field. It is the recognition of this need that inspired us to write this textbook.

The book is primarily designed for the first course in international business, directed to undergraduate and graduate (MBA) students who have completed entry-level courses in the functional areas. It could be used in a one- or two-semester course, as outlined in the Instructor's Manual. The book should also prove useful as a secondary source in courses on international economics, international finance, international marketing, and international management. To make the text more challenging to graduate students, we recommend that students be required to do supplementary reading. To this end, we have provided each chapter with a list of suggested readings that include many diverse and current publications in the field.

All the materials in the text have been tested in international business classes at University of North Texas. Students' feedback has been incorporated to improve the presentation.

## DISTINCTIVE TEXT FEATURES

The following features distinguish this text from others in the field:

## Depth of Coverage

The presentation of often-ignored theories, including comparative labor costs theory, the theory of overlapping demand, the technological gap theory, the Prebisch theory, and the eclectic theory of production, make this text more comprehensive than most. Because many international business texts are weak in their coverage of economics, many instructors are forced to assign supplementary readings in international economics. These supplementary readings are usually aimed at economics majors and, therefore, are often difficult for business students to understand. For this reason, we have included such key economic concepts as elasticity, economies of scale, opportunity cost, and value added in an easily accessible manner.

As a result of the increasing importance and attention being given to the study of technological forces and technology transfer and social responsibility and ethical issues facing multinational corporations, we include a complete, separate chapter on each of these topics.

In addition, exporting, countertrade, global strategy, the impact of culture and religion on international business, and Mexican in-bond industry *(maquiladoras)* are among other topics that receive more coverage than in most textbooks.

## Application of Theories

Theories are discussed along with numerous real-life examples and case studies to illustrate their relevance and application to real-world situations. For example, currency devaluation and the J-curve effect are presented along with a discussion of the devaluation of the U.S. dollar in September 1985, the discussion of the theory of mercantilism is presented with the example of "high tech-mercantilism" that is practiced in France today, and the presentation of the Prebisch theory includes a demonstration of its usefulness in studying the import substitution policies that are practiced by Latin American countries such as Colombia, Peru, and Chile.

## Global Strategic Orientation

We devote two chapters (13 and 14) to the topic of global strategic management, in which we make students aware of the importance of the formulation and implementation of an integrated strategy and its role in enhancing a multinational corporation's chances for success and survival. This complex topic is covered in a step-by-step approach that aids comprehension. Because of the in-depth coverage of this subject, we have divided it into two chapters 13 and 14. As a result, those instructors who prefer to put a lesser emphasis on this topic may omit Chapter 14 or parts of it.

We have also taken a strategic approach in discussing the operational aspects of MNCs. For example, international marketing management and strategy, international financial management and strategy, and international operations management and strategy are covered in separate chapters.

## ORGANIZATION OF THE TEXT

The text consists of four parts subdivided into 21 chapters. Part One focuses on the economic framework of international business, where international trade and foreign direct investment theories, international monetary system, balance of payments, and the foreign exchange market are discussed. Included in this part are two current events that have been subject to much discussion in academic circles: the crash of the U.S. stock market on Monday, October 19, 1987, and the challenges that are posed by the complete integration of the European Community (EC) in 1992.

Part Two deals with the environmental aspects of international business, including coverage of environmental, legal, political, sociocultural, and technological forces.

Part Three elaborates on the strategic and operational processes of international business. Topics include patterns of involvement, global strategy formulation, international marketing strategy, international human resource management and organizational structure, operations management strategy, and financial management strategy.

Part Four draws attention to social aspects of international business, including social responsibility and ethical issues and host-home conflicts. Among the topics covered is the transborder data flow (TDF) problem. Given the economic and noneconomic implications of TDF, its importance as a subject of study is crucial. This part concludes the book with a look at the future of international business.

Each chapter begins with the main learning objectives of the chapter and concludes with a detailed summary, a number of questions, and a list of suggested readings.

Each part of the book ends with a number of real and fictional cases in international business, including three comprehensive cases at the end of the book. The real cases describe a situation faced by an individual or an organization whose identities are known. They typically include a chronology of significant events, summaries of important financial and nonfinancial data, statements of opinions of experts and employees, and information about competitors and industry. Some fictional cases present situations that have actually taken place using all the facts but not real names, locations, or other attributes that are not essential to the problem and the decision-making process. Other fictional cases, however, are descriptions of situations that are made up to resemble but not actually to portray real events. Regardless of their nature, cases provide students with an opportunity to use the principles and theories presented in the text in decision-making situations.

The text concludes with a complete glossary for easy access to the terminology used in international business.

## SUPPLEMENTARY MATERIALS

To aid instructors we have developed a comprehensive support package that includes:

The **Instructor's Manual/Test Bank With Transparency Masters** by the authors, includes answers to the end-of-chapter questions and cases along with lecture openers, learning objectives, and lecture notes. Additionally, it provides a list of videocassettes on subjects related to international business, in-class exercises, guidelines for case analysis, and a listing of sources for research in international business. The manual also contains 50 transparency masters of key text figures and tables. The test questions have been class tested and include more questions than any other competing textbook. There are 40 multiple-choice questions, 30 true/false questions, and 30 fill-in-the-blank questions, with answers, for each chapter.

The test bank is available on Harpertest, a highly acclaimed microcomputerized test generation system that allows you to create fully customized tests. It features full word-processing capabilities, "help" screens, and a password option to protect data and is free to adopters on request for the IBM-PC and compatibles.

## ACKNOWLEDGMENTS

A comprehensive textbook on international business could not be written without the help of individuals who offer their valuable time and talents. Our students at both St. Lawrence University and University of North Texas have been instrumental in providing feedback and contributing to many of the cases presented in this book. We are grateful to all of them. We would also like to thank the students in the international business operations classes at University of North Texas who used the material in this book in the form of class notes and who provided invaluable feedback over the past four years.

We are indebted to B.R. Baliga (Texas Tech University), James E. McConnell (SUNY, Buffalo), and Brian Toyne (University of South Carolina) who read the manuscript and provided us with constructive criticism and valuable advice.

We thank our colleagues at St. Lawrence University, Wendell Brown, Thomas Coburn, Peter Fitzrandolph, Ernest Oliveri, David Richardson, Sally Stevens, and Jeffrey Young, and at University of North Texas, Rose Knotts, Martin Rosenfeldt, Carl Swanson, and Fredrik W. Williams, for being supportive and helpful at different stages of the process.

Several typists, editors, and students were extremely helpful in assisting us with the preparation of both the text and the Instructor's Manual. They are: Gail Colvin, Melissa Frisbee, Steven Frisbee, Lynn Jensen, Laurie Olmstead, and Karen Pcolar at St. Lawrence University and Pat Watkinson, Janice Wilson, Kris Roberts, Anis Kashani, and Chinny Tan at University of North Texas.

Our deepest thanks go to our families and friends who had to sacrifice on so many occasions so that we could work on this project. Our love and thanks to Dorothy Thurman Asheghian and Chinny Tan (who read every page of the manuscript and provided us with important comments), Daniel Thurman Asheghian, Laila Thurman Asheghian, and Alex Eric Ebrahimi. We made it!

PARVIZ ASHEGHIAN
BAHMAN EBRAHIMI

# About the Authors

**Parviz Asheghian** (Ph.D., Georgia State University) is associate professor of economics at St. Lawrence University. Professor Asheghian has taught a number of courses in both economics and business, including international business and international economics/finance.

Dr. Asheghian has served for several years in the private and public sectors of the Iranian economy and has done extensive research on the subject of international business. His major research interests are in the areas of foreign investment and multinational corporations, foreign exchange market, and productivity and efficiency analysis. His work has been published in a number of journals, including *Journal of International Business Studies, The Quarterly Review of Economics and Business, Managing International Development, Journal of Economic Development,* and *Portfolio: International Economic Perspectives.*

Professor Asheghian also serves on the editorial boards of several scholarly journals, including *Technology and Development, Global Development Report, Journal of Development and Cooperation, Journal of Third World Development,* and is a member of the Academy of International Business, the American Economic Association, the Eastern Economic Association, the Financial Management Association, and the World Academy of Development and Cooperation.

**Bahman Ebrahimi** (Ph.D., Georgia State University) is assistant professor of management at University of North Texas. Professor Ebrahimi has taught undergraduate and graduate courses in international business, policy/strategic management, and graduate management seminars. He has also been involved in his family-owned import/export business and has served as a consultant to many organizations.

Dr. Ebrahimi's major research interests are in the areas of strategic management, strategy implementation, cross-cultural management, and power in organizations. His work has been published in a number of journals, including *Journal of Applied Vocational Behavior, Advances in International Comparative Management,* and *Infortrade Report.*

Professor Ebrahimi has been an active member of several professional organizations, including the Academy of International Business, Academy of Management, the Decision Sciences Institute, and Kappa Chapter—University of North Texas (Honor Society for International Scholars).

# Introduction

*T*oday, the competition for goods and services has gone far beyond national boundaries. We have entered a new age of global competition that is characterized by a one-world market. In this market, as manufacturers "go global," so must the suppliers of raw materials, as well as distributors, bankers, accountants, lawyers, and brokers. Successful corporate managers are increasingly treating the whole world as their domain for securing sources of supply as well as demand. It is estimated that the sales between foreign subsidiaries of the same company may account for roughly 25 percent of global trade. Such estimates underline that the competitiveness of business in this age is beyond the grasp of any purely domestic company. In such a competitive environment, the life cycles of different products are getting shorter, and it is costlier and harder to develop new products. This makes the jobs of today's corporate managers more challenging. To turn these challenges into opportunities, today's managers need to develop products and bring them to the global markets much faster than ever before.

Although globalization is not a new phenomenon, what is different today is the speed and the extent of growth in global markets. There are two major factors that have contributed to this growth. First, advancements in communication and transportation have resulted in the enormous expansion in international trade and investment. As a result, for major advanced countries, the percentage of gross national product (GNP) that is absorbed by foreign trade has roughly doubled since 1960. Second, long-term increases in the GNP per capita, coupled with higher life expectancy and greater education in some less developed countries (LDCs) have increased their role in global markets.* For example, Brazil, Hong Kong, Singapore, and South Korea now rank among the top 20 exporters of manufactured goods. In 1965, no LDCs were even included in the top 30. The increasing importance of LDCs in the global markets has decreased the power of advanced countries in dominating these markets.[1]

Just as business operations have global implications, so does a country's overall economic activity. No country operates in an economic vacuum. A nation's production, consumption, inflation, interest rates, investments, technology, and all the other variables that affect its economic system are influenced by the economies of other nations. For example, the U.S. budget deficit, running at about an annual rate of $200 billion in the 1980s, has given rise to a chain of events that have affected the economies of other nations. The high budget deficit has fueled inflationary expectations, and has forced the U.S. government to pursue tighter monetary policies. It has also meant a higher demand for credit by the U.S. government to finance the deficit. These factors have caused the U.S. interest rates to rise, and higher interest rates in the United States, as compared to other industrial nations, have encouraged the movement of short-term funds from those countries to the United States. The increased inflow of short-term funds into the United States caused overvaluation (appreciation) of the dollar. This, in turn, has expanded the U.S. imports and restrained exports, leading to a trade deficit that was running at an annual rate of more than $100 billion in the 1980s. These series of events have raised protectionist sentiments in the United States and have put pressure on the government to use measures to restrict imports. The protectionist measures, in turn, have further intensified the debt problems of less developed countries.[2]

Aware of the global implications of the above events, and to mollify the protectionist sentiment in the United States, the major industrial nations (the United States, Japan, West Germany, Britain, and France) collectively decided to devalue the U.S. dollar in September 1985. The cheaper dollar, however, makes Japanese and European exports to the United States more expensive.

---

*Following the United Nations definition, in this textbook we define LDCs (also referred to as "developing countries") as those market economies located in Latin America, the Caribbean, Africa, Asia, Oceania, and the island of Malta in the Mediterranean Sea. Exceptions to this definition are the countries of Israel, Japan, Australia, New Zealand, and South Africa.[3]

This caused these countries to fight back by devaluing their own currencies.[4] The possibility that the United States may respond by further devaluing the dollar shook the confidence of the foreign investors in the U.S. market. They feared that with the depreciating dollar the value of their investment, as measured in terms of their home currency, would continue to decline.*[5] This caused some foreign investors to pull out of the U.S. stock market. Some other investors who had heavily invested in the United States became effectively paralyzed. They found themselves "too deeply invested to pull out, yet too worried to resume buying."[6]

The chain of events that started with the U.S. budget deficit contributed to the crash of the U.S. stock market on Monday, October 19, 1987. On this so-called Black Monday, the Dow–Jones industrial average fell nearly two times as far as it did on Black Friday of 1929, wiping out $500 billion in wealth in a few hours. Within hours of the collapse of the U.S. stock market, the European and Asian markets were falling fast, experiencing an unprecedented decline in their stock prices and losing billions of dollars.[7]

As a less dramatic example of the interrelationship among economies of nations, cheaper labor costs in LDCs such as Brazil, China, Hong Kong, India, Mexico, Philippines, South Korea, Taiwan, and some southern African countries have caused many multinational corporations (MNCs) in advanced countries to move their manufacturing plants to those nations. This has caused labor unions in advanced countries to resist foreign imports. Their members have feared the loss of jobs or lower wages.

Today, the spread of industrialization and industrial innovation is leading the world economy into a new era. In this new era, significant economic and technological considerations are forcing the movement of traditional industries to LDCs and creating newly industrialized countries (NICs). This, in turn, is triggering a reallocation of resources in the industrial nations from the traditional capital-intensive industries to the new knowledge and service intensive industries. Such changes are causing and are expected to cause various economic problems for advanced nations, such as unemployment and corporate bankruptcy.

These events, leading to new global business environments, are expected to drastically change the nature of international business and have profound impact on corporate strategy. An example of these changes is the complete economic integration of the European Community (EC) in 1992, which will have significant impact on global competition.** Global environments are more complicated, more dynamic, and more unpredictable than domestic ones. This calls for managers who welcome the challenge of coping with the complexity of the political, economic, social, technological, and competitive elements of the

---

*The devaluation of the U.S. dollar makes the foreign investor's home currency relatively more expensive. As a result, each dollar that is invested before devaluation would command smaller amounts of the domestic currency after devaluation.

**This topic will be discussed in Chapter 4.

continually changing global environments. This demands better training in the field of international business, and it requires a broad comprehension of different factors that shape our global environments. We start our exploration of international business in this chapter by reviewing some of the most basic concepts that are needed for a better understanding of this subject.[8]

## DEFINITION OF INTERNATIONAL BUSINESS

*International business* can be defined as those business transactions among individuals, firms, or other entities (both private and public) that occur across national boundaries. These activities include the movement of goods, that is, the importing and exporting of commodities; the transaction of services such as management, accounting, marketing, finance, and legal services; the investment of capital in tangible assets such as manufacturing, agriculture, mining, petroleum production, transportation, and the communications media; and transactions in intangible assets, such as trademarks, patents, and the licensing of manufacturing technology.

As the above definition implies, the field of international business is a broad area of study that covers a wide range of activities. These activities, which take place between different sovereign nations, each one with its own specific environment, give rise to the tremendous problems with which a firm in international business must deal. Dealing with these problems requires an understanding of the environmental variables that affect international business. These variables are economic, political, legal, sociocultural, technological, and geographic. Although such environmental variables are often beyond a firm's control, their recognition allows the manager to work more effectively within the constraints posed by these variables. This necessitates a working knowledge of other academic disciplines besides business, such as economics, political science, history, geography, law, anthropology, sociology, and psychology.

Along with a knowledge of the environmental variables, the successful operation of an international business necessitates familiarity with other important subjects such as management, marketing, finance, and accounting. Such knowledge allows us to deal with operational variables that affect different functions of an international business. Figure 1.1 portrays the environmental variables that affect international business operations, which in turn affect the way by which each business function is performed.

Although the variables portrayed in Figure 1.1 will be explained in detail throughout the textbook, an overview of their related academic disciplines will enable us to better appreciate the contribution that these disciplines have made to the subject of international business.

Economics provides us with the most basic information that is needed to engage in international business. Data on unemployment, inflation, and economic growth are essential knowledge that one needs to know before operating in a foreign country. Economics also helps us to analyze different issues that are raised in the process of international business. For example, it enables us to

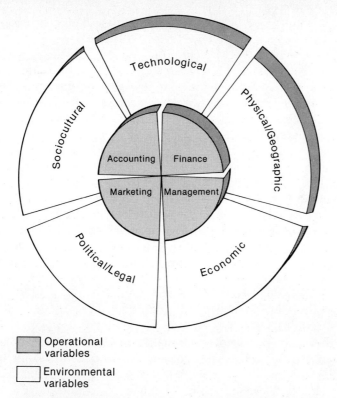

**Figure 1.1** Operational and environmental variables affecting international business

measure the costs and benefits of engaging in international business from the viewpoints of both the host and the home countries. In fact, a special field of economics, the study of *international trade,* concentrates mainly on the analysis of the flow of commodities among countries. Because international trade, that is, the exports and imports of goods and services, is an integral part of international business, an understanding of it is crucial for the successful operation of an international business.

Political science, which involves the study of governing institutions and their environments, plays a significant role in international business. For example, the existence of political stability is a significant prerequisite for the initiation and continuation of foreign operations by a firm. Take the case of Iran, whose prerevolutionary reputation as "the island of stability" in the Middle East gave rise to the rapid growth of American foreign investment. However, the emergence of its new anti-American government, which occurred after the 1979 revolution, resulted in the complete withdrawal of the U.S. investment in that country.

History, the study of ideas and institutions that existed in the past, enables us to better understand the process of international business at the present time. For example, as we explain later in Chapter 2, the mercantilist ideology, which prevailed in Europe between the sixteenth and eighteenth centuries, is still practiced today, in less extreme terms, in France.

Geography provides us with general information on the quantity, quality, and location of both plentiful and scarce resources. It also informs us of the geographical barriers that affect the channels of communication and distribution of goods and services in the world's economy. Different countries are endowed with different quantities and qualities of resources, depending, in part, on their geographic locations. This means the total resource cost to produce a good in one country could be lower than producing the same good in another country. These geographical differences give rise to the production of different goods and services in different countries. International business helps different countries produce those commodities that are the most efficient for them to produce (that is, the ones they can produce most cheaply). It also helps countries import those commodities that are less efficient for them to produce (or those they cannot produce). This enables all people to consume a better quality and larger quantity of goods and services. Many of us would find our standard of living deteriorating if we were denied access to Saudi Arabian oil, Colombian and Brazilian coffees, Central American bananas, French wines, Ceylonese tea, and the host of other products that can be obtained only through international business.

Law, either national or international, provides the rules of conduct for engaging in international business. These laws cover a wide range of activities that affect the operation and profitability of a firm. Tax regulations, employment regulations, the percentage of local partnerships allowed, the percentage of the total product that must be produced locally, and the labeling and packaging requirements for certain products are examples of laws that a manager of a firm should know before engaging in international business. In some cases these laws are so extreme that they make legal international business impossible. For example, the production and the sale of alcoholic beverages are forbidden in Islamic countries such as Saudi Arabia and Iran.

Knowledge of anthropology, sociology, and psychology is important in conducting international business because these disciplines help us to understand a culture better. A culture consists of a set of beliefs, values, attitudes, and practices of a group of people who live in a given environment. An understanding of these cultural factors allows us to comprehend the acceptable and the unacceptable modes of behavior in a given society. For example, drinking alcohol at social occasions is an acceptable behavior in Western cultures; however, it is outlawed in most Islamic countries. Consequently, because international business involves different nations, all of its facets, especially marketing and management, are affected by differences in cultural factors.

Management generally has three main tasks. These are (1) setting up a plan for the business, (2) executing this plan, and (3) evaluating and controlling the plan that is under operation. This involves organization, production, and the motivation and direction of personnel. Because of the existence of cultural differences in an international setting, the job of a manager is more complicated and necessitates an understanding of the cultural differences that may relate to personnel management. There may be different approaches to motivation, compensation, and collective bargaining practices. For example, providing a sense of job security may be an important factor for motivating an Indian worker. However, building a sense of loyalty seems to be more effective in inspiring a Japanese worker.

Marketing is concerned with those business functions that place the manufactured goods and services in the hands of consumers. To fulfill these functions, decisions must be made with regard to pricing, promoting, packaging, and distributing products and services. Because international business involves different nations, each one with its own cultural, social, political, legal, economic and environmental variables, decisions should be made within the constraints imposed by these significant factors. This requires a knowledge of the cultural environment in which the firm is operating. What is acceptable and workable in one society may not work in another. For example, a television advertisement that shows a woman in a swim suit is acceptable in a country like the United States; however, such an advertising strategy is impossible in Saudi Arabia, where a woman is required to be "under the veil."

Finance deals with the management of the flow of funds, according to some plan by a given firm. On an international scale the task of financing extends to include issues such as exchange rates, the balance of payments, speculation, and capital markets. A workable knowledge of these issues, as we explain in other chapters, is a prerequisite for the successful operation of a multinational corporation.

Accounting is concerned with the recording, classifying, reporting, and interpreting of financial activities in monetary terms of individuals, businesses, governments, and other entities. Accounting helps us to understand the financial position of a firm. For example, a company's balance sheet provides us with information on assets, liabilities, and owner's equity. The income statement of a firm provides us with the results of management's operations and decisions. It furnishes information on whether or not a firm has made profits or losses in a given year. In international business, accounting further helps us by translating into meaningful terms the financial statements that are provided in foreign countries. This allows one, as the manager of an international business, to better comprehend and compare the activities of a firm in a different nation.

## HISTORY OF INTERNATIONAL BUSINESS

International business has a history that dates back to ancient times. Forty centuries ago, Greek, Mesopotamian, and Phoenician merchants engaged in international business through the exportation and importation of goods and services. The major motivating force that led them to take the higher risk involved in doing business internationally was (just like today) the prospect of higher profits that could be secured from that kind of operation. However, systematic international business did not start until around the fifth century B.C. About this time, Greek merchants started to export cheap, mass-produced products. This was an important step towards the expansion of international business. Prior to this period, international business was mainly limited to the exportation and importation of luxury items. This event contributed to the expansion of international business and the emergence of Greece as the center of international business activities. It also allowed a greater degree of economic specialization by the trading nations.

With the development of the Roman Empire around the second century B.C., the center of international business activities gradually shifted to Rome. This movement was the result of a number of factors that facilitated the flow of goods and services to and from the empire. Chief among these were the free movement of people and goods in Rome, a safer Mediterranean Sea protected from piracy, and the expansion of new roads. In this era, trade further flourished with the development of private banks. These banks, which transferred credit within the empire, accepted deposits and made loans.

The decline of the Roman Empire had a great impact on international business. Civil wars made traveling unsafe and discouraged the movement of people and commodities. This resulted in the loss of distant markets for many businesses. Additionally, high taxes, imposed by the government, in part, for the support of the army, contributed to the decline of business activities. Consequently many industries shrunk and international business became virtually impossible. Following the fall of Rome, the center of business activities shifted to Constantinople, which became the trading center for east–west and north–south routes. Meanwhile, in the West, the Catholic Church became the dominant institution and the main deterrent for business activities. The Church did not view money-making as a virtuous activity, but rather as greed.

The rebirth of international business activities in the West started with the Crusade of the eleventh century. Crusaders contributed significantly to the revival of business activities by rediscovering the Eastern supply of goods and by stimulating an increasing Western demand for them. Crusaders helped Italian cities like Genoa and Venice to replace Constantinople as the leading trade center of the world. These cities witnessed the development of credit, banking, and the joint stock company, which further facilitated the expansion of international business.

By the end of the fifteenth century, the center of international business had gradually moved from the Mediterranean to Western Europe. Spain and Portugal replaced Venice and Genoa as the focal points of international commercial activities. Later, with the wars of independence from Spanish authority, Holland became the major trading center of Western Europe, channeling most European trade through its seaports.

In the early sixteenth century mercantilist ideology came into play. As we will explain in detail in Chapter 2, mercantilists maintained that for a country to be powerful it should encourage exports and discourage imports. A related proposition to mercantilists' thought was the idea of establishing colonies to enhance the wealth of the mother country. England, France, Holland, Portugal, and Spain established colonies to take advantage of raw materials that existed in other lands. By controlling their colonies they maintained monopolistic rights over colonial trade, and they were able to turn that trade to their own advantage.

The next phase in the development of international business started with the Industrial Revolution in Europe in the eighteenth century. In this era, the emergence of large industrial corporations resulted in mass production and dictated an expansion of the market for goods produced on an international scale. It also called for a larger source of supply of raw materials, energy, and labor to keep pace with the growing demand for industrial goods. As Europeans became more and more involved in industrial production, it resulted in the production of less food. Thus, they began to import large amounts of agricultural products, which were obtained in return for their manufactured goods. Consequently, specialization in production became an inevitable economic reality demanding a further increase in international business activities and an expansion in foreign markets.

The late eighteenth century witnessed yet another expansion in the domain of international business. During this period, a number of companies began expanding their operations by establishing branch offices in foreign countries. Alfred Nobel, the Swedish entrepreneur, started his first foreign plant in Hamburg, Germany, in 1866. The Singer company established a plant in Glasgow, Scotland, in 1867. Fredrick Bayer founded dye factories in Russia in 1876, in France in 1882, and in Belgium in 1908.

A recent stage in the history of international business is the emergence of the United States as the world's leader in this field. Beginning in the twentieth century New York City started to replace London as the center for commercial and financial activities of the world. This was the result of the changes that took place in the world concurrent with World War I and World War II.

Beginning with World War I, the need to supply the allies with the equipment for war stimulated U.S. industry. During the 1920s, the automotive, machine tool, petroleum, and chemical industries experienced rapid growth. The United States became the single most important economic leader in the world. Capital continued to flow after World War I from the United States for humanitarian assistance and to her allies.

World War II was another important stage in the development of the U.S. international business. U.S. direct investment in foreign countries grew rapidly—mainly in Canada and Europe—accounting for roughly 70 percent of the net foreign direct investment in the world during the postwar period through the 1960s. However, following this period the relative share of the U.S. foreign direct investment in the world gradually declined, reaching the approximate levels of 63 percent in 1970, 54 percent in 1975, and 44.5 percent in 1980.*[9]

Starting with the 1970s the picture of international business began to change. Advances in communication media, speedier worldwide travel made possible by jet age technology, and lower costs of production in developing

---

*As we explain later in this chapter, foreign direct investment involves an investment in the equity securities of a foreign firm that is large enough to exert effective control over the firm.

countries resulted in the expansion of international business. In this period, West Germany, the United Kingdom, other European countries, Canada, and Japan started catching up with the United States. Japan's rapid growth in the automobile and steel industries, for example, placed that country's corporations on the list of the 50 largest corporations in the world.

Recent years are also a period during which activities of LDCs in the area of international business have been increasing. Many companies from LDCs (such as Argentina, Brazil, Hong Kong, India, South Korea, and Taiwan) have engaged in foreign direct investment, mainly in manufacturing in other LDCs. Because of their "scaled-down" and relatively more labor-intensive technology, and their lower managerial and overhead costs, these companies have been able to produce relatively low-cost products. These products have successfully competed in the world market, mainly on the basis of their lower prices.

All of these events have contributed to the weakening position of the United States as the world leader in international business. Later in this chapter we use data to provide further explanations regarding the position of the United States in the world of international business.[10]

## THE DIFFERENCE BETWEEN INTERNATIONAL AND DOMESTIC BUSINESS

International business is the outgrowth of domestic business. In fact, most major corporations that are active in the international scene today started their operations in the domestic market. For example, major Japanese automobile manufacturers, such as Toyota, Nissan, and Honda, started their operations at home in Japan. With the expansion of their domestic market, they started to export to other countries. As the magnitude of their operations grew, they found it profitable to set up their plants and equipment in other countries such as the United States. Although international business is an extension of domestic business, it is significantly different from the latter, mainly due to the environmental and operational variables that we discussed earlier. The diversity that exists between countries with regard to their currency, inflation rates, interest rates, accounting practices, cultures, and government regulations is among the many factors that explain the complexity of international business as compared to domestic business.

All countries have their own currency. This means, for example, a British exporter of Rolls Royce automobiles who receives U.S. dollars in return likes to convert the proceeds into British pounds. These kinds of transactions involve the foreign exchange market, as we will explain in detail in Chapter 7. These transactions further add to the complexity of international business.

The variations in interest rates, inflation rates, and tax rates have a significant impact on the profitability of a firm that is operating in a foreign country. For a firm that is borrowing and investing in a foreign country, higher interest rates, tax rates, and inflation rates mean higher cost of operation and the lower profitability. On the other hand, for a firm that is depositing money in a foreign bank, higher interest rates mean a higher return.

All the variables that affect the performance of international business may change in reaction to the world's market forces of demand and supply or to the changing political stability of a host country. As a result, an international business is generally faced with a relatively higher risk than a similar domestic business. The financial risk stems from differences in interest rates, exchange rates, and inflation rates that exist among countries. On the political scene, a firm is faced with the risk of expropriation or harassment, which might result from nationalization or xenophobia. Risk might also arise from varying tax laws that govern the operations of a business in a different country.

Although international business is generally riskier than domestic business, in some cases risk could be reduced by going international. For example, the risk of losing the entire investment of a firm in one market—the domestic market—can be reduced by diversification, that is, investing in several markets, both domestic and international.

Generally, the manager of an international business is faced with much higher risks than the manager of a similar domestic business. Risks stemming from environmental and operational variables often provide the manager of an international business with a more challenging job. However, the manager may also benefit from international business by reducing risks. To be successful the manager of an international business must take all of the variables and their related risks into account, optimizing the objectives of the firm.

## DEFINITION OF MULTINATIONAL CORPORATION

A multinational corporation (MNC) is the principal actor in international business. There is no consensus among scholars with regard to the definition of MNC. Differences in definitions stem from the different types of MNCs, each type following a specific purpose. Consequently each definition is based on a given criterion that is considered to be indicative of the purpose of that type of MNC. Three major criteria have been used in the definition of MNCs: (1) structural criterion, (2) performance criterion, and (3) behavioral criterion.

Using the *structural criterion,* an MNC can be defined by two approaches. In the first approach, multinationality is defined by the number of countries in which a firm is operating. This means that a firm has its base in a country, say the United States, and operates in a number of other countries. In the second approach, ownership characteristics are used as the basis for definition. Since the term "multi" means "many," the multinational firm refers to a firm that is owned or operated by individuals from many nations. Thus an MNC can be defined either by the nationality of the owners or by the nationality of the top management.

If the first definition is adopted, this means that an MNC is a firm that makes stock available to all the countries in which it is operating. If the second definition is adopted, it means that a firm could be considered an MNC if its top management is composed of people from various countries. It is assumed that such individuals would have a worldwide outlook and would be less prone to follow the interest of any specific nation.

Using *performance* criterion, the MNC can be defined on the basis of the absolute amount or the relative share of assets, of number of employees, of sales, or of earning in a foreign country. According to the absolute measure, a firm is considered an MNC if it has allocated a "certain amount" of its resources to its foreign operations. By the relative measure, a firm is considered an MNC if it allocates a "significant portion," that is a very large percentage, of its resources to foreign operations. This measure implies that the magnitude of the foreign operations of a firm is so significant that it depends on other countries for its growth and financial stability.

Using *behavioral criterion,* a firm can be classified as multinational if its top management "thinks internationally." In this definition it is assumed that because the MNC is concerned with more than one country, its top management sees the entire world as the domain of their operation. Thus the international manager is considered as a person who searches for investment opportunities in the world market, rather than being confined to the domestic market.[11]

In this book we define **multinational corporation** (MNC) as a group of corporations that is operating in different countries but is controlled by its headquarters in a given country. We refer to the country that houses the headquarters of an MNC as the *home* country and to other countries as *host* countries. We maintain that the ownership of MNCs can be public, private, or mixed.

## FOREIGN DIRECT INVESTMENT AND PORTFOLIO INVESTMENT

One must differentiate between the terms *portfolio investment* and *foreign direct investment.* The main criterion for differentiating between the two is control. **Portfolio investment** is merely a financial investment that does not exert control over the assets of the firm in question. This can involve investment in debt securities, that is, bonds, or a small amount of investment in equity securities, that is, stocks of a firm. **Foreign direct investment (FDI)** is an investment that results in control of a firm by the investor. This can involve an investment in equity securities of a firm that is large enough to exert effective control over the firm.

The amount of equity securities that is needed to classify an investment as either portfolio or FDI is a subject that is open to debate. In practice, the amount is arbitrarily set by different countries, depending on their perception of effective control. The U.S. Department of Commerce, for example, considers FDI as any investment by an individual or a firm in a foreign company that represents more than 10 percent of the outstanding stock of that company. The percentage chosen by other nations varies, and it is usually higher than 10 percent.

It should be noted that FDI does not necessarily involve the movement of capital from a host to a home country. In fact FDI can be financed in a number of other ways. As a foreign investor, one could finance an investment by (1) selling technology to affiliates in a foreign country and investing the proceeds in that country, (2) raising the needed capital locally, (3) reinvesting the firm's foreign earnings in that country, or (4) using the management service fees that are earned in a foreign country. Thus the important characteristic of FDI is not how the investment is financed but the control that it confers. It is the word "control" that differentiates FDI and portfolio investment. Portfolio investment does not involve control and is undertaken solely as a means for obtaining capital gain, rather than engaging in entrepreneurial activities.

## THE SIGNIFICANCE OF INTERNATIONAL TRADE AND INVESTMENT IN THE WORLD ECONOMY

The importance of international trade and investment in the world economy can be viewed from three different angles. First, international trade and investment activities provide us with a variety of goods and services that exist in the world. In this context, we become citizens of the world and are no longer confined to the products produced in our own country. As an American, for example, we can buy a Honda or Toyota car, a Sony VCR, an Olivetti typewriter, a Pierre Cardin tie, a pair of Italian shoes, Canada's Molson beer, and the list goes on. But more important, international trade and investment allow us access to raw materials that we need for our industries. For example, the United States lacks deposits of chromium, tin, and tungsten that are important for certain industrial processes. Second, as the result of international trade and specialization, as will be explained in detail in Chapter 2, the efficiency of the world's production increases. This allows countries that are relatively more efficient in the production of certain commodities to concentrate their effort in the production of such goods. They can then export what they cannot consume, importing from other nations what they cannot produce. In this way a better quality and a larger quantity of goods can be produced at lower prices. Thus we can enjoy, for example, French wines and Persian rugs all over the world for low prices. Third, international trade and investment provide a source of income and employment for the countries involved. In the United States, for example, exports contribute to $1 out of every $7 of goods produced and generate one out of every nine manufacturing jobs.[12]

As a rough measure of the importance of international trade in a country's economy, we can compare the percentages of exports and imports to the gross national product (GNP) of the country in question. Also, to recognize the real significance of a country's trading position in the world, we can measure the ratios of its exports and imports to the world's total exports and imports.* Table

---

*Measuring the importance of trade by the percentage of exports and imports to GNP may omit the role of illegal trade.

1.1 portrays the trade positions of the major industrialized countries in the world. As this table indicates, the United States, accounting for a 12.32 percent share of the world export market, holds the largest share, followed by West Germany, Japan, France, and the United Kingdom.

The overall trade position of the United States in the world has declined over the years, losing ground to countries such as West Germany and Japan. This can be detected from Table 1.2. As this table indicates the share of the United States in the world exports market, which was 17.427 percent in 1950, declined to 15.867 percent in 1965, 13.157 percent in 1975, and 10.923 percent

**Table 1.1  THE TRADE POSITIONS OF THE MAJOR INDUSTRIAL COUNTRIES IN THE WORLD, 1984**
Billions of Dollars

| Country | Imports | Exports | GNP | M/GNP | X/GNP | M/W | X/W' |
|---|---|---|---|---|---|---|---|
| United States | 341.179 | 217.890 | 3662.8 | 9.31 | 5.95 | 18.52 | 12.32 |
| Germany | 153.007 | 171.728 | 557.083 | 27.46 | 30.26 | 8.30 | 9.71 |
| Japan | 136.176 | 169.700 | 1166.519 | 11.67 | 14.55 | 7.39 | 9.59 |
| France[a] | 115.714 | 96.694 | 530.632 | 21.80 | 18.22 | 6.42 | 5.66 |
| United Kingdom | 104.863 | 93.772 | 373.156 | 28.10 | 25.10 | 5.69 | 5.30 |
| Netherlands | 62.295 | 65.863 | 111.069 | 56.08 | 59.29 | 3.38 | 3.72 |
| Italy | 84.225 | 73.318 | 313.367 | 26.88 | 23.97 | 4.57 | 4.14 |
| Canada | 79.760 | 90.291 | 318.465 | 25.045 | 28.35 | 4.32 | 5.10 |

[a]data for 1982

M = Imports; X = Exports; W = World Imports; W' = World Exports

*Source: International Financial Statistics,* vol. 38, no. 12, December 1985.

**Table 1.2  THE RELATIVE SHARES OF THE MAJOR INDUSTRIAL COUNTRIES IN THE WORLD EXPORTS MARKET, 1950–1986**
Percentage

| Country | 1950 | 1965 | 1975 | 1986 |
|---|---|---|---|---|
| United States | 17.427 | 15.867 | 13.157 | 10.923 |
| Canada | 5.118 | 4.869 | 4.145 | 4.507 |
| Japan | 1.398 | 4.870 | 6.791 | 10.593 |
| France | 5.223 | 5.865 | 6.463 | 6.280 |
| West Germany | 3.377 | 10.324 | 10.971 | 12.231 |
| Italy | 2.044 | 4.149 | 4.186 | 4.916 |
| Netherlands | 2.394 | 3.684 | 4.261 | 4.077 |
| United Kingdom | 10.720 | 7.959 | 5.283 | 5.377 |

*Source:* Calculated by the authors from the data provided in the *International Financial Statistics: Yearbook, 1987,* pp. 116–117.

in 1986. During the same period Japan's share rose from 1.398 percent in 1950 to 10.593 percent in 1986. West Germany's share increased from 3.377 percent in 1950 to 12.231 percent in 1986.

The weakening trade position of the United States over the years can be contributed to three factors. First, countries such as Japan have captured a greater share of the world market. Second, the U.S. firms have concentrated their activities in foreign direct investment (FDI). Third, a stronger U.S. dollar has made American goods more expensive abroad, causing an increase in U.S. imports and a decrease in U.S. exports. Table 1.3 provides us with data on the direction of trade in the world. As this table indicates, the bulk of exports in the world is undertaken by the advanced (developed) countries. According to this table the share of the world's total exports are 70.6 percent for developed countries, 18.7 percent for less developed countries (LDCs), and 10 percent for socialist countries. Additionally, of the total amount exported by developed countries, 69.5 percent went to the developed countries themselves, 24.9 percent went to LDCs, and 4.5 percent went to socialist countries. This means that, overall, the advanced industrial nations are the major trading partners for most goods and services that are traded internationally. However, one must not underestimate the importance of LDCs in providing export markets for advanced countries. For example, until the recent increase in their debt-service ratio, the Latin American countries provided the highest growth market for U.S. exports. Mexico, an LDC, is the third most important trading market for the United States.

Table 1.3   SHARE OF WORLD EXPORTS BY DESTINATION IN 1982
            (In Percent)

| | Destination of exports | | |
|---|---|---|---|
| Origin of exports | Developed countries | Less developed countries | Socialist countries |
| World | 70.6 | 18.7 | 10 |
| Developed Countries[a] | 69.5 | 24.9 | 4.5 |
| Less Developed Countries[b] | 67.1 | 28.7 | 3.8 |
| Socialist Countries[c] | 28.6 | 13.1 | 3.5 |

[a]Developed countries include the industrialized market economies of Western Europe, North America, South Africa, Australia, and New Zealand.

[b]Less developed countries include market economies of Latin America, the Caribbean, Africa, Asia, Oceania, and Malta in the Mediterranean Sea. Exceptions are Israel, Japan, Australia, New Zealand, and South Africa, which are developed countries.

[c]Socialist countries include the industrialized, centrally planned economies of Eastern Europe. Also included are China, Mongolia, the Democratic People's Republic of Korea, and Vietnam.

*Source:* Adapted from United Nations Conference on Trade and Development, *Handbook of International Trade and Statistics: 1984 Supplement,* pp. 68–69.

As international trade is dominated by the world's advanced industrial nations, so also is FDI led by these countries. Table 1.4 shows the outflows and inflows of foreign direct investment by major industrial countries. As this table indicates, the United States is the major investor and the major recipient of foreign direct investment in the world. This position is followed by the United Kingdom, Japan, West Germany, Italy, Canada, France, and the Netherlands. A comparison of data for 1970 and 1983 reveals that the position of the United States as the world's leading foreign investor has been weakening. In fact, the United States is the only country experiencing a negative rate of growth (−35 percent) for the direct investment outflows. It is also interesting that during the same period, the United States shows the highest rate of growth of foreign direct investment inflows (669 percent) of any country. This simply means that FDI activities of the United States abroad have been decreasing, whereas other countries have continued to increase their investment in the United States. The growing amount of FDI in the United States can be attributed, among other factors, to the relative market size in the United States, the declining labor costs relative to other rich nations, the relative abundance of raw materials, and the restrictions on the importation of certain products to the United States. These factors, which encourage a firm to invest in another country, will be more fully discussed in later chapters.

Tables 1.5 and 1.6 provide us with more detail on the activities of the United States with regard to FDI. As Table 1.5 shows, Canada is the major recipient of the U.S. FDI abroad, accounting for 21.6 percent of the total. The next largest recipient is the United Kingdom, which accounts for 13.8 percent.

Table 1.4   THE OUTFLOW AND INFLOW OF FOREIGN DIRECT INVESTMENT INVOLVING MAJOR INDUSTRIAL COUNTRIES
Millions of Dollars

| | 1970 | | 1983 | | Percentage change | |
|---|---|---|---|---|---|---|
| Countries | Outflows | Inflows | Outflows | Inflows | Outflows | Inflows[a] |
| United States | 7,590 | 1,469 | 4,881 | 11,299 | −35 | 669 |
| France | 374 | 622 | 1,760 | 1,795 | 370 | 188 |
| Germany | 873 | 595 | 2,908 | 1,130 | 233 | 90 |
| Italy | 109 | 606 | 2,205 | 1,229 | 1,922 | 103 |
| Netherlands | 551 | 536 | 1,529 | 648 | 177 | 21 |
| United Kingdom | 1,310 | 871 | 3,656 | 4,769 | 179 | 447 |
| Japan | 355 | 94 | 3,612 | 416 | 917 | 342 |
| Canada | 301 | 386 | 2,049 | 162 | 580 | −81 |

[a]Last column calculated by the authors.

*Source:* Derived from *International Economic Indicator,* U.S. Department of Commerce, International Trade Administrator, March 1984, pp. 54–55.

Table 1.5   U.S. FOREIGN DIRECT INVESTMENT ABROAD AT YEAR END 1984
              Millions of Dollars

| | All industries | Petroleum | Manufacturing | Other industries[a] |
|---|---|---|---|---|
| All countries | 233,412 | 63,319 | 93,012 | 77,081 |
| Developed Countries | 174,057 | 40,616 | 72,866 | 60,575 |
| Canada | 50,467 | 11,614 | 21,467 | 17,386 |
| Europe | 103,663 | 24,714 | 43,661 | 35,288 |
| Belgium | 5,288 | 587 | 2,829 | 1,872 |
| Denmark | 1,380 | 745 | 279 | 356 |
| France | 6,478 | 495 | 4,187 | 1,796 |
| Germany | 15,231 | 3,192 | 9,362 | 2,677 |
| Greece | 202 | — | 68 | — |
| Ireland | 4,427 | 53 | 3,691 | 683 |
| Italy | 4,998 | 810 | 3,264 | 924 |
| Luxembourg | 454 | — | 255 | — |
| Netherlands | 8,262 | 3,228 | 3,347 | 1,687 |
| United Kingdom | 32,145 | 10,949 | 12,654 | 8,542 |
| Other European | 24,796 | 4,561 | 3,726 | 16,509 |
| Japan | 8,374 | 2,100 | 4,120 | 2,154 |
| Australia, New Zealand & South Africa | 11,554 | 2,189 | 3,617 | 5,748 |
| Developed Countries | 53,932 | 18,417 | 20,146 | 15,369 |
| Latin America | 2,094 | 5,940 | 15,665 | 6,489 |
| Other Africa | 6,247 | 4,485 | 508 | 1,254 |
| Middle East | 3,435 | 1,205 | 260 | 1,970 |
| Other Asia & Pacific | 16,156 | 6,787 | 3,714 | 5,655 |
| International | 5,423 | 4,285 | — | — |

[a]Others include trade, banking, finance, insurance, real estate, mining, smelting, transportation, communications, and public utilities.

*Source:* Derived from *The Survey of Current Business,* vol. 65, no.6, June 1985, p.30.

It is also interesting to note that the developed countries' share of the U.S. FDI abroad is 74.5 percent. This means American FDI is directed toward large developed nations, as American trade is. Table 1.6 shows the FDI activities of other countries in the United States. According to this table, the United Kingdom is the major investor in the United States, accounting for 23.87 percent of the total. Other major investors in the United States are the Netherlands, Japan, Canada, and West Germany. A comparison between developed and developing countries in Table 1.6 also shows that developed  countries, accounting for 86.33 percent of the total investment, have a far greater amount of investment in the United States than do developing countries that account for only 13.67 percent of the total.

Table 1.6    FOREIGN DIRECT INVESTMENT IN THE U.S. AT YEAR END 1984
Millions of Dollars

| | All industries | Petroleum | Manufacturing | Other industries[a] |
|---|---|---|---|---|
| All Countries | 159,571 | 24,916 | 50,664 | 83,991 |
| Developed Countries | 137,751 | 24,181 | 45,151 | |
| Canada | 14,001 | 1,419 | 3,888 | 8,694 |
| Europe | 106,567 | 22,897 | 38,684 | 44,986 |
| Belgium | 2,559 | — | 495 | — |
| France | 6,502 | — | 5402 | — |
| Germany | 11,956 | −1 | 4,431 | 7,526 |
| Italy | 1,614 | — | 340 | — |
| Luxembourg | 751 | — | 74 | — |
| Netherlands | 32,643 | 9,878 | 12,470 | 10,295 |
| United Kingdom | 38,099 | 10,917 | 9,347 | 17,835 |
| Denmark, Greece, & Ireland | 725 | — | 138 | — |
| Other Europe | 11,7+8 | 340 | 5,988 | 5,390 |
| Japan | 14,817 | −178 | 2,262 | 12,733 |
| Australia, New Zealand, & South Africa | 2,366 | 43 | 317 | 2,006 |
| Developing Countries | 21,820 | 735 | 5,512 | 15,574 |
| Latin America | 15,516 | 695 | 5,287 | 9,534 |
| Middle East | 5,159 | 15 | 94 | 5,050 |
| Other Africa, Asia, & Pacific | 1,146 | 25 | 131 | 990 |

[a]Others include trade, banking, finance, insurance, real estate, mining, smelting, transportation, communications, and public utilities.

Source: Derived from The Survey of Current Business, vol. 65, no.6, June 1985, p. 32.

## THE WORLD'S MAJOR MULTINATIONAL CORPORATIONS

Table 1.7 shows the 50 largest industrial corporations on the basis of their total sales in 1987. Among these countries the United States, with 20 firms, has the largest number of MNCs in the world, accounting for about 47 percent of total sales. Out of the 20 American firms, 7 are engaged in petroleum refining and the rest manufacture motor vehicles, computers, chemicals, electronic equipment, aerospace equipment, tobacco, food, and cosmetics. Other developed nations on this list are the Netherlands, the United Kingdom, Japan, Italy, France, West Germany, and Switzerland. As this table indicates, the majority of these MNCs belong to developed countries. The list includes only two developing countries—Brazil and South Korea. A comparison of the 1987 and 1986 rankings provides us with useful information regarding the relative performance of each MNC during 1987. For example, it indicates that the major auto

**Table 1.7  THE 50 LARGEST INDUSTRIAL CORPORATIONS RANKED BY SALES**

| Rank '87 | Rank '86 | Company | Headquarters | Industry | Sales $ Millions | Profits $ Millions |
|---|---|---|---|---|---|---|
| 1 | 1 | General Motors | Detroit | Motor vehicles | 101,781.9 | 3,550.9 |
| 2 | 3 | Royal Dutch/Shell Group | London/The Hague | Petroleum refining | 78,319.3 | 4,725.8 |
| 3 | 2 | Exxon | New York | Petroleum refining | 76,416.0 | 4,840.0 |
| 4 | 4 | Ford Motor | Dearborn, Mich. | Motor vehicles | 71,643.4 | 4,625.2 |
| 5 | 5 | International Business Machines | Armonk, N.Y. | Computers | 54,217.0 | 5,258.0 |
| 6 | 6 | Mobil | New York | Petroleum refining | 51,223.0 | 1,258.0 |
| 7 | 7 | British Petroleum | London | Petroleum refining | 45,205.9 | 2,280.1 |
| 8 | 12 | Toyota Motor | Toyota City (Japan) | Motor vehicles | 41,455.0 | 1,699.6 |
| 9 | 11 | IRI | Rome | Metals | 41,270.0 | 146.5 |
| 10 | 8 | General Electric | Fairfield, Conn. | Electronics | 39,315.0 | 2,915.0 |
| 11 | 13 | Daimler-Benz | Stuttgart | Motor vehicles | 37,535.5 | 970.2 |
| 12 | 10 | Texaco | White Plains, N.Y. | Petroleum refining | 34,372.0 | (4,407.0) |
| 13 | 9 | American Tel. & Tel. | New York | Electronics | 33,598.0 | 2,044.0 |
| 14 | 14 | E.I. du Pont de Nemours | Wilmington, Del. | Chemicals | 30,468.0 | 1,786.0 |
| 15 | 18 | Volkswagen | Wolfsburg (W. Ger.) | Motor vehicles | 30,392.7 | 242.1 |
| 16 | 19 | Hitachi | Tokyo | Electronics | 30,332.2 | 617.3 |
| 17 | 27 | Fiat | Turin | Motor vehicles | 29,642.8 | 1,830.2 |
| 18 | 25 | Siemens | Munich | Electronics | 27,462.9 | 649.6 |
| 19 | 15 | Matsushita Electric Industrial | Osaka | Electronics | 27,325.7 | 862.4 |
| 20 | 16 | Unilever | London/Rotterdam | Food | 27,128.8 | 1,278.6 |
| 21 | 21 | Chrysler | Highland Park, Mich. | Motor vehicles | 26,257.7 | 1,289.7 |
| 22 | 22 | Philips' Gloeilampenfabrieken | Endhoven (Neth.) | Electronics | 26,021.2 | 316.9 |
| 23 | 17 | Chevron | San Francisco | Petroleum refining | 26,015.0 | 1,007.0 |
| 24 | 26 | Nissan Motor | Tokyo | Motor vehicles | 25,650.5 | 123.9 |
| 25 | 31 | Renault | Paris | Motor vehicles | 24,539.7 | 613.7 |
| 26 | 20 | ENI | Rome | Petroleum refining | 24,242.5 | 483.6 |
| 27 | 23 | Nestlé | Vevey (Switzerland) | Food | 23,625.9 | 1,224.8 |

Table 1.7 (*Continued*)

| Rank '87 | '86 | Company | Headquarters | Industry | Sales $ Millions | Profits $ Millions |
|---|---|---|---|---|---|---|
| 28 | 29 | BASF | Ludwigshafen (W. Ger.) | Chemicals | 22,383.7 | 584.7 |
| 29 | 24 | Philip Morris | New York | Tobacco | 22,279.0 | 1,842.0 |
| 30 | ● | CGE (CIE Générale D'Électricité) | Paris | Electronics | 21,204.3 | 304.8 |
| 31 | 33 | Elf Aquitaine | Paris | Petroleum refining | 21,186.4 | 690.2 |
| 32 | 35 | Samsung | Seoul | Electronics | 21,053.5 | 249.3 |
| 33 | 28 | Bayer | Leverkusen (W. Ger.) | Chemicals | 20,662.2 | 833.3 |
| 34 | 32 | Hoechst | Frankfurt | Chemicals | 20,558.1 | 766.6 |
| 35 | 42 | Toshiba | Tokyo | Electronics | 20,378.1 | 213.8 |
| 36 | 30 | Amoco | Chicago | Petroleum refining | 20,174.0 | 1,360.0 |
| 37 | 41 | Peugeot | Paris | Motor vehicles | 19,658.2 | 1,116.1 |
| 38 | 43 | Imperial Chemical Industries | London | Chemicals | 18,232.8 | 1,245.8 |
| 39 | ● | Honda Motor | Tokyo | Motor vehicles | 17,237.7 | 516.2 |
| 40 | 38 | United Technologies | Hartford | Aerospace | 17,170.2 | 591.7 |
| 41 | 40 | Occidental Petroleum | Los Angeles | Food | 17,096.0 | 240.0 |
| 42 | 39 | Procter & Gamble | Cincinnati | Soaps, cosmetics | 17,000.0 | 327.0 |
| 43 | 45 | Atlantic Richfield | Los Angeles | Petroleum refining | 16,281.4 | 1,224.3 |
| 44 | 34 | RJR Nabisco | Atlanta | Tobacco | 15,868.0 | 1,209.0 |
| 45 | 44 | Petrobrás (Petróleo Brasileiro) | Rio de Janeiro | Petroleum refining | 15,640.5 | 171.5 |
| 46 | 36 | Boeing | Seattle | Aerospace | 15,355.0 | 480.0 |
| 47 | ● | NEC | Tokyo | Electronics | 15,325.1 | 94.0 |
| 48 | 46 | Tenneco | Houston | Petroleum refining | 15,075.0 | (218.0) |
| 49 | ● | Nippon Steel | Tokyo | Metals | 14,639.8 | (69.7) |
| 50 | ● | Volvo | Göteborg (Sweden) | Motor vehicles | 14,576.0 | 730.4 |
| | | TOTALS | | | 1,504,492.5 | 56,735.1 |

● Not on last year's list

*Source: Fortune,* August 1, 1988. pp. D3–D4. Reprinted by permission from The FORTUNE Directory; © 1988 Time. Inc.

manufacturers in the world experienced a good year. This is because their ranking in terms of sales either stayed the same or improved. As Table 1.7 shows, Japanese car makers experienced a remarkable year. Toyota Motor entered the top 10, and for the first time Honda Motor entered the top 50.

In concluding this chapter we may emphasize that in today's world no country, whether developed or less developed, can live in isolation. Where the global economy is profoundly affected by international business activities, we have become, in a sense, citizens of the world. As informed citizens we need to understand the elements that affect international business and, hence, our own economic well-being. A prerequisite for this understanding is familiarity with the institutions and the theoretical frameworks that are the subject of the forthcoming chapters.

## SUMMARY

1. International business can be defined as those business transactions among individuals, firms, or other entities (both private and public) that occur across national boundaries.
2. International business is affected by two different sets of variables. These are environmental variables and operational variables.
3. The understanding of environmental variables requires a working knowledge of other academic disciplines, including economics, political science, history, geography, law, anthropology, sociology, and psychology.
4. The comprehension of operational variables necessitates a familiarity with accounting, finance, management, and marketing on an international level.
5. International business dates back to ancient times. Forty centuries ago Greek, Mesopotamian, and Phoenician merchants engaged in international business through the exportation and importation of goods and services.
6. Systematic international business started around the fifth century B.C., when Greece became the major center for international commercial activities.
7. With the passage of time, Greece lost its position as the center of international business activities. This position shifted to a number of places, including Rome, Constantinople, Genoa, Venice, Western Europe, and finally the United States.
8. Although the United States stands as the major participant in international business today, its position is gradually weakening. The change in the economic picture, which started early in the 1970s, has meant the United States is faced with stiff competition from Japan and Western Europe in the world market.
9. The difference between international and domestic business is mainly due to the environmental and operational variables. The variations that exist among countries with regard to currencies, inflation rates, interest rates, accounting practices, cultures, and government regulations are among the factors that differentiate international business from domestic business.
10. There is no consensus among scholars with regard to the definition of multinational corporation (MNC). Different definitions are based on different criteria that are considered to be indicative of the purpose and the type of MNC.
11. Using a structural criterion, the MNC can be defined by the number of countries

in which a firm is operating or by the nationalities of its owners and/or top management.

12. Using a performance criterion, an MNC can be defined on the basis of the absolute amount or the relative share (percentage) of assets, number of employees, sales, or earnings in a foreign country.

13. Using a behavioral criterion, a firm can be classified as an MNC if its top management "thinks internationally."

14. In this book, an MNC is defined as a group of corporations that is operating in different countries but is controlled by its headquarters in a given country.

15. The main criterion for differentiating between portfolio investment and foreign direct investment is the amount of control of the company the investment allows.

16. Foreign direct investment can be financed by (1) selling technology to affiliates in a foreign country and investing the proceeds in that country; (2) raising the needed capital locally; (3) reinvesting the firm's foreign earnings in that country; or (4) using the management service fees that are earned in a foreign country.

17. The importance of international trade and investments in the world economy can be viewed from different angles. First, they provide us with a variety of goods and services that exist in the world. Second, they result in greater specialization in the world, causing the world's manufacturing efficiency to increase. Third, they provide a source of income and employment for the countries involved.

18. To roughly measure the importance of international trade in a country's economy we can compare the percentages of exports and imports to the GNP of the country in question.

19. To recognize the relative significance of a country in the world's trade we can measure the ratios of its exports and imports to the total world exports and imports.

20. International business is dominated by the world's major industrial countries. The United States is the world's major exporter, the major investor and the major recipient of foreign direct investment.

21. The overall trade position of the United States has declined over the years, losing ground to countries such as Japan and Western European countries.

## QUESTIONS

1.1 Explain the changing pattern of the overall international business position of the United States in the last two decades. In your answer include a discussion of the growth of FDI in the European countries and Japan. What do you think the patterns of FDI will look like in the future?

1.2 Why is an understanding of international business important to you as a business major student?

1.3 The major objective of all firms, whether domestic or international, is to make a profit. To achieve this goal, can we apply the same techniques and concepts we use for domestic firms to the MNCs? Discuss.

1.4 International business has a long history that dates back to ancient times. Why has so much attention been directed to this subject in recent years?

1.5 Do you think that environmental variables that affect international business in LDCs are, in general, different from those that affect international business in advanced countries? Discuss, giving appropriate examples.

# *Map Portfolio*

The enclosed maps provide additional information regarding the relative significance of international trade and multinational corporations in different nations. They illustrate the number and location of different countries in the world (*The World of States*), the relative trade power of each country (*Trade Power*), and each "country's share of total sales by the world's top 500 industrial companies" (*Big Business*).

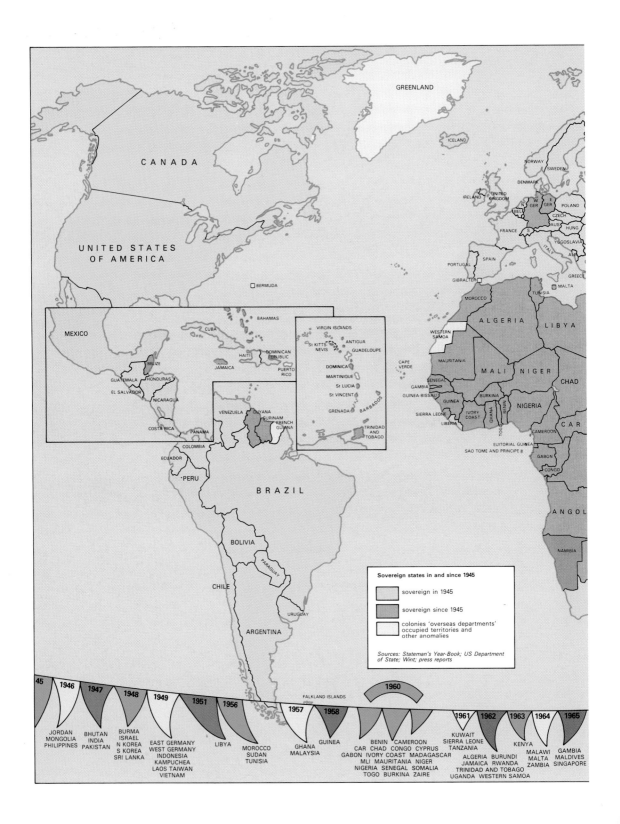

GREENLAND

CANADA

ICELAND

UNITED STATES
OF AMERICA

BERMUDA

NORWAY
SWEDEN

DENMARK

IRELAND UNITED
KINGDOM

FRANCE

N S
GER

E
GER

BEL

POLAND

CZECH
AUS
HUNG

YUGOSLAVIA

ITALY

PORTUGAL  SPAIN

GREECE

GIBRALTAR

MALTA

MEXICO

BAHAMAS

CUBA

JAMAICA

HAITI
DOMINICAN
REPUBLIC

PUERTO
RICO

BELIZE

GUATEMALA    HONDURAS

EL SALVADOR

NICARAGUA

COSTA RICA      PANAMA

VIRGIN ISLANDS

St KITTS    ANTIGUA
NEVIS     GUADELOUPE

DOMINICA

MARTINIQUE

St LUCIA

St VINCENT

GRENADA    BARBADOS

TRINIDAD
AND
TOBAGO

MOROCCO

WESTERN
SAMOA

MAURITANIA

SENEGAL

GAMBIA

GUINEA-BISSAU

GUINEA

SIERRA LEONE

LIBERIA

IVORY
COAST

CAPE
VERDE

ALGERIA

TUNISIA

LIBYA

MALI      NIGER

CHAD

BURKINA

GHANA

TOGO

BENIN

NIGERIA

CAR

CAMEROON

EQUITORIAL GUINEA

SAO TOME AND PRINCIPE

GABON

CONGO

VENEZUELA   GUYANA

SURINAM
FRENCH
GUIANA

COLOMBIA

ECUADOR

PERU

BRAZIL

BOLIVIA

PARAGUAY

CHILE

URUGUAY

ARGENTINA

ANGOLA

NAMIBIA

FALKLAND ISLANDS

**Sovereign states in and since 1945**

sovereign in 1945

sovereign since 1945

colonies 'overseas departments'
occupied territories and
other anomalies

*Sources: Stateman's Year-Book; US Department
of State; Wint; press reports*

| 45 | 1946 | 1947 | 1948 | 1949 | 1951 | 1956 | 1957 | 1958 | 1960 | 1961 | 1962 | 1963 | 1964 | 1965 |

JORDAN
MONGOLIA
PHILIPPINES

BHUTAN
INDIA
PAKISTAN

BURMA
ISRAEL
N KOREA
S KOREA
SRI LANKA

EAST GERMANY
WEST GERMANY
INDONESIA
KAMPUCHEA
LAOS TAIWAN
VIETNAM

LIBYA

MOROCCO
SUDAN
TUNISIA

GHANA
MALAYSIA

GUINEA

BENIN  CAMEROON
CAR CHAD CONGO CYPRUS
GABON IVORY COAST MADAGASCAR
MLI MAURITANIA NIGER
NIGERIA SENEGAL SOMALIA
TOGO BURKINA ZAIRE

KUWAIT
SIERRA LEONE
TANZANIA

ALGERIA BURUNDI
JAMAICA RWANDA
TRINIDAD AND TOBAGO
UGANDA WESTERN SAMOA

KENYA

MALAWI
MALTA
ZAMBIA

GAMBIA
MALDIVES
SINGAPORE

Since the Second World War the number of independent states has grown from 72 to 168. The proliferation continues.

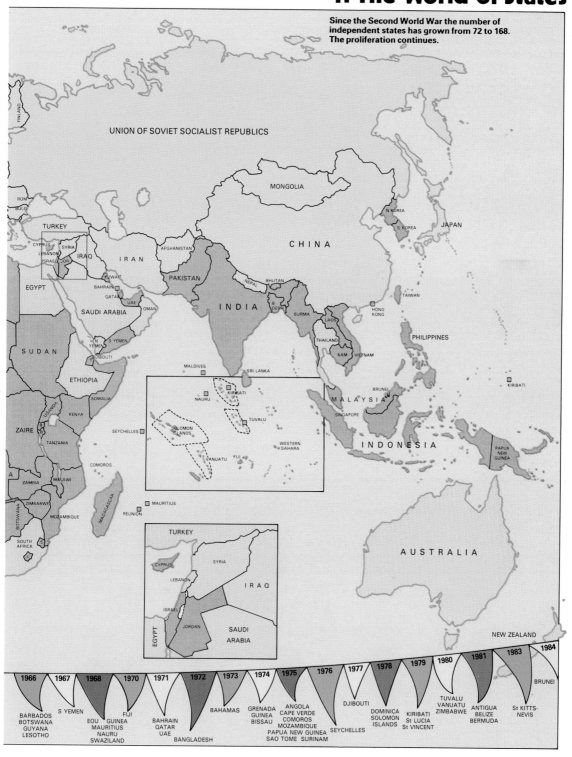

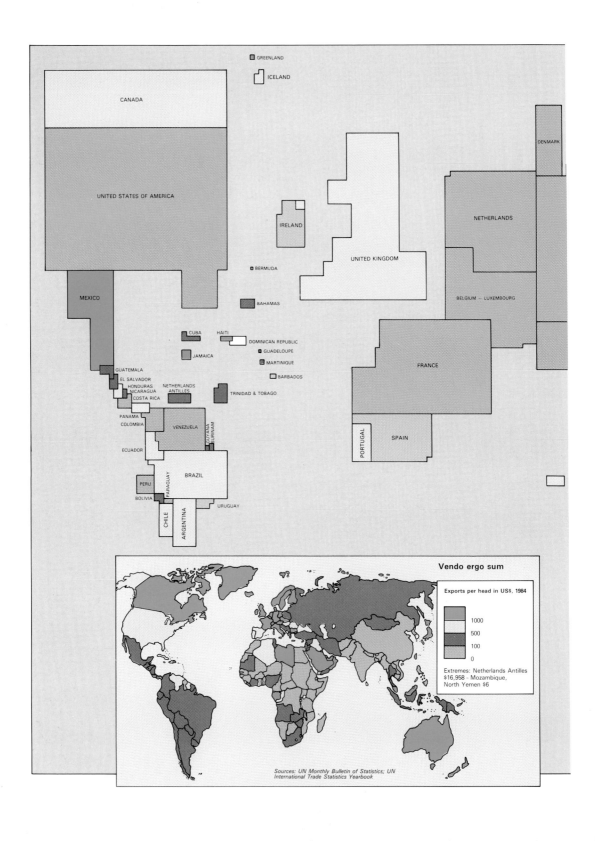

GREENLAND

ICELAND

CANADA

DENMARK

UNITED STATES OF AMERICA

NETHERLANDS

IRELAND

UNITED KINGDOM

BERMUDA

MEXICO

BAHAMAS

BELGIUM – LUXEMBOURG

CUBA   HAITI

DOMINICAN REPUBLIC

JAMAICA

GUADELOUPE

MARTINIQUE

FRANCE

BARBADOS

GUATEMALA

EL SALVADOR

HONDURAS

NICARAGUA

NETHERLANDS ANTILLES

COSTA RICA

TRINIDAD & TOBAGO

PANAMA

COLOMBIA

VENEZUELA

GUYANA

SURINAM

PORTUGAL

SPAIN

ECUADOR

BRAZIL

PERU

PARAGUAY

BOLIVIA

URUGUAY

CHILE

ARGENTINA

**Vendo ergo sum**

Exports per head in US$, 1984

1000
500
100
0

Extremes: Netherlands Antilles
$16,958 - Mozambique,
North Yemen $6

*Sources: UN Monthly Bulletin of Statistics; UN*
*International Trade Statistics Yearbook*

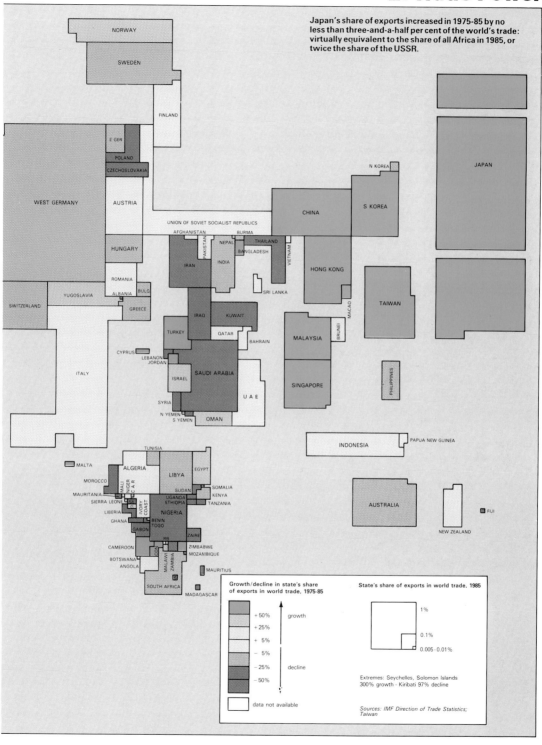

Japan's share of exports increased in 1975-85 by no
less than three-and-a-half per cent of the world's trade:
virtually equivalent to the share of all Africa in 1985, or
twice the share of the USSR.

Growth/decline in state's share
of exports in world trade, 1975-85

+ 50%    growth
+ 25%
+ 5%
− 5%
− 25%    decline
− 50%

data not available

State's share of exports in world trade, 1985

1%

0.1%

0.005 - 0.01%

Extremes: Seychelles, Solomon Islands
300% growth - Kiribati 97% decline

Sources: IMF Direction of Trade Statistics;
Taiwan

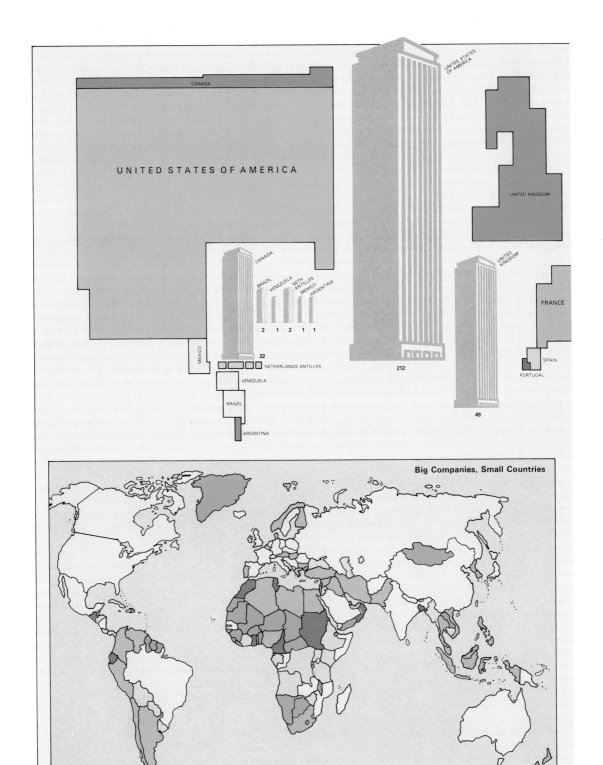

CANADA

UNITED STATES OF AMERICA

UNITES STATES
OF AMERICA

UNITED KINGDOM

CANADA

BRAZIL
VENEZUELA
NETH
ANTILLES
MEXICO
ARGENTINA

2  1  2  1  1

MEXICO

22

NETHERLANDS ANTILLES

VENEZUELA

BRAZIL

ARGENTINA

UNITED
KINGDOM

212

49

FRANCE

SPAIN

PORTUGAL

**Big Companies, Small Countries**

**The world's top 500 industrial companies have sales roughly equivalent to nine-tenths of the US gross national product.**

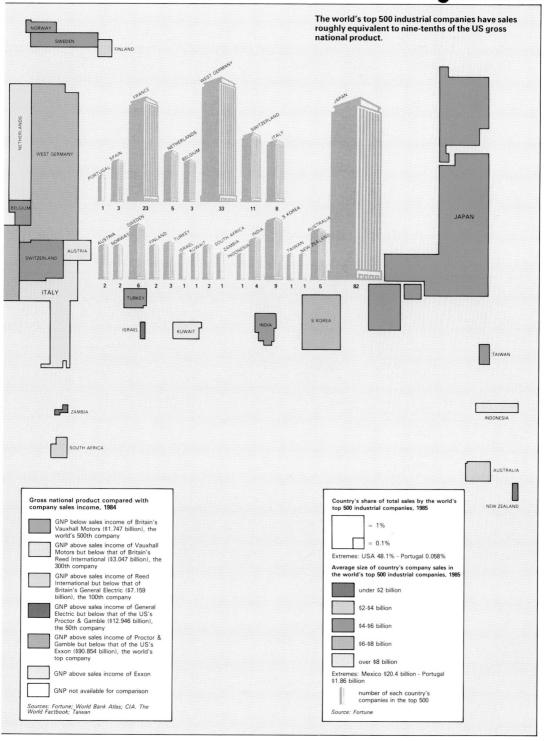

**Gross national product compared with company sales income, 1984**

- GNP below sales income of Britain's Vauxhall Motors ($1.747 billion), the world's 500th company
- GNP above sales income of Vauxhall Motors but below that of Britain's Reed International ($3.047 billion), the 300th company
- GNP above sales income of Reed International but below that of Britain's General Electric ($7.159 billion), the 100th company
- GNP above sales income of General Electric but below that of the US's Proctor & Gamble ($12.946 billion), the 50th company
- GNP above sales income of Proctor & Gamble but below that of the US's Exxon ($90.854 billion), the world's top company
- GNP above sales income of Exxon
- GNP not available for comparison

*Sources: Fortune; World Bank Atlas; CIA. The World Factbook; Taiwan*

**Country's share of total sales by the world's top 500 industrial companies, 1985**

- = 1%
- = 0.1%

Extremes: USA 48.1% - Portugal 0.058%

**Average size of country's company sales in the world's top 500 industrial companies, 1985**

- under $2 billion
- $2-$4 billion
- $4-$6 billion
- $6-$8 billion
- over $8 billion

Extremes: Mexico $20.4 billion - Portugal $1.86 billion

- number of each country's companies in the top 500

*Source: Fortune*

0 - 15 million
15 - 50 million
50 - 100 million
100 + million
Data not available

1.6 Differentiate between portfolio investment and FDI.

1.7 Compare the different criteria that are used in the definition of international business. Refer to Table 1.7 and explain what criterion is used in identifying firms as MNCs. Why do you think such a criterion is used as opposed to others?

## NOTES

1. "Entering A New Age of Boundless Competition," *Fortune,* March 14, 1988, pp. 40–48.
2. Franklin R. Root, "Some Trends in the World Economy and Their Implications for International Business," *Journal of International Business Studies* (Winter 1984): 19–23.
3. United Nations Conference on Trade and Development, *Handbook of International Trade and Development Statistics,* 1984 Supplement.
4. "Big-Five's Attempt to Deflate the Dollar Is Losing Steam; Can They Win the War?" *The Wall Street Journal,* 12 December 1985, p. 34.
5. "The Plunge in Stocks Has Experts Guessing About Market's Course," *The Wall Street Journal,* 19 October 1987, p. 1.
6. "Anguish Abroad: Foreign Ardor Cools Toward U.S. Stocks After Market's Dive," *The Wall Street Journal,* 26 October 1987, p. 1.
7. "How Bad? The Economy Will Have to Struggle to Avoid a Recession," *Business Week,* 2 November 1987, pp. 42–43; "How the Bull Crashed Into Reality," *Business Week,* 2 November 1987, pp. 48–50.
8. Root, "Some Trends in the World Economy."
9. United Nations Center on Transnational Corporations, *Transnational Corporations in World Development,* (London: Graham & Trotman, 1985), p. 207.
10. William A. Dymsza, "Trends in Multinational Business and Global Environment: A Perspective," *Journal of International Business Studies* (Winter 1984): 25–46.
11. Yair Aharoni, "On the Definition of a Multinational Corporation," *The Quarterly Review of Economics and Business* 11 (Autumn 1971): 27–37.
12. U.S. Department of Commerce, International Trade Administration, *Current International Position* (May 1983), p. 1.

## SUGGESTED READINGS

Abernathy, William J., Kim B. Clark, and Alan M. Kantrow. "The New Industrial Competition." *Harvard Business Review* 59 (September–October 1981): 68–81.

Aharoni, Yair. "On the Definition of a Multinational Corporation." *The Quarterly Review of Economics and Business* 11 (Autumn 1971): 27–37.

Dunning, John H. *International Production and the Multinational Enterprise.* London: Allen & Unwin, 1981., Chap. 1.

Fishwick, Frances. *Multinational Companies and Economic Concentration in Europe.* New York: Praeger, 1982.

Freeman, Orille L. *The Multinational Company: Instrument for World Growth.* New York: Praeger, 1981.

Hart, Thomas, Michael E. Porter, and Eileen Rudden. "How Global Companies Win Out." *Harvard Business Review* 60 (September–October 1982): 98–108.

UN Commission on Transnational Corporations, *Transnational Corporations in World Development: A Re-examination.* New York: United Nations, 1978.

Vernon, Raymond. *Sovereignty at Bay: The Multinational Spread of United States Enterprises.* New York: Basic Books, 1971.

Wilkins, Mira. *The Emergence of Multinational Enterprise: American Business Abroad from the Colonial Era to 1914.* Cambridge, Mass.: Harvard University Press, 1971.

———. *The Maturing of Multinational Enterprise: American Business Abroad from 1914 to 1970.* Cambridge, Mass.: Harvard University Press, 1971.

World Bank. *World Development Report 1983.* New York: Oxford University Press, 1983.

# The Economic Framework of International Business: Theories and Institutions

**B**ecause international business involves different nations, each with its own independent economic system, it is affected significantly by global economic events. An understanding of these events requires a knowledge of the concepts, the institutions, and the causal relationships between different variables that shape our global economic environment every day. Equipped with a knowledge of global economic events, the MNC manager is better prepared to evaluate the opportunities and limitations that are not found at home.

In this part we explain fundamental concepts, theories, and institutions that affect our international economic environment within which all business firms must operate. This allows us to answer some of the main questions that are raised in international business:

1. Why do nations trade?
2. What are the gains from trade?
3. Why do firms invest in a foreign country?
4. What are international trade barriers? How do they affect the free flow of goods and services across the national boundaries?
5. What are the main institutions that affect international business?
6. How does the international monetary system operate?
7. What is the significance of a country's balance of payments? How is it interpreted?
8. How is the exchange rate determined?

Part One, therefore, is intended to provide a comprehension of the global economic environment and the way that it operates.

# Chapter 2

# International Trade Theories

*T*he world of international business is extremely complicated. It includes many nations with different cultural, economic, and social backgrounds. Such complexity is further amplified by the fact that all nations are economically related to each other in one way or another. For example, the increase in oil prices by the Organization of Petroleum Exporting Countries (OPEC) in 1973, from $2.59 to $11.65 per barrel, was felt by almost everyone in the world. In the United States this resulted in an increase in oil prices and fueled inflation for years to come. As a consequence, the entire economic picture of the United States took on a new dimension. Foreign trade, investment, consumption, and government spending were all affected.

In the area of foreign trade, for example, the demand for fuel-efficient

Japanese cars increased. In the meantime demand for the U.S. manufactured automobile, the "gas guzzler," declined. This contributed to the gloomy picture of the U.S. automobile industry in the 1970s, as evidenced by the bankruptcy crisis of one of the major automobile manufacturers, Chrysler Corporation, which the U.S. government finally "bailed out." In the area of investment, the U.S. automobile manufacturers were forced to retool their industry in order to respond to the ever-increasing demand for small cars. In the area of consumption, many consumers changed their driving habits and rebudgeted their income to account for the higher fuel cost. Other industrialized nations in the world experienced similar problems in facing what was then the deepest recession since the depression of the 1930s. Oil-producing nations, however, became richer overnight and found themselves confronted with the whole range of opportunities that were setting the stage for new prosperity and the host of economic problems that could accompany it.

The decline in oil prices, starting in the early 1980s, has once again changed the economic picture of the world. This has caused some of the oil-producing nations to face one of the most serious economic crises that they have ever experienced. One of these nations, Mexico, is on the brink of bankruptcy and is unable to pay its huge debt. Two other nations, Iran and Iraq, who needed additional funds to finance their war, have been badly hurt by their shrinking oil revenues. Yet, in desperation, they kept cutting their oil prices in order to capture a larger portion of the market, worsening their economic conditions in the long run.

In the West, aided by the lower oil prices in the early 1980s, the United States was enjoying one of the lowest inflation rates it had ever experienced, contributing to the increase in consumption and investment. Yet, the United States is still struggling to resolve its balance of trade deficit (an excess of imports over exports), especially with regard to Japan, which continues to capture a large percentage of the U.S. market, mainly because of its success in producing high quality goods. The recent crash of the U.S. stock market, as we explained in Chapter 1, has opened up a new chapter in the U.S. economy. Its whole impact remains to be seen in the future.

As the previous example indicates, an increase or decrease in the price of one commodity, such as oil, creates such an enormous chain of events that it makes the analysis of all the causal relationships virtually impossible. In this situation, one finds a mass of data that is unmanageable and meaningless without a theoretical framework. To be able to use these data and to discover an orderly relationship between different economic variables, it is necessary to develop a theory. A **theory** is an abstraction of reality and is based on certain simplifying assumptions. In our example of the rise and then decline of oil prices, rather than trying to examine all the variables involved, we may concentrate on a few of them. For instance, we may ask what happens to the quantity demanded of oil as the result of an increase or decrease in the price of oil, assuming that all other things that affect the demand for oil stay constant. Such an assumption would allow us to simplify and to abstract from the myriad data related to the impact of a change in the price of oil. In fact every theory, whether in the biological, physical, or social sciences, uses the same approach, simplifying and making assumptions, and actually distorting reality. Such a methodology allows the development of a theory that, if it holds up under empirical testing, would provide us with the understanding of diverse empirical data. It will allow us to predict the future course of events with a reasonable degree of certainty.

In summary, we use theories to arrive at conclusions about the real world. A theory is an abstraction from reality and is based on certain simplifying assumptions. The test of the usefulness of a theory is its power to predict. We continue to use a given theory until certain events show it to be false. In this case a new theory could replace the old one.

Having realized the importance of theory we devote this chapter to a discussion of international trade theories. An understanding of these theories is significant because international trade is the first stage of the international operations of an enterprise. At this stage, a firm starts to export to a foreign country, and if successful, this might lead to other forms of international operation: franchising, licensing, wholly owned subsidiary, joint venture arrangements, management contracts, and turn-key operations.* For example, the decisions by companies such as International Business Machines (IBM), General Motors (GM), or General Electric (GE) to manufacture overseas were based on their desire to enhance their investment in markets that were previously served by exportation of goods from the United States.

Thus, an understanding of international trade theories is a prerequisite to the understanding of international business. This knowledge helps us answer some of the most important questions that are raised in international business:

1. Why do nations trade?
2. What are the gains from trade?
3. What type of commodities should a nation export and import?
4. What is the importance of technology in determining the patterns of trade between countries?
5. Why do some LDCs prefer to produce manufactured goods rather than raw materials and agricultural products?

In this chapter we study some of the most fundamental theories of international trade and explain their implications for an international manager.

## THEORY OF MERCANTILISM

The systematic study of international trade started in the era of mercantilism that prevailed in Europe between the sixteenth and eighteenth centuries. During this time modern nation-states were beginning to develop. The basic idea of mercantilism was that wealth is a necessary condition for national power.

---

*These concepts will be fully explained in Chapter 12.

National power is, in turn, enhanced by the increase in specie, that is, gold and silver coins. Thus, for a country which lacks gold and silver mines, the only means of acquiring gold and silver is by encouraging exports and discouraging imports.

The problem with mercantilist ideas was that they confused the concept of wealth with the acquisition of precious metal. Because they assumed that wealth was limited, they concluded that one nation's gain from trade was achieved only by another nation's loss.

David Hume, the eighteenth-century British economist, essayist, historian, and philosopher, criticized mercantilism and showed that there is a self-correcting mechanism, called the specie-flow mechanism, that makes mercantilist policies self-defeating. He explained that as a nation increases its exports and accumulates more gold and silver coins (that is, money), the money supply in the economy increases. An increase in the money supply creates an inflationary effect and increases domestic prices. Increase in domestic prices makes domestic goods more expensive for foreigners to buy, resulting in a decrease in exports. On the other hand, an increase in domestic prices makes foreign produced goods relatively cheaper than domestic ones, causing imports to increase.[1] With imports rising and exports falling, the country's money supply (supply of precious metals) will decline.

Although mercantilistic ideas have continued to be criticized by later economists, such as David Ricardo and Adam Smith, some of their teaching is still practiced in a lesser degree today. For example, in an attempt to take away some of the world economic power and leadership of the United States, France, under General Charles de Gaulle, adopted policies to increase French exports and discourage imports, particularly from the United States. Additionally, he demanded that the United States settle the payment deficit with France in gold. The mercantilist policy instituted by de Gaulle is still followed by his successors, in a less extreme fashion.[2] Today, socialists have created a France in which key industries and banks are nationalized. As a result, about one-third of France's productive capacity and 70 percent of its high-tech electronic industries are under the control of the government. Today, the government intervention in France's economy has reached a level that was practiced in the seventeenth century. Some authors have called the present governmental practice of France "high-tech mercantilism."[3]

## THEORY OF ABSOLUTE ADVANTAGE

The theory of absolute advantage was developed by Adam Smith. Smith was a leading advocate of free trade who recognized the significance of specialization and division of labor. His theory of absolute advantage states that two countries could benefit from trade if, due to natural or acquired endowments, they could provide each other with a product cheaper than it could be produced at home. This means that the total resource cost to produce a good in one country is absolutely less than the resource cost to produce the same good in another country. Thus, according to this theory, each country should specialize in the production of the goods that it can make most efficiently, that is, the goods that can be made most cheaply.

Absolute advantage might be the result of natural endowment or acquired endowment. Natural endowment includes factors that are related to climate, soil, and mineral resources. For example, some nations have petroleum and others do not. Bananas can be produced cheaply in Central America because of its tropical climate. Acquired endowments include special skills and technology. The defensive AWAC planes are produced by the United States. Saudi Arabia produces oil. Thus, according to the theory of absolute advantage the United States should export AWAC planes to Saudi Arabia, and Saudi Arabia should export petroleum to the United States. France should export wine to Sweden, and Sweden should export lumber to France. Japan should export electronic robots to Iran, and Iran should export petroleum to Japan.

The concept of absolute advantage can be explained numerically by a simple example. Let us assume that (1) two countries, England and Portugal, are both able to produce two goods, cloth and wine, (2) there are no transportation costs between these countries, (3) competitive conditions prevail, (4) labor is the only factor of production and thus the only cost of production, (5) labor is freely mobile within countries but not between countries, and (6) there is no government intervention. The following hypothetical example (Table 2.1) shows the production resulting from 1 day (8 hours) of labor.

According to Table 2.1, Portugal's absolute advantage is in the production of wine, because 1 day of labor produces 10 gallons of wine in Portugal as compared to 5 gallons of wine in England. England's absolute advantage is in the production of cloth, because 1 day of labor produces 10 yards of cloth in England as compared to 5 yards in Portugal. Thus, it is sensible for England to specialize in the production of cloth and export it to Portugal, importing wine. The reverse is true for Portugal.

We may now introduce the concept of opportunity cost to show the extent by which each country benefits from trade. The *opportunity cost* is the value of the benefit foregone when choosing one alternative rather than another. In our example, it simply means that which a nation would have to give up of one good when choosing to produce another good. For example, the opportunity cost of 1 gallon of wine in England is 2 yards of cloth, because 1 day of labor can produce either 10 yards of cloth or 5 gallons of wine.

Table 2.1  PRODUCTION FROM ONE DAY OF LABOR AT
          FULL EMPLOYMENT

|          | Cloth output (yards per day) | Wine output (gallons per day) |
|----------|------------------------------|-------------------------------|
| England  | 10                           | 5                             |
| Portugal | 5                            | 10                            |

Both countries could gain from trade if they specialize and exchange wine for cloth at a relative price ratio of 1:1, that is, by trading 1 gallon of wine for 1 yard of cloth. As a result, England can employ more of its resources to produce cloth, and Portugal more of its resources to produce wine. England can export 1 yard of cloth for 1 gallon of wine, as opposed to trading 1 yard of cloth for ½ gallon of wine at home, thereby gaining ½ gallon of wine for each yard of cloth exported. In the same manner, Portugal could gain ½ yard of cloth for each gallon of wine exported to England.

In summary, the theory of absolute advantage suggests that

1. The higher the level of specialization by a country, according to its absolute advantage, the more there would be a potential gain from trade.
2. Both trading partners would gain from trade in such a situation.

The above conclusions are in contrast with mercantilist thoughts which imply one country's gain from trade is achieved by another country's loss.

## THEORY OF COMPARATIVE ADVANTAGE

The theory of absolute advantage examined previously showed the effects of trade when each trading partner had an absolute advantage in the production of only one commodity. A more complicated case emerges when a country could produce both goods with an absolute advantage, that is, at a lower cost than the other country. David Ricardo first demonstrated this case in his theory of comparative advantage. He showed that both trading nations can benefit from trade even when one of the nations has an absolute advantage in the production of both commodities. In terms of our previous example of two countries, England and Portugal, and two goods, cloth and wine, Ricardo's theory can be explained by the use of Table 2.2. As this table indicates, England has an absolute advantage in the production of both commodities. One day of labor produces 60 yards of cloth and 30 gallons of wine in England as compared to 10 yards of cloth and 20 gallons of wine in Portugal. This might lead one to think that trade is not advantageous for England. Yet, trade is still profitable to both countries, because the relative cost of production in both countries is different. The cost ratios shown in the table show how cloth and wine are exchanged in each country before trade takes place. As Table 2.2 indicates, before trade 2 yards of cloth in England can be exchanged for 1 gallon of wine.

Table 2.2   PRODUCTION FROM ONE DAY OF LABOR AT FULL EMPLOYMENT

|  | Cloth output (yards per day) | Wine output (gallons per day) | Cost ratio (cloth to wine) |
| --- | --- | --- | --- |
| England | 60 | 30 | 2:1 = 2.0 |
| Portugal | 10 | 20 | 1:2 = 0.5 |

In other words, 1 yard of cloth commands ½ gallon of wine in England. In Portugal, on the other hand, 1 yard of cloth is exchanged for 2 gallons of wine. This shows that cloth is relatively cheaper in England, while wine is relatively cheaper in Portugal. If England exports 1 yard of cloth to Portugal it could receive 2 gallons of wine, as opposed to ½ gallon at home. If Portugal exports 1 gallon of wine to England it could receive 2 yards of cloth, as opposed to ½ yard at home. Therefore England should export cloth to Portugal and Portugal should export wine to England. However, as the wine exports of Portugal enter England, the supply of wine in England will increase and the price will fall. Similarly, in Portugal, the cloth imports from England will increase its supply, decreasing its price. This process continues until the price ratios in England and Portugal will become equal to each other. In other words, trade would equalize the relative prices in these two countries. At this new price, it pays for both countries to specialize in the production of the commodity in which they have a comparative advantage. England specializes in the production of cloth and Portugal specializes in the production of wine. In this way both countries would export the extra commodity that they produce at home and import the commodity that they would not produce.

Thus, according to the theory of comparative advantage, if one country could produce each of the two goods more efficiently than another country, and could produce one of these goods more efficiently than the other, it should specialize in that commodity and export that commodity in which it is comparatively more efficient, that is, the commodity in which it has the greatest absolute advantage. The less efficient nation should specialize in and export the commodity in which it is comparatively less inefficient, that is, the commodity in which it has the least disadvantage.

## HECKSCHER-OHLIN THEORY

Ricardo's theory of comparative advantage assumes that domestic differences in natural or acquired endowment give rise to differential factor productivities that provide the basis for trade among nations. This implies that the primary determinant of the basis for trade is factor productivity.*

Eli Heckscher and Bertil Ohlin, two Swedish economists, argued that international differentials in supply conditions explain the direction of international trade. They explained that supply includes not only factor productivities but factor endowments as well.† Their ideas gave rise to the development of a theory that considers factor endowment as the primary cause of international trade.

---

*The term "factor productivity" refers to the productivity of the factors of production. For example, labor productivity is measured as output per day in Table 2.1.

†The term "factor endowment" refers to the relative abundance of factors of production in a country. For example, some countries have more capital relative to labor (they are capital abundant); other countries have more labor relative to capital (they are labor abundant).

According to this theory the price differentials among nations are related to two factors: (1) differences in relative endowments of the factors of production that exist among countries, and (2) differences in the intensities of factor usage in the production of different commodities. Given these circumstances the Heckscher-Ohlin (H-O) theory states that each country should export those commodities that use its abundant factor more intensively, importing goods that use its scarce factor more intensively.* This means, for example, countries that have an abundance of labor, such as India or Hong Kong, should export commodities such as cloth, which require a labor-intensive technology. On the other hand, a capital-abundant country like the United States should export commodities such as airplanes and electronic computers, which require capital-intensive technology.

## LEONTIEF PARADOX

In 1953, Professor Wassily Leontief provided the first major attempt to empirically examine the Heckscher-Ohlin theory. Using the U.S. trade data for 1947, he analyzed the capital to labor ratio for some 200 export industries and import-competing industries. He found that the capital to labor ratio for the U.S. export industries was lower than that of its import-competing industries. In other words, his results suggested that the United States exported goods that were relatively labor intensive and imported commodities that were relatively capital intensive. Given that the United States was considered to be a capital-abundant and a labor-scarce country at the time of the study, Leontief's results seemed to contradict the H-O theory, which predicted that a capital-abundant country would export relatively capital-intensive goods. To further examine the H-O theory, Leontief did another study, using 1951 data, and again he found that U.S. exports were relatively less capital intensive than U.S. imports. To explain the paradox, Leontief argued that the United States is two to three times more efficient than other countries. If the labor supply in the United States were adjusted to account for this efficiency, the United States could actually be considered a labor-abundant nation.

Leontief's paradoxical conclusion gave rise to similar studies for other countries. For example, a case study of Japan, by Tatemoto and Ichimura in 1959, suggested that Japanese exports were capital intensive and its imports were relatively labor intensive. Because Japan was believed to be a labor-abundant country at the time of the study, the paradox was repeated. However a more careful analysis of the patterns of Japanese exports revealed that Japanese exports to less developed countries (LDCs) tended to be relatively capital intensive, whereas its exports to advanced countries—the United States and Western

---

*The term "factor" here refers to the factors of production, for example, capital and labor. A factor of production could be abundant (cheap) or it could be scarce (expensive).

countries—tended to be labor intensive. This explanation seems to conform to the H-O theory, because Japan is a relatively labor-abundant country as compared to the United States, and it is relatively capital-abundant in comparison to its LDC trading partners.

## COMPARATIVE LABOR COSTS THEORY

The empirical investigation of the H-O theory started by Leontief and followed by many other economists raised questions about the theory's applicability. This led some economists to explain the international trade patterns in terms of a comparative labor costs theory. The idea behind this theory is the realization that the unit labor cost of each commodity is determined by two factors, namely, labor productivity and wage level. Thus, according to this theory, when comparing two countries' exports, both of these factors should be taken into consideration.

If two countries, A and B, have the same wage level but country A has a relatively higher labor productivity, this means that country A can produce the same product more cheaply than country B. This is because an hour of labor in country A produces more output than an hour of labor in country B. This, in turn, causes the cost per unit of the product to decrease.

Even a country that has both higher wage levels and higher labor productivity can still produce a good more cheaply than another country, if the overall difference in productivity could more than offset the overall difference in wage rates. For example, suppose that countries A and B are producing a commodity that requires only labor. Country A pays $10 an hour for labor, and spends 1 hour to produce 1 unit of the commodity. Country B pays only $5 an hour. However it takes this country 3 hours to produce 1 unit of the same commodity. Although the wage rate is higher in the more efficient country, country A, its cost of production ($10 $\times$ 1 = $10) is lower than country B ($5 $\times$ 3 = $15).

One of the earliest empirical studies of the comparative labor costs theory was done by the British economist G. D. A. MacDougall in 1950. He chose a sample of 25 separate industries in the United States and the United Kingdom, and compared their labor productivities and wage rates. His analysis showed that:

1. The U.S. labor productivity was greater than it was in the United Kingdom (see Table 2.3).
2. On average, the U.S. wage rates were two times as high as U.K. wage rates.

Given the above results, one would expect that the United States' share of world export markets should be greater than the United Kingdom's share in those industries where the U.S. labor productivity was more than two times greater than the United Kingdom's labor productivity. One would also expect a higher share of export markets for the United Kingdom in those industries

**Table 2.3   UNITED STATES AND UNITED KINGDOM PREWAR OUTPUT PER WORKER AND QUANTITY OF EXPORTS IN 1937**[a]

**U.S. outputs per worker more than twice United Kingdom:**

| | | |
|---|---|---|
| Wireless sets and valves | U.S. exports | 8 times U.K. exports |
| Pig iron | U.S. exports | 5 times U.K. exports |
| Motor cars | U.S. exports | 4 times U.K. exports |
| Glass containers | U.S. exports | 3.5 times U.K. exports |
| Tin cans | U.S. exports | 3 times U.K. exports |
| Machinery | U.S. exports | 1.5 times U.K. exports |
| Paper | U.S. exports | 1 times U.K. exports |

**U.S. output per worker 1.4 to 2.0 times the United Kingdom:**

| | | |
|---|---|---|
| Cigarettes | U.K. exports | 2 times U.S. exports |
| Linoleum, oilcloth, etc. | U.K. exports | 3 times U.S. exports |
| Hosiery | U.K. exports | 3 times U.S. exports |
| Leather footwear | U.K. exports | 3 times U.S. exports |
| Coke | U.K. exports | 5 times U.S. exports |
| Rayon weaving | U.K. exports | 5 times U.S. exports |
| Cotton goods | U.K. exports | 9 times U.S. exports |
| Rayon making | U.K. exports | 11 times U.S. exports |
| Beer | U.K. exports | 18 times U.S. exports |

**U.S. output per worker less than 1.4 times United Kingdom:**

| | | |
|---|---|---|
| Cement | U.K. exports | 11 times U.S. exports |
| Men's/boys' outer clothing of wool | U.K. exports | 23 times U.S. exports |
| Margarine | U.K. exports | 32 times U.S. exports |
| Woolen and worsted | U.K. exports | 250 times U.S. exports |

[a]Exceptions (U.S. output per worker more than twice the British, but U.K. exports exceed U.S. exports): electric lamps, rubber tires, soaps, biscuits, matches.

*Source:* G. D. A. MacDougall, "British and American Exports: A Study Suggested by the Theory of Comparative Costs," reprinted in Caves and Johnson, eds., *Readings in International Economics* (Homewood, Ill.: Irwin, 1968), p. 554.

where the United Kingdom's labor was more than half as productive as compared to the United States.

According to the data presented in Table 2.3, out of 25 industries that were investigated by MacDougall, 20 followed the expected outcome. The United States' share of the export market was largest when the labor productivity was at least two times as great as the U.K. productivity. By relating export patterns to wage levels and productivity MacDougall's comparative cost theory added a new dimension to the factor endowment theory. However, this theory, like its predecessors, is not without its limitations. One of its major limitations is that it relates the export patterns to labor, ignoring the impact of other factors of production. Another problem with the theory is that it does not account for differences in product quality. For example, one reason for the popularity of Japanese cars in the United States is their superior quality, as compared to similar American cars. Thus, in using the theory of comparative cost one should incorporate the above factors before explaining a country's comparative position.

## THEORY OF OVERLAPPING DEMAND

The thrust of the H-O theory, as we explained earlier, is based on the premise that the trading partners are dissimilar with regard to their factor endowments. It is this dissimilarity on the supply side that gives rise to trade between different nations. Thus, in applying this theory to the real world, one would expect that the main bulk of international trade would be undertaken between the labor-abundant developing countries and the capital-abundant industrialized countries. Unfortunately, however, the empirical evidence presented since World War II provides results that are contradictory to the H-O theory. It was shown that international trade basically involved the industrialized nations, which traded their manufactured goods with each other. This finding casts further doubt on the validity of the H-O theory and its ability to explain the trade in manufactured goods. Thus, the stage was set for the development of a new theory by a Swedish economist, Staffan Linder.

According to Linder, the main element that causes trade in manufactured goods is domestic demand conditions. The production and sale of a product start first in a domestic market, where the demand and the market conditions are familiar to the producer. It is the domestic demand that gives rise to the production and allows the producer to grow large enough to be able to compete in foreign markets.

Because the decision to produce is initially based on local demand conditions, it is reasonable to assume that trade would take place between countries that have similar demand conditions for their manufactured goods. In other words, the entrepreneur tries to minimize the risk of unknown factors by operating in countries where demand patterns are very similar to the domestic market. Thus, according to Linder, trade in manufactured goods is mainly attributed to the existence of overlapping demand among the trading partners.

To provide further explanation of the theory of overlapping demand, Linder regarded income as the main variable that gives rise to demand. He explained that tastes and preferences for a certain commodity materialize only when they are supported by income. It follows that, according to the overlapping demand theory, international trade in manufactured goods would be undertaken by countries that have similar income levels. Thus the more similar two countries are with respect to income, the greater the potential would be for mutual trade in manufactured products.

## TECHNOLOGICAL GAP THEORY

The inability of the H-O theory to explain trade in manufacturing was first noticed by Irving Kravis. His work, along with other authors, underlined the importance of technology in explaining the patterns of trade between countries.

We explained earlier that according to the H-O theory each country should export the commodities that use its abundant factors more intensively. Thus, according to the theory, a labor-abundant country, paying relatively low wages, should export labor-intensive commodities. However, Kravis's empirical investigation of the H-O theory provided contradictory results. He learned that in virtually every country studied the exporting industries were those that paid the highest wages. To explain this contradiction, Kravis maintained that each country would, in essence, export the commodity that its entrepreneurs could best develop. If a country has cheap labor to produce, say, pocket calculators, but lacks the innovators, entrepreneurs, and skilled labor to develop this product, then production and exportation of the product would not take place. In other words, what counts for a country that wants to export a technically advanced product is its technological superiority over its trading partners.

The pioneering work of Kravis was followed by the research of a number of writers, giving rise to the technological gap theory. M. Posner introduced the concept of *imitation lag* to elaborate on the possibility of international trade between countries. He divided the lag into two components: the **demand lag**, and the **reaction lag**. When new products are imported into a country, it would take time for a demand to develop. This is because the new foreign goods may not be a perfect substitute for existing domestic goods and consumers may be unfamiliar with the new product. The demand lag is the time needed for the development of the demand for newly exported goods. The reaction lag is the time it takes for the local entrepreneur to react to the competition from abroad by starting his/her own local production. The difference between these two lags causes international trade to take place. A manufacturer might export a commodity to a nation when the demand lag is shorter than the reaction lag.

In his study, Gary Haufbauer used the concept of *imitation lag* to explain the pattern of trade in synthetic materials. He found that a country's share of exports in synthetic materials could be explained by the imitation lag and the market size.

Ranking countries according to their imitation lags, he learned that new synthetics were introduced rather consistently in countries at the top of the rank and then exported to other countries down the rank. The spread of the technology caused the movement of production of new synthetics down the rank, displacing the exports of the top countries. Top countries, however, then engaged in the development and exportation of new products.

Gordon Douglass used the concept of imitation lag to explain the patterns of export in motion pictures from the United States. He argued that once a country was a leader in a given product it would have a continuing advantage in related products. The United States pioneered in many film innovations and was successfully able to continue its exportation by incorporating product innovations such as the "talkies," color movies, and wide-screen movies, which were not yet available in other countries. After a lag, when the technology became commonplace, it was observed that the United States might or might not continue her exportation of movies, or trade might move in both directions.

In summary, the empirical findings of the technological gap theory support the view that technology is the most significant element in explaining the pattern of international trade. As these findings suggest, the production and exportation of a product starts in a technologically advanced country like the United States. As the technology becomes commonplace and the country starts losing its export market for that product, a new product is developed and the same pattern is followed as with the old product.

The technological gap theory is similar to the product life cycle theory, which is explained in the next section. These two theories are consistent with each other, and both see technology as the most significant factor in explaining patterns of international trade.

## PRODUCT LIFE CYCLE THEORY

Product life cycle theory, which was initially known as "product cycle," was pioneered by Raymond Vernon. The theory was further developed by Louis Wells, who applied it to marketing and used the term "product life cycle." According to this theory manufactured goods pass through a product life cycle. During this cycle a country like the United States, which is initially an exporter, would eventually lose its export market and become an importer of the product. On the basis of this theory we can divide the life of a product into five stages: (1) new, (2) expansion, (3) maturity, (4) sales decline, and (5) demise. Figures 2.1(a) and 2.1(b) illustrate the stages of a product life cycle. In both figures time is measured on the horizontal axis. Figure 2.1(a) shows how the U.S. sales volume, measured on the vertical axis, changes over time.

Figure 2.1(b) shows the net exports, measured on the vertical axis, of different countries over time. At the first stage a firm in an advanced country, say the United States, innovates a product at the time $t_0$, and begins its production and sale in the U.S. local market. At this stage the firm has a virtual monopoly over the new product in the world market. As the firm's operation expands and foreign demand is developed, the firm takes advantage of its economies of scale and exports the product to other nations at the time $t_1$. By the time the product enters its third stage, at time $t_2$, the income and the product familiarity abroad have increased. Higher demand for the product overseas induces some entrepreneurs, or companies in other industrialized nations (that is, in Canada, the European nations, and Japan), to take advantage of the situation and start production. In some cases, some of the U.S. manufacturers may start building their production facilities abroad in order to protect their share of the market, which could be in danger of being lost due to tougher competition in the foreign market. As foreign producers become larger and their ability to pro-

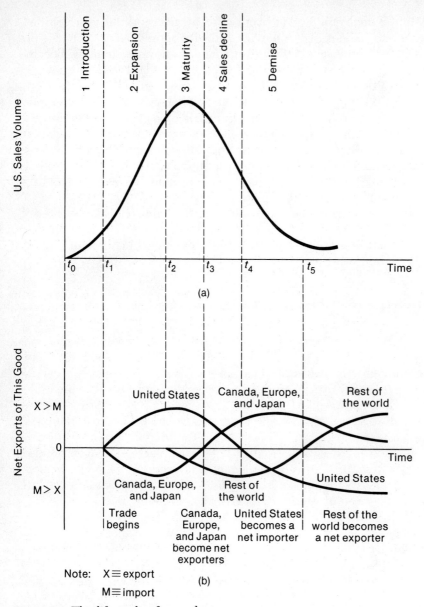

**Figure 2.1** The life cycle of a product

*Source:* Adapted from Louis T. Wells, Jr., ed., *The Product Life Cycle and International Trade* (Boston: Division of Research, Harvard Business School, 1972), p.15. Reprinted by permisssion of Harvard Business School Press.

duce at a lower cost increases, they would become net exporters of the product at the time $t_3$. This would bring the product to its fourth stage. By this time the production has become increasingly standardized. Firms in other nations take advantage of the economies of scale that were previously available to the U.S. manufacturers. This would enable them to cut their costs, causing the United States to lose its competitive advantage and become a net importer of the product at time $t_4$. At the final stage, at time $t_5$, the product is so commonplace that it would be exported from low income, less developed countries to higher income, advanced countries. This happens because the lower wage rates in LDCs would outweigh the superior technology of the advanced countries.

The product life cycle theory has provided a convincing explanation of the pattern of world trade in manufactured goods, and the pattern of foreign direct investment, for the early post–World War II period. During this period, the research and development activities of the United States led to the innovation and production of new products. Later, as the market expanded, these products were exported to other countries. Eventually, demand for these products increased to a level that was sufficient to support local production facilities in other countries. At this stage, as competition in foreign markets became tougher, the U.S. share of the exports market was threatened. In response, the U.S. multinational corporations either shifted their production facilities to low-cost countries, or allowed local firms in those countries to take over production. This resulted in the production by the low-wage LDCs of some products, which were then exported back to advanced countries.

Much production by multinational corporations is not initiated by an innovation, as the theory leads us to believe, but takes place due to a cost advantage. The theory does not explain the reason why MNCs invest abroad instead of, for example, engaging in a contractual agreement or licensing. Additionally, much of foreign investment by MNCs, especially in the raw materials industries, does not seem to follow a product life cycle.[4]

## IMMISERIZING GROWTH

As we discussed earlier, according to the theory of comparative advantage each country should specialize in and export the goods in which it is comparatively more efficient than its trading partner. Because the comparative advantage of most of the less developed countries lies in the production of the primary products, they should, according to the theory, specialize in and export these products. Around the mid-1950s, however, economists presented cases that showed that the pursuit of the dictates of the theory of comparative advantage actually makes the LDCs worse off, or the pursuit "immiserizes" them. The possibility of "immiserizing growth," which was emphasized by Jagdish N. Bhagwati, was later studied by Harry Johnson and Carlos Diaz Alejandro. Through their work, the concept of immiserizing growth came to be known as an expansion of the factor supply or productivity that makes a nation worse off. The possibility of immiserizing growth occurs when an increase in the supply of a tradeable good tends to decrease its price in the world market. If the magnitude of the price decrease is large enough, it might have an adverse effect on the exporting country, thereby worsening its welfare.

Take the case of Brazil, which is the world's largest coffee bean exporter. Assume a technological advance in coffee bean production is introduced to this country. This would encourage an individual coffee bean grower to take advantage of the situation and increase production and sales. Because all farmers might behave in this fashion, their collective action may result in a considerable increase in output. Given that Brazil has a large share of the world's coffee bean market, and given an inelastic demand for coffee beans, the expansion of the coffee bean supply by Brazil results in a lower world price for coffee beans. If the magnitude of this price decline is large enough to outweigh the increase in the quantity supplied, the Brazilian's revenue from coffee bean exports would decrease. In this way, Brazil's own improvements in the technology, and the resulting increases in the supply, make Brazil's terms of trade (the amount of goods exported per unit imported) worse off. When this happens additional international trade would actually worsen Brazil's economic welfare rather than improve it.

Several conditions are necessary for immiserizing growth to occur:

1. The world's demand for the country's exports must be inelastic, such that an expansion in the quantity of exports results in a large decline in price.
2. The country's economic growth must be biased toward the export sector.
3. The country's economy must be dependent on international trade to the extent that a decline in world prices for its exports could outweigh the gains possible from being able to supply more of the product.

Although immiserizing growth might have taken place for an LDC like Brazil, it does not seem very prevalent in the real world, but it is a possibility. And if it does occur, it would bring with it unpleasant results. Because immiserizing growth takes place only in the presence of an inelastic demand, it is possible for a country to exploit this inelasticity by imposing optimum tariffs and taxes on exports. The success of such a strategy depends on the market power exercised by the country in question; and the market power, in turn, is limited by the existence of potential new entrants into the world market.

## PREBISCH THEORY

The possibility of the existence of immiserizing growth in the LDCs gave rise to a new argument that questioned the wisdom of pursuing policies that were based on the theory of comparative advantage. Raul Prebisch, a Latin American economist, and others in the early 1960s, argued that the LDCs, primarily exporters of agricultural products and raw materials, facing an inelastic demand in their export markets, were not gaining and would not gain from trade with the advanced countries.* Because the prices of these products relative to manufactured goods had been declining and unstable, Prebisch and others argued, the terms of trade had been deteriorating for these countries. They also believed that the initial export by an LDC to an advanced country would bring a higher gain to the advanced country, alleging that the advanced country is in a more advantageous position.

Given the above arguments, their policy recommendation to the LDCs was that

1. They should decrease the resources that are used for the output and export of their primary product sector.
2. They should expand the resources that are used in their modern and industrial sector.
3. They should restrict the import of the industrial goods into their countries, replacing these imports with goods produced domestically.
4. They should demand a decrease in the trade barriers that are imposed upon them by the advanced countries against their industrial products.

The Prebisch theory created a great deal of controversy, especially regarding the validity of the facts that were presented in its support. The theory was based on data related to the long-run movements of the British terms of trade from the late 1800s to the end of the 1930s. Questions have been raised concerning the adequacy of such data. To be sure, the British terms of trade did improve, whereas the terms of trade of its trading partners declined during the period. However, it is argued that the British export and import structure was unique and as such it does not lend itself to generalization about the deterioration of the terms of trade of today's LDCs. Additionally, such data do not provide proper allowance for quality changes that occur for a product. The evidence shows that the quality of primary products usually stays fairly constant, whereas the quality of manufactured products keeps on improving as time goes by. For example, the quality of Brazilian coffee beans is almost the same as it was years ago, whereas a 1989 model of an IBM computer is much more sophisticated than a 1970 model. Thus, if the quality changes are taken into consideration, one could argue that the terms of trade of the LDCs may not have deteriorated over time. In other words, the reason that an LDC exported more primary products per unit of manufactured goods over time could be related to the relative rising value of the manufactured goods as compared to the value of primary products over the same time. In our example, the quality of the Brazilian coffee beans has stayed fairly constant. Because in a competitive market a relatively higher quality commodity commands a relatively higher price, then more Brazilian coffee beans must be exported per unit of the IBM computer imported into Brazil.

To date, the evidence indicates that periods of worsening terms of trade

---

*Both income elasticity of demand and price elasticity of demand for primary products are low.

have alternated with periods of improving terms of trade. Thus, it is believed that policymakers should not discourage investment on the primary products on the grounds that these sectors inevitably face unfavorable price trends, for this may not happen. Research has also shown that, contrary to the Prebisch theory, in some cases the gain from the initial opening of trade accrued mainly to the primary product exporters in the LDCs, as opposed to their trading partners in the advanced countries.

With all its controversies, the Prebisch theory has had an enormous impact on the economic policies of the LDCs, especially those in Latin America. Many of these countries, such as Colombia, Peru, and Chile, have vigorously followed the policies of *import substitution*—substituting domestic production of manufactured goods for the exportation of raw materials. Such policies, implemented by the imposition of taxes and tariffs on the importation of manufactured goods from abroad, have resulted in high production costs, for domestically manufactured goods. For example, in Colombia, Peru, and Chile the production costs of vehicles ran two to three times higher than the costs of similar vehicles in the international market. As we explain later in Chapter 4, policies of indiscriminate import substitution have proven to be self-defeating. Such policies, which give rise to inefficient and costly production, would result in losses for both consumers and producers, thereby reducing the world's welfare.

## THE RELEVANCE OF INTERNATIONAL TRADE THEORIES FOR INTERNATIONAL BUSINESS

Trade theories have important implications for international business. These theories have been developed in response to a need, that is, a desire to predict the future course of events with a reasonable degree of accuracy. The understanding of these theories helps to explain the rationale for the pursuit of the different trade policies by different nations over time. For example, the theory of mercantilism, developed in the sixteenth century, is practiced today, in less extreme terms, by France. In another example, the Prebisch theory set the foundation for the adherence to the import substitution policies that are followed by many LDCs today, such as Colombia, Peru, and Chile.

Trade theories are useful in providing a framework that can assist business persons or government authorities in formulating their international trade policies. For a business person, the life cycle theory, for instance, can provide a framework that is helpful in scrutinizing products that are likely candidates for export. As the life cycle theory suggests, the newly developed products that have a high technological base, such as a personal computer, are more apt to be marketable in a high-income advanced country than in an LDC. Trade theories can also help the government authorities in an LDC by providing them with guidelines regarding the direction that their trade should follow. For example, if a labor-abundant LDC plans to enhance its exports, it should concentrate on the production of standardized products because, according to the life cycle theory, these products will generate more exports than other products.

Trade theories enable us to understand the implications of a country's decisions regarding different international economic issues, allowing us to better plan a corporation's future strategy. For example, trade theories tell us that, under certain conditions, the devaluation of a country's currency, that is, the lowering of the value of its currency in terms of other currencies, will cause its export prices to fall and its import prices to rise. This would lead to an increase in its export volume and a decrease in its import volume, improving the country's balance of payments.* From the international business standpoint, this means that the country's export market would improve and would warrant a strategy of expanding production activities abroad. A case in point is the recent devaluation of Chinese currency in February 1986. This devaluation, which lowered the value of the currency 13 to 14 percent against other major currencies, is expected to encourage the existing corporations in China to enhance their export activities, and also to attract more foreign investors.[5]

In summary, trade theories are useful in assisting an international manager, or a government authority, in formulating policies with regard to international business. These theories are also helpful in understanding the hows and whys of different policies that are undertaken by people involved in international business. It is important to keep in mind that these theories are abstractions from reality and, as such, they provide us with a framework that may be helpful in the analysis of international business. To be useful, such a framework should be employed along with the additional information that is gathered in the real world with regard to a given problem.

## SUMMARY

1. A theory is an abstraction from reality and is based on certain simplifying assumptions. The test of the usefulness of a theory is its power to predict. We continue to use a given theory until certain events falsify it. When this happens, a new theory replaces the old one.
2. The basic idea of mercantilism is that wealth is a necessary condition for national power. National power is, in turn, enhanced by the increase in specie. Thus, for a country that lacks gold and silver mines the only means of acquiring gold and silver is by encouraging exports and discouraging imports.
3. The theory of absolute advantage states that each country should specialize in goods that it can produce most efficiently, that is, goods that it can make most cheaply.
4. According to the theory of comparative advantage, if one country could produce each of the two goods more efficiently than another country, and could produce one of these goods more efficiently than the other, it should specialize in that commodity and export that commodity in which it is comparatively more efficient, that is, the commodity in which it has the greatest absolute advantage. The less efficient nation should specialize in and export the commodity in which it is comparatively less inefficient, that is, the commodity in which it has the least disadvantage.
5. According to the H-O theory, each country should export those commodities that

_____

*As we will explain in Chapter 6, the balance of payments is a statement that shows the amount of foreign currency that was pumped into and out of a nation's economic system in a given period of time—usually a year.

use its abundant factor more intensively, importing commodities that use its scarce factor more intensively.

6. Leontief's paradox provided the first major challenge to the H-O theory. His study suggested that the United States exports goods that are relatively labor intensive and imports goods that are capital intensive.

7. The idea behind comparative labor costs theory is the realization that the unit labor cost of each commodity is determined by two factors, that is, labor productivity and wage level. Thus, according to this theory, when comparing two countries' exports, both of these factors should be taken into consideration.

8. The theory of overlapping demand states that international trade in manufactured goods would be undertaken by countries that have a similar demand and income level. Thus, the more similar two countries are with respect to demand and income, the greater the potential would be for trade between them in manufactured products.

9. According to the product life cycle theory, manufactured goods pass through five different stages: (a) new, (b) expansion, (c) maturity, (d) sales decline, and (e) demise. During the life cycle of a product, a country like the United States that is initially an exporter of the product would eventually lose its export market and become an importer of the product.

10. The technological gap theory relates the trade between nations to the existence of the technological gaps among them. According to this theory, it is the technological superiority of a country that gives it an advantage in securing export markets.

11. According to Posner, the possibility of international trade between nations could be explained by the *imitation lag*. This lag is composed of the *demand lag*, and the *reaction lag*. The demand lag is the time that is needed for the development of demand for a newly exported good. The reaction lag refers to the time that it takes for the local entrepreneur in the importing country to react to the competition from abroad by starting local production. The difference in time between these two lags causes the international trade to take place.

12. Immiserizing growth is an expansion of factor supply or productivity that makes a nation worse off when it exports the goods it specializes in producing.

13. According to the Prebisch theory, because world prices for primary products have been declining and unstable, the terms of trade for LDCs have deteriorated over time. Thus, LDCs should restrict the import of industrial goods into their countries, replacing these imports with goods produced domestically.

14. Trade theories have important implications for international business. The understanding of these theories is significant because (a) they explain the rationale for the pursuit of the different trade policies undertaken by different nations over time; (b) they are useful in providing a framework that can assist a business person or a governmental authority in formulating their international trade policies; and (c) they enable us to understand the implications of a country's decisions regarding different international economic issues, allowing us to plan better the corporation's future strategy.

## QUESTIONS

2.1 Compare the theory of comparative advantage and the theory of absolute advantage.

2.2 Explain the difference between the H-O theory and the theory of comparative advantage.

**2.3** Briefly discuss the mercantilist's ideas with regard to international trade. Give an example of this theory as it exists today. What are fallacies of this theory?

**2.4** Explain the Leontief paradox. Has the theory proven to be correct?

**2.5** Graphically illustrate and verbally explain the product life cycle theory. Explain the usefulness of this theory for the manager of an MNC. Give examples of nations that have gone through stages of the product life cycle.

**2.6** Explain the Prebisch theory. What is the basis of this theory? What are the policy implications of this theory? Give examples of countries that are in one way or another following the Prebisch recommendations.

**2.7** Discuss the usefulness of trade theories for business, using real life examples.

**2.8** As you recall, in Chapter 1, using Table 1.3, it is pointed out that advanced industrial nations are the major trading partners for most goods and services that are traded internationally. Which one of the theories that we explained in Chapter 2 is in accord with the above statement? Explain this theory and elaborate on its implications for LDCs.

**2.9** Assume that a two-country trading world consists of France and Costa Rica. The following table explains the amount of output produced by each country:

| | | Output of | |
| | Labor input | Wine | Beef |
| Country | (days) | (gallons) | (pounds) |
|---|---|---|---|
| France | 2 | 140 | 70 |
| Costa Rica | 2 | 20 | 60 |

**(a)** Which country, if any, has an absolute advantage in production? A comparative advantage? Explain.

**(b)** In what commodity does each country specialize?

**(c)** What are gains from trade?

# NOTES

1. David Hume, "Of Money," *Essays* (London: Green, 1912), vol. 1, p. 319; See also Eugene Rotwein, *The Economic Writings of David Hume* (Edinburgh: Nelson, 1955).
2. Alan M. Rugman, Donald J. Lecraw, and Laurence D. Booth, *International Business: Firm and Environment* (New York: McGraw-Hill, 1985), pp. 26–27.
3. Donald A. Ball and H. Wendell McCulloch, Jr., *International Business: Introduction and Essentials*, 2nd ed. (Plano, Tex.: Business Publications, 1985), p. 61.
4. H. Ian Giddy, "The Demise of the Product Cycle Model in International Business Theory," *Columbia Journal of World Business* (Spring 1978): 90–97.
5. "China Devalues Its Currency 13.6% Against U.S. Dollar to Aid Its Economy," *The Wall Street Journal*, 7 July 1986, p. 17.

## SUGGESTED READINGS

Bhagwati, J. N. "Immiserizing Growth." *Readings in International Economics.* Homewood, Ill.: Irwin, 1967.

Douglass, G. K. "Product Variation and International Trade in Motion Pictures." Ph.D. diss., Massachusetts Institute of Technology, Cambridge, Mass., 1963.

Grubel, Herbert G. *International Economics,* rev. ed. Homewood, Ill.: Irwin, 1982.

Hecksher, E. "The Effects of Foreign Trade on Distribution of Income." *Economisc Tidskrift* 21 (1919): 497–512.

Hufbauer, G. C. *Synthetic Materials and the Theory of International Trade.* Cambridge, Mass.: Harvard University Press, 1966.

Johnson, H. G. *Economic Policies Toward Less Developed Countries.* New York: Praeger, 1967.

Kravis, I. B., and R. E. Lipsey. *Price Competitiveness in World Trade.* New York: National Bureau of Economic Research, 1971.

Leontief, W. "Domestic Production and Foreign Trade: The American Capital Position Reexamined." *Proceedings of the American Philosophical Society* 97 (September 1953).

Linder, S. B. *An Essay on Trade and Transformation.* New York: Wiley, 1981. Chap. 3.

McDougall, G. D. A. "British and American Exports: A Study Suggested by the Theory of Comparative Costs." *Economic Journal* 6 (1951): 697–724.

Ohlin, Bertil. *Interregional and International Trade.* Cambridge, Mass.: Harvard University Press, 1933.

Posner, M. "International Trade and Technical Change." *Oxford Economic Paper* 13 (October 1961): 323–341.

Prebisch, R. *Toward a New Trade Policy for Development.* New York: United Nations, 1964.

Salvatore, D. *Theory and Problems of International Economics.* New York: McGraw-Hill, 1985. Chaps. 1–2.

Smith, Adam. "An Inquiry into the Nature and Causes of the Wealth of Nations." In Allen R. William, ed., *International Trade Theory: Hume to Ohlin.* New York: Random House, 1965.

Vernon, R. "International Investment and International Trade in the Product Life Cycle." *Quarterly Journal of Economics* 80 (May 1966): 190–207.

Vernon, R., ed. *The Technology Factor in International Trade.* New York: National Bureau of Economic Research, 1970.

Wells, L. T. "A Product Life Cycle for International Trade." *Journal of Marketing* 32 (July 1968): 1–6.

Wells, L. T., ed. *The Product Life Cycle and International Trade.* Boston: Division of Research, Graduate School of Business Administration, Harvard University, 1972.

# Theories of Foreign Direct Investment and the Multinational Corporation

*B*efore the emergence of multinational corporations, private capital crossed national boundaries only in the form of portfolio investment. The real drive toward foreign direct investment (FDI) started in the 1920s. With the depression of the 1930s, FDI experienced some set backs, but recovered somewhat in the late 1930s. World War II was an important stage in the development of FDI. As we explained in Chapter 1, the United States emerged from the war as the world's main economic power. The United States' FDI grew rapidly, accounting for roughly 70 percent of the net FDI during the postwar period through the 1960s. Following this period the relative share of the United States' FDI in the world declined, reaching the level of 44.5 percent in 1980. For other countries, rapid expansion in their FDI did not occur until about 1965 because these countries were busy re-

building their domestic economies after World War II and did not have sufficient funds to invest significant amounts outside their borders.

In the late 1980s, the United States was still the major foreign direct investor in the world. Other major foreign direct investors were the United
Kingdom, Japan, West Germany, Italy, Canada, France, and the Netherlands.
Although FDI from advanced countries accounts for about 98 percent of the
total value of FDI in the world, LDCs such as Argentina, Brazil, Hong Kong,
and Singapore are emerging as the fastest-growing foreign investors in the
world.[1] As a result, most of the world's major firms, from both advanced
countries and LDCs, have significant amounts of foreign direct investment.
These investments include all kinds of business activities in different industries, ranging from extractive industry to manufacturing industry and service
industry. The significance of FDI in international business can be inferred
from the United States alone, where sales from products produced in foreign
countries are many time greater than the sales of exported U.S. domestically
produced goods.

Chapter 2 provided us with a theoretical explanation of international
trade, that is, the export and import of goods and services. The inadequacy
of international trade theories to explain all the facets of international business has led some theoreticians to develop theories that specifically deal with
the subject of foreign direct investment and MNCs. The complexity of this
subject has caused experts from different fields, such as economics, finance,
and management, to study the subject. These theoreticians have developed
theories that have emphasized their own area of expertise, leading to a better understanding of various complex issues that are raised in the study of
international business. However, this development has also made it more
difficult to reach a unified theory of international business that is accepted by
the experts from various fields. At this point, most theoreticians feel that
more research is needed before a unified theory of FDI and MNCs can be
agreed upon.

In this chapter, we first review the main theories of FDI. Second, we discuss
some of the major theories concerning MNCs. Both kinds of theories have been
developed in the free market capitalist economies by theoreticians who are
receptive, for the most part, to both FDI and MNCs. Third, we provide an
explanation of the Marxist theory that is used as a means for opposing both FDI
and MNCs.

## FOREIGN DIRECT INVESTMENT THEORIES

We defined the concept of FDI in Chapter 1. The question to ask at this point
is "Why do firms invest in a foreign country?" In answering this question, we
review the two major theoretical contributions in the field of FDI and explain
their relevance to the real world.

## Theory of Capital Movements

The earliest theoreticians, who assumed that a perfectly competitive market does exist, considered FDI as a form of international capital movement. Capital moves across national boundaries in different ways. International capital movements can occur through purchases and sales of outstanding bonds and stocks, through different short-term credit instruments, and through FDI.

According to the theory, international capital movements, and hence FDI, could be explained in terms of *differential profit,* or differential interest rates found in different countries. In other words, the theory postulated that a firm crossed its national boundaries to earn a higher interest income or profit in a foreign country as compared with what could be earned at home. Thus, FDI was considered to be a form of international capital movement. It differed, however, from other forms of international capital movement, such as transactions in bonds and stocks, in that it was accompanied by different degrees of control, technology, and management brought by the foreign investor.

In 1960, the economist Stephen Hymer wrote a pathbreaking doctoral dissertation and laid the foundation for the modern theories of FDI.[2] A few years later, in the late 1960s, Charles Kindleberger provided the first comprehensive survey of the literature of FDI along the lines explained by Hymer. Kindleberger elaborated on the inadequacy of the assumption of perfect competition in the analysis of FDI, and he asserted that FDI could not exist under such an assumption. He explained that, in a perfectly competitive market, domestic firms could purchase the needed capital through capital markets that specialize in capital movements. This is preferable to purchasing the needed capital through firms that specialize in the production and distribution of goods and services. Thus, for a firm to undertake FDI, it must possess an advantage over the domestic firms that are operating in the host countries. In other words, there must be some imperfections in the market. He then concluded that "in a world of perfect competition for goods and factors, direct investment cannot exist."[3]

Today, Hymer's early insights into the determinants of FDI have remained unshaken. Although contributions by different specialists in the fields of industrial organization, management, and international finance have increased our understanding of FDI in general, and MNCs in particular, the assumption of market imperfections remains an integral part of theories of FDI and MNCs. We devote the rest of this section to an explanation of this important theory.

## Market Imperfections Theory

This theory provides a further step in the explanation of FDI. The market imperfections theory asserts that the decision of an MNC to undertake foreign direct investment stems from its desire to capitalize on certain advantages that are not available to domestic firms that are operating in the host country.

An MNC beginning operations in a foreign country is at a disadvantage when compared to indigenous (local) firms. The managers of an indigenous firm are familiar with their national environment. They know the economy, the politics, the history, the laws, the geography, and the culture of their country. The managers of a foreign firm, however, can obtain the same knowledge, but only at a cost. In addition, managers of foreign firms face added risks that are not shared by the indigenous firms. These risks include the uncertainty of operating in a foreign exchange market, the fears of a political takeover of their business, and the additional costs of operating at a long distance from home, such as higher insurance premiums and transportation costs.

Despite the above disadvantages, a foreign firm also enjoys a number of advantages that are not shared by the local firm. These advantages may be superior management skills, better technology, better economies of scale, a greater knowledge of the world market, and a better financial network.*

According to the market imperfections theory, the advantages must be greater than the disadvantages or the foreign firms would incur losses and not operate in a foreign land. Furthermore, these advantages must be transferable within the firm and across the national boundaries.

Theoretically, these advantages stem from the existence of imperfections in the market, and this is where the theory gets its name. Market imperfections arise when some of the underlying assumptions of perfect competition are violated. In the theoretical world of perfect competition, it is assumed that (a) a large number of firms are producing homogeneous products, (b) free entry and exit exist in the industry for both buyers and sellers, (c) perfect and free knowledge prevails in the market, and (d) all factors of production are perfectly mobile. In the real world, however, these assumptions do not hold, and, as a result, some firms acquire competitive advantages over others. These advantages are referred to as "ownership specific advantages" or "firm-specific advantages." These advantages are internal to the firm and consist of tangible and intangible assets that are under the firm's control. Two examples of tangible assets are (1) availability of specific markets or raw materials not accessible to other firms, and (2) larger firm size, which leads to economies of scale, and lower production costs, which in turn hamper competition. Intangible assets include trademarks, brand names, patents, management skills, marketing skills, and so forth, which would give a firm a competitive edge over others and enables it to achieve greater market power.

The market imperfections theory helps us to speculate about industries that are likely candidates for the expansion of either indigenous or international operations. This approach alone, however, is not capable of answering many questions that are raised in the area of foreign investment. For example, it does not tell us why a firm has to invest in a foreign country in order to take

---

*Economies of scale refers to decreases in the long-run average costs of a firm as the size of its plant is increased.

advantage of its competitive edge. As we will explain in Chapter 12, other forms of international business, such as licensing, franchising, management contracts, and so forth, would also allow a firm to exploit its advantages.

An application of the market imperfection theory is seen in its usefulness in explaining horizontal and vertical integration. **Horizontal integration** means the merger of firms that are producing similar products under one ownership. The products could be close substitutes, such as gasoline produced by different plants, or comparable products, such as aluminum cans and bottles. The purpose of integration is to form a line of products that can be sold through the same selling and distribution channels, thereby increasing the profit. On an international scale, horizontal integration means the production of goods in the foreign country that are similar to those manufactured at home. The motive for integration is to gain better from the firm-specific advantages. Chrysler, GM, Volkswagen, Toyota, Honda, General Tire and Rubber, and Pfizer are examples of firms that produce products in foreign countries that are similar to those manufactured at home.

**Vertical integration** means a merger of firms engaged in different stages of production and distribution under one ownership. Vertical integration could be either forward or backward. **Forward integration** means extending operations into the buyer's market. For example, a potato grower could vertically integrate by extending its activities to include the selling, marketing, and distribution of potatoes. **Backward integration** means expanding operations into the suppliers' market. Using the same example, it means that the firm that is engaged in selling potatoes would take over production of potatoes as well. Internationally, as with horizontal integration, the motive behind vertical integration is to augment the firm-specific advantages. The oil industry is a prime example of vertical integration. This industry is dominated by a small number of international firms such as Exxon, Mobil, and Texaco. The firms in this industry frequently engage in vertical integration to bring extraction, transportation, refining, and distribution under their control. This allows them to fully utilize their firm-specific advantages and also provides them with a secure source of both supply and demand. Such security would permit them to operate refineries to their potential, minimizing costs that arise from an underutilized capacity.

## THEORIES OF THE MULTINATIONAL CORPORATION

According to our discussion of FDI theories, the decision of a firm to invest can be explained in the context of market imperfections. Although market imperfections still represent the basis for the theoretical development of the MNC, theoreticians have recently shifted their attention toward developing a global theory of the multinational firm that also accounts for the internal organization of a firm.[4]

In this section we study three of the major theories of the MNC.

## Internalization Theory

The internalization theory is an extension of the market imperfection theory. For a firm to have a competitive edge in an imperfect market, it must have some advantages over other firms. Internalizing means keeping those advantages within the firm in order to maintain this competitive edge. Externalizing, on the other hand, means making those advantages available to others in return for some gain, usually money. As an example, assume you are the manager of a local restaurant and your success in business is due to your knowledge of a special recipe. Obviously one way for you to capitalize on this knowledge is to externalize it; that is, you can make the knowledge available to others in return for some money. As you know, however, if such an action is taken, then naturally your competitive position would be weakened and your profits would decline. Additionally, it is very difficult for you to know the monetary value of your knowledge. Because of this uncertainty you may decide to "internalize" your knowledge, that is, to keep it to yourself. Methods for internalization would include secrecy, patents, copyrights, or family networks. As we explain later, internalization also explains vertical and horizontal integration when they are used to reduce risk and to increase the efficiency of an MNC's operation.

On an international level, MNCs regularly engage in internalization to more fully capitalize on their firm-specific advantages. Chief among these advantages is knowledge. An MNC obtains knowledge by either experience or research and development. Knowledge may include skills or technologies that are used in the management and production processes of the MNC. Knowledge is considered an intermediate good that is used in the production of final goods. As such, it is an intangible asset to the firm. To be competitive in the world market, MNCs try to establish property rights over their acquired knowledge. In other words, they internalize their knowledge rather than sell it. This prevents the potential rivals at home or abroad from having access to the MNC's knowledge. With such knowledge the rivals could threaten the competitive advantage of the MNC.

Besides knowledge, other factors induce a firm to internalize. Among these factors are transaction costs, buyers' uncertainty, quality control, foreign exchange control, taxes and tariffs imposed by the government, and regulations governing FDI. For example, some MNCs engage in internalization by vertical integration in order to reduce risks and to increase efficiency. In fact many European and American MNCs have integrated backward to minimize risks of variations in quantity, quality, and the price of their inputs. They have also engaged in internalization by forward integration to reduce the risks associated with sales volume and price. Consider the Iranian revolution of the late 1970s that drastically reduced the outflow of oil from that country. MNCs involved in that part of the world could survive because their integration simply allowed them to adjust to the situation, thus preventing disruption in their worldwide activities.

## Appropriability Theory

This theory is based on the assumption that the eminent feature of MNCs is their ability to specialize in the creation of technology. Technology is created by MNCs at five different stages: (1) discovery of a new product, (2) development of a product, (3) generation of the production function, (4) market generation, and (5) appropriability.[5]

The term *appropriability* comes from the word "appropriable," which means "that can be appropriated" "to take for one's own or exclusive use."[6] According to appropriability theory, after generating a technology, a firm should be able to appropriate the resulting benefits. If this were not possible, the firm would not be able to bear the cost of technology generation and thus would have no incentive to create new technology. The theory also asserts that MNCs specialize in the creation of technologies that are transmitted more efficiently through their internal channels than through market mechanism. The use of internal channels enables firms to appropriate the technology they generate—technology that would otherwise be lost to firms. Furthermore, MNCs prefer to produce sophisticated technologies even to the extent that they may be detrimental to the users of the technology. This is because MNCs are more successful in appropriating the return from sophisticated technologies, as compared with simple technologies. Ultimately, however, there is a decline in the production of new technology. This situation creates a technology cycle at the industry level. In this cycle, industries producing information at a fast rate are considered young. As the industry ages and matures, the amount of information and the rate at which it is generated decline. As a result of this the optimum industry size diminishes.

The appropriability theory provides an explanation for the tendency of MNCs to engage in takeover activities. This approach considers takeovers of a host country's plants and equipment as the normal result of the growth of a MNC to an optimum firm size at the beginning stage of an industry's life cycle.

In summary, the appropriability theory is similar to the internalization theory in terms of creating an internal market (internal channels) for exploiting the firm-specific advantage. The appropriability theory accentuates the potential returns from technology generation and the ability of the MNC to appropriate such returns.

## Eclectic Theory of International Production

This theory was developed by John Dunning in an attempt to build a general theory that is based on the firm-specific advantages and the location-specific advantages. More specifically, this theory maintains that for an MNC to invest abroad three advantages must be present. These are (1) firm-specific advantages, (2) internalization advantages, and (3) location-specific advantages.

**Firm-specific advantages**, as we explained earlier in this chapter, result from tangible and intangible resources that are owned by a firm. These resources, exclusive to the firm, would enable it to have a comparative advantage over other firms. For a firm to become an MNC, however, it should possess **internalization advantages** as well. This means that the firm must have a desire and an ability to internalize (use) its firm-specific advantages, rather than externalizing (selling) them through licensing, management contracts, and so forth. This, of course, is achieved by serving a foreign market. But a firm can serve a foreign market by extending its activities to include either exportation or production in a foreign country. For production to take place, the foreign country should have some **location-specific advantages** from the viewpoint of the firm. In other words, there should exist some natural resources, or perhaps a low-cost labor force, making it profitable for a firm to locate its production facilities abroad instead of at home.

The eclectic theory suggests that, given a firm-specific advantage, internalization and competitiveness are positively correlated. In other words, the MNCs that are able to internalize their activities the most are more competitive in the world market. MNCs usually engage in the kinds of internalization that are most appropriate to their market conditions, to their input combination, and to the policies of the countries with which they are dealing. For example, the theory predicts that internalization would be greater for MNCs that come from countries with minimal raw materials than from those with abundant materials.

In summary, the eclectic approach suggests that knowledge alone does not give the MNC a competitive edge over rivals. Instead, the firm's willingness to internalize this knowledge rather than sell it to others contributes to its success. The utilization of this knowledge in a host country is a prerequisite for FDI to take place.

The eclectic theory provides an explanation of the pattern of international production on a country-by-country basis. For an MNC to invest in a foreign country, both firm-specific advantages and location-specific advantages must be present. The MNC favors investment in that country where it is most profitable to internalize its monopolistic advantages. Otherwise, it would be preferable for the MNC to serve that foreign country through exports or licensing.

## MARXIST THEORY

Karl Marx considered history as a logical process, which is changed mainly in response to economic activities. In providing his economic interpretation of history, he distinguished among three stages of development of a capitalist enterprise: the investment expansion, the concentration of power, and the growth of the world market.

Marx believed that the economic environment in a capitalist society is such that it forces capitalist entrepreneurs to constantly expand their operations. He wrote the following:

Moreover, the development of capitalist production makes it constantly necessary to keep increasing the amount of the capital laid out in a given industrial undertaking, and competition makes the imminent laws of capitalist production to be felt by each individual capitalist, as external coercive laws. It compels him to keep constantly extending his capital, in order to preserve it, but extend it he cannot, except by means of progressive accumulation.[7]

As the process of capital expansion continues, Marx explained, it gives rise to an increasing concentration of capital by fewer and fewer capitalists. In the meantime, such a concentration, by itself, calls for more capital accumulation. The process of concentration, he maintained, appears in two different shapes, which are interrelated. The first is the dissemination of large-scale production, and the second is the enlargement of enterprise via takeover and expansion. Marx explained that the organizational structure that is more appropriate to capital expansion is a joint-stock company—what today we call a corporation.

Marx maintained that the world market is vital to the existence of the capitalists and provides the basis for capitalist production. Capitalism rose in the commercial revolution of the sixteenth and early seventeenth centuries. It provided an international market in the world. The expansion of this market, which was based on the need of Western European countries, fueled further the expansion of capitalist enterprises and facilitated the transition from feudalism to capitalism.

Having explained the three stages of capitalist enterprise development, Marx considered MNCs as the final chapter of this development process. The three stages of investment expansion, concentration of power, and the growth of the world market would lead to the monopolization of capital, which is the result of increasing competition among capitalists. At this stage the small capitalist either weakens or is taken over by a few larger ones, or as Marx put it, "one capitalist always kills many."[8] Marx implied that a final stage would follow the monopolization of capital. It was left to V. I. Lenin, however, the founder of Russian communist ideology in the early twentieth century, to elaborate on this stage. Lenin argued that concentration and monopolization of capital would lead to an economic system that is controlled by "finance capital." This is the stage in which large banks in cooperation with huge monopolies control and manipulate the masses. The expansion of these giants would necessitate their penetration into foreign markets. This is achieved by crossing national boundaries and forming international companies (MNCs), which would then control the market and resources of other nations. When this happens the economy has reached the highest and final stage of capitalism, which is called "capitalistic imperialism."

Marx's followers, such as Paul Baran, Paul Sweezy, Harry Magdoff, and Stephen Hymer, have all considered FDI as a vehicle for transferring riches from the poor nations to the wealthy countries. They believe that MNCs would tear the social and political fabrics of the LDCs and destroy the possibility of their self-sufficiency, making them dependent on the advanced countries. This is achieved by the hierarchical division of labor and a tendency to centralize the decision-making process in a few key cities located in the advanced countries. As a result, the rest of the world would be confined to a lower level of activity and income. Thus the present mold of income inequality and dependency would worsen, and the relationship between different countries would be based on "superior" and "subordinate," and "head office" and "branch plant."

In analyzing the political consequences of the MNCs, Stephen Hymer takes a very pessimistic view. He sees that MNCs are faced with unavoidable nationalistic rivalry between the major capitalist countries, with the economic challenge of the socialist bloc countries, and with threats from the LDCs. He specifically emphasizes that "One could easily argue that the age of multinational corporations is at its end rather than its beginning."[9]

The Marxist theory has attracted the attention of many political groups as a rationale for opposing MNCs. Consequently, some countries, such as Cuba, have gone so far as to break their economic ties with the capitalist economics of the West. Evidence shows, however, that as the result of their actions these same countries have suffered from stagnation by reducing or severing their economic relations with the West.

The economic thoughts of Marx have been criticized on many grounds. With regard to large corporations specifically, an economic historian writes "Marx failed to recognize, however, that the large corporation, while facilitating the concentration of control, has at the same time been instrumental in diffusing property among many capitalists."[10] In fact, evidence shows that countries such as Taiwan and South Korea have experienced a healthy economic growth and a more equitable income distribution while they have been highly dependent on the United States and other capitalist countries for their trade and investment.*

In today's world, pragmatism has undermined the philosophical ideologies of the Marxist sympathizers. This is evident by the operation of multinational enterprises by the Soviet Union and Eastern European countries in nonsocialist countries. Even more important, a significant shift in the People's Republic of China's economic policies followed the demise of Mao Tse-tung in 1976. Since then the Chinese have reversed their policies with regard to FDI, openly inviting Western entrepreneurs to invest in their country.

We may conclude this section by stating that theories about foreign direct investment and the multinational corporation, like trade theories, are abstractions from reality. As such, they help us to understand the "why" and the "how" of FDI and the MNC. One must be careful, however, not to read too much into theories. It should be kept in mind that these theories provide only some comprehension of the general elements that explain FDI and the MNC. To be sure, these theories should be employed along with the additional data that are

---

*Both Taiwan and South Korea have experienced a real per capita income growth of over 6 percent per year during the 1960s and 1970s.

gathered in the real world, when trying to answer the questions that are raised by FDI and MNC.

## SUMMARY

1. According to the theory of capital movements, international capital movements, and hence FDI, could be explained in terms of *differential profit,* or differential interest rates found in different countries.
2. In the late 1960s, the inadequacy of the assumptions about perfect competition in the analysis of FDI was recognized. It was concluded that market imperfection is the prerequisite for FDI.
3. According to the market imperfection theory, for a firm to undertake FDI, it must have a comparative advantage over the existing firms in the host country.
4. The competitive advantages of a foreign firm, as compared with a domestic firm, might be found in superior managerial skills, better technology, better economies of scale, a greater knowledge of the world market, and a better financial network.
5. The competitive advantages are referred to as "ownership advantages" or "firm-specific advantages." These advantages are internal to the firm and consist of the tangible and intangible assets that are under the firm's control.
6. Horizontal integration means the merger of firms that are producing similar products under one ownership.
7. Vertical integration means the merger of firms that are engaged in different stages of production under one ownership.
8. Vertical integration could be either forward or backward. Forward integration means extending operations into the buyer's market. Backward integration means expanding operations into the supplier's market.
9. The internalization theory is an extension of the market imperfection theory. In this theory it is assumed that a firm would capitalize on its knowledge by internalizing it, that is, by keeping it to itself.
10. On an international level, MNCs regularly engage in internalization to more fully capitalize on their firm-specific advantages.
11. According to the appropriability theory, MNCs prefer to produce sophisticated technologies, instead of simple ones, because they are more successful in appropriating the return from these technologies.
12. According to the eclectic theory it is not the possession of knowledge alone that gives an MNC a competitive edge over its rivals, but its willingness to internalize this knowledge rather than sell it.
13. Karl Marx distinguished among three stages of capitalist enterprise development. These stages are investment expansion, concentration of power, and the growth of the world market.
14. According to the Marxist theory, the three stages of capitalist enterprise development would eventually result in monopolization of capital, which in turn leads to an economic system that is controlled by "finance capital." When this happens, the economy has reached the highest and final stage of capitalism—capitalistic imperialism—in which MNCs come into existence.
15. The economic thought of Marx has been criticized on many grounds. In today's

world, pragmatism has undermined the philosophical ideologies of Marxist sympathizers.

## QUESTIONS

3.1 Compare the appropriability theory and the internalization theory.

3.2 As an MNC manager, how could you benefit from the eclectic theory when investing in a foreign country?

3.3 Distinguish between horizontal integration and vertical integration, and give examples of industries that have experienced integration. Are the motives behind horizontal and vertical integration the same? Explain.

3.4 Discuss the major shortcomings of trade theories in explaining foreign direct investment and MNCs.

3.5 The existence of superior managerial and marketing skills is a necessary, but not a sufficient, condition for international integration. Do you agree with this statement? Discuss.

3.6 Compare the Marxist theory with the theories of FDI and MNCs as they have developed in the free market capitalist economies. How does the Marxist view of FDI and MNC differ from the free market view? What are the implications of each of these views regarding international business?

## NOTES

1. "Guess Who Is Creating the World's Newest Multinationals," *The Wall Street Journal,* 12 December 1983, p. 26.
2. Stephen H. Hymer, "The International Operation of National Firm." Ph.D. diss. Massachusetts Institute of Technology, 1960.
3. Charles P. Kindleberger, *American Business Abroad: Six Lectures on Direct Investment* (New Haven, Conn.: Yale University Press, 1969), p. 13.
4. A. V. Calvet, "A Synthesis of Foreign Direct Investment Theories and Theories of the Multinational Firm." *Journal of International Business Studies* (Spring/Summer 1981):43–59.
5. Stephen P. Magee, "Technology and the Appropriability Theory of the Multinational." In Jagdish Bhagwati, ed., *The New International Economic Order* (Cambridge, Mass.: Massachusetts Institute of Technology Press, 1976).
6. *Webster's New Dictionary of the American Languages,* 2nd ed. (New York: Simon & Schuster, 1980), p. 68.
7. Karl Marx, *Capital,* 3 vols. (Moscow: Progress Publisher, 1975), vol. 1, p. 555.
8. Ibid., p. 714.
9. Stephen H. Hymer, "The Multinational Corporation and the Law of Uneven Development," In Jagdish Bhagwati, *Economics and World Order: From the 1970s to the 1990s* (London: Macmillan, 1972), p. 131.
10. H. William Spiegel, *The Growth of Economic Thought* (Englewood Cliffs, N.J.: Prentice-Hall, 1971), p.475.

## SUGGESTED READINGS

Aggarwall, Ray. "Investment Performance of U.S. Based Multinational Companies: Comments and a Perspective on International Diversification of Real Assets." *Journal of International Business Studies* (Spring/Summer 1980):98–104.

Aliber, Robert Z. "A Theory of Direct Foreign Investment." In Charles P. Kindleberger, ed. *The International Corporation.* Cambridge, Mass.: Massachusetts Institute of Technology Press, 1970.

Asheghian, Parviz. "Foreign Direct Investment and Its Economic Impact in a Less Developed Country: The Case of Iran." *Managing International Development* (July/August 1984):38–51.

Calvet, A. L. "A Synthesis of Foreign Direct Investment Theories and Theories of the Multinational Firm." *Journal of International Business Studies* (Spring/Summer 1981):43–59.

Caves, Richard E. *Multinational Enterprise and Economic Analysis.* Cambridge, Mass.: Harvard University Press, 1980.

Dunning, John H. *International Production and the Multinational Enterprise.* London: Allen & Unwin, 1981. Chap. 2.

Errunza, V. R., and L. W. Sanhet. "The Effects of International Operation on the Market Value of the Firm: Theory and Practice." *Journal of Finance* (May 1981): 401–417.

Hirsch, S. "An International Trade and Investment Theory of the Firm." *Oxford Economic Papers* 28 (1976).

Hood, Neil, and Stephen Young. *The Economics of Multinational Enterprise.* New York: Longman, 1979.

Hymer, Stephen H. *The International Operations of National Firms: A Study of Direct Investment.* Cambridge, Mass.: Massachusetts Institute of Technology Press, 1976.

Hymer, Stephen H., and Robert Rowthorn. "Multinational Corporations and International Oligopoly: The Non-American Challenge." In Charles P. Kindleberger, ed., *The International Corporation: A Symposium.* Cambridge, Mass.: Massachusetts Institute of Technology Press, 1970.

Knickerbocker, Fredrick T. *Oligopolistic Reaction and Multinational Enterprise.* Boston: Division of Research, Graduate School of Business Administration, Harvard University, 1973.

Levy, Haim, and Marshall Sarnat. "International Diversification of Investment Portfolio." *The American Economic Review* (September 1970): 668–675.

Magdoff, Harry. "The Multinational Corporation and Development—A Contradiction!" In David E. Apter and Louis W. Goodman, eds., *The Multinational Corporation and Social Change.* New York: Praeger, 1976.

Magee, Stephen D. "Information and the Multinational Corporation: An Appropriability Theory of Direct Investment." In Jagdish N. Bhagwati, ed., *The New International Economic Order.* Cambridge, Mass.: Massachusetts Institute of Technology Press, 1977.

Rugman Alan, M. *International Diversification and the Multinational Enterprise.* Lexington, Mass.: Lexington Books, 1979.

———. "Internalization as a General Theory of Foreign Direct Investment." *Welwirtschaftliches Archiv* 116 (June 1980):365–379.

# Chapter
## 4

# National Policies Affecting International Trade

$T$he discussion of international trade theories, presented in Chapter 2, led us to the conclusion that free trade is the most efficient way of allocating the world's scarce resources. We learned that if countries specialize according to their comparative advantage, not only do they benefit as participants of trade, but also world output is maximized. In spite of the convincing arguments for free trade, however, governments have interfered with the free flow of goods and services by imposing tariff and nontariff barriers.

Although the majority of economists favor free trade and oppose any kind of trade barriers, they carefully discuss the exceptional cases that might warrant trade restrictions. In this chapter we first explain tariff and nontariff barriers to trade; second, we describe the major international

schedule provides a single tariff for a given good, irrespective of the exporting country in question. A multiple column schedule tariff, however, differentiates between countries by applying lower rates to countries with which treaty agreements have been arranged.

Although specific and ad valorem tariffs basically serve the same goal, they each have advantages and disadvantages. Since a specific tariff is calculated as a certain amount of money per unit of the product imported, for example $0.07 per pound, it is easy to measure and administer. However, a shortcoming of this tariff is that the level of protection that it gives to domestic goods changes negatively with variation in the prices of imported products. In other words, the lower the prices of the imported products, the higher the level of protection. For example, if we impose a specific tariff of $10 per bicycle imported, then imports valued at, say, $200 would be more discouraged than imports valued at $250. This is because $10 is a higher percentage of $200 (5 percent) than it is of $250 (4 percent). As a result, at the time of a business recession abroad, when the value of imported goods declines, the amount of protection provided by a specific tariff increases. However, at the time of inflation abroad, when the value of imported products increases, the protective power of the specific tariff decreases.

In comparison to a specific tariff, an ad valorem tariff has the advantage of distinguishing between products with different values and assigning tariffs according to those values. Thus, a 10 percent ad valorem tariff on imported bicycles assigns a $20 tariff on a $200 bicycle and a $25 tariff on a $250 bicycle.

Another superiority of an ad valorem tariff, as compared with a specific tariff, is that it provides a constant degree of protection for the domestic products, irrespective of variations in their prices over time. For example, if the tariff rate is 10 percent, the duty on an imported product of $100 would be $10. If the price of the product increases, say, to $200, the duty would be $20. On the other hand, if the price of the product decreases to, say, $50, the duty would be $5. In other words, the amount of tariff paid is always equal to 10 percent of the value of the product. Thus, an ad valorem tariff has the advantage of assigning duty in proportion to the value of the product in question. Consequently, ad valorem tariffs provide a constant degree of relative protection, irrespective of variations in the prices of the commodities in question.

## Effective Rate of Protection

As we already know tariffs are imposed on imported goods in order to protect the domestically produced goods from foreign competition. A tariff raises the price of an imported good and makes the domestically produced good more attractive to the residents of the country that imposes the tariff. The level of protection that is provided by a tariff is a measure of the degree to which domestic prices can rise above foreign prices without forcing domestic producers out of the market.

Since tariffs could be imposed not only on final goods but also on intermediate goods, firms are affected by tariffs on their inputs into the production process as well as on their outputs, that is, the products they sell. For example, an automobile producer is affected not only by tariffs on cars but also by tariffs on steel, rubber, glass, and the electronic devices that are used in the production of those cars. Consequently, the tariff rates published in a country's tariff schedule, referred to as the **nominal tariff rates**, do not always provide us with the real measure of protection afforded to the commodity in question. This is because the nominal tariff rates are aimed only at the final products. It is necessary to calculate an **effective rate**, which takes into account not only tariffs on the final product but also on inputs used to make that product.

Consider the production of video cassette recorders (VCRs). Assume that the foreign producer can manufacture this product in its entirety and export it for $400. The domestic producer, however, has to buy the component parts from abroad and assemble them at home. Assume that the domestic manufacturer pays $240 for the component parts and that the cost of assembly is $160. Then the production cost for the domestic manufacturer is $400. Since at this price the domestic manufacturer is not making any profit, assume that the government steps in and imposes a 20 percent tariff on the importation of VCRs from abroad. As a result, the price of the imported VCR would rise to $480, allowing the domestic manufacturer to sell VCRs at this price and make an $80 profit on each VCR sold.* Although the nominal rate of protection is 20 percent, we cannot say that the domestic producer is afforded a 20 percent protection. This is because the component parts enter the country duty free.

As Table 4.2 shows, if free trade existed, the imported VCR could enter the country for $400. But at this price the domestic producer can only add $160 to the cost of the components, making zero profit on domestically produced VCRs. However, the protective tariff would allow the domestic producer to add up to $240 ($160 for assembly costs and $80 for profit) to the costs of component parts and still be competitive with the $480 price of the imported VCR. In other words, the effective rate of protection is $(240 - 160)/160 = 0.5$. This means that the domestic **value added**, that is, the price of the final product minus the cost of the imported inputs, could increase to a level of 50 percent over what might exist without the tariff. In the above example, the value added before tariff was $160 ($400 - $240), which was raised to $240 ($480 - $240), a 50 percent increase. In other words, the nominal tariff rate of 20 percent imposed on the final imported product resulted in an effective degree of protection equal to 50 percent, two and one-half times the nominal rate.

Given the above example, we can define the **effective rate of protection** as the percentage increase in the domestic value added of a product as the result of tariffs.†

---

*In this example we are assuming that all intermediaries (middlemen) receive zero profit.

†Generally the effective rate of protection can be calculated by the use of a formula, as demonstrated in the Appendix to this chapter.

Table 4.2   THE EFFECTIVE RATE OF PROTECTION

| Imported VCRs | | Domestic VCRs | |
| --- | --- | --- | --- |
| Parts | $240 | Parts | $240 |
| Assembly cost and profit | 160 | Assembly cost | 160 |
| | | Profit | 80 |
| Nominal tariff | 80 | | |
| Import price after tariff | 480 | Domestic price after tariff | 480 |

## NONTARIFF TRADE BARRIERS

There are many different ways a government could restrict trade without using a tariff. In fact, the trade policies of many countries in recent years have called for the replacement of tariff trade barriers with nontariff barriers. Such replacement by major industrial countries has occurred as they have progressively reduced tariff rates and eliminated quotas under the auspices of the General Agreement on Tariffs and Trade (GATT), which we will explain later in this chapter. This has caused nontariff trade barriers to emerge as the main obstacle to the benefits of international free trade. The lowering of tariff rates has been likened to the emptying of a swamp. The lower water level has disclosed all the snags and stumps (nontariff barriers) that must be cleaned up to make the swamp easy to cross.

In this section we survey some of the main nontariff barriers that affect international free trade. These include quotas, subsidies, taxes, and other diverse measures (such as customs procedures, foreign exchange restrictions, and regulations involving labeling, health, safety, and shipping). We also study dumping, that is, a form of international price discrimination that restricts international free trade.

### Quotas

A quota is the limitation set on the number or quantity of a given commodity that crosses national boundaries. Depending on whether a good is imported or exported, the quota is referred to as an import quota or an export quota.

**Import Quotas**   Import quotas are the most prevalent form of nontariff trade barriers. Like import tariffs, the purpose of import quotas is the protection of domestic industries. The imposition of a quota on a foreign product limits its supply and causes its price to rise. This would make the domestic product relatively cheaper, strengthening its competitive position in the market. Three major types of quotas can be specified; these are unilateral quotas, bilateral or multilateral quotas, and tariff quotas.

The **unilateral quota** is a quota that is imposed by an importing country without negotiation or consultation with exporting countries. Since the imposition of this type of quota does not consider the opinions of the exporting countries that are affected, it may result in tension, antagonism, or retaliation by those countries. Sugar imports into the United States provide an example of a commodity that is subject to a unilateral quota.

**Bilateral or multilateral quotas** are imposed by an importing country after consultation or negotiation with the exporting countries. Since the decisions to impose these quotas involve the opinions of exporting countries, it tends to enhance the cooperation of these countries, facilitating the successful operations of the quota system. Countries have used this type of quota with such commodities as textiles, footwear, and automobiles. For example, in 1979 the United States negotiated agreements with Taiwan and the Republic of South Korea to set a limit on the number of color televisions that could be imported from these countries into the United States.[1] As another example, in 1979 the United States and Japan signed an agreement to limit Japanese imports of textile into the United States. This agreement, which was amended in 1982, gradually grew to include 20 categories of textile.[2]

A **tariff quota** combines the characteristics of both a tariff and a quota. It sets a limit on the quantity of a given commodity that can enter a country at a given rate of custom duty (tariff) or at no duty. Any additional quantities that are imported above the limit are subject to higher custom duty rates.

Export Quotas   Export quotas, by imposing limitations on the number of goods that could be exported, are another way that a nation can restrict the free flow of international trade. In the extreme case, export quotas ban the importation of a product into a country. The three main purposes of export quotas are the following:

1. To ensure the availability of a certain amount of a good, which may be in short supply for domestic use. For example, during the 1980s the exportation of certain foodstuffs was banned by the Islamic Republic of Iran, which had been facing food shortages due to its war with Iraq.
2. To control the supply of certain commodities, on the national and international level, in order to manipulate their prices. For example, beginning in 1982, Saudi Arabia, Kuwait, Libya, and the United Arab Emirates individually restricted their production of oil. These four members of the Organization of Petroleum Exporting Countries (OPEC) reduced their production by 60 percent from 1979 levels in order to set the price of oil at a higher level.
3. To check the exportation to hostile nations of goods that are significant from a strategic point of view. For example, the United States bans the exportation of some sophisticated electronic devices and computers to the Soviet Union. Also, the exportation of military hardware to Iran, which is considered an unfriendly nation, is prohibited by the U.S. government.

The United States is so sensitive about the export of strategic goods to the Soviet bloc nations that it may even impose trade sanctions against foreign firms that violate this rule. For example, such sanctions were proposed by the U.S. Congress against Toshiba Machine of Japan and Kongsberg Vaapenfabrikk of Norway. These firms had shipped machine tools for making ultraquiet submarine propellers to the Soviet Union.[3]

Export quotas can also be classified as unilateral, bilateral, or multilateral. A **unilateral export quota** is established without the prior consent of the trading nations. A **bilateral or multilateral export quota**, however, is initiated by agreements between trading nations.

## Voluntary Export Restraints

Since there is a general agreement among most trading nations not to impose quotas, except in special cases, there is reluctance to use them. Consequently, importing nations usually request their exporting trading partners to voluntarily restrain their exports. Exporting nations are naturally reluctant to set a limit on their exports. The imposition of this type of quota, therefore, implies that the importing nation has threatened to impose even tougher restrictions if voluntary cooperation with quota is not undertaken. For example, in 1981, the U.S. automakers and the United Auto Workers (UAW) asked Congress and the Reagan administration to impose quotas on the imports of Japanese automobiles. The purpose was to limit the sales of Japanese automobiles in the U.S. market in order to allow the troubled U.S. automakers to stay competitive and operate profitably. It was hoped that this would give the U.S. automakers a chance to retool their factories and to produce new cars that could successfully compete with the Japanese automobiles, when quotas on the Japanese cars were lifted. In response to the demand of automakers the Reagan administration came up with a compromise. Rather than impose quotas on Japanese imports, the U.S. government got the Japanese to agree to voluntarily limit their exports to the United States to 1.68 million cars a year.* This agreement was extended for four years. The fourth year quota, which set a limit of 1.85 million cars a year, expired on March 31, 1985.[4] On March 28, 1985, the Japanese government, however, announced that it would continue the voluntary restraint for at least another year, but at a higher level of 2.3 million cars a year. Again, in January 1987, Japan told the United States that it would extend the restraint of 2.3 million cars a year to March 1988.[5] In 1989 the quota was still in effect, and it was expected that if and when the quota is lifted, the Japanese share of the U.S. market would increase. In other words, the American auto manufacturers would face the same stiff competition from Japan as they did before the imposition of the initial quota in 1981. Thus, it seems that the quota has not resolved the real problem, that is, the inability of the U.S. auto industry to effectively compete in the world market. According to consumer surveys Japanese cars have consistently outscored American cars in terms of quality and customer satisfaction. It seems that

---

*Imposing quotas on just one country, that is, Japan, would have been in violation of GATT, as we explain later.

what the U.S. auto industry really needs is a free and competitive market that would force the U.S. entrepreneur to innovate, to cut costs, and to improve efficiency, thereby producing high quality cars that could effectively compete in the international market.

## Comparison of Tariffs and Quotas

Both tariffs and quotas are protectionist means that are used to raise the prices of foreign goods relative to domestic goods. This allows the domestic producers to more effectively compete with the foreign producers of similar goods. The main differences between tariffs and quotas are the following:

1. Quotas are more effective tools in restraining trade flow than are tariffs. An import duty raises the domestic price, but it does not limit the quantity of goods that can be imported into a country. Consequently the degree of protection provided by a tariff, as the result of a higher price, is determined by the market mechanism. However, by imposing an absolute limit on the quantity of imported goods, a quota entirely forecloses the market mechanism adjustment and provides us with a certain and precise restraining tool.

2. A disadvantage of quotas is that their use may lead to a domestic monopoly of production of the good and higher prices. Since a domestic firm knows that foreign firms cannot surpass their quotas, it may increase its prices. Tariffs, however, do not necessarily induce monopoly power because no limit is set on the number of goods that can be imported into the country.

3. Since quotas are more effective in restricting the trade flow than tariffs, they are more effective tools for bargaining and retaliation.

4. Quotas might be easier to administer than tariffs. The imposition of tariffs requires statutory legislation, which is a time-consuming process. Consequently, quotas are better suited for application by nations in emergency situations.

5. Quotas are more restrictive than tariffs and suppress competition. Tariffs call for some degree of competition.

6. Quotas might be more harmful than tariffs to an importing nation if they give monopoly power to exporters. For example, in the early 1960s, in an attempt to ease protectionist sentiments in the United States, the government persuaded the foreign suppliers of the U.S. textile and steel producers to impose "voluntary export restraint" quotas to limit their exports to the United States. Accordingly, these foreign suppliers were forced into dividing the limited quota of their exports to the U.S. market among themselves. This led these foreign suppliers, who were previously competing with each other, to collude and charge the U.S. importers the full U.S. price, rather than the lower, competitive world price. Consequently, the United States not only experienced the same losses as it would with an identical tariff, but it

also sustained additional losses due to its inability to keep the price markup at home.[6]

## Subsidies

Subsidies are indirect forms of protection that are granted by national governments to domestic producers. Subsidies are given to either export-competing industries or to import-competing industries. The main purpose of subsidizing some of the home industries is to improve the international trade positions of a country either by diminishing its dependence on imports or by earning more foreign exchange by enhancing its exports. Subsidies enable domestic firms to export their products at prices lower than what is really needed to cover their costs or provide them with desired profits. This allows the less efficient domestic producer to more successfully compete against the more efficient foreign producers in the international market for exported goods.

Subsidies take different forms. The simplest form of a subsidy is direct cash payments by the government to the producer after the sales have been completed. However, since such direct subsidies for manufactured goods are prohibited by the General Agreement on Tariffs and Trade (GATT), nations committed to GATT may resort to other forms of subsidies to reach the same goal. These forms include special privileges that might be granted by a government to its exporters, such as low interest loans, special insurance arrangements, and tax concessions. For example, to encourage U.S. exports, the Export-Import Bank of the United States grants direct loans and guarantees insured loans to foreign buyers of American goods and services.

As another example, in subsidizing small export companies, the Japanese government announced a plan to provide a subsidy package that includes low interest loans, relaxed credit rules, and the consideration of loans to these companies without collateral.[7]

Governments may also buy a firm's surplus products at a relatively high price and export it at a low price. This is a policy that has been followed by the U.S. government in implementing the farm price support program.

Regardless of the way that a subsidy is granted, its economic effect, like a tariff, is the loss of economic efficiency and a higher cost for consumers. As a result, society as a whole loses on two accounts because of subsidies: first, by financing the subsidy's direct cost, and, second, by paying the higher price that results from the imposition of the subsidy. Additionally, since a subsidy replaces the law of comparative advantage, the gains from international specialization and division of labor are also diminished.

## Taxes

The free flow of international business is also disturbed by taxes, not only by those taxes imposed on traded goods themselves but also by the differential tax structures of trading nations. In the most extreme case, firms set up their operations in foreign countries mainly because of the lower taxes in those nations as compared with their own countries. For example, many U.S. banks have set up their offices in places such as the West Indies and Panama, which have lower tax rates than the United States. As another example, the relatively low taxes in Hong Kong are a contributing factor in attracting foreign capital to that island.

As a protective device, taxes can be used to encourage exports or to discourage imports. On the export side, one device is to exempt exports from the value-added tax. Devised by the French economists, the *value-added tax* is a tax imposed on the value that is added at each stage of the production of a given good. Thus the tax paid by the producer at each stage of production is proportional to the value added to the product at that stage.

Another device is to give a foreign tax credit to a firm in order to prevent double taxation of its income by both the domestic and the foreign government. To achieve this goal some countries, such as Japan, exempt the foreign earnings of the subsidiaries of their MNCs from taxes. However, some other countries, like the United States, allow a firm's foreign taxes to be deducted from its domestic tax liabilities. Of course, no matter what technique is used, the granting of tax credits is like a subsidy and causes a government to give up part of its revenue to a foreign nation.

Excise taxes and processing taxes can also be used to discourage the importation of certain products. *Excise taxes* are duties that are collected when goods pass through customs. Processing taxes, levied on certain semifinished goods and raw materials, are duties that are collectable upon the first domestic processing. As a protective device, the imposition of these taxes on imports raises the prices of imported goods. This causes the competitive position of domestic goods to improve, thus boosting their sales.

### Other Nontariff Trade Barriers

Besides quotas, subsidies, and taxes, there are other forms of nontariff trade barriers, which are often well disguised and appear in the form of government policies and regulations. They may be classified into three major categories: government purchasing policies, administrative and technical regulations, and foreign exchange rate controls.

**Government Purchasing Policies**   Since governments are significant buyers in the international market, they have enormous power in affecting the flow of international goods and services. In pursuing their protectionist policies, governments usually require that preferences be given to domestic rather than foreign sellers regarding government purchases. For example, in the United States, according to the Buy American Act, established U.S. agencies have to give a 6 percent price advantage to domestic suppliers. This price advantage raises to 12 percent in the case of a business that is located in a small or depressed area, and to 50 percent for defense contracts. This law was still in effect during the late 1980s.

**Administrative and Technical Regulations**   There are large numbers of administrative and technical regulations that are imposed by national governments on imports. Although some of these regulations may be imposed with no intention of restricting trade, they may have the effect of import restrictions.

   *Government Health and Safety Standards*   An example of these standards are the U.S. pollution control standards, which call for mandatory antipollution control devices and prohibit the sale of foreign cars that do not meet these requirements. This makes the foreign cars relatively more expensive, causing a potential decrease in foreign car imports to the United States. As another example, in Japan, pharmaceuticals and medical equipment are subject to such a rigorous safety inspection that it might take months or years for the products to be tested. Usually, during the time it takes for these tests to be completed, Japanese manufacturers are given samples of the product by the government. This enables them to produce their own brand of the product before the foreign brand is allowed to enter the Japanese market.[10] As yet another example, auto inspectors are so strict in Japan that they reject 80 percent of the cars that are imported from abroad.[11]

   *Marketing and Packaging Standards*   An example of the standards are the Canadian regulations that require canned foods to be packed in can sizes established by the Canadian government. This means that some foreign food manufacturers, who pack their products in can sizes different from those specified by the Canadian government, would not be able to export their products to Canada. Consequently, the overall potential import of canned goods into Canada decreases. As another example, Denmark requires that all soft drinks be sold in returnable bottles. This regulation discriminates against foreign exporters, such as the French mineral water producers, who find it too expensive to collect the returnable bottles for refilling in France.

   *Custom Procedures and Valuation*   The government of the importing country could discriminate against a product or an exporting country by simply delaying the importation process by undue inspection or by disagreeing on the invoice value of the product. For example, instead of using the invoice value of a product for calculating its duty, they might use the domestic wholesale price, the retail price, or an estimated price based on what it might cost to produce the product at home. Consequently, they may come up with a price that is higher than the invoice price and charge the exporter a higher duty than is justified. In dealing with this problem most industrial countries since 1980 have agreed upon a standard procedure for the determination of values, in order to give foreign suppliers a fair chance.

**Foreign Exchange Control**   By intervening in the foreign exchange market, as we will explain in Chapter 7, a government can reduce the amount of imports. This is achieved by devaluing the national currency so that each unit of national currency is worth less foreign currency in exchange. This causes import prices to rise. For example, consider the export of Beck's beer from Germany to the United States. The beer costs two German marks per bottle in Germany. If we ignore transportation costs and assume that there are no quotas or tariffs and that each U.S. dollar equals two German marks, then the value of Beck's beer in the U.S. market would be one dollar per bottle. If the U.S. devalues the dollar so that each U.S. dollar commands only one German mark, then the value of the beer in the United States would be equal to two dollars. In other words, the devaluation of the U.S. dollar causes the price of Beck's beer to increase. This in turn would lead to a lower quantity of Beck's beer demanded, causing the amount of the beer imported to decrease.

Another method used to reduce imports is to employ multiple exchange rates. With this method a country assigns separate official exchange rates for different commodities that are either imports or exports. Most less developed countries today use this method in order to ensure that essential goods are imported while nonessential goods are discouraged. These countries assign a low exchange rate for essential imports, such as raw materials or capital goods, and set a high exchange rate for nonessentials, such as luxury goods.

## Dumping

**Dumping** is the practice of selling a product at below cost, or at a lower price in a foreign market as compared with the domestic market. The practice of dumping can take three different forms, known as sporadic, predatory, and persistent dumping.

**Sporadic dumping** occurs when a firm with surplus inventories sells its product in a foreign market at below cost or at a price that is lower than what is charged in the domestic market. This form of dumping occurs occasionally and is practiced in order to dispose of the firms' unexpected surplus that has resulted from either mismanagement or unpredictable changes in supply and demand conditions. In this case, to protect its domestic industry, the importing country can impose temporary tariff duties to neutralize the impact of sporadic dumping. However, since this kind of dumping is of a temporary nature and its impact on international trade is insignificant, most governments do not choose to impose tariff duties for protection purposes.

**Predatory dumping** is practiced when a firm temporarily sells its product at below cost or at a lower price in a foreign market with the intention of weakening or driving its competitors out of the market. If this is successful, the firm raises the price of the product after competition has been eliminated. As the result, the firm would then gain monopoly power over the product and would be able to set a new price that is high enough to compensate for the losses that occurred during the dumping practice. To be successful the firm should be able to prevent new entrants from coming into the market long enough to enjoy a monopoly profit from sales.

**Persistent dumping**, or international price discrimination, goes on continually. This form of dumping occurs when a monopolistic firm consistently sells its product at below cost or at a lower price abroad than at home. The purpose of this kind of dumping is to maximize the firm's profit, and it may occur when a firm's foreign demand for its products is relatively more elastic than its domestic demand.* Persistent dumping is also practiced when a firm, which is exporting, absorbs its fixed costs at home and is able to price its exports such that the foreign price covers only its variable costs.

In summary, sporadic dumping is the "occasional" sale of a product at below cost, or at a lower price in a foreign market, in order to dispose of a firm's unexpected surplus. Predatory dumping is the "temporary" sale of a product at below cost, or at a lower price in a foreign market, with the purpose of driving foreign producers out of the market, and then raising the price after competition is eliminated. Persistent dumping is the "continual" sale of a product at below cost or at a lower price in a foreign market for the purpose of profit maximization.

Over the years many countries have been accused of dumping their products in the United States. For example, an investigation in 1970 showed that Sony was selling its Japanese made TV sets for $180 in the United States while charging its domestic consumers $333 for the same model. Other examples of dumping in the United States include the dumping of Japanese steel and German Volkswagens. Also the Japanese were accused of dumping their computer chips in the U.S. market in 1986. U.S. companies complained that the Japanese manufacturers of computer chips were engaged in predatory pricing practices. These complaints prompted the talks that led the United States and Japan to sign a "semiconductor trade agreement," on July 31, 1987. According to this agreement, minimum prices were set for certain Japanese made chips sold in any nation other than Japan.[8] Another example is the case of one of the Canadian firms, that accused both the United States and Japan for dumping their hypodermic needles into Canada.[9]

Since dumping of a product into a country puts its import-competing firms at a disadvantage, the governments of many countries have enacted antidumping regulations that usually involve a remedial tariff. The purpose of this tariff is to neutralize the undesirable effect of the lower dumping price on domestic firms. In the United States, the Anti-Dumping Act of 1921 rules that a tariff equal to the price differential (domestic price compared with foreign price) be imposed against the dumper, for as long as dumping continues.

The international antidumping code negotiated during the Kennedy round

---

*The demand for a product in a foreign market is expected to be more elastic than in a domestic market because foreign buyers have more options in purchasing a product than domestic buyers. Consequently, foreign buyers are more responsive to price changes than domestic buyers. In other words, a 1 percent increase in the price of a product would cause a relatively higher decline in the quantity demanded in the foreign market as compared with a 1 percent increase in the price in the domestic market. This situation allows the entrepreneur to engage in price discrimination by charging higher prices in the less elastic (less responsive) domestic market as compared with the foreign market.

of trade liberalization (1962–1967) incites the importing countries to impose a fixed duty that is high enough to offset the harm to the domestic country's import-competing firms that is caused by the dumper's lower prices.

In practice, when dumping charges can be proved, most accused firms usually decide to increase their prices rather than pay antidumping duties. For example, in response to dumping charges, both Volkswagen in 1976 and Sony in 1977 raised their prices in order to avoid the imposition of antidumping duties on their products in the United States.

## INTERNATIONAL ORGANIZATIONS AND AGREEMENTS AFFECTING INTERNATIONAL TRADE

In this section we study the major international organizations and agreements that affect international trade. First, we explain international cartels. Second, we describe economic integration. Third, we discuss the major trade associations in LDCs. Fourth, we discuss the Organization for Economic Cooperation and Development. Finally, we elaborate on the General Agreement on Tariff and Trade (GATT).

### International Cartels

**An international cartel** can be defined as an organization that is composed of firms in the same industry, but from different countries, who agree to limit their outputs and exports in order to influence the prices of their commodities and to maximize their profits.

International cartels existed in railway services and in the tobacco business as early as 1880s. The postwar period has witnessed international cartel arrangements in industries involved in oil, steel, sugar, coffee, and farm products.

Today, the most successful international cartel is OPEC (the Organization of Petroleum Exporting Countries), which was formed on September 14, 1960, in reaction to unilateral cuts in crude oil prices by the international oil companies. The objectives of OPEC, as stated by the five original members (Iran, Iraq, Kuwait, Saudi Arabia, and Venezuela), were to stabilize oil prices and to unify the petroleum policies for the member countries. During the 1960s and the 1970s this organization expanded rapidly, and enrolled eight additional members (Qatar, Indonesia, Libya, Abu Dhabi, Algeria, Nigeria, Ecuador, and Gabon). Although this 13-member international cartel had been able to win a few concessions in the 1960s and 1970s, its power did not come to full flower until 1971. In that year, according to the Teheran Agreement, OPEC countries won concessions that allowed them to participate in the process of setting the posted prices of oil. Subsequently, they succeeded between 1973 and 1974 in quadrupling the price of crude oil, setting the stage for the energy crisis of the early 1970s.

In general, the successful operation of a cartel depends on four major factors, namely, the factors of supply, demand, price, and the degree of homogeneity among members. More specifically, to effectively operate a cartel, one needs to satisfy the following conditions:

1. To be able to control a large percentage of the world's supply of an essential commodity.
2. To face an inelastic demand for a commodity that has only a few substitutes.
3. To have members who have similar revenue requirements, facilitating the establishment of an optimum price.
4. To have members with similar backgrounds in such areas as culture, religion, race, language, and political ideology.

Because OPEC has fulfilled most of the above requirements, it has been able to survive for a quarter of a century. However, since the power of a cartel to control the market lies in the unification of its members, and since each member country has its own national objectives, it is not always easy for them to reach a common goal. Consequently, cartels are inherently unstable and are usually expected to collapse in the long run. Even in the case of OPEC, which has successfully operated for many years, there are now signs of its deterioration, evidenced by the lack of cooperation among its member countries. Today, its members do not honor the production quotas that they had agree upon. As a result, the cartel members do not even know exactly how much oil the OPEC members really produce.[12] Two prominent members, Iran and Iraq, were engaged in a war, and the rest of the member countries could not agree on a common pricing policy. Saudi Arabia presses for a relatively low price in order to discourage conservation efforts, substitution, and technological progress that might replace oil. Indonesia, Iran, Nigeria, and Venezuela, however, desire a relatively high price to maximize their short-run revenue.

## Economic Integration

Economic integration is an agreement among nations to decrease or eliminate tariffs. Depending on the terms and the intensity of the agreement, economic integration can be classified as a preferential trade arrangement, a free trade area, a customs union, a common market, or an economic union.

**Preferential Trade Arrangements**　　A preferential trade arrangement is an agreement among participating nations to lower trade barriers. The classical example of a preferential trade arrangement is the British Commonwealth preference scheme, which was formed in 1932 by the United Kingdom.

**Free Trade Area**　　A free trade area is an agreement among nations that removes trade barriers while allowing each member nation to define its own barriers on trade with nonmembers. The European Free Trade Association (EFTA) provides the best example of a free trade area. This association was formed in 1960. Initially it included Austria, Denmark, Norway, Portugal, the United Kingdom, Sweden, and Switzerland. Later, the Faroe Islands, Finland, and Iceland joined this association. Britain and Denmark left the EFTA when they became members of the European Community (EC).

**Customs Union**  A customs union allows the lowering or abolishing of trade barriers among member countries, and it adopts a unified system of tariffs against nonmembers. An example is the **Zollverein**, a customs union established in 1834 by a number of small sovereign German states. This customs union preceded the political unification of Germany, which was achieved in 1870. By removing trade barriers through much of Germany, the Zollverein was an important factor in German unification.

The formation of a customs union may lead to both positive and negative effects for the nations involved. These effects are measured in terms of trade creation and trade diversion, respectively. By eliminating trade barriers among member countries, a customs union might make it cheaper for some member countries to import some of their products from other members rather than producing these products domestically. This is referred to as **trade creation**, which occurs when there is a shift from a high-cost producer inside the union to a low-cost producer also inside the union. Trade creation increases the welfare of the member countries because it leads to specialization in production according to factor endowment and comparative advantage.

By adopting a unified system of tariffs against nonmembers, a customs union makes imports from outside of the union relatively more expensive. **Trade diversion** occurs when lower-cost imports from a country that is not a member of the customs union are replaced by a higher-cost imports of a member country. In other words, trade diversion occurs when there is a shift from low-cost producers outside the union to high-cost producers inside the union. Trade diversion decreases the welfare of member countries because it goes against specialization in production.

The European Community (EC), as we will explain later, provides us with examples of both trade creation and trade diversion. Bela Balassa, an economist, has found that the manufacturing sector of the EC portrays trade-creation effects, whereas the agriculture sector of the EC shows trade-diversion effects. In the manufacturing sector, evidence of substantial trade creation is found in the chemical, fuel, machinery, and transportation equipment industries. In the agriculture sector, trade-diversion effects are especially strong in the beverage, tobacco, raw material, and food industries. According to the study, Britain and West Germany are the two countries that have felt the main impact of trade diversion because, before joining the EC, both of these countries imported a significant portion of their food from the cheapest sources overseas. After joining EC, however, they had to import these supplies from high-cost sources within EC.[13]

**Common Market**  A common market is a more complete form of a customs union. It combines the characteristics of a customs union with the elimination of barriers against the movement of capital and labor among member countries.

An example of a common market is the European Community (EC), which was previously referred to as the European Economic Community (EEC), or European Common Market (ECM). The EC was formed in 1958 by Belgium, France, Italy, Luxembourg, West Germany, and the Netherlands. In 1973, Denmark, Ireland, and the United Kingdom joined the EC. Greece joined in 1981, and Portugal and Spain joined in 1986.

The first objective of the EC is the abolishment of all restrictions on traded goods (industrial or agricultural) and the establishment of common external tariffs against nonmember countries. The second objective is the free movement of labor and capital among its member countries. Although these objectives have been achieved for the most part, there are still some restrictions on the movement of certain labor in the EC at the professional and technical levels.

Overall, the EC members have been very cooperative and have stayed together in protecting their market. For example, in response to the loss of jobs and sales to the United States and Japan, the EC announced a fivefold increase in its industrial research expenditures to boost its competitive position. Additionally, it called on Japanese automakers to voluntarily restrain their exports to the EC as a whole.[14] In 1987, upon request of its members, the EC opened up an antidumping investigation against the Japanese, suspected of dumping semiconductors, and against the South Koreans, suspected of dumping compact disc players, on the European market.[15]

*The EC After 1992* The cooperative efforts of the EC members are expected to reach a zenith in 1992. At their 1985 summit in Milan, the EC members endorsed the "White Paper" that established a detailed legislative program for complete economic integration by 1992. According to the EC commission president, it was necessity that gave rise to the "White Paper," rather than idealism. Under competitive pressure from American and Japanese companies, both in domestic and international markets, Europe found itself struggling with persistently high unemployment. This set the stage for the birth of the "White Paper," the basic thrust of which is the removal of the whole series of trade barriers. These trade barriers can be classified in three major categories: (1) physical barriers—for example, customs procedures and the related paperwork; (2) technical barriers—such as conflicting commercial laws and technical regulations; and (3) fiscal barriers—such as differing excise taxes and value-added taxes. The dismantling of these trade barriers, resulting in a single EC home market, is not only challenging and rewarding for Europeans; it also has global economic implications.

For the EC members the removal of the barriers will stimulate both supply and demand. From the supply standpoint, the removal of the barriers means tougher competition in the Community. EC businesses faced with the pressure of new rivals in the previously protected markets are forced to cut prices. From the demand side, the decrease in prices means an increase in the quantity demanded, which, in turn, encourages the EC businesses to expand their output. The increased competition in the Community also means that EC businesses are forced to cut costs by more efficient use of their resources, and to make products that better suit the European and global markets.

Besides its impact on supply and demand, removal of the barriers will affect the economy at large. Public deficits are expected to decrease as a result of an economically more prosperous Community. The decline in prices, as explained earlier, is expected to ease inflationary pressure, thus ensuring economic growth without harming the EC's external trade status. The inflation-free growth, along with the removal of the barriers, raises the prospect of job creation, thus decreasing unemployment for the Community members.

From the global standpoint, a more dynamic EC will stimulate worldwide competition, and, as trade theories suggest, global welfare will increase.

Not only will 1992 present the EC members with a wave of opportunities; it will also provide their businesses and governments with new challenges.

For EC businesses, the removal of the barriers means the end of protectionism and the beginning of tougher competition; this means downward pressure on profits that result from monopoly power and protectionism. It also means that businesses have to adopt new strategies that capitalize on the expanded market's increased opportunities for innovation and economies of scale.

For EC governments, 1992 means the time by which they must have fulfilled their obligations to enact legislations supporting the objectives of the "White Paper." This outlines 300 items of legislation for the removal of physical, technical, and fiscal barriers before the deadline. After achieving the objectives of the "White Paper," the governments must help to maintain them by giving clear signals of their commitment to businesses.

The success of the EC in the 1990s depends on cooperation among the businesses and the governments involved. Such cooperation is complicated by the Community's diverse cultural and economic picture. The Community is composed of 12 countries, 10 cultures, 9 official languages, 12 currencies, and 12 sets of requirements on border controls.* All of this demands an institutional adjustment entailing a stronger European monetary system, capable of dealing with problems that may arise.

With the prospect of 1992, some firms are about to alter their strategies. The European companies are engaging in mergers, establishing joint ventures, and investing as never before in expectation of a new economic boom. It is interesting to note that some European companies are not only expanding in Europe, but they are also looking for opportunities in the United States. For the U.S. firms, 1992 has meant revival of their activities in Europe, which had drastically declined due to trade barriers. Subsidiaries incorporated in the EC will gain from the dismantling of the barriers to the same extent as do European firms. The U.S. MNCs that are already established in the EC have devised strategies to take advantage of opportunities offered by the 1992 target. Many smaller firms have considered a possible future in the Community. Such con-

---

*Added to this is resistence for some political elites who see 1992 as a threat to their authority.

cerns are not only shared by the European and American firms but by all non-EC countries, especially Japan. Evoked by anticipation of a unified European market, all these events have inflicted tremendous pressure on the European politicians to see that the goal of the "White Paper" is achieved on time.

**Economic Union**  An economic union is the most complete form of economic integration. This kind of integration goes one step further than the common market and calls for the harmonization or unification of the fiscal, monetary, and tax policies of the member nations. An example of an economic union is Benelux, which includes Belgium, Luxembourg, and the Netherlands. This economic union, which was formed during the 1920s, is now a part of the EC.

## Major Trade Associations Among the LDCs

The triumph of the EC has inspired some of the LDCs to engage in economic integration with the intention of helping their own economic development. LDCs have embarked on this cooperative movement, in part, as a defensive reaction to the regional economic integration in Europe which began in the late 1950s and early 1960s. This has resulted in the emergence of different trade associations among the LDCs, some of which have met with scant success.

One factor that has contributed to the failure of some of these trade associations has been the uneven distribution of gains among their members. With most of the benefits accruing to the relatively more developed nations in the group, other nations in the LDC group have been discouraged and consequently withdrawn from the association.

Another factor in the dissolution of these associations is the reluctance of many LDCs to surrender part of their sovereignty to a trade association. Also there is an inadequacy of transportation and communications among the LDCs. The natures of their economies make them compete for the same world market, discouraging trade association agreements.

The major trading associations among LDCs are the following:

1. The Andean Common Market (ANCOM), established by Bolivia, Colombia, Chile, Ecuador, and Peru in 1969. In 1976 Chile left the ANCOM, and in 1973 Venezuela joined this market. ANCOM is a subgroup of LAFTA, which is listed subsequently, and its main policy is to restrict foreign-owned investment.
2. The Association of Southeast Asian Nations (ASEAN), established by Indonesia, Malaysia, the Philippines, Singapore, and Thailand in 1967.
3. The Caribbean Free Trade Association (CARIFTA), established in 1968 by Antigua, Barbados, Bolivia, Colombia, Dominica, Ecuador, Grenada, Guyana, Jamaica, Montserrat, Peru, St. Lucia, St. Vincent, Trinidad, Tobago, and Venezuela. In 1973 this was changed into the Caribbean Common Market (CARICOM) and was extended to include the Bahamas, Belize, St. Kitts-Nevis-Angullia.
4. The Central American Common Market (CACM) is a customs union

that was established by Costa Rica, El Salvador, Guatemala, Honduras, and Nicaragua in 1960.

5. The East African Community (EAC) was established by Kenya, Tanzania, and Uganda in 1967. Due to the political upheaval in Uganda, this association lost its effectiveness, and it was consequently dissolved in 1977.

6. The Economic Community of West African Nations (ECOWAS) was established by Benin, Gambia, Ghana, Guinea, the Ivory Coast, Mali, Mauritania, Niger, Nigeria, Rwanda, Senegal, Togo, and Upper Volta in 1965.

7. The Latin American Free Trade Association (LAFTA) was established by Argentina, Bolivia, Chile, Colombia, Ecuador, Mexico, Paraguay, Peru, Uruguay, and Venezuela in 1960. This association was relatively successful in extending tariff reductions to its members until the mid-1960s. Following that date, however, the nationalist views of some of its members made further tariff reductions difficult. In 1980 the members of LAFTA signed a treaty to form a new association called the Latin American Integration Association (LAIA). This association established new objectives for tariff reductions and other policies that are to be followed in integrating the economies of its members.

## The Organization for Economic Cooperation and Development

The Organization for Economic Cooperation and Development (OECD) is an organization that provides an important channel for multilateral cooperation in the world today. OECD was established in Europe in 1961. Although most members of this organization are European nations, it also includes the major industrial countries of Australia, Canada, Japan, New Zealand, and the United States. The major objectives of the OECD are (1) to assist its member countries in pursuing policies that promote economic and social welfare and (2) to coordinate and encourage members' assistance to the LDCs.

To help its members with trade issues the OECD has organized three committees, each dealing with a specific problem. These committees are the Development Assistance Committee, the Executive Committee Special Session, and the Trade Committee.

The Development Assistance Committee deals with the transfer of funds to the LDCs. The Executive Committee Special Session is concerned with the coordination of the economic policies of the member countries. Finally, the Trade Committee is responsible for (1) discussing current issues and (2) studying the long-term trade policies of member countries.

An important contribution of OECD to international cooperation is the issuance of a code of conduct regarding the operation of MNCs. The purpose of this code is to help MNCs enhance their contributions to international cooperation, while minimizing the problems that arise from their operation. Specific provisions provided by the code say that a MNC should consider national balance-of-payments and credit objectives in formulating its financial activities, advance national scientific and technological goals, disclose complete information regarding the taxes, observe the national standards with regard to labor practices and working conditions, refrain from discrimination in employment, avoid engaging in activities that might adversely affect competition by unfair practices, and regularly make public important operational and financial information.

Although the above code of conduct is not legally enforceable, it has been publicly accepted by most MNCs and has become an increasingly important element that affects the activities of MNCs.

## The General Agreement on Tariffs and Trade

The General Agreement on Tariffs and Trade (GATT) is an international organization that was created to promote freer international trade. The formation of this organization was an attempt to combat the worldwide trade restrictions that had contributed to the post–World War II economic recession.

Established in 1947 by 23 countries, including the United States, GATT was expanded over the years. In 1986 it had 92 members from virtually all the advanced countries, many LDCs, and several communist countries of Eastern Europe.[16] The principal policies governing the operations of GATT are as follows:

1. Nondiscrimination. This principle dictates that each member country should impose the same tariff rates on all of the GATT members. This tariff rate is referred to as the most favored nation (MFN) rate. According to the MFN system, changes in tariff rates agreed upon between any two GATT countries must also be applied to other GATT countries as well. For example, if the United States increases the tariff rate on Italian guitars from, say, 17 percent to 20 percent, it should also impose the same rate on all other countries who export guitars. There are two exceptions to this principle. The first exception is made in regard to associations of economic integration. This means that countries that belong to customs unions, free trade areas, or international trading associations can impose lower tariff rates on their member countries than those levied on nonmember countries. The second exception applies to a nation's trade relationship to its former colonies. For example, under this exception the British Commonwealth preferences are retained under GATT.

2. Reduction of tariffs by negotiation. The negotiations to reduce tariffs and nontariff barriers have been one of the most important activities of GATT. These negotiations have been accomplished by GATT's sponsorship of periodic conferences referred to as "rounds." The first major round is known as the *Kennedy round,* which was initiated by the United States in 1962 and completed in 1967. This round led to an agreement for the reduction of tariff rates for industrial products by a total of 35 percent from their 1962 level, with the tariffs to be phased out in five years. Overall, the Kennedy round proved to be

successful and resulted in the most significant tariff reduction since GATT came into existence.

The second major round is known as the *Tokyo round,* which was formally opened in Tokyo in 1973 and was concluded in 1979. The primary goal of the Tokyo round was the elimination of nontariff trade barriers. Since under the previous round many tariffs were either removed or significantly decreased, many nations had used nontariff trade barriers to pursue their own protectionist policies. The Tokyo round demanded tariff reductions from member countries and called for a code of conduct that would prevent legitimate domestic policies from turning to nontariff trade barriers. The Tokyo round ruled that industrial countries' tariffs had to be cut by an overall average of 33 percent over an eight-year period. This included tariff cuts of 31 percent for the United States, 27 percent for the European Common Market, and 28 percent for Japan.

Overall, the major achievement of the Tokyo round is in its unification of the international community in dismantling the nontariff barriers for the first time. Obviously, the success of the round will depend on how governments will follow in actual practice the nontariff codes that they have agreed upon.

Since 1947, seven rounds have been completed and the eighth round of negotiation, referred to as the **Uruguay round,** which started in 1986, should be completed by 1990. The four major issues for this round of negotiations are (1) nondiscrimination; (2) a further clarification or new rules on distinguishing between "border" measures (such as taxes on international trade) and "nonborder" measures (such as subsidies); (3) the widening trade gap between advanced countries and LDCs; and (4) determining GATT's role in the future.

**3.** Forum for discussions in resolving trade disputes. In resolving trade disputes between different nations GATT acts as an international court of law, and, as such, plays a significant role in the world of international free trade. Before the establishment of GATT, trade disputes between two nations could not be resolved through a formal channel by the intervention a third party. Consequently, trade disagreements between nations went on for years and often resulted in retaliation and trade wars. Today, if two countries cannot settle their dispute by negotiation, they can appeal to GATT for a decision. Accordingly, GATT will assign a committee of experts from different countries to investigate the problem and make recommendations to the parties involved. If these recommendations are not followed, GATT rules for countermeasures to be taken against the nation deemed to be at fault.

So far, there have been very few disputes referred to GATT, some of which were never resolved. For example, in the middle of 1962 the EC members increased their duties on poultry imports, which came mostly from the United States, resulting in a 63 percent decline in U.S. poultry exports to the EC member countries. This set the stage for what became known as the "chicken war." Since bilateral negotiations between these two parties did not resolve the problem, the case was taken to GATT. GATT ruled that the United States had experienced a loss of $26 million and should be compensated by withdrawing concessions to EC if a settlement could not be reached. Although both sides accepted the ruling, they were still unable to resolve the "chicken war." Thus in January 1965, the United States imposed high retaliatory tariffs against the EC on imports of brandy, dextrine, potato starch, and trucks. Although in this example GATT was not effective in eliminating EC duties on poultry, it did limit the extent of the U.S. retaliation and precluded the EC from employing counterretaliatory measures. In fact, the existence of GATT has been a deterrent to trade wars between nations, and it has caused trading partners to try to solve their disputes rather than await GATT rulings. For example, in 1975 the United States protested the granting of subsidies by EC to the producers of certain cheeses. As a result, a compromise was reached when the EC chose to temporarily suspend its export rebate payments, that is, the cash subsidies given to the cheese exporters, and the United States decided not to impose countervailing duties against the EC.

A more recent example is a dispute between the United States and Canada. In 1982, the United States filed a complaint with GATT regarding the performance requirements imposed on new U.S. foreign investments in Canada. According to these requirements foreign companies had to (1) give preference to the purchase of Canadian goods over imported goods and (2) meet certain export requirements. In the 1982 GATT ruling, it was decided to drop the first requirement but to maintain the second requirement.

## ARGUMENTS FOR PROTECTION

Our discussion of the law of comparative advantage in Chapter 2 showed that free international trade results in the most efficient utilization of the world's scarce resources. Although the law of comparative advantage and the benefits of free international trade have never been successfully refuted, many nations, under pressure by special interest groups, have reverted to protectionism. Protectionist policies have been followed by both advanced countries and LDCs. Examples of advanced countries who have pursued protectionist policies include Canada, Japan, France, the United Kingdom, and the United States. Brazil and Colombia are examples of many LDCs that have vigorously pursued protectionist policies. The results of such policies have been higher prices for the consumers and a net national loss for the society that adopts protectionism. For example, it was estimated that the 29.3 percent average tariff on apparel imports into the United States had cost American consumers $2.7 billion in higher prices in 1981.[17]

The history of different nations is replete with the lobbying of corporate executives, union leaders, and political groups who have sought protectionism and argued that their case is special and demands immediate attention. Most of their arguments can be classified into one of six categories: the infant industry argument, the national security argument, the diversification argument, the wage and employment protection argument, the balance-of-trade argument, and the infant government argument.

## Infant Industry Argument

The infant industry argument asserts that since a new and underdeveloped industry cannot survive competition from abroad, it should be protected temporarily with high tariffs and quotas on imported goods. It is hoped that this protectionism will allow the industry to grow and would enable it to become technically more efficient so that it could successfully compete with foreign industries.

The infant industry argument can be attributed to Alexander Hamilton, the first secretary of the treasury of the United States. In his famous Report on Industry and Commerce, published in 1791, he articulated the economic problems of the time and recommended the use of tariffs to enhance the development of industry and to foster the growth of the U.S. economy. This report set the stage for the imposition of tariffs for a number of industries during the nineteenth and twentieth centuries. Since the infant industry argument pleads only for a temporary protection and does not deny the validity of free trade, it is more widely accepted by economists as a theoretically sound argument. However, in practice, economists have realized that there are four major shortcomings associated with this argument.

First, it is not necessarily true that an infant industry needs protection to get started. Some new industries could even displace the less dynamic, older ones through effective management, marketing, and financial policies. Even if an industry is unprosperous now, it might be expected to gain sufficient profit in the future to outweigh the present costs. It should be able to borrow capital now and survive the initial rough period, and thus it does not need protection.

Second, if an industry is protected it could lose its incentive to effectively compete with the exporting nation's mature industries, and because of this it may never grow to maturity.

Third, this argument assumes that the government can effectively identify those industries that deserve protection. The historical evidence shows, however, that it is very difficult for a government to make the right choice in deciding which industry to protect. For example, the U.S. wool industry, which was chosen for protection by the U.S. government in the early nineteenth century, has not yet grown out of its infancy stage.

Fourth, even if the government can make the right choice of an industry to protect, it could still be argued that protection against imports is not a sound decision. In this case, if an infant industry must be protected from foreign competition, a subsidy may be a more appropriate means of protection than a tariff or a quota. This is because tariffs and quotas lead to higher prices for the domestic consumers, whereas subsidies tend to increase output as well as reduce costs. Additionally, since subsidies are visible and must be periodically voted on by the representatives in government, they are less likely to turn into permanent protection.

## National Security Argument

According to the national security argument, a nation that is dependent on foreign sources of essential supplies would be vulnerable at a time of war, when the flow of such supplies could be blocked by its enemies. England, as an example, in both world wars had its imports of food and raw materials curtailed by the German navy. It is argued, then, that a country needs to impose tariffs on some crucial goods that are needed for war and defense in order to promote their domestic production and ensure their continued availability.

In the United States such an argument has been used from time to time by the leaders of various industries who have appealed to the U.S. government for protection against foreign competition. For example, during the 1960s, Roger Blough, the chairman of the board of U.S. Steel Corporation, used this argument in front of a congressional committee. He argued that since a strong industrial steel industry was necessary for a modern defense, the United States could not rely on importation of steel from countries that are close to the Soviet Union or the People's Republic of China. For this reason he argued that the steel industry should be protected by trade barriers.

On the surface, the national security argument is persuasive and makes sense. However, it suffers from the following shortcomings:

**1.** Although this argument has many economic implications, it is a political and military argument rather than an economic one. Such an argument, therefore, should not be settled by input from those who have personal business interests at stake in protectionism.

**2.** Since most producers consider their products essential for the national security, it is very difficult for the government to specify certain industries as truly warranting protection. In fact, in the United States, the producers of many ordinary products, such as plastics, electronics, umbrellas, candles, and gloves, have asked for protection on the basis of national security.

**3.** Apart from the above considerations, if some protection is necessary, direct subsidies are preferable to tariffs and quotas (as is the case with infant industries).

## Diversification Argument

Many of the LDCs of today are dependent on a single commodity for their economic survival. Such single commodities are Bolivia's tin, Burma's rice, Chile's copper, Costa Rica's coffee, and Panama's bananas. Since a significant portion of these countries' income is based on the exportation of one product, fluctuations in the demand for that product could lead to severe economic instability. To prevent such an episode, according to the proponents of the diversification argument, these countries should follow protectionist policies in order to encourage the establishment of different industries. Developing a number of different industries will provide for greater economic stability and growth, without a reliance on a single product.

There is some truth in this argument. For example, a decline in oil prices in the 1980s crippled economies that concentrated on the production of this product. A case in point is Mexico, which is faced with a staggering and overdue international debt, bringing that country to the brink of bankruptcy.

The problems with the diversification argument are as follows:

1. It is not an argument which is applicable to the advanced countries such as the United States or Canada, which are already diversified.
2. The argument takes for granted that the government, rather than the private sector, can more effectively recognize the diversification needs of the economy. Such a presumption goes against the rationale of competition and the workings of the market mechanism, and it may lead to an inefficient and unnatural diversification, which might be costly for the nation.
3. This argument assumes that a great reliance on manufacturing ensures stability in export earnings. The evidence shows, however, that there has not been any significant difference between the stability of export earnings of the LDCs who support diversification and the stability of export earnings of the advanced countries. For example, the data show that Japan's advanced economy has experienced more year-to-year instability than most LDCs' economies have experienced since World War II.[18]

### Wage and Employment Protection Argument

According to this argument, high-wage countries such as the United States or the United Kingdom cannot compete effectively with the low-wage countries and hence they should impose tariffs or quotas to protect their workers from the products made by low-wage workers overseas. This argument is very popular and has been endorsed by both American business leaders and the American labor movement, which has actively pursued protectionism since the late 1960s. Their efforts have resulted in protective controls in industries that employ a large number of people such as the apparel, automaking, steel, sugar, and textiles industries.

The opponents of the wage and employment protection argument present the following criticisms and qualifications:

1. The cheaper labor abroad might lead only to a cheaper wage cost, but not necessarily to cheaper production costs. This is because labor is not the only factor of production. Other factors of production, such as capital and land, are also significant cost components of a product. Consequently, depending on the relative proportion of resources used in the production of a commodity, products can be classified as labor intensive, capital intensive, or land intensive. Thus low-wage countries might have an advantage over high-wage countries only with respect to labor-intensive commodities, that is, products for which wages are a large percentage of the total production costs.

**2.** Even in the case of labor-intensive products, high-wage countries could still compete effectively with low-wage countries for two reasons. First, fringe benefits and government-imposed bonuses are much higher in some low-wage nations, such as China, Chile, and Mexico. Thus, if we add these fringe benefits to the hourly wage rates, the wage differential between high-wage and low-wage countries diminishes, and may become insignificant. Second, the labor efficiency in high-wage countries is usually higher than in low-wage countries. Thus the higher labor efficiency in high-wage countries might compensate for the lower wage levels in low-wage countries.

## Balance of Trade Argument

The balance of trade of a nation, which is a simpler version of the balance of goods and services discussed in Chapter 6, is a statement that shows the money value of all merchandise imported and exported. According to the proponents of the balance of trade argument, tariffs or quotas are necessary because they encourage a favorable balance of trade. It is argued that such a surplus is desirable because it means that a country is selling relatively more products abroad than it is buying from abroad. This, in turn, would lead to a higher level of income, employment, and production for the domestic economy.

Although the above argument seems to be persuasive it ignores the following points:

**1.** In the long run, protectionism might lead to retaliation from another country and make a country worse off. If an industry that is threatened by imports obtains tariff protection against another country, that country might in turn impose duties against that industry's exports. If this happens, more jobs might be lost because of a decrease in exports than are gained by reducing competing imports.

As an example of this, the U.S. lumber industry complained that Canada is unfairly subsidizing its softwood lumber industry. This issue gave rise to protectionist sentiment in the U.S. Congress and caused President Reagan to impose a 35 percent tariff on imports of Canadian-made cedar shades and shingles. It was also expected that the United States would impose countervailing duties of $2.9 billion a year on the Canadian softwood exports, if the subsidization charges against Canada were proven.[19] In its turn, reacting to the U.S. move, the Canadian government imposed import duties on the U.S. exports of books and other publications, and on certain computer parts and semiconductors. As this example indicates, protectionism did not resolve the underlying problems of either of these two nations. Its only outcome was to hinder the trading relationship of these two friendly nations.

**2.** Import duties lead to higher prices for consumers who have to pay for inefficient domestic producers. From an economic standpoint this leads to misallocation of scarce resources. This is because, in the long run, protectionism encourages the reallocation of resources out of more productive industries into the less productive (protected) industries, causing costs to increase and comparative advantages to decrease.

## Infant Government Argument

According to this argument, a nation that is young and has no alternative means of raising the needed funds for its economic development should use import and export duties as a crucial source of public revenue.

Although this argument, like its predecessors, goes against the free trade notion, it is widely accepted by economists on the grounds that it may contribute to the economic growth of the LDCs.

For many poor LDCs the main impediment to economic development is caused by the inability of their governments to raise the necessary funds for rendering essential public services, such as housing, education, road construction, and water management. Although revenue could be generated through taxes on income, property, consumption, and production, these taxes are difficult to measure and administer. Additionally, even if these taxes could be adequately measured, since the main problem of most LDCs is that they are poor, the amount of revenues generated would not be sufficient for launching the development programs. By just patrolling the border with a few custom officials, however, revenue can be collected easily by imposing duties on imports and exports. This, in fact, is a practice that is followed by many LDCs, who get roughly between 25 percent and 60 percent of their revenue from customs duties.

In summary, the infant government argument is valid only when an LDC that has no other source of revenue uses import and export duties to finance its economic development programs and does not use import and export duties as a protectionist device.

We conclude this chapter by stating that, as a general rule, protectionist policies should be avoided. Such policies fuel inflation and raise costs to consumers by increasing the domestic prices of the protected products. Such policies misallocate scarce resources by encouraging producers to shift their production activities from products that they can produce more efficiently to those that they produce less efficiently. For example, in an effort to improve its economy, Mexico, a country that has been burdened with heavy foreign loans, started to dismantle its protectionist barriers in 1985. At that time, there were more than 5,000 items that were subject to restrictive import licenses. In 1987, there were fewer than 500 such items. During this two-year period (1985–1987) the government subsidies were also reduced and tariffs were cut from as high as 100 percent to about 40 percent. As a result of these policies, the Mexican economy became more competitive. The increased competition forced the Mexican producers to improve the quality of their products. These freer trade policies greatly contributed to the Mexican economic recovery, which, in 1987, seemed to be moving towards "an impressive economic turnaround."[20]

As another example, it is estimated that the U.S. trade barriers on manufactured goods is costing the American consumers more than $50 billion a year, or $450 for every individual who is working. In the clothing industry alone, the U.S. protectionist policies have resulted in more than a doubling of prices compared with what they would have been if the United States had not had trade barriers.[21] The protectionist price policies in the steel industry under President Carter cost consumers about $100 million a year for more than three years. These policies saved, temporarily, 12,000 steelworking jobs. However, the cost of each job saved to the consumer was more than $80,000 a year, which is more than what the job actually paid.[22] Although these policies were enacted presumably to save American jobs, economists believe that no jobs have been saved on a permanent basis.

What seems to be needed in the case of the U.S. manufacturing is a freer trade that causes the inefficient manufacturers to drop out of the market and encourages the productive producers to make products that are of high quality and can compete in the international market. For example, a U.S. steel industry executive writes that "it is only during periods of intense competitive pressures, such as the one we have seen since 1982, that modernization accelerates, along with the closing of antiquated facilities that cannot be modernized or be environmentally acceptable. . . . The steel industry's problem is not in what steelworkers are paid, but in their lack of productivity."[23] As Japanese manufacturers have demonstrated, the popularity of their automobiles in the world market is due not to their government's protectionism but to the excellent quality of their cars, which, despite rising prices, has kept them in high demand throughout the world.[24]

## SUMMARY

1. A tariff is a tax or customs duty that is imposed on the importation or exportation of a product that is crossing national boundaries.
2. Depending on the purpose for which tariffs are imposed, they can be classified as protective tariffs or revenue tariffs. Protective tariffs are levied to protect the home industry from foreign competitors. Revenue tariffs are imposed by governments to raise tax revenues.
3. Depending on the way in which tariffs are calculated, they can be classified as specific tariffs, ad valorem tariffs, or compound tariffs. A specific tariff is expressed in terms of a fixed amount of money per unit of the imported product. Ad valorem tariffs are expressed in terms of a percentage of the total value of the imported commodity. Finally, a compound tariff is a combination of a specific tariff and an ad valorem tariff.
4. The effective rate of protection can be defined as the percentage increase in the domestic value added of a product as the result of tariffs.
5. Nontariff trade barriers include quotas, subsidies, taxes, and other diverse measures (such as customs procedures, foreign exchange restrictions, and regulations involving labeling, health, safety, and shipping) that restrict free international trade.
6. A quota is the limitation set on the quantity of a commodity that crosses the national boundaries. Depending on whether a good is imported or exported, the quota is referred to as an import quota or an export quota.

7. The main differences between tariffs and quotas are (a) Quotas are more effective tolls in restricting trade flow than are tariffs; (b) a disadvantage of quotas is that their use may lead to domestic monopoly of production; (c) since quotas are more effective in restricting the trade flow than tariffs, they are more effective tools for bargaining and retaliation; (d) quotas might be easier to administer than tariffs; (e) quotas are more restrictive than tariffs and suppress competition; and (f) quotas might be more harmful than tariffs to an imposing nation if they give monopoly power to exporters.

8. Subsidies are indirect forms of protection that are granted by a national government to domestic producers. Subsidies are given to either export-competing industries or import-competing industries.

9. Besides quotas, subsidies, and taxes, other nontariff trade barriers can be classified into three major categories: (a) government purchasing policies, (b) administrative and technical requirements, and (c) exchange rate controls.

10. Dumping is the practice of selling a commodity in a foreign market at below cost, or at a cheaper price than the price that is charged in the domestic market.

11. Sporadic dumping occurs when a firm with surplus inventories sells its product in a foreign market at below cost, or at a price that is lower than what is charged in the domestic market.

12. Predatory dumping is practiced when a firm charges a lower price than its competitors in the foreign market with the intention of weakening them or driving them out of the market.

13. Persistent dumping occurs when a firm consistently sells its product at below cost, or at a lower price abroad than at home.

14. An international cartel is an organization that is composed of firms in the same industry but from different countries who agree to limit their outputs and exports in order to influence the prices of the commodities they produce and to maximize their profits.

15. The most successful international cartel is the Organization of Petroleum Exporting Countries (OPEC). This organization, formed in 1960, is composed of 13 oil-producing nations.

16. Economic integration is an agreement by some nations to have discriminatory decreases in tariffs or to eliminate tariffs among themselves.

17. Depending on the terms and intensity of the agreements, economic integration can be classified as a preferential trade arrangement, a free trade area, a customs union, a common market, or an economic union.

18. A preferential trade arrangement is an agreement among participating nations for lowering trade barriers among them.

19. A free trade area is established by an agreement between nations that removes trade barriers among members, while allowing each member nation to define its own barriers on trade with nonmembers.

20. A customs union is an organization that allows for the lowering or abolishing of trade barriers between member countries, and that adopts a unified system of tariffs against nonmembers.

21. The formation of a customs union may lead to both trade creation and trade diversion. Trade creation occurs when there is a shift from a high-cost producer inside the union to a low-cost producer also inside the union. Trade diversion occurs when lower-cost imports from a country that is not a member of the customs union is replaced by the higher-cost imports of a member country.

22. A common market is a more complete form of a customs union. It combines the

characteristics of a customs union with the elimination of barriers on the movement of capital and labor among member countries.

23. The cooperative efforts of the EC members are expected to reach a zenith in 1992. At their 1985 summit in Milan, the EC members endorsed the "White Paper" that established a detailed legislative program for complete economic integration by 1992.

24. The basic thrust of the "White Paper" is the removal of the whole series of trade barriers. These trade barriers can be classified into three major categories: (a) physical barriers; (b) technical barriers; and (c) fiscal barriers.

25. An economic union is the most complete form of economic integration. This kind of integration goes one step further than a common market and calls for the harmonization or unification of the fiscal, monetary, and tax policies of the member nations.

26. The major trade associations among LDCs are the Andean Common Market (ANCOM), the Association of Southern Asian Nations (ASEAN), the Caribbean Free Trade Association (CARIFTA, Changed to CARICOM in 1973), the Central American Common Market (CACM), the East African Community (EAC), the Economic Community of West African Nations (ECOWAS), and the latin American Free Trade Association (LAFTA, changed to LAIA in 1980).

27. The Organization for Economic Cooperation and Development (OECD) is an organization that provides an important channel for multilateral cooperation in the world today. The major objectives of the OECD are the following: (a) to assist its member countries in pursuing policies that promote economic and social welfare, and (b) to coordinate and encourage members' assistance to LDCs. OECD has also issued a code of conduct for the operations of MNCs.

28. The General Agreement on Tariffs and Trade (GATT) is an international organization that was created to promote freer international trade.

29. The principal policies governing the operations of GATT are the following: (a) nondiscrimination in matters of trade, (b) the reduction of tariffs by negotiation, and (c) the establishment of a forum for discussions in resolving trade disputes.

30. The six major arguments for protection are the following: (a) infant industry, (b) national security, (c) diversification, (d) wage and employment protection, (e) balance of trade, and (f) infant government.

## QUESTIONS

4.1 Differentiate between tariff and nontariff barriers.

4.2 Compare subsidies and tariffs. Explain the disadvantages of each of these forms of protection.

4.3 The textbook presents six arguments for protection:
   a. Give a recent example of protectionism that fits under one of these arguments.
   b. Do you think that protectionism is justifiable under the circumstances explained in your example? Explain.
   c. Which of the arguments for protection do you think are more relevant for your country today?

4.4 Tariffs are more effective as a protective device than subsidies. This is because tariffs generate revenue, whereas subsidies require revenue. Do you agree with these statements? Discuss.

4.5 The American workers are wrong to think they need protection from imports in order to save their jobs. Do you agree with this statement? Discuss.

4.6 Dumping is good for my country because it means some foreigners are subsidizing our consumption. Do you agree with this statement? Discuss.

4.7 Explain the difference between a customs union and a free trade association.

4.8 Compare sporadic, persistent, and predatory dumping.

4.9 Assume the production of $1000 worth of garments in England requires $500 worth of cloth. The nominal tariff rates of importing these products into the United States are for cloth, 10 percent, and for garments, 25 percent. Given these data, calculate the effective rate of protection of the garment industry in the United States. Show the details of your work.

4.10 Given the existence of tension between some of the OPEC members, it is evident that it will break up in the 1990s. Do you agree with this statement? Discuss.

## APPENDIX 4.1 Formula for Calculating the Effective Rate of Protection

The effective rate of protection can be calculated by the use of the following formula:

$$R_e = \frac{T_f - rT_m}{1 - r}$$

Where:

$R_e$ = the effective rate of protection.
$T_f$ = the nominal tariff rate on the final product.
$r$ = the ratio of the value of the imported input to the value of the final product (the import price without tariff).
$T_m$ = the nominal tariff rate on the imported input.

Plugging the Table 4.2 data into the formula, we get:

$$R_e = \frac{0.2 - (0.6)(0.0)}{1 - 0.6} = 0.5$$

## NOTES

1. Office of the Special Representative for Trade Negotiations, *Press Release No. 269,* 17 January 1979.
2. "U.S. Is Taking a Tough Approach To Limit Japan's Textile Exports," *The Wall Street Journal,* 13 January 1986, p. 31.
3. "U.S. Asks Allies To Curb Exports To Soviet Union," *The Wall Street Journal,* 24 June 1987, p. 22.
4. "Japan's Export Increase Will Heighten Pressure on U.S. Automaker's Profit," *The Wall Street Journal,* 29 March 1985, p. 2

5. "Japan to Extend Curb on Exports of Cars to U.S.," *The Wall Street Journal*, 27 January 1987, p. 39.

6. Charles P. Kindleberger and H. Peter Lindert, *International Economics*, 6th ed. (Homewood, Ill.: Irwin, 1978), pp. 150–152.

7. "Japan Plans to Subsidize Small Export Companies," *The Wall Street Journal*, 2 December 1985, p. 24.

8. "Hurdle Is Cleared in Move to Penalize Japanese Chipmakers for Dumping," *The Wall Street Journal*, 2 December 1985, p. 24; "Falling Chips: Semiconductor Accord With Japan Fails to Aid U.S. Firms as Intended," *The Wall Street Journal*, 12 February 1987, pp. 1, 10.

9. "Canadians Investigate Charges of Dumping Hypodermic Needles," *The Wall Street Journal*, 11 November 1985, p. 32.

10. Michael Doan, "New Protectionism: A Threat to U.S. Trade," *U.S. News and World Report*, 1 February 1982 pp. 51–52.

11. Ibid.

12. "As OPEC's Members Produce Above Quota, Big Data Gap Widens," *The Wall Street Journal*, 24 November 1987, pp. 1, 18.

13. Bela Balassa, *The Theory of Economic Integration* (Homewood, Ill.: Irwin, 1961).

14. "Europeans Mull Major Research Boost to Compete with U.S., Japanese Firm," *The Wall Street Journal*, 10 June 1986, p. 32; "Japan Concern on Autos Is Linked to German Sales," *The Wall Street Journal*, 12 June 1986, p. 32

15. "EC Opens Anti-Dumping Investigations Against Japanese and South Koreans," *The Wall Street Journal*, 7 July 1987, p. 24.

16. "General Agreement on Tariffs and Trade—GATT." In *The Europa Year Book*, 3 vols. (London: Europana, 1987), vol. 1, p. 59.

17. "A Global Trade War on the Way?" *U.S. News & World Report*, 1 March 1982, pp. 57–58

18. Joseph D. Coppock, *International Instability: The Experience After World War II* (New York: McGraw-Hill, 1982), Chap. 4.

19. "Lumber Probe Is Not Expected to Fuel Dispute: U.S. to Play Down Action on Trade Complaint on Canadian Softwood," *The Wall Street Journal*, 9 June 1986, p. 8; "Canadian Dollar Falls 1% Against U.S. Currency: Concern over Trade Dispute Pulls Down Canada Unit," *The Wall Street Journal*, 3 June 1986, p. 34

20. "Fading Prospects? Mexico's Turnaround of Sagging Economy Now Seems Imperiled," *The Wall Street Journal*, 23 November 1987, pp. 1, 19.

21. "As Free-Trade Bastion, U.S. Isn't Half as Pure as Many People Think," *The Wall Street Journal*, 1 November 1985, p. 1

22. "Protectionism Ensures Stagnation," *The Wall Street Journal*, 21 August 1987, p. 22.

23. Ibid.

24. U.S. Congress, Office of Technology Assessment, *U.S. Industrial Competitiveness: A Comparison of Steel, Electronics and Automobiles* (Washington, D.C.: U.S. Government Printing Office, 1981), p. 47.

## SUGGESTED READINGS

Aho, Michael C., and Jonathan D. Arouson. *Trade Talks: America Better Listen*. New York: Council on Foreign Relations, 1985.

Anjaria, Shailendra J. "A New Round of Global Trade Negotiations," *Finance and Development,* June 1986, pp. 2–5.

Anjaria, S. J., et al. *Trade Policy Developments in Industrial Countries.* Washington, D.C.: International Monetary Fund, 1981.

Baldwin, Robert E. *The Multilateral Trade Negotiations.* Washington, D.C.: American Enterprise Institute, 1979.

Bergsten, Fred C., and William R. Cline. "Trade Policy in the 1980's: An Overview." In William R. Cline, ed., *Trade Policy in the 1980s.* Washington, D.C.: Institute for International Economics, 1983.

Blackhurst, Richard, et al. *Trade Liberalization, Protectionism, and Interdependence.* Geneva: General Agreement on Tariffs and Trade. Special Paper on International Economics, No. 7. Princeton, N.J.: Princeton University Press, 1965. Chap. 4.

Bruynes, Lee. "Europe in 1992 and Beyond: Phillips Looks to the Future," *Europe,* October 1988, pp. 18–19.

Buchan, David. "E.C. Will Abolish Restriction of Capital Movements," *Europe.* July/August 1988, pp. 18–20.

Cohen, Robert B. "The Prospects for Trade and Protectionism in Auto Industry." In William R. Cline, ed., *Trade Policy in the 1980s.* Washington, D.C.: Institute for International Economics, 1983.

European Community. *Europe.* Monthly. Luxembourg: Commission of the European Communities.

European Community. *General Report on the Activities of Community.* Annual. Luxembourg: Commission of the European Communities.

European Free Trade Association. *EFTA: What It Is, What It Does.* Current Edition. Geneva: Secretariat of Free Trade Association.

General Agreement on Tariffs and Trade. *Focus.* Monthly. Geneva, Switzerland: General Agreement on Tariffs and Trade Information Service.

General Agreement on Tariffs and Trade. *GATT: What It Is, What It Does.* Geneva: General Agreement on Tariffs and Trade. Latest edition.

Griffin, James, and David Teece. *OPEC Behavior and World Oil Prices.* London: Allen & Unwin, 1982.

Hufbauer, Clyde. "Subsidy Issues After Tokyo Round." In William K. Cline, ed., *Trade Policy in the 1980s.* Washington, D.C.: Institute for International Economics, 1983.

Hufbauer, Gary C., et al. *Trade Protectionism in the United States: 31 Case Studies.* Washington, D.C.: Institute for International Economics, 1986

Jackson, John H. "GATT Machinery and Tokyo Round Agreements." In William K. Cline, ed., *Trade Policy in the 1980s.* Washington, D.C.: Institute for International Economics, 1983.

Kerr, A. *The Common Market and How It Works.* New York: Pergamon Press, 1977.

Longworth, R. C. "U.S. Begins Assesing Impact of 1992 Market Deadline," *Europe,* May 1988, pp. 14–15.

MacAvoy, Paul. *Crude Oil Prices: As Determined by OPEC and Market Fundamentals.* New York: Harper & Row, Ballinger Books, 1982.

Mosetting, Michael D. "The Implications of 1992 for U.S. Business," *Europe,* December 1988, pp. 18–20.

Organization for Economic Cooperation and Development. *The Impact of the Newly Industrializing Countries on Production and Trade In Manufacturers.* Paris: Organization For Economic Development and Cooperation, 1979.

Paolo, Ceddhini. *The European Challenge 1992.* Brookfield, VT: Grower, 1989.

Rohson, Peter. *The Economics of International Integration.* London: Allen & Unwin, 1980. Chaps. 2 and 3.

Spellman, James D. "1992 Prompts Unprecedented Wave of Mergers," *Europe,* December 1988, pp. 35–39.

Swann, D. *The Economics of the Common Market.* Baltimore, Md.: Johns Hopkins University Press, 1975.

United States International Trade Commission. *Annual Report.* Washington, D.C.: U.S. Government Printing Office. Annual.

Waltt, Alan W. "The Need for New GATT Rules to Govern Safeguard Actions." In William K. Cline, ed., *Trade Policy in the 1980s.* Washington, D.C.: Institute for International Economics, 1983.

"Will Montreal Talks Resolve Trade Issue?" *Futures: Magazine of Commodities and Options,* December 1988, p. 42.

# The International Monetary System

*B*ecause each sovereign nation has its own currency, it is essential to maintain a workable system of international payments that facilitates trade between different countries. Ideally, such a system would be composed of an international central bank that would handle an international money which would be accepted by all nations. Practically, however, because sovereign nations like to manage their own monetary systems, rather than trusting an international central bank, it has been necessary for them to engage in various cooperative arrangements. These arrangements, which involve rules, procedures, customs, instruments, and the organizational setting, are referred to as the international monetary system.

Because the international monetary system has been continually changing, its comprehension necessitates an understanding of the major events that have shaped its present form. The purpose of this chapter is to provide us with a basic knowledge of the history of the international monetary system. This will help us to understand the present institutional setting of the international monetary system and the way that it influences the foreign exchange market.

## THE GOLD COIN STANDARD

In earlier times, when the volume of foreign trade was insignificant and was confined mainly to a few luxury items, the international payments were made chiefly in gold and silver. Gold and silver values were determined by their market prices at the time that the payments were made. With the increase in the volume of international trade in the nineteenth century, however, it became necessary to devise a unified method of international payments that could be accepted by all countries. This meant the development of a system that could not affect the free interaction of market forces and would not be subject to control by any government. The quest for such a system resulted in the development of the gold coin standard, or, simply, the gold standard. The essential characteristics of the gold coin standard were the following:

1. A country's unit of currency (such as the U.S. dollar, the British pound, or the German mark) was defined by law in terms of a fixed weight of gold. For example, one U.S. dollar was equated to 23.22 grains of fine gold, and one British pound was defined as containing 113 grains of fine gold.
2. Gold itself, either in bullion or in coins, was permitted to be exported or imported without any restrictions.
3. The national currency and gold coins could be freely converted into each other at the defined rate. Also, the government was obligated to exchange gold for paper money, or vice versa, at the defined rate.
4. There were no restrictions imposed on the coinage of gold.
5. Gold coins were considered as full legal tender for all debts.

Because national currencies were defined in terms of a fixed amount of gold, this meant that the exchange rates had to be stable and could only fluctuate within a very narrow limit known as the gold export point and the gold import point. To clarify, consider our previous example of the U.S. dollar and the British pound. Because one U.S. dollar was equal to 23.22 grains of fine gold, and one British pound was equal to 113 grains, then one British pound was equal to 4.86 U.S. dollars ($113 \div 23.22 = 4.86$). Given that the cost of shipping and insurance of 113 grains of gold between New York and London was almost $0.02 (2 cents) in 1930, the exchange rate of one U.S. dollar fluctuated between $4.84 and $4.88 to the British pound at that time.

The reason for this fluctuation is that under this system gold could be sold at two different rates: at the fixed legal rate defined by the government, or at the market rate defined by the demand and supply for gold. Thus, if the market rate of the British pound increased, say, to $4.89, it would have been cheaper for a U.S. importer to obtain 113 grains of gold for $4.86 at the legal rate from the U.S. Treasury. The importer could then ship the gold to London to settle payments to a British exporter. Because 113 grains of gold in England was accepted as one British pound, the U.S. importer would have had to pay $4.88 for a British pound ($4.86, the legal rate, plus $0.02 shipping), instead of the higher market rate of $4.89, thus saving $0.01 on each British pound bought. With similar reasoning, if the market rate fell, say, to $4.83, a British importer could obtain 113 grains of gold for each British pound, and then ship the gold to New York at a cost of $0.02 for each 113 grains shipped. Because 113 grains of gold was equal to $4.86 in New York, the importer was in effect getting $4.84 ($4.86, the legal rate, minus $0.02 shipping) for each British pound instead of the lower market rate of $4.83, thus saving $0.01 on each 113 grains of gold shipped.

In the previous example, $4.88 and $4.84 were known as the "gold points," $4.88 being referred to as the "gold export point," and $4.84 being known as the "gold import point." Thus the gold points were equal to the legal rate, plus or minus the cost of shipping gold. These gold points set an upper and a lower limit within which the exchange rate could fluctuate. In our example, gold would be exported from the United States when the market rate rose above the gold export point ($4.88) and imported when it fell below the gold import point ($4.84). Consequently, the exchange rate remained stable within the limits set by the gold points.

The gold standard system provided an automatic adjustment mechanism that corrected for the deficit or surplus in the balance of payments.* Because each country's money supply was composed of either gold itself or paper money backed by gold, a surplus in the balance of payments of a country meant a rise in the money supply, which resulted in higher domestic prices. This, in turn, caused exports to decrease and imports to increase, thus reducing the surplus in the balance of payments. A deficit in the balance of payments of a nation meant a decrease in the money supply. The fall in the money supply, in turn, resulted in lower domestic prices, which caused exports to increase and imports to decrease, thus reducing the deficit in the balance of payments.

The gold standard system prevailed mainly from 1880 to 1914. With the outbreak of World War I in 1914 the system was disrupted, but it continued its existence on a somewhat modified basis until the early 1930s. The gold standard system is linked to classical economic theory. Consequently, the automatic adjustment in the balance of payments was based on the classical theory of income and employment which assumed that (1) there was full employment of

---

*As we will explain in detail in Chapter 6, the balance of payments of a country is an accounting statement that shows all the transactions of a country with the rest of the world. If, as the result of these transactions, a country is pumping more money out of its economy than it is pumping in, it has a balance of payments deficit. If the reverse is true, the country would have a balance of payments surplus.

resources, and thus a rise in the quantity of money could ensure an increase in the general price level, and (2) prices and wages were flexible.

Given these assumptions, allowing the money supply to correct for the balance of payments problem meant that a country could not employ monetary policy to achieve full employment without creating inflation. This is because classical economists believed that there were automatic forces in the system that established full employment without inflation. Under these classical assumptions, no depression could be prolonged. However, the Great Depression of the 1930s proved the contrary, and with it emerged Keynesian economics, which explained that (1) the assumption of full employment was a special, rather than a general case; and (2) the assumption of price and wage flexibility was not valid for our modern economic system. This meant that the government had to intervene in the economic system to ensure full employment and combat depression rather than waiting for automatic forces to take effect, as classical economists recommended. Thus, although the gold standard had the desirable feature of exchange stability, it subjected the domestic economy to the undesirable processes of deflation or inflation. In other words, it provided external stability at the expense of the internal instability. With the Great Depression, the stage was set for the abandonment of this monetary standard. As a result, it was formally abandoned by the United Kingdom in 1931, by the United States in 1933, and by other countries in the following few years.

## THE GOLD BULLION STANDARD

Following the abandonment of the gold coin standard in the 1930s, the United States and most of the other advanced countries adopted the gold bullion standard.

Under the gold bullion standard, the nation's unit of currency was defined in terms of a fixed weight of gold. However, unlike the gold coin standard, gold did not circulate within the domestic economy. Gold was used only to meet two purposes: (1) to meet the needs of different industries, such as in dentistry and in jewelry manufacture and (2) to settle international transactions between different nations. Thus, for the most part, the impact of gold on the monetary system was neutralized. In other words, gold was demonetized, except for any possible indirect influence that might result from transactions between national governments.

By replacing the gold coin standard with the gold bullion standard, it was hoped that these countries could effectively manage their money rather than leave it to market forces and becoming subservient to market forces. It was hoped that this new system would restore confidence in their currencies at the national and international levels. The 1930s, however, witnessed a period of great instability in the world, as nations struggled to export their unemployment by the use of competitive currency devaluations, trade restrictions, and export subsidies. These practices resulted in declining international trade and contributed to further unemployment. Such events paved the way for the establishment of a new international monetary system known as the gold exchange standard.

## THE BRETTON WOODS SYSTEM AND THE GOLD EXCHANGE STANDARD

In 1944, in response to the chaos in the international financial system which started in the early 1930s, representatives of the United States, the United Kingdom, and 42 other nations met at Bretton Woods, New Hampshire, to decide on a new international monetary system. Their efforts resulted in the creation of the Gold Exchange Standard System and the establishment of two supporting institutions, known as the International Monetary Fund (IMF) and the International Bank for Reconstruction and Development (IBRD), or the World Bank.

Under the Gold Exchange Standard System the value of the U.S. dollar was fixed in terms of gold, that is, one U.S. dollar was equated to $\frac{1}{35}$ ounce of gold. This meant that the United States had to exchange on demand dollars for gold at a rate of $35 per ounce of gold, without any limitation or restrictions. Other nations' currencies, however, were fixed to the *dollar* and thus, indirectly, to gold. It was also decided that other nations should be ready to defend their currencies if their values moved 1 percent above or below their par (official) value. This meant if a nation's currency depreciated by more than 1 percent of its par value, it had to sell its dollar reserves to buy its own currency in order to prevent its further depreciation.* On the other hand, if a nation's currency appreciated by more than 1 percent of its par value, it had to purchase dollars in order to prevent its further appreciation.† Thus the Gold Exchange Standard System combined exchange rate stability with some flexibility. The incorporation of the stability into the system stemmed from the inclination to avoid the chaotic conditions that had existed before.

Because the main rationale of the Bretton Woods system was to prevent the recurrence of the events of the Great Depression of the 1930s, nations were prevented from imposing additional trade restrictions. Additionally, it was agreed that the existing trade barriers had to be lifted gradually under GATT sponsorship through multilateral negotiations. Restrictions on liquid capital flows, however, were allowed in order to enable nations to protect their currencies against the instability that could result from large flows of international money.

---

*Depreciation means a decrease in the value of one currency in terms of another currency (the dollar).

†Appreciation means an increase in the value of one currency in terms of another currency (the dollar).

# THE INTERNATIONAL MONETARY FUND

To achieve its goals, as we explained earlier, the Bretton Woods agreement gave birth to the International Monetary Fund (IMF). This institution, which started operations on March 1, 1947, with a membership of 30 countries, grew rapidly, and by 1986 included 151 members. With the exception of Switzerland, practically all the free world's nations have joined the IMF. From the Eastern European countries only Yugoslavia, Romania, and Hungary joined the IMF. Although the Soviet Union participated in the Bretton Woods conference, it decided not to join. The reasons given for the reluctance of some of the socialist countries to join the IMF are related to (1) the veto power that is granted to the United States with regard to some important decisions, (2) the reporting requirement that forces members to make statements with regard to their gold and foreign exchange interests and requires them to hold part of their interest in the United States where the IMF is located; and (3) the provisions that allow the members to have access to the IMF resources.

In 1986, the Soviet Union was considering joining the IMF and the World Bank. Such a move is believed to be part of the modernization policies that are being carried out under the new leader of the Soviet Union, Mikhail Gorbachev. However, Soviet experts believe that "it will be years before the Soviets get a foot in the door."[1]

The IMF was set up to pursue two main objectives. First, the IMF was to ensure that nations will follow the agreed set of rules for conduct in engaging in international business, and, second, the IMF was to assist nations with temporary balance of payments deficits by providing them with borrowing facilities.

The IMF was financed by its members. Upon joining the IMF, a nation had to subscribe to a quota, which was based on its relative economic significance and the level of its international business activities. The size of members' quotas, which reflected voting ability and borrowing capacity from the Fund, has been revised several times. For example, in 1944 the United States was assigned the largest quota of 31 percent. By 1986 this quota had decreased to 20 percent. In 1986 the quota of the United Kingdom was about 7 percent; West Germany 6 percent; France 5 percent; and Japan 4.7 percent.

Initially, upon joining the IMF, a member country had to pay 25 percent of its quota in gold (called gold tranche) and the remaining 75 percent in its own currency. Beginning with the year 1978, the Fund no longer required the payment of 25 percent of a quota in gold. Now, such payment could be made in "reserve tranche," that is, either in currencies acceptable to the IMF or in Special Drawing Rights (SDRs), which will be explained later.

Under IMF rules, a member country could borrow from the IMF an amount equal to 25 percent of its quota in any given year. Any borrowing above this subscription requires the IMF's approval, and it is granted only for resolving a country's balance of payments problems.

Today the IMF stands as a powerful international institution whose strength stems from (a) its ability to grant or deny loans beyond the reserve tranche of its member nations; (b) the requirement that its permission must be obtained for more than a 10 percent devaluation of a currency; and (c) the ruling that joining the IMF is a prerequisite for membership in the World Bank. Two examples of activities of IMF include the approval of a $452 million loan to Nigeria to support that nation's move to trade liberalization in 1986,[2] and the approval of two loans to the Philippines in 1986.[3]

## SPECIAL DRAWING RIGHTS

The Special Drawing Right (SDR) is one of the most significant inventions of the IMF. During the 1960s the world was experiencing an international liquidity problem.* As we will explain later, during this period the United States was facing a balance of payments deficit. The confidence in the U.S. dollar, which was used as a significant international reserve, that is, international medium of exchange, was shaken. As a result, there was widespread expectation that the dollar would not continue to supply the needed international reserve.†

At the 1967 annual meeting of the IMF Board of Governors in Rio de Janeiro, the Special Drawing Right emerged as a new reserve asset to supplement the international reserves of gold and foreign exchange. SDRs are bank accounts in the IMF. Each country can use its own money to buy SDRs from the IMF, according to its quota. In this manner, each country's bank account in the IMF is credited for the amount of SDRs purchased. The SDRs can then be used by each country to settle its accounts with other nations. In other words, SDRs entitle their holder nations to draw out any kind of money that they need and pay off their debts to other nations. Because the IMF sells SDRs to all countries, it ends up with bank accounts in all currencies that can then be sold to different countries in return for their SDRs. Thus, SDRs are not backed by gold or any other currency. They are accepted by all nations just because they have agreed to do so. SDRs are employed only by the central banks of nations in order to resolve their balance of payments problems; they are not used in private business transactions. At the 1967 meeting of the IMF in Rio de Janeiro, the initial allocation of SDRs, distributed to member nations according to their quotas in the IMF, totaled 9.5 billion. Table 5.1 shows the total allocation of SDRs and their distribution among major industrial countries and developing countries in 1986.

The value of one SDR was initially equal to $1.00, but following the devaluation of the U.S. dollar in 1971 and 1973, its value continued to rise. Because the dollar's trouble was transmitted to the SDRs, beginning in 1974, the IMF de-

---

*International liquidity is the world's supply of gold, foreign exchange, and other assets that are used in settling the balance of payments deficit among nations.

†The term "international reserve" refers to gold, foreign exchange, and other assets that act as an international medium of exchange and are set aside (reserved) by a nation in settling its balance of payments deficit.

Table 5.1 QUOTAS FROM IMF MEMBERS

| Countries | Millions of SDRs | Percentage* |
|---|---|---|
| All Countries | 89,305.1 | 100.00 |
| Industrial Countries: | 56,089.0 | 62.81 |
| United States | 17,918.3 | 20.06 |
| United Kingdom | 6,194.0 | 6.93 |
| West Germany | 5,403.7 | 6.05 |
| France | 4,482.8 | 5.02 |
| Japan | 4,223.3 | 4.73 |
| Canada | 2,941.0 | 3.30 |
| Italy | 2,901.1 | 3.25 |
| Netherlands | 2,264.8 | 2.54 |
| Belgium | 2,080.4 | 2.33 |
| Austria | 775.6 | 0.87 |
| All others | 6,904.0 | 7.73 |
| Developing Countries: | 33,216.1 | 37.19 |
| Africa | 5,778.1 | 6.47 |
| Asia | 9,220.3 | 10.42 |
| Europe | 2,987.5 | 3.34 |
| Middle East | 7,269.1 | 8.14 |
| Western Hemisphere | 7,961.1 | 8.91 |

*This column was calculated by the authors.

Source: International Monetary Fund, International Financial Statistics 39 (July 1986):22–23

cided to use a weighted average of a "basket" of 16 major currencies to establish the value of the SDR.

Although SDRs are not used to settle private dealings, they are utilized as the "money unit" in some international transactions. For example, Suez Canal tolls are stated in SDRs. However, this does not mean that the payments for the tolls are actually paid in SDRs, but in terms of the national currency. The tolls are first figured out in SDRs. Then the amount of payments in national currency is determined on the basis of the exchange rate between the SDR and the national currency.

# THE WORLD BANK

The International Bank for Reconstruction and Development (IBRD) or the World Bank, as we explained earlier, was established in 1944 by the participating nations at the Bretton Woods conference.

Initially, this bank was set up mainly to provide loans for post–World War II reconstruction. Today, however, the bank's major function is to provide financial resources for the implementation of development projects, such as communication systems, dams, and transportation networks in the LDCs. The bank has more than 151 member nations. Membership in the bank is achieved by the purchase of shares of stock. The United States, having purchased about one-third of the bank's stock, represents the major stockholder of the World Bank.

The strength of the World Bank as an international financial institution stems not only from its capital stock but also from its ability to raise money through the sale of bonds. These bonds are considered very safe and are widely accepted because they are backed by the credit of all the participating nations up to a level equivalent to 100 percent of their quotas.

The expansion in the activities of the World Bank has led to the establishment of two institutions, the **International Financial Corporation** (IFC) and the **International Development Cooperation Agency (IDCA)**.

The IFC was established in July 1956 in order to provide capital and managerial assistance to private businesses of LDCs. The IDCA was created in 1979 by the World Bank to make "soft loans," that is, loans on much easier terms than the World Bank would normally make. The purpose of these loans is to help the financing of the development projects of LDCs. Unlike the regular World Bank's loans, these loans are much riskier, and for this reason they may not be repaid. However, the IDCA takes this risk if it believes there is a good chance that the loan would successfully stimulate the development process of the LDC in question.

## THE DEMISE OF THE BRETTON WOODS SYSTEM

The main cause of the demise of the Bretton Woods system was the United States balance of payments deficits. As we explained earlier, the Bretton Woods system gave rise to the Gold Exchange Standard System that considered dollars as gold and adopted the dollar as the international reserve currency that backs the values of other currencies in the world. Such a strategy was feasible because the United States was in a good financial position and was ready to exchange gold for dollars at the official rate of $35 an ounce. The financial strength of the United States was reflected in its 1945–1949 balance of payments surplus. Beginning in 1950, as the European and Japanese economies were becoming stronger, the U.S. balance of payments surplus turned into a deficit. However, up to 1957, the deficit was relatively small and averaged only $1 billion a year. The United States could easily survive such a deficit because (1) the dollar was used as the international currency, and thus many nations were willing to hold on to it rather than exchange it for gold, (2) the United States had enough gold reserve and stood by ready to exchange dollars for gold at the official rate of $35 an ounce, and (3) nations preferred to hold dollars instead of gold because dollars could earn interest.

Beginning in 1958, the U.S. balance of payment deficit, which was averaging $1 billion a year during the 1950–1957 period, tripled and averaged $3 billion a year. This was followed by a huge capital outflow and high inflation, which further intensified the U.S. balance of payments problem. As a result, the confidence in the dollar was shaken, and beginning in 1968 the United States was experiencing a so-called *dollar crisis.* Foreigners, who felt that the devaluation of the U.S. dollar was inevitable, were no longer holding on to their dollars as a stable international money, but were exchanging them for gold. As a result, the U.S. gold reserve decreased to the point that it began to be smaller than the foreign-held dollar reserves. To alleviate the problem and to discourage foreigners from demanding gold for their dollars, the United States invented the so-called Roosa bonds. These were interest-bearing treasury bonds with a guaranteed exchange rate. They were designed to persuade foreigners to hold on to their dollars by insuring that there would be no decrease in their value if the dollar were devalued. This was achieved by denominating the bond in a foreign currency, say the German mark, and guaranteeing the exchange rate. This meant, for example, that a German could buy a Roosa bond with $100 and the bonds would be payable, at the guaranteed exchange rate of $1.00 = DM 2.5, in deutsche marks, being worth DM 250. Unfortunately, however, this scheme did not resolve the problem and the U.S. gold reserve continued to decline to the extent that in 1970 it had reached one-fourth of the dollar reserves that were held by foreigners. To deal with the problem, in 1970, and early 1971, the United States tried to get nations with trade surpluses to revalue their currencies. However, such efforts proved to be fruitless, and the U.S. balance of payments deficit kept rising, reaching the level of $12 billion in the first half of 1971. By this time confidence in the dollar was badly shaken, and this forced President Nixon to suspend the convertibility of dollars into gold on August 15, 1971, breaking the Bretton Woods system. Concurrent with this decision, the United States launched wage and price controls and imposed a temporary 10 percent tariff on imports, to be abolished after the necessary currency realignments were made.

## THE SMITHSONIAN AGREEMENT

The Nixon action of August 15, 1971, resulted in a floating dollar. This means that the exchange rate (the price) of the dollar was to be determined by the market forces of demand and supply. In other words, dollars were to be exchanged at the rate that foreign banks were willing to pay for them. However, this situation did not last for long. In December 1971, in an attempt to shape once again the international monetary system, the representatives of the "big ten" trading nations met at the Smithsonian Institution in Washington, D.C. At this meeting it was agreed to officially devalue the dollar by changing its gold price from $35 to $38 an ounce. At the same time, the German mark was appreciated by about 17 percent and the Japanese yen by about 14 percent against the dollar. Other nations' currencies were appreciated by smaller amounts. It was also decided to increase the band of fluctuation from 1 percent, existing under the Bretton Woods system, to 2.25 percent. Additionally, the United States lifted its 10 percent tariff on imports that were imposed on August 15, 1971.

Because under this system the U.S. dollar continued to be inconvertible into gold, the international monetary system was still, in principle, under the *dollar standard.* Nixon considered the Smithsonian agreement as the most important monetary arrangement in world history and vowed that he would never again devalue the dollar.

The Smithsonian arrangement seemed to work well for about one year. The United States was still under wage and price controls and the value of the dollar seemed to be under control. However, in 1972, the United States was once again faced with a huge balance of payments deficit amounting to $10 billion. It was becoming obvious that the Smithsonian agreement was not working and another devaluation had to take place. In January 1973, President Nixon relaxed the control over prices and wages. This contributed to the collapse of confidence in the dollar. These situations led to another official devaluation of the dollar, which was announced in February 1973. The dollar still remained inconvertible into gold; however, its official price was changed from $38 to $42.22 an ounce.

## THE PRESENT INTERNATIONAL MONETARY SYSTEM

The devaluation of February 1973 did not succeed in resolving the dollar crisis. Given that the dollar had been devalued two times since 1971, the possibility of another devaluation was speculated. When such speculation reached its high point in March 1973, the major industrial nations decided to let their currencies float. Britain, Canada, Japan, Italy, Switzerland, and the United States let their currencies float independently. France, West Germany, and the original members of the EC decided to maintain relatively fixed exchange rates internally, but to let their currencies float jointly against the dollar and other dollar-tied currencies. The managed floating exchange rate system was born.

Under the freely fluctuating exchange rate system, as we explained earlier, the price of a currency is defined by the interaction of the market demand and supply for it. Thus, if there is a shortage of a country's currency, then the exchange rate (the price of that currency) increases. On the other hand, if there is a surplus of a nation's currency, its exchange rate (the price of that currency) declines. This free movement of exchange rates, incurring in response to the market forces of demand and supply, is what brings the balance of payments of nations into equilibrium. In other words, a country's balance of payments surplus or deficit is automatically resolved by the appreciation or depreciation, respectively, of its currency. In a freely floating exchange rate system, governments do not intervene in the foreign exchange market. Because in March 1973 governments did not want to surrender to the market forces the entire control over a variable as important as the exchange rate, a freely floating exchange rate system seemed to be undesirable. As a result, the managed floating exchange rate system was adopted. Under this system governments could intervene in the foreign exchange market in order to serve their national exchange rates policies.* To coordinate these policies, informal guidelines were established by the IMF.

Because the managed floating exchange rate system was not a planned system, and it was forced on the world by the demise of the Bretton Woods system, it was met with skepticism. Critics could not see how market forces could manage the international monetary system, when the carefully planned system had collapsed. Thus, from the beginning, serious efforts were made to design rules to govern the float. It was hoped that such rules would prevent countries from pursuing competitive exchange rate depreciation to stimulate their exports, returning the world to the chaotic conditions that had existed in the 1930s. Fortunately, however, the system worked well and was formally recognized by the 1976 Jamaica Accords. The rules of managed floating exchange rates were formalized by the IMF. According to these rules, nations are allowed to intervene in the foreign exchange market in order to smooth out short-run fluctuations, without trying to change the long-run pattern of the exchange rates. The Jamaica Accords also allowed the countries the option of a foreign exchange rate regime so long as their activities did not disturb the normal trade patterns and the operation of the world economy.

To show its determination in eliminating gold as an international reserve asset, the IMF sold one sixth of its gold holdings between 1976 and 1980. Additionally, the official price of gold was abandoned, and it was decided that the IMF would no longer engage in gold transactions between its members. Thus, the gold tranche became reserve tranche.† Starting in 1974, the IMF started to measure all reserves and other official transactions in SDRs rather than in U.S. dollars.

According to Table 5.2, in 1986, nine different exchange rate regimes were chosen by different members of the IMF. As this table shows, in 1986, 31 nations, or roughly 21 percent of the total IMF members, had pegged their currencies to the U.S. dollar. This indicates that the U.S. dollar is still considered a significant international reserve asset.

Thus, today nations have a large degree of flexibility and can select the exchange rate regime that best fits their economic conditions. In general, major

---

*The terms "clean floating" and "dirty floating" have been used by some commentators to describe floating exchange rate systems. The term "clean floating" is synonymous with the term "free floating." As we explained before, in a free (clean) floating exchange rates system, exchange rates are determined by the interaction of the market forces of demand and supply. The term "dirty floating" refers to the managing of a country's exchange rate system with the objective of attaining goals other than just smoothing out the short-run fluctuations. For example, a country may intervene in the foreign exchange market to depreciate its currency in order to expand its exports.

†Although gold was abolished as an international reserve asset, the IMF decided to measure its gold asset at the pre-1971 official price of $35 or 35 SDR per ounce.

**Table 5.2   DIFFERENT EXCHANGE RATE REGIMES USED BY THE IMF MEMBERS**

| Classification status[a] | Number of countries | Percentage of countries[f] |
|---|:---:|:---:|
| Currency pegged to U.S. dollar | 31 | 20.90 |
| French franc | 14 | 9.45 |
| Other currencies | 4 | 2.70 |
| SDR | 12 | 8.10 |
| Other currencies composite[b] | 32 | 21.62 |
| Flexibility limited vis-à-vis single currency[c] | 5 | 3.37 |
| Cooperative arrangement[d] | 8 | 5.41 |
| Adjusted according to a set of indicators[e] | 5 | 5.40 |
| Managed floating | 21 | 14.19 |
| Independently floating | 16 | 10.80 |
| Total | 148 | 100 |

[a]Excluding the currency of Democratic Kampuchea.

[b]Composite currencies which are pegged to various baskets of currencies of member's own choice, as distinct from SDR basket.

[c]Exchange rate of all currencies have shown limited flexibility in terms of the U.S. dollar.

[d]Refers to cooperative arrangement maintained under the European monetary system.

[e]Includes exchange rate arrangements under which the exchange rate is adjusted at relatively frequent intervals, on the basis of indicators determined by the respective member countries.

[f]This column is calculated by the authors.

*Source:* International Monetary Fund, *International Financial Statistics* 39 (July 1986): 20.

industrial countries and countries that are faced with a relatively high inflationary strain have adopted a more flexible exchange rate regime than the regime chosen by the highly specialized economies of the small LDCs. All countries still require international reserves in order to defend their currencies by ironing out the short-run vacillations in their exchange rates. Although most of the international reserves used in the defense of national monies are composed of convertible currencies, the future will call for the use of SDRs. It is expected that the amount of SDRs that are allocated to each country by the IMF will increase in the future.

## THE EUROPEAN MONETARY SYSTEM

The exchange rate instability that started with the collapse of the Bretton Woods system caused the original six member countries of the EC to cooperate in designing a system that provides them with a greater monetary stability. In March 1972, they decided to let their currencies float jointly against the U.S. dollar within a range of 2.25 percent around the par value, instead of the 4.5

percent agreed upon in December 1971. This decision was referred to as the *"European Snake"* and was in effect until March 1973.

In an attempt to revive the European Snake and narrow the band of exchange fluctuations between its members, in March 1979 the EC established the European Monetary System (EMS). The membership of this system included Belgium, Denmark, France, Ireland, Italy, Luxembourg, the Netherlands, and West Germany. Britain was the only EC member that decided not to join.

The objective set by the EMS members was "closer monetary cooperation leading to a zone of monetary stability in Europe."[4] To achieve this objective the following features were incorporated into the EMS:

1. A unit of currency known as the *European Currency Unit* (ECU) was created. This currency unit, which resembles an SDR is a weighted average of the nine EC currencies and is used for accounting purposes among the EMS members.*

2. The par value or the central rate of each currency is defined in terms of ECUs, and countries can intervene to prevent movements of their currencies greater than 2.25 percent above these values. Countries whose exchange rates were previously floating against other members' currencies were allowed a greater fluctuation band of 5 percent, instead of 2.25 percent. Among EMS members, Italy is the only country that decided to use this option and was qualified to do so.

3. To provide short-term credit for intervention purposes the EC members established the European Monetary Corporation Fund (EMCF). This corporation allocates ECUs to member nations in return for 20 percent of their gold and dollar reserves.

Because members of the EMS were allowed to follow their own independent monetary policy, the EMS has had difficulty in achieving its objective of monetary stability. In fact, the members' differential inflation rates caused the EMS to undertake seven realignments of exchange rates from its formation in March 1979 to March 1983. Since 1983, however, the EMS seems to have been more successful in achieving exchange rate stability among the currencies of its members. Exchange rate fluctuations of the members' currencies have, in general, been smaller than the fluctuations of other major currencies. The recent success of EMS in maintaining relative stability can be largely attributed to the implementation of restrictive monetary and fiscal policies in those member countries, such as France and Italy, that face high inflation rates. However, the existence of inflationary differentials between EMS members warranted another realignment of currencies. This was achieved in July 1985 by depreciating the central rate of the Italian lira against other member currencies by about 8 percent.[5]

---

*Although Britain did not join the EMS, its currency was used in the calculation of the ECU.

## FIXED VERSUS FLEXIBLE EXCHANGE RATES

The breakdown of the Bretton Woods system and the Nixon action of August 15, 1971, allowing the dollar to float, that is, to freely fluctuate, set the stage for the debate over fixed versus flexible exchange rates. Although a compromise was reached and the present system of the managed float was born, the debate over the relative merits of these two systems continues.

The major arguments presented by the advocates of the flexible (freely fluctuating) exchange rate system are the following:

1. In general, the flexible exchange rate system is more efficient than the fixed exchange rate system because under the flexible exchange rate system only the exchange rate is required to change in order to correct the balance of payments disequilibrium (surplus or deficit). Although balance of payments equilibrium could be achieved under the classical gold standard system, as we explained earlier, such a system is based on the assumption of price flexibility. This means that instead of relying on one price, that is, the exchange rate, we should rely on all prices to bring adjustment. From an economic standpoint this is inefficient. In addition, the assumption of price flexibility presented by classical economists is far removed from the reality of today's world.

2. Because the flexible exchange rate system automatically adjusts when disequilibrium in the balance of payments occurs, a nation does not need to worry about its external balance and it can concentrate its resources in pursuing its internal economic goals, such as economic growth, full employment, and price stability.

The main arguments advanced by the proponents of the fixed exchange rate are the following:

1. Because the fixed exchange rate system is not subject to wide day-to-day fluctuations that occur under the freely fluctuating exchange rate system, it involves a lower degree of uncertainty as compared with the flexible exchange rate system. The lower uncertainty under this system reduces risk and increases the volume of international business and investment.

2. Speculators would have a more destabilizing effect under a flexible exchange rate system than under a fixed exchange rate system because, given a flexible exchange rate system, when the price (the exchange rate) of a foreign currency is increasing, the speculators would buy more of it, expecting that the price would continue to rise. The higher demands of the speculators would push the price even higher, intensifying the price rise. With a similar argument, when the price of a foreign currency is falling, the speculators would sell their foreign currencies, pushing the price further down.

3. Fixed exchange rates are not as prone to inflationary pressures as are flexible exchange rates because under a fixed exchange rate system the deficit in the balance of payments of a nation leads to international reserve losses and forces

a nation to control its excessive inflationary pressures.* The fixed exchange rate system thus gives the nation some price sensitivity. In a flexible exchange rate regime, however, where the balance of payments deficits are automatically corrected by changes in exchange rates, such a sensitivity does not exist. As a result, the government authorities are more prone to excessively stimulate the economy in order to enhance the possibility of their reelection, thereby achieving their political goals.

The debate over the flexible versus fixed exchange rate systems continues, and the experts have not yet reached a unanimous opinion on this issue. However, the present monetary system, which represents a compromise between the two extremes of flexible and fixed exchange rate systems, seems to have served well so far. A merit of this system, as we discussed earlier, is its flexibility, which allows a nation to choose the exchange rate system that best suits its economic conditions. This has facilitated cooperation among nations and has contributed to the smooth operation of the international monetary system. Nevertheless, there are some people—notably Secretary of Housing and Urban Development Jack Kemp—who still argue for the return of the gold standard system and its resultant fixed exchange rate system.

## SUMMARY

1. The international monetary system refers to the rules, procedures, customs, instruments, and the organizational setting that provide a workable system of international payments among different countries, and that facilitates international trade among them.
2. The gold coin standard was a monetary standard that: (1) defined a country's unit of currency in terms of a fixed weight of gold; (2) permitted gold metals to be exported or imported without any restriction; (3) allowed the conversion of the national currency into gold and vice versa at the defined rate; (4) imposed no restrictions on the coinage of the gold; and (5) considered gold coins as the full legal tender for all debts.
3. Gold points referred to the limit within which the exchange rate could fluctuate. These points were equal to the legal rate plus or minus the cost of shipping gold. The upper and lower gold points for a country were called the gold export point and the gold import point, respectively.
4. The gold bullion standard was a monetary standard under which a nation's unit of currency was defined in terms of a fixed weight of gold. However, unlike the gold coin standard, gold did not circulate within the domestic economy. For the most part, therefore, the impact of gold on the monetary system was neutralized; that is, gold was demonetized.

---

*The control of inflation amounts to a lowering of domestic prices as compared with foreign prices. The lower prices of domestic goods and services causes their foreign demand to increase. This leads to more foreign exchange earnings for the country and thus improves the balance of payments deficit of the home country.

5. The Bretton Woods system was established in 1944 by agreements among the representatives of the United States, the United Kingdom, and 42 other nations who met at Bretton Woods, New Hampshire, to decide on a new international monetary system.

6. The Bretton Woods agreement resulted in the creation of the Gold Exchange Standard System and its two supporting institutions, known as the International Monetary Fund (IMF) and the International Bank for Reconstruction and Development (IBRD), or the World Bank.

7. Under the Gold Exchange Standard System (a) the value of the U.S. dollar was fixed in terms of gold; (b) other nations' currencies were fixed to the dollar and, therefore, indirectly to gold; and (c) nations were required to defend their currencies if their values moved 1 percent above or below the par value (the official value).

8. The IMF was set up to achieve two main purposes. These were (a) to ensure that nations would follow the agreed upon set of rules of conduct in engaging in international business; and (b) to assist nations with temporary balance of payments deficits by providing them with borrowing facilities.

9. Special Drawing Rights (SDRs) were invented by the IMF members in its 1967 annual meeting in Rio de Janeiro. SDRs are bank accounts in the IMF and are allocated among member nations according to their quotas. The SDRs entice holder nations to draw out any kind of money that they desire to settle a country's balance of payments problem.

10. The World Bank was initially set up by the IMF to provide loans for the post–World War II reconstruction. Today, the bank's major function is to provide financial resources for the implementation of development projects in the LDCs.

11. The main two supporting institutions of the World Bank are the International Financial Corporation (IFC) and the International Development Cooperation Agency (IDCA). The IFC was established in July 1956 to provide capital and managerial assistance to private businesses in LDCs. IDCA was created in 1979 to make "soft loans."

12. The Smithsonian agreement was reached by the representatives of the "big ten" trading nations at the Smithsonian Institution in Washington, D.C., in December 1971. This agreement, which was an attempt to shape the international monetary system once again, resulted in the devaluation of the dollar from $35 to $38 per ounce of gold.

13. The managed floating exchange rate system has been in effect since March 1973. Under this system the exchange rate of a currency is determined by the market forces of demand and supply. However, a nation is allowed to intervene in the market in order to smooth out short-run fluctuations, without trying to change the long-run pattern of the exchange rate.

14. The present international monetary system allows nations to have a large degree of flexibility in choosing the exchange rate that best fits their economic situation. In 1986 there were nine different exchange rate regimes chosen by different countries.

15. The European Snake refers to the decision of the original six members of the EC to let their currencies float together against the U.S. dollar within a range of 2.25 percent around the par value.

16. The European Monetary System (EMS) was established in March 1979. The objective set by the EMS members is "closer monetary cooperation leading to a zone of monetary stability in Europe."

17. The merits of the flexible exchange rate system, according to its proponents, are that (a) it is more efficient than the fixed exchange rate system, and (b) it enables a nation

to concentrate its resources in pursuing its internal economic goals rather than worrying about its external trade position.

18. The main arguments advanced by the proponents of the fixed exchange rate system are that (a) it leads to a lower degree of uncertainty than the flexible exchange rate, (b) it causes speculators to have a less destabilizing effect on the exchange rate, and (c) it is not as subject to inflationary pressures as are flexible exchange rates.

## QUESTIONS

5.1 Why do you think the managed floating exchange rate system has been chosen over the freely fluctuating exchange rate system, or the fixed exchange rate system?

5.2 Given the 1987 crash of the stock market in the United States and the worldwide inflationary trends, what do you think is the prospect for returning to the gold standard and the resulting fixed exchange rate regime?

5.3 Compare fixed exchange rate and flexible exchange rate systems. Which system do you think provides more freedom to governments in pursuing an independent monetary policy? Explain.

5.4 What are the two supporting institutions that were established by the Bretton Woods agreement? Name these and briefly describe their main objectives.

5.5 As we mentioned in the introduction to this chapter, an international monetary system should ideally be composed of an international bank that handles an international money that would be accepted by all nations. What do you think is the advantage of such a system? What is the disadvantage of such a system?

5.6 One of the disadvantages of a flexible exchange rate is that it is prone to inflation. Explain why this might be the case, in general, and why it is especially true for countries that are heavily dependent on trade for their basic necessities.

5.7 Elaborate on the role of SDRs in the international monetary system. What purpose do they serve? What rights do they give to their holders? How are their values determined today?

5.8 Explain how exchange rates were established under the gold standard. How did the gold points determine the range within which the foreign exchange rates fluctuated?

5.9 Compare the overall status of U.S. balance of payments in the 1950s and 1960s. Why didn't the deficit pose any problems in the early 1950s but became problematic in the 1960s? Given the experience of the 1960s, do you think that the dollar was overvalued or undervalued in the international market? Could you suggest ways that might have remedied the problem?

## NOTES

1. "The Soviets Consider Joining IMF, World Bank," *The Wall Street Journal,* 15 August 1986, p. 19.
2. "World Bank Approves Loan to Nigeria to Aid Nation's Bid to Liberalize Trade," *The Wall Street Journal,* 17 October 1986, p. 33.

3. "IMF Approves 2-Loan Package for Philippines," *The Wall Street Journal,* 27 October 1986, p. 32.
4. International Monetary Fund, *Annual Report 1979* (Washington D.C.: International Monetary Fund, 1979), p. 40.
5. International Monetary Fund, *Annual Report 1985* (Washington D.C.: International Monetary Fund, 1985), pp. 35–36.

## SUGGESTED READINGS

Aliber, R. Z. *The International Money Game.* New York: Basic Books, 1973.

Artus, J. R., and J. H. Young. "Fixed and Flexible Rates: A Renewal of the Debate." *International Monetary Fund Staff Papers.* Washington, D.C.: International Monetary Fund, December 1979, pp. 654–698.

Bordo, M. D. "The Classical Gold Standard: Some Lessons for Today." *Federal Reserve Bank of St. Louis Review.* May 1981.

Chrystal, K. Alec. *International Money and the Future of SDR.* Essays in International Finance Series, No. 128. Princeton, N.J.: Princeton University Press, 1978.

Cohen, B. J. *The European Monetary System: An Outsider's View.* Essays in International Finance Series, No. 142. Princeton, N.J.: Princeton University Press, December 1981.

De Uries, M. *The International Monetary Fund, 1966–1971.* Washington, D.C.: International Monetary Fund, 1976.

Eithier, W., and A. J. Bloosfield. *Managing the Managed Float.* Essays in International Finance Series, No. 112. Princeton, N.J.: Princeton University Press, October 1979.

Hosefield, J. K. *The International Monetary Fund, 1945–1965.* Washington, D.C.: International Monetary Fund, 1969.

International Monetary Fund. *Annual Report.* Washington, D.C.: International Monetary Fund. Annual.

International Monetary Fund. *IMS Survey.* Washington, D.C.: International Monetary Fund. Bi-monthly.

Machlup, Fritz. *Remaking the International Monetary Systems: The Rio Agreement and Beyond.* Baltimore, Md.: Johns Hopkins University Press, 1968.

McKinnon, R. I. *Money in International Exchange: The Convertible Currency System.* New York: Oxford University Press, 1979.

Solomon, R. *The International Monetary System, 1945–1976: An Insider's View.* New York: Harper & Row, 1976.

Storm, R. *The Balance of Payments: Theory and Economic Policy.* Chicago: Aldine, 1973. Chap. 3.

Triffin, R. *Our International Monetary System: Yesterday, Today, and Tomorrow.* New York: Random House, 1968.

# Chapter 6

# The Balance of Payments

*E*very year the residents of a country engage in numerous transactions with the residents of other nations. Such transactions, which take different forms and range from the export and import of goods and services to foreign aid and to gifts, give rise to the inflow and outflow of foreign exchange between a nation and the rest of the world. Because the huge volume of such transactions as presented by myriad accounting data is hard to understand and interpret individually, it is necessary to classify and aggregate the data into a simple accounting statement known as the balance of payments.

In this chapter we describe the balance of payments accounting system and explain the methodology for interpreting the different accounts included in this statement. In achieving these objectives, first we define the concept of the balance of payments. Second, we present the U.S. balance of payments as an example. Finally, we discuss the usefulness of the balance of payments from the standpoints of a country and of a business person.

## DEFINITION OF THE BALANCE OF PAYMENTS

The balance of payments (BOP) can be defined as an accounting statement that shows the summary of all the transactions between the residents of a nation and the residents of all other nations during a given period of time. In other words, the BOP indicates the amount of foreign currency that was pumped into and out of a nation's economic system in a given period. This definition, although straightforward, requires some clarification. First, the period of time for which a balance of payments is prepared is usually a calendar year. However, the United States and some other countries also provide their BOP data on a quarterly basis. Second, the term "transactions" here refers to (1) exports and imports of goods, services, and assets for which payments are usually made and (2) gifts and unilateral transfers for which no payments are made. Third, the term "residents" refers to individuals, business firms, and government agencies that are legally residing in the country in question. By this definition, diplomats, military personnel, temporary migrant workers, and tourists are considered residents of the countries from which they come. Similarly, a corporation is regarded as the resident of the country in which it is incorporated. However, the foreign subsidiaries of such corporations are considered the residents of the countries in which they are located. Although some of these definitions are arbitrary, they do not pose a problem because the rest of the accounting items are adjusted to them.

## THE BALANCE OF PAYMENTS ACCOUNTING

The balance of payments is an accounting statement that, like other accounting statements, is based on a double-entry bookkeeping system. There are four major accounting statements that are prepared by each business firm. These are the income statement, the balance sheet, the statement of retained earnings (or the capital statement in the case of a proprietorship), and the statement of changes in financial position (SCFP). Among these statements, the SCFP for a business firm resembles the BOP for a nation. For a given period the SCFP for a firm presents (1) the sources of funds, that is, it shows where the funds came from; (2) the uses of funds, that is, how the funds were spent; and (3) the net cash which is the difference between the two preceding items. In the same manner, the BOP shows where the nation's foreign exchange came from (the sources of funds in the case of the SCFP) and where it went (the uses of funds in the case of the SCFP). However, the BOP is not identical to the SCFP. The major difference between them is that some transactions, mainly the exchange of different kinds of real financial assets, are included in the BOP but are not included in the SCFP. Additionally, while debit and credit entries are recorded simultaneously in a business firm's records, they are often entered independently in international accounting records. This results in a time lag between debit and credit items and causes discrepancies between them. Such discrepancies, included in the BOP as **errors** and **omissions** or **statistical discrepancy,** do not exist in a firm's statements. The inclusion of the errors and omissions causes the sum of debit items in the balance of payments to be equal to the sum of credit items, as it should be in the case of all financial statements.

## Debit and Credit Items

The balance of payments is an international accounting statement, and, like any other accounting statement, it is based on the concepts of debits and credits. Thus, international transactions presented in this statement are entered as either debits or credits.

*Credit items* in the balance of payments involve the receipt of payments from foreigners. Thus, they give a nation more foreign currencies or reduce a foreign nation's holdings of domestic currency. *Debit items,* on the other hand, involve payments to foreigners. These are transactions that use up a nation's foreign currencies or increase a foreign nation's holdings of domestic currency. In a nation's BOP, credit items are recorded with a positive sign (+) and debit items are entered with a negative sign (−).

To clarify the concepts of debit and credit, consider the U.S. balance of payments, which is a financial statement that shows the summary of all debit and credit items between the residents of the United States and the residents of the rest of the world. What happens to the U.S. balance of payments when Americans buy cars from Japan, buy cameras from Germany, or fly to Canada on a Canadian airline? All these transactions involve payments to foreigners, providing them with more U.S. dollars, and hence are considered as debit items. What about foreigners buying American automobiles, IBM computers, or flying on an American airline? These transactions involve payments from foreigners, causing a decrease in foreign nations' holdings of the U.S. dollar, and hence are recorded as credit items in the balance of payments. What if the United States lends money to an LDC? This transaction represents a debit item, because it involves payments of the U.S. dollar to foreigners. Finally, what if some British entrepreneurs invest in Chrysler Corporation by buying some of its stock? This is a credit item because it involves payments from foreigners, causing the British to decrease their dollar holdings.

In summary, the imports of goods and services, unilateral transfers (gifts) given to foreigners, and capital outflows are recorded as debits because they result in payments to foreigners. However, exports of goods and services, unilateral transfers (gifts) received from foreigners, and capital inflows are recorded as credit items because they result in the receipt of payments from foreigners.

Before proceeding to the next section, it is necessary to clarify the concepts of capital "outflows" and capital "inflows" as they are used in U.S. government publications.

*Capital outflows* can be defined in two forms:

1. An increase in a country's assets abroad. For example, when an American buys the stocks of a German company, there is an outflow of capital from the United States because it involves payments to foreigners.
2. A decrease in foreign assets in a country. For example, when a British MNC sells its subsidiary in the United States to Americans, there is an outflow of capital from the United States because it involves payments to foreigners.

*Capital inflows* can be defined in two forms:

1. An increase in foreign assets in a country. For example, when a Saudi Arabian sheik buys the stock of GM, there is an inflow of capital to the United States because it involves the receipt of payments from foreigners.
2. A decrease in a country's assets abroad. For example, when a U.S. citizen sells stock of Triumph in England there is a capital inflow because it involves the receipt of payments from foreigners.

## Major Accounts in the Balance of Payments

The items presented in a balance of payments can be broken into three major categories. These are the current account, the capital account, and the compensating (reserve) account.

The **current account** includes those transactions that do not result in any future obligations. The **capital account** includes those transactions that do involve future obligations. In the previous examples, the United States lending of money to an LDC and the British investment in the Chrysler Corporation represent capital account items. This is because both of these transactions create future obligations, that is, the LDC's loan has to be repaid, and the investment in Chrysler creates either profits or losses over time. Other preceding examples, involving the purchase of goods and services by Americans from foreigners and vice versa, represents current account items, because they do not create any future claims or obligations. In general, current account items are caused by (1) the purchasing and selling of goods and services from and to foreigners; and (2) unilateral transfers, that is, remittances and grants that are given to or received from foreigners free of charge. Capital account items result (1) when a country invests in foreign nations or when foreign nations invest in that country; (2) when a nation provides loans to foreigners or when it receives loans from foreigners; and (3) when a nation deposits money in foreign banks or when foreigners deposit money in the country's local banks.

**Compensating (reserve) account** items are a nation's holdings of foreign convertible currencies, gold, and SDRs, which are used by its monetary authorities to intervene in the foreign exchange market to resolve its balance of payments problem. To be sure, because a nation's own currency is not considered as foreign exchange, by definition, it is not included in the reserve items. Compensating items resemble the cash or near cash holdings of a private company, which provides it with the potential of settling its financial obligations. Because reserve transactions are undertaken only between governments, they are carried out by central banking systems such as the U.S. Federal Reserve system or the Bank of England. A nation's own currency does not constitute foreign exchange because it is not, by definition, included in the reserve items.

## Double-Entry Bookkeeping

As we already know, modern accounting is based on the principle of double-entry bookkeeping. According to this principle, each transaction is recorded two times, once as a credit (cr.) and once as a debit (dr.). This is because every single transaction has two sides that must be recorded. For example, the payment of $500 in wages to a company's workers results in a $500 increase in wages expense (the wages expense account is debited for $500) and a $500 decrease in cash (the cash account is credited for $500).

A nation's balance of payments is an accounting statement, so it is subject to the principle of double-entry bookkeeping that is employed in the preparation of all other accounting statements.

For example, assume that the United States exports $1,000 of merchandise to France and is paid with French francs equivalent to $1,000. Because the U.S. exports causes receipts from foreigners (the French), it is recorded as a credit (+) item. As we explain in Chapter 7, the payments and/or receipts for exports and imports are achieved through the foreign exchange market and involve certain documents. In this chapter, however, we ignore these details for the sake of simplicity, to better concentrate on the concepts of double-entry bookkeeping. The payment itself represents a short-term capital outflow from the United States.* This is because the receipt of francs by the United States represents an increase in American claims against French goods and services. This is equivalent to an increase in the U.S. assets abroad and, by definition, it is a short-term capital outflow. This transaction is recorded in the BOP of the United States as the following:

---

*Short-term capital refers to financial obligations that are either payable on demand or have less than a year maturity. Long-term capital, on the other hand, refers to financial obligations that have a maturity of one year or more. Examples of short-term capital include (1) demand deposits (checking accounts), (2) time deposits (saving accounts), (3) short-term government securities, (4) short-term promissory notes of corporations, and (5) short-term bank loans. Examples of long-term capital are long-term government or corporate securities and commercial bank certificates of deposit.

|  | Dr. | Cr. |
| --- | --- | --- |
| Short-term capital outflow | $1,000 | |
| Merchandise exports | | $1,000 |

Now assume that the United States imports $500 of merchandise from Germany and pays for it with the U.S. dollar. This transactions is represented in the U.S. BOP as the following:

|  | Dr. | Cr. |
| --- | --- | --- |
| Merchandise imports | $500 | |
| Short-term capital inflow | | $500 |

In the above transaction, the merchandise imports is debited because it represents a payment to foreigners. The payment itself is considered as short-term capital inflow because this transaction results in an increase in Germany's holding of the U.S. dollar. In other words, it represents an increase in Germany's claim against U.S. goods and services. This is equivalent to an increase in foreign assets in the United States, and, by definition, it is a short-term capital inflow.

As another example, suppose that an American resident spends $3,000 while vacationing in Mexico. This transaction resembles the import of merchandise. This is because the expenditure of $3,000 by an American in Mexico involves payments to foreigners, and hence it is recorded as the following:

|  | Dr. | Cr. |
| --- | --- | --- |
| Imports on travel services | $3,000 | |
| Short-term capital inflow | | $3,000 |

Merchandise imports is debited because it represents a payment to foreigners. The payment itself is credited because it represents an increase in foreign holdings of U.S. dollars.

As a fourth example, assume that the U.S. State Department gives $1,500 to an LDC as a gift (unilateral transfer). This transaction is recorded as the following:

|                              | Dr.      | Cr.      |
| ---------------------------- | -------- | -------- |
| Unilateral transfer          | $1,500   |          |
| Short-term capital inflow    |          | $1,500   |

In the above transaction, unilateral transfer is debited because it involves payments to foreigners. The payment itself is credited as capital inflow, because it represents an increase in foreign holdings of the U.S. dollar.

As a fifth example, assume that a U.S. resident buys the stocks of Japan's Sony Corporation for $5,000 in cash. This transaction is recorded in the U.S. balance of payments as the following:

|                              | Dr.      | Cr.      |
| ---------------------------- | -------- | -------- |
| Long-term capital outflow    | $5,000   |          |
| Short-term capital inflow    |          | $5,000   |

In the above transaction, long-term capital outflow is debited because the purchase of stocks increases the United States' assets abroad. The short-term capital inflow is credited because the payment itself represents an increase in the foreign holdings of the U.S. asset, that is, the U.S. dollar.

Assuming that the above items are the only transactions that have taken place in the United States for a given year, we can present the U.S. balance of payments as the following:

|                              | Dr.       | Cr.       |
| ---------------------------- | --------- | --------- |
| Merchandise imports          | $    500  |           |
| Merchandise exports          |           | $  1,000  |
| Imports of travel services   | 3,000     |           |
| Unilateral transfers         | 1,500     |           |
| Long-term capital            | 5,000     |           |
| Short-term capital, net      |           | 9,000     |
| Total                        | $ 10,000  | $ 10,000  |

In the above statement, the $9,000 for short-term capital is obtained by algebraically adding up the five short-term capital entries −$1,000 + $500 + $3,000 + $1,500 + $5,000), and the rest of the entries are reported as they were recorded before.

Although all the debit items and credit items were recorded simultaneously in this example, in practice, the BOP is prepared by reporting different items separately. However, as we mentioned before, this does not pose a problem because the equality of debits and credits is maintained by the inclusion of an account referred to as "errors and omissions" or "statistical discrepancy."

## THE U.S. BALANCE OF PAYMENTS

In this section, we provide a detailed explanation of the U.S. balance of payments (BOP), and explain the relationship between its different items.

### The Significance of the U.S. Balance of Payments

The significance of the U.S. BOP, as compared with other countries, is due to the important role played by the United States in the world economy. Today, approximately 90 percent of the world's trade and investment is denominated in U.S. dollars. Also, under the present international monetary system, as we explained before, many countries' currencies are still pegged to the U.S. dollar. Finally, as we explained in Chapter 5, the United States stands as the country with the highest share of SDRs in the world. As Table 5.1 indicated, the United States accounted for 20.06 percent of the market value of the total SDRs allocated by the IMF in 1986.

Given the above facts, it is necessary for an international manager to understand the U.S. BOP because any change in this statement reflects a change in the U.S. economy and the dollar, indirectly influencing the operation of any international firm.

### The U.S. Balance of Payments Statistics

Table 6.1, presenting a summary of the U.S. international transactions for 1985, provides data on the United States BOP. The complete statements of the U.S. international transactions for the years 1984 and 1985 are presented in Table 6.2.

According to Table 6.1, the United States exported $359,702 million of goods and services in 1985. Out of this total, $213,990 million represented merchandise exports, that is, physical goods such as automobiles, computers, chemicals, and so forth. The rest ($145,712 million) accounts for exports of services; these are travel services rendered by the United States to foreigners, fees and royalties received by the United States from its foreign affiliates, and interest and dividends gained from the U.S. foreign investment abroad.

Besides the exports of goods and services of $359,702 million in 1985, the United States transferred (exported free of charge) $58 million to foreign countries under U.S. military grants programs.

**Table 6.1  SUMMARY OF THE U.S. INTERNATIONAL TRANSACTIONS FOR 1985**
**(Millions of Dollars)**

| | |
|---|---:|
| Exports of goods and services | 359,702 |
|   Merchandise | 213,990 |
|   Services | 145,712 |
| Transfers of goods and services under U.S. military grants, net | 58 |
| Imports of goods and services | −462,581 |
|   Merchandise | −338,279 |
|   Services | −124,302 |
| U.S. military grants of goods and services, net | −58 |
| Unilateral transfer (excluding military grants of goods and services), net | −14,784 |
|   U.S. government grants | −11,246 |
|   U.S. government pensions and other transfers | −1,612 |
|   Private remittances and other transfers | −1,926 |
| U.S. assets abroad, net (increase/capital outflow [−]) | −38,183 |
|   U.S. official reserve assets, net | −3,858 |
|   U.S. government assets, other than official reserve assets, net | −2,628 |
|   U.S. private assets, net | −31,697 |
|     Direct investment abroad | −19,091 |
|     Foreign securities | −7,871 |
|     U.S. nonbank claims | na |
|     U.S. bank claims | −5,926 |
| Foreign assets in the U.S., net (increase/capital inflow [+]) | 123,108 |
|   Foreign official assets in the U.S., net | −1,908 |
|   Other foreign assets in the U.S., net | 125,016 |
|     Direct investment in the U.S. | 16,254 |
|     U.S. Treasury and other U.S. securities | 71,622 |
|     Nonbank liabilities | na |
|     Bank liabilities | 40,610 |
| Allocation of special drawing rights | 0 |
| Statistical discrepancy | 32,738 |
| Memoranda: | |
|   Balance on merchandise trade | −124,289 |
|   Balance on goods and services | −102,879 |
|   Balance on goods and services and remittances | −106,418 |
|   Balance on current account | −117,664 |
| Transactions in official reserve assets: | |
|   Increase(−) in U.S. official reserve assets, net | −3,858 |
|   Increase(+) in foreign official assets in the U.S. | −2,056 |

*Source:* U.S. Department of Commerce, *Survey of Current Business* (Washington, D.C.: U.S. Government Printing Office, March 1986), p. 36.

**Table 6.2   U.S. INTERNATIONAL TRANSACTIONS, YEARS 1984–1985**
Millions of Dollars

| Line | (Credits +; debits −) | 1984 | 1985 |
|---|---|---|---|
| 1 | Exports of goods and services | 362,021 | 359,702 |
| 2 | Merchandise, adjusted, excluding military | 219,916 | 213,990 |
| 3 | Transfers under U.S. military agency sales contracts | 10,086 | 9,293 |
| 4 | Travel | 11,386 | 11,655 |
| 5 | Passenger fares | 3,023 | 2,993 |
| 6 | Other transportation | 13,799 | 14,342 |
| 7 | Fees and royalties from affiliated foreigners | 6,530 | 6,817 |
| 8 | Fees and royalties from unaffiliated foreigners | 1,585 | 1,695 |
| 9 | Other private services | 7,463 | 7,576 |
| 10 | U.S. Government miscellaneous services | 624 | 885 |
|  | Receipts of income on U.S. assets abroad: |  |  |
| 11 | Direct investment | 23,078 | 35,292 |
| 12 | Other private receipts | 59,301 | 49,883 |
| 13 | U.S. Government receipts | 5,230 | 5,281 |
| 14 | Transfers of goods and services under U.S. military grant programs, net | 190 | 58 |
| 15 | Imports of goods and services | −457,965 | −462,581 |
| 16 | Merchandise, adjusted, excluding military | −334,023 | −338,279 |
| 17 | Direct defense expenditures | −11,851 | −11,338 |
| 18 | Travel | −16,008 | −17,043 |
| 19 | Passenger fares | −6,508 | −7,385 |
| 20 | Other transportation | −14,666 | −16,303 |
| 21 | Fees and royalties to affiliated foreigners | −187 | 159 |
| 22 | Fees and royalties to unaffiliated foreigners | −329 | −366 |
| 23 | Private payments for other services | −3,762 | −3,967 |
| 24 | U.S. Government payments for miscellaneous services | −2,133 | −2,287 |
|  | Payments of income on foreign assets in the United States: |  |  |
| 25 | Direct investment | −10,188 | −9,013 |
| 26 | Other private payments | −38,543 | −35,453 |
| 27 | U.S. Government payments | −19,769 | −21,306 |
| 28 | U.S. military grants of goods and services, net | −190 | −58 |
| 29 | Unilateral transfers (excluding military grants of goods and services), net | −11,413 | −14,784 |
| 30 | U.S. Government grants (excluding military grants of goods and services) | −8,522 | −11,246 |
| 31 | U.S. Government pensions and other transfers | −1,591 | −1,612 |

**Table 6.2** (*Continued*)

| Line | (Credits +; debits −) | 1984 | 1985 |
|------|------------------------|------|------|
| 32 | Private remittances and other transfers | −1,300 | −1,926 |
| 33 | U.S. assets abroad, net (increase/capital outflow (−)) | −20,447 | −38,183 |
| 34 | U.S. official reserve assets, net | −3,131 | −3,858 |
| 35 | Gold | | |
| 36 | Special drawing rights | −979 | −897 |
| 37 | Reserve position in the International Monetary Fund | −995 | 908 |
| 38 | Foreign currencies | −1,156 | −3,869 |
| 39 | U.S. Government assets, other than official reserve assets, net | −5,516 | −2,628 |
| 40 | U.S. credits and other long-term assets | −9,619 | −7,219 |
| 41 | Repayments on U.S. loans | 4,483 | 4,435 |
| 42 | U.S. foreign currency holdings and U.S. short-term assets, net | −380 | 156 |
| 43 | U.S. private assets, net | −11,800 | −31,697 |
| 44 | Direct investment | −4,503 | −19,091 |
| 45 | Foreign securities | −5,059 | −7,871 |
| 46 | U.S. claims on unaffiliated foreigners reported by U.S. nonbanking concerns | 6,266 | n.a. |
| 47 | U.S. claims reported by U.S. banks, not included elsewhere | −8,504 | −5,926 |
| 48 | Foreign assets in the United States, net (increase/capital inflow (+)) | 97,319 | 123,108 |
| 49 | Foreign official assets in the United States, net | 3,424 | −1,908 |
| 50 | U.S. Government securities | 4,857 | −939 |
| 51 | U.S. Treasury securities | 4,690 | −610 |
| 52 | Other | 167 | −329 |
| 53 | Other U.S. Government liabilities | 453 | 148 |
| 54 | U.S. liabilities reported by U.S. banks, not included elsewhere | 663 | 372 |
| 55 | Other foreign official assets | −2,549 | −1,489 |
| 56 | Other foreign assets in the United States, net | 93,895 | 125,016 |
| 57 | Direct investment | 22,514 | 16,254 |
| 58 | U.S. Treasury securities | 22,440 | 20,910 |
| 59 | U.S. securities other than U.S. Treasury securities | 12,983 | 50,712 |
| 60 | U.S. liabilities to unaffiliated foreigners reported by U.S. nonbanking concerns | 4,284 | n.a. |
| 61 | U.S. liabilities reported by U.S. banks, not included elsewhere | 31,674 | 40,610 |
| 62 | Allocations of special drawing rights | | |

**Table 6.2** (*Continued*)

| Line | (Credits +; debits −) | 1984 | 1985 |
|------|----------------------|------|------|
| 63 | Statistical discrepancy (sum of above items with sign reversed) | 30,486 | 32,739 |
| 63a | *Of which* seasonal adjustment discrepancy | | |
| | Memoranda: | | |
| 64 | Balance on merchandise trade (lines 2 and 16) | −114,107 | −124,289 |
| 65 | Balance on goods and services (lines 1 and 15) | −95,945 | −102,880 |
| 66 | Balance on goods, services, and remittances (lines 65, 31, and 32) | −98,836 | −106,418 |
| 67 | Balance on current account (lines 65 and 29) | −107,358 | −117,664 |
| | Transactions in U.S. official reserve assets and in foreign official assets in the United States: | | |
| 68 | Increase (−) in U.S. official reserve assets, net (line 34) | −3,131 | −3,858 |
| 69 | Increase (+) in foreign official assets in the United States (line 49 less line 53) | 2,971 | −2,056 |

*Source:* U.S. Department of Commerce, *Survey of Current Business* (Washington, D.C.: U.S. Government Printing Office, March 1986), p. 36.

The imports of goods and services of the United States amounted to (−)$462,581 million. Out of this total, (−)$338,279 million accounts for merchandise imports, including different items such as automobiles, petroleum, textiles, television sets, VCRs, and so forth. The rest (−$124,302 million) represents imports of services, that is, travel services purchased by the U.S. residents from foreigners, fees and royalties paid by the United States to foreigners, and dividends and interest paid by the United States on foreign investment in the United States.

In 1985, the unilateral transfer made by the United States is broken down into two categories: (1) the net U.S. military grants of goods and services of (−)$58 million given to foreign governments, and (2) the net unilateral transfers (excluding military grants of goods and services) of (−)$14,784 million given to foreigners.* The (−)$14,784 million included net U.S. government grants of (−)$11,246 million to foreign countries, net U.S. government pensions and other transfers of (−)$1,612 million given to foreign nations, and net pri-

---

*Note that the $58 million in military grants have appeared twice in the balance of payments, once with a positive sign (credit item), and once with a negative sign (debit item). This transaction resembles the merchandise exports; however, it should be clear that (1) instead of debiting "short-term capital outflow" to show the payments for goods, the "U.S. military grants of goods and services" is debited; and (2) instead of crediting merchandise exports to show the transfer of goods, the "transfer of goods and services" under U.S. military programs is credited.

vate remittances and other transfers of (−)$1,926 million given to foreign nations. Private remittances and other transfers refer to gifts made by individuals and nongovernmental institutions to foreigners. Examples include monies sent back home by migrant workers and a contribution that is made by a U.S. resident to relief funds in LDCs. Because the sign of all the items of the unilateral transfers in the U.S. BOP is negative, it indicates that the U.S. residents sent more money abroad than they received.

The U.S. assets abroad increased by the net amount of (−)$38,183 million, as indicated by the negative sign (debit) of this capital outflow item. This amount included a net increase of (−)$3,858 million in the U.S. official reserve assets, a net increase of (−)$2,628 million in the U.S. government assets other than official reserve assets, and a net increase of $31,697 million in the U.S. private assets abroad.

The (−)$31,697 million net increase in the U.S. official assets abroad itself is composed of (−)$19,091 million increase in the U.S. direct investment abroad, a (−)$7,871 increase in the U.S. holdings of foreign securities, and an increase in the U.S. bank liabilities of (−)$5,926 million.*

The foreign assets in the United States increased by the net amount of $123,108, as shown by the positive sign (credit) of this capital inflow item. This amount includes a net decrease of (−)$1,908 million in foreign official assets in the United States, and a net increase of $125,016 million in other foreign assets in the United States. The $125,016 million itself is composed of a $16,254 million increase in the amount of foreign investment in the United States, a net increase of $71,622 million in the U.S. Treasury and other U.S. securities held by foreigners, and a net increase of $40,610 million in the U.S. bank liabilities to foreigners.†

To find the overall credit balance for the U.S. international transactions, we add up all the items with the positive signs as follows:

| | |
|---|---:|
| Exports of goods and services | $359,702 million |
| U.S. military grants, net | 58 million |
| Foreign assets in the United States, net | 123,108 million |
| Total Credit | $482,868 million |

To find the overall debit balance for the U.S. international transactions, we add up all the items with the negative signs as follows:

---

*These last three figures do not add up to $31,697 million because the data on the U.S. nonbank claims were not available.

†These last three figures do not add up to $125,016 million because the data on nonbank liabilities were not available.

| | |
|---|---|
| Imports of goods and services | (−)$462,581 million |
| U.S. military grant | (−)58 million |
| Unilateral transfer | (−)14,784 million |
| U.S. assets abroad, net | (−)38,183 million |
| Total Debits | (−)$515,606 million |

Because the total amount of debit items, (−)$515,606 million, is greater than the total amount of credit items, (+)$482,868 million, by $32,738 million, it is necessary to record an entry called **statistical discrepancy**. This entry is needed to ensure that the sum of debit items in the BOP is equal to the sum of credit items (including the statistical discrepancy). The reason for the existence of this statistical discrepancy, as we mentioned earlier, is that the debit and the credit entries are not recorded simultaneously, causing a time lag between debit and credit items. Also, some transactions may have been valued either incorrectly or may not have been reported at all. The rest of the items recorded in the U.S. balance of payments are discussed next.

### The Major Accounts in the U.S. Balance of Payments

The balances of the three major accounts, the current account, the capital account, and the official reserve account, can be derived from the data presented in the U.S. BOP (Table 6.1).

The memoranda section of this table presents four different balances. Each of these balances is attained by algebraically adding up all the relevant credit (+) items and debit (−) items and reporting the results. The fourth item shows that the balance of the current account was (−)$117,664 for 1985. As we already know, the current account is the sum of all purchases and sales of goods and services and unilateral transfers. In fact, this figure can be calculated from Table 6.1 by adding up the balance of goods and services (−)$102,879 million and the unilateral transfer (−)$14,784. According to our calculations, the balance of the current account turns out to be (−)$117,663 [(−)$102,879 + (−)$14,784 = (−)$117,663] rather than (−)$117,664, which is reported in Table 6.1. This difference is due to the rounding of figures to the nearest million by the U.S. Department of Commerce, as reported in Table 6.1.

The U.S. capital account balance can be calculated by algebraically adding up the U.S. assets abroad (excluding reserve assets) and foreign assets in the United States (excluding reserve assets). From Table 6.1, the U.S. assets abroad, excluding reserve assets, is (−)$34,325 million, which is calculated as (−)$38,183 − (−)$3,858. The foreign assets in the United States, excluding reserve assets, is (+)$125,016 million, which is calculated as (+)$123,108 − (−)$1,908. Thus, the U.S. capital account balance is (+)$90,691 million, which is calculated as (−)$34,325 + (+)125,016.

Finally, the official reserve account balance can be calculated from the last two items provided in the memoranda. According to the first item, in 1985, there was a net increase in the U.S. official assets of $(-)\$3,858$ million. In the meantime, there was a net decrease in foreign official assets in the United States of $(-)\$2,056$. The algebraic sum of these, that is, $(-)\$5,914$ million, is the balance on the U.S. official reserve account.

## MEASURES OF BOP DEFICITS AND SURPLUSES

As we explained earlier, the inclusion of a statistical discrepancy item always causes the balance of payments to balance. This means that the sum of debit items in the BOP is always equal to the sum of credit items. However, from an economics standpoint, concepts of surplus and deficit have been developed to measure disequilibrium in the BOP. The method for presenting a measure of surplus and deficit is to divide transactions in the BOP into two major groups known as autonomous and accommodating items. **Autonomous items**, referred to as **above-the-line items**, are regarded as those transactions that take place for their own sake, irrespective of the balance of payments position. These include all transactions that take place in response to business conditions at home and abroad. The rest of the items in the BOP are referred to as **accommodating items**, or **below-the-line items**. These transactions, also referred to as compensating items, are viewed as items that could be used to compensate for the BOP surplus or deficit.

Depending on the type of transactions included in autonomous and accommodating items, different methods could be used for defining BOP surplus or deficit.

Before May 1976, the U.S. BOP showed different balances. These were (1) the balance on goods and services; (2) the balance on goods, services, and remittances; (3) the balance on the current account; (4) the balance on the current account and long-term capital (basic balance); (5) the net liquidity balance; and (6) the official reserve transactions balance.

The name of these balances indicates the kinds of transactions that are considered to be autonomous. For example, in defining the **balance of goods and services**, "goods and services" are considered as autonomous transactions. By this definition, the surplus or deficit measures the country's achievement as an international trader. The second item, the **balance of goods, services, and remittances**, is similar to the first item, except that it considers remittances, that is, U.S. government pensions and private remittances, as autonomous transactions as well. The third item, the **current account balance,** goes one step further than the second item and includes U.S. government grants as autonomous transactions. The balance presented by this account resembles the net profit of a business enterprise that results from its current operations.

The **basic balance** considers the current account items and long-term capital transactions as autonomous. The purpose of presenting this balance is to measure the underlying structural changes in a country's balance of payments. In other words, the basic balance measures the long-run trends in a nation's BOP. Such trends are not affected by short-run economic conditions such as interest rates, exchange rates, and monetary policies. However, they are influenced by long-run changes in international competition, factor productivity, factor endowment, and so forth.

The net **liquidity balance** is more complete than the basic balance, considering nonliquid short-term capital flows such as loans and acceptances as autonomous. The term **liquidity** refers to money or assets that could quickly be exchanged for money. Thus, the net liquidity balance emphasizes the international liquidity position of a country. In other words, it shows the amount of domestic currency (dollars) that have been accrued to foreigners as the result of autonomous transactions. Under the system of gold standards that existed before 1971, therefore, the holders of the U.S. dollars could demand gold in return for their dollars, and the net liquidity balance was a measure of pressure on the U.S. international reserve asset, that is, the U.S. gold reserve.

The **official reserve transactions balance (ORT)** considers all private international transactions as autonomous. This would leave only the net official reserve position as an accommodating (compensating) account. The net official reserve position includes reserve assets (gold and convertible currencies) and changes in liabilities to foreign official agencies.

Under a fixed exchange rate system, reserve assets are needed by a country to finance its BOP deficits. The ORT was provided by the United States to reflect such a pressure on its BOP.

In 1976, three years after the United States adopted the managed floating exchange rate system, it was realized that the preparation of all of these balances were not necessary. The major reason behind this decision was the recognition that under the system of managed floating, pressure on the dollar is transmitted to the foreign exchange market, causing its value to fluctuate. In this system, the official reserve is only used to set the dollar value at a desired level by intervening in the foreign exchange market. Thus, the loss of the official reserve is not an indicator of the exact size of the BOP deficit (surplus), but it is a measure of the degree of government intervention in the foreign exchange market.

As Table 6.1 indicates, in 1985 the United States calculated only four partial balances that were reported in the memoranda of the BOP. These were (1) the balance on merchandise trade; (2) the balance on goods and services; (3) the balance on goods, services, and remittances; and (4) the balance on the current account. But, for the reason discussed earlier, the official reserve transactions balance, the basic balance, and the net liquidity balance were not published. However, they could be easily derived from the BOP, and their understanding is necessary because they still appear in writings on international finance. Given the present international monetary system, these concepts should be interpreted with caution and must be supplemented with the analysis of the exchange rate.

# THE INTERNATIONAL INVESTMENT POSITION

The international financial status of a country could be further evaluated by an accounting statement known as the international investment position (IIP) or, as it is often referred to, the "balance of international indebtedness." This statement presents the total amount and distribution of a country's assets abroad and foreign assets at home at a given point in time. IIP is useful in providing us with information that could be utilized in projecting the future flow of income generated from the country's foreign investments.

In comparison to a nation's BOP that shows the "flow," that is, the rate of change of goods, services, and capital over a given period of time, the IIP provides us with the "stock" of a nation's foreign assets and liabilities at a given point in time (namely, the end of a year).

Although more attention is paid to the BOP, usually the two statements are interrelated and are analyzed together. In fact, the IIP provides us with the stock that corresponds to flows given by the capital account and reserve items recorded in the BOP. Theoretically speaking, if we add a nation's capital flows during the current year to its IIP at the end of the preceding year, they should give the IIP of the nation at the end of the current year. In reality, however, this is not the case due to measurement problems.

Table 6.3 shows the IIP of the United States at the end of selected years, 1970–1985. The *net international investment position* (NIIP) in the United States, that is, Item A in the table, is obtained by subtracting the foreign assets in the United States (Item C) from the U.S. assets abroad (Item B). Because at the end of the year 1985 foreign assets in the United States ($1,059,807 million) are greater than U.S. assets abroad ($952,367 million), this would give the United States a negative number for the U.S. net international position of (−)$107,440. This negative NIIP experienced by the United States in 1985 is the first to occur since 1919, when assets and liabilities started to be compiled in a systematic fashion.

The decrease in the U.S. NIIP, which has been occurring for the last few years, is depicted by Item A in Table 6.3 for the years 1981 through 1985. This decrease is related to the relatively higher growth of foreign assets in the United States as compared with the growth of the U.S. assets abroad during the period 1970–1985. Foreign assets in the United States grew by 891 percent (from $106,912 million in 1970 to $1,059,807 million in 1985), whereas the U.S. assets abroad grew only by about 476 percent (from $165,385 million in 1970 to $952,367 million in 1985).

The increase in foreign assets in the United States is caused by several interrelated factors: (1) the relatively high yields on U.S. securities; (2) the relatively high interest rates in the United States as compared with other industrial nations; (3) the relatively higher economic growth in the United States as compared with other countries; and (4) the strong U.S. demand for foreign funds.

One of the factors that has contributed to the worsening of the NIIP of the United States is foreign direct investment (FDI). Although U.S. FDI abroad

Table 6.3  INTERNATIONAL INVESTMENT POSITION OF THE UNITED STATES AT THE END OF SELECTED YEARS, 1970–85
Millions of Dollars

| | 1970 | 1975 | 1980 | 1981 | 1982 | 1983 | 1984 | 1985 |
|---|---|---|---|---|---|---|---|---|
| A. Net International Investment Position of the U.S. | 58,473 | 74,240 | 106,037 | 140,704 | 136,200 | 88,494 | 4,384 | −107,440 |
| B. U.S. Assets Abroad | 165,385 | 295,100 | 606,867 | 719,687 | 824,875 | 874,053 | 898,187 | 952,367 |
| U.S. Official Reserve Assets | 14,487 | 16,226 | 26,756 | 30,075 | 33,957 | 33,748 | 34,933 | 43,185 |
| Gold | 11,072 | 11,599 | 11,160 | 11,151 | 11,148 | 11,121 | 11,096 | 11,090 |
| SDRs | 851 | 2,335 | 2,610 | 4,095 | 5,250 | 5,025 | 5,641 | 7,293 |
| Reserve Position in the IMF | 1,935 | 2,212 | 2,852 | 5,054 | 7,348 | 11,312 | 11,541 | 11,947 |
| Foreign Currencies | 629 | 80 | 10,134 | 9,774 | 10,212 | 6,289 | 6,656 | 12,856 |
| Other Government Assets | 32,143 | 41,804 | 63,545 | 68,451 | 74,333 | 79,250 | 84,636 | 87,418 |
| U.S. Private Assets | 118,755 | 237,070 | 516,586 | 621,161 | 716,585 | 761,055 | 778,618 | 821,764 |
| Direct Investment Abroad | 75,480 | 124,050 | 215,375 | 228,348 | 207,752 | 207,203 | 212,994 | 232,667 |
| Foreign Securities | 20,892 | 34,913 | 62,653 | 63,452 | 75,672 | 84,270 | 89,997 | 114,147 |
| Other Private Assets | 22,383 | 78,107 | 238,538 | 329,361 | 433,161 | 469,582 | 475,627 | 474,950 |
| C. Foreign Assets in the U.S. | 106,912 | 220,860 | 500,830 | 578,983 | 688,675 | 785,559 | 893,803 | 1,059,807 |
| Foreign Official Assets | 26,151 | 86,910 | 176,062 | 180,425 | 189,109 | 194,599 | 199,127 | 202,308 |
| Direct Investment in the U.S. | 13,270 | 27,662 | 83,046 | 108,714 | 124,677 | 137,061 | 164,583 | 182,951 |
| Other Foreign Assets in the U.S. | 67,491 | 106,228 | 241,722 | 289,844 | 374,889 | 453,899 | 530,093 | 674,548 |

Source: U.S. Department of Commerce, Survey of Current Business (Washington, D.C.: U.S. Government Printing Office, June 1986), p. 28.

($232,667 million in 1985) is still greater than the FDI in this country ($182,951 million in 1985), the latter has experienced a much faster growth. As Table 6.3 indicates, during the 1970–1985 period, the growth of the U.S. FDI abroad was 208 percent (from $75,480 million in 1970 to $232,667 million in 1985), as compared with the growth of the FDI in the United States, which was about 1278 percent (from $13,270 million in 1970 to $182,951 million in 1985).

## THE USEFULNESS OF THE BOP

The information provided by the BOP is useful for both government authorities and business persons.

From the government standpoint, the BOP can be utilized in planning a country's commercial, fiscal, and monetary policies. Different items recorded in the BOP can help the government authorities to analyze the nation's economic relations with other countries. For example, they can look at the current account to assess the normal channels of receipts and payments from current economic activities. As a second example, they can study the long-term capital transactions inflow to assess the country's comparative advantage in investment opportunities. Third, they can determine the country's ability to intervene in the foreign exchange market by looking at its official reserve transactions account.

From the business standpoint, the BOP is affected by and also affects business activities. The influence of business activities on BOP stems from the fact that the major items recorded in the BOP are generated by business. These items include imports and exports of goods and services; inflows and outflows of capital; receipts and payments of dividends, fees, royalties, and rents from foreign operations.

The business activities are also affected by the BOP because it is an indicator of a country's economic health. If a country is experiencing a BOP deficit, it is important for a business person to know what corrective action could be chosen by the government authorities to alleviate the problem. If the corrective action chosen by the government is devaluation of the national currency, then exports may be expected to rise and imports may be expected to fall.* However, if the corrective action calls for imposition of import tariffs or quotas, then the importation of certain raw materials and goods can be expected to fall. Because each of these policy options has different implications for business operations, it is important for the manager of an MNC to know which options might be chosen so that he or she can adjust the company's strategy accordingly.

---

*The devaluation of a national currency causes its value to decrease as compared with foreign currencies. Thus, if the German mark is devalued, its value in terms of the U.S. dollar would decrease. This means that each mark commands less dollars (or each dollar commands more marks). As a result, the value of Germany's products in terms of the dollar would decrease. However, the value of its imports in terms of the dollar would increase. This may lead to higher exports and lower imports for Germany, improving its BOP deficit.

## SUMMARY

1. The balance of payments (BOP) can be defined as an accounting statement that shows the summary of all the transactions between the residents of a nation and the residents of all other nations during a given period of time (usually a calendar year).

2. The inclusion of the errors and omissions account in the BOP causes the sum of debit items in this statement to be equal to the sum of the credit items.

3. Credit items in the BOP involve the receipt of payments from foreigners. Thus they give a nation more foreign currencies, or they reduce a foreign nation's holdings of domestic currencies. These items include the exports of goods and services, unilateral transfers received from foreigners, and capital inflows.

4. Debit items in the BOP involve payments to foreigners. These are transactions that use up a nation's foreign currencies or increase foreign holdings of the domestic currency. These items include imports of goods and services, unilateral transfers given to foreigners, and capital outflows.

5. Capital outflow can be defined as (a) an increase in a country's assets abroad, or (b) a decrease in foreign assets in a country.

6. Capital inflow can be defined as (a) an increase in foreign assets in a country, or (b) a decrease in a country's assets abroad.

7. The major accounts in the BOP are the current account, the capital account, and the accommodating (compensating) account.

8. Current account includes those transactions that do not result in any future obligations. These transactions include (a) purchases of goods and services from foreigners; and (b) unilateral transfers, that is, remittances and grants that are given to foreigners for free.

9. Capital account includes those transactions that involve future obligations. These transactions include (a) investing in foreign nations, (b) providing loans to foreigners, and (c) depositing money in foreign banks.

10. Accommodating (compensating) accounts include a nation's holdings of foreign convertible currencies, gold, and SDRs that are used by its monetary authorities to intervene in the foreign exchange market in resolving its balance of payments problems.

11. The method for presenting a measure of surplus or deficit in the BOP is to divide transactions into two major groups known as autonomous items and accommodating (compensating) items.

12. Autonomous items, referred to as "above the line" items, are those transactions that take place for their own sake, irrespective of the BOP position. These include all transactions that take place in response to business conditions at home and abroad. The rest of the items in the BOP are referred to as accommodating (compensating) items or "below the line" items. These transactions are viewed as items that could be used to finance the BOP surplus or deficit.

13. Before May 1976, the U.S. BOP showed six different balances. These were (a) the balance on goods and services; (b) the balance on goods, services, and remittances; (c) the balance on current account; (d) the balance on current account and long-term capital (basic balance); (e) the net liquidity balance; and (f) the official reserve transactions balance.

14. The names of the balances in the BOP indicate the kinds of transactions that are considered to be autonomous.

15. Since 1976, every year the United States has calculated only four partial balances

that are reported in the memoranda of the BOP. But the basic balance, the liquidity balance, and the official reserve transactions balance are no longer reported. However, they could be easily derived from the BOP, and they still appear in writings on international finance.

16. The international investment position (IIP) or the balance of international indebtedness is a statement that presents the total amount and the distribution of a country's foreign assets at a given time (namely, the end of a year).

17. The increase in foreign assets in the United States in recent years is caused by (a) the relatively high yields on the U.S. securities, (b) relatively high interest rates in the United States as compared with other industrialized nations, (c) the relatively higher economic growth in the United States as compared with other countries, and (d) the strong U.S. demand for foreign funds.

18. The information provided by the BOP is useful for both government authorities and business persons. From the government standpoint, the BOP can be utilized in planning a country's commercial, fiscal, and monetary policies. From a business person's perspective, the BOP is useful because it is an indicator of a country's economic health, which must be considered in planning any firm's strategies.

## QUESTIONS

6.1 Explain the concept of the double-entry bookkeeping system. Why does the application of this system to the balance of payments result in an entry called "statistical discrepancy"?

6.2 Explain the method that is used for presenting a measure of surplus or deficit in the balance of payments.

6.3 What balances were presented by the United States to measure the balance of payments deficit prior to May 1976? What balances are presented now, and why?

6.4 Describe the pattern of the net international position of the United States in recent years. What factors have shaped this pattern? Explain.

6.5 Use the most recent copy of the U.S. balance of payments, printed in the current issue of the *Survey of Current Business,* to answer the following questions:
   a. Does the United States have a deficit or a surplus in its current account? What is its size?
   b. Explain how the balances shown in the memoranda section are determined.
   c. Explain how the statistical discrepancy was determined.

6.6 Show how each of the following items is debited or credited in the U.S. balance of payments:
   a. The importation of $1,000 worth of goods by a U.S. resident from a German resident who has agreed to be paid in six months.
   b. The payment by a U.S. resident with a check that is drawn on his or her German bank account after the six-month period has expired.
   c. The purchase of $5,000 worth of the stock of Mercedes-Benz in Germany by a U.S. resident.
   d. The transfer of $2,000 in cash as a gift by a U.S. resident to a relative in Germany.
   e. The receipt of a $500 dividend by the U.S. resident from Mercedes-Benz in Germany.

6.7 What is the difference between a country's balance of payments and its international investment position? Is it possible for a country to have a balance of payments deficit and, at the same time, strengthen its international economic status? Explain.

## SUGGESTED READINGS

Asheghian, Parviz. "The Impact of Devaluation on the Balance of Payments of Less Developed Countries: A Monetary Approach." *Journal of Economic Development* (July 1985):143–151.

Congdon, Tim. "A New Approach to the Balance of Payments." *Lloyd's Bank Review.* No. 146 (October 1982):1–14.

Gray, Peter H. *International Trade, Investment, and Payments.* Boston: Houghton Mifflin, 1979.

International Monetary Fund. *Balance of Payments Manual,* 4th ed. Washington, D.C.: International Monetary Fund, 1977.

International Monetary Fund. *Balance of Payments Yearbook.* Washington, D.C.: International Monetary Fund. Annual.

Johnson, Harry G. *Money, Balance of Payments Theory and the International Monetary Problem.* Princeton, N.J.: Princeton University Press, 1977.

Johnson, Harry G. *The Monetary Approach to the Balance of Payments.* Winchester, Mass.: Allen & Unwin, 1975.

Kuwayma, Patricia H. "Measuring the United States Balance of Payments." *Monthly Review.* Federal Reserve Bank of New York (August 1975):183–194.

Stern, Robert M., et al. *The Presentation of the U.S. Balance of Payments: A Symposium.* Essay in International Finance Series, No. 123. Princeton, N.J.: Princeton University Press, 1977.

United States Department of Commerce, Office of Business Economics, *Survey of Current Business.* Washington, D.C.: U.S. Government Printing Office. March, June, September, and December issues.

Whitman, Marina. "The Payments Adjustment Process and the Exchange Rate Regime: What Have We Learned?" *American Economic Review* (May 1975): 133–136.

# The Foreign Exchange Market

One of the significant factors that differentiates international business from domestic business is the existence of different national currencies. In domestic transactions only one currency is used. For example, the dollar is used in the United States, while the deutsche mark, dinar, franc, pound, and yen are employed as currencies of West Germany, Kuwait, France, England, and Japan, respectively. In international transactions, however, two or more currencies are involved. For example, an American importer who wants to purchase French wine possesses the dollar, while the French exporter who makes the sale demands francs in return. Thus, there are two currencies involved, and this necessitates the existence of a mechanism that allows the settlement of this international transaction so that both parties' requirements are met. Such a mechanism is provided in the form of the foreign exchange market.

The purpose of this chapter is to provide us with a basic understanding of the foreign exchange market. First, we define the concept of the foreign exchange market. Second, we describe the instruments that are used in the market. Third, we elaborate on the functions of commercial banks in the foreign exchange market. Fourth, we discuss different types of foreign exchange transactions. Fifth, we describe the Eurocurrency market. Finally, we provide an explanation of international banking.

## DEFINITION OF THE FOREIGN EXCHANGE MARKET

The **Foreign Exchange Market** (FEM) can be defined as a market within which individuals, business firms, and banks purchase and sell foreign currencies and other debt instruments. In this definition the term *market* does not refer to any centralized meeting place, nor does it involve any one country. For example, the foreign exchange market for any currency, say the U.S. dollar, consists of all locations where the dollars are purchased and sold for other national currencies. These locations include Amsterdam, Frankfurt, Hong Kong, London, Milan, New York, Zurich, Paris, and Toronto. Trading between these locations is not subject to any formal requirements for participation and is usually performed over the telephone or through the telex.

## FUNCTIONS OF THE FOREIGN EXCHANGE MARKET

The principal function of the FEM is the provision of a mechanism by which funds from one nation and currency are transferred to another nation and into another currency. In this manner the FEM performs a clearinghouse function. It brings together parties who want to exchange their currencies and enables them to clear their balances on the basis of the market exchange rate.

The participants of the FEM are commercial banks, the commercial banks' customers, and central banks. The transactions undertaken by these parties can be classified into four levels: (1) the transactions between commercial banks and their customers, (2) the indirect transactions between commercial banks themselves through their brokers, (3) the transactions between these banks and their foreign subsidiaries, and (4) the central bank transactions.

At the first level, tourists, investors, exporters, and importers purchase and sell foreign currencies from and to commercial banks. The demand for foreign currencies originates when tourists go abroad, when a firm imports goods and services from abroad, when an indigenous firm invests in other countries, and so on. The supply of foreign currencies, however, stems from the expenses of foreign tourists in a country, the foreign investment in a nation, the exports of goods and services by a country, and so on. A nation's commercial banks provide the clearinghouse that brings together those who demand and those who supply foreign currencies, allowing foreign exchange transactions to take place.

At the second level, commercial banks deal indirectly with each other through foreign exchange brokers who act as intermediaries. The purpose of these transactions is to allow commercial banks to even out the flow of foreign exchange among themselves. Anytime a commercial bank does not have its desired amount of foreign currency, it can turn to a foreign exchange broker to purchase additional foreign currency or sell its unwanted surplus. Thus, foreign exchange brokers act as wholesalers of foreign currencies, operating in an interbank market where commercial banks deal in foreign currencies.

At the third level, commercial banks deal with their overseas branches. This allows them to match the demand for foreign currencies with the supply of foreign currencies in their banking system. In the United States, although several banks engage in foreign exchange transactions, it is the major New York banks that usually carry out transactions with foreign banks. Other banks in the United States maintain a correspondence relationship with the New York banks in order to meet their foreign exchange needs.

At the fourth level, the nation's central banks engage in foreign exchange transactions in order to control the value of their currencies. As we already know, under the managed floating exchange rate system, if the demand for a foreign currency in a country exceeds the supply of that currency, it causes the price of that currency (measured in terms of domestic currency) to rise. To set the price at a desired level, the nation's central bank could sell that foreign currency, causing its price to decline. On the other hand, if the demand for a foreign currency falls short of its supply, its prices would decline. In this case, the central bank could buy that foreign currency, causing its price to rise to the desired level.

## FOREIGN EXCHANGE INSTRUMENTS

Because residents of all countries want to be paid in their own currencies when dealing in international business, different financial means are needed to make such payments possible. These means, referred to as foreign exchange instruments, are written or printed financial documents that allow the payment of funds from one country and one currency to another country and another currency. Chief among these instruments are cable (telegraphic) transfers, commercial bills of exchange (commercial drafts), bank drafts, and letters of credit.

In what follows, we first provide an explanation of these instruments, and we then elaborate on certain documents that must accompany these instruments in any export transaction.

### Cable Transfers

The cable (telegraphic) transfer is the most important financial instrument that is used in international business. A cable transfer is an order that is transmitted by a bank in a country to its foreign correspondent in another country, instructing its correspondent bank to pay out a specific amount to a designated person or account. For example, consider an American importer in New York who is importing £50,000 worth of scotch whiskey from a British exporter in London. At an exchange rate of $2 = £1, the American importer could pay for the scotch whiskey by buying a cable transfer for £50,000 from a local bank, say his/her bank in New York, paying $100,000 (plus any bank service charges) to the bank. The bank in New York then calls its correspondent bank in England to transfer £50,000 from its account into the exporter's account. The main advantage of cable transfer is the speed by which payments are made. Normally the funds are transferred within one or two days following the transaction.

## Commercial Bills of Exchange

A commercial bill of exchange is a written order by an exporter (the drawer) to an importer (the drawee), instructing the importer to pay on demand, or on a certain date, a specified amount of money to a designated party (the payee). The payee could be either the exporter, or a local bank where the exporter has an account. A bill of exchange that is payable on presentation to the drawee is referred to as a **sight bill**. A bill that is payable at some future date is known as a **time bill**. A time bill is usually expressed in terms of the "days after sight," such as a "30-day sight bill," or a "60-day sight bill."

Using the previous example, if the payment for the scotch whiskey import were to be made by a commercial bill of exchange, the British exporter (the drawer) instructs the American importer (the drawee) to transfer the stated amount (£50,000) at a given time, for example, 30, 60, or 90 days after all the scotch whisky bottles are delivered to New York. The transfer is made to a designated bank in England or directly to the British exporter. An example of a 60-day time draft (the term *time draft* is synonymous with the term *time bill*) used in this transaction is shown in Figure 7.1.

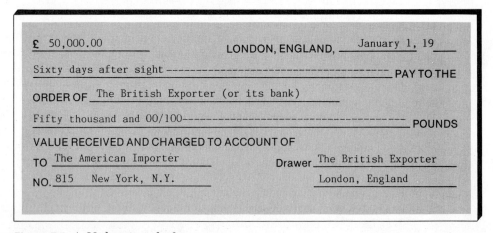

| £ 50,000.00 | LONDON, ENGLAND, _____January 1, 19____ |
| Sixty days after sight ------------------------------------- PAY TO THE |
| ORDER OF _The British Exporter (or its bank)_____ |
| Fifty thousand and 00/100------------------------------------ POUNDS |
| VALUE RECEIVED AND CHARGED TO ACCOUNT OF |
| TO _The American Importer_____ | Drawer _The British Exporter_____ |
| NO._815   New York, N.Y._____ | London, England |

**Figure 7.1** A 60-day time draft

When a commercial bill of exchange is presented to the drawee, the willingness to honor the bill is expressed by writing "accepted" on the face of the bill, followed by the date and the signature of the drawee. The bill then becomes an acceptance and is legally binding. The accepted bill is called *trade acceptance*. The exporter may hold the trade acceptance until the maturity date or sell it at a discount to his or her local bank, to some other banks, or to an acceptance dealer.

## Bank Drafts

A bank draft is similar to a commercial bill of exchange in the sense that it is a written order by a drawer to a drawee instructing him or her to pay, on demand or at a certain date, a specified amount of money to a payee. The major difference between these two financial instruments is that in the case of the bank draft, the drawee is a bank rather than an importer. In other words, a bank draft directs the exporter to receive payments directly from a bank designated by the importer. Usually this involves a bank in the importer's country instructing its correspondent bank in the exporter's country to pay the specified amount to the exporter. Thus, a bank draft is also a check.

Using our previous example of scotch whisky imports, if a bank draft is used as the payment instrument, then the drawee would be the American importer's designated bank (that is, the London-based correspondent bank of the importer's bank in New York) rather than the importer.

As in the case of a commercial bill of exchange, the willingness of the drawee (the bank in this case) to honor the bill is declared by writing "accepted" on the face of the bill. An accepted bank draft is referred to as a *bank acceptance*. Like a trade acceptance the bank acceptance could either be held until maturity or sold at a discount.

## Letters of Credit

A letter of credit is a document that is issued by an importer's bank declaring that payments should be made to an exporter regarding a specific shipment of commodities, accompanied by the shipment documents. In comparison to the bill of exchange, a letter of credit is a safer document in the sense of assuring payment at a certain date. In the case of a bill of exchange there is always the possibility that the importer would not make the payment to the exporter at the specified time. The letter of credit, however, has the guarantee of the importer's bank obliging that bank to accept the bill when it is presented.

Using our first example, if the British exporter of scotch whiskey is not sure of the creditability of the American importer, the exporter could request a letter of credit. In this case the American importer would request a local bank, say his/her bank in New York, to issue a letter of credit in favor of the British exporter. The bank in New York then informs the British exporter that it has issued a letter of credit on the exporter's behalf. This allows the British exporter to draw a bill of exchange against the bank in New York, rather than against the American importer. When the bill is accepted by the bank it becomes a *bank acceptance.* The exporter could then endorse the bank acceptance and sell it at a discount in the money market.

When the letter of credit is guaranteed by the importer's bank, the exporter still bears the risk of revocation of the letter of credit by that bank. There is also the risk of the importer's bank failing and the risk of nonpayment that might result from new exchange restrictions. To avoid these risks the exporter may request a "confirmed," or a "irrevocable," letter of credit. A *confirmed* letter of credit means that the payment is guaranteed not only by the importer's bank but also by the exporter's bank as well. In our example, the British exporter could draw a bill of exchange on a local bank, say his/her bank in London, for £50,000 and this bank is obliged to confirm the bill. If the bill is a sight bill the exporter would be paid immediately by the bank in London. However, if the bill is a time bill, the exporter would receive a bank acceptance that could easily be sold at a discount in the money market.

## OTHER MEANS OF PAYMENT

In addition to payment through foreign exchange instruments, an exporter has the option of dealing with an importer either on a cash basis or on an open account basis. *Cash payment* is especially attractive when the exporter is not sure of the creditworthiness of the importer and considers the transaction too risky. An *open account* is usually used when a parent-subsidiary relationship exists between the exporter and importer, or when the exporter is confident of the creditability of the importer. When this option is chosen the exporter simply ships the merchandise to the importer, along with the necessary documents, without any prior payment or obligation by the importer.

## EXPORT SHIPMENT PROCESS

The payment for an export transaction is settled through a documentary draft. A documentary draft is a draft that is accompanied by certain documents. An importer cannot secure the possession of the imported goods unless these documents are released to him or her. The documents are released to the importer, upon his or her acceptance or payment of the draft, giving the importer the right to claim the goods at the port of entry. Two types of documentary drafts may be used. If the exporter has no question about the creditworthiness of the importer, a **documentary-acceptance (D/A) draft** is used. In this case, the documents are released to the importer upon his or her acceptance of the draft. However, if the exporter does have questions about the creditworthiness of the importer, a **documentary-on-payments (D/P) draft** is used. In this case, the documents are released to the importer upon his or her payment of the draft.

Typically, documents that are used in an export transaction include: the commercial invoice, bills of lading, and the marine insurance certificate. The **commercial invoice** is a document that shows the price of merchandise that is being traded. The **bill of lading** is a document that provides evidence of the shipment of a commodity. This is the most important document because it gives the holder the right to control the goods in question. The **marine insurance certificate** is a document showing that the shipped merchandise has insurance coverage.

To further our understanding of an export order and the way that these documents are employed in the process, let us use our whiskey example and assume that payment will be made by a 60-day time draft. Given this example, the exportation of scotch whiskey and the payment for it (as illustrated in Figure 7.2) involve the following several steps:

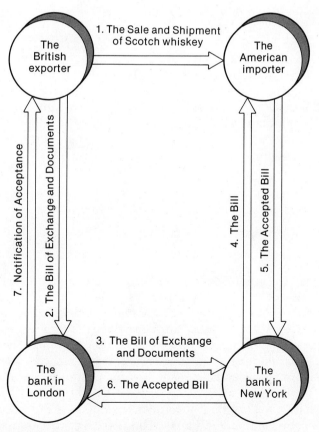

**Figure 7.2** The export shipments process of whiskey

1. The British exporter sells the scotch whiskey to the American importer and ships the bottles to New York.
2. At the same time, the British exporter draws a bill of exchange against the American importer, payable 60 days after sight, and sends the bill along with its supplementary documents (the commercial invoice, the bill of lading, and the marine insurance certificate) to the local bank, the bank in London.
3. The bank in London in turn mails the bill and all the documents to its correspondent bank in the United States, say the bank in New York.
4. When all the scotch whiskey bottles are delivered, the bank in New York presents the bill to the American importer for acceptance.
5. The American importer either pays the bill (if a D/P draft is used) or accepts the bill (if a D/A draft is used) and returns it to the bank in New York. The importer then receives the bill of lading from the bank, which gives the importer the right to claim the scotch whiskey bottles at the port of entry.
6. The bank in New York returns the accepted bill to the bank in London.
7. The bank in London informs the exporter that the accepted bill has been received.

Upon the acceptance of the bill by the importer, the exporter can endorse and sell the bill to either an investor or to the local bank (the bank in London) at a discount. In this case the bank (or the investor) assumes a financial function; that is, after 60 days it presents the bill to the American importer for payment. Of course, the exporter also has the option of holding the bill until its maturity. In this case, the exporter would receive the full face value of the bill rather than the discounted amount.

## THE FUNCTIONS OF COMMERCIAL BANKS IN THE FOREIGN EXCHANGE MARKET

The parties involved in international trade seldom transact directly with each other. Rather, as our previous examples have shown, they usually deal with commercial banks that are located in their own countries. Commercial banks, therefore, are the main channels through which foreign exchange transactions take place. In performing their roles in the foreign exchange market, commercial banks render three main services through their international departments: (1) purchasing and selling of foreign currencies, (2) lending, and (3) collecting.

The purchasing and selling of foreign currencies are the most common task performed by commercial banks. The need for such transactions arises from many sources. First, tourists entering and leaving a country need to exchange their currencies. Second, exporters generate a supply of foreign currency and a demand for local currency. Third, importers generate a demand for foreign currency and a supply of domestic currency. Finally, a person or a firm that plans to invest in a foreign country needs to purchase foreign currency.

The lending services provided by commercial banks to their international customers take different forms, ranging from direct payment to a customer to discounting a customer's draft. In making such loans, banks use different lending instruments that are available to them. Examples include the importer's letter of credit, discussed earlier, and a bank draft that has been discounted.

The collections services rendered by commercial banks provide means by which the international payments between residents of a country and the residents of the rest of the world take place. Using our previous example of scotch whiskey, payment for the sale would usually be made through a commercial bank located in either New York or London.

## FOREIGN EXCHANGE TRANSACTIONS

Foreign exchange transactions take place between commercial banks and their customers, and among commercial banks themselves who buy and sell foreign currencies either locally or internationally. Today, foreign exchange transactions are made through a network of telephones, computers, cables, and communications satellites that allow the foreign exchange market "to follow the sun" around the globe. Consequently, commercial banks located in major financial centers such as New York, London, Tokyo, and Rome can instantaneously contact each other and close a foreign exchange deal verbally over the phone. What these banks exchange are, in effect, bank deposits denominated in different currencies. For example, a Chicago bank selling U.S. dollars to a German bank is, in effect, purchasing a deposit from that bank that is denominated in German marks. This would give the Chicago bank the right to draw a check on the German bank for the amount of the deposit denominated in marks. It would also give the German bank the right to draw a check on the Chicago bank for the amount of the deposit denominated in U.S. dollars.

The speed by which these transactions take place contributes to the constant fluctuation in the exchange rates. This fluctuation makes dealing in the foreign exchange market a risky business. To deal with foreign exchange risks one could choose to transact either in the spot market or in the forward market. One could also engage in either hedging or speculation.

In this section, we first explain foreign exchange risks and then discuss the choices that are open to an individual for dealing with these risks.

### Foreign Exchange Risks

As we already know, foreign exchange rates are determined by the interaction of demand and supply in the foreign exchange market. A nation's demand and supply of foreign exchange shifts (increases or decreases) over time, causing fluctuations in foreign exchange rates. Among the factors that cause the shifts in the demand and supply of foreign exchange are changes in the relative rates of interest in different nations, the different growth and inflation rates in different nations, the devaluation of a nation's currency, the changes in tastes for foreign and domestic products at home and abroad, the changes in relative incomes of different nations, and the expectation of changes in different economic variables, such as interest rates, inflation, and so on.

For example, the higher interest rates in a nation, as compared with other countries, may encourage the movement of short-term funds to that nation, leading to the appreciation of its currency. As we explained in Chapter 1, this is in fact what occurred in the United States in the late 1970s and early 1980s contributing to the U.S. trade deficit.

As another example, if Germany's taste for Japanese products increases, assuming that other things that affect demand and supply for Japanese products stay constant, Germany's demand for Japanese yen would increase (the demand curve would shift to the right). This would lead to an increase in the exchange rate, that is, to a depreciation of the German mark.

As a third example, a lower inflation rate in Germany than in Japan, assuming other things stay constant, makes Germany's products cheaper in Japan. This leads to an increase in Germany's supply of Japanese yen (the shift of the supply curve to the right) and would lead to a decrease in the exchange rate, that is, to an appreciation of the German mark.

Given the numerous economic variables that affect the world economy, great variations occur in exchange rates on a daily basis. Figure 7.3 portrays the exchange rate movements for seven major industrial countries, the so-called Group of Seven (G-7), from 1980 to 1987.

In Figure 7.3, with the exception of the United States, the exchange rate movements for each country are represented with two different curves. One of the curves (the solid line curve) is based on the measurement of the exchange rate in terms of the U.S. dollar. The other curve is drawn on the basis of the effective exchange rate index. The effective exchange rate index is used to indicate the extent to which the external value of a nation's currency moves relative to other nations' currencies. This index measures the value of a given currency in terms of the weighted average of 17 major currencies.* According

---

*The number of countries included in the calculations of the index may vary according to the agency that undertakes the computations. For example, the Federal Reserve Bank of Cleveland, Ohio, includes only ten countries (see, for example, the Federal Reserve Bank of Cleveland, *Economic Trends,* August 1987, p. 21). The weights take into consideration factors such as the size of trade flows and the relevant price elasticities of exchange rate changes (see The Federal Reserve Bank of St. Louis, *International Economic Conditions* (October 1987), p. 5.

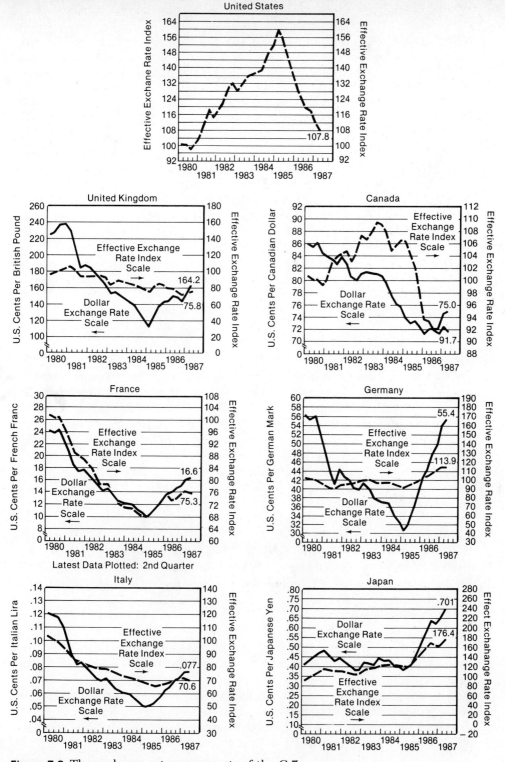

**Figure 7.3** The exchange rate movements of the G-7

*Source:* The Federal Reserve Bank of St. Louis, *International Economic Conditions* (October 1987): 2–3.

to the figure, the U.S. dollar values of Canadian dollars, French francs, German marks, Italian lira, and Japanese yen continued to decline during the period 1980–1985, indicating the appreciation of the U.S. dollar. However, following the devaluation of the dollar in 1985, as we explain later, the value of these currencies in terms of the U.S. dollar started to rise.

As Figure 7.3 indicates, large fluctuations in exchange rates occur for any currency. These variations give rise to three different types of risks: transaction exposure, translation exposure, and economic exposure. **Transaction exposure** arises when individuals and institutions expect to make payments or to receive funds that are denominated in a foreign currency. **Translation exposure** is a measure of how exchange rate fluctuations affect the recording and reporting of a company's financial position in its financial statements. **Economic exposure** is related to the total impact of fluctuating exchange rates on a firm's profitability.

In Chapter 17 we provide a further explanation of these three types of risks. In what follows, we elaborate on the ways by which one can deal with transaction exposure.

### The Spot Market

The **spot market** is a foreign exchange market in which foreign currencies are purchased and sold for immediate delivery, that is, within two business days after the day that the transaction is agreed upon. This two-day period is needed to allow the traders to instruct their respective commercial banks to make the necessary transfers in their accounts. The spot price of foreign exchange, determined by the demand and supply, is subject to constant fluctuations due to appreciation or depreciation of different currencies against each other. Foreign exchange quotations are usually made in two different ways: (1) in terms of the amount of the domestic currency that is needed to buy a unit of foreign currency; and (2) in terms of the amount of foreign currency that is needed to buy a unit of domestic currency.

Table 7.1 indicates the spot price (or rate) for different currencies in terms of the U.S. dollar for Friday March 17, 1989, and for Thursday March 16, 1989. For example, next to West Germany we find that the spot rate was $0.5329 = DM 1 on Friday and $0.5346 = DM 1 on Thursday. On the same line we find that the spot rate was DM 1.8762 = $1.00 on Friday, and DM 1.8705 = $1.00 on Thursday.

Today, most of the foreign exchange transactions take place in the spot market and the payment instruments usually used in this market are cable transfers and "on sight" drafts.

The advantage of dealing in the spot exchange market is the immediate delivery of the foreign currency at the current exchange rate. As a result, one can avoid the risk of fluctuations in the exchange rate that results from the delivery of the foreign currency at a future date.

## Table 7.1  FOREIGN EXCHANGE RATES

| Country | U.S. $ equiv. | | Currency per U.S. $ | |
|---|---|---|---|---|
| | Fri. | Thurs. | Fri. | Thurs. |
| Argentina (Austral) | .026171 | .026171 | 38.21 | 38.21 |
| Australia (Dollar) | .8190 | .8170 | 1.2210 | 1.2239 |
| Austria (Schilling) | .07573 | .07599 | 13.20 | 13.15 |
| Bahrain (Dinar) | 2.6518 | 2.6518 | .37710 | .37710 |
| Belgium (Franc) | | | | |
|   Commercial rate | .02545 | .02553 | 39.29 | 39.16 |
|   Financial rate | .02535 | .02543 | 39.44 | 39.31 |
| Brazil (Cruzado) | 1.0101 | 1.0101 | .99000 | .99000 |
| Britain (Pound) | 1.7145 | 1.7190 | .5832 | .5817 |
|   30-Day Forward | 1.7105 | 1.7149 | .5846 | .5831 |
|   90-Day Forward | 1.7035 | 1.7077 | .5870 | .5855 |
|   180-Day Forward | 1.6961 | 1.6993 | .5895 | .5884 |
| Canada (Dollar) | .8357 | .8354 | 1.1965 | 1.1970 |
|   30-Day Forward | .8346 | .8343 | 1.1981 | 1.1985 |
|   90-Day Forward | .8320 | .8316 | 1.2019 | 1.2024 |
|   180-Day Forward | .8281 | .8278 | 1.2075 | 1.2079 |
| Chile (Official rate) | .0040726 | .0040726 | 245.54 | 245.54 |
| China (Yuan) | .268672 | .268672 | 3.7220 | 3.7220 |
| Colombia (Peso) | .002785 | .002785 | 359.00 | 359.00 |
| Denmark (Krone) | .1366 | .1372 | 7.3155 | 7.2880 |
| Ecuador (Sucre) | | | | |
|   Floating rate | .001926 | .001926 | 519.00 | 519.00 |
| Finland (Markka) | .2310 | .2297 | 4.3280 | 4.3525 |
| France (Franc) | .1576 | .1579 | 6.3450 | 6.3310 |
|   30-Day Forward | .1578 | .1581 | 6.3370 | 6.3225 |
|   90-Day Forward | .1581 | .1585 | 6.3250 | 6.3088 |
|   180-Day Forward | .1586 | .1591 | 6.3020 | 6.2845 |
| Greece (Drachma) | .006337 | .006361 | 157.80 | 157.20 |
| Hong Kong (Dollar) | .128254 | .128209 | 7.7970 | 7.7985 |
| India (Rupee) | .0650618 | .0650618 | 15.37 | 15.37 |
| Indonesia (Rupiah) | .0005750 | .0005750 | 1739.00 | 1739.00 |
| Ireland (Punt) | 1.4340 | 1.4340 | .6973 | .6973 |
| Israel (Shekel) | .5503 | .5503 | 1.8170 | 1.8170 |
| Italy (Lira) | .0007278 | .0007291 | 1374.00 | 1371.50 |
| Japan (Yen) | .007598 | .007682 | 131.60 | 130.00 |
|   30-Day Forward | .007635 | .007726 | 130.96 | 129.42 |
|   90-Day Forward | .007708 | .007797 | 129.72 | 128.24 |
|   180-Day Forward | .007823 | .007908 | 127.82 | 126.44 |
| Jordan (Dinar) | 1.8968 | 1.8968 | .5272 | .5272 |
| Kuwait (Dinar) | 3.4542 | 3.4542 | .2895 | .2895 |
| Lebanon (Pound) | .002061 | .002061 | 485.00 | 485.00 |
| Malaysia (Ringgit) | .36297 | .36304 | 2.7550 | 2.7545 |
| Malta (Lira) | 2.9325 | 2.9325 | .3410 | .3410 |

Table 7.1 (*Continued*)

| Country | U.S. $ equiv. | | Currency per U.S. $ | |
|---|---|---|---|---|
| | Fri. | Thurs. | Fri. | Thurs. |
| Mexico (Peso) | | | | |
|   Floating rate | .0004417 | .0004417 | 2264.00 | 2264.00 |
| Netherland (Guilder) | .4729 | .4742 | 2.1145 | 2.1085 |
| New Zealand (Dollar) | .6150 | .6145 | 1.6260 | 1.6273 |
| Norway (Krone) | .1465 | .1470 | 6.8220 | 6.8010 |
| Pakistan (Rupee) | .05208 | .05208 | 19.20 | 19.20 |
| Peru (Inti) | .0008460 | .0008460 | 1182.00 | 1182.00 |
| Philippines (Peso) | .048309 | .048309 | 20.70 | 20.70 |
| Portugal (Escudo) | .006516 | .006516 | 153.45 | 153.45 |
| Saudi Arabia (Riyal) | .2666 | .2666 | 3.7505 | 3.7505 |
| Singapore (Dollar) | .5154 | .5158 | 1.9400 | 1.9385 |
| South Africa (Rand) | | | | |
|   Commercial rate | .3920 | .3926 | 2.5508 | 2.5468 |
|   Financial rate | .2451 | .2451 | 4.0800 | 4.0800 |
| South Korea (Won) | .0014858 | .0014858 | 673.00 | 673.00 |
| Spain (Peseta) | .008576 | .008602 | 116.60 | 116.25 |
| Sweden (Krona) | .1561 | .1563 | 6.4030 | 6.3945 |
| Switzerland (Franc) | .6182 | .6215 | 1.6175 | 1.6090 |
|   30-Day Forward | .6206 | .6239 | 1.6111 | 1.6028 |
|   90-Day Forward | .6253 | .6282 | 1.5990 | 1.5917 |
|   180-Day Forward | .6329 | .6352 | 1.5798 | 1.5741 |
| Taiwan (Dollar) | .03602 | .03602 | 27.76 | 27.76 |
| Thailand (Baht) | .039339 | .039339 | 25.42 | 25.42 |
| Turkey (Lira) | .0005130 | .0005130 | 1949.00 | 1949.00 |
| United Arab (Dirham) | .2722 | .2722 | 3.6725 | 3.6725 |
| Uruguay (New Peso) | | | | |
|   Financial | .002022 | .002022 | 494.50 | 494.50 |
| Venezuela (Bolivar) | | | | |
|   Floating rate | .02547 | .02547 | 39.25 | 39.25 |
| W. Germany (Mark) | .5329 | .5346 | 1.8762 | 1.8705 |
|   30-Day Forward | .5348 | .5364 | 1.8698 | 1.8642 |
|   90-Day Forward | .5381 | .5396 | 1.8582 | 1.8532 |
|   180-Day Forward | .5433 | .5443 | 1.8406 | 1.8369 |
| SDR | 1.30364 | 1.30511 | 0.767082 | 0.766221 |
| ECU | 1.11378 | 1.11487 | | |

Special Drawing Rights (SDR) are based on exchange rates for the U.S., West German, British, French and Japanese currencies. Source: International Monetary Fund.

European Currency Unit (ECU) is based on a basket of community currencies. Source: European Community Commission.

*Source:* Reprinted by permission of *The Wall Street Journal,* Monday, March 20, 1989, p. C10, © Dow Jones & Company, Inc. 1989. All rights reserved.

## The Forward Market

The **forward market** is a type of foreign exchange market in which foreign currencies are purchased and sold for future delivery. In other words, it involves an agreement between two parties to purchase or sell a given amount of foreign exchange at a specified date in the future at a rate agreed upon when the agreement is first made. This rate is called *forward* rate and is usually quoted for one month, three months, or six months. Although forward contracts for longer periods are not common, they can be arranged for delivery at any specified period of time up to one year, and occasionally up to three years. For example, one could agree to buy DM 1,000 six months from today at 2DM = $1. At the time that this agreement is reached, the seller has to deliver only 10 percent of the marks (DM 100) to the buyer as a security margin. The rest of the deutsche marks are delivered at the agreed rate after the six-month period has elapsed. Thus, after this period, the buyer would end up with DM 1,000 for $500, regardless of what the spot rate is at that future time.

Why do forward markets exist? Return to our previous example of an American importer in New York importing $100,000 worth of scotch whiskey from a British exporter in London. Let us assume that the British exporter and the American importer have agreed to settle the payment in the U.S. dollar, using a 60-day time draft. The British exporter draws a $100,000 60-day time draft against the American importer. Given that the existing exchange rate is £1 = $2.00, the $100,000 would be equal to £50,000. Thus, if the exchange rate does not change after the 60-day period is over, the British exporter would receive £50,000 for the scotch whiskey exported. However, if at the end of the 60-day period the exchange rate increases to say £1 = $2.50, then the British exporter would lose £10,000. This is because at the new rate the $100,000 draft is worth only £40,000 ($100,000 ÷ $2.50 = £40,000). On the other hand, if the exchange rate decreases to, say, £1 = $1.25, the British exporter would gain £30,000 ($100,000 ÷ $1.25 = £80,000).

In the above example, it is the British exporter who takes an exchange risk in the foreign exchange market. This risk stems from getting paid in a foreign currency, that is, the U.S. dollar. Therefore, the British exporter would either lose or gain, depending on the exchange rate at the end of the 60-day period. In this case the American importer faces no exchange risk because the payment is made in the U.S. dollar. However, if the agreement had called for payment in British pounds, it would have been the American importer who would have faced the risk and not the British exporter.

To avoid the above risk, the *forward* or the *future* exchange market can be used. Thus, if the payment is to be made in the U.S. dollar, the British exporter could sell the $100,000 for pounds forward at the time that the transaction agreement is reached. To do this, the British exporter could make a contract with the local bank, the bank in London. Accordingly, the British exporter agrees to sell $100,000 for pounds to the bank in London after six months at a forward rate that is agreed upon at the time when the agreement is reached.

Similarly, if the payment is to be made in the British pound, the American importer could avoid the risk by entering the forward market. The importer can purchase the £50,000 for U.S. dollars 60 days forward from a local bank.

As the above example indicates, the reason that trading partners enter the forward market is to avoid the risk of fluctuations in the foreign exchange rates. Because exporters and importers dealing in the forward market make transactions mainly through their local commercial banks, the foreign exchange risk is transferred to those banks.

The commercial banks can minimize the foreign exchange risk by matching forward purchases from exporters with forward sales to importers. However, because the supplies and the demands of forward currency transactions by exporters and importers usually do not coincide, the banks assume some of the risk.

If the bank engages in speculations, as we explain in the next section, a higher level of risk would be realized. Most banks do not choose to engage in speculation; instead, they prefer to make their profit on the difference between the buying and selling prices of foreign currencies in which they exchange. For example, a bank may buy a £50,000 bill for $100,000, while selling such a bill for £50,500, making a £500 profit.

Today, forward markets exist only for the currencies of the major industrial countries. Forward contracts are not available for most LDCs' currencies. Also, it is difficult to obtain a forward contract in any currency for more than a year ahead. The reason there are forward contracts for only a few currencies is the banks' desire to avoid the higher risk associated with dealing in the exchange of all currencies.

Table 7.1 gives the forward rate for various currencies with respect to the U.S. dollar for Friday March 17, 1989, and Thursday March 16, 1989. For example, on the next three lines under West Germany, for Friday, we find the 30-day forward rate ($0.5348 = DM 1), the 90-day forward rate ($0.5381 = DM 1), and the 180-day forward rate ($0.5433 = DM 1).

If the forward rate is higher than the current spot rate, the foreign currency is considered to be at a *forward premium* as compared to the local currency. However, if the forward rate is lower than the current spot rate, the foreign currency is considered to be at *forward discount*. In our previous example of West Germany (Table 7.1), because the spot rate on Friday is $0.5329 = 1 DM and the 180-day forward rate is $0.5433 = 1 DM we say that the deutsche mark is at a six-month forward premium with respect to the U.S. dollar.

## Hedging

Because the exchange rate changes, any future payments or receipts involve a foreign exchange risk. To avoid this risk one could engage in hedging. **Hedging** against a foreign currency means making sure that one neither owns nor owes in that currency. Hedging can take place either in the spot market or in the forward market, usually in the latter.

Using our previous example of scotch whiskey exports from England to the United States, let us assume this time that payment has to be made in British pounds for £50,000. In this case, it is the American importer who takes the exchange risk. Thus, if the present spot market rate of the pound is £1 = $2, then the current dollar value of payment would be $100,000. However, if after 60 days the spot rate changes to, say, £1 = $1.25, the dollar value of the payment would be $62,500. On the other hand, if the 60-day spot rate changes to say £1 = $2.50 the dollar value of the payment would be $125,000. Thus, the importer could gain or lose, depending on the spot rate of the 60-day bill in the market. However, because the American importer does not want to take such a gamble, the importer could hedge against the exchange risk by either buying or borrowing £50,000 at the present spot rate of £1 = $2, and depositing the proceeds in an interest-earning bank account for 60 days until the payment is due. If the American importer chooses to borrow the £50,000, the cost involved in this transaction is the difference between the higher interest rate that has to be paid on the borrowed funds and the lower interest rate that would be earned from depositing the funds in the bank for 60 days. If the importer uses his or her own money to buy the £50,000, the transaction cost is the difference between the opportunity cost of the money used and the interest rate that would be earned from depositing this fund in a bank for 60 days.*

As the above example indicates, covering exchange risk through the spot market involves either a borrowing cost or the cost of tying up one's money for a period of time (60 days in the example). To avoid this risk one could hedge in the forward market rather than in the spot market. In this way the need for borrowing or tying up a certain amount of money for a period of time is eliminated. For example, the American importer could buy the British pounds in forward market for delivery in 60 days at today's 60-day forward rate. Thus if the 60-day forward rate is £1 = $2.20 the importer has to pay $110,000 (£50,000 × $2.20) in 60 days for the £50,000. Consequently, the hedging would cost the importer $10,000 or 10 percent of $100,000 for the 60-day period.

Today, hedging usually takes place in the forward market. This enables the international traders to avoid the uncertainty of the foreign exchange market, enhancing the flow of trade and investment throughout the world. Hedging is especially helpful to MNCs that have to deal in large amounts of foreign currencies of different countries every day.

## Speculation

The opposite of hedging is speculation. In contrast to a hedger, who tries to avoid the foreign exchange risk, the speculator purposely undertakes risk in expectation of a profit. Like hedging, speculation can take place in either the spot market or the forward market. Also, as in the case of hedging, speculators usually operate in the forward market.

---

*The opportunity cost is the value of the benefit forgone by depositing money in the bank account instead of using it in the best available alternative.

A speculator engages in the spot market by predicting the fluctuations in the spot rate. Thus, if a speculator expects the spot rate of a foreign currency to fall, the speculator would borrow that currency for, say, 30 days, and immediately exchange it for the domestic currency at the current spot rate. The speculator could then deposit the domestic currency in an interest-earning bank account. After the 30-day period is over, the speculator could pay off the loan by using the bank deposit of domestic currency to purchase the foreign currency at the going spot rate. At that time, if the new spot rate is lower than the previous spot rate, as the speculator predicted, a differential revenue is realized. But this speculation also involves a differential cost of the higher interest rate paid on foreign currency borrowed as compared with the interest earned from domestic currency deposited in the bank. Thus, the speculator would make a profit if the differential revenue is greater than the differential cost.

With a similar argument, if a speculator expects the spot price of a foreign currency to rise, the speculator could borrow domestic money and purchase the foreign currency at the current spot rate and hold it in an interest-earning bank account for resale in the future. Again, if the speculator's predictions come true, and if the differential revenue is greater than the differential cost, a profit is realized.

As an example, assume that the current spot rate on the pound is $2.00 = £1, and a speculator believes that the spot rate of the pound in one month will be $1.98 = £1. The speculator could borrow, say £1,000, at the annual interest rate of 13 percent, and immediately sell those pounds at the going spot rate of $2.00 per pound, receiving $2,000. The speculator then deposits these dollars in a bank account at an annual rate of 12 percent. After one month the speculator would earn $20.00 ($2,000 × 12/100 × 1/12) interest on the account. Thus, the speculator would have $2,020 (principal + interest). If the speculator was correct in predicting the spot rate, the speculator could then sell $2,020 at the new spot rate of $1.98 = £1, receiving £1,020.20 (2,020/1.98 = 1,020.20). Out of this amount the speculator spends £1,010.83 to pay off the loan [£1,000 for the principal plus £10.83 for the interest (£1,000 × 13/100 × 1/12 = £10.83)], realizing £9.37 (£1,020.20 − £1,010.83) profit.

Thus, speculation in the spot market requires the speculator to either use his or her own funds or to borrow money. To avoid this requirement, speculation, like hedging, usually takes place in the forward market. For example, if a speculator anticipates that the spot rate of a foreign currency will be higher in, say, 60 days than its present 60-day forward rate, the speculator could purchase a certain amount of that foreign currency 60 days forward. After the 60-day period has elapsed, the speculator receives the delivery of the foreign currency at the agreed forward rate. If the speculator was correct in predicting the exchange rate, the agreed upon forward rate would be lower than the going spot rate. In this case, the speculator could sell the foreign currency immediately, realizing a profit. If the speculator was wrong in predicting the exchange market, the forward rate would be higher than the spot rate, resulting in a loss for the speculator.

For example, assume that the 60-day forward rate of the pound is $2.00 = £1, and the speculator expects the spot rate of the pound in 60 days to be $2.05 = £1. The speculator then purchases say £1,000 forward for delivery in 60 days. After 60 days the speculator gets the delivery of £1,000, paying $2,000 (£1,000 × $2.00). At this time, if the new spot rate was $2.05 = £1, as the speculator predicted, he or she could sell the £1,000 delivered for $2,050, making a $50 profit.

If a speculator purchases a foreign currency, in either the spot or forward market, with the intention of selling it later at a higher future spot rate, it is said that the speculator is taking a *long position* in that currency. However, if a speculator borrows or sells a foreign currency forward with the intention of purchasing it at a future lower price, to either pay off the foreign currency borrowed or to deliver the foreign currency sold forward, it is said that the speculator is taking a *short position.*

Speculation can be either stabilizing or destabilizing. **Stabilizing speculation** refers to the purchase of a foreign currency when its domestic price (the exchange rate) is declining, in the anticipation that it will soon increase, thus generating a profit. Stabilizing speculation also refers to the sale of a foreign currency when its domestic price is rising, in the anticipation that it will soon decline. Stabilizing speculators, by smoothing changes in the foreign exchange market, render a useful function. This is due to the law of demand and supply. When the domestic price of a foreign currency is falling, stabilizing speculators purchase that foreign currency. This increases the quantity demanded of that foreign currency, causing its domestic price to increase. On the other hand, when the domestic price of a foreign currency is rising, they sell that currency. This increases the quantity supplied of that currency, causing its domestic price to decrease.

**Destabilizing speculation** refers to the sale of a foreign currency when its domestic price is falling, in anticipation that it will decrease even lower in the future. Destabilizing speculation also refers to the purchase of a foreign currency when its domestic price rises, in the anticipation that it will increase even higher in the future. Destabilizing speculators, by magnifying the exchange rate fluctuations, disrupt the flow of international business. This is because of the law of demand and supply. When the domestic price of a foreign currency is falling, destabilizing speculators sell that currency. This increases the quantity supplied of that currency, causing its price to fall even further. On the other hand, when the domestic price of a foreign currency is rising, they purchase that currency. This increases the quantity demanded of that foreign currency, causing its price to rise even further.

Speculators are usually individuals or firms that undertake the risk of speculation in anticipation of high profit. However, banks, importers, exporters, and any other individual who expects payments in a foreign currency can engage in speculation. The speculation by exporters and importers usually involves *leads* and *lags* in payments. These refer to the few months' leeway in which one gets paid for exports or pays for imports. For example, if an American exporter who gets paid in British pounds expects the exchange rate to rise, the exporter would try to delay the payment (a *lag*) by extending credit to the importer. On the other hand, if an American importer who has to pay in British pounds expects the exchange rate to rise, the importer would try to pay as soon as possible (a *lead*).

## Swaps

A **swap** is an arrangement by which two parties exchange one currency for another and agree that, at a certain date in the future, each party receives from the other the amount of the original currency that was given up at the time that swap took place.

The swap was initiated by the U.S. Federal Reserve system ("the Fed") in 1962. At that time, the United States was experiencing a balance of payments deficit, causing the confidence in the U.S. dollar to be badly shaken and the short-term capital to flow out of the dollar into stronger currencies. In order to help to offset this outflow of funds, the U.S. Federal Reserve system agreed with several European central banks to enter into reciprocal currency arrangements, that is, swap arrangements. According to these arrangements, which are still practiced today, the central banks of different countries can swap their currencies with each other in order to help finance their temporary payments disequilibriums. For example, if the U.S. Federal Reserve system is short of British pounds, it can ask the central bank of England to provide them, with the understanding that the swap will be repaid within a given period of time, usually within 3 to 12 months. In the same manner, if the Bank of England needs the U.S. dollar it could enter into a swap arrangement with the U.S. Federal Reserve system.

Swap arrangements have been used by the central banking system of many nations as a means for intervening in the foreign exchange market. For example, swaps are used by the U.S. Federal Reserve system to collect the surplus of dollars from foreign central banks. These surpluses are in excess of what these banks usually hold, and if they are not collected by the Fed, they would be sold in the foreign currency market, depreciating the dollar. Although a swap is a temporary arrangement that has to be repaid after a certain time period, it does buy time. This would allow the Fed to make other arrangements to resolve the foreign exchange disequilibrium problem.

Since the adoption of the managed floating exchange rate system in 1973, the popularity of swap arrangements as a credit instrument, as compared with the IMF drawing facilities, has been increasing. The rise in popularity is due to several factors. First, swap arrangements involve minimal administrative red tape and can be executed very quickly. Second, borrowing from the IMF, in excess of 50 percent of a nation's quota, may require substantial justification, whereas swap arrangements are made unconditionally. Third, borrowing from the IMF is relatively costly for the borrowing nation as compared with the swap arrangements. Finally, a substantial borrowing from the IMF by a nation is visible and may be interpreted as a symptom of an unhealthy economy, inducing destabilizing speculations.

At the corporate level, swap arrangements can be classified into currency swap and credit swap.

**Currency swap** is an arrangement between two firms to exchange one currency for another, reversing the exchange at a future date. Currency swap usually takes place between an MNC's parent company and its subsidiary company. For example, a subsidiary of an American MNC that is located in Mexico and needs the U.S. dollar could enter into a swap arrangement with its parent company in the United States. Accordingly, the subsidiary could swap pesos (the Mexican currency) with the U.S. dollar and agree to reverse the exchange at some future date. Because this arrangement allows the firms to avoid the use of the foreign exchange market, they escape the possibility of loss that might result from fluctuations in the exchange rates.

**Credit swap** is an arrangement between a firm and a foreign central bank or commercial bank to exchange one currency for another, reversing the exchange at a future date. Credit swap is often used by MNCs when their subsidiary operates in a country in which either no forward exchange market exists, or where it is difficult to obtain local credit. For example, assume that an American firm has a subsidiary in Kuwait that is in need of funds. The U.S. parent company can make a contract with a local bank in Kuwait. According to this contract, the U.S. parent company deposits a certain amount of dollars in the Kuwait bank for a given period of time. In return for this dollar deposit the Kuwait bank makes a loan in an equivalent amount of dinar, at a specified rate of interest, to the U.S. subsidiary. At the end of the time period, the U.S. subsidiary pays off the dinar loan to the Kuwait local bank. The Kuwait bank, in turn, returns the original dollar amount to the U.S. parent company. The swap arrangement can also be used to overcome the blockage of funds remittance, as we will explain in Chapter 17.

The advantage of this swap arrangement is that it does not expose the parent company to an exchange loss that might result from fluctuations in the foreign exchange market. In other words, after the loan period is expired, the U.S. parent company receives the original amount of dollars deposited, irrespective of the going exchange rate.

The cost of this arrangement is the opportunity cost that accrues to the U.S. parent company as a result of depositing those dollars in a Kuwait bank at no interest. In this transaction the parent company gains only if the opportunity cost is less than the benefit that accrues to the subsidiary. The subsidiary in its turn benefits only if the cost of interest paid to the Kuwait bank is less than the expected rate of return on those dinars invested in the subsidiary, plus the losses or gains associated with the currency fluctuations.

## Arbitrage

**Arbitrage** refers to the simultaneous purchase of a currency in one market, where it is cheaper, and sale in another market, where it is more expensive, in order to profit from differences in spot exchange rate quotations. This is a riskless process that results in equalization of exchange rate quotations in different monetary centers.

For example, assume that the spot price of the pound is £1 = $1.50 in New York and £1 = $1.55 in London. An arbitrager can buy pounds at $1.50 in New York, and immediately sell them for $1.55 in London, thus realizing a revenue of $0.05 per pound. Although $0.05 per pound seems insignificant, on £2 million the revenue would be $100,000, which can be gained with only a few minutes' work. The arbitrager has also to pay for the transfer cost, that is, the cost of overseas phone calls and the overhead cost associated with arbitrage activities. Because these costs are very small compared to the revenue, the arbitrager usually realizes a substantial profit.

If there are only two currencies traded between two financial centers, as in the above example, the arbitrage is referred to as **two-point arbitrage**. However, if there are three currencies traded between three financial centers, the arbitrage is known as **triangular** or **three-point arbitrage**. These two forms of arbitrage follow the same principle. However, in practice, two-point arbitrage is more prevalent than three-point arbitrage.

As we mentioned earlier, the arbitrage activities result in equalization of the exchange rates in different monetary centers. This happens because arbitragers raise demand for the foreign currency in the financial center where the currency is cheaper, causing the price of that currency to rise. At the same time, they raise the supply of foreign currency in the financial centers where the currency is expensive, causing the price of that currency to fall. Thus, arbitrage activities result in the equalization of exchange rates for currencies, leading the international financial center toward a unified market.

## DEVALUATION

**Devaluation** is a deliberate increase in the foreign exchange rate (the value of foreign currencies in terms of the domestic currency) of a nation by its monetary authorities. The purpose of devaluation is to improve the balance of payments deficit of the country in question. By increasing the domestic price of foreign currencies, devaluation makes the value of the home country's exports, measured in terms of the foreign currencies, cheaper, causing these exports to rise. The higher foreign currency prices also mean that the value of the home country's imports are more expensive, causing imports to fall. Thus, if devaluation is successful, the increase in exports and decrease in imports will improve the balance of payments.

Under the fixed exchange rate system, devaluation is achieved by changing the par value of the currency in question. For example, as we explained in Chapter 5, the United States devalued the dollar in December 1971 and in February 1973 by decreasing the par value of the dollar in terms of gold in order to resolve the balance of payments problems.

Under the managed floating exchange rate system, a nation can devalue its currency by simply buying another nation's currency through its central bank. Because this action raises the demand for that foreign currency, it would cause its value to increase in terms of the domestic currency. Additionally, because all currencies interact in the foreign exchange market, the decline in the value of the nation's currency in terms of another currency, would lead to the depreciation of its value relative to other currencies. For example, since 1971, the Japanese government has repeatedly bought a tremendous volume of U.S. dollars in order to hold down the value of its currency, that is, the yen. The Japanese government has used this policy, apparently, to make the U.S. exports relatively expensive abroad, giving an edge in price advantage to the Japanese exports.

Beginning with the 1980s, the popularity of devaluation as a policy tool has increased in many nations. In order to increase their exports and decrease their imports, many countries have cheapened their currencies. For example, since 1982 Brazil has devalued its currency by 99 percent, Indonesia by 62 percent, and Mexico by 97 percent.[1]

Devaluation of country A's currency in terms of country B's currency means revaluation of country B's currency in terms of country A's currency. For example, if the U.S. dollar is devalued against the Japanese yen, making yen more expensive for Americans to buy, then the Japanese yen would be revaluated against the U.S. dollar, making the U.S. dollar cheaper for the Japanese to buy. If this is the case, the U.S. exports would increase (imports would decrease), whereas Japanese exports would decrease (imports would increase). As a result, the U.S. balance of payments would be improved at the expense of the Japanese balance of payments. Thus, the stage is set for a trade war between these two countries. A case in point is the recent devaluation of the U.S. dollar on September 22, 1985. On that date, the United States persuaded Japan, West Germany, Britain, and France to agree to devalue the U.S. dollar in an effort to mollify protectionist sentiments that then existed in the U.S. Congress. Although this action was approved by this so-called Group of Five countries, in practice they did not continue to cooperate with each other. The U.S. dollar did decline, but the U.S. trade deficit continued to stay at a record high. At the same time, exporters in Japan and West Germany continued to suffer from the cheap dollar, losing profits. Given this situation, Japan and European countries decided to fight back by devaluating their own currencies in turn. They did this by buying dollars to boost its price. The magnitude of their purchases can be inferred from the tremendous increase in the net foreign government purchases of the U.S. government securities. This figure, which was $10 billion in the first quarter of 1986, rose to $52 billion in the second quarter.[2] Nevertheless, against these odds, the U.S. dollar continued to depreciate against major currencies, and beginning with September 1987 the U.S. balance of trade started to show signs of improvement.*[3]

## J-Curve Effect

As our preceding discussion indicates, devaluation of a currency affects a country's balance of trade by its net impact on import expenditures and export

---

*Balance of trade is part of a country's balance of payments. It measures the difference between merchandise exports and imports. If the value of exports is greater than the value of imports, a favorable balance of trade exists. If, however, the value of imports exceeds the value of exports, an unfavorable balance exists.

receipts. If a country devalues its national currency by, say, 5 percent, its import prices initially rise by 5 percent in terms of the domestic currency. As a result the quantity demanded of imports would fall according to the home demand elasticities. At the same time, export prices would fall by 5 percent in terms of foreign currency. As a result, the quantity demanded of exports would increase according to the foreign demand elasticities. However, for devaluation to take effect time is needed to induce changes in the volume of exports and imports. In other words, there is a time lag between devaluation and its ultimate effect on the balance of trade. One popular explanation of this time lag is referred to as the "J-Curve effect."

According to the J-Curve effect, with devaluation the trade balance worsens first, before it gets better. This is, in fact, where the theory got its name. The letter "J" corresponds to the initial worsening of the trade balance (a downturn) before the forthcoming improvements take place (an upturn). This is because the initial effect of devaluation is to increase import expenditures. Import expenditures (quantity of imports × price of imports) initially rise because there is an increase in import prices, whereas, at the same time, import quantity remains unchanged due to prior commitments. However, with the passage of time, the quantity of imports decreases while the quantity of exports increases. As a result the trade balance improves. Figure 7.4 illustrates a J-curve, indicating the time path of the response of the trade balance to devaluation. As this figure indicates, the shape of the curve resembles the letter J (slightly askew).

An example of the J-Curve effect is the 1967 devaluation of the British pound. It took approximately two years before this devaluation had a significant

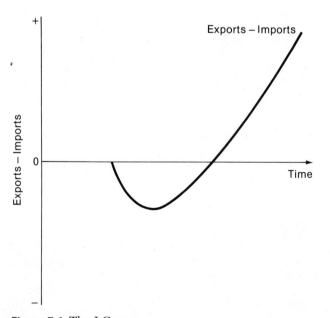

**Figure 7.4** The J-Curve

effect on the British trade balance. As another example, the devaluation of the U.S. dollar occurred in September 1985, but the U.S. trade balance continued to deteriorate for two years, before it started to show signs of improvement in September 1987.[4]

In interpreting the J-Curve effect, one must note that it is often difficult to separate the currency-trade relationship depicted by the curve from other economic variables that affect a nation's trade balance.

## THE EUROCURRENCY MARKET

The Eurocurrency market is the principal international money market. This market provides an important source of debt financing for MNCs. Eurocurrencies are currencies that are deposited outside the country of their origin. For example, the U.S. dollars deposited in French commercial banks, or in a French branch of an American bank, are referred to as Eurodollars. Similarly, a British pound deposited in a West German commercial bank is called a Eurosterling. Other Eurocurrencies are Dutch guilders, French francs, German marks, Japanese yen, and Swiss francs.

The Eurocurrency market is the outgrowth of the Eurodollar market. As the name of the Eurodollar implies, it was initially the dollar that was deposited in Europe. Subsequently, however, other major currencies followed the dollar's path in being deposited outside their countries of origin, and the concept of Eurocurrency was born. Although the "Euro" prefix implies that these currencies are deposited in Europe, the market is no longer restricted to Europe. In fact, these currencies are deposited in non-European international monetary centers such as Hong Kong, Kuwait, Singapore, and Tokyo. However, the Eurodollar is still the major form of Eurocurrency and accounts for 75 to 80 percent of the market.

Table 7.2 shows the size of the Eurocurrency market in the late 1970s and early 1980s. As the table indicates, the size of this market, as measured by total liabilities, grew from $946 billion in 1978 to $2,481 billion in 1985, that is, by about 162 percent. In the meantime, the Eurodollar, as a percent of the total gross liabilities in all Eurocurrencies, grew from 73 percent in 1978 to 81 percent in 1985, that is, by about 11 percent. This shows that the significance of the Eurodollar as the major currency in the Eurocurrency market continues to increase.

### The Growth of the Eurodollar Market

The development of the Eurodollar market started in the 1950s when the U.S. dollar was occupying a prominent position in the world economy, replacing the British pound as the leading international reserve currency. One of the main factors that contributed to the development of the Eurodollar market was "Regulation Q" of the United States Federal Reserve system. This regulation imposed a ceiling on interest rates that the United States banks could pay on

**Table 7.2  EUROCURRENCY MARKET SIZE**[a]

Billions of Dollars (Rounded to the Nearest $5 Billion) at the End of Period

| | 1978 | 1979 | 1980 | 1981 | 1982 | 1983 | 1984 June | 1984 Sept. | 1984 Dec. | 1985 March |
|---|---|---|---|---|---|---|---|---|---|---|
| Gross Liabilities to: | | | | | | | | | | |
| Nonbanks | $187 | $219 | $278 | $372 | $432 | $479 | $503 | $492 | $500 | $508 |
| Central banks | 86 | 122 | 128 | 112 | 91 | 88 | 88 | 94 | 96 | 96 |
| Other banks | 673 | 904 | 1,172 | 1,470 | 1,645 | 1,711 | 1,769 | 1,763 | 1,787 | 1,877 |
| Total | $946 | $1,245 | $1,578 | $1,954 | $2,168 | $2,278 | $2,360 | $2,349 | $2,383 | $2,481 |
| Eurodollars as percent of total gross liabilities in all Eurocurrencies | 73% | 72% | 76% | 79% | 80% | 81% | 81% | 81% | 82% | 81% |
| Dollar liabilities of foreign branches of U.S. banks as percent of total gross liabilities in all Eurocurrencies | 24% | 22% | 20% | 19% | 18% | 17% | 16% | 15% | 15% | 15% |

[a]Based on foreign liabilities of banks in major European countries, and in the Bahamas, Bahrain, the Cayman Islands, Panama, Canada, Japan, Hong Kong, and Singapore.

*Source:* The Federal Reserve Bank of St. Louis, *International Economic Conditions* (October 1985). p. 8.

time deposits. Because this regulation did not apply to dollars deposited in Europe, it caused U.S. residents and foreigners to deposit their dollars in London, which in the late 1950s was paying interest rates that exceeded the levels set by Regulation Q in the United States. This induced the major U.S. banks to instruct their overseas branches to bid for dollars by proposing higher interest rates than those offered in the United States. The dollars collected by these branches were then sent to the parent offices of these banks in the United States, which could in turn lend such funds in the domestic market.

Another factor that gave rise to the growth of the Eurodollar market was related to the fear, by some depositors, that their deposits in the United States might be confiscated in the case of an international conflict. This was especially feared by the Soviet Union, whose dollar holdings were confiscated by the United States during World War II. Consequently, the Soviet Union was among the first customers of the Eurodollar market who felt that it was safe to hold dollar deposits in Europe, mainly in London, where the United States has no jurisdiction.

The growth of the Eurodollar market was also fueled by the willingness of the European traders in dollars, who found it convenient to deal in London instead of New York due to the uniformity of time zones for the European countries. This made it possible to expand trading hours per day, which had been previously limited to only a few hours a day when the U.S. and European banks were open at the same time.

Finally, the growth of the Eurodollar market was accelerated in the 1970s by three main factors: (1) a sharp increase in the OPEC nations' oil revenue, causing significant balance of payments surpluses for these countries; (2) an expansion in the volume of world trade; and (3) the lifting of restrictions on bank transactions on Eurocurrencies.

## Financial Activities of the Eurocurrency Market

As a financial center, the Eurocurrency market represents two major submarkets: the interbank market, in which banks provide credit to each other, and a market for commercial customers who seek funds from these banks in order to finance their trade and investment.

The Eurocurrency market deals in *short-term* and *medium-term* credit. A short-term Eurocurrency loan has a maturity of less than six months. A medium-term Eurocurrency loan has a maturity of three to seven years. There is also a *Eurobond market,* which handles long-maturity loans of 15 or 20 years. Bank loans provided through this market carry a variable rate of interest that is calculated by adding a margin to the London Interbank Offered Rate (LIBOR). LIBOR is the rate of interest that is used between the banks when they provide loans of Eurocurrencies to each other.

Financial activities that are undertaken by the Eurocurrency market have significant implications for international finance. By enabling different countries to deal with each other in one center, the Eurocurrency market increases the financial interdependence of these countries. As a result, it enhances the financial interaction between different nations, facilitating world trade and investment. However, it is argued that the movement of currency by a country in and out of unregulated markets complicates the central bank's task in controlling the money supply. Thus, the Eurocurrency market might interfere with a country's plan to achieve its predetermined monetary objective.

According to a ruling enacted on December 3, 1981, the U.S. banks were permitted to receive deposits from overseas and reinvest them abroad. Also, foreign deposits in the United States were exempted from the interest rate ceilings, and from reserve and insurance requirements. As a result of this ruling, the U.S. banks have been able to compete directly in the Eurodollar market, capturing a large percentage of the market.

## INTERNATIONAL BANKING

International banking refers to those banking activities that cross national boundaries, facilitating the flow of money between different countries. These banking activities are essential elements of the growth of international business, without which MNCs would not have been able to expand as much as they have to date. International banks not only provide MNCs with debt financing from local and international markets, but they also ensure the timely flow of the existing corporate resources.

The development of international banking has occurred in response to the expansion of international business operations. To meet the overseas needs of their domestic clients, commercial banks started by establishing international departments. These departments arranged for reciprocal deposits with their correspondent commercial banks that were located in countries where the bulk of their transactions took place.

With further developments in international business activities in the 1960s, the correspondent commercial bank relationship appeared to be inadequate for handling the needs of MNCs. Thus, many banks established branches in foreign countries or took over existing foreign banks. The first reason for this development was that various U.S. control measures were instituted in the 1960s. These measures, which were designed to control the U.S. balance of payments, encouraged U.S. banks to develop branches overseas. One such measure was the Interest Equalization Tax (IET) that was introduced in 1963 and eliminated in 1974. According to IET, an excise tax was imposed on the purchase of foreign securities by the U.S. citizens, discouraging the outflow of funds from the United States to foreigners. As a result, foreign borrowers had to look outside the United States for funds. Another such measure was the Direct Investment Program, which was initiated in 1968. This measure set a limit on the amount of money that a parent company in the United States could send to its subsidiaries overseas. As a result, U.S. firms were forced to demand more overseas assistance from their banks in transferring funds overseas.

The second major reason for the development of international banking was the expansion of the Eurocurrency market, which provided a large unregulated source of funds for MNCs. This was especially important to the U.S. banks, which could borrow in the unregulated market and provide loans to U.S. firms which, due to various U.S. control measures instituted in the 1960s, were forced to seek assistance overseas.

The third major stimulant to international banking has been the growing demand for funds from the LDCs. This was especially significant when oil prices quadrupled in the 1973–1974 period, exerting tremendous pressure on the world financial system. There was concern as to how non–OPEC LDCs, which could previously finance their deficit by foreign direct investment and foreign debt, would be able to survive the crisis. However, international banking came to the rescue. The surplus funds deposited by the OPEC LDCs into the international banking system were loaned to the non–OPEC LDCs, who could use these funds to finance their foreign currency needs.

The fourth major factor that was instrumental in the development of international banking is the Edge Act which was passed in the United States in 1919. This act was a reaction to the restrictions set by the Federal Reserve Board Regulations. According to these regulations, the U.S. banks are not allowed to get involved in activities abroad that are not permitted in the United States. However, the Edge Act permitted the organization of the so-called Edge Act Corporations by the U.S. banks. This allowed Edge Act Corporations of the U.S. banks to engage in any banking activities that were permitted in the local market of foreign countries. As a result, the U.S. banks became more effective in competing against local banks in foreign countries.

The fifth major factor in the development of international banking is the decision by the Federal Reserve Board in December 1981 to allow U.S. banks to set up their International Banking Facilities (IBFs) within the United States. Before this decision was made, the U.S. banks had to set up their IBFs in London and the Caribbean in order to take advantage of the Eurodollar market. Therefore, part of the U.S. dollar business was shifted abroad. The 1981 decision was made to increase the flow of the U.S. dollar business back to the United States, free from most domestic requirements.

The pattern of international banking in the 1980s can be characterized by two factors: (1) the increased competition among international banks, and (2) the inability of some foreign governments to pay off their huge debts.

The increased competition among international banks in the 1980s could be attributed to the declining oil revenues for the OPEC nations. This decline not only reduced the funds that these nations could provide to the Eurodollar market, but also it encouraged them to manage their own money instead of relying on Western international banks.

The inability of some foreign governments to meet their loan obligations can be attributed to the decline of oil prices and the general slowing down of the world economy in the 1980s. A case in point is Mexico, which because of a sudden decline in its oil revenue has found itself on the brink of bankruptcy and is unable to meet its loan obligations.

We close this chapter by noting that MNCs are among the major participants in the foreign exchange market. Their activities, along with some other major participants such as the central banks, fuel the constant fluctuations of the foreign exchange rates. Although such fluctuations offer a range of opportunities for MNCs, they also enhance the risks of engaging in international business. This has contributed to the development of forecasting methods that are based on various economic theories of exchange rate determination. Some of the forecasting techniques that are used in international business will be discussed in Chapters 11 and 14.

## SUMMARY

1. The foreign exchange market can be defined as a market within which individuals, business firms, and banks purchase and sell foreign currencies and other debt instruments.

2. The transactions undertaken by the participants of the foreign exchange market can be classified into four levels: (a) the transactions between commercial banks and their customers, (b) the indirect transactions between commercial banks through their brokers; (c) the transactions between these banks and their foreign subsidiaries; and (d) central bank transactions.

3. Foreign exchange instruments are written or printed financial documents that allow the payments of funds from one country and one currency to another country and another currency. Chief among these instruments are cable (telegraphic) transfers, commercial bills of exchange (commercial drafts), bank drafts, and letters of credit.

4. A cable transfer is an order that is transmitted by a bank in a country to its foreign correspondent in another country, instructing its correspondent bank to pay out a specific amount of money to a designated person or account.

5. A commercial bill of exchange is a written order by an exporter (the drawer) to an importer (the drawee) instructing the importer to pay on demand, or at a certain date, a specified amount of money to a designated party (the payee).

6. A bill of exchange that is payable on demand to the drawee is referred to as a sight bill. A bill that is payable at some future date is known as a time bill.

7. A bank draft is similar to a commercial bill of exchange because it is a written order by a drawer to a drawee instructing him or her to pay on demand, or at a certain date, a specified amount of money to a payee. The major difference between these two major financial instruments is that in the case of the bank draft, the drawee is a bank rather than an importer.

8. A letter of credit is a document that is issued by an importer's bank, declaring that payments will be made to an exporter regarding a specific shipment of commodities, accompanied by the required shipment documents.

9. Commercial banks render three main services through their international departments: (a) purchasing and selling of foreign currencies; (b) lending; and (c) collecting.

10. The spot market is a type of foreign exchange market in which foreign currencies are purchased and sold for immediate delivery, that is, within two business days after the transaction agreement.

11. The forward market is a type of foreign exchange market in which foreign currencies are purchased and sold for future delivery.

12. If the forward rate is greater than the current spot rate, the foreign currency is considered to be at a "forward premium" as compared with local currency. How-

ever, if the forward rate is smaller than the current spot rate, the foreign currency is considered to be at a "forward discount."

13. Hedging against a foreign currency means making sure that one neither owns nor owes in that currency. Hedging can take place in either the spot market or the forward market.

14. Speculation is the opposite of hedging. In contrast to a hedger who tries to avoid the foreign exchange risk, the speculator purposely undertakes risk in the expectation of a profit. Like hedging, speculation can occur in either the spot market or the forward market.

15. If a speculator purchases a foreign currency in either the spot market or the forward market with the intention of selling it later at a higher future spot rate, it is said that the speculator is taking a "long position."

16. If a speculator borrows or sells a foreign currency forward with the intention of purchasing it at future lower prices, to either pay off the foreign currency borrowed, or to deliver the foreign currency sold forward, it is said that the speculator is taking a "short position."

17. A swap is an arrangement by which two parties exchange one currency for another and agree that, at a certain date in the future, each party receives from the other the amount of the original currency that was exchanged at the time that the swap took place.

18. Currency swap is an arrangement between two firms to exchange one currency for another, reversing the exchange at a future date.

19. Credit swap is an arrangement between a firm and a foreign central bank or a commercial bank to exchange one currency for another, reversing the exchange at a future date.

20. Arbitrage is simultaneously purchasing a currency in one market, where it is cheaper, and selling it in another market, where it is more expensive, in order to profit from the differences in spot exchange price quotations.

21. If there are only two currencies traded between two financial centers, the arbitrage is referred to as two-point arbitrage. However, if there are three currencies traded among three financial centers, the arbitrage is known as triangular or three-point arbitrage.

22. Devaluation is a deliberate increase in the foreign exchange rate (the value of foreign currencies in terms of the domestic currency) of a nation by its monetary authorities.

23. The purpose of devaluation is to improve the balance of payments deficit of the country in question.

24. Under the fixed exchange rate system, devaluation is achieved by changing the par value of the currency in question.

25. Under the managed floating exchange rate system, a nation can devalue its currency by simply buying another nation's currency through its central banks.

26. According to the J-Curve effect, with devaluation the trade balance worsens at first, before it improves. The letter "J" corresponds to the initial worsening (downturn) of the trade balance before the forthcoming improvement (upturn) takes place.

27. Eurocurrencies are currencies that are deposited outside the country of their origin.

28. The factors that have contributed to the growth of the Eurodollar market are (a) Regulation Q of the United States Federal Reserve system; (b) the fear by some depositors that their deposits in the United States might be confiscated in the case of international conflict; (c) the convenience for Europeans of dealing in London

instead of New York, due to the uniformity of time zones for the European countries; (d) the sharp increase in the OPEC nations' oil revenue; (e) the expansion in the volume of world trade; and (f) the lifting of restrictions on bank transactions in Eurocurrencies.

29. As a financial center the Eurocurrency market represents two major submarkets. The interbank market, in which banks provide credit to each other, and a market for commercial customers, who seek funds from these banks in order to finance their trade and investment.

30. Bank loans provided through the Eurocurrency market carry a variable rate of interest that is calculated by adding a margin to the London Interbank Offered Rate (LIBOR).

31. LIBOR is the rate of interest that is used between the banks when they provide loans of Eurocurrencies to each other.

32. International banking refers to those banking activities that cross national boundaries, facilitating the flow of money between different countries.

33. Factors that have contributed to the development of international banking are (a) the various control measures that were instituted in the 1960s, encouraging U.S. firms to develop branches overseas; (b) the expansion of the Eurocurrency market; (c) the growing demand for funds from the LDCs; (d) the Edge Act of 1919, which permitted the organization of so-called Edge Act Corporations by U.S. banks; and (e) the decision of the U.S. Federal Reserve Board in December 1981 to allow U.S. banks to set up their International Banking Facilities (IBFs) within the United States.

## QUESTIONS

7.1 Differentiate between spot exchange rate and forward exchange rate.

7.2 Compare hedging and speculation and explain why they usually take place in the forward market.

7.3 Contrast stabilizing speculation and destabilizing speculation. How can a speculator take a short position? A long position?

7.4 Differentiate between currency swap and credit swap, and explain why central banks use swap arrangements today.

7.5 Compare two-point arbitrage and triangular arbitrage, and elaborate on the impact of arbitrage activities on the exchange rates of different monetary centers.

7.6 Explain how devaluation is achieved under (a) the fixed exchange rate system and (b) the managed floating exchange rate system. Give an example of a recent devaluation, explaining its possible impact on the economy.

7.7 What is the relationship of the J-Curve to the time path of devaluation? Explain.

7.8 An American exporter is expected to receive £100,000 from a British importer two months from now. The spot rate is $2.05 = £1.00, and the 60-day forward rate is $2.00 = £1.00. Given this information, how can the American exporter hedge his or her foreign exchange risk? How can the British importer hedge his or her foreign exchange risk?

7.9 Assume that you are the manager of an MNC that is importing coffee beans from Colombia. It is expected that pesos (the Colombian currency) will change in value soon. How do you manage your leads and lags if the pesos rise in value? If the pesos fall in value?

7.10 Suppose you are a speculator and the 60-day forward rate is $2.00 = £1.00. Given this information, how would you speculate in the forward market if you believe that the spot rate in two months would be $2.08 = £1.00? How much would you earn if you were correct? How would you speculate in the forward market if you believe that the spot rate in two months would be $1.98 = £1.00? How much would you earn if you were correct?

7.11 Suppose you are an arbitrageur who is facing the following exchange rates:

London: $2 = £1

Toronto: Fr 15 (French francs) = £1

Milan: Fr 6 (French francs) = $1

Given these data, explain how you can engage in triangular (three-point) arbitrage. How much profit will you make?

## NOTES

1. "Nation's Devaluations of Currencies Spark a Global War," *The Wall Street Journal,* 22 December 1986, pp. 1, 15.
2. Ibid.; "Big-Five Attempt to Deflate the Dollar Is Losing Steam; Can They Win the War?" *The Wall Street Journal,* 12 December 1985, p. 34.
3. "Trade Deficit Shrank in Month," *The Wall Street Journal,* 13 November 1987, p. 3.
4. Ibid.

## SUGGESTED READINGS

Aliber, Robert Z. "International Banking: Growth and Regulation." *Columbia Journal of World Business* (Winter 1975):9–16.

———. *The International Business Money Game.* New York: Basic Books, 1979.

Asheghian, Parviz. "Impact of Devaluation on the Balance of Payments of Less Developed Countries: A Monetary Approach." *Journal of Economic Development* (July 1985): 143–151; Reprinted in *Portfolio: International Economic Perspectives,* No. 3 (1987).

———. "Currency Devaluation: A Comparative Analysis of Advanced Countries and Less Developed Countries." *Quarterly Review of Economics and Business* (Summer 1988): 61–70.

———, and William G. Foote, "Exchange Rate Devaluation: A Monetary Model and Empirical Investigation." *Eastern Economic Journal.* (April–June 1988): 181–187.

Bell, Geoffrey. *The Eurodollar Market and the International Financial System.* New York: Wiley, 1973.

Booth, Lawrence D. "Hedging and Foreign Exchange Exposure." *Management International Review* (Spring 1982):26–42.

Eimzing, P. *The Dynamic Theory of Forward Exchange.* London: Macmillan, 1967.

Eiteman, David, and Arthur Stonehill. *Multinational Business Finance,* 3rd ed. Reading, Mass.: Addison-Wesley, 1982.

Fieleke, Norman S. "The Rise of the Foreign Currency Futures Market." In Robert E. Baldwin and J. David Richardson, ed., *International Trade and Finance: Readings,* 3rd ed. Boston: Little, Brown, 1986. pp. 437–440.

Gendreau, Brian. "New Markets in Foreign Currency Options." In Robert E. Baldwin and J. David Richardson, ed., *International Trade and Finance: Readings,* 3rd ed., Boston: Little, Brown, 1986. pp. 441–450.

Gidny, Ian H. "Measuring the World Foreign Exchange Market." *Columbia Journal of World Business* (Winter 1979):36–48.

———. "Why It Doesn't Pay to Make a Habit of Forward Hedging." *Eurocurrency* (December 1976):23.

Jacques, Laurent L. "Management of Foreign Exchange Risk: A Review Article." *Journal of International Business Studies* (Spring/Summer 1981):81–103.

Kubarych, R. M. *Foreign Exchange Markets in the United States.* New York: The Federal Reserve Bank, 1978.

McKenzie, G. *Economics of the Eurodollar Market.* London: Macmillan, 1976.

Melvin, Michael. *International Money and Finance.* New York: Harper & Row, 1985, Chap. 1.

Park, Yoon S. *The Euro-bond Market: Function and Structure.* New York: Praeger, 1974.

Revey, Patricia A. "Evolution and Growth of the United States Foreign Exchange Market." *Federal Reserve Bank of New York Quarterly Review* (Autumn 1981):32.

Stockes, Houston H., and Hugh Neuberger. "Interest Arbitrage, Forward Speculation and the Determination of the Forward Exchange Rate." *Columbia Journal of World Business* (Winter 1979):86–98.

# Case I: 1

# China Opens Its Doors to the West*

## INTRODUCTION

During the last few decades we have seen the world become a smaller, more interdependent place. With the advancement of technology and the expansion of the communications industry, international trade has become easier and much more manageable. With the rapidly growing world population and the ever increasing scarcity of the world's raw materials, international trade has become of fundamental importance to future global economic growth and international political stability. Given the scarcity of the world resources the importance of the People's Republic of China as a country that holds one of the most untapped resources for international trade and modernized development becomes apparent. The People's Republic of China (PRC) will prove to be an oasis for many multinational corporations as it gradually opens its doors to foreign trade.

## HISTORY

The year 1949 marked the formal establishment of the People's Republic of China. The communists seized power and brought with them radical reforms and an ideology unprecedented in the history of Chinese culture. During the 1950s, China was greatly dependent on the Soviet Union, its communist brother. Mao Tse-tung, chairman of the Central Communist Party (CCP), stated in his famous address to the Soviet Union's Seventh CCP Central Committee that it was China's purpose to approach the international arena from an anti-imperialist stance by following the leadership of the Soviet Union, their only genuine friend. "Dependence on the Soviet Union during the 1950s produced one of the most remarkable technology transfers in modern history."[1] With the help of the Soviets, large-scale socialist construction was undertaken to industri-

---

*This case initially was written by William Cowan of St. Lawrence University as a term project under the supervision of Professor Asheghian, who has subsequently revised it for inclusion in this textbook.

alize a country whose semifeudal, semicolonial society had been dominated by stagnant productive ·forces that for centuries had been based on primitive agriculture and handicraft industries.

The period of harmony between the Soviets and the Chinese did not last long, however. Differences over ideology, politics, and policies on economic reform and development reached a peak in 1958–1959, bringing about an almost overnight withdrawal of the Soviet Union influence from China.

In the wake of the Sino-Soviet split, a radically new approach was taken by the Chinese concerning international involvement. Being left on the brink of economic collapse by the Soviets was a bitter experience for the Chinese and dramatized to them the high potential costs of dependence on any one country or any one source of supply.[2] The doctrine of self-reliance was instituted and became the new guideline. Self-reliance did not construe complete or absolute self-sufficiency. Self-reliance called for China to rely primarily on its own efforts, manufacturing the products needed by society whenever and wherever possible. And self-reliance meant continued economic growth, given the country's human, material, and financial resources.

The doctrine of self-reliance paralleled the ultra-left-wing movement known as the "Cultural Revolution," which peaked in 1967. The radical policies and actions by Lin Biao and the Gang of Four, who led the revolution, caused already strained foreign relations to become worse. The radicals in power supported strong economic nationalism, resistance to foreign influences, and reliance on domestic innovations for economic and technical development. This led to China's failing to fulfill export contracts, to attacks on foreign embassies, and to outbreaks of antiforeign hysteria, further damaging economic relations.

The beginning of the 1970s saw normality finally return to China as the government began to realize that the costs of continued isolationism would hurt economic growth. The policies of self-reliance became modified to coincide with the new goals of accelerated economic growth and industrialization. In 1972, President Nixon visited China and began the "opening" of China. The Chinese put forth a new trade offensive, and relations between China and the West steadily improved. The new policy of trade expansion, however, did not proceed without debate. The radicals held that increasing foreign dependence and relaxing the self-reliance policies were actions promoted by profiteers and were a sellout to foreign capitalism and imperialism.

In October of 1976, the Gang of Four were arrested, and the pragmatists came to control China's destiny. Deng Xiaoping's push for rapid modernization embarked China on a massive acquisition of Western technology and machinery. An initial trickle of business contracts in mid-1977 was followed by an upsurge of contracts, which began in May 1978 and continued through December. This resulted in the importation of $6.9 billion worth of plants and equipment in 1978 alone.[3] However, the deficit and lack of capable technicians to handle the massive influx of technology led the overzealous Ministry of Finance to suspend many late 1978 contracts while they reevaluated their open door policy. This resulted in major cancellations including a $14 billion Jidong steel project with West Germany and two nuclear power plants from France.[4]

By early 1979 the government reaffirmed its commitment to modernization through an open door policy of trade liberalization and expansion. The underdeveloped state of China's foreign trade was due primarily to the underdeveloped state of her economy, which limited the amount of merchandise available for export and, consequently, the amount China could import from other countries due to balance of payments concerns. To cope with the problems involved with foreign investment in China, the government established an array of organizations to control and monitor trade. The Foreign Investment Control Commission was established to supervise approval of foreign trade offers. The Chinese International Trust and Investment Corporation was founded to act as a goodwill agency and promote international commerce in the PRC. Also established were the Import-Export Control Commission and the State General Administration of Exchange Control.

## INTERNATIONAL ARRANGEMENTS

China has made a substantial move toward furthering its international economic involvement. The main arrangements used in China to conduct international business can be categorized as joint venture, cooperative enterprise, and compensation trade.

### Joint Venture

By 1981, 28 joint ventures had been approved and established. China strictly followed a policy of import substitution, purchasing plants and equipment that produced goods that had been imported from abroad. This policy, coinciding with that of self-reliance, was aimed at making China less dependent upon the "outside" world. The Chinese government promoted joint ventures by doing the following:

1. The government required only a minimum of 25 percent financing of a project by a foreign entity, much lower than the traditional 50 percent required by some countries, such as Japan.
2. The government set no upper limit to the percentage being financed by the foreign entity.
3. The government granted two to three year tax holidays to encourage investment.

By the end of 1981, total investments in joint ventures had risen to $240 million.[5]

Since 1981, China has worked with the United Nations Industrial Development Organization (UNIDO) to advertise over 130 investment opportunities for small- to medium-size joint ventures, bringing an expected $900 million in foreign investment into the country.[6]

An important industry that relies on joint venture arrangements in China is oil prospecting and exploration. The movement for modernization in China has created enormous demands for foreign exchange, and the Chinese are looking toward the petroleum industry to play a critical role in financing their balance of payments problems through the sales of petroleum products. The costs of developing an efficient petroleum industry are staggering, and China has relaxed its self-reliance policies and invited Japanese and Western oil companies to participate in China's oil development, especially in areas of prospecting and exploration. The China Petroleum Company, a government-run organization that oversees the oil industry in China, has signed several joint prospecting and exploration contracts with major world oil companies. China's offshore oil deposits in the Bohai Gulf and the Northern Gulf of the South China Sea are expected to produce hundreds of millions of barrels of oil annually once they are developed. Some 300 field joint ventures are presently being negotiated by businesspersons from over 30 countries.[7]

The historical problems with joint ventures in China have been price controls implemented by the government and preset wage levels. However, the Chinese are slowly granting greater freedom in the marketplace, and these issues are being addressed.

## Cooperative Enterprise

A cooperative enterprise, also known as contractual ventures, differs from a joint venture in that it is owned and operated by the Chinese. An investor from another country contributes whatever resources he or she wants and draws a percentage of the profits according to the value of what has been invested. Since 1980, more than 300 cooperative enterprises have been established, primarily situated in the special economic zones. Foreign input here is valued at approximately $500 million.

## Compensation Trade

This is an arrangement under which the Chinese produce goods with the equipment and technology supplied by foreign corporations. The Chinese pay off the value of the equipment and technology by selling the goods produced back to the suppliers.[8] This type of investment has brought over $300 million in investment in China from foreign entities, including such American corporations as the Boston-based Gillette Company.[9]

# CHINA'S MAIN TRADING PARTNERS

China's significant trading partners are Japan, the United States, and Western Europe.

## Japan

Japan has benefited from China's open door policy more than any other nation in the world. China buys more goods from its island neighbor than from any other country, accounting for Japan's 26 percent control of China's nearly $50 billion worth of world trade in 1984.[10] Anti-Japanese sentiments are prevalent throughout China ever since the occupation of China by Japan during the war years of the 1930s and 1940s. It is therefore surprising that Japan's control of the Chinese market is so strong. Several reasons for this, however, can be pointed out. First, the Japanese have made extensive efforts in filling China with corporate offices and personnel. Compared with the fewer than 100 U.S. corporate offices in Beijing, there are more than 250 Japanese companies and banks, many with dozens of salespersons, engineers, and support staff.[11] In addition, the Western MNCs have typically limited their offices in China to the major cities, whereas Japan has made great efforts to have offices throughout the country.

Among other Japanese advantages are their efficient use of trading companies to organize package deals when trading with China. "If China wants to modernize a plant, it would take 10 to 20 American companies offering different machines to close the deal. The Japanese utilize a trading company who puts the whole package together, including financing, shipping, insurance and engineering."[12] It is no wonder that the Japanese are able to negotiate many trade contracts using this efficient method.

There also exists a cultural tie that links these two countries. Japan's location and its cultural affinity with China through religion, language, and customs offer an advantage with which the rest of the world is unable to compete. Intangibles, such as proper seating arrangements at business meetings and bowing manners when greeting someone, are new and unfamiliar to Western business society, but are familiar to the Japanese and have contributed to their success.

The future of the Sino-Japanese trading relations is not clear. Continued trade will enhance China's modernization prospects, but there is increasing sentiment that Japan must increase actual investment in China or retaliatory sanctions against the Japanese may result.

## The United States

Unlike the Japanese domination, the United States has not been able to capture a significant percentage of China's foreign trade.[13] The historic visit of President Nixon to China in 1972 laid the foundation for the present Sino-American relations.[14] U.S. trade volume has expanded from a relatively small amount in 1971 to $6 billion in 1984.[15] With the opening of China, many U.S. businesspersons envisioned extremely rapid U.S. integration into their markets. China's growth has been substantial, but it has fallen short of the original expectations of many Western businesspersons. Although the initial surge of U.S. investment in China was tremendous, things cooled off as U.S. businesses realized that China was short on cash for purchases, had a low ability to manage the vast technological transfer programs planned, and had a reputation for quick decisions to cancel already signed contracts. China and the United States formed the Joint Commission on Commerce and Trade to focus on these trade problems and to search for their solutions. In addition to the previously mentioned issues, other problems being addressed are the following:

1. China's lack of copyright laws
2. China's lack of patent control in the chemical industry
3. China's profit limit laws
4. China's lack of commercial law.

Many of these issues have been addressed and reforms are being implemented.

The composition of trade between China and the United States has remained relatively steady for the last decade. U.S. imports from China were predominantly foodstuffs, tobacco, and textiles. The U.S. exports to China have been in two main areas. Approximately 80 percent of the United States' exports to China has been agricultural goods, such as wheat, to supplement the enormous food supply required for that nation. The second major category of exports has been one-time purchases, such as huge equipment deals or transfers of technology, which are used for specific projects.

It is likely that Sino-American trade will further expand throughout the 1990s and into the twenty-first century. The U.S. Congress, through its 1982 Export Trading Company Act, is attempting to ease antitrust policies to encourage more investment in China. The Chinese government is also making strides in freeing the market place to encourage modernization, which will expand their international trade involvement.

### Western Europe

During the 1960s and 1970s, four of China's 12 leading trading partners were in Western Europe.[16] Chinese exports to Western Europe were mainly foodstuffs, textiles, and light manufactured goods; while their imports from Western Europe were predominantly machine tools, chemicals, and finished steel products. China views Western Europe as an alternative to its traditional major trading partners, the United States and Japan. They have worked diligently to enhance relations with the Western European nations, and they have a strong desire to continue increasing trade in this sector.

## BALANCE OF PAYMENTS

Unlike many countries in the world, China managed from 1949 to 1979 to maintain a balance of trade from a gross perspective. They experienced trade deficits during the years of 1951–1955, 1960, 1974–1975, and 1978–1979, but these were offset by surpluses during 1956–1973 and 1976–1977.[17] China's requirements for modernization and industrialization demand massive expenditures abroad to import the necessary goods and technology. These massive expenditures place great strain on their balance of payments. China's main hope is for successful, rapid expansion of its petroleum industry to significantly counteract the balance of payments trend toward deficits. Through large-scale exportation of their petroleum products, China hopes to offset large portions of its balance of payment deficits, which are expected to increase throughout the 1990s.

## LOOKING INTO THE FUTURE

China seems to be the "wild card" of the new global economy. Its emergence as a modernizing, industrial nation shall have profound effects on the rest of the world. It appears that before long China will become one of the global leaders in the export of energy. Their petroleum reserves have been estimated at 50 to 80 billion barrels (compared to Saudi Arabia's reserves of 163 billion and the U.S. reserves of 27 billion).[18] China's huge population and abundant, untapped natural resources give it much potential for tremendous future economic growth.

It seems clear now that the ultimate success of China's development program depends on modifying guidelines and principles of communist ideology.

## NEW DEVELOPMENTS

The Chinese government has tried to remake Chinese Communism by launching a series of bold economic reforms since 1979. But a decade later, the tide of history is sweeping China with much greater force than that country's leadership could ever have imagined. The leadership thought they could open the bottle halfway, allowing self-interest to enliven the economy without permitting political freedom. They were wrong. Suddenly the decaying socialist state is under siege by a dynamic new China with a mind of its own.[19] It seems that the genie is out of the bottle.

The mindless power struggles among the Chinese leadership and between the Army units, and the bloody confrontation with the Chinese people in the streets of Beijing and dozens of other Chinese cities, makes it clear that the old China is headed for fundamental change. It seems that China has entered a delicate and dangerous period. Neither the Chinese government nor foreign observers see this confrontation ending anytime soon. Many experts foresee government paralysis, civil unrest, and possibly much worse.[20] The question is whether or not these events unravel a decade of hard-earned economic progress and undo the open-door relations with the West.

## QUESTIONS

1. Why does a communist country like China open its door to capitalist entrepreneurs? Discuss.
2. Suppose you are the manager of an MNC that is planning to open a plant in China. What factors do you consider?
3. Why do you think the Japanese are more successful in China than the Americans?
4. What are the principle arrangements employed in China for conducting international business? Explain.

5. What do you think will happen in China, and how will it affect that country's relations with the West?

## NOTES

1. Chu-yuan Cheng, *China's Economic Development: Growth and Structural Change* (Boulder, Colo.: Westview Press, 1982), p. 448.
2. Ibid., p. 449.
3. Ibid., p. 451.
4. Ibid., p. 452.
5. Arnold Chao, "Economic Readjustment and the Open-Door Policy," in Lin Wei and Arnold Chao, eds., *China's Economic Reforms* (Philadelphia: University of Pennsylvania Press, 1982), p. 209.
6. "China Thinks Small to Woo Investors Back," *Business Week,* 17 May 1982, p. 44.
7. Arnold Chao, "Economic Readjustment and the Open-Door Policy," p. 211.
8. Ibid., p. 210.
9. "China Thinks Small . . . ," *Business Week,* p. 44.
10. Barry Kramer, "Master Merchants: Japanese Dominate the Chinese Market with Savvy Trading," *The Wall Street Journal,* 18 November 1985, p. 1.
11. Ibid.
12. Ibid.
13. Percy Timberlake, "China as a Trading Nation," in Nelville Maxwell, ed., *China's Road to Development* (Oxford: Oxford University Press, 1982), pp. 575–586.
14. Cheng, *China's Economic Development,* p. 468.
15. Kramer, "Master Merchants: Japanese Dominate . . . ," *The Wall Street Journal,* p. 1.
16. Cheng, *China's Economic Development,* p. 468.
17. Ibid., p. 474.
18. Hunter Lewis and Donald Allison, *The Real World War* (New York: Coward, McCann, and Geoghegan, 1982), p. 132.
19. "China Begins A New Long March," *Business Week,* 5 June 1989, p. 38.
20. James P. Sterba, Adi Ignatius, and Robert S. Greenberger, "Class Struggle: China's Harsh Actions Threaten to Set Back 10-Year Reform Drive," *The Wall Street Journal,* 5 June 1989, pp. A1, A8.

## SUGGESTED READINGS

Anders, Stephen. *China's Industrial Revolution.* New York: Pantheon Books, 1977.

"Arco's Deal with China Is a Tough Act to Follow." *Business Week,* 4 October 1984, pp. 44–44.

Cheng, Chu-yuan. *China's Economic Development.* Boulder, Colo.: Westview Press, 1982.

"China Begins A New Long March." *Business Week,* 5 June 1989, p. 38.

"China Thinks Small to Woo Investors Back." *Business Week,* 17 May 1982, p. 44.

"China Unloads a Pile of Surplus Imports." *Business Week,* 6 September 1982, p. 44.

"China Update." *Business Week,* 14 May 1984, p. 44.

"Communism in Turmoil: Special Report on China and the Soviet Union," *Business Week,* 5 June 1989, pp. 52–87.

Elliot, Dorinda, and Maks Westerman. "Why Beijing Is Hungry for U.S. Food Companies." *Business Week,* 24 December 1984, p. 43.

"The Greatest Leap Yet Toward a Free Market." *Business Week,* 14 November 1984, p. 45.

Ho, Sam P. *China's Open Door Policy: The Quest for Foreign Technology and Capital.* Vancouver, B.C.: University of British Columbia Press, 1984.

Ignatius, Adi. "People's Republic: Chinese Communism Faces a Crossroads as the Masses Speak." *The Wall Street Journal,* 19 May 1989, pp. A1, A6.

Keidel, Albert. "China: Gaining Efficiency Through Western Ways." *Business Week,* 24 May 1982, pp. 172–174.

Kramer, Barry. "Japanese Dominate the Chinese Market with Savvy Trading." *The Wall Street Journal,* 18 November 1985, pp. 1, 26.

Lewis, Hunter, and Donald Allison. *The Real World War.* New York: Coward, McCann, and Geoghegan, 1982.

Maxwell, Nelville. *China's Road to Development.* Oxford: Oxford University Press, 1975.

Office of the Group of 30 for the Study Group on Foreign Direct Investment. *Foreign Direct Investment 1973–1987: A Survey of Foreign Direct Investment.* Washington, D.C.: U.S. Government Printing Office, 1984.

Sterba, James P. "Whither China? Bungled Effort to End Protests Leaves Nation in Danger of Anarchy." *The Wall Street Journal,* 30 May 1989, pp. A1, A12.

Sterba, James P., Adi Ignatius, and Robert S. Greenberger. "Class Struggle: Chinas's Harsh Actions Threaten to Set Back 10-Year Reform Drive." *The Wall Street Journal,* 5 June 1989, pp. A1, A8.

U.S. Department of Commerce. International Trade Administration. *Investment Climate in Foreign Countries.* Washington, D.C.: U.S. Government Printing Office, 1983.

Wang, George C. *Economic Reform in the PRC.* Boulder, Colo.: Westview Press, 1982.

Wei, Lin, and Arnold Chao. *China's Economic Reforms.* Philadelphia: University of Pennsylvania Press, 1982.

# Case I: 2

# To Protect or Not to Protect:
# That Is the Question*

When President Reagan was first elected, he strongly promoted a free foreign trade policy. For example, in the 1984 Economic Report of the President, Mr. Reagan wrote:

> I remain committed to the principle of free trade as the best way to bring the benefits of competition to American consumers and businesses. It would be totally inappropriate to respond by erecting trade barriers or by using taxpayers' dollars to subsidize exports.[1]

Although President Reagan preached this hands-off policy, his political and legal actions showed that he intended to protect U.S. industries that he felt were important to the economic and social well-being of the United States. Trade legislation in the steel, textile, and motorcycle industries were prime examples of the Reagan administration's protectionist actions.

One main argument of the administration for protectionism was its desire to sustain a diversified economy in the United States. An example of this type of protection of an industry by the Reagan administration is the legislation passed in the motorcycle industry. Harley-Davidson is the only American motorcycle maker still in production. In the past few years its profits fell greatly because Japanese heavy motorcycle producers were dumping their cheaper products on the U.S. market. Japan could produce the motorcycles more cheaply, mainly because of their lower labor costs. As Harley-Davidson was just about to fold, the company made a request to the administration for some type of protection. Because Reagan felt it was important to keep motorcycles in production in the United States and to keep the U.S. economy more

---

*This case initially was written by William W. Saltonstall of St. Lawrence University as a term project under the supervision of Professor Asheghian, who subsequently revised it for inclusion in this textbook.

diversified, he imposed a 49.9 percent tariff on heavy motorcycles entering the nation. The result of the tariff was a 10 to 15 percent rise in the price of imported motorcycles.[2] Harley-Davidson has since managed to keep up production and stay semicompetitive in the motorcycle market because of Reagan's protectionist act.

National security was another Reagan argument for protectionism. National security was a high-priority objective in the Reagan administration, as was evidenced by the continual increases in military spending witnessed during his administration. Mr. Reagan advocated protection of several industries that he felt were important to American national security. The U.S. steel industry is indispensable with respect to national security. Steel is a material used in the production of almost all weaponry and other military-related commodities. Competition from West Germany, the Netherlands, Japan, and several other nations had been taking its toll on the U.S. steel industry. The president, feeling this industry to be vital to the United States' security, initiated several protectionist actions to allow U.S. steel producers to stay competitive in the international market. In 1984, the U.S. carbon steel industry filed several petitions to the government explaining its persistent losses and their effects on the country, such as an increase in unemployment if the industry were to fold. Reagan responded by sending Commerce Secretary Malcolm Baldrige to negotiate with European steel producers. This resulted in the imposition of quotas on imported carbon steel into the United States. Reagan also continued the protection that the Ford administration induced in 1976 in the form of tariffs for the specialty steel industry.[3] Following this protectionist measure, the U.S. steel industry has continued to survive, and the Reagan administration believed that such policies strengthened the U.S. national security.

Reagan argued for protectionism as necessary for maintaining wages and full employment. A case in point is the U.S. automobile industry. In recent years the U.S. auto industry has experienced a large decrease in its sales. One factor contributing to the sales decline of the U.S.-produced cars has been the supply of cheap labor available in competing foreign nations. Japan is a prime example, where lower wages allow the Japanese producers to lower the selling price of their cars in the U.S. market. In 1984, to deal with these situations, the Reagan administration negotiated a three-year trade agreement with Japan in which Japan agreed to abide by the restraints that were requested by the Reagan administration.[4] Reagan's motive in this agreement was to keep the U.S. car industry competitive with foreign competition. He also wished to avoid high unemployment levels that would occur if U.S. automobile plants were shut down.

Finally, an important Reagan argument for protectionism was the desire to lessen the U.S. trade deficit. Given the huge balance of payments deficit in the United States, the Reagan administration protectionist policies aimed to restrict imports from countries such as Japan in order to restore the equilibrium in the balance of payments.

## QUESTIONS

1. What theoretical arguments supported President Reagan's commitment to free trade? Explain.

2. The Reagan administration used different arguments to impose protectionist measures. Are these arguments justifiable? Discuss. What are other arguments that call for protectionist policies? Explain.

3. Give examples of products that you know have enjoyed protection by the United States or another government. Can you pinpoint the reasons for the imposition of such protection?

## NOTES

1. Lee Hamilton, "Free Trade: Rhetoric vs. Reality," *Christian Science Monitor*, 25 April 1984, p. 14.
2. Ibid.
3. M. Weidenbaum, and M. Munger, "Protectionism: Who Gets Protected," *Consumers Research Magazine* 66 (October 1983): 16–17.
4. John Destler, "Why Reagan Is a Free Trade Villain," *New York Times*, 18 March 1984, p. F3.

## SUGGESTED READINGS

Destler, John. "Why Reagan is a Free Trade Villain." *New York Times*, 18 March 1984, p. F3.

Forsythe, David. *American Foreign Policy in an Uncertain World.* Lincoln: University of Nebraska Press, 1984, p. 203.

Friedman, Milton. *Free to Choose*, New York: Harcourt Brace Jovanovich, 1980.

Garten, Jeffrey. "America's Retreat from Protectionism." *New York Times*, 16 June 1985, p. F3.

Hamilton, Lee. "Free Trade: Rhetoric vs. Reality." *Christian Science Monitor*, 25 April 1984, p. 14.

"How to Foil Protectionism." *Fortune*, 21 March 1983, p. 76.

Kinsley, Michael. "Keep Trade Free." *The New Republic*, 11 April 1983, p. 10.

McKenzie, Richard. "Low Wages in Foreign Countries Do Not Fully Explain Imports." *Consumer Research Magazine*, October 1983, pp. 18–19.

Mouat, Lucia. "Reagan Nominee Sees Danger in Rising Trade Protectionism." *Christian Science Monitor*, 11 April 1985, p. 3.

Pine, Art. "Can Reagan Resist Protectionist Forces?" *The Wall Street Journal*, 30 July 1984, p. 1.

"The Protection Racket." *The Wall Street Journal*, 20 December 1984, p. 26L.

Putka, Gary. "Western Europe Sees U.S. Protectionism Looming, and Warns It Would Retaliate." *The Wall Street Journal,* 13 March 1985, p. 38.

Richey, Warren. "U.S. Trade Commissioner Urges U.S. Industries to Forego Protectionism." *Christian Science Monitor,* 12 October 1984, p. 6.

Weidenbaum, M., and M. Munger. "Protectionism: Who Gets Protected?" *Consumers Research Magazine,* October 1983, pp. 16–17.

# U.S.–Soviet Trade and the Impact of Perestroika[*]

## INTRODUCTION

The Soviet Union is currently going through some major changes in its political system and economic policy. The Soviet leader, Mikhail Gorbachev, is pushing for a new openness, or *glasnost,* in the Soviet government. These changes will surely affect the United States and Russian trade relations. We will analyze the past U.S.–Soviet trade relations and attitudes and then try to determine what effects these new Russian policies will have on future trade.

## U.S. TRADE WITH THE SOVIET UNION

In 1959, Nikita Khrushchev boasted that the Soviet economic output would overtake and surpass that of the United States. However, economic problems in the Soviet Union, such as agricultural and industrial shortages, forced that country to continue its imports from the West, especially from the United States. Soviet imports from the United States, which seldom totaled more than $100 million before the 1970s, reached the level of $162 million in 1971, and $541 million in 1972. In 1973, the United States was the biggest noncommunist exporter to the Soviet Union, with almost $1.2 billion in exports.

The chief products that the United States exports to the Soviet Union are agricultural. In fact, the USSR accounted for about one-fourth of American grain exports in 1979. Table I:3.1 shows the U.S. trade status with the Soviet Union.

The drastic increase in trade in 1973 was the result of a severe drought in Russia. Russia had wanted to make a political statement to the United States

---

[*]This case was initially written by Anne La Taste of University of North Texas as a term project under the supervision of Professor Ebrahimi, who has subsequently revised it for inclusion in this textbook.

Table I:3.1   U.S.–SOVIET TRADE
              STATUS: SELECTED
              ANNUAL U.S.
              EXPORTS TO USSR
              Millions of Dollars

| Year | Total manufactured and agricultural products |
|------|--------------------|
| 1971 | 162 |
| 1972 | 541 |
| 1973 | 1,186 |
| 1974 | 511 |
| 1975 | 1,835 |
| 1980 | 1,513 |
| 1984 | 3,284 |
| 1985 | 2,423 |
| 1986 | 1,248 |

*Source:* U.S. Bureau of the Census, "Highlights of U.S. Export and Import Trade," FT 990, monthly.

and demonstrate how it could be independent from the economy of the United States. Although a drought is something that cannot be predicted or controlled, government policies can be controlled, and Soviet policies had led them steadily to a point of inefficiency and low productivity. These policies have contributed to past U.S. exports to Russia.

Political forces have seemed to govern the trade between the United States and the USSR. Americans have boycotted Soviet-made products and held distrustful views about the Soviet government. In 1951, the "most favored nations" status was withdrawn from all communist countries. Although several communist countries have been reinstated since then, high tariffs remain for others. The U.S. grain trade restrictions to Russia are another example of political influences on trade. Despite these trade barriers, Americans have traded profitably with the Soviet Union. It seems that Americans have always wanted to trade with the USSR but the trade restrictions kept getting in the way.

Between 1972 and 1975, General Electric had a $250 million contract with Russia for the manufacture of gas turbine compressors. Honeywell had a $65 million computer contract. Companies were willing to take low profits in "first deal" contracts in order to reap greater profits in the future. Although the wariness that Americans feel toward the Soviet Union has not disappeared, financial considerations have become as important as political factors.

Russians have been willing to trade with Americans because of the benefits they would receive. The state-owned industries in Russia have not operated for profit and have been inefficient. These inefficiencies in Russia have led to shortages of goods and services, allowing industries in the United States to increase their exports to the Soviet Union.

Besides agricultural products, many technological agreements have existed between American companies and the Soviet Union. Some agreements have included exchanges of technology in mining machinery, power generation, ship building, telecommunications, and aircraft computers. Russia has benefited considerably from trade with the United States. It has gained foreign technology, and the Soviet people have become accustomed to imported material goods.

## REASONS FOR REFORM

What are the reasons for the current economic reforms in the Soviet Union? Has the past trade with the United States led to these Russian reforms? Will the reforms lead to increased U.S.–Soviet trade? The answers to these questions are in the existence of shortages in that country. Without doubt the new reforms are due to the Soviet's faltering economy. Productivity is low and bureaucratic inefficiencies are running rampant. In recent years, the Soviet economy has grown at only half the 4 percent rate that it did during the early postwar period.

Gorbachev gave his reasons for the reforms in a speech in the beginning of February 1987. He stated that:

1.  Disregard of the law, report padding, bribe taking, sycophancy, and the encouragement of todayism have had a deleterious effect on the moral atmosphere of the society.
2.  Soviet policymaking has grown rife with conservative sentiments, inertia, a tendency to brush aside everything that does not fit into conventional patterns, and an unwillingness to come to grips with outstanding socioeconomic problems.
3.  The growth of alcohol and drug abuse and a rise in crime have become indicators of the decline of social morality.
4.  There were no firm obstacles placed in the path of dishonest, pushy, greedy people intent on personal gain from their party membership.[1]

The new reforms, referred to as *perestroika* (restructuring), call for major changes in the Soviet economic policies. Gorbachev insists, however, that the basic communist philosophy will not be violated.

## PERESTROIKA

The new reforms of perestroika are meant to bring the Russian economy back into shape. Capitalistic practices are being used as a means of reaching that objective. As one writer puts it, the Soviets are "inching down the capitalistic road."[2] The Soviet government is now allowing free enterprise but for many years the "underground economy" had been helping to meet the demands of the Russian consumers. In fact, Soviet experts believed that 40 percent of Russian household services were performed by illegal moonlighters of the underground economy. Now, it seems that this flourishing underground economy will be brought above ground and under control. The government's revenues will benefit, no doubt, by these newly taxable enterprises. Another example of capitalistic tendencies taking over is that some Soviet companies are now allowing their employees to be paid according to a percentage of the profits made by the business.

These reforms are being seen in other ways too. Democratization seems to be creeping into the system. Gorbachev is asking that secret ballot elections be held for certain offices. It is reported that "Gorbachev wants to halve the 50,000 employee staff of Gosplan, the central planning agency, and cut the number of Moscow ministries from around 80 to 20."[3] Democracy is seen in other ways too. Employees can vote out their managers if they feel this will increase their productivity. This drastic from-the-bottom-up approach to management is certainly a change for the Russians.

Advocates of these new reforms are calling for even more drastic measures, such as allowing a certain amount of unemployment and allowing businesses to go bankrupt. Many feel that these reforms are only a drop in the bucket. Others feel that the changes are too great. Despite support, Gorbachev still faces much opposition.

## OPPOSITION

Gorbachev is facing opposition from the system and from society. He admits that "between the people who want these changes, dream of these changes, and the leadership, there is an administration layer: the apparatus of the ministries, the party apparatus, which does not want to be deprived of certain rights connected with privileges."[4] The people who dislike these reforms have defeated prior attempts at reform. Other experts believe that Gorbachev will have a tough time defeating the corrupt groups that have been so powerful in the past and that do not want to lose that power now.

There have been no significant results from perestroika so far. In Moscow, state stores remain virtually devoid of decent consumer products including food, clothing, and luxury items. The average Soviet citizen spends his or her days standing in lines, seeking the scraps of perestroika Mr. Gorbachev keeps promising. In a recent survey, a third of the people polled believed that long lines for food would not disappear "during their lifetime, if ever." The only visible result from reform is that officials are now willing, even eager, to criticize past policies, engage in discussion and give the impression of "new thinking."[5]

By January 1989, the Soviet economy worsened. Budget deficits were estimated to exceed $120 billion. Shortages of consumer products remained rampant and the sale of illicit goods in black markets flourished.[6]

In March of 1989, the first relatively free election in 70 years took place in the Soviet Union. In that election, dozens of old-guard Communist Party leaders were defeated and many non-Party members were elected to the Supreme Soviet Congress.[7]

The events in the Soviet Union seem to point in an opposite direction to those that are taking place in the neighboring communist country: the People's Republic of China. It seems that in the Soviet Union *Glasnost* (political openness) has been relatively successful, but *Perestroika* (economic reform) has not been effectively implemented. China, however, has been successful in implementing economic development, but has not been willing to open its political arena to reforms.

## QUESTIONS

1. What opportunities may the United States face if Gorbachev is successful in implementing his reforms? What threats?
2. What might happen to the Russian economy if these reforms are successful?
3. How might social and moral reforms help the Soviets become more productive?
4. What effects do you think perestroika will have on U.S.–Soviet trade?

## NOTES

1. William Doerner, "The Call to Reform," *Time,* 9 February 1987, pp. 28–30.
2. James O. Jackson, "Inching Down the Capitalist Road," *Time,* 4 May 1987, p. 42.
3. Peter Galustzka, "Gorbachev Is Making a Bold Bid," *Business Week,* 29 June 1987, p. 49.
4. Doerner, "The Call to Reform," pp. 28–30.
5. Karen E. House, "The '90s & Beyond: Communist Giants Are Too Burdened at Home to Lead Much Abroad," *The Wall Street Journal,* 4 February 1989, pp. A1, A7.
6. "Gorbachev's Reforms: Will They Work?" *Business Week,* 5 June 1989, p. 57
7. Ibid.

## SUGGESTED READINGS

Black, Cyril E., et al. *Common Sense in U.S.–Soviet Trade.* Washington, D.C.: American Committee on East–West Accord, 1979.

"Communism in Turmoil: Special Report on China and the Soviet Union," *Business Week,* 5 June 1989, pp. 52–87.

Doerner, William. "The Call to Reform." *Time,* 9 February 1987, pp. 28–30.

Galustzka, Peter. "Gorbachev Is Making a Bold Bid," *Business Week,* 29 June 1987, p. 49.

Goldman, Marshal. *Detente and Dollars.* New York: Basic Books, 1975.

House, Karen E. "The '90s & Beyond: Communist Giants Are Too Burdened at Home to Lead Much Abroad," *The Wall Street Journal,* 6 February 1989, pp. A1, A7.

Jackson, James. "Inching Down the Capitalist Road," *Time,* 4 May 1987, p. 42.

*New York Times,* 1 April 1987, p. A8.

# Machine Outil S.A.: Foreign Exchange Risk Management

On April 26, 1973, Messieurs Volny-Martin, President Directeur-Général, and Leberre, Directeur Financier, respectively, of Machine Outil, S.A. (MOSA), a Swiss machine tool manufacturer, were trying to decide how they should manage the foreign exchange risk arising from a potential $60 million contract with the Soviet Union. The company had been negotiating this order with the Soviet Committee for Science and Technology (SCST) in Moscow. This order, the equivalent of SFR 180 million, would be the largest single contract that this firm had ever considered undertaking.

## THE COMPANY

MOSA had been founded in 1876. The company remained independent until the early 1960s when Globcon, Inc., a diversified American corporation, acquired 92 percent of the outstanding equity. This represented Globcon's only investment in the machine tool industry. MOSA manufactured a complete range of single and multiple spindle lathes, including both mechanically and numerically controlled models. The machines were designed by the firm's Systems Development Department to meet the specific needs of each client. The major part of MOSA's sales was to the automotive industry, and its lathes were used by every major automobile manufacturer in the world.

Sales volume had increased from SFR 245 million in 1970 to SFR 290 million in 1972. However, due to severe price competition in the industry, profits had fallen from 9.6 percent of sales in 1970 to 2.1 percent in 1972. Until the second half of 1972, the firm had always enjoyed a large backlog of orders which, over the past seven years, had never been less than 14 months and was often as much as 18 months. From the design stage to finished machine, production took an average of eight months. Since the relatively long delivery time

*Source:* Copyright © July 1979, Helmut Lipfert, Lee Remmers, Greg Thompson, INSEAD, Fontainebleau, France. This case was printed in Carlson, Remmers, Hekman, Eiteman, and Stonehill. *International Finance: Cases and Simulation.* Reading, Mass.: Addison-Wesley Publishing Co., 1980, pp. 63–68.

sometimes resulted in lost orders, MOSA's president had for some time tried to convince the New York headquarters to agree to an increase in manufacturing capacity, but without success. The major reason for Globcon's refusal was the forecast by its Corporate Planning Department that the machine tool industry would suffer a decline in orders from the OECD countries until at least 1975. This prediction appeared to have been partially confirmed, for by March 1973, MOSA's order backlog fell to 10 months. The latest forecast showed that sales volume to OECD countries would not be much over SFR 200 million for all of 1973. As a result, company management had been particularly anxious to obtain a part of the $350 million order for machine tools needed for a new truck plant in the Soviet Union.

MOSA had five principal competitors in its markets, one each in the United States, Germany, United Kingdom, France, and Italy. Of these, the American and German firms were of considerable size. The recent price competition in this industry was partially due to the U.S. manufacturer, which, benefiting from the recent realignments in the value of the dollar, had become an important factor in the international market. In addition, faced with a weakening demand in its domestic market, this company had been obliged to reduce employment by about 30 percent. This would have been even more severe had it not been for a number of export orders obtained at prices below cost of manufacture. Therefore, as a result of both lower volume and prices, almost all companies in the industry, including MOSA, were suffering losses by the spring of 1973.

## FOREIGN EXCHANGE POLICY

MOSA had long pursued very conservative policies in managing its finances and foreign exchange positions. Funds were raised only on the Swiss credit markets, which offered the lowest interest rates obtainable anywhere; foreign exchange risk was covered by entering into forward contracts taken to mature on the purchase contract payment dates. These forward contracts were arranged on the same day that the machine purchase contract was invoiced. MOSA usually found that its clients would not agree to be invoiced in Swiss francs, especially during recent months, for it was widely feared that the Swiss would follow the German example and revalue their currency. Machine purchase contracts were normally priced using the forward rate (quoted in Zurich) for that maturity which corresponded to the months in which payments were specified. In addition, MOSA policy was to add 0.6 percent per month to the base price from the date the machine purchase contract was signed until the month of delivery.

Whenever it became apparent that the actual payment date would deviate from the date specified in the machine purchase contract (and, therefore, from the maturity of the forward contracts), it was strict company policy to prolong the original forward contract by means of a swap* regardless of the cost. The chief financial officer, M. Leberre, believed that the higher the cost

---

*A swap is the purchase or sale of currency *spot* against the sale or purchase of currency forward.

of prolonging a forward contract (in terms of the forward discount*) the more necessary it was to do so. Short-term interest rate differentials, according to M. Leberre, were influenced by speculative international capital flows. Therefore, he reasoned, speculation in a currency that usually precedes a change in parities would be reflected in the forward premium or discount. With one exception some three years earlier, the highest prolongation cost to date had been 0.9 percent of the machine purchase contract amount.

This exception involved a payment of 8.6 million French francs in 1969 for machines sold to the Continental Motor Company for a plant north of Bordeaux. The machines had been delivered and installed as planned, and M. Leberre had every reason to believe that the payment, covered by a forward contract, would be made on August 15, 1969, the date specified in the contract. Since most of the Continental staff were on holiday during August, the payment date slipped by, and despite M. Leberre's frantic efforts, actual payment was not made until September 4. On August 27, the French franc was devalued by 11.2 percent. Although MOSA's post-devaluation swaps (between August 27 and September 4) had produced a small gain (0.1 percent of contract volume), the cost of daily and weekly swaps from August 15 to August 26 had amounted to 2.1 percent of the value of the machine purchase contract. The MOSA management decided not to press Continental Motors for payment of the loss for fear of jeopardizing future orders. However, steps were taken by MOSA to avoid recurrence of such an event in the future.

## THE SOVIET TRUCK PLANT CONTRACT

MOSA enjoyed a longstanding relationship with the SCST, which had looked to the Swiss firm as a dependable supplier of high-quality products. During the five-year period from 1968 to 1972, sales to the Soviet Union had ranged from SFR 9 million to SFR 28.5 million per year, averaging 8.6 percent of MOSA's total sales volume.

Upon completion of a machine or group of machines, but prior to shipment, the usual practice had been for a small team of Soviet technicians to verify that the performance was as specified in the contract. This took place in Switzerland at the firm's manufacturing facilities. After acceptance by the Soviet team, payment in U.S. dollars had always been made within one week. Provided that the machine had been completed as originally planned and made available to the Soviets for their performance trials, the actual payment date usually conformed closely with the planned payment. On some occasions, however, engineering and production delays occurred, causing significant differences between planned and actual payments.

---

*Due to relatively low interest rates in Switzerland and the reputation of the Swiss franc as a "hard currency," forward foreign exchange had almost always sold at a discount against the Swiss franc.

On April 18, 1973, a four-man MOSA negotiating team in Moscow reported that there was a reasonably good chance for the firm to sell up to $60 million worth of machine tools to the Soviets for delivery between April 1974 and March 1975. A tender would have to be submitted by April 30. The bid would be binding, at a fixed dollar price, and would be accompanied by a delivery guarantee provided by a major Swiss or American bank. The SCST would announce its decision on May 31, 1973. Although the MOSA sales team had met frequently with representatives from the SCST during early April, and had survived long evening gatherings with them consuming prodigious quantities of vodka and caviar, by April 15 when the report was sent, it remained very uncertain how much, if any, of the total contract they could expect. They were able to learn that the toughest competition would come from the U.S. machine tool manufacturer referred to earlier; this firm had the advantage of bidding in its own currency, thus avoiding any exchange risk.

At Globcon corporate headquarters in New York, great interest had been expressed in the Soviet contract. Since its Swiss affiliate was currently operating at a loss, with its backlog of orders dwindling and future sales prospects poor, and because its cost structure included a high proportion of overheads, the contract was considered at headquarters to be of crucial importance to the future of MOSA.

In order to improve the chances of being awarded all or part of the contract, Messieurs Volny-Martin and Leberre decided to modify their usual pricing policy. They would base their bid on the minimum catalog price less 5 percent, and would not include any allowance for inflationary cost increases or foreign exchange risk. Minimum catalog prices were calculated on the basis of total cost at full plant capacity plus a 10 percent markup. They believed that the economies of scale gained from such a large contract (12 machine tool units of the same type were involved—a situation not previously enjoyed by the firm) would about offset cost increases due to inflation. Finally, the exchange rate to be used for the bid would be the spot middle rate on April 30, 1973.

On April 20, spot dollars (middle rates) were quoted in Zurich between SFR 2.9950 and 3.0050.* Forward dollar rates were quoted as follows:

| Maturity | Forward discount |
| --- | --- |
| 1–3 months | .030 SFRs per $ per month |
| 4–6 months | .027 SFRs per $ per month |
| 7–12 months | .024 SFRs per $ per month |
| 13–17 months | .021 SFRs per $ per month |
| 18–36 months | .018 SFRs per $ per month |

*For purpose of the case study, the rates shown above are assumed, that is, are not the actual rates on the date indicated.

Assuming that MOSA would be able to make delivery as specified in the contract, and that it would receive the entire contract, payment dates and amounts would be as follows:

| | |
|---|---|
| June 1, 1974 | $ 10 million |
| October 1, 1974 | $ 16 million |
| December 1, 1974 | $ 14 million |
| February 1, 1975 | $ 8 million |
| May 1, 1975 | $ 12 million |

Shareholder equity of MOSA was SFR 30 million. Of this amount, SFR 12 million were retained earnings. Hidden reserves (i.e., the difference between actual and book values of the firm's assets) were estimated at over SFR 20 million.

## FOREIGN EXCHANGE RISK—THE ALTERNATIVES

There had been a marked change of attitude among officials at the Swiss Central Bank in Berne during the past four weeks. Whereas they had previously resisted the idea of allowing a change in the value of the Swiss franc, many observers believed that the Central Bank officials had decided to try to put a stop to the influx of foreign currencies and would revalue the franc or permit its float upward in the very near future. Messieurs Volny-Martin and Leberre believed that the prospective contract should be hedged for the month of May, the period between submission of the bid and its eventual acceptance or rejection in total or part.

One way to protect themselves during the bid period was to take a one-month forward contract to mature on May 31 at the .03 SFR per dollar forward discount. In considering this, M. Leberre pointed out that this would "cost" MOSA SFR 1.8 million on a $60 million forward contract. Moreover, he argued, it would be completely lost in the event that they were not awarded any of the contract. He also suggested that the expected dollar payments specified in the contract (see above) be covered immediately by forward contracts of the same amount and maturity. He considered that, in the event the contract was not received or only partially received, he would have time to reduce or eliminate the exposed positions with relatively little risk or loss.

M. Volny-Martin believed that a better way to obtain the necessary foreign exchange protection would be to borrow Eurodollars, convert them into Swiss francs which could be used to finance MOSA operational needs with the remainder being placed on deposit to earn back some of the dollar interest expense. The dollar payments from the contract would then be used to repay the Eurodollar loans. For this operation, the banks would probably ask for the guarantee of the parent company.

In discussing this alternative with M. Volny-Martin, M. Leberre was convinced that its cost would be practically the same as that of the forward contract, but agreed to consider it carefully. After some thought he came up with a variation in which they would borrow Eurodollars at maturities of 12, 18, and 24 months and invest them in long-term Swiss franc bonds. This should result in a lower cost of covering the exchange risk than provided by the forward contract. However, M. Leberre had realized that this idea involved some interest rate risk. If bond yields rose over time, the bonds would fall in value.

Several days later, an officer of MOSA's bank in Lausanne suggested yet another alternative to M. Leberre. He pointed out that since the cost of covering forward was the result of the interest rate differential between the Swiss franc and the U.S. dollar, a narrowing of this differential would reduce the cost of forward contracts. Therefore, he proposed they should cover forward the outstanding amounts of the contract by means of a series of one-month contracts until such time that the interest rate differential was significantly smaller. At that time they could then take out forward contracts with maturities that would coincide with the contract payment dates. Since the present Swiss franc-dollar interest rate differential was at an all-time high and because some of their banking contacts expected the differential to narrow late in the year or by early 1974, M. Leberre thought this idea to have considerable merit.

Three days before submission of the bid, Messieurs Volny-Martin and Leberre were expected to obtain final approval from the Globcon top management. Although they were confident that the price quoted in the bid would be approved without serious discussion, they were still unsure as to what foreign exchange exposure alternative they should propose. They were also debating whether to ask Globcon to help pay the cost of covering the foreign exchange risk including the possible additional cost of swaps needed to cover a payment delay. After all, they reasoned, the parent company should profit from its Swiss investment in the case where the Swiss franc rose in value against the dollar.

## QUESTIONS

1. If you were in charge of the decision to protect MOSA against foreign exchange risk, which alternative would you choose and why?
2. Should Globcon help to pay the cost of covering the foreign exchange risk? Why?

## SUGGESTED READINGS

Eiteman, David K., and Arthur I. Stonehill. *Multinational Business Finance.* 5th ed. Reading, Mass.: Addison-Wesley, 1989, Chaps. 4, 5, and 6.

Folks, William R., Jr., and Raj Aggarwal. *International Dimensions of Financial Management.* Boston, Mass.: PWS-Kent, 1988, Chaps. 3, 4, and 5.

Madura, Jeff. *International Financial Management.* St. Paul, Minn.: West, 1986, Chaps. 8, 9, and 10.

Melvin, Michael. *International Money and Finance.* New York: Harper & Row, 1985, Chaps. 1, 2, 3, 7, and 8.

Weston, J. Fred. *Guide to International Financial Management.* New York: McGraw-Hill, 1977, Chaps. 8 and 10.

# *PART* TWO

# Environmental Aspects of International Business

In Chapter 1, we stated that an international business is affected by a host of environmental variables that influence the day-to-day operations of the business. Chief among these variables are economic, political/legal, sociocultural, technological, and physical/geographic factors. Dealing with these variables, as we explained before, necessitates an understanding of other academic disciplines, such as economics, political science, history, geography, law, anthropology, sociology, and psychology.

The purpose of Part Two is to provide a deeper understanding of some of these and other environmental variables and the way in which they affect international business. Such knowledge will better enable us to comprehend the customs, the code of conduct, and the written and unwritten laws and regulations that govern the business environment of a host country. Some of the main questions that are answered in this part are:

1. What factors make up environmental forces?
2. How can an international manager deal with environmental forces?
3. What legal and political conditions govern the international business activities? What are the implications of these conditions for an MNC?
4. What are the elements of the sociocultural environment? What is the impact of these elements on an MNC?
5. What is technology? What variables affect the choice of technology by an MNC? What is the relationship of technology with culture?

Part Two, therefore, is designed to provide a more detailed perspective on the environmental variables that affect international business operations.

# Broad Environmental Factors Facing an MNC

$A$ host of external factors influence a firm's choice of directions and actions, and ultimately, its internal conditions. The survival and success of a firm depend on how it relates to the largely uncontrollable factors that shape its environment. These outside factors can lead to positive conditions—opportunities—or to negative constraints—threats—to a firm. Although this is true for firms both domestically and internationally, the task of matching the firm to its environment is more difficult in an international setting. This chapter focuses on the broad environmental issues faced by a multinational company. First, we briefly introduce broad environmental forces. Second, we discuss the nature of international business environments. Third, we elaborate on forces that shape these environments.

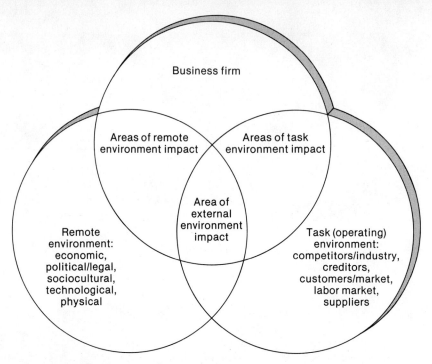

**Figure 8.1** A firm's external environment

*Source:* Adapted from J. A. Pearce II and Richard B. Robinson, Jr., *Strategic Management: Strategy Formulation and Implementation,* 3rd ed. (Richard D. Irwin, Inc., Homewood, Ill., 1988), p. 100.

Fourth, we show models of the domestic environment and the international environment. Fifth, we list sources of international business information. Finally, we discuss environmental assessment.

## BROAD ENVIRONMENTAL FORCES

Generally speaking, the environmental forces can be divided into two inter-related sets of factors: those in the remote environment and those in the task environment.* Figure 8.1 depicts the impact of these two sets of factors on a business firm.

We will briefly explain the differences between these two sets of factors. A more in-depth coverage of all these factors will be presented later in this chapter.

---

*The distinction between remote and task environments is adapted from John A. Pearce II and Richard B. Robinson, Jr., *Strategic Management: Strategy Formulation and Implementation,* 4th ed. (Homewood, Ill.: Irwin, 1988), chap. 4.

## Remote Environment

**Remote environment** consists of those factors outside the boundaries of a firm. These factors greatly influence a firm, but the firm has little or no reciprocal influence on these factors. The remote environment consists of economic, political/legal, sociocultural, technological, and physical/geographic factors.

## Task Environment

The **task environment** refers to the factors in the immediate operating environment that confront and influence an MNC as it attempts to attract or acquire needed resources or to market profitably its products or services. Among the most important factors in the task environment are a firm's competitive and industry position, customer and market conditions, and its relationship with its suppliers, its creditors, and its labor market.

# INTERNATIONAL BUSINESS ENVIRONMENTS

The environment of international business is composed of three major parts. These are the domestic environment (the home country), the foreign environments (which is the domestic environment of the host countries), and the international environment. Figure 8.2 shows that as a firm operates internationally it passes through an international environment, which is composed of a diverse set of economic, legal, and political forces, before entering foreign environments. These various international environmental forces may hinder or help a firm's overseas operations. Like a tourist traveling from one country to another, an MNC faces economic, political, social, and other constraints not faced in domestic operations.

## The Domestic Environment

The **domestic environment** consists of all the remote and task factors that are found in the home country. The domestic managers are most familiar with these factors. Such factors not only affect the domestic operations but also the overseas activities. The economic, political, and social conditions at home might prompt the government to provide incentives or to curtail foreign investment or exports. For example, when the government faces a shortage of foreign currency, restrictions may be placed on transfer of funds out of the country. Such is the case in Iran, Mexico, and Venezuela. This would limit the overseas expansion possibilities for MNCs based in these countries. On the other hand, when domestic unemployment is high, an MNC with production facilities overseas may be faced with import restrictions. For example, in 1986, the Egyptian government issued a series of import restrictions by imposing tariffs.[1]

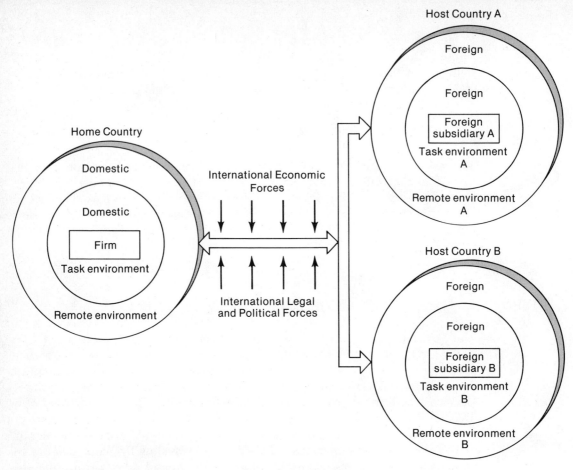

**Figure 8.2** The basic model of international operations

## The Foreign Environments

The **foreign environments** refer to all the remote and task factors that are encountered in the foreign nations in which an MNC operates.

The same remote factors and task factors that exist in the domestic environment are encountered in foreign environments, except that they occur in foreign nations. Although the same environmental categories apply, their nature and values can be quite different from those found in the domestic environment. Within the domestic environment, many of the factors which an executive faces remain constant: a single currency, a reasonably homogeneous and familiar culture, a common language, and a well-developed infrastructure. Such factors are expected, accepted, and often ignored. In international operations, however, there are few fixed factors or constraints. Of course, the differences, opportunities, and threats vary depending largely on the host country's conditions. There are vast differences between foreign environmental conditions found in certain countries and those found in the domestic environment. While the differences between the foreign environmental conditions in some other countries, when compared with the conditions in the domestic environment, may be minimal. For example, for a Western MNC, political differences are greatest when it operates in Eastern bloc countries, whereas cultural differences might be greater in most of the Asian or African countries.

Another aspect of the foreign environmental factors is the difficulty in assessing and forecasting their values. Lack of familiarity and information about environmental conditions in a foreign country often leads to incorrect assessments and forecasts. In foreign environments, political/legal factors are probably the most difficult to assess. An example of this is the sudden political change during the Iranian revolution, which caught most political analysts by surprise. In some developing nations political coups d'etat are commonplace. A coup d'etat may change a pro-foreign investment government into an anti-foreign investment government overnight.

The unfamiliarity of international executives with local conditions, the higher uncertainty, and the multiplicity of the factors involved in foreign operations require a more complex decision-making process. Nevertheless, despite the difficulties, the managerial positions involving international business decisions can be very challenging and rewarding.

### International Environment

An **international environment** is created from the interaction between the domestic and the foreign environments. The international environment is composed of a set of diverse economic, legal, and political forces. Included in this environment are international organizations such as the United Nations and its agencies, regional organizations like the European Community (EC), and international industrial organizations such as the Organization of Petroleum Exporting Countries (OPEC). These organizations are usually formed on the basis of industry agreements or on the basis of regional or international agreements such as GATT (General Agreement on Tariffs and Trade). We have discussed many of these organizations in earlier chapters.

In summary, we note that an MNC has to encounter three distinct sets of environments: the domestic environment, the foreign environments, and the international environment. Although the domestic and foreign environments are unique, similar factors can be used in their assessment. In other words, each environment, although different, consists of remote forces and task forces.

We now turn to an in-depth discussion of remote and task environments.

## REMOTE ENVIRONMENT

As we explained earlier, the remote environment consists of those forces outside the boundaries of the firm. The remote environment consists of factors such as economic, political/legal, sociocultural, technological, and physical/

geographic. These factors present a firm with a host of opportunities, threats, and constraints. Few organizations possess capabilities to exert any meaningful reciprocal influence over these forces. For example, when the interest rates are high and automobile sales are low, an individual automaker may provide sales incentives (lower automobile loan interest rates, rebates, and so forth) and boost its sales. However, the same automaker would not be able to lower the national interest rates, despite its success in increasing its own sales.

A more recent example is the increase in the strength of the U.S. dollar in the early 1980s, which, as we discussed in Chapter 1, contributed to the U.S. balance of payments deficit. Although some U.S. exporters were able to maintain or even increase their overseas sales through effective marketing strategies, none could significantly reduce this deficit or influence the value of the U.S. dollar. Still another example is the improved political conditions in China and the better relations between China and the United States before the pro-democracy movement was crushed in June 1989. These improvements had led to opportunities for U.S. manufacturers and exporters to enter or broaden their operational base in China, a vast and almost untapped market. No single American firm could have created the same set of opportunities.

## Economic Factors

Economic factors refer to the variables that affect the state and direction of the economy in which a firm operates. The MNC must understand the economic trends of the societies in which it operates or wishes to operate. The significance of economic factors and their impact on international business are discussed throughout this textbook. Thus, a detailed explanation of economic factors is not presented in this section. The following list includes some of the main economic factors that the MNC must consider:

1. The stage of business cycle in the country in question must be considered; that is, is the country in a period of depression, recession, economic recovery, or prosperity.
2. The inflationary or deflationary trends in price levels must be studied. In case of severe inflation, wage and price controls may be enacted.
3. The monetary policies, that is, the level of money supply and monetary stability must be understood.
4. The fiscal policies, that is, the level of government spending and taxation must be analyzed.
5. The balance of payments surplus or deficit should be studied.
6. The economic growth—the rate of change of a country's GNP—must be predicted.
7. The interest rates, the unemployment level, and the inflation rate need to be studied.
8. The possible depreciation or appreciation of the currency should be predicted.

## Political/Legal Factors

National or federal, state or provincial, and local governments directly affect how businesses operate. Governments regulate and legislate matters dealing with direct foreign investment, foreign ownership, contract laws, quotas and tariffs, wage and price controls, equal employment opportunity requirements, local employment requirements, job safety and health standards, pollution control standards, and so forth. These laws can change how businesses run on a day-to-day basis.

Government actions can increase an MNC's opportunities or constraints, sometimes at the same time. Governments can provide greater ease of operations or opportunities for more business. The following are a few examples of such government activities:

1. The demands that government makes for products and services through government contracts can create, maintain, enhance, or eliminate many market opportunities. The Russian gas pipeline to Europe provided MNCs, such as Dresser Industries, with multimillion-dollar contracts. The huge amounts of petro-dollars enabled oil-rich OPEC countries to make many purchases and grant many contracts to MNCs.

2. Host governments can subsidize and provide incentives to encourage MNCs to operate in their countries. For example, the Egyptian government initiated an open-door policy toward foreign investment in 1974, providing tax holidays of up to eight years for foreign companies starting industrial operations in Egypt.[2]

3. Home country governments can subsidize exports or provide incentives, such as low-interest loans, for exports. For example, the U.S. government provides tax incentives to exporters.

4. Changes in government policy, both at home and abroad, can lead to an increase in opportunities and in new business for firms. For example, on October 4, 1987, the United States and Canada signed an agreement that opened the 4,000-mile border to "almost free trade." It is expected that this agreement will lead to new sets of opportunities for both countries and their MNCs.

If MNCs are willing to research the political/legal environment and respond to changes, their business may increase.

Each nation has unique political/legal conditions. There are many variations of government intervention in international business. An MNC must deal with several levels of government. When entering a foreign nation, a firm may face a broad spectrum of national laws and regulations concerning international trade and foreign investment. There may be national transportation agencies, state or provincial agencies that regulate the production and distribution of the firm's products, and local or municipal harbor authorities.

Host government approval and support are vital to an MNC's success. Massey-Ferguson's operation in Turkey provides an example of the importance of this approval. The company entered into a 51 percent joint ownership venture with a local partner to produce tractors. Massey-Ferguson reportedly failed to fully assess the implications of the economic and political constraints and the government stability in Turkey. For success, the company needed strong government support, which never materialized. Consequently problems arose, and the joint venture was terminated in 1970.[3]

The legal and political aspects of international business will be discussed fully in Chapter 9.

## Sociocultural Factors

**Sociocultural factors** refer to the beliefs, values, attitudes, and lifestyles of the societies in which an MNC operates. These factors originate from the cultural, demographic, ecological, educational, ethnic, and religious conditioning of the members of a society. They are shared by the members and are passed from one generation to the next through a learning process. Therefore, sociocultural forces are dynamic. The constant change in sociocultural factors is the result of human efforts to control and to adapt to environmental conditions in order to satisfy human needs and wants.

To be effective in a foreign country, the international manager needs to understand the local culture. Knowing what to do is as important as knowing what not to do. Even the rejection of a cup of coffee while negotiating a deal with a Saudi Arabian business person may cause major problems. Understanding and managing the sociocultural factors are probably the most important tasks for an MNC and its executives to do.

Chapter 10 will present an in-depth discussion of the sociocultural context of international business.

## Technological Factors

The MNC must be aware of basic technological changes that lead to innovations in the particular industry (or industries) in which it operates. Such changes can mean the development of new raw materials and improvements in products, processes, or productivity. **Basic technology** refers to breakthroughs in technology that have profound effects throughout many industries. These include the development of lasers, computer chips, genetic engineering and farming procedures, communications networks, synthetic fibers, synthetic fuels, and robots. For example, industrial robots have revolutionized the auto industry and have greatly increased productivity. As another example, the development of synthetic fuels, along with improvements in their economic use, can bring about their use as a substitute for crude oil as a source of raw material in the electric power industry. As a third example, consider how computers have changed the space industry over the years. The use of self-repairing computers aboard the Voyager 2 space probe is only one example of the impact of computers in this area. Such sophistication makes the technology used in the spacecraft of the 1960s seem like horse and buggy technology.

The state of the art may be dynamic and change rapidly (as in the telecommunication and computer industries), or it may be stable and very slow to change (as in the manufacturing of consumer goods). Staying abreast of techno-logical change is vital for maintaining a competitive edge. A productive re-search and development (R&D) department is needed to transform basic tech-nology into **applied technology** and to develop new products and processes for the firm. Changes in technology (external or internal) influence product life cycles, production processing, and marketing strategies.

Business firms usually are able to change the nature of their applied tech-nology through in-house R&D or by purchasing the technology from other firms. However, very few businesses have the capability and the resources to engage in basic technological research. Basic technological advances usually are the result of research efforts carried out by the government, major research centers and universities, and highly innovative business firms. This is the reason for including basic technological forces in the almost uncontrollable remote environmental factors.

New product or process technologies can be protected by patents and copyrights. Such protection can give an MNC a competitive edge. For example, new drug patents enable pharmaceutical companies to enjoy profits by en-abling them to be the sole producers of a medicine over a period of many years. When such protection expires, competition from other companies may make it less profitable to produce that medicine.

In developing a new technology a firm must be careful in assessing the strengths of its competitors and in assessing the usefulness of that technology in generating revenues. For example, when the Gillette Company developed a superior stainless steel razor blade, it feared that such a superior product might mean fewer replacements and sales. Thus, the company decided not to market it. Instead, Gillette sold the technology to Wilkinson, a British garden tool manufacturer. Because Gillette thought that Wilkinson would use the tech-nology only in the production of garden tools, it did not restrict its use in the razor blade market. However, when Wilkinson Sword Blades were introduced and sold quickly, Gillette understood the magnitude of its mistake. Only supe-rior marketing skills and experience enabled Gillette to recover eventually.[4] In summary, the development, utilization, and protection of superior technology are important in providing a competitive advantage for a firm.

Technological forces and related issues unique to international operations, such as technology transfer and the utilization of proper technology, will be discussed in Chapter 11.

## Physical/Geographic Factors

No two countries have identical physical environments. The territorial size, geographic location, natural resources, climate, rivers, lakes, and forests of the country make up the physical environment of the international business. Envi-ronmental factors in any nation are affected by many physical forces, which greatly influence the sociocultural, the political, the economic, and the market-ing or distribution factors. The physical environment also shapes cultural char-acteristics, such as race and language, and it determines land use, transporta-tion, logistics, and commercial flows.

The geographic location can explain the political environment of a nation. For instance, political instability is characteristic of many countries in certain regions of the world, such as those in Central America or in the Middle East. As another example, Japan, which has communist neighbors like China and the Soviet Union and is in close proximity to the Korean Peninsula, must maintain a balanced political relationship with both the Eastern bloc and the Western nations.

Deserts, forests, lakes, mountains, plains, and rivers constitute the **topography** of a nation. Topography influences the distribution of products, separates markets, and at times necessitates adaptations of a product or its packaging. Topography also affects the climate of a country, which in turn influences the storage and transportation of products. For example, Quaker Oats uses special vacuum-sealed tins to protect its products from damage in hot and humid climates.

Population distribution is also affected by the climate and topography. In mountainous countries with plains and deserts, such as Iran or Turkey, climate variations from region to region are quite drastic. For example, during the summer season, one can find snow-covered mountains in northern Iran and temperatures of well over 100°F in the south. In those countries, population concentration tends to exist in the plains and is often close to scarce water reserves.

Inland waterways, such as the Amazon River in South America, the Nile in Africa, and the Rhine in Europe, can usually accommodate transportation and connect markets. Climate may also affect an MNC's product mix. The same firm may sell heaters in some countries, air conditioners in other locations, and central heating and cooling systems in still other areas. Production and storage costs may also be higher if the product has to withstand extreme heat or very humid conditions.

Firms with seasonal product offerings may face threats from unforeseen weather changes. For example, the lack of snow in the winter of 1978 in the United States forced ski resorts and manufacturers of snow-making and snow-removal equipment to change their market forecasts and strategies. As a result, one company diversified into lawn mowers. As another example, drought conditions, especially in LDCs, can catch food processors with inadequate supplies. Abnormal weather conditions on sea and on land can paralyze transportation, which is likely to be expensive for an MNC.

In order to assess climate conditions, some businesses employ meteorologists or use the services of climate-forecasting companies. For example, Sears and Roebuck uses in-house weather forecasters to decide on inventories for weather-sensitive merchandise, such as air conditioners, heaters, and snow tires. Oceanroutes is a company that provides climate-forecasting services. Through plotting weather and sea conditions, this company decides on the best routes for steamship lines so that time and fuel costs are minimized.

An effective MNC manager should scan the geographic environment to seek opportunities and to become aware of threats. In other words, he or she should try to determine if conditions are better elsewhere for achieving the MNC's objectives. A manager may search the environment for locations for additional outlets, or the manager may search the environment for areas in which to relocate (either in the same region or in a new region). Such changes might mean the relocation of headquarters, plants, or operational locations. Decisions concerning the addition of other countries to be served may be made. Examples include Volkswagen's business entry into North America, Northern Electric's addition of the United States to its Canadian business, or Coca Cola's entry into China.

# TASK ENVIRONMENT

As we explained earlier, the task environment refers to the forces in the immediate operating environment that confront an MNC as it attempts to attract or acquire needed resources or to strive to profitably market its products or services. A firm's competitive and industry position, its customer/market condition, and its relations with its sources of resources, that is, with its suppliers, creditors, and workers, constitute its task environment. Usually a firm, through its actions and choices, can influence, but not entirely control, the conditions in its task environment. Thus, an MNC can be much more proactive when formulating strategies and plans for its task or immediate environment than it can when dealing with its remote environment.

## Competitive and Industry Factors

An MNC's executive must examine the state of competition and the industry conditions that the firm faces in each country. This may determine whether or not the company will retain its business in a given market. It also indicates what strategies the firm needs to follow in pursuing its business. In this section we discuss the analysis of the competition and of the industry as task environment factors.*

**Industry Analysis**   The word **industry** refers to a group of firms that produce products and services that are close substitutes for each other. The firms in an industry are drawn into competitive rivalry to serve much the same needs of similar buyers. Examples of such industries are automobile, banking, shoe, steel, and textile.

For successful operation of an MNC in a competitive environment, its executives should accurately appraise and understand industry conditions globally and on a country-by-country basis. Such an analysis would accomplish the following:

1. Analyze the strategically relevant features of the industry's structure. These features include the numbers and sizes of rival firms, the market leaders and

---

*For a more extended discussion of these topics, see Michael E. Porter, "How Competitive Forces Shape Strategy," *Harvard Business Review* vol. 59, no. 2 (March/April 1979), pp. 137–45; and Michael E. Porter, *Competitive Strategy: Techniques for Analyzing Industries and Businesses* (New York: Free Press, 1980), Chaps. 1, 3, 8, 13, and App. B.

the extent of their dominance, the customers and the buying side of the market (to be discussed later), the channels of distribution, the extent of vertical integration in the industry, the ease of entry into and exit from the industry, the size and geographical boundaries of the industry, and other characteristics peculiar to the industry.

**2.** Analyze the direction in which the industry is moving and the factors behind the industry evolution. The stages of the product (or service) life cycle, as discussed in Chapter 2, lead to fundamental changes in an industry. Important changes in the industry structure influence long-term investment opportunities and necessitate strategic adjustments by an MNC. Many of the broad environmental factors influence the evolution of industries.

**3.** Analyze the underlying economic characteristics of the industry. These characteristics include capital requirements, cost structure, economies of scale, normal profit margins, internal cash flow, pricing practices, price-cost structures under various capacity utilization levels, break-even conditions, and so forth. Such revenue-cost-profit considerations establish constraints upon the ability of an MNC to operate in a given industry.

**Competitive Analysis**  There are three factors that need to be examined about competition: the entry and exit of major competitors, the availability of substitutes and complements for current products and services, and the major strategic changes by current competitors.[5]

**1.** Analyze the entry and exit of major competitors in the industry. An MNC should ask these questions regarding competition: How has the competition changed? Are there new competitors entering the market? Are old ones leaving? For instance, the economic impact of competition from the low-cost, more efficient steel producers from Korea and Japan on U.S. steel manufacturers is an example of competition from new entrants to the market. Potential competition can come from those firms that can overcome entry barriers inexpensively, companies that can gain from the synergy upon entering the industry, firms whose competition in the industry can be an extension of their current strategy, and firms that can integrate forward or backward if they enter the industry. Mergers and acquisitions may introduce stronger competitors in an industry. For instance, many industry analysts believe that the surge in mergers and acquisitions in the U.S. airline industry will lead to the formation of about eight strong mega-airlines in the United States.

**2.** Analyze the availability of substitutes. The availability of quality and less costly substitute products and services affects the profitability and success of the firm in the markets in which it operates. For example, the construction of a new dam and the electric power that it generates can reduce the demand for fuel used in power plants. This can negatively affect MNCs involved in the oil business in a given country. On the positive side, a ban on artificial sweeteners, such as saccharin, will increase the demand for an MNC's sugar products.

**3.** Analyze the major strategic changes of current competitors. A strategic shift by major competitors is probably the most important factor to be studied by an

MNC manager. For example, the introduction of an unconditional 2,500-hour or a 2-year guarantee under normal use for its light bulb by Westinghouse caused major concern for GE and other competitors. Aggressive competition from IBM, Savin, SCM, Kodak, and other copier manufacturers necessitated reaction by Xerox, a company that once had such a dominant competitive position in this business that it could ignore the competition altogether.

Figure 8.3 presents a framework for competitor analysis. Analyzing a competitor based on this model leads to the development of a *competitor's response profile*. The first component of the model includes a diagnosis of each competi-

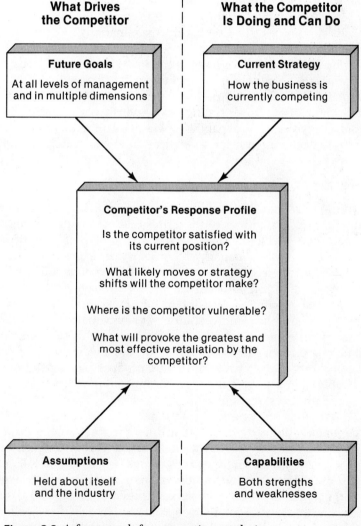

**Figure 8.3** A framework for competitor analysis

tor's *future goals.* This will enable an MNC's executives to understand the driving force behind its competitor's future course of action.

The second component involves an examination of a competitor's *assumptions* regarding itself, the industry, and the other companies in the industry. This will identify biases or blind spots that may creep into a competitor's perception of its environment. These spots are areas that a competitor will ignore completely (such as a strategic move), will perceive incorrectly, or will recognize slowly. Knowing these blind spots will help a firm to choose moves that have less chance of causing immediate retaliation by its competitors. Knowing these blind spots will also help to find moves for which reaction, when it comes, is not effective.

The third key component of a competitor's profile includes statements of the *current strategy* of the competitor. Such strategy always exists and must be identified. This process requires careful examination of a competitor's activities and behaviors.

The final component of a competitor analysis deals with a realistic appraisal of the *competitor's capabilities,* including the competitor's strengths, weaknesses, and resources. A competitor's goals, assumptions, and current strategy will determine the nature, timing, and intensity of its probable actions and reactions. A competitor's capabilities will determine its ability to move or respond strategically in reaction to environmental or industry events.

## Customer/Market Factors

Perhaps the most valuable result of conducting a task environmental analysis is gaining an understanding of the firm's customers and learning their needs and wants. The development of a customer profile of present and potential buyers enables an MNC manager to anticipate changes in the size of the market, to allocate resources, to respond to the forecasted shifts in consumer demand patterns, and to plan the strategic operations of the firm.

A **customer profile** should contain information on the geographic, demographic, psychographic, and consumer behavior patterns of the buyers. The first component of a customer profile is **geographic factors**. The importance of geographic boundaries in international business was discussed earlier. As our discussion showed, the attraction that a product has for the buyer can vary considerably due to geography. For example, air conditioners do not sell well where temperatures average 70°F or below.

As the second component of a customer profile, **demographic factors** are the most commonly utilized variables for differentiating among customer groups. These variables are descriptive characteristics through which customer segments can be identified, and they include age, sex, family size, lifestyle, income, marital status, occupation, education, religion, race or ethnic background, social class, and nationality. Data on these variables are reasonably easy to collect, to quantify, and to forecast in advanced nations. In LDCs the collection of such data may prove to be quite difficult. In addition, whatever data are available in these countries may not be very accurate.

Among other demographic factors are the **primary demand factors,** which are associated with the general population in a given country. The following primary demand factors are the most important:

**1.** Population growth rate and shift. The number of people in a market can greatly influence the demand for products and services. Larger populations may mean larger numbers of potential buyers. The population in many LDCs is growing, leading to new opportunities for MNCs. Shifts in population also affect the concentration of marketing efforts. In advanced countries, population concentrations are shifting from city centers to the suburbs. The development of new shopping centers and malls in suburban areas is a response to this shift. In many LDCs, the migration of people from rural to urban areas means an expansion of the more readily accessible markets in the cities.

**2.** Age shift. Shifts in the age distribution change primarily demand for product and services. As birthrates decline and health care improves, there will be more older people and fewer babies in the market. This may mean that the demand for products and services targeted for the elderly will increase, whereas those for babies will decline. For example, in order to deal with a declining infant population in the 1970s, Johnson & Johnson started advertising the use of its baby shampoo for adults. As a second example, in order to deal with age shift, soft drink companies target their commercials toward different age groups.

**3.** Income distribution. The distribution of wealth and income in a country has a profound effect on the purchasing capabilities of its population. In some nations, a minority group (based on social status, race, political ties, and so forth) commands a major share of the wealth and income. This is true in many LDCs. As a result, a large portion of the population is incapable of purchasing many products or services.

The third component of a customer profile is **psychographic factors.** A psychographic examination is the measurement of the personality and lifestyle of present and prospective buyers. It is an important component of a customer profile. Some of the variables that are used in psychographic examination include the physical activity, the compulsiveness, the conservatism, the authoritarianism, the leadership orientation, and the ambition of the buyers.

Finally, data regarding **consumer behavior** should be collected to complete the customer profile. This information includes (but is not limited to) the usage rates, the benefit expectancies, the product awarenesses, the end uses, the brand loyalties, and the sensitivities to marketing factors (price, quality, service, advertising, sales promotion) of customers.*

## Sources of Resources: Suppliers, Creditors, and Labor Factors

An MNC relies on its suppliers, creditors, and the labor market for essential financial services, raw materials, equipment, labor, and other services on a regular basis. Dependable relationships between a firm and the sources of its

---

*For a more comprehensive discussion, the reader is referred to Philip Kotler, *Marketing Management: Analysis of Planning and Control,* 6th ed. (Englewood Cliffs, N.J.: Prentice-Hall, 1988).

resources are necessary for smooth operations and long-term survival. Good relationships are vital—especially when a firm must make special requests. These requests may be for favorable prices or credit terms, faster deliveries, smaller or larger than usual order quantities. The MNC should assess the strength of these relationships.

A successful firm needs to attract and retain capable employees. The nature of the labor component of the task environment heavily influences the personnel policies (recruitment, selection, promotion, and so forth) of a business. Several factors affect the MNC's access to the needed human resources. The most important of these include the host country's policies regarding the employment of natives and nonnatives, the local employment rates, the ready availability of needed knowledge and skills, the local wage levels, and the reputation of the business as an employer. The management of human resources will be discussed in Chapter 15.

In addition to the immediate relationships with suppliers, creditors, and labor sources, and the bargaining power with sources over the cost and availability of resources, an MNC executive must examine the long-term trends regarding their availability and cost. An MNC's manager should assess the long-term cost and availability of raw materials, subassemblies, energy, money, and labor.

In summary, an MNC needs to face a broad set of environmental factors. The environment of an MNC consists of two sets of factors: those in the remote environment and those in the task or immediate environment. The remote environment includes economic, political/legal, sociocultural, technological, and physical/geographic factors. The task environment consists of competitive/industry, customer/market, and sources of resources—suppliers, creditors, and labor. An MNC has to face these remote and task factors both at home—the domestic environment—and in foreign nations—the foreign environments. In addition, unlike a domestic firm, an MNC faces a set of diverse economic, legal, and political forces that shape its international environment. Environmental factors can lead to positive conditions—opportunities—or to negative constraints—threats—to an MNC. The survival and success of an MNC depend on how it relates to the largely uncontrollable factors that shape its environment.

## DOMESTIC ENVIRONMENT MODEL

Figure 8.4 shows the business relationships that exist when a firm operates only in its home (domestic) environment. The firm sends into this environment a stream of goods and services, information, pollution, wages, salaries, taxes, and so forth. Meanwhile, all firms are influenced by constraints in their remote and task environments. For domestic firms, some of these environmental conditions are constants (such as the currency and the language) and require little if any attention.

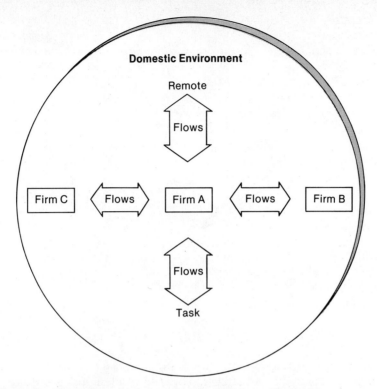

Flows: Goods, services, funds, people, information, and technology.

Remote: Economic, political/legal, sociocultural, technological, and physical/geographic.

Task: Competitor/industry, customer/market, supplier, creditor, and labor.

**Figure 8.4** Domestic environment model

*Source:* Adapted from Christopher Korth, INTERNATIONAL BUSINESS, 2nd ed., © 1985, p. 14. Reprinted by permission of Prentice-Hall, Inc., Englewood Cliffs, NJ.

## INTERNATIONAL ENVIRONMENT MODEL

Figure 8.5 depicts a basic model of international business operations. Firms A and B, located in two different countries, engage in some form of business interchange. The crossing of national borders complicates the picture. The terms of interchange are governed by international institutions and agreements. The interchange may be enhanced by the existence of trade incentives or curtailed by the enactment of trade barriers between the nation-states. Unlike the interchange between two domestic firms, the existence of trade barriers or incentives may not be based on purely economic rationality.

Even the local elements of the environment become more complex as

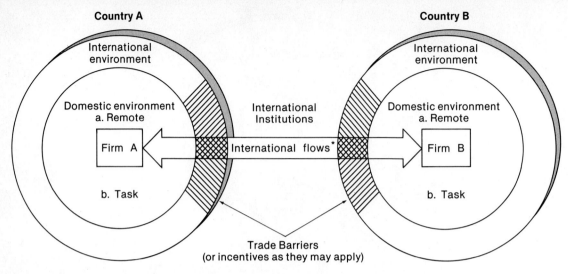

\* International flows include goods, services, funds, people, information, and technology.

**Figure 8.5** International environment model

particular international environmental forces confront the firms in addition to the interchange process itself. These local elements are quite different from those faced by the domestic firm and include international organizations (that may govern, aid, or hinder international activities), international laws and systems, foreign currencies, and so forth.

When a firm's involvement overseas progresses far enough to become truly multinational, it is not only affected by the host countries in which it operates, but the MNC may also affect those host countries in turn.

## SOURCES OF INTERNATIONAL BUSINESS INFORMATION

The box on page 219 presents a list of sources that may be used in gathering information regarding environmental forces with which an MNC must deal. If a company can afford the resources (time, expense, and psychological commitment), it should independently gather primary data on the specific market in which it operates or plans to enter. In other cases, a firm may use secondary (published) sources of data or commission another firm to conduct its market research. The box on page 219 provides a list of sources from which published information is available. In addition, the appendix at the end of this chapter provides a bibliographical list of selected sources of international business data.

# Sources of International Business Information

**U.S. Government**

Industry trade lists

World traders data reports

*Commerce Business Daily*

*Marketing Handbook*

Overseas business reports (by countries)

U.S. Trade Center reports

*Foreign Commerce Handbook*

*Export Statistics Profile*

Market share reports

Global market surveys

Foreign economic trends

Foreign trade statistics

Foreign market reports

U.S. embassies

**International Organizations**

United Nations' *Statistical Yearbook*

Organization for Economic Cooperation and Development

Pan American Union

European Community

International Monetary Fund

Andean Pact

*The World Book*

Pan-Arab Research Center

**Foreign Governments/Private Agencies**

Government censuses and statistical services

Chamber of Commerce

Industry trade associations

Consultants

Consulates in the United States

Universities

Research centers/institutes

Japanese External Trade Organization (JETRO)

**Standard Reference Sources/Services**
Business International: weekly news service

*Business America*

*Investing Licensing & Trading Conditions Abroad*

*Financing Foreign Operations*

CIS

*Statistical Reference Index*

*Europe Yearbook*

*Exporters' Encyclopedia*

*International Financial Statistics Yearbook*

Predicasts

*World-Product-Casts*

*World-Regional-Casts*

*Statesman's Yearbook*

World Bank

*World Tables*

*World Development Report*

**Trade, Business, and Service Organizations**

**International and foreign marketing research agencies**

**Trade associations**

**Service companies, e.g., international banks, customs services**

## ENVIRONMENTAL ASSESSMENT

This chapter has described the MNC as being influenced by three environments: domestic, foreign, and international. The domestic and foreign environments consist of remote and task factors. The international environment includes forces acting for and against trade or foreign direct investment across national borders. These factors and forces and their components are not easily identifiable or mutually exclusive. They do not influence all situations. In fact, the environment of international business is so turbulent, and these factors and forces are so dynamic and interactive that the influence of any single element cannot be totally disassociated from the impact of other elements. A multinational executive can be frustrated in attempting to monitor and to anticipate the changing influences of the environment. Different external factors affect different strategies at different times with varying impacts.

By monitoring and forecasting these environmental factors, MNCs and their executives can find opportunities and threats and determine their nature, their relationships, and their impacts. The uncertainty and ambiguity associated with these external forces and their influence on the firm should not prevent the effective executive from searching for the realities of the environment. Resourcefulness and psychological commitment to environmental analysis are necessary ingredients in the development of a proactive and effective global strategy. The development of such a strategy will be discussed in Chapters 13 and 14.

We conclude this chapter by stating that MNCs must respond to the environments of nations in which they operate. MNCs should not attempt to determine these environments. Indeed, most environmental factors are decided and shaped by the home and the host countries and the international conditions, rather than by an MNC. The complexity and scope of international business suggest that environmental analysis must be far-reaching indeed. While overseas political risk for MNCs may be greater in LDCs, greater volatility is sometimes found in advanced nations and may be more significant. Sudden changes in trade restrictions or currency exchange rates, or politically motivated embargoes, and so forth, can be as damaging to an MNC as coups d'etat or revolts. Because the stakes may be higher in advanced nations, the ultimate losses may be greater if trouble arises. Effective multinational managers should examine the opportunities and the threats throughout the world.

## SUMMARY

1. An MNC's survival and success depend on how it relates to a host of uncontrollable external factors constituting its environment. The complexity and scope of these environmental factors suggest that they should be carefully and extensively analyzed.

2. In general, the environmental forces can be divided into two interrelated sets of

factors, those in the remote environment and those in the task or immediate environment.

3. The remote environment consists of factors which originate beyond the control of any single firm. They include economic, political/legal, sociocultural, technological, and physical/geographic factors. These factors present opportunities, threats, and constraints for the MNC, with the organization rarely possessing the strength to exert any meaningful reciprocal influence over these elements.

4. The task environment refers to the factors in the immediate competitive situation, which confront an MNC with many challenges when it attempts to attract needed resources or to strive to profitably market its products or services. These factors are competitive and industry, customer and market, supplier, creditor, and labor sources. An MNC has some reciprocal impact on these factors.

5. Unlike a purely domestic firm, which faces the environment in one reasonably familiar nation, an MNC deals with domestic, foreign, and international environments. The domestic environment consists of all the remote and task elements based in the home country. Foreign environments refer to the remote and task elements that exist in the host (foreign) countries. The international environment consists of organizations and systems overseeing international business transactions. The forces in these three environments influence the MNC and its executives.

6. Economic factors refer to the condition and the direction of the economy.

7. Political/legal factors refer to the forces that regulate and legislate the way businesses are run.

8. Sociocultural factors relate to the beliefs, values, attitudes, and lifestyles of the societies in which the multinational company operates.

9. Technological changes lead to innovations (of products, of materials, of processes, and in productivity) in a particular industry.

10. Territorial size, geographic location, natural resources, climate, topography, rivers, lakes, and forests form the physical/geographic component of the remote environment.

11. An industry is defined as a group of firms with similar products and services competing for the same customers. An effective industry analysis should include an examination of the strategic features of its structure, its future direction, and the underlying economic characteristics of the industry.

12. Analysis of the competition should examine the following: the entry and exit of major competitors; the substitutes and complements for current products and services; and the major strategic changes by current competitors.

13. A customer profile should be developed to highlight their needs and wants. This profile should contain geographic, demographic, psychographic, and consumer behavior information about present and prospective buyers. Primary market (demand) information, such as population growth and shift data, age shift data, and income distribution data should also be gathered.

14. The MNC should examine the strength of its relationship with its sources of resources—suppliers, creditors, and labor. The international executive should also assess the long-term trends in the availability and cost of raw materials, subassemblies, energy, money, and labor.

15. Environmental assessment is the process of monitoring, examining, and anticipating the changing influences of the turbulent environment that an MNC faces. An MNC must respond to the environments of the nations in which it operates. The complexity and scope of international business suggest that environmental analysis must be far-reaching indeed.

## QUESTIONS

8.1 What is meant by environment of international business? How does this environment affect the success and ultimate survival of an MNC? Discuss.

8.2 Briefly discuss the two sets of environmental factors and the components of each factor.

8.3 Outline and discuss a number of economic forces that influence an MNC more strongly than they do a domestic firm.

8.4 Choose a factor of the remote environment and fully explain its impact on the MNC.

8.5 Why is it as important to know what not to do as it is to know what to do when you are conducting business with people of a different culture?

8.6 Discuss the impact of physical and geographic factors on international marketing.

8.7 How does analysis of the competition and the industry fit into the picture for formulating an MNC's global strategy?

8.8 What is the difference between the environment of a purely domestic business and a truly multinational firm?

8.9 What are the most important environmental issues that an MNC should concentrate on?

8.10 Choose an MNC with which you are familiar. Conduct an environmental assessment for this company. Explain your rationale for your assessment in terms of the key environmental conditions and your evaluation of those conditions.

## APPENDIX 8.1: Selected Sources of International Business Data

Business International Corporation. *Master Key Index.* Quarterly. New York: Business International Corporation.

*Business International.* New York: Business International Corporation.

*Business Latin America.* New York: Business International Corporation.

*Business Europe.* New York: Business International Corporation.

*Business Asia.* Hong Kong: Business International Asia/Pacific.

*B. I. Money Report.* New York: Business International Corporation.

*Eastern Europe Report.* Geneva: Business International, S.A.

Business International. *Research Reports* (periodic country and functional studies). New York: Business International Corporation.

Business International. Updated reference services (for doing business):

*Financing Foreign Operations.* New York: Business International Corporation.

*Investing, Licensing, and Trade Conditions Abroad.* New York: Business International Corporation.

Commission of the European Communities. *List of Periodicals* (Irregular). Luxembourg: Commission of the European Communities Library.

Commission of the European Communities. *Systematic Catalogue of Books* (Irregular). Luxembourg: Commission of the European Communities Library.

*Computer-Readable Data Bases: A Directory and Data Sourcebook.* 2 vols. White Plains, N.Y.: American Society for Information Sciences, 1985.

Conference Board. *Cumulative Index* (Annual). New York: The Conference Board.

Delphos, William A. *Washington's Best-Kept Secrets: A U.S. Government Guide to International Business.* New York: Wiley, 1983.

*Demographic Yearbook* (Annual). New York: United Nations Statistical Office.

*Directory of United Nations Databases and Information.* New York: United Nations, 1985.

*Encyclopedia of Geographic Information Sources,* 3rd ed., Detroit: Gale Research, 1978.

*Encyclopedia of the Third World.* New York: Facts on File.

Ernst & Ernst. *International Business Series* (Irregular). New York: Ernst & Ernst.

*Export Today* (Bimonthly). Washington, D.C.: SIRCo International.

*Euromoney* (Monthly). London: Euromoney Publications.

*F & S International* and *F & S Europe* (Annual). Cleveland: Predicasts.

*Financial Times International Business Yearbook* (Annual). London: Financial Times Yearbook.

*Foreign Economic Trends and Their Implications for the U.S.* Washington, D.C.: U.S. Department of Commerce.

Gallatin Publications. *Gallatin Business Intelligence* and *The Gallatin Letter.* New York: Gallatin International Business Service, Coply International.

Hoopes, David S., ed. *Global Guide to International Business.* New York: Facts on File, 1983.

*Index to International Business Publications* (Irregular). Washington, D.C.: U.S. Department of Commerce.

*InfoNational InfoTrade Report: International Business Insights and Opportunities* (Bimonthly). Dallas, Tex.: InfoNational.

*InfoTrade Data Services: InfoSearch and InfoTrade Online.* Customized Data Services. Dallas, Tex.: InfoNational.

*International Bibliography: Information Documentation* (Quarterly). New York: Bowker & Unipub.

*International Bibliography of Economics* (Annual). London and New York: Tavistock.

*International Executive* (triannual). Hastings-on-Hudson, N.Y.: The International Executive.

*International Financial Statistics Yearbook.* Washington, D.C.: International Monetary Fund.

*International Marketing Data and Statistics,* 9th ed., Detroit: Gale Research, 1984.

International Monetary Fund. *Balance of Payments Yearbook* (Annual). Washington, D.C.: International Monetary Fund.

International Monetary Fund. *Direction of Trade* (Monthly). Washington, D.C.: International Monetary Fund.

International Monetary Fund. *International Trade Statistics* (Monthly). Washington, D.C.: International Monetary Fund.

*International Trade Reporter: Export Shipping Manual.* Washington, D.C.: Bureau of National Affairs.

*International Yearbook and Statesmen's Who's Who* (Annual). Kingston, England: Kelly's Directories.

Kruzas, Anthony. *Encyclopedia of Information Systems and Services,* 4th ed. Detroit: Gale Research, 1981.

*Management Administration and Productivity: International Directory of Institutions and Information Sources.* Washington, D.C.: International Labor Office, 1981.

MeKeirle, Joseph O., ed. *Multinational Corporations: The E.C.S.I.M. Guide to Information Sources.* Brussels, Belgium: European Center for Study of Information on Multinational Corporations, 1977.

*OECD Catalogue of Publications* (Biennial with supplements). Paris: OECD.

*OECD Economic Surveys* (Annual). Paris: OECD.

*OECD Financial Statistics* (Annual with supplements). Paris: OECD.

*Overseas Business Reports* (Irregular). Washington, D.C.: U.S. Department of Commerce.

*Political Risk in Thirty-Five Countries.* London: Euromoney, 1984.

Public Affairs Information Service. *Bulletin* (Weekly). New York: H. W. Wilson.

*Statesman's Yearbook, The* (Annual). New York: Macmillan, St. Martin's Press.

*Statistical Yearbook.* New York: Statistical Office of United Nations.

*Survey of Research on Transnational Corporations.* New York: United Nations Centre on Transnational Corporations.

*Ulrichs International Periodicals Directory, Vol. I & II.* New York: Bowker.

*UNDEX: United Nations Documents Index* (ten per year). New York: United Nations.

*UN Statistical Yearbook* (Annual). New York: United Nations.

*U.N.E.S.C.O. Statistical Yearbook* (Annual). Paris: United Nations Educational, Scientific, and Cultural Organization.

*User's Guide to the Information System on Transnational Corporations.* New York: United Nations, 1980.

U.S. Bureau of the Census. *U.S. Exports.* Washington, D.C.: U.S. Government Printing Office.

U.S. Bureau of the Census. *U.S. General Imports.* Washington, D.C.: U.S. Government Printing Office.

U.S. Department of Commerce. *Business America: The Magazine of International Trade.* Washington, D.C.: U.S. Department of Commerce, International Trade Administration.

U.S. Department of State. *Background Notes.* Washington, D.C.: U.S. Department of State.

*World Trade Annual.* New York: Walker.

*Yearbook of Industrial Statistics* (Annual). New York: United Nations.

*Yearbook of International Trade Statistics* (Annual). New York: Statistical Office of the United Nations.

*Yearbook of National Accounts Statistics.* New York: United Nations.

## NOTES

1. "Prospects of Profits: Egypt," *Business International,* 14 July 1986, p. 222.
2. *Fortune,* October 1987, pp. 137–138.
3. David A. Ricks, *Big Business Blunders: Mistakes in Multinational Marketing* (Homewood, Ill.: Dow Jones–Irwin, 1983), p. 121.
4. Ibid., pp. 123–124.
5. W. F. Glueck and L. R. Jauch, *Business Policy and Strategic Management,* 4th ed. (New York: McGraw-Hill, 1984), pp. 94–153.

## SUGGESTED READINGS

Jauch, L. R., and W. F. Glueck. *Business Policy and Strategic Management,* 5th ed. New York: McGraw-Hill, 1988. Chap. 3.

Kolde, E. J. *Environment of International Business,* 2nd ed. Boston: Kent, 1985. Chap. 1.

Pearce, J. A. II, and R. B. Robinson, Jr. *Strategic Management: Strategy Formulation and Implementation,* 4th ed. Homewood, Ill.: 1988. Chap. 4.

Porter, M. E. "How Competitive Forces Shape Strategy." *Harvard Business Review,* vol. 59, no. 2 (March/April 1979), pp. 137–145.

———. *Competitive Strategy: Techniques for Analyzing Industries and Competitors.* New York: Free Press, 1980. Chaps. 1, 3, 8, 13, and Appendix B.

———. *Competitive Advantage: Creating and Sustaining Performance.* New York: Free Press, 1985. Chaps. 1, 9.

Ricks, D. A. *Big Business Blunders: Mistakes in Multinational Marketing.* Homewood, Ill.: Dow Jones–Irwin, 1983.

Ronen, S. *Comparative and Multinational Management.* New York: Wiley, 1986. Chap. 9, pp. 345–392.

Terpstra, V., and K. David. *The Cultural Environment of International,* 2nd ed. Cincinnati: South-Western Publishing, 1985.

———. *International Dimensions of Marketing,* 2nd ed. Boston, Mass.: Kent, 1985. Chap. 2.

Thompson, A. A., Jr., and A. J. Strickland III. *Strategic Management: Concepts and Cases,* 4th ed. Plano, Tex.: Business Publications, 1987. Chap. 4.

# Chapter 9

# The Legal and Political Aspects of International Business

*T*he **legal and political aspects of international business** refer to those conditions that govern international business activities and the settlement of trade disputes among MNCs, host nations, and other interested parties.

There is no single international legal and political system. The legal and political environment of international business consists of the laws, the political ideologies, and the judicial systems (the courts) of the individual countries and also a limited number of regional and international laws, treaties, and institutions. The MNC is faced with at least as many legal and political environments as the number of nations in which it operates. In addition to the national legal and political systems and philosophies, each nation maintains its own independent court system. In the absence of an international legal system, there are certain agreements, treaties, and codes among most nations that cover limited areas of international business operations.

The purpose of this chapter is to provide a broad understanding of the legal and political aspects of international business. First, we define and discuss the concept of law. Second, we elaborate on variations that exist among legal systems. Third, we explain the relationship between the home and the host countries' legal and political systems. Fourth, we discuss the concept of international law. Fifth, we cover guidelines for negotiations, contracts, and dispute resolution. Sixth, we elaborate on the variations in political systems. Finally, we define the concept of legal and political risk and discuss its forecasting.

## IMPLICATIONS FOR THE MNC

The problem of settling private trade disputes, though not unique to the international business field, is especially magnified by increased government interference, the existence of different laws, and the question of jurisdiction in an international setting. International business trade disputes are more difficult to avoid than domestic ones because they involve both foreign and domestic laws and practices. There is a greater likelihood of miscommunication and misinterpretation of foreign and international laws than domestic laws. In addition, the problem may be compounded by the political instability and changes within the countries where an MNC operates.

When a dispute occurs in international transactions, the settlement, the arbitration, and the litigation are complicated not only by the distance between parties, but also by the differing trade customs and laws. Another problem is deciding which laws will apply and which courts have **jurisdiction** over the dispute. Should the home country, the host country, or the international laws and judicial systems decide the case? By definition, the MNC's operation extends beyond national borders and thus beyond the jurisdiction of individual nations. This results in much confusion, uncertainty, and conflict as to the applicability of different laws to an MNC. This complicates the formulation of global strategies in general, and legal strategies in particular.

Home countries are frustrated when they try to extend their control and regulate their MNCs' overseas activities. Host countries fear that MNCs can and do (at times) break with impunity their national regulations and laws.

The field of international law and politics is complex and fascinating. However, a complete coverage is far beyond the scope of this chapter. Here we will explore some pressing legal and political issues the MNC faces.

## LAWS

**Laws** are rules established by authority, custom, or social agreement. Such rules govern the behavior and relationship among the people in a society. The laws of a society are a reflection of its attitudes, culture, religion, and traditions. As a result, each country's legal system differs somewhat from that of every other nation. In addition to written formal laws, some laws are indigenous or unwritten. In some countries, the legal system is dominated by unwritten law, such as tribal law.

Laws represent the expression of the political will of a nation, and therefore the political and legal systems of a country are closely related.

## Variations in National Legal Systems

As noted earlier, the laws of a nation reflect its culture. Because culture differs among nations, many national legal systems exist. Commercial and noncommercial laws, therefore, are rarely the same between any two nations. As an MNC executive, you need to be aware of the differences between the laws of your native country and those of the nations to which you are assigned. In this section we will discuss five major legal systems that exist in the world today. These are common law, civil or code law, religious law, communist law, indigenous (tribal, unwritten) law.

Few nations have a truly pure legal system. Most national laws have evolved from a mixture of many legal systems. A nation's legal system reflects the cultural borrowing of law through contact with other cultures, the historical and colonial background, the religious and moral norms, the economic and political philosophy, and the tribal and ethnic traditions.

**Common Law**   Also known as community law, common law originated after the domination of England by the Normans in A.D. 1066. Common law was based on unwritten principles and precedents set by customs, usages, and previous rulings. Recently commercial law has been recognized as a special area of the common law system. Commercial law, like all other common laws, is based on long-standing customs as well as on court decisions. Property rights are based on ownership established by usage.

Today, more than 25 countries follow a common law system. This includes countries that have been associated with the British legal philosophy. In addition to the United Kingdom, Canada and the United States are examples of countries governed by this system.

**Civil or Code Law**   In this legal system, the laws are grouped into civil, commercial, and criminal laws. Each part of the judicial system has its own administrative structure and set of laws. Each group of laws is a compilation of identical laws, or similar subject matter laws that form a code. Civil law originated from the influence of the old Roman law and later from the Napoleonic code. Today, over 70 countries in the Western world follow this legal system. France is an example of a country that is governed by civil or code law.

**Religious Law**   A few of the world's countries follow religious law. For example, Saudi Arabia follows a strict Moslem legal and political system. As will be explained in Chapter 10, Moslem law is based on the teachings of the Koran (the Moslem holy book) and Sharia (Islamic law), as interpreted by religious leaders. Laws not defined by the historical sources of the Shari'a are left to decisions, according to government regulations and by Islamic judges. Islamic commercial law is not drastically different from other legal systems. One of the major differences is the prohibition of usury—the giving and receiving of interest on borrowed money. This prohibition influences banking and financing practices.

Few countries follow a purely religious law. Nevertheless, religious influence is apparent in many legal systems. For instance, Judeo-Christian principles have had a major influence on the legal systems in the Western world. Today, the legal systems of over 30 nations are dominated by religious law.

**Communist Law**  The Eastern bloc countries follow communist law. As was discussed in Chapter 3, Karl Marx was the father of communist ideology. According to Marx, communism was the final stage of historical development and in the end would result in a classless society. Modern communism is quite different from this ideal and pure classless society. Communism in its present format cannot even be considered as a transitory stage toward Marx's final stage of history.

Communist systems vary from the bureaucratic collectivism of the Soviet Union to the more free-enterprise supplemented system of communism in Yugoslavia. Marxist-Leninist ideology is subscribed to in differing degrees by communist countries. Marxism-Leninism provides an ideological guideline for various economic systems, legal and political philosophies, and institutions. Private MNCs from noncommunist countries are barred from establishing production plants in communist countries. However, MNCs can still do business with many of these countries through state agencies.

In a communist system the basic economic decisions regarding "what," "how much," "for whom," and "when" to produce are made by a central planning body. Allocation of resources among different industries is made according to state-formulated plans. Factors of production such as land, capital, and plants are owned by the state, and prices are established by the government as well.

These state economic plans are usually formulated annually and for five years in advance. Foreign trade is conducted within these plans, and it should, therefore, conform to the plans' objectives and priorities. The amount of foreign exchange available for foreign trade is based on these plans. In addition to this limiting factor, the state has a foreign trade monopoly. Most or all of the foreign trade is carried out by specialized state agencies. Each agency is responsible for all the exports and imports of certain goods. This system provides tremendous resources at each trading agency's disposal, and it gives them a strong bargaining power in dealing with MNCs. National central banks and specialized foreign trade banks finance foreign trade. Commercial law is based on state ownership and control, and thus it is restrictive and prohibitive for the MNCs trading with communist nations. Today, more than a dozen countries follow some form of communist law. A country that is governed by communist law is the Soviet Union.

It should be pointed out that a dual structure exists in all the societies that utilize the Marxist-Leninist system. In these systems the government structure is duplicated by a corresponding party structure. In order to do business in one of these countries it is necessary to work with not only the relevant ministry or company, but the party organization as well. Another interesting point is the use of terminology. None of the systems refer to themselves as communist. They are all, as they admit, still at the stage of socialism. Former Premier Nikita Khrushchev contended that the Soviet Union had reached the stage of advanced socialism. But this statement has been downplayed in the last few years because he also had said the Soviet Union would achieve communism by the early 1980s. The distinction between communist law and other laws may be seen by examining excerpts of the Soviet constitution.[1]

**Indigenous Law**   Indigenous law includes tribal and unwritten laws. There are no countries with pure indigenous law. However, tribal law is mixed with other legal systems in about 30 nations.

Table 9.1 provides a breakdown of nations based on the five legal systems described here.

Table 9.1   NATIONAL LEGAL SYSTEMS IN THE WORLD

| | |
|---|---|
| Civil law systems | |
| Pure civil law countries | 32 |
| Mixed civil law countries | 39 |
| Total countries with civil law characteristics | 71 |
| Common law systems | |
| Pure common law countries | 7 |
| Mixed common law countries | 19 |
| Total countries with common law characteristics | 26 |
| Moslem law systems | |
| Pure Moslem law countries | 2 |
| Mixed Moslem law countries | 28 |
| Total countries with Moslem law characteristics | 30 |
| Communist law Countries | 12 |
| Indigenous law systems (tribal, unwritten law) | |
| Pure indigenous law countries | 0 |
| Mixed indigenous law countries | 30 |
| Total countries with indigenous law characteristics | 30 |

*Source:* Adapted from: Arthur S. Banks and Robert B. Textor, *A Cross-Polity Survey* (Cambridge, Mass.: Massachusetts Institute of Technology Press, 1963), pp. 115–117.

## THE LEGAL AND POLITICAL ENVIRONMENT

The legal and political environment of international business consists of the home country laws and political system (for example, the U.S. laws and political system for a U.S.–based MNC), the host country laws and political systems (that is, the laws and political conditions of nations in which an MNC operates overseas), and the international law and political climate (that is, the collection of agreements, treaties, and conventions between two or more nations). The legal and political factors are a part of the remote environment, which we discussed in Chapter 8.

### Home Country's Legal and Political System

A major element of the legal and political environment of international business is the law and political conditions of the home country. This means the MNC is affected by a large number of domestic laws. For example, Control Data Corporation (CDC), based within the U.S. legal and political framework, was denied a license to export a Cyber 76 Computer to Russia in 1977. This limited CDC's operations internationally. Another example is the U.S. ban in 1986 on the operations of U.S. MNCs in Libya, because of political tensions between the two countries.

As we discussed in earlier chapters, most MNCs start as domestic firms. This means that the international headquarters which normally has the largest concentration of the MNC's assets, usually remains in the home country. As a result, the home country government has the greatest control over the multinational company. The home country government's control may originate from the following three sources:

**1.** The headquarters of the multinational are under its legal jurisdiction. Being incorporated in the home country, the home government can take legal actions affecting the entire MNC. Through its conduct and its regulations, the home nation can change financial flows, alter patterns of trade, control technology transfer, establish the competitive structure of the industry, change the patterns of intracompany pricing and relationships, and restrict the movement of people.

**2.** The MNC's top executives are usually citizens of the home country. As a result, there are generally close relationships and contacts among the MNC's top executives and the home country's government officials. All are usually from the same sociocultural background and members of the same "establishment." They easily move back and forth between the public sector and private industry.

**3.** The greatest concentration of assets and the headquarters of the MNC are usually located in the home country, but the subsidiaries of the MNC are incorporated in host countries and are subject to their laws.[2]

When the home country government tries to control the parent company as well as its overseas subsidiaries, conflict may arise. As a result, the MNC may end up in the middle of a conflict. On one hand, the home country government attempts to extend its control to the MNC's foreign subsidiaries. On the other hand, the host nation, based on its territorial authority, wishes to regulate and control the subsidiary located within its borders. For example, when the Russians invaded Afghanistan in 1979, the U.S. government attempted to put political and economic pressure on the Soviet government to show its displeasure with the invasion. The Carter administration banned trade with the Soviet Union. In addition, the U.S. government sought cooperation from its European allies; the allies refused. In accordance with this ban, the U.S. government ordered U.S.–based MNCs and their overseas subsidiaries to comply. U.S. MNCs found themselves in the middle of an international conflict. Dresser Industries, the U.S. manufacturer of oil and gas-drilling equipment, along with its subsidiaries in Europe, was faced with a dilemma. U.S. laws prevented them from completing their contractual obligations to the Russians. At the same time, the European governments, which were also affected by these contracts, were pressuring the subsidiaries to complete the projects. Eventually the United States prevailed.

## Foreign Laws and Political Systems

**Foreign laws and political systems** refer to the legal and political climate, the rules, and the institutions of the host nations in which an MNC conducts business. Because of cultural variations, we find great diversity among the laws and political ideologies of different nations. Because the societies have different attitudes toward the behavior of their people and organizations, they form different laws to regulate that behavior.

If one examines the large volume of laws pertaining to business in only one nation, and then the corresponding regulations pertaining to business in other nations, one realizes the complexity that the legal differences between nations pose for the MNC. The importance of the host nation's laws to an MNC executive lies not so much in international business transactions as in conducting the business of the MNC in that particular foreign country. The problems result from the differences in laws between the home and host countries. The development of international and regional laws is slowly lessening these national differences. However, true standardization of laws influencing international business is still some time in the future.

The following are some of the areas of legal concern for the executives of MNCs:

**Financial Considerations**   These include laws governing capital formation, stock issuance, stock market transactions, the exchange of goods and money, and profit conversion.

**Structural Considerations**   These involve laws concerning proprietorships, partnerships, different types of corporations, and franchises.

**Ownership Considerations**   These include regulations concerning the percentage of foreign ownership allowed by the host country.

**Location of Business Considerations**   These involve zoning laws and statutes that govern location decisions by the MNC in the foreign country.

**Foreign Direct Investment (FDI) Considerations**   These consist of regulations facilitating, restricting, or prohibiting some or all of the business activities by citizens or MNCs from certain countries, including the granting of preferred trade status to a nation or special tax breaks for FDI. For example, in 1987 the United States and Canada signed an agreement that opened their 4,000-mile border to "almost free trade."[3] As another example, Canada controls foreign direct investment by an institution called the Foreign Investment Review Agency (FIRA).

**Taxation Considerations**   These involve both tax laws and tax rates. For instance, Japan has the highest effective corporate tax rate in the world, over 50 percent. Japan also has the steepest progressive individual tax system.[4] Taxes include excise or value added taxes, personal income taxes, sales taxes, and corporate taxes. Most governments use their power of taxation to regulate, control, facilitate, or restrict business activities, foreign trade, and foreign direct investment.

**Industrial Property Protection Considerations**   These include laws regarding patents, trademarks, copyrights, and trade secrets. Over 100 nations have laws regulating patents (which protect inventors' new discoveries) and trademarks (which protect a distinctive name, symbol, or device). The scope and enforcement of protection vary from country to country. The duration of protection can vary from 10 to 20 years. On the other hand, the absence of protection in some nations provides havens for counterfeiters and trademark pirates. For example, some of the southeast Asian countries tend to ignore patents and trademarks. As a result, every year counterfeiters produce millions of dollars' worth of "designer" clothes, watches, and computer equipment and software.

Over the past decade, international product counterfeiting has affected an increasing number of industries. Originally, counterfeiting was a problem mainly associated with elite consumer products (Calvin Klein jeans, Cartier jewelry, Apple personal computers, and so forth). Today, however, counterfeiting affects insecticides, fertilizers, aircraft parts, and prescription drugs.[5] The International Trade Commission estimates that counterfeiting cost U.S. companies more than $40 billion in lost exports, domestic sales, and royalties.[6]

The U.S. government and industry groups have been taking steps to fight counterfeiting. In a comprehensive effort, the United States is close to establishing a global consensus on a code. This code would protect intellectual property rights, including trade secrets. If negotiations are successful, this code would be enforced by the General Agreement on Tariffs and Trade (GATT).[7]

**Antitrust Considerations (In Most Capitalist Nations)**   These involve laws against monopolies and price-fixing. On the other hand, some countries permit the cooperation of competing firms in foreign markets. For instance, as we will discuss in Chapter 12, the passage of the Webb-Pomerene or Export Trade Act of 1918 by the U.S. Congress deliberately permitted the cooperation of competing firms in export trade, that is, in foreign countries. This act says that the cooperation of competitive firms in the development of foreign markets will not lead to their prosecution for breaking antitrust laws. In other words, firms that compete domestically can collaborate in exporting. This law was designed to make American firms stronger and more competitive in world markets.

**Corrupt Practices and Bribery Considerations**   These consist of laws that distinguish payoffs and bribery from customary gifts or facilitating payments. The practice of giving expensive gifts or making monetary payments to high-level government officials is more common in some countries than others. Making payments or gift giving in return for favors, permits, or large orders is considered bribery in most nations. The existence and pervasiveness of bribery worldwide are shown by the number of words for bribes and bribery used in different countries, for example, *baksheesh* (in Arab countries), *dash* (in West Africa), *grease* (in the United States), *la bustarella* (in Italy), *mordida* (in Latin America), *pot de vin* (in France), and *roshveh* (in Iran). For example, in some countries you may find a sign posted in an office that reads, "Please refrain from bribing the clerk."

As a result of exposed bribery scandals by U.S. MNCs during the 1970s, the U.S. Congress enacted the **Foreign Corrupt Practices Act (FCPA)**. Corporate bribery was called "unnecessary," "bad practice," and "ethically repugnant." The FCPA does not clearly distinguish between the so-called legal grease payments and actual bribes. The U.S. Justice Department has suggested that they may prosecute some grease payments anyway. Experts disagree whether the FCPA puts U.S. MNCs at a disadvantage against other MNCs that make such payments in host countries. One has to keep in mind that gift giving (not for favors in return) under certain conditions is a customary practice and an integral part of some cultures. For example, in Arab countries and in Iran gift giving is a custom that is usually expected on the first visit.

**Personnel and Labor Considerations**   These involve laws regulating collective bargaining, worker participation in management (co-determination), safety and health on the job, employment and compensation, and restrictions on the number of **expatriate** (nonnative) managers allowed to run an MNC's subsidiaries. For example, in 1988 the U.S. Equal Employment Opportunity Commission (EEOC) and Honda of America Manufacturing, a subsidiary of Honda Motor Company of Japan, resolved a federal discrimination complaint. According to this settlement, Honda agreed to give 370 blacks and women a total of $6 million in back pay. Although Honda did not admit to wrongdoing, the EEOC action put a spotlight on sensitive questions about the hiring practices of Honda.[8]

**Marketing Considerations**   These include product regulations that control the amount of physical and chemical ingredients and their purity, safety, and performance. Packaging and contents disclosure laws are also considerations for MNCs. For example, the U.S. government has made the manufacturers of all-terrain vehicles (ATVs) make refund payments to their customers. ATVs are small, motorized vehicles with three or four tires, generally used for recreation. Since 1982, ATVs have been implicated in more than 800 deaths and more than 275,000 injuries. About half of these casualties have been children under age 16.[9]

Price control laws are present in one form or another in most nations. Although price-fixing among competitors is illegal in the United States, some countries allow price agreements among competitors under certain conditions. A common law governing pricing is called resale-price maintenance (rpm). Because of the difficulties in enforcing rpm, the trend is away from its utilization, but some nations still use rpm. Another common practice is the establishment of price controls. Price controls can be nationwide. For example, price freezes in France under the Mitterrand administration were nationwide. An example of limited price control is Japan's price control of rice. Price ceilings or margins are frequent mechanisms for price controls.

There are differences in legislation governing distribution channels, distribution contracts, the legality of exclusive distribution in a country, and so forth. For example, door-to-door selling is illegal in France.

One of the most controversial elements of international business is advertising and promotion. It is subject to a great deal of control. In addition to legal controls, advertising industries in many nations have self-regulating codes. Regulations can deal with the message and its truthfulness. There are controls on comparative advertising—the famous taste test ads and similar ads. Regulations may also ban the advertising of certain products or impose restrictions on sales promotions and gimmicks, such as contests, deals, and premiums. For example, laws in Finland prohibit the advertising of alcohol, obscene literature, political organizations, religious messages, and weight-reducing drugs. As another example, comparative advertising is illegal in Iran.

**Environmental Protection Considerations**   These include laws governing waste disposal, air and water pollution, the use of pesticides, and so forth. For example, in the United States the Environmental Protection Agency (EPA) monitors activities of firms with regard to environmental safety.

**Movement of Goods Considerations**   These include laws regulating or restricting the movement of goods into or out of the country, that is, exports and imports controls, as we explained in Chapter 4.

**Technology Transfer Considerations**   These involve regulations pertaining to the transfer of technology across national borders. For example, as we explained in Chapter 1, the exportation of strategic goods to the Soviet Union is prohibited by the U.S. government.

**Contract Enforcement Considerations**　These involve the laws concerning the enforcement of contracts between private parties, between MNCs and the government or government-owned companies (such as those in communist countries or LDCs).

## Enforcement

An MNC executive should be interested in how foreign laws are enforced, as well as in the laws themselves. Many laws never get enforced. An executive should also consider the degree of impartiality found in the justice system. Is the justice system in the host country impartial in judging disputes between a foreign subsidiary and a domestic company? Some courts are known for favoring domestic firms and parties over MNCs. In these countries, laws gradually assume a bias against the MNC. The knowledge of the foreign laws and their enforcement (impartial or discriminatory) is essential in evaluating the legal and political climate. A multinational executive should realize that he or she must usually turn to the national law (domestic or foreign) whenever and wherever conflicts arise and disputes have to be settled.

## International Law

**International law** governs relations between independent nations. It differs from national law because no single legislative body formulates international law. International law is a collection of agreements, conventions, and treaties between two or more nations. When the involved nations are located in the same region, such laws are called **regional law**. Treaties between two countries are **bilateral**, among three nations, **trilateral**, and among more than three states are **multilateral**. There are certain differences between national law and international law:

**1.** Unlike national law, international law does not reflect national cultures. It represents intercultural differences, adjustments, and cultural borrowings.

**2.** The domain and coverage of the national law and international law are different. National laws and legal systems govern the behavior of that particular nation's citizens, residents, and both the domestic as well as foreign organizations conducting business within its boundaries. International law governs the relations among nations. It covers political and military agreements, as well as commercial activities such as international trade, foreign direct investment, and contracts.

**3.** National laws have enforcement mechanisms that international laws usually lack. The World Court is a prestigious, but inactive, juridical body in international law. International law is dependent on sovereign nations for its enforcement. One country alone cannot enforce the terms of an agreement or a law against another country. Politics, political isolation, and military force have been used at times to enforce international agreements. The Russian invasion of Czechoslovakia in 1968, and the pressure put on Poland by Russia to take drastic action against the Solidarity movement are examples of use of force in enforcement of bilateral and regional treaties.

**4.** International law also covers the activities of international organizations (The United Nations and its agencies, the World Bank, the International Monetary Fund, and others), multinational corporations, and human rights. Of course, there are still many aspects of international business that are not covered by international law.

Technological developments (in information processing, in telecommunications, and in transportation) and the growth of international business have increased some common concerns and problems among nations. International law has grown rapidly in response to these common concerns and new problems. International organizations, such as the United Nations Centre for the Transnational Corporations, have attempted to improve the body of international law needed to deal with MNCs and international business transactions.

International laws cover an ever-increasing number of countries and subjects. Traditionally, international law was only formulated by, and protected the interests of, the Western world. Nowadays, international law recognizes the cultural, economic, and political diversity of all the nations involved. As a result, more attention is given to protecting the legitimate right of all sovereign nations and their citizens.

## Jurisdiction

MNCs often concern themselves about whether or not a nation's laws stop at its territorial borders. In the absence of a controlling and truly enforceable international law, should extraterritorial national laws, that is, national laws applicable outside national borders, regulate MNCs? Many national courts, including those in the United States, have tried to project their power outside their national territory. Other government agencies have also tried to extend their power outside their borders. The U.S. Treasury Department has asserted that the Internal Revenue Service (IRS) has the power to "examine any . . . data relevant or material" to a tax return. This IRS code was applied to a Japanese company's U.S. subsidiary that had filed a tax return in the United States. The IRS required the Japanese parent company to surrender its business records for inspection.[10]

In another controversial act, the U.S. Commerce Department, under the authority of the Export Administration, ordered not only American subsidiaries in Europe but also certain European companies to refrain from fulfilling the contracts to supply the equipment needed to build the Soviet Union's Siberian-European gas pipeline. This was an obvious attempt to extend American laws and regulations extraterritorially.

International law gives nations the opportunity to argue about a proper extraterritoriality. The **International Court of Justice (ICJ)**, located in The Hague, the Netherlands, has left the matter of extraterritorial law primarily to the discretion of nations involved in disputes.

According to the ICJ, **jurisdiction** is defined as the capacity of a nation under international law to prescribe or to enforce a rule of law extraterritorially. The ICJ has asserted that a nation has jurisdiction over business transactions in its territory, except as limited by treaty or other regional or international agreement. In other words, a nation has jurisdiction whenever such jurisdiction does not come into conflict with a principle of international law.

## OBSTACLES TO INTERNATIONAL NEGOTIATIONS AND CONTRACTS

Differences in cultures, trade customs, and legal codes necessitate careful attention to the negotiation of contracts involving parties from different nations. The language barrier can be a significant obstacle to negotiations. Even people from English-speaking nations use different dialects, which can occasionally bring about misunderstanding in negotiations and in contract formulation. Naturally, each negotiating party prefers to use the language whose nuances they know best. You can either use a common language, such as English or French, or use an interpreter. If you use a common language native to one of the parties, the other party will have difficulty in expression and in understanding. If the common language is not native to either party, difficulties may even be greater. As we will discuss in Chapter 10, it is not only the spoken language but also the unspoken body language that must be understood in negotiations. Certain hand gestures and body movements, while quite acceptable in one culture, may be offensive or misunderstood in another culture. Thus, some important body language movements are rarely an appropriate communications aid in international negotiations.

The use of interpreters can severely slow the pace of negotiations and add another element of difficulty. The interpreter may yet be another source of error. He or she can take an unwanted active role as opposed to just interpreting what is said in the negotiations, thus causing difficulties. Anyone who has been an interpreter knows how difficult and exhausting it is to keep up with the conversation, especially when emotions are at a high level, negotiations are progressing at a fast pace, and issues are tangled. Even if an accurate, efficient, and impartial translator exists, other translation problems may arise. A Chinese replying "yes" in answer to a question may not be answering "yes" in the sense of agreement, but may merely be saying, "Yes, I understand the question." As another example, to a Japanese the English word "maybe" means no. By using maybe instead of no, the Japanese saves face for himself or herself, as well as for the other party.

The specificity of the legal language used in agreements and contracts can lead to other problems. Contracts and agreements usually are, and should be, drawn by qualified legal experts (attorneys). Lawyers from some countries, such as the United States and the Soviet Union, tend to use careful language that spells out the full extent of each party's rights and duties. This practice may prove risky when dealing with lawyers from other nations who tend to lean toward more generally worded contracts. For example, attorneys in Japan tend to leave it to the parties to supply the details, whereas in Germany, the courts are left with a wide range in which to interpret generally worded agreements. To the Japanese, a contract relationship is shaped as mutual understanding is developed. Thus, a detailed and thoroughly drafted agreement introduced during negotiations with a Japanese executive may lead to distrust and resentment. A German negotiator, knowing the dislike of German courts for exhaustively worded contracts, may not sign such a contract.

The United States is a legally oriented society. American lawyers play an important role and are influential participants in many international business transactions. Three-fourths of the attorneys in the world work in the United States.[11] Many American attorneys assume that the lawyers on the other side will balance things out in the contract. This may prove to be an erroneous assumption in international negotiations because the opposite party's negotiating team may not contain a lawyer, or if it contains one, the lawyer may be a minor participant in the negotiations.

Acceptable contract clauses in one country may be unacceptable in another nation. For instance, French courts routinely, and German courts occasionally, enforce penalty clauses that are not legally enforceable in the United States. Unfair contract terms are prohibited by statute in England. One-sided contracts can cause suspicion in Japan, or they may lead to hostility in negotiations with a party from a developing nation because it may resemble the LDC's past exploitations by developed nations. In some countries in the Middle East or Africa, it is common to have "boycott" clauses in contracts. A *boycott clause* prohibits parties from doing business with certain blacklisted persons or countries, such as prescribed in the Arab boycott of Israel. Such boycott clauses are illegal in the United States.

In summary, careful consideration should be given to the many differences among nations in the negotiation processes. Potential problems and areas of misunderstandings are many. As the saying goes, "Forewarned is forearmed."

## DISPUTE SETTLEMENT

A procedure for dispute settlement should be arranged in writing before the contract is signed. Because an international agreement is in effect over a long period of time, it can be expected to bring about differences in interpretation between the parties from time to time. An effective international contract should contain an efficient and simple mechanism for resolving "interpretative differences." Periodic informal meetings to discuss such differences are highly recommended.

If informal and mutual discussions or negotiations fall short of resolving disputes, one or more of the parties may seek either arbitration or litigation.

## Dispute Settlement by Arbitration

**Arbitration** is the process of seeking judgments on disputed issues from a neutral third party that is acceptable to both contentious parties. Dispute settlement by arbitration is usually voluntary. If the contract includes an arbitration clause then the parties proceed with arbitration. In the absence of such a clause, parties can voluntarily submit the dispute to arbitration by unbiased expert arbitrators or business people who are familiar with trade disputes.

Many international disputes are not about matters of law but involve disputes over factual matters. The questions of law are usually of secondary importance. Settlement by litigation is usually costly and time consuming, and it may bring the business relationships to a standstill. Juries and judges may lack appropriate knowledge and may be inclined to compromise in order to settle disputes. Commercial arbitration can be less costly, quicker, and less disruptive. Arbitration may also provide a more intelligent understanding of the nonlegal points involved in the trade dispute. As a result, arbitration is becoming more popular every day.

## Dispute Settlement by Litigation

Litigation is the process of bringing legal suit against another party in a court of law to redress alleged wrongdoing. The International Court of Justice (ICJ) is the primary body that hears the suits brought by one country against another. It is a United Nation's agency located at The Hague in the Netherlands. The fifteen ICJ judges are drawn from all of the major legal systems in the world. They are each qualified to be appointed to the highest judicial positions in their respective countries. If a host nation violates international law, an MNC can take its grievance before the ICJ. Only sovereign nations of the world may be parties in a proceeding before the ICJ. The Court gives judgments against or in favor of the disputing countries. Judgments may include monetary damages or injunctive relief for the plaintiff. If needed, judgments can be enforced by referring them to the United Nations Security Council, consisting of the so-called superpowers, for appropriate action. Such action may include the use of military force against a noncompliant nation.

Because only sovereign nations can bring actions before the ICJ, a home country needs to represent the MNC involved. For example, the United States represented its MNCs in their suits against the Iranian government in the early 1980s. The home nation, of course, has discretion over espousing the MNC's claim. The home country government also need not pay the MNC any damages awarded by an ICJ judgment. Some nations have laws mandating state representation for rightful claims of their citizens and corporations before the ICJ, and for forwarding the awarded damages to them.

Some international disputes may qualify for litigation in host country courts, home country courts, or in a court in a third country. For example, after the disastrous Union Carbide chemical plant leak in Bhopal, India, attempts were made by the Indian government to try the lawsuits against Union Carbide in the U.S. courts. This was because the U.S. courts have a tendency to grant large settlement rewards in such cases. However, Union Carbide argued that because the accident took place in India, the Indian courts should have jurisdiction over the suits. As we will discuss in the Union Carbide case in Part Four of this book, the dispute was finally settled when the Indian Supreme Court ordered Union Carbide to pay $470 million to that government.

Litigation in some national courts may lead to surprises for an MNC executive. The following are some of the difficulties that an MNC may face in host country courts:

1. Courts in some countries may not be immune to political persuasions. For instance, in socialist countries, courts may be expected to deliver "socially just" judgments.
2. In certain nations, international business disputes are heard only in special courts or tribunals. Different procedures may apply and different names, such as a "commercial" court or a "foreign investment grievances board," may be used.
3. Legal appeal procedures may be nonexistent or may take peculiar forms. Appeals may have to be presented to the top political person in the country.
4. It may be difficult to provide personal testimony or documents that are outside the host country, but are nevertheless required by the local court. Document certification may also be a problem.

In summary, international business dispute settlement in a national court can be time-consuming, expensive, frustrating, and full of surprises for an MNC. Once a judgment is made, recognition and enforcement of judgments by one nation may prove difficult in another nation.

## VARIATIONS IN POLITICAL SYSTEMS

The political environment of international business includes the home and host countries' attitudes toward business enterprises. The legal environment is generated from this political climate. The legal and political environment constitutes the "rules of the game." These rules and regulations facilitate or restrict the operations of an MNC across national boundaries.

Political systems are based on certain ideological beliefs. Thus, the variations in political systems prevalent in different nations stem from these ideological beliefs. Such beliefs lead to the different ways that nations organize and perform their economic activities. The spectrum of ideological beliefs ranges from laissez-faire capitalism to totalitarian communism. Today, no country represents a purely laissez-faire capitalistic system, nor is there one formated as a purely communist nation. Each country has a set of economic and political institutions that enacts its basic ideological beliefs. For success, an MNC must be familiar with the ideological beliefs and the economic and political systems of the countries in which it operates.

As we mentioned earlier, pure forms of economic and political systems do not exist. Thus, it is necessary to think of a spectrum of systems ranging from those that rely heavily on market mechanisms for the allocation and the distribution of goods and services to those that rely on central (government) planning for allocation and the distribution activities. On the market end of the spectrum falls the United States with its reliance on individual initiative, private ownership of property, the profit motive, competition, and a relatively minimal amount of governmental control of the whole process. On the other end of the spectrum lies the Soviet Union with its centrally planned economy. The state and the Communist party are synonymous in this country. The state has a monopolistic power over all resources, and production is carried out by the state-owned farms and factories.

Between the two extremes (the United States and the Soviet Union) are countries with various mixtures of market mechanisms and central planning. For example, Hungary and Yugoslavia are centrally commanded economies that rely on market mechanisms for some economic activities. As another example, Japan is a market economy that relies on some public ownership of business, with extensive economic participation by the government.

In some of the LDCs, the government owns and controls some of the factors of production. There are shortages of capital, skilled labor, management, and technology in many of these countries. Unlike communist nations, many of these countries permit foreign direct investment and seek economic aid from the advanced nations and international organizations (such as the IMF and the World Bank). Examples include prerevolutionary Iran and the Philippines.

## LEGAL AND POLITICAL RISK

Legal and political factors are particularly significant to the operation and strategy of MNCs. Because these firms operate within the jurisdiction of more than one government, they increase the risk of having their operations affected by some form of government initiative. Through their political ideologies and legislative power, governments are able to influence and alter their country's business environment. Such actions may include regulations that influence a firm's ability to compete. Or, even more drastically, such regulations may change the ownership of company's assets.

Unlike their purely domestic counterparts, MNCs enjoy a certain amount of mobility. One of the strategic choices open to MNCs includes its national location and the different legal and political environments which that may bring. The legal and political environment becomes a strategic variable, that is, part of an MNC's strategic decision-making process.

Host governments view MNCs in a special category. Although an MNC's subsidiary may be incorporated under national (host country) laws, its foreign ownership links and its classification as a foreign firm may subject it to special regulations and government actions, different from those influencing domestic firms. In addition to legal and political events within a host country, the MNC may also be influenced by a change in the political relationship between the host country and the home country or some other country.

The possibility of change in a legal and political environment, which may have an impact on the operations and the economic well-being of an MNC, is called the **legal and political risk** (LPR). The effect of a possible change could be either negative or positive. However, in practice, the main focus is on possible negative effects. In other words, legal and political risk more narrowly refers to the government-associated hazards of doing business in a foreign country.

**Legal and political risk strategy** refers to the process of forecasting legal and political events in order to protect the MNC against loss or to help the MNC take advantage of the opportunities that result from such events. LPR strategy also helps MNCs recover compensation after an adverse event has taken place.

## Legal and Political Risk Factors

There are a number of actions through which host governments can influence an MNC's operations and economic well-being. These actions are designed to control the real or imagined dangers of foreign direct investment and to curtail an MNC's power. Such actions range from nondiscriminatory interference to expropriation or destruction.

**Nondiscriminatory Interference**   This mildest form of regulation is not particularly aimed against foreign-controlled subsidiaries. Joint ventures, management, or licensing agreements between local firms and MNCs may also be influenced by these actions. Examples of nondiscriminatory interference include enacting certain currency regulations or making currency inconvertible, requiring local (host country) management, enforcing price regulations, and requiring use of only local raw materials or product components.

**Discriminatory Interference**   These actions are designed to favor local firms over MNCs. Examples of discriminatory interference include restricting the amount of ownership by foreign individuals or firms, such as only allowing joint ventures with local (host country) citizens or firms; restricting the number of expatriate managers allowed to work for the MNC; requiring special fees or taxes; requiring an excessive number of permits or documents; restricting the allocation of government sales contracts; and enacting price controls against imports.

**Indigenization of Capital**   These actions include discriminatory sanctions designed to pressure an MNC, to prevent its profitable operation, and finally, to put it out of business. Purely nationalistic or political reasons, or the creation of more opportunities or profits for local firms, are the motives behind such sanctions. Indigenization of capital may include a **creeping or slow expropria-**

**tion,** preventing an MNC's capital or profits from leaving the country. Or it may involve levying high taxes, royalties, or other charges against an MNC to make its operations unprofitable. There may also be claims against the MNC for compensation for past inequities.

**Loss of Assets**    This is accomplished through outright takeover of the MNC's assets by the host country. This can take place by expropriation of a few MNCs, the nationalization of an entire industry, or the socialization of the whole country. Another violent but rare practice is the destruction of foreign-owned assets.

**Expropriation** is the official seizure of foreign property of an MNC by a host government. Seized property can then be used in the public interest. According to international law, expropriation is the right of sovereign states, but prompt compensation at fair market value in convertible currencies is supposed to be awarded to the MNC. In practice, negotiations, court proceedings, and appeals delay the promptness of the compensation. Fair market value is another point of disagreement between the MNC and the host government. An MNC usually wants "going-concern" value, whereas a host government is usually willing to pay only the depreciated book value. A host government may also not have enough convertible currency reserves to pay the agreed upon settlement. For instance, the takeover of the U.S.–owned copper mining subsidiaries in Chile in 1971 was eventually settled only after the overthrow of the Allende government in 1973. In 1968, the government in Peru took over International Petroleum Company (Exxon) and a few other companies. Partial compensation was not agreed to until 1974.

**Nationalization** refers to the transfer of ownership of an entire industry from private to public, that is government ownership. This is a nondiscriminatory measure that leads to nationalization of all domestic and foreign-owned firms in an industry. For example, some of the firms and industries in Iran were nationalized after the overthrow of the Shah in 1979. Another example is nationalization of some French industries and banks in the late 1970s.

**Socialization** or **communization** is the nationalization of all the industries in a country. The socialization of Cuba after the Cuban revolution is an example.

Of course, the milder cases of government interference in international business are very common. It is the more severe acts that concern an MNC the most. In 1974, the Economic and Social Council to the Secretary-General of the United Nations conducted a study of the takeovers of foreign firms. They reported 875 takeover cases during the period from 1960 to 1974. It is interesting that two-thirds of the cases were carried out by only ten countries.[12] Another study surveyed the expropriation of U.S. and British firms during the period from World War II to 1970. The extractive industries (petroleum, plantation agriculture, and mining), the service trades, commercial banking, and insurance businesses were the targets of most takeovers of both American and British firms. The manufacturing sector faced the lowest number of takeovers.[13]

There is no accurate account of the dollar volume of assets involved in these takeovers. However, estimates do exist, and the value of the U.S. subsidiaries taken over between 1961 and 1975 was estimated by one study to be between two to three billion dollars. Nevertheless, the monies lost in takeovers are said to be minimal compared with the large amount of foreign direct investment committed by the U.S. multinationals.[14] Table 9.2 shows the summary of the results of this study.

Table 9.2  SUMMARY OF FOREIGN TAKEOVERS OF U.S. FIRMS

| | Number | Percent | 1946–60 | 1961–66 | 1967–71 | 1972–73 |
|---|---|---|---|---|---|---|
| Total, all industries and regions | 170 | 100 | 12 | 22 | 79 | 57 |
| | | | | (percent of the total for the period indicated) | | |
| **By industry** | | | | | | |
| Extractive | 69 | 41 | 50 | 50 | 39 | 37 |
| Financial | 32 | 19 | — | 5 | 28 | 18 |
| Manufacturing | 51 | 30 | — | 27 | 27 | 40 |
| Utilities | 18 | 10 | 50 | 18 | 6 | 5 |
| **By region** | | | | | | |
| Latin America | 93 | 55 | 83 | 59 | 44 | 61 |
| Africa | 51 | 30 | 17 | — | 51 | 16 |
| Middle East | 14 | 8 | — | 32 | 4 | 7 |
| Asia | 12 | 7 | — | 9 | 1 | 16 |
| **By form of takeover** | | | | | | |
| Expropriation | 103 | 60 | 67 | 95 | 63 | 42 |
| Intervention/requisition | 25 | 15 | — | — | 14 | 25 |
| Renegotiation of contract | 20 | 12 | — | — | 8 | 25 |
| Forced sale | 22 | 13 | 33 | 5 | 15 | 8 |
| **By selectivity of takeover** | | | | | | |
| Entire industry: mixed | 21 | 12 | 33 | — | 8 | 19 |
| Entire industry: foreign | 68 | 40 | 42 | 68 | 38 | 28 |
| Selected firms: no industry specification | 25 | 15 | 8 | — | 21 | 16 |
| Selected firms within a specific industry | 56 | 33 | 17 | 32 | 33 | 37 |
| **By political/economic circumstances** | | | | | | |
| Leftist change in government | 81 | 48 | 17 | 41 | 65 | 33 |
| Right or center nationalist | 7 | 4 | 17 | — | 6 | 2 |
| Natural resource sovereignty | 35 | 20 | 33 | 41 | 4 | 32 |
| Mature and standardized product | 47 | 28 | 33 | 18 | 25 | 33 |

*Source:* Robert G. Hawkins, Norman Mintz, and Michael Provissiero. "Government Takeovers of U.S.–Foreign Affiliates." *Journal of International Business Studies* (Spring, 1976), p. 9.

In assessing legal and political risk, the MNC must not only focus on country-specific factors, but also be concerned with company and industry factors. In other words, a firm should develop legal and political risk forecasts and strategies that are based on (1) the legal and political conditions of the host nations, (2) the industry's characteristics, and (3) the nature and conditions of the MNC's subsidiaries in those foreign nations.

## LEGAL AND POLITICAL RISK FORECASTING

The main purpose of **legal and political risk (LPR) forecasting** is to predict the likelihood of future legal and political events. An MNC must be prepared for, and respond to, slow as well as sudden changes in the home and host countries' legal and political environments. LPR forecasts fall into two categories. The first category involves anticipations about evolutionary (slow) change in the current legal and political system. The second category includes forecasts aimed at major discontinuities and events that may take place in the political system. These sudden changes often accompany radical changes in the government. We continue this section with a brief description of these two categories.

### Evolutionary Legal and Political Change

An MNC should assess and understand the existing legal and political environment, and forecast its future actions and directions of change. Examples of evolutionary legal and political change include alterations in government domestic regulations, in attitudes toward foreign trade and FDI, in economic policies (fiscal and monetary), in balance-of-payments and exchange rates policies, in relations with other governments, and in the peaceful transition of government.

### Major Discontinuous Political Change

Sudden change in the political system, such as the overthrow of the government by a coup d'etat or revolution is the major source of political risk. This kind of event changes major assumptions underlying all of an MNC's plans and strategies, and can pose a threat to its economic well-being or continued existence in a host country. Of course, not all such events are negative, and, at times, new opportunities can be created.

Usually, every change is bound to benefit some, while adversely affecting others. For instance, after the revolution in Iran, American and some European MNCs suffered and eventually had to withdraw from that country. As a result, a vacuum was created. The Japanese and other so-called friendly nations and their MNCs filled the gap and benefited from the change.

## Forecasting Methods

Understandably, MNC managers want advance notice of political discontinuity. They would like to know in advance what changes might lead to major adverse political events. Such knowledge can be gained from legal and political risk (LPR) forecasts. An MNC often acquires or commissions from private-sector firms LPR forecasts. These forecasts are called business environment risk information reports, and they are prepared by companies such as Frost and Sullivan's Political Risk Services, Price Waterhouse, Global Risk Assessments, and Control Risk (in London). Overall, such forecasts are concerned with predicting the stability of legal and political systems and the possibility that the present rules of the game might be changed.

Legal and political risk forecasting is an art. Despite the crucial role that such forecasts play in assessing the investment worthiness of host countries, this art of forecasting remains in its infancy. Indexes of political stability formulated by political scientists tend to be unreliable about the future and unclear about their implications for MNCs. The more sophisticated forecasts using sophisticated information-processing technology (computer modeling) usually leave the critical judgments up to the user of the information. The complex nature of such events; the problems in obtaining complete, accurate, and current information; and the biases embedded in external and in-house information are contributing factors to the vagueness of political forecasting. Four approaches can be suggested in forecasting political interference.

**Grand Tours** This involves an assessment visit to the potential host country by an executive or a team from an MNC. The investigating team meets with local businesspersons and government officials. The findings are then reported to the headquarters' management. Such "first-hand" impressions can be superficial, and the visit may be carefully orchestrated by the eager host country officials.

**The Old Hands or Expert Opinion** This approach relies on the advice of outside consultants who are familiar with the host country. These experts could be academicians, other businesspersons, diplomats, journalists, or politicians from the home or host nation. The advice of these experts is usually an improvement over the "instant expert" advice of the grand tour team members. This is the traditional method of legal and political risk forecasting, but there are obvious hazards in this approach. Government officials associated with the host nation may have personal reasons to encourage continued foreign direct investment (FDI) in their country. Even company executives, with everything to gain personally from a new expansion, can be overly optimistic about the legal and political environment. For example, few experts anticipated the overthrow of the Shah of Iran. Even President Carter referred to Iran under the Shah as "the island of stability"—just before the Shah's downfall! Conscious or unconscious bias may play a role.

**Delphi Techniques (Surveys)** In this approach outside experts or MNC executives are surveyed. Initially, a checklist of legal and political variables similar to

**Table 9.3  CHECKLIST FOR LEGAL AND POLITICAL RISK FORECASTING**

**Legal Environment**

Type of legal system

Judicial system load

Appeal procedure

History of discriminatory practices against foreign citizens and firms

Contract enforcement practices

Compensation award procedure

Stability of legal system

Arbitration practices

Stability of implementation of laws, regulations, and rules

Current revisions in administrative procedures

Existence of specialized structures for rule making, implementation, and adjudication (such as tribunals)

**Political Environment**

Form of government

Length of leadership in power

History of government stability

Political party fractionalization

Party political platform

Volatility of electorate

Irregular leadership changes

Popular support for leadership

Role of military in politics

Religious, ethnic, or ideological splits

Intolerance and unwillingness to compromise among political groups

Amount of political participation allowed through elections, political parties, labor or trade unions

Amount of political participation allowed or tolerated through demonstrations, propaganda, lobbies, professional associations, and other informal interest groups

Actual participation in political activities

Political competition

Constitutional changes

**Internal Stability**

Prospects for domestic political violence

Demonstrations

Riots

Political strikes

Purges

Terrorism

Assassinations

Government crises

History of discontinuous political changes

History of military coups d'etat

Prospects for adverse economic effects from emerging political change

Guerrilla warfare

Internal security forces per 1000 population

The capability of the political system to punish certain behavior or reinforce other behavior (coercion)

**Table 9.3** (*Continued*)

**External Political Relations**
  Prospects of border warfare
  Geographical tension spillovers
  Regional political alliances
  Economic warfare
  Threat of large-scale war
  Military-related violence
  Diplomatic crises
  Trade disputes
  External threats to supplies or markets
  Labor disputes
  Alliances
**Socioeconomic factors**
  Ethnolinguistic fractionalization
  Percentage growth in per capital GNP
  Per capita income
  Percentage growth in per capita energy consumption
  Income distribution
  Wealth distribution
  Economic crises
  Balance of payments situation
  Inflation rate
  Exchange rate volatility
  Exchange regulations
  Controls on repatriation of capital and profits
  National debt

those in Table 9.3 is formed. Next, the group of experts rank these variables and form a composite index of legal and political risk using the weighted average of these variables. Finally, countries are ranked, based on these composite indexes. Such forecasts are developed on the basis of the country (country-specific forecasts) or the firm (firm-specific forecasts) which consider firm and industry characteristics. An MNC can develop its own in-house forecast or use independent organizations' indices and rankings. One such independent forecast is the Business International Index, which was originally constructed by F. T. Haner.

**Quantitative Methods**  Recently, there has been a growing interest in using advanced statistical and computer modeling techniques in forecasting legal and political risk for MNCs. These techniques are similar to the techniques used in economic forecasting. Like the leading economic indicators used to forecast economic change, certain variables that are casually related with drastic political change are used to predict discontinuous political change. Most of these statistical and computer models, however, fall short of predicting firm-specific (micro) future events from their larger forecasts about country-specific (macro) changes. In other words, countrywide political instability need not to mean that there is a great danger of expropriation for an MNC. Firm-specific characteristics may play a very important role on the actual outcome of the legal and political risks of an MNC.[15]

With the growing amount of political instability in different parts of the world, the popularity and importance of LPR forecasting have increased over the years. Many governments and MNCs still remember being caught by surprise and hurt by the unanticipated revolution that toppled the Shah of Iran in 1979. This is only one example that reminds MNCs that surprises can be expensive. The field of LPR assessment has been concerned with broad social revolution and discontinuous political change in LDCs. The best strategy to cope with such sudden change is not to invest in the first place in a foreign country if high risk exists. Secondly, the parent company should divest its holdings in risky host countries. In the case that a new investment is necessary, the MNC should demand a higher premium for its participation in the project. To protect itself, the parent company can also buy insurance or establish a reserve to offset potential losses.

## LEGAL AND POLITICAL RISK STRATEGY

As we defined earlier, legal and political risk strategy refers to the process of forecasting legal and political events in the hope of protecting the MNC against loss or in the hope of helping the MNC to take advantage of any benefits from such events. Finally, the LPR strategy hopes to recover compensation after an adverse effect has taken place.

Discontinuous political change, while not the greatest source of damage to MNCs, still accounts for about 30 percent of the total losses due to host government actions. Much greater loss is due to the business-as-usual events in host countries that do not lead to social revolution or other drastic changes. These actions are rational or semirational attempts by host governments to achieve greater control, independence, or economic benefits. In such situations, LPR forecasts should focus on the vulnerabilities of specific projects.

The management of LPR in such settings requires the use of experimental corporate strategies that also truly qualify as global strategies. Of course, there are some specific strategies that an MNC can use to manage legal and political risk. Some of these strategies are used before the actual direct foreign investment takes place, and some strategies are followed after investment. Table 9.4 depicts a list of such strategies.

We conclude this chapter by stating that the political, economic, and technological interdependence of the nations in today's world has resulted in record high international business activities. As MNCs and international business operations penetrate all parts of the world, new legal questions and problems are introduced and new laws are formulated to deal with them. Laws are developed to facilitate and encourage international business as well as to regulate and

Table 9.4  LEGAL AND POLITICAL RISK STRATEGIES

| Before Investing | After Investing |
|---|---|
| Internal hedging | Internal hedging |
| Minimization of local equity | |
| Local borrowing | Good-citizen policy |
| Local equity (joint ventures) | Increase in technical contribution |
| Management contract | Negotiation and arbitration |
| Franchising | Internal reserve |
| International vertical integration | |
| Production integration | |
| Marketing integration | |
| International supply sourcing | |
| External hedging | External hedging |
| Government insurance (OPIC in U.S., BFCE-Coface in France, ECGD in U.K.) | Private insurance (Lloyd's of London) |
| Private insurance (Lloyd's of London) | International investment codes |
| Host government guarantees | Divestment |

*Source:* Adapted from Bernard Marois, "Comment G'erer le Risque Politique lie a' vos Operations Internationales," Collection L' Exportateur, C.F.C.E., Paris, 1981.

govern this business. As a result, both the realm of international business activity as well as the law dealing with this business have become increasingly complex. The legal systems of today must respond to the increased volume of trade, the diverse environmental problems, the new marketing practices, and the new financing procedures. The legal system must also respond to the diverse demands for economic development and for stability from all the nations and MNCs involved.

The relevant question in managing legal and political risk can be stated as the following: Given a set of strategic choices available to an MNC, what is the best legal and political strategy? An MNC executive needs to formulate the best strategy for generating a profit over the relevant time horizon. A manager should not merely gain maximum legal and political security. Legal and political expertise should be employed in a consulting capacity, not as the final architect of an international business relationship. Thus, the MNC should not start with a legal and political strategy in its international operations. Legal and political as well as marketing, production, financial, management, ownership, personnel, and control strategies should conform to an overall corporate global strategy. The topic of global strategic management will be discussed in Chapters 13 and 14.

## SUMMARY

1. The legal and political aspects of international business refer to the legal and political conditions that govern international business activities and the settlement of trade disputes among MNCs, host nations, and other interested parties.
2. There is no single international legal and political system. The legal and political environment of international business consists of the political ideologies, laws, and judicial systems (such as the courts) of the individual countries. It also consists of a limited number of regional and international laws, treaties, and institutions.
3. Laws reflect the culture and represent the political will of a nation. Laws are the rules established by authority, custom, or agreement. They can be written, formal, indigenous, or unwritten (tribal).
4. Cultural, economic, and political variations have resulted in five legal systems in the world. Common law is based on unwritten principles and precedents established through custom, usage, and previous rulings. Civil or code law is based on grouping similar laws into a code under the headings of civil, commercial, and criminal law. Religious law (such as Moslem law) follows the guidelines and teachings of a religion. Communist law is based on the Marxist-Leninist ideology of the public ownership of production factors and the control of distribution mechanisms based upon state-formulated economic plans. Indigenous law includes tribal and unwritten law.
5. The legal and political environment of an MNC consists of the home country laws and political system, the host countries' laws and political systems, and the international laws and political climate.
6. Foreign laws and political system refer to the legal and political climate, the rules, and the institutions in the host nation in which the MNC conducts business. Because of cultural variations, we find great diversity among the laws and political ideologies of different nations.
7. The knowledge of foreign laws and their enforcement (whether or not they are impartial or discriminatory laws) is essential in evaluating the legal and political climate. The MNC executive must realize that the national law (domestic or foreign) frequently decides international trade disputes.
8. International law is a collection of agreements, conventions, and treaties between two or more independent nations. Technological developments in information processing, in telecommunications, and in transportation and the growth of international business have brought new problems and common areas of concern under international law.
9. Jurisdiction is defined as the capacity of a nation under international law to prescribe or to enforce a rule of law. There is no clear agreement among nations about which country's laws apply and which court should have jurisdiction over international business disputes.
10. Because of differences in cultures, trade customs, and legal codes, careful attention should be given by an MNC manager to negotiations and contracts involving international parties.
11. A procedure for dispute settlement and for resolving "interpretive differences" should be arranged in writing before an international business contract is enacted. In the absence of such a procedure, or if the procedure fails, arbitration by an expert arbitrator or litigation by a court can be used. Litigation can take place in national

courts (those of the home or host country, or a third country) or in the International Court of Justice.

12. The political environment of international business includes the attitudes toward business enterprise in the home and host nations. The legal environment is generated from the political climate. Political systems are based on certain ideological beliefs. On one end of the ideological spectrum is laissez-faire capitalism, and on the other end is pure communism. Because there is no pure ideological system, all nations lay somewhere in between these two extremes.

13. The possibility of change in the legal and political environment of a country that has an impact on the operations and economic well-being of an MNC is called the legal and political risk (LPR).

14. Legal and political risk strategy refers to the process of forecasting legal and political events in order to protect the MNC against loss (or to help the MNC take advantage of opportunities) that result from such events. LPR strategy also helps MNCs recover compensation after an adverse event has taken place.

15. Host governments may take a number of legal and political actions against the MNC. These actions may range from nondiscriminatory interference to the loss of an MNC's assets. Loss of assets may take three forms. Expropriation is the official seizure of foreign property by a host government. Nationalization is the transfer of the ownership of an entire industry from private to public (government) hands. Socialization or communization is the act of nationalization of all the industries in a country.

16. There are four approaches to legal and political risk forecasting. These are assessments of the country by (a) the grand tour, (b) the expert opinion, (c) the Delphi techniques, and (d) the quantitative techniques.

17. The legal and political strategy should be a part of a corporation's global strategy. In other words, the MNC should be concerned with a legal and political strategy that fits in with its overall strategic choices.

## QUESTIONS

9.1 What is meant by the legal and political aspects of international business? Why are they important? What role do they play in international business?

9.2 Choose a pair of legal systems and fully research their characteristics. Discuss the major differences in these two legal systems.

9.3 What are the three dimensions of the legal and political environment of international business? Why does the home country government have the greatest control over the MNC?

9.4 Discuss international law. What makes international and national law different? What would be the impact on international business of the creation and the enforcement of a well-developed international law.

9.5 Why is it difficult to decide who has jurisdiction over international business disputes?

9.6 Discuss the major barriers in international negotiations and contracts. Can you think of other problems?

9.7 How are international business disputes settled?

9.8 What are the major problems of conducting business in the Eastern bloc countries? Discuss.

9.9 What is meant by legal and political risk? What are the most severe and economically devastating legal and political risks for MNCs? Why?

9.10 Choose a developing nation and develop a legal and political assessment of that country. Would you recommend that an electronics manufacturer establish an assembly plant in this country? Why?

# NOTES

1. "Constitution (Fundamental Law) of the Union of Soviet Socialist Republics," *Soviet Life,* no. 1 (256), January 1978.
2. Jack N. Behrman, "The Multinational Enterprise and Nation States: The Shifting Balance of Power." In Ashook Kapoor and Philip D. Grub, ed., *The Multinational Enterprise in Transition* (Princeton, N.J.: Darwin Press, 1972), p. 412.
3. "A Free-Trade Milestone: The U.S.–Canada PACT on a Scale with the EC," *Business Week,* 19 October 1987, pp. 52–53.
4. *Business Week,* 7 July 1986, p. 20.
5. R. F. Bush, P. H. Bloch, and S. Dawson, "Remedies for Product Counterfeiting," *Business Horizons,* January–February 1989, pp. 59–65.
6. Eduardo Lachica, "Trade Thievery: U.S. Companies Curb Pirating of Some Items But by No Means All," *The Wall Street Journal,* 6 March 1989, pp. A-1, A-8.
7. Ibid.
8. "Blacks, Women at Honda Unit Win Back Pay," *The Wall Street Journal,* 24 March 1988, p. 2.
9. "Agency, in Switch, Backs U.S. Plan on ATV Dispute," *The Wall Street Journal,* 21 December 1987, p. 25.
10. *The New York Times,* 5 February 1983, p. 10.
11. Adam Anderson, "Manager's Journal: Why There Are So Few Lawyers in Japan," *The Wall Street Journal,* 9 February 1981.
12. Economic and Social Council to the Secretary-General, *Permanent Sovereignty Over Natural Resources* (New York: United Nations, September 1974), pp. 1–3.
13. Frederick J. Truitt, "Expropriation of Foreign Investment: Summary of the Post–World War II Experience of American and British Investors in Less Developed Countries," *Journal of International Business Studies* (Fall 1970), pp. 21–34.
14. Robert G. Hawkins, Norman Mintz, and Michael Provissiero, "Government Takeovers of U.S. Foreign Affiliates," *Journal of International Business Studies* (Spring 1976), pp. 3–15.
15. R. J. Rummel, and David Heenan, "How Multinationals Analyze Political Risk," *Harvard Business Review* (January/February 1978), pp. 67–76.

# SUGGESTED READINGS

Eiteman, David K., and Arthur I. Stonehill. *Multinational Business Finance.* 5th ed. Reading, Mass.: Addison-Wesley, 1989. Chap. 8.

Kahler, Ruel. *International Marketing.* 5th ed. Cincinnati: South-Western, 1983. Chap. 7, pp. 101–124.

Kahler, Ruel, and Ronald L. Kramer. 4th ed. *International Marketing,* 5th ed. Cincinnati: South-Western, 1983. Chap. 16.

Keegan, Warren J. *Multinational Marketing Management.* 3rd ed. Englewood Cliffs, N.J.: Prentice-Hall, 1984. Chap. 6.

Leontiades, James C. *Multinational Corporate Strategy: Planning for World Markets.* Lexington, Mass.: Lexington Books, D.C. Heath, 1985. Chap. 13, pp. 153–166.

Moran, Theodore H., ed. *Multinational Corporations: The Political Economy of Foreign Direct Investment.* Lexington, Mass.: Lexington Books, D.C. Heath, 1985. Chap. 5, pp. 107–118.

Ronen, Simcha. *Comparative and Multinational Management.* New York: Wiley, 1986. pp. 359–365, 390–391.

Terpstra, Vern. *International Dimensions of Marketing,* 2nd ed. Boston: Kent, 1988.

———. *International Marketing.* 4th ed. Chicago: Dryden Press, 1987. Chap. 5.

———. *The Cultural Environment of International Business.* Cincinnati: South-Western, 1978. Chap. 7, pp. 219–251, Chap. 8, pp. 252–280.

Terpestra, V., and K. David. *The Cultural Environment of International Business,* 2nd ed. Cincinnati: South-Western, 1985. Chap. 8.

Vernon, Raymond, and Louis T. Wells, Jr. *Economic Environment of International Business.* 4th ed. Englewood Cliffs, N.J.: Prentice-Hall, 1986.

Walter, Ingo, and Tracy Murray, eds. *Handbook of International Business,* 2nd ed. New York: Wiley, 1988, Chaps. 7, 21, 24, 25, 26, 27, 28.

Wilson, Donald T. *International Business Transactions.* St. Paul, Minn.: West, 1984. p. 49, Chap. 6, pp. 113–130, Chap. 10, pp. 258–289, pp. 290–292, Chap. 15, pp. 383–421, Chap. 16, pp. 422–437.

# The Sociocultural Context of International Business

*B*ecause the MNC has to operate in different host countries, a comprehension of the sociocultural context is essential for its successful operations. The importance of understanding cultures—as well as understanding the similarities and differences between cultures—is clear when one looks at the multitude of blunders MNCs and their executives have made because of insensitivity to cultural differences.[1]

An Oriental folktale dramatizes the consequences of cultural differences:

> Once upon a time there was a great flood, and involved in this flood were two creatures, a monkey and a fish. The monkey, being agile and experienced, was lucky enough to scramble up a tree and escape the raging waters. As he looked

down from his safe perch, he saw the poor fish struggling against the swift current. With the very best of intentions, he reached down and lifted the fish from the water. The result was inevitable.[2]

Undesirable, sometimes disastrous consequences can occur when international managers assume that people in different cultures think, feel, and act the same way they do. Ignorance of cultural differences is not only unfortunate, it is bad business.

The purpose of this chapter is to provide us with a broad understanding of the sociocultural elements and their impact on international business and MNCs. First, we define the concepts of society, social systems, and culture. Second, we discuss the impact of the culture and its elements on international business and MNCs.

## SOCIETY AND SOCIAL SYSTEMS

Society can be defined as a system whereby people live together in organized communities. Society includes all aspects of economic and social activity. The legal and political systems, the religion, the mores, the educational system, the language, the demographics, and the technology are all parts of a society.

The internal set of beliefs and values in a society results in a cohesive link among its groups and it parts that make it distinct from other societies. The characteristics of societies, however, do not remain static. This is especially true in the ever-changing, dynamic world of the present time. The spread of communications, information processing, and technological advancements in transportation have brought the people of the world closer, resulting in increased interaction and cultural borrowing among societies. These developments have made the world a *global village.* However, great differences in attitudes, beliefs, and ideologies still exist. Some societies have been greatly transformed, whereas others have kept traditional values. For example, as a result of technological advancements, rapid changes have occurred in the heterogeneous American society. The process of change in a homogeneous or more traditional society, such as China or Japan, has been slower. This can be attributed to the stronger ties of the Chinese and Japanese people to a single culture, religion, and political system. Only since Mao's Cultural Revolution and since the slow ideological revitalization of China in the early 1980s has China at last broken ties with tradition and made fast progress toward economic development.

All facets of international business are affected by cultural variations. Thus, crosscultural recognition, understanding, education, training, and development are essential for those in managerial positions with MNCs.

## CULTURE

There is no general agreement among anthropologists with regard to the definition of culture. We define **culture** as "a cognitive frame of reference and a pattern of behavior transmitted to members of a group from previous generations of the group."[3] From this definition, "culture" involves several dimensions of behavior:

1. A psychological dimension in learning and in using a mind-set common to the group.
2. A social dimension in the interaction among group members.
3. A historical dimension in the transmission of mind-sets and practices across generations of a group.[4]

Despite differences of opinion regarding a definition of culture, there are three dimensions of culture on which agreement exists:

1. Culture is not "innate," but it is "learned."
2. Different aspects of culture are "interrelated"; that is, if you change one aspect of culture everything else is also affected.
3. Culture is "shared" and, in effect, it "defines" the boundaries of different groups.[5]

## THE IMPACT OF CULTURE ON MNC OPERATIONS

The sociocultural environment and its elements have a significant influence on the MNC. These influences are greatest on the functions of the MNC that directly interact with the public. The influences are less on MNC activities that do not interact with the public. For example, the accounting and finance functions are the least affected by sociocultural influences, whereas marketing is probably the most affected. In different cultural settings, the marketing strategies involving product design, packaging, promotion, and pricing should be altered to reflect variations in cultural attitudes and values.

The influence of cultural factors on an MNC's operations also depends on the firm's level of interest and involvement in the culture. An MNC might only be selling its products, exporting them from the home country or a third country, or the products might be produced in a foreign country by licensing the production operation to a local manufacturer. On the other hand, a complete commitment to production and to marketing in the host country may characterize the level of involvement of the MNC. It is obvious that the degree of the impact of culture on the firm in different functional areas varies according to the level of involvement of the MNC. The greater the MNC's involvement in and dependence on the host culture, the greater the need for an MNC manager to understand the sociocultural environment.

Due to the interaction between a foreign firm and a host country's environment, a foreign firm also has some degree of control over parts of its environment. The organization can manipulate environmental conditions by providing employment and training for the local people, by transferring technology, and by producing and promoting new products. Of course there are limitations to the impact of the firm on the host country's environment. Usually larger conglomerates are able to alter the sociocultural conditions more than the smaller, less-involved companies.

## ELEMENTS OF THE SOCIOCULTURAL ENVIRONMENT

In order to understand the complex phenomenon of culture and cultural differences, one should study the elements of culture. In the midst of confusion and disagreement about culture, one may find some commonalities in all cultures. These commonalities are referred to as **cultural universals**. Unfortunately, there is no consensus among anthropologists with regard to the elements that can be considered as cultural universals. A classical list of 73 cultural universals is provided by the anthropologist George P. Murdock.[6]

These cultural universals include calendar, cleanliness training, courtship, division of labor, education, ethics, etiquette, food taboos, gestures, greetings, hospitality, joking, language, mealtimes, population policy, property rights, religious rituals, status, and trade.

Let us begin with providing some examples of how a few of these cultural universals influence business operations, then we will discuss a few important sociocultural elements at length.

Because different calendars and holidays exist in different countries, misunderstandings in meeting plans, production schedules, and delivery dates can easily arise unless care is taken on both sides. For example, in Moslem countries Friday is the weekend and the usual day off. As another example, in Iran the first day of Spring—usually March 21—is celebrated as the first day of a new year. Festivities for the new year can last up to 13 days, and banks and government agencies are closed for a period of five days.

In areas of high illiteracy, packaging and advertising the product become a challenge. Labels in such areas usually picture what the package contains. An unfortunate experience of a company that exports baby food to an African nation exemplifies this problem. The company used a label showing a picture of a baby and stated verbally the type of baby food in the jar. Unfortunately for the company, the people looked at the labels and interpreted them as meaning the jars contained ground-up babies. Terrible sales followed.[7]

The American family is nuclear and is usually an independent unit. In many other countries, however, there may be an extended family system with several generations held together through the father's side (patrilineal) or through the mother's side (matrilineal). At times nepotism is the standard practice. The family looks out for itself. If the father is working, he wants to get a job for his son, or his nephew, or his distant cousin. All working members of a family may be employed by the same company. Even if an **expatriate** manager (a manager working in a country other than his or her own) of an MNC is not happy with this practice, he must accept it as normal and routine in that country.

The role of the U.S. government in industrial relations has traditionally been very influential. While supporting free and decentralized collective bargaining, some labor union practices in the United States are defined as contrary to national interest and declared illegal. These include union recognition strikes, the closed shop (where workers must belong to the union-before being hired by the company), and secondary boycotts. Other employment practices, such as equal employment opportunity for all citizens, safety and health standards, social security benefits, and unemployment compensation are legally mandated. Similar to those in the United States, the labor laws in West Germany are quite influential and extensive.

In contrast, British industrial relations are characterized by relative absence of legal structuring and legal constraints. Unions are voluntary associations. Collective bargaining agreements are not contracts and have no legal status. In Japan, however, legislation is fairly extensive. An MNC faces quite different levels of laws and regulations in different countries, and procedures for handling legal business disputes vary widely depending on the country.

Cultural influences on industrial relations systems are also evident. One notes the orderly, almost regimented logic of German systems as compared with the classic liberalism of the system found in the United Kingdom. Paternalism is evident in Japan. In contrast, company-oriented unionism is predominant in America's more competitive, free enterprise industrial society.

Many other cultural differences can cause misunderstandings. For example, an expatriate manager may translate a funny and decent joke, and yet find his local (host country) associates offended by the joke. The expatriate must be careful with teasing for it is entirely possible for a foreigner who speaks the home country language to still not understand ordinary humor in the foreign language. An entirely innocent joke may backfire. Ethnic jokes can be especially offending.

Hospitality styles differ among cultures. A businessman in the Middle East may spend half an hour discussing all kinds of social matters and offering tea, coffee, or other drinks before discussing business. Around noon he may issue an invitation to his house for lunch. He knows that his family is always ready for unannounced guests. There will be plenty of food, or, if not, they will manage by ordering food from a restaurant. Business will not be discussed until after a short nap and a cup of tea or coffee. Around 4:30 P.M., business may start. If you refuse his offers or act impatiently, you are most likely to offend him. Consequences could be disastrous.

Sexual restrictions, differences in sex roles, and the relationships between the sexes can be a source of trouble. Americans are used to patting the shoulders of coworkers of the opposite sex when they want to show their appreciation or happiness. Innocent touching, hugging, or embracing can backfire in cultures where these acts are forbidden. Even kissing a girlfriend or wife in public can lead to resentment, if the culture disapproves. Such is the case in many Islamic countries such as Saudi Arabia and Iran. Some Americans have been criticized for their insensitivity to local cultures. Practices that seem natural at home may be unacceptable or even seem like hostile acts in other cultures.

Many failures overseas are attributable to poor human relations, and often they are the result of ignorance of local attitudes and cultural values. Failures may also result from an inappropriate transfer of Western management methods. Technical competence is not enough. Understanding and communicating with the host culture mean respecting the people involved and working with them in ways that are familiar to them. As the saying goes, "When in Rome do as the Romans do."

## LANGUAGE AND COMMUNICATION

Language is the primary means of communication and penetrates all dimensions of a culture. It reflects the nature, mental processes, and values of each culture. Language is a form and medium of communication, not merely a collection of sounds, words, and phrases. Language also reflects human behavior and the culture from which it originates. Learning a language well really means learning the culture, and learning the language facilitates understanding and communicating with a culture and its people. Language can be defined as the following:

> The aspect of human behavior that involves the use of vocal sounds in meaningful patterns and, when they exist, corresponding written symbols to form, express, and communicate thoughts and feelings.[8]

Languages are distinguishing factors among cultures, and linguistic divisions are usually indicative of social, cultural, and political differences among groups. In some countries several languages exist. For example, in Europe, short physical distances between countries and changing national borders have established different cultural groups with different languages within the borders of several countries. In Belgium, for instance, there are three national languages: Flemish in the north and French and German in the south. Switzerland is characterized by four language groups representing four cultures. Canada has English- and French-speaking cultural groups. The situation is more drastic in some African and Asian countries. There are 14 official languages and 80 dialects in India. In Iran, Persian (Farsi) is the official language, while Turkish, Kurdish, Baluchi, Armenian, and many other dialects represent cultural variations. In Nigeria, it may not be possible to communicate with the people of a nearby tribe or locality with one's own native language.

To facilitate communication, a few **lingua francas** (common languages) have developed. For example, the most widely used lingua franca in India, and until recently the only official one, was English. Today, Hindi and English are the two official languages in India. Generally, former colonies adopt the language of their one-time rulers as the lingua franca, such as the Spanish spoken in Latin America and the French spoken in Africa. At times, however, these official languages are not good substitutes for the first language of the people, and for that reason they are less effective for an MNC manager's day-to-day operations or marketing programs.

It is always helpful, if not crucial, to at least attempt to converse in the local language. Language training must be an integral part of the cultural training for MNC executives on overseas assignments. It is essential not only to learn the vocabulary, the grammar, and the sentence structure of a language, but also to acquire the mental processes necessary to communicate well in a foreign cultural setting. The ability to speak a language is not enough. One must have the linguistic competence to recognize the meaning of idiomatic expressions, which are quite different from the meanings of words found in a dictionary. Thus, effective communication should not be taken for granted just because a manager becomes familiar with a language.

Communication occurs at a certain time, in some place, using certain mediums, and in a cultural context. Effective communication requires an understanding of and a sensitivity to all of these contextual elements. Because of the reputation of English as the common language worldwide and the physical isolation of the United States, the majority of the people in the United States have little exposure to other languages. This lack of language training can pose serious problems and bring about blunders for American MNCs.

There have been attempts to develop an international language. One such attempt was the development of **Esperanto**, a simple language to facilitate communication across cultural boundaries. The idea was to use Esperanto as a common language in all business circles. Dr. Lazarus Ludwig Zamenhof, the developer of this language, thought that a worldwide language could bring countries closer together and promote peace. In this language the word "esperanto" means "hope." He combined many languages to form words that are easy to learn and remember. The rules of grammar, punctuation, and spelling are simple enough to learn in about one hour.

Today, Esperanto is spoken around the world, especially in Europe, but many more people need to learn to speak this language before it becomes a truly worldwide language. There are also other so-called international languages that have not received widespread acceptance.

Written language differences can also cause problems in international operations. For example, a laundry detergent manufacturer faced problems when it ignored writing differences in another language. When the company initiated its promotional campaign in the Middle East, on its advertising displays it pictured the soiled clothes on the left, the box of detergent in the middle, and the clean clothes on the right. But because the people from the Middle East write and read from right to left, many of them interpreted the message to indicate that the detergent actually soiled the clothes.[9]

Of course, communication problems are not limited to corporations or their executives. World political leaders are not immune to such blunders:

> Former President Carter's speech in Poland will long be remembered for his incorrectly translated appreciation of the Polish woman (whom his translator said he "lusted for"). Former President Kennedy, in a major speech in Berlin, tried to say he was proud to be from Berlin but actually remarked that he was proud to be a jelly-filled donut (a "Berliner"). Other well-known people have mangled public introductions terribly by using incorrect titles and names. It seems that if there is a way to say something incorrectly, some poor soul has managed to do so.[10]

It is obvious that word by word translations without regard to cultural meanings can be very risky. Even words in the same language can have different meanings in different nations, and meanings of words can differ in different regions of the same country. It is best to use a double translation procedure. The original message should first be translated by a native speaker to his own tongue and then translated back to the original language by a foreigner to compare it with the original.

Many MNCs have faced problems in translating brand names or promotional messages into a foreign language. For example, the Kentucky Fried Chicken advertising slogan of "Finger Lickin' Good," was originally translated into Chinese to mean "So good you suck your fingers." Not a very appealing thought to the Chinese. As a second example, when a Japanese knife maker introduced its product in the United States it printed a warning label on the knife which read, "Caution: Blade extremely sharp keep out of children." The Japanese have also tried to sell a hair product called "Blow-up" and a baby soap named "Skinababe" in the United States. As another example, when Coca-Cola entered the China market, the shopkeepers developed their own slogan signs that in Chinese calligraphy translated as "Bite the wax tadpole," or "Beat the mare with wax." Coca-Cola had to research over 40,000 Chinese characters to find a variation that read "May the mouth rejoice."[11]

## Low- and High-Context Cultures

It is useful to distinguish between low- and high-context cultures when dealing with crosscultural communication.[12] Communication in a high-context culture is conducted so that most of the information is internalized in the person or in the physical context. One needs to understand these hidden codes and messages in the context of the conversation and the body language. In **high-context** cultures feelings are not explicitly expressed. It is assumed that the other party understands the sentiments without discussion. An expatriate in a high-context culture needs to read between the lines. One needs to know the context of the communication to understand it, because the context is where much of the information is. Examples of high-context cultures include Asia (Japan), the Middle East, and Africa.

Communication in a **low-context** culture is in the form of explicit codes and messages. In these cultures spoken words with explicit meanings are more dominant. Feelings are explicitly expressed in words. People in low-context cultures are usually more outspoken and expressive than the people from high-context cultures. Examples of countries with low-context cultures include Switzerland, Germany, Scandinavia, and the United States.

When managers from low- and high-context cultures engage in communication, the potential for misunderstanding is the greatest. For instance, an American may be looking for the meaning in a message—what is said. At the same time, a Japanese may be looking for the meaning in what is not said—in the silences and the pauses. An American may try to be articulate and accurate, whereas a Japanese may try to receive messages that often do not have to be said directly.

## Nonverbal Communication

Not all communication is written or spoken. People communicate with more than words when they speak. **Nonverbal language** involves body postures, eye contact, and many more "silent" communications. Facial expressions and body movements add more meaning to the spoken messages sent to others.

Table 10.1 depicts some of the important forms of nonverbal communication.

It is difficult if not impossible to make generalizations about differences in nonverbal communication and body language across different cultures. It is best to provide some examples. For instance, avoidance of eye contact by a local employee might be interpreted as an evasive behavior by a scolding expatriate manager. However, the employee might consider such a behavior as an expression of respect toward the manager. In Japan, looking subordinates in the eye is considered judgmental and punitive. On the other hand, when a subordinate looks a superior in the eye, he or she may be showing hostility. Americans like and trust people with direct eye contact. Arabs also like eye contact.[13]

Another element of cultural difference is the language of space. For exam-

Table 10.1   NONVERBAL COMMUNICATION PATTERNS

| Nonverbal communication form | United States | Some other countries |
|---|---|---|
| Appearance: clothing, grooming | Dress for success | Not as important, or offensive |
| Timing of verbal utterances | Prompt exchanges | Slower response time |
| Act of touch in conversation | Much less | More |
| Body and hand movements | Very little hand movement | Much hand movement (for example, among the Italians) |
| Use of eye contact | Much utilized | Avoidance |
| Action of smelling | Avoidance of odors | Use of odors to convey messages |
| Relative position between people | Face-to-face conveys friendship | Face-to-face means confrontation |
| Nonverbal aspects of speech: tones, accents, quality, and variety of voice | Less emotional; loud voice is sign of anger | More emotional loud voice is normal (as in the Middle East) |
| Bodily positions | Certain postures indicate friendly, hostile, superior, or other attitudes | |
| Physical distance | Further apart | Closer in Middle East and in Latin America |

ple, standing too far away in one culture might give the feeling of coldness or lack of trust, whereas standing too close in another culture might mean aggressiveness or hostility. When Americans talk to each other, they usually stand a little more than an arm's length apart. In the Middle East and South America, people stand much closer when they speak. Therefore, an American may feel uncomfortable when conversing with a person from these cultures. As the American backs off, as they usually do, the Latin American perceives this backing away as rejection. As another example, in the United States many offices are structured so that employees have their own individual rooms, so they "can think." In the United States, space, like time, is compartmentalized and used. In addition, space, like time, indicates status; that is, more important people have more space. Generally, more powerful managers have larger offices, which are higher up in the office building, with larger windows. In countries such as Japan there are no individual offices, and subordinates and superiors work side by side in the same large office. Unlike in the United States, in Japan "sitting near the window" signifies those employees who are being retired.[14]

It is advisable not to gesture with hands in many cultures. In parts of Asia gestures and slight hand movements may make people nervous. "Thumbs up" is considered vulgar in Ghana and in Iran, with the same meaning that raising the middle finger signifies in the United States. Body language is more than gestures. It includes the way one stands, sits, taps one's fingers, crosses legs, or tenses facial muscles. Unfortunately, these small but important body messages are difficult to translate across cultures.

The expatriate manager needs to learn how to walk into a room, greet, sit, and communicate verbally and nonverbally. The small details of social etiquette and body language are extremely important to the conduct of business. This is because these details establish the tone and set the scene for conversation. Awkwardness may not necessarily foil a deal, but the absence of awkwardness is definitely an advantage.[15]

## Barriers to Communication

Of all the elements of a culture, communication is probably the most critical, and it is the cause for many major problems between cultures. MNCs and their executives should be able to establish good communication with customers, suppliers, employees, the public, and the governments in the countries where they do business.

Figure 10.1 depicts potential communication barriers in international marketing. As the figure indicates, because of language and other cultural differences, messages can be translated incorrectly. Government regulations and economic or taste differences may be ignored by the MNCs. MNCs are both senders and receivers of information. Improper or ineffective communication either sending or receiving can cause problems and even failures for MNCs.

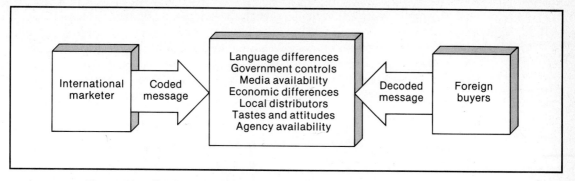

**Figure 10.1** Barriers to communication

*Source:* From Vern Terpstra, *International Dimensions of Marketing,* 2nd ed. (Boston: PWS-KENT Publishing Company, 1988), p. 156. © by PWS-KENT Publishing Company. Reprinted by permission of PWS-KENT Publishing Company, a division of Wadsworth, Inc.

# RELIGION

**Religion** is a major element and mainspring of culture. On a macro level, religion affects the language, social structure, economic system, and a host of other sociocultural elements. On a micro level, religion is frequently responsible for the behavior of the individuals and groups in a society. Therefore, in order to understand any of the sociocultural elements and the individual behavior that results from them, or in order to understand their impact on an MNC, one must understand religion. Understanding religion means understanding the most intimate convictions within humankind.

Understanding religion provides the best insight into the internal or mental behavior that is manifest in the external aspects of the culture. A working knowledge of some of the major religions will help the MNC executive to better understand why people's attitudes and behaviors vary from one culture to another. There are many religions, with varying numbers of followers, that have diverse impacts upon economic and business activities. In the following sections a few of the major religions of the world will be discussed. The coverage will not be theological or comprehensive, but will attempt to illustrate a few ways these religions may affect international business and MNCs.*

## Animism

Animism, currently practiced in some African and Latin American societies, is probably the oldest religion on earth. In Latin America, animism is characterized by the worship of natural phenomena, both animate and inanimate. The

---

*For a more detailed coverage of world religions, the reader is referred to the suggested readings at the end of this chapter.

worshipper of animism believes that the world can be controlled by ritual and that substances have magical properties. For example, a visual representation of a person can be used to control that person. In animism, anything unfamiliar is credited to magic. In animistic societies, problems are usually credited to the evil spirits. If these spirits are not exorcised, it can lead to misfortunes such as defective products, machinery breakdowns, and accidents.

Because animism is practiced primarily in some LDCs, magic is often given the credit for advanced technology. Vern Terpstra, who spent a number of years in Zaire, had an opportunity to see the persistence of animism along with modern educational activities. He writes:

> First, traditional witchcraft and the casting of spells were occasionally practiced. Second, reactions to European products and practices were often based on a magical interpretation. As one instance, a number of Africans affected the wearing of glasses. Because many Europeans wore glasses, it was felt that the wearing of glasses enhanced the intelligence of the wearer. As another instance, dispensaries established by Europeans were quite successful in replacing the witch doctor, because the white man's medicines, especially penicillin, were obviously better "magic" than the "dawa" of the witch doctor. Some consumer goods marketers in Africa have not hesitated to imply that possession of their products gives magical qualities to the owners. Of course, the same is occasionally true of marketers on American TV.[16]

The result of the animistic beliefs is the establishment of a traditional, slow-changing, backward-looking culture. Because of these qualities, MNC managers find difficulty operating in such a culture. The success or failure of a firm is often dependent upon its managers' understanding of these religious foundations.

## Brahmanic Hinduism

Hinduism, the primary religion of India, is thought to be about 3,000 years old. In 1980, there were about 583 million (13.39 percent of the world population) Hindus.*

Hindus believe that the creation of the world is a continuing process shared by men. Three gods carry out this continuous creation. At the end of each cycle or age in creation, Shiva (the destroyer god) destroys the old world. Brahma (god of creation) creates a new world. During the age or cycle, Vishnu (the savior) in the form of a human being or in some other form, with special powers, comes to aid humans when they face problems they cannot solve. This cosmic cycle is the basis for the philosophy of *reincarnation.*

As with other religions in India, in Hinduism nothing is permanent. Life is

---

*For a discussion of Hinduism and other religions of Asia the reader should consult Kenneth L. Woodward, "Religions of Asia," *Modern Maturity,* December 1984–January 1985, pp. 72–78; and Vern Terpstra and Kenneth David, *The Cultural Environment of International Business,* 2nd ed. (Cincinnati: South-Western, 1985), Chap. 4.

an illusion. Because everything is in the constant process of birth, death, and reincarnation, time is considered to be cyclical. This is in contrast to the Western view of time as abstract and limited. For this reason, specific time schedules are not followed in Hinduism.

In Hinduism, every person has a specific place in life and specific responsibilities. Each person is born with certain abilities and in a place because of his past actions and attitudes. This philosophy establishes the foundation for the *caste system,* which is the base for the whole pattern of society. A caste is a rigidly exclusive social class. These are heridatary classes into which Hindu society is divided. Castes are the basis for social division of labor. The highest caste, the Brahmins (the intellectual and priestly caste), is followed by the warriors (the landlords and politicians), the merchants, the peasants, and the untouchables (the outcastes).

There are many changing subgroups within each caste. An individual is born into a caste, and his position and job are inherited. One can move to a higher caste only in subsequent lives. A person can be punished by being reincarnated into a lower caste. The worst form of punishment by the gods is to reincarnate someone as an animal. In ordinary social life in India, caste lines underlie real injustices and strong prejudices. Many people recognize these injustices and efforts are being made to eliminate them. The Indian government forbids discrimination based on birth within a particular caste. With all the efforts to eliminate inequalities, discriminatory practices still exist. In certain instances the expatriate manager must recognize these conditions. For instance, it is risky to appoint a person of a lower caste to a supervisory position over members of higher castes.[17] The main function of the caste system is to preserve the status quo in Indian society.

The **baradari** or "joint family" is another characteristic of Hinduism. Traditionally, marriages are arranged in India. The bride joins the groom's family after marriage. Thus, families are enlarged through marriages. Eventually, an enlarged baradari or joint family evolves. The eldest member of the family has chief authority over this joint family. The older women have authority over the younger. The family council consists of the elders, who provide advice and consent to all members. The youth grow up to respect this hierarchy of authority, thinking and behaving in terms of extended joint family.

Baradari plays a role in the business world. If a member of the family gains fame and fortune, he is to remember the family and share his success, or help other members along their path to success.

Baradari may lead to nepotism. If the father works for a company, he will seek employment for his son and nephew, or even for distant family members. This practice may mean a stronger sense of loyalty to the company, but it also increases favoritism. The international manager needs to be aware of this "baradari" philosophy. A manager may anger and create resentment in many employees if he or she disciplines or fires a family member.

Restrictions on the freedom of women in Hinduism are based on the Hindu belief that an individual must have committed a sin during a former life to be born as one. As was pointed out earlier, marriages are arranged. A woman can not remarry if widowed, but a man may. Such unequal treatment of the sexes influences the role of women in the business world in India. An MNC should be careful in assigning women to executive positions in cultures dominated by Hinduism. Despite all these restrictions, the more contemporary women in India are well educated and are increasingly involved in many facets of modern Indian life.

## Buddhism

About 650 B.C., Buddhism arose as a reformation of Hinduism. Followers of Buddhism are concentrated in southeastern and eastern Asia from India to Japan. About 6.29 percent of the world population or 274 million people are Buddhists. Buddhist philosophy is based on Hinduism, but it has discarded much of Hinduism's dogma and ceremonial functions. The stress is on tolerance and spiritual equality.

Buddhism is based on philosophies of a prince named Gautama, who then became the Buddha, the "awakened one." Buddhism—the religion of those seeking to be awakened—is open to anyone. After Gautama became enlightened, he described the so-called Middle Path as the path to happiness. This path represents a middle ground between two extremes. At one extreme is the life of sensual indulgence. At the other extreme is the life of drastic asceticism or self-mortification. Both extremes lead to out-of-balance living and are to be avoided. Neither extreme releases one from suffering, and release from suffering is the true goal of life. Neither extreme is wise or brings about happiness. To find the Middle Path to harmonious and balanced living, one must search thoughtfully—not spend time in wordy arguments. He or she must explore and experiment. Buddha said, "Happiness he who seeks may win, if he practice the seeking."[18] Buddha opposed the caste system by opening his teachings to everyone.

Buddhism is based on the four *Noble Truths* that leads to the *Holy Eightfold Path.* The way to happiness is found in these eightfold paths. As a result of the lifelong following of this complicated and demanding ethical system, the adherent to the Holy Eightfold Path achieves *Nirvana.* Nirvana has a double meaning. On the one hand, it suggests the extinction of all craving, resentment, and covetousness, and therefore it leads to happiness. On the other hand, it is a release from all future reincarnations, the end of the "Round of Becoming." This is the ultimate goal of Hindu and Buddhist, alike. To cease to desire for everything, including material possessions, has adverse effects on acquisitiveness, achievement, and affluence. Devoted Buddhists, therefore, are less concerned with material possessions and try to follow the Eightfold Path.

Certain consequences follow for MNCs that are operating in such environments. Workers may be less inclined to work hard and might be harder to motivate. Marketing efforts may be less productive because of the lack of enthusiasm for new products and material possessions. Spiritual inclinations are stronger than the motives to acquire wealth, work achievement, or consumer goods. In addition, Buddhist monks can be influential in shaping political and social action since workers pay attention to these monks. An MNC executive in these environments needs to be aware of and sensitive to these Buddhists philosophies.

## Judaism

With its central teaching that the love of a unique God goes hand in hand with the love of one's fellow human, Judaism has probably influenced more lives and religious beliefs throughout history than any other religion. For instance, two other major religions—Christianity and Islam—are founded on Judaism.

Throughout thousands of years of wandering and persecution, Jews have remained intensely loyal to their religion. Currently, about 17 million people (0.39 percent of the world's population) practice this religion.

Abraham, believed to be the father of Judaism, thought that God took a special interest in human destiny and hopes. The founder of Judaism, Moses, clarified this idea of a personal God. Jews believe that God revealed the laws of life (the *Ten Commandments*) to Moses on Mount Sinai. Moses is given credit for clarifying a collection of laws on religious practice, behavior, and diet.

Jewish people have always looked for a future time when all humans, governments, and societies would reflect God's righteousness. This future time has been called *Kingdom of God.* At that time, God's righteous rule would extend over the earth and all humankind. More traditional Jews believe that Messiah, a selected person, will bring this kingdom. Many contemporary Jews believe every person is a messiah, and can advance righteousness. This gradually will bring the kingdom. Although Christians and Jews alike hope for a "Kingdom of God," their beliefs are expressed differently.

Liberal Jews are interested in living rightly now. Jews are more achievement oriented than Buddhists. Many tend to be well educated and are successful in professional careers and in the business world.

Orthodox (traditional) Jews are very strong in their traditions and their worship of God. They normally live in their communities, so they may better keep their religious practices and dietary laws. For example, they keep strict Sabbath on Saturdays and follow all the Mosaic laws, including dietary restrictions. Their way of life is different and sometimes difficult to understand for non-Jews, leading to complaints and persecutions. They have suffered throughout history and are probably the most displaced religious group. The MNC executive needs to understand, respect, and consider these special practices and laws when working in orthodox Jewish communities.

## Christianity

Christianity, an approximately 2,000-year-old offshoot of Judaism, also emphasizes a personal god who has made a great sacrifice for mankind. According to Christian theology, God sent his only begotten son, Jesus Christ, to earth so that he could redeem mankind through his own suffering and death.

Like other religions, Christianity has different sects. In the year 1980, there were about 1,433 million Christians in the world (about 33 percent of the world's population). This consisted of 809 million Roman Catholics, 349 million Protestants, 124 million Eastern Orthodox believers, and about 155 million followers in other groups.

A *Protestant* is a person who belongs to one of many sects of Christianity that separated from the Catholic Church during the Protestant Reformation in the sixteenth century.

The result of the Reformation was a greater emphasis on the individual and his or her actions, instead of the Roman Catholic emphasis on ritual and contemplation. In Protestantism one glorifies God through one's "calling" (one's life task) and through hard work. Also, hard work was evident by achievement. Thrift and frugality were necessary in order not to use the produced wealth selfishly. It was the duty of Protestants to accumulate wealth, to utilize it as an investment, and to increase production.

In Catholicism, money-making secular activities were considered to be socially, morally, and religiously unacceptable, even dangerous. Secular work, however, was considered a religious duty in Protestantism. The fruits of such hard work—production and income—were considered to be signs of God's approval of such endeavors. Consequently, money-making through hard work became a religious duty and was well accepted. The income, however, was not to be spent entirely for personal consumption. Money was to be saved for capital formation and investment. This philosophy led to the rise of the so-called capitalistic Protestants. The Protestants were also required to tithe, giving one-tenth of their income to the church to please and glorify God. The *Protestant work ethic* refers to this view of work as a moral virtue. According to the Protestant work ethic it is a religious duty to glorify God through hard work and thrift.[19]

## Islam

The word *Moslem* means "submitter." *Allah* is God. *Islam* means "submission to Allah's (God's) will." Moslems believe in submission to Allah because it brings peace and fulfillment. Moslems worship only Allah (God). The terms "Mohammedan" and "Mohammedanism," implying worship of Mohammed (the prophet), have been incorrectly used to refer to Islam, the religion. Mohammed claimed to be an ordinary man to whom God spoke through His angels. Allah understood man's need for direction, so, He established three means to reveal His will to man: the *prophets,* the *Koran* (the book of revelations), and the *angels.*

A Moslem must pray five times daily, at specific times: at sunrise, at noon, in midafternoon, at sunset, and at nightfall. The call for prayer is heard in Islamic countries at these times. This is the chief religious discipline, and the means to spiritual purification. The foreign manager of an MNC should know that work needs to be stopped during these prayer times in Moslem countries. Fasting is a means of purifying the physical body. During the month of Ramadan all believers, except those excused for physical conditions or for special activities, are expected to fast. No eating, no drinking, no smoking, and no sexual activity is allowed from dawn to sunset.

The Moslem year is lunar based on the moon cycles. A lunar year is ten to eleven days shorter than a solar year. As a result of this, Ramadan, the month of fasting, can fall in any season. In summer, when the days are hot and long, fasting is a severe test of faith. Moslems believe that in addition to purifying the body, fasting is a test of self-control and an act of sympathy toward the poor. Occasionally, food is consumed before dawn or after sunset. As a result of Ramadan rituals, the sales of some products fall drastically and factory output is at its lowest during Ramadan.

Islam is not only a religion, but also an economic, political, and social system based on the *Koran* and *Sharia* (Islamic law) as interpreted by religious orders. Islamic philosophy influences the total society, both social life and individual behavior. The Koran and the Sharia give instruction for conduct in all facets of life, from an individual's diet to social justice.

Islam forbids the consumption of alcohol and pork. It prohibits any form of sex outside marriage. Usury, the charging of interest on borrowed money, is not allowed, and this prohibition restricts some modern banking practices. Traditionally, women have a restricted role in some Islamic countries.

In 1980 there were about 723 million Moslems (16.6 percent of the world population). Moslems reside mainly in Asia and Africa. The highest concentration of the followers is in the Middle East. The majority of Moslems are *Sunnis* (traditionalists). Only about 10 percent of all Moslems are *Shiites.* They are the majority groups only in Iran and Iraq. But even with such a small number of followers, the Shiites are a strong political force in the Middle East. It was the Iranian Shiite clergy who led the revolution, causing the downfall of the Shah of Iran in 1979.[20] In the past, the split between the Sunnis and Shiites has led to occasional conflict. However, the brotherhood of Islam (regardless of sect differences) is a strong bonding factor among Moslems worldwide.

Shiites usually practice a more orthodox and fundamental type of Islam. Fundamentalists normally reject Western ideology and practices.[21] Moslems are sensitive about their religion. The expatriate manager needs to be aware of this sensitivity and understand the Moslems devotion to Islam. The manager needs to incorporate their rituals into his or her managerial practices.

## Confucianism

Although this is not a religion as such, it is a widely held philosophy that has shaped the Chinese norms of social and individual ethics and morality for thousands of years. It is an ethical system that is based on the teachings of the Chinese philosopher Confucius, who taught that all people possess unselfish love for others. The cultivation of this love is itself a reward. This emphasis on love and a gentle decorum accounts for such Chinese customs as courteous bowing, deference to elders, and politeness. Similar to the Protestant work ethic, the *Confucian work ethic* glorifies hard work and practice of thrift.

## Shintoism

Shintoism, the indigenous religion of Japan, has no founders or book of principles. Shintoism is based on legends that trace the founding of Japan back to a cosmic act. Accordingly, Shintoism gave the Japanese emperors divine status. Although there is no theology or organized worship, thousands of Japanese go to Shinto shrines every day.

In summary, religion is the spiritual side of a culture and the culture's approach to the supernatural. It provides meaning and motivation to life beyond the mere material aspects. Religion may lead people to great heights of new accomplishment, or it may lock them into a static past. Religion can unify diverse national cultures. The *World Christian Encyclopedia* provides a census of all the religions in the world. About two-thirds of this encyclopedia covers detailed statistics on all the world religions broken down country by country. An examination of these national statistics along with economic, trade, and other information are necessary for any multinational executive who is interested in working in a particular country. Table 10.2 shows the breakdown of the world's population into different religious groups.

**Table 10.2   ADHERENTS IN MILLIONS AND AS A PERCENTAGE OF THE WORLD POPULATION**

| | In the year 1900 | | In the year 1980 | | In the year 2000 | |
|---|---|---|---|---|---|---|
| | | % | | % | | % |
| Literate Religions | | | | | | |
| Buddhist | 127 | 7.84 | 274 | 6.29 | 359 | 5.73 |
| Christian | 558 | 34.44 | 1,433 | 32.90 | 2,020 | 32.27 |
| Roman Catholic | 272 | 16.79 | 809 | 18.58 | 1,169 | 18.67 |
| Protestant and Anglican | 153 | 9.44 | 345 | 7.92 | 440 | 7.03 |
| Eastern Orthodox | 121 | 7.47 | 124 | 2.85 | 153 | 2.44 |
| Other | 12 | 0.74 | 155 | 3.56 | 258 | 4.12 |
| Hindu | 203 | 12.53 | 583 | 13.39 | 859 | 13.72 |
| Jewish | 12 | 0.74 | 17 | 0.39 | 20 | 0.32 |
| Muslim | 200 | 12.35 | 723 | 16.60 | 1,201 | 19.19 |
| New Religions | 6 | 0.37 | 96 | 2.20 | 138 | 2.20 |
| Other* | 13 | 0.80 | 17 | 0.39 | 61 | 0.97 |
| Nonliterate Religions | | | | | | |
| Chinese Folk Religion | 380 | 23.46 | 198 | 4.55 | 158 | 2.52 |
| Tribalist and Shamanist | 118 | 7.28 | 103 | 2.37 | 110 | 1.76 |
| Nonreligious and Atheist | 3 | 0.19 | 911 | 20.92 | 1,334 | 21.31 |
| World Population | 1,620 | 100.00 | 4,355 | 100.00 | 6,260 | 100.00 |

*Including Sikh, Confucian, Shinto, Baha'i, Parsi

*Source: World Christian Encyclopedia* (Oxford: Oxford University Press, 1983), in Vern Terpstra, and Kenneth David, *The Cultural Environment of International Business*, 2nd ed. (Cincinnati, OH: South-Western, 1985), p. 82.

## Religion and International Business

Throughout the ages, great events have happened in the name of religion. Examples include the enslavement of the Hebrews, the Islamic conquests, the Christian crusades, Western colonialism, and even the present fighting among religious groups in Lebanon. Social and political movements have been more successful when they have been supported or justified by religious philosophy. The division of independent India in 1947 into primarily Hindu India and Moslem Pakistan was an example of a social and political movement with a basis in religion. As another example, the social and civil discontent against the Shah of Iran became more mobilized after it was supported by the Islamic fundamentalists. This led to the Shah's eventual overthrow and the establishment of an Islamic Republic.

Many crosscultural studies have shown that religion is one of the strongest determinants of economic and business activity both on a macro level and on a micro level. As a result, international business is affected by religious beliefs in a number of ways. First, religion can impose spiritual and moral norms on a culture, and thus affect business and economic activity. The subordination of impulse, greed, and selfishness to moral conduct is the norm in most religions. Buddhism imposes strict limits on the desire and the craving for possessions, and on selfish enjoyment of any kind.

Second, business activity can conflict with religious holidays or ceremonies. There is a difference in the sabbath day among countries with different religions. It is on Sundays for Christians, Saturdays for Jews, and Fridays for Moslems. The slowing down of business activities and worker productivity during Ramadan (the fasting month) in Moslem countries is significant. Third, religion can also impose economic norms. For example, the Protestant work ethic justifies hard work and economic achievement. Finally, international business can lead to modernization, which may be in conflict with religious beliefs and traditions. Exposure to Western cultural values can bring about uncertainties in the religious and cultural traditions of many countries. For example, in Saudi Arabia the religious values are not in agreement with the modern Western way of life.

We close this section by giving the following specific examples of the impact of religious beliefs on the business world:

**1.** The social and economic role of women in a culture is affected by religion. Women may be restricted from working beside men in certain job positions. This is true in some Islamic countries, such as Saudi Arabia. Women's roles as consumers may also be limited.

**2.** Religious holidays might bring about an increase or a decline in the consumption of certain items. During Christmas in Western countries, there is an increase in gift giving and food consumption. In Moslem countries sales of cigarettes decline during Ramadan. The MNC must be sensitive to the holy days and the holidays in formulating their work schedules and marketing programs.

**3.** Religious dietary restrictions, or encouragements, also affect consumption patterns. There are taboos against the consumption of pork for Jews and Moslems, and beef for Hindus. Islam forbids the consumption of alcohol.

**4.** Some religions subscribe to the concept of destiny or fate—a belief that one can not alter or change one's future. Hindus, Buddhists, and some Moslems believe in fate. Western cultures believe in the mastery of individual human over his or her destiny. As a result, there is an emphasis on planning in the West. Many Moslems believe that things will happen only if God wants them to happen. The term *Insha-Allah,* meaning "God willing" or "If God desires," is often heard in Islamic countries to express this belief.

**5.** The Hindu caste system restricts participation of members of some castes in certain economic activities. The caste system represents the lines that separate market segments. It also affects personnel and management policies and practices.

**6.** Baradari, the Hindu joint family, encourages nepotism in family business. As a result, family rank is usually more important than performance or other considerations in obtaining job assignments.

**7.** Some religions, such as animism, are more conservative and bound by tradition. People believing in such a religion can express fear and hostility toward technological changes and new products. An MNC must understand the logic of such religious beliefs and learn to deal with them.

**8.** Religious beliefs about magic, witchcraft, and curses can prevent or limit certain business activities. In parts of Asia, ghosts, fortune telling, palmistry, and soothsayers are an integral part of life and must be dealt with in business activities. In certain instances business deals will be delayed in anticipation of the proper religious time to conduct business, or they might be abandoned entirely because of superstitious beliefs.

**9.** Religious organizations and institutions play an important role in economic activities. The influence of Islamic mosque in the Middle East and the Catholic Church in the West should not be ignored. Organized religious groups can block or encourage the introduction of new products and technology, depending on their religious view of the new developments.

Religion has a major influence on the attitudes, beliefs, values, and motivations of the people and their culture. Ignoring religious beliefs can drastically reduce the production or the sales of products and cause disastrous failures for the MNC. Differences between the religious beliefs of an MNC manager and those of other people can lead to frustration for the manager, but an expatriate manager should understand and be sensitive to these differences. He or she must adapt the business activities of the MNC to these religious factors.

## ATTITUDES AND VALUES

Every culture has a set of attitudes and values that influences the behavior of the culture's members and establishes norms for their social conduct. Values perform as priorities for the sorting out of codes of behavior. Based on these priorities, a person in the culture selects one behavior or set of goals over others. Many of these attitudes and values have a religious foundation. The choices of behavior, therefore, imply moral judgment. Examples of values and attitudes can be seen in the baradari (the joint family) of Hinduism and in the Buddhist emphasis on piety, both of which have economic implications.

An international manager often finds a conflict between his or her values and the values of others from different cultural backgrounds. One serious problem is the ethnocentric attitudes of members of different cultures; each member believing that his or her value is the correct, logical, and best one. As a result of this kind of attitude an individual might believe that what works at home should work in a foreign culture. He or she, therefore, ignores environmental differences. **Ethnocentrism** refers to the belief that one's culture is superior to the culture of others. This may lead to stereotyping of others, misunderstandings, and conflict. In international surroundings, a manager must never take other peoples' beliefs for granted or consider his or her own beliefs to be the best. In this section attitudes and values will be discussed.

## Attitudes Toward Material Culture

**Material culture** refers to the objects and things made and used by humans. A house is an excellent symbol of American material culture. It is a good measure of material worth—the larger and better the house, the richer the owner. The study of material culture deals with the way products are made, that is, with *technology.* It also deals with the questions of "when," "what," and "for whom" to produce, that is, with *economics.* Material culture affects the types of products and the quality of the products demanded. It also affects the level of the demand for these goods.

For example, the consumption ethic, which began with mass production in the United States, is the cornerstone of the American material culture. As another example, the Protestant work ethic is concerned with work, achievement, and thrift.

As we will explain in Chapter 11, the technological aspect of material culture has resulted in major differences between the industrially developed and the less-developed countries. This difference is referred to as the "technology gap." References to industrialized countries, developing nations, agricultural societies, and less-developed countries refer to different material cultures. The economic organization and the technological level of a society are strong determinants of its behavior.

Differences in material culture usually necessitate product and marketing adaptations by an MNC. Marketing strategies that are concerned with the product, the package, the promotion, and the price should be modified to fit the material culture of a specific market.

## Attitudes Toward Work and Achievement

Different cultures attach varying values to work and achievement, just as they attach different attitudes to material culture. Again, one should not assume or expect orientations toward work and achievement to be the same everywhere. People generally work hard for what they consider worth working for. These values and priorities vary not only from nation to nation but also from region to region, and from culture to culture within the same country.

Accumulation of wealth and material objects is a measure of achievement in many cultures. McClelland, in his historical cross cultural studies, has found differing societal values toward achievement among different nations. In addition, his studies have shown that society's attitude toward achievement is a major determinant of a country's economic performance. That is, countries with higher levels of achievement motive accomplish higher economic performance.[22]

While operating in different parts of the world, an MNC executive needs to understand the attitudes of the local population toward work and achievement. Usually, if the right incentives are provided, the people will be motivated and will work hard. Otherwise, they may see no reason to meet the MNC executive's expectations. Providing job security and employment opportunities for the working members of the joint family may be the best motivators in India. On the other hand, building a sense of loyalty and commitment may motivate Japanese workers. Other cultures may expect higher pay or more challenging work.

## Attitudes Toward Time

Attitudes toward time vary from culture to culture. Each culture has a different attitude about the importance of time and punctuality. This can be a source of frustration and misunderstanding for an MNC's manager. For example, Americans like to be on time and finish business within a definite time frame. In the Middle East, however, a visitor may be kept waiting, or there may be a long delay before the conversation leads to business matters. The Middle Easterner may take time to get to know the visitor before approaching business matters. But once the business conversation gets underway, there is no limit on the amount of time spent on it.

The reason for such a difference in attitudes toward time is due to the contrast between traditional and modern values regarding time. Time orientations were traditionally more concrete. These older orientations were based on the alternations and cycles observed in nature: day and night, and the change in the seasons. These alternations and cycles were the base for production and for religious rituals. Time was viewed as cyclical. The measurement of time was based on recurring natural events such as the movement of the sun (the solar calendar), phases of the moon (the lunar calendar), the four seasons, and so forth. As a result of this cyclical view, time was considered to be replaceable and it was not measured very precisely. This orientation toward time still exists in some LDCs as well as in some subcultures of the more advanced countries. Even in the United States, people in the smaller towns and rural areas may have a time orientation that is more concrete than is found among people in the fast-paced big cities.

The more modern the attitude toward time, the more abstract and precise it becomes. Time is measured as a linear and nonrepetitive sequence. It is the artificial and precise movements of the clock that indicate the exact time in modern societies. Abstract time became the norm for economic activity and a way of life after the Industrial Revolution. The abstract orientation toward time is a linear conception that leads to an emphasis on future and long-term planning. This emphasis on long-term planning is the basis for scheduling activities.

When dealing with members of other cultures, one must recognize the differences in attitudes toward time. A person who is accustomed to an abstract, linear, and forward-looking time orientation may have difficulty adapting his or her attitudes to fit the different time orientations of other people. Important contracts and business deals may be lost if one rushes to do business too soon, or misinterprets delays in getting down to business.

In general, Westerners are more precise about time and are more punctual, whereas many Latins are more casual about time. Middle Easterners can also be more relaxed about time. Of course, exceptions are possible in any culture. In some cultures, promptness and time consciousness are determined by age and status. Subordinates and younger people are expected to be on time, whereas the boss or the elder may be the last to arrive. In some countries days are managed by sunrise and sunset. Appointments are scheduled for sometime tomorrow or next week, instead of for an exact hour and minute.

## Attitudes Toward Change

The MNC usually acts as an agent of change. It brings new technology and management practices as well as new products and marketing strategies to a host country. Under many circumstances, the introduction of new practices and the changing of old traditions can lead to resistance by the native people. The degree of resistance to change differs depending upon the society. Some societies are more tradition bound and less receptive to change. American managers who are used to customers accepting change are surprised by the lack of acceptance of new products in some other parts of the world. This may be because the United States is a relatively young nation and has less attachment to traditions than more traditionally oriented societies. In more traditional countries there is a reverence for old methods, proven products, and accepted practices.

Modernization, as it is known to the Western world, is a cultural import and is alien to the non-Western regions of the world. One must not judge everything based on Western criteria. Westerners often assume that others have, or should have, the same economic values as they do. This leads to frustration on their part, and resentment on the part of people from the East.

Usually slow, incremental change is more easily accepted than rapid change. The international manager must be aware of this and use it to his or her advantage. The closer the new idea is to the traditional cultural attitudes and values, the more quickly it will be accepted. People who will be affected by the change need to recognize the advantages of the new over the old before they will accept the new. Overall, the new idea should be consistent with the traditions. It should be shown to be a better idea, and it should be introduced slowly and in an orderly fashion.

## Attitudes Toward Risk

Associated with change is uncertainty and potential risk. Accepting change, therefore, depends on the amount of risk a person is willing to take. In traditional and conservative societies there is a greater reluctance to take the risk associated with trying something new. The innovator may experience resentment from peers, customers, and the public. Change may also be counter to religious beliefs and thus create the potential for religious persecution against those who accept the change. The social risks associated with innovation are in addition to the entrepreneurial or the normal business risk of innovation.

In agrarian societies, the farmer may be reluctant to try a new seed, a new method of farming, or modern machinery. This reluctance may be due to the fear of the unknown and the high risk associated with the possibility of a disastrous crop resulting from the use of new products and procedures. There is evidence that rural merchants, fishermen, and artisans are more modern and less tradition bound than rural farmers.

Much of new technology transferred from the developed nations to the less-developed countries fails. This is because MNCs have not been sensitive to the local environment and the cultural traditions. This lack of sensitivity usually leads to a lack of acceptance of the innovations or a disappointing performance by such innovations.

When introducing an innovation the MNC should (1) examine the social, cultural, and environmental impacts of the change; (2) determine the social, cultural, and environmental obstacles to the change and then establish a planned process of slow change and adaptation to this value orientation; (3) test and evaluate the innovation in terms of the host country's culture and environmental conditions; (4) demonstrate the advantages and effectiveness of the innovation in the host country; (5) accept that technological innovations are usually more easily accepted than social, political, or cultural innovations; and (6) examine and find local cultural values and attitudes that are supportive of the innovation, in order to go with the grain of the local culture rather than against it.

## Attitudes Toward Decision Making

Patterns of decision making can be either objective or subjective. In objective decision making, relevant information is collected from all persons who possess it and decisions are made based on a rational or semirational analysis of the data gathered. Subjectivity in decision making, on the other hand, may mean that the personal judgment of an elder or a senior executive may be the sole criterion on which a decision is made.

Because of the high degree of respect for authority in some societies, the subjective style of decision making by an individual is the social norm. Usually no request is made for an explanation of the rationale and the reasons behind such a decision. This would only indicate a lack of confidence in the person's judgment. The elder or executive is also expected to be knowledgeable enough so as not to seek information from subordinates or other people. Thus, the hierarchical rank or age of the person may be the most important element in the decision-making process. Decisions are based on individual skills and emotions rather than the objective analysis of the facts by many people.

The number of people who can be involved in the decision-making process is also the source of another cultural variation in decision making. Decisions can be made by one individual, that is, autocratically, or by a number of people in a democratic, participative fashion. Research findings show that participative, group decisions are usually of better quality, have higher acceptance levels, and are easier to implement. But such decisions can take longer to make. Some cultures, such as the Japanese, adhere to the group consensus decision-making style to a greater degree.[23]

## Attitudes Toward Family

The family is the basic social institution. In the United States, the family usually includes the parents and the unmarried children living in a household. In many other countries the family unit is extended to include all the relatives (by blood or by marriage). The Hindu joint family (baradari) discussed earlier is a prime example of such a large, *extended family.* The extended family, however, does not need religious sanction to exist. In many LDCs this type of family unit exists and serves several vital socioeconomic roles. The extended family serves as a vehicle for mutual protection, for psychological and moral support, and for economic insurance in times of need or in old age. In today's modern world, it also serves as a way to obtain business contacts or employment opportunities.

In some countries members of three generations live together in a household, most of the time very happily. In Latin America, the work group usually consists of family members. People use their mother's as well as their father's surname. In nations where the extended family exists, business people frequently explore family ties before starting business matters. If family ties are known, the possibility for the development of a better business deal is usually enhanced. The notion of the extended family is in direct contrast to the *nuclear family* or the single-parent households found in the United States.

The concept of extended family can bring stability to the society, as is the case in Japan. Or it can ensure a stable class or caste system, as is the case in India. The extended family also provides trusting relationships. People may purchase higher-priced items (especially durable goods) from a distant cousin because of the family ties. The best job opportunities may be filled with relatives regardless of their merits. Often consumption decisions are made in a different manner than in the Western nations. Family members may pool their resources and respect an older member's suggestions and decisions in making large purchases. Along with the benefits obtained from the extended family come high expectations on the part of the individual. A family member is expected to respect the elderly, to abide by their authority, and to support them. Instead of the Social Security system found in the United States, family members can depend on the family to support and take care of them in their old age. The family acts as a source of unemployment or disability insurance. No-interest loans can usually be obtained from other family members. People come to help other family members in case of illness or disaster. Fulfilling one's responsibilities toward the family has priority over obligations to the employer. This may interfere with the employment practices of the MNC because it might mean sudden absence from the work place by a native worker to tend to a family crisis. Overall, the extended family is a way to use the relationships and dependencies for the benefit of all members of the family.

### Attitudes Toward Authority

Based on the hierarchical structure represented in extended families, respect for authority is usually greater in the more traditional societies. This leads to a near reverence of authority figures. Extended family members usually do not question the decisions of the head of the household and the elders. There is no physical distance between the different age groups in these societies and generations might live together under the same roof. However, the status differences based on age differences are strong and visible. Older age means higher rank in the hierarchical structure of the family.

In the United States, senior citizens usually live apart from other generations. The generation gap is influential. The youth-oriented culture of the United States seems to have a negative attitude toward the old age. Respect for the aged is relatively less than it is in the more traditional nations. Different age groups, such as senior citizens or teenagers, form different economic subcultures with their own consumption patterns and purchasing capabilities.

The differences in family structures and in attitudes toward authority in various cultures have led to differences in authority orientations in the workplace. In countries with extended family units, the hierarchical rankings are more distinct, and the respect for the higher-ranked person is much stronger. The manager is expected to know the answers, or at least act as if he or she does. Autocratic managerial decision making is generally expected and accepted in most of these nations. The decisions made by the manager are respected and followed. Questioning the rationale behind decisions usually means disrespect and shows doubt about a manager's knowledge and judgment. An exception is found in Japan with its strong adherence to consensus style decision making.

## COPING WITH CULTURAL DIFFERENCES

The expatriate managers of an MNC have a special need for cultural sensitivity in coping with cultural differences. Foreign job assignments are usually major transitional experiences and are often accompanied by culture shock. **Culture**

**shock** is the anxiety one experiences when facing a new and different culture, with its new characteristics and expectations. During this traumatic period of culture shock, a person finds that his or her familiar cultural characteristics and expectations do not work in the new setting.

Let us recall the Oriental folktale mentioned earlier. For the average person, being in a new cultural setting is like being a "fish out of water," experiencing anxiety, stress, and frustration. The problem is further aggravated if the person has an ethnocentric orientation, that is, a belief that his or her culture is superior to other cultures.

We conclude this chapter by providing ten tips that a person may employ to deal with sociocultural differences and with the stress and tension of culture shock wherever and whenever it may be confronted:

**1.** Be culturally prepared. Forewarned is forearmed. Individual and group study and training should be undertaken. Such study and training should help the person to understand cultural characteristics in general, as well as the cultural specifics of the host nation to be visited.

**2.** Learn local communication complexities. Language training should be an essential part of the cultural preparation program. At least some basic aspects of the language should be mastered. The role of the nonverbal elements of culture should not be ignored.

**3.** Mix with the host nationals. It is essential to mix and socialize with the people from the host country, both before departure and after arrival.

**4.** Be creative and experimental. Learn from mistakes, try new ways, take risks, and experiment. Do not be afraid of failure.

**5.** Be culturally sensitive. A visitor will be more accepted if he or she is culturally sensitive. Be aware of customs and traditions. Watch people and act as they do. Never stereotype the people or criticize their way of life.

**6.** Recognize complexities in the host culture. Try to avoid making quick, simplistic evaluations of situations in a foreign country. Most societies are composed of different ethnic or religious groups and different social classes or castes. There are also differences between geographical regions and rural and urban settlements.

**7.** Perceive yourself as a culture bearer. You represent your own culture in a foreign country. In other words, you are an ambassador of your culture in a foreign country. Because you also assess everything in a host culture through your own cultural background, bias on your part is easy. A visitor's upbringing and culture and his or her lack of understanding of a host culture can lead to misunderstandings as well as to personal conflicts.

**8.** Be patient, understanding, and accepting of yourself and your hosts. One must be more tolerant and flexible in unfamiliar situations. Have a healthy curiosity. Be willing to face inconveniences, and be patient when answers or solutions are not forthcoming or are difficult to obtain.

**9.** Be most realistic in your expectations. Avoid overestimation of your own capabilities or those of your hosts. Unrealistic expectations of a crosscultural experience can lead to disappointment and frustration.

**10.** Accept the challenge of intercultural experiences. Anticipate, savor, and face the challenge to adapt to your new cultural experience. Be flexible and allow yourself to modify your habits, attitudes, values, tastes, relationships, and pleasures as a way to personal growth and fulfillment.[24]

## SUMMARY

1. Society is a system whereby people live together in organized communities. Society includes all aspects of economic and social activity. The legal and political systems, the religion, the mores, the educational system, the language, the demographics, and the technology are all parts of a society.
2. Culture is the common cognitive frame of reference and the pattern of behavior shared by the members of a society, and culture is transmitted to members of a group from previous generations of the group.
3. There are as many as 73 dimensions to the sociocultural environment. These dimensions are called cultural universals. Only a few important dimensions were discussed in this chapter.
4. Language is the primary means of communication and penetrates all dimensions of a culture. Communication can be both verbal and nonverbal. Verbal language refers to written as well as oral forms of communication. Nonverbal language involves the unspoken word as opposed to the spoken word. It also includes body language. Language differences can cause serious problems in international business operations.
5. Religion is a major element and mainspring of culture. It is an inner determinant of many of the external manifestations of culture. It affects the language, the social and economic structure, and a whole host of other sociocultural elements. Religion strongly influences the behavior of the individuals and the groups in a society. In this chapter a few of the major religions and their influences on international business were discussed.
6. Material culture refers to the objects made and used by humans. The study of material culture deals with the way products are made, that is, with technology. It also deals with the questions of "when," "what," and "for whom" products are made, that is, with economics.
7. Different cultures attach different values to work and to achievement.
8. Attitudes toward time vary from culture to culture. Traditional cultures consider time to be concrete, repetitive, and replaceable. The modern orientation toward time is to regard it as abstract, precise, linear, and nonrepetitive. Thus, different values are attached to time spent on business deals in different countries.
9. Some cultures are more open to changes in life-styles, procedures, products, and technology than other cultures.
10. Acceptance of change depends on the amount of risk a person is willing to take. In traditional and conservative societies there is a greater reluctance to take the risks associated with trying the new.
11. In the more traditional societies, the subjective style of decision making is dominant, whereas in modern cultures the objective style is more common.

12. Extended family structures are the norm in traditional cultures, with many different family members and their families living together in the same household.
13. Based on the hierarchical structure found in extended families, respect for authority is usually greater in more traditional societies.
14. Culture shock is defined as the psychological anxiety one experiences when facing a new and different culture with its new characteristics and expectations. Strategies to prevent culture shock and to manage the experience of cultural differences were presented.

## QUESTIONS

10.1 How do the elements of the sociocultural environment affect the operations of an MNC?

10.2 Define culture and describe its characteristics. Discuss the impact of cultural differences on the multinational company and its managers.

10.3 Discuss cultural barriers in communication. What are their implications for international marketing? Have you personally faced communication problems with persons from other cultures? What were the reasons for the lack of communication? How can these cultural barriers to communication be overcome? Discuss.

10.4 Give additional examples of how religious beliefs affect the way people live. Discuss the way businesses operate in cultures with different religions.

10.5 How do attitudes toward change affect the way an expatriate approaches his or her foreign job assignment? You should consider the individual manager's attitude as well as the host country's attitude toward change in answering this question.

10.6 After graduating from college you are offered a job with a multinational company with the potential for a foreign assignment after two years. What considerations would you think of in deciding to accept or reject this job offer? Discuss.

10.7 Assume that you have accepted the job described in Question 10.6. How would you prepare yourself and your family for such an assignment?

10.8 Has this course in international business affected your sensitivity to and understanding of cultural differences? How? Has it helped you better cope with these differences? Discuss.

## NOTES

1. David A. Ricks, *Big Business Blunders: Mistakes in Multinational Marketing* (Homewood, Ill.: Dow Jones-Irwin, 1983).
2. Don Adams, "The Monkey and the Fish: Cultural Pitfalls of an Educational Advisor," *International Development Review,* vol. 2, no. 6 (1960), p. 22.
3. M. E. Beres and J. D. Portwood, "Explaining Cultural Differences in the Perceived Role of Work: An International Cross-Cultural Study," in G. W. England, A. R. Negandhi, and B. Willport, eds., *Cross-Cultural Studies on Organizational Functioning* (Kent, Ohio: Kent State University Press, Comparative Administration Research Institute, 1979).
4. Ibid.
5. Edward T. Hall, *Beyond Culture* (Garden City, N.Y.: Anchor Books, 1976), pp. 13–14.

6. George P. Murdock, "The Common Denominator of Cultures," in Ralph Linton, ed., *The Science of Man in the World Crises* (New York: Columbia University Press, 1945), pp. 123–142.

7. David A. Ricks, *Big Business Blunders,* p. 31.

8. Peter Davies, ed., *The American Heritage Dictionary of the English Language,* paperback edition (New York: Bell, 1976).

9. David A. Ricks, *Big Business Blunders,* p. 55.

10. Ibid., pp. 13–14.

11. Lennie Copeland and Lewis Griggs, *Going International: How to Make Friends and Deal Effectively in the Global Marketplace* (New York: Random House, 1985), p. 11.

12. Edward T. Hall, *Beyond Culture,* pp. 79–82.

13. Lennie Copeland and Lewis Griggs, *Going International,* pp. 110–112.

14. Ibid., pp. 16–17.

15. Ibid., pp. 99–118.

16. Vern Terpstra, *The Cultural Environment of International Business* (Cincinnati: South-Western, 1984), pp. 34–35.

17. Vern Terpstra and Kenneth David, eds., *The Cultural Environment of International Business,* 2nd ed. (Cincinnati: South-Western, 1985), p. 89.

18. F. H. Ross and Tynette Hills, *The Great Religions by Which Men Live* (Greenwich, Conn.: Fawcett, 1986), p. 53.

19. Max Weber, *The Protestant Work Ethic and the Spirit of Capitalism* (London: Allen & Unwin, 1930; New York: Scribner, 1958).

20. Kenneth L. Woodward, "Religions of Asia," *Modern Maturity,* December 1984–January 1985, pp. 75–78.

21. "Sunnis? Shiites? What's That Got to Do with Oil Prices?" *Forbes,* 12 April 1982, pp. 88–99.

22. David C. McClelland, *The Achieving Society* (Princeton, N.J.: D. Van Nostrand, 1961); David C. McClelland, "Business Drives and National Achievement," *Harvard Business Review* (July–August 1962), pp. 92–112.

23. S. P. Sethi, N. Namiki, and C. L. Swanson, *The False Promise of the Japanese Miracle: Illusions and Realities of the Japanese Management System* (Boston: Pitman, 1984).

24. P. R. Harris and R. T. Moran, *Managing Cultural Differences,* 2nd ed. (Houston, Tex.: Gulf, 1987), pp. 212–215.

## SUGGESTED READINGS

Adams, Dan. "The Monkey and the Fish: Cultural Pitfalls of an Educational Advisor." *International Development Review,* vol. 2, no. 2, (1969), pp. 22–24.

Anderson, James N. D. *The World's Religions.* London: Inter-Varsity Fellowship of Evangelical Unions, 1950.

Andreski, Stanislav, ed. *Max Weber on Capitalism, Bureaucracy and Religion: A Selection of Texts.* London: Allen & Unwin, 1983.

Batton, Thomas R. *Communities and Their Development.* New York: Oxford University Press, 1957.

Bellah, Robert N. (ed.). *Religion and Progress in Southeast Asia.* Ann Arbor: University of Michigan Press, 1965.

Beres, M. E., and J. D. Portwood, "Explaining Cultural Differences in the Perceived Role of Work: An International Cross-Cultural Study." In G.W. England, A.R. Negandhi, and B. Willport, eds., *Cross-Cultural Studies on Organizational Functioning.* Kent, Ohio: Kent State University Press, Comparative Administration Research Institute, 1979.

Copeland, L., and L. Griggs. *Going International: How to Make Friends and Deal Effectively in the Global Marketplace.* New York: Random House, 1985.

Hall, Edward T. *Beyond Culture.* Garden City, N.Y.: Anchor Books, 1976.

Harris, P. R., and R. T. Moran. *Managing Cultural Differences,* 2nd ed. Houston, Tex.: Gulf, 1987.

Kroeber, Alfred L., and Clyde Kluckhohn. "Culture: A Critical Review of Concepts and Definitions." *Papers of the Peabody Museum of American Archeology and Ethnology.* Cambridge, Mass.: Harvard University Press, 1952., vol. 47, no. 1. Vintage edition. New York: Knopf, 1963.

Lester, Robert C. *Theravada Buddhism in Southeast Asia.* Ann Arbor: University of Michigan Press, 1972.

Miner, John B., Jeffry M. Wachtel, and Bahman Ebrahimi. "The Managerial Motivation of Potential Managers in the United States and Other Countries of the World: Implications for National Competitiveness and the Productivity Problem." *Advances in International Comparative Management,* vol. 4 (August 1989), pp. 147–170.

Negandhi, A. R.. "Cross-Cultural Management Studies: Too Many Conclusions, Not Enough Conceptualization." *Management International Review,* vol. 14, no. 6 (1974), pp. 59–67.

———. "Cross-Cultural Management Research: Trend and Future Directions." *Journal of International Business Studies* (Fall 1983), pp. 17–38.

Ouchi, William G. *Theory Z: How American Business Can Meet the Japanese Challenge.* Reading, Mass.: Addison-Wesley, 1981.

———. *The M-Form Society: How American Teamwork Can Recapture the Competitive Edge.* Reading, Mass.: Addison-Wesley, 1984.

Phatak, A. V. *International Dimensions of Management,* 2nd ed. Boston: Kent, 1988.

Radhakrishnan. *The Hindu View of Life.* London: George Allen & Unwin, 1961.

Ricks, David A. *Big Business Blunders: Mistakes in Multinational Marketing.* Homewood, Ill.: Dow Jones-Irwin, 1983.

Roberts, K. H. "On Looking at an Elephant: An Evaluation of Cross-Cultural Research Related to Organizations." *Psychological Bulletin,* 74 (1970), pp. 327–350.

Ross, Floyd H., and Tynette Hills. *The Great Religions by Which Men Live.* Greenwich, Conn.: Fawcett, 1986.

Sethi, S. P., N. Namiki, and C. L. Swanson. *The False Promise of the Japanese Miracle: Illusions and Realities of the Japanese Management System.* Boston: Pitman, 1984.

Slater, Robert. *World Religions and World Community.* New York: Columbia University Press, 1968.

"Sunnis? Shiites? What's That Got to Do with Oil Prices?" *Forbes,* 12 April 1982, pp. 88–99.

Terpstra, Vern. *The Cultural Environment of International Business.* Cincinnati: South-Western, 1978.

———. *International Dimensions of Marketing,* 2nd ed. Boston: Kent, 1988.

———. *International Marketing,* 4th ed. Chicago: Dryden Press, 1987.

Terpstra, Vern, and Kenneth David, eds., *The Cultural Environment of International Business,* 2nd. ed. Cincinnati, Oh.: South-Western, 1985, Chap. 4.

Tylor, Edward B. *Primitive Culture.* London: Murray, 1871.

Weber, Max. *The Protestant Work Ethic and the Spirit of Capitalism.* London: Allen & Unwin, 1930; New York: Scribner, 1958.

———. *The Religion of China: Confucianism and Taoism.* Glencoe, Ill.: Free Press, 1949.

———. *The Religion of India: The Sociology of Hinduism and Buddhism.* Glencoe, Ill.: Free Press, 1958.

———. *Ancient Judaism.* Glencoe, Ill.: Free Press, 1952.

Woodward, Kenneth L. "Religions of Asia." *Modern Maturity,* December 1984–January 1985, pp. 72–78.

# Chapter 11

# Technological Forces and Technology Transfer

*T*echnology is one of the most important factors that has contributed to economic well-being in the advanced countries, and it has helped maintain our present standard of living. Technological improvement has enabled us to reduce our working hours, to increase production efficiency, to improve our working conditions, and to enhance the flow of the goods and services that we produce. In manufacturing, for example, about three decades ago an ammonia plant was capable of producing 150 tons of ammonia a day; in 1970, it could produce 1,500 tons a day; and in the early 1980s it could produce 3,000 tons of ammonia in a single day.[1] In agriculture, for example, technological innovations over the last generation have significantly increased the productivity of labor and land in the U.S. agricultural sector. In the production of corn, for instance, from 1910 to 1914, each acre of land required 35.2 hours of labor to produce 26 bushels of corn. From 1972 to 1982, however, each acre of land required only 3.4 hours of labor to produce 105.3 bushels of corn. Such improvements have drastically changed the structure of the U.S. agricultural sector over time. The U.S. agriculture sector has been transformed from a relatively labor-intensive system to a relatively capital-intensive one. As a result, in the late 1980s there were about 2.2 million farms in the United States, as compared with roughly 5.5 million farms 60 years ago, which is a 60 percent decrease. The number of workers in the agriculture sector has declined substantially.[2]

Presently, there is not a single day that goes by without news of some type of technological progress that will affects our lives. The invention of computer chips, for example, has had an enormous impact on production, education, and health care, to name just a few areas affected. The introduction of robots in many factories has reduced the need for labor. The use of VCRs and microcomputers has become commonplace in our homes, businesses, and schools. The advancements in medical technology have contributed to longevity in our society.

Unfortunately there is a negative side to our technological progress. The introduction of nuclear weapons has completely changed the balance of power in the world and has made the destruction of the human race a real possibility. Factories using modern technologies have polluted our air and water, contributing to the causes of cancer, birth defects, and other health-related problems. Despite this, we have come to rely on more technology to resolve the problems that are created by the technology in the first place. For instance, in the area of military technology, the Reagan administration announced research on "Star Wars" technology to combat the possibility of nuclear attack. To fight pollution, we use high-tech antipollution devices. It seems that our passion for technological advancement is a never-ending process.

In the past, most technologies have been developed by the advanced industrial nations, spreading to other countries only after different time lags. For example, the Industrial Revolution that started in England in the eighteenth century later spread to North America and Western Europe in the nineteenth century, and finally to Japan and Russia in the early twentieth century. However, this process has not yet been completed and many LDCs in Africa, Asia, and South America are still using the pre–Industrial Revolution technologies. As a result, the LDCs have become technologically dependent on the advanced nations for their economic growth and development. To obtain the needed technology, many LDCs have turned to the international market as a channel for modern technology transfer.

Theoretically, foreign direct investment (FDI) in the LDCs is perceived not only as a source of capital inflow but also as a vehicle for acquiring modern technology and the necessary managerial know-how that these countries require for their development. Following World War II, when a shortage of capital existed, FDI was emphasized as a significant source for providing the needed capital for LDCs. As shortage of capital was slowly resolved, however, and as many development efforts that were based solely on capital failed, the technology transfer role of FDI became the center of attention.

Having realized the importance of FDI as a vehicle for technology transfer, it has become evident that much of the success of investment projects depends on the selection of *appropriate technology,* that is, a technology that better fits the economic and social environment of the country in question. What may be appropriate technology for the capital-abundant United States, however, may be totally inappropriate for a labor-abundant country like India. Thus, it is necessary for an MNC to adapt its technology to the national environment of the country in which it operates.

The purpose of this chapter is to provide us with a broad understanding of the issues that are raised when technology is transferred through international business. First, we define the concept of technology and discuss its different classifications. Second, we describe the variables that affect the choice of technology. Third, we explain the modes by which technologies are transferred, and we elaborate on the strategies that are used in choosing among these modes of technology transfer. Fourth, we describe the major methods that are used in technological forecasting. Fifth, we discuss the relationship between technology and culture. Finally, we study the role of technology in the process of economic development.

## DEFINITION OF TECHNOLOGY

**Technology** can be defined as the method or technique for converting inputs to outputs in accomplishing a specific task.

In the above definition, the terms "method" or "technique" are used to mean not only the knowledge, but also the skills and the means for accomplishing a task. Thus, technological innovation taken in this context refers to the increase in knowledge, the improvement in skills, or the discovery of a new or improved means that extends our ability to achieve a given task.

Because the inputs of production can be combined in different proportions to produce the same type of output, we have different technological alternatives in the production of a given product. For example, a table can be built in many different ways. A primitive technology would use labor with handtools to get the job done. A highly advanced technology would use a computer to design the table, to organize an assembly line, and to employ the skills of trained laborers using power tools to accomplish the task. Between these two extremes, one could picture a wide variety of combinations of laborers and machines, each representing a specific level of technology. At one extreme, when a primitive technology is used, the technology is referred to as "labor-intensive" or "capital-saving." The other extreme represents "capital-intensive" or "labor-saving" technology. As we move from the labor-intensive extreme to the capital-intensive extreme, we create different production alternatives by simply increasing the capital intensity of our production technology.

## CHOICE OF TECHNOLOGY

As our preceding discussion indicated, different technological alternatives can be used for the production of a given type of product. The question to ask, then, is what alternative should be chosen? To answer this question, one must take into consideration the variables that affect the choice of technology. Chief among these variables are the costs of capital and labor, the availability of technological alternatives, the size and growth of the market, and the obsolescence of the existing technology.

### The Cost of Capital and Labor

What determines a firm's choice to use a relatively capital-intensive technology or to use a relatively labor-intensive technology? Obviously, a firm attempts to achieve the lowest possible production cost when producing a given product. As a result, the choice of technology will depend on the relative cost of labor as compared with the cost of capital. Thus, given two alternative methods of production, if labor is relatively more expensive than capital, assuming everything else is the same, the firm would use a more capital-intensive technology. On the other hand, if capital is relatively more expensive than labor, the firm would use a labor-intensive technology. This means a firm that operates in an advanced country like the United States, which has an abundance of capital, should use a relatively capital-intensive technology. However, a firm that is located in an LDC, like India, should use a relatively labor-intensive technology.

The research and development (R&D) efforts of the United States in recent decades are indicative of the choice of technology on the basis of the relative cost of capital and labor. Given the relative scarcity of labor in the United States, these R&D efforts have resulted in the development of technologies that are largely labor saving, that is, capital intensive. However, today, when the relative scarcity of natural resources is expected to increase, as we will explain in Chapter 21, there are signs that some of the U.S. industries are shifting away from labor-savings to natural resource–saving technologies, that is, those technologies that reduce the amount of natural resources needed in the production of different goods.

### The Availability of Technological Alternatives

The choice of technology by a firm is affected by the commercial feasibility of the technology and the availability of technological alternatives to the firm. These, in turn, depend on the industry in which a firm is operating. In some industries, numerous technological alternatives exist from which a firm can choose its desired production technique. For example, in the textile industry the production process is broken down into a number of different operations, each allowing trade-offs between capital and labor. In other industries, however, there may be only a very few alternatives from which a firm can choose. For example, in the petroleum industry, the refinery of raw materials is achieved by the distillation process, using heat to separate different products. In this process, there is little room for intervention. Consequently, the substitution of capital for labor is not feasible in the basic distillation process.

## The Size and the Growth of the Market

Because the objective of a firm is the production of a product that can be sold for a profit, the market size and its growth are among the most significant factors that should be taken into consideration in choosing a technology. Given that the demand for the products of an MNC is generated by both the domestic and the foreign markets, the size and the potential growth of these markets are important factors that should guide the MNC in choosing the technology that produces products in the quantity and of the quality that are warranted by these markets. Thus, it is necessary for us as managers of MNCs to have some knowledge of the market size and the share of the market that could be captured by our company. If the market is too small, and we choose a relatively large size plant, then our plant has to operate under its capacity. This unused plant capacity, leading to a higher production cost and higher prices, erodes our competitiveness in the marketplace. On the other hand, if our market is too large, and we choose a relatively small-size plant, we would not be able to satisfy the market demand and would lose some of our customers to our rivals. Thus, it is important to gather as much information about the market as is possible. Such information should include data on the total sales in the market, the rate of market growth, the price of substitutes and complimentary goods, the labor training costs, the labor relations problems, the government regulations, and information on major competing firms with regard to their market share, product quality, customer satisfaction, and distribution channels. Such information not only guides us to choose the optimum plant size but also allows us to define the right price for the product—a price that covers our full cost and yields the desired rate of return on the invested capital.

## The Obsolescence of the Existing Technology

Because in any industry the introduction of a new invention might result in the obsolescence of the existing technology, it is important for us as managers of MNCs to predict the possibility of such an occurrence before undertaking an investment project. This prediction is helpful in guiding us to select those technologies that would generate sufficient revenues to justify their initial costs before they become obsolete. Take the case of the textile industry, which has gone through numerous innovations regarding each specific production operation. A recent study lists 40 different innovations in textile machinery, and it shows the number and the nature of the innovations for each specific production operation. According to this study, there have been six different innovations regarding fiber preparation. For example, one of the innovations, called the automatic hopper feeder, was introduced in West Germany in 1959 and was later used by Automatic Material Handling, Inc., in 1973, leading to the obsolescence of the existing technology.[3] To ensure that the expected revenue justifies the initial cost of the product, any firm investing in the textile industry prior to 1959 should have tried to predict the possibility that the existing process would become obsolete at a certain time. But what about those firms who have already invested in an old technology when a new technology is introduced? Should a firm that uses the nonautomatic hopper feeder convert to the automatic one? To answer this question one needs to undertake a cost-benefit analysis, taking into consideration the initial cost of the equipment, the cost of labor, the cost of capital, the cost of discarding the old equipment, and the expected additional revenue that would be generated by the new technology as compared with the old technology. If revenues are greater than the costs, then the firm should use the new technology, otherwise it should continue to use the old technology.

The question of obsolescence in the selection of technology has become even more significant and pressing in today's world since the computer has tremendously changed the speed at which new innovations are introduced.

## TECHNOLOGY TRANSFER

One of the potential benefits of MNCs to host countries, especially LDCs, is their ability to generate and transfer technology to these countries. Aware of the importance of technology in the process of economic development, many LDCs have considered it to be an important consideration in deciding to favor foreign direct investment. For example, a government official in prerevolutionary Iran stated that:

> Since our development plan reserves a high place for the private sector, the role of foreign private investment in this sector is very important. For it should also bring with it administrative and managerial skills, innovations and entrepreneurship to our private sector, creating a true and genuine partnership, but also laying the foundation for self-sustained and sound expansion.[4]

Technology transfer is a complex, time-consuming, and costly process that is composed of many stages. This process ranges from research and development to product planning and design. It includes labor training, quality control, management practices, marketing skills, and service supports. The successful implementation of such a process demands continuous communication and requires close cooperation between the parties involved. Unfortunately, however, both home and host countries have raised questions regarding the potential benefits of technology transfers to the LDCs. This has led to controversy and conflict between home and host countries, further complicating the management of MNCs.

## Home Countries' Reactions to Technology Transfer

Home countries have often reacted against the export of technology on the ground that it is harmful to their economic base. They argue that the establishment of production facilities by MNCs' subsidiaries abroad decreases their export potential. Additionally, they claim, because some of the MNCs' imports come from their subsidiaries abroad, the volume of imports to the home country increases. Given the decrease in exports and increase in imports for the home countries, it is argued that the availability of jobs in the home country will be diminished. It is also argued that by providing technological know-how to foreign nations, a country might lose its international competitiveness in the world. This in turn leads to the loss of GNP, causing the rate of economic growth of the home country to diminish.

The above arguments have caused some groups, especially labor unions, to oppose the expansion of MNCs to foreign countries. In the United States this has been especially a sensitive issue in recent years. Many U.S. MNCs have chosen to set up plants in countries such as Mexico, Singapore, and Taiwan in order to take advantage of the cheaper labor costs in these countries. These plants are used to assemble U.S.–made components into products that are then exported back to the United States. For example, in 1982 some U.S. automobile manufacturers set up assembly plants in Mexican border towns to make cars using the U.S. parts and inexpensive Mexican labor.[5] As another example, Zenith Radio Corporation closed its television plant in Sioux City, Iowa, in 1979, and set up plants in Mexico and Taiwan.[6] Such incidents have caused a bitter confrontation between MNCs and labor unions, whose members have been asked to accept wage cuts in order to keep jobs at home. The U.S. labor unions have blamed MNCs not only for exporting jobs abroad, but also for exploiting foreigners by paying them low wages.

## Host Countries' Reactions to Technology Transfer

The subject of technology transfer by MNCs has been a more touchy and sensitive issue in the host countries than it has been in the home countries. Suspicion of MNCs, fueled by the fear of technological dependency, has caused the residents of many host countries, especially laborers, to persuade their governments to enact regulations that control the activities of these corporations. For example, in the hope of upgrading the skill level of jobs in Canada, the Canadian government has encouraged MNCs to locate their entire operation of one line of their product in Canada. As another example, Japan has feared that MNCs, through their superior technology, might dominate their local firms. As a result, Japan has restricted the flow of technology through MNCs by "taking the foreign investment package apart," that is, by buying capital, management, and technology separately, rather than acquiring them together through the MNC.

Although the positive role of MNCs in technology transfer has been met with skepticism from both advanced countries and LDCs, the role of the MNCs has created more heated debates and has stirred more controversy in the LDCs as compared with the advanced countries. This has led some economists to question the possible advantages of technology transfers by MNCs to LDCs. Two types of criticisms can be differentiated concerning MNC transfer of technology.

The first criticism is related to the monopolistic nature of MNCs. It is argued that an MNC that is transferring technology to an LDC can dictate conditions that are favorable to its own interest. This is due to the MNC's monopolistic power over the technical and managerial know-how, the capital, and the foreign exchange (currency) that is transferred to the LDC through its investment. Consequently, it is argued, the real cost to LDCs of obtaining foreign private technical knowledge may well be higher than it first appears. For example, a study of U.S. subsidiaries abroad finds that these subsidiaries are established mostly in industries that are oligopolistic in nature, and that their purpose is to protect a market that previously was served by exports.[7]

The second criticism is related to the type of technology that is transferred. It is argued that the technology that is transmitted through the multinational corporation is not "appropriate" for conditions that exist in LDCs. In comparison with advanced countries, LDCs are mostly located in the tropical and subtropical zones and, therefore, have a climate different from the advanced countries. Their factors of production are locally available in quite different proportions. Educated managers, skilled workers, technicians, and professionals are relatively scarce. Given these conditions, if a technology that is designed for an advanced country is transferred to an LDC, it will have a distorting effect on the LDC's economy as a whole. To avoid this problem, it is necessary for the MNC to adapt its technology to the conditions that exist in the LDC. However, it must be realized that technology is not transferred in a vacuum. The successful transfer of technology and its adaptation to the national environment of an LDC not only depends on the willingness and the ability of the MNCs, but also on the absorptive capacity of the recipient host country and its relationship with the MNC. The lack of technical and managerial skills needed to operate a successful manufacturing process, the existence of small and stagnant markets, and the restrictive government policies in LDCs are among factors that have provided serious obstacles to the process of technology transfer and adaptation. Consequently, although MNCs have been the means of some technology transfer in a few cases, they have not, in general, performed this task up to their potential.[8] For example, a study of U.S. MNCs in LDCs found that these corporations adapted their technologies, in some degree, to meet the factor proportion problem, that is, the relative abundance of labor to capital of the LDC in question. It was also found that American firms had more of a tendency to get by without some of the most automatic devices as compared with the local firms. This was related to the American reliance on their own technical know-how and training abilities.[9] As another example, in a study of Latin America it was learned that the Latin American companies usually took the same approach as the foreign firms in selecting a production technique. Often Latin American companies utilized the capital-intensive techniques that were developed in advanced countries. The use of the capital-intensive techniques, according to the study, was mostly related to the lack of skilled labor in Latin America. The study also emphasizes that the MNCs had not tried to design labor-intensive techniques that could solve, partially, the unemployment problem of Latin America.[10] As a third example, in a study of Brazil it was found that MNCs were reluctant to fully adapt their technology to the conditions prevailing in Brazil. According to the study, the failure of the MNCs to adapt their technology to Brazil was related to their unwillingness to do an adequate search in Brazil's "permissive environment," that is, an environment that allowed MNCs to operate profitably without fully adapting their technologies to the national environment of Brazil.[11]

### Reconciling Host and Home Countries' Reactions

The question to ask at this point is whether or not the host countries and the home countries are both correct in their negative views of technology transfer. Theoretically speaking, as our discussion of trade theories in Chapter 2 indicated, free trade would lead to a maximization of the world's economic welfare. Thus, we could argue that as long as technology is flowing from the donor to the recipient country in a perfectly competitive market, free from government intervention, both countries would benefit. However, because in actual market settings both government intervention and market imperfections exist, disturbing the free flow of technology, there is reason to believe that both the recipient host and donor home countries might not benefit from the process of technology transfer. Thus, what seems to be needed is the absence of government intervention, allowing the free forces of market demand and supply to direct the flow of technology transfer, as is dictated by the precepts of the comparative advantage theory of trade. Unfortunately, however, what seems to be theoretically right is not implemented in a practical way. This is due to noneconomic variables, such as xenophobia, nationalistic ideology, and labor union demands, that enter the decision-making process, each playing a significant role in the process of technology transfer.

## MODES OF TECHNOLOGY TRANSFER

The transfer of technology through international business depends on the patterns of international involvement, which are fully described in Chapter 12. These patterns provide us with the modes of technology transfer. These modes of transfer include the export of goods and services, licensing, turnkey operations, management contracts, franchises, joint ventures, and wholly owned subsidiaries. Among these modes, the wholly owned subsidiaries are potentially the best means of technology transfer to LDCs. This is because they provide not only the technology needed for successful operation, but also the knowledge and the skills that are required for the actual production to take place.

## TECHNOLOGY TRANSFER STRATEGIES

Given that the international transfer of technology can take different modes, the question to ask at this point is what mode should be chosen by the MNC? The answer depends on the relative cost and the feasibility of technology transfer. These, in turn, are determined by four interrelated factors: (1) the sophistication of the technology, (2) the national environments of the home and host countries, (3) the characteristics of the MNC, and (4) the characteristics of the domestic firms.

### The Sophistication of the Technology

If a product is relatively new or it involves a highly sophisticated technology, an MNC is more apt to establish a wholly owned subsidiary rather than choose other modes of technology transfer. This is because the MNC has full ownership and, therefore, full control over its subsidiary. This enables the corporation to better protect and internalize those technologies that have been obtained through its own substantial research and development expenditures.

### The Environments of the Home and Host Countries

The existing laws and the competitive environment in both the home and the host countries have a bearing on the technology transfer mode that is chosen by the MNC. Many MNCs move their production facilities abroad in order to protect a market that is in danger of being lost either due to the takeover of the market by competitors or because the tax structure of the host or home country makes such a move profitable.

The choice of technology transfer modes by MNCs is especially limited in the LDCs. These countries that usually lack the technical and managerial know-how, yet they often insist on national ownership and staffing. Consequently, most LDCs, such as Kuwait and United Arab Emirates, do not even allow the establishment of wholly owned subsidiaries in their countries. These countries usually set percentage ceilings on the foreign equity that can be invested in each firm of an industry. They also may limit foreign direct investment in joint ventures.

### The Characteristics of the MNC

The financial capability of an MNC and its top executive strategy with regard to long-run profit maximization are important elements that affect the choice of the technology transfer modes. If the top executives view technology as an essential ingredient of the MNCs marketing-manufacturing package, and if they believe that such a strategy would lead to long-run profit maximization, then a wholly owned subsidiary is preferred over other modes of technology transfer. The top executive view with regard to long-run profit maximization can be formulated in terms of the cost-benefit analysis.

Different investment projects are expected to generate different costs and revenues, leading to different profits. At one extreme, the exporting mode could be chosen. This alternative is relatively costless because it does not require investment in equipment and machinery in a foreign country. On the other extreme, the wholly owned subsidiary could be chosen, involving the commitment of financial and managerial resources for a long period of time. Which alternative should be chosen? This depends on the expected profit from these projects and the attitudes of the top executives with regard to risk. If the top executives are risk takers, they would choose the mode that is expected to have the higher risk and the higher profit. On the other hand, if they are risk averters, they would select the mode that is expected to involve lower risk and lower profit.

## The Characteristics of Domestic Firms

The size, the degree of competitiveness, and the ability of the domestic firms to absorb the imported technology are among the factors that affect the choice of the technology transfer mode by the MNC. For example, when an MNC plans to invest in an LDC, foreign direct investment might be the preferable mode of technology transfer, due to problems in exporting technology to such countries. However, in advanced countries, where domestic firms are capable of imitating an imported technology, licensing arrangements might be preferable to foreign direct investment. Additionally, licensing might be suitable for relatively small corporations that do not have the necessary capital, management, or experience to get involved in foreign direct investment.

## PRICING OF TECHNOLOGY TRANSFER

Because the market for technology is highly imperfect and the pricing information is not readily available, the pricing decisions for technology transfer represent a complex issue. This complexity is further amplified by the existence of different compensation packages from which an MNC can choose. These packages range from simple royalties and licensing fees to more comprehensive agreements that include additional payments to the licensor for technical assistance and other services rendered. Other payments to the licensor might be made based on profits, on goods supplied by the licensor, on dividends from an equity share granted by the licensee, and on tax savings resulting from the agreement.

Given the complexity of the pricing of international technology transfer, and the lack of a standard model for negotiation, the success of the MNC's manager in dealing with a nonaffiliated foreign buyer of technology depends on his or her negotiating skills and bargaining power.

## Transfer Pricing

The issue of the pricing of technology transfer is further complicated by what is known as transfer pricing. *Transfer pricing* refers to the pricing of goods and services that pass between either a parent company and its subsidiaries or between the subsidiaries themselves. Because transfer prices are set by the corporate family when dealing with each other, they may not reflect the market prices. Often a market price for a particular good or service may not even exist. As a result, an MNC may use transfer pricing to minimize taxes or to overcome foreign exchange controls that prohibit the repatriation of funds.

Because tax rates are different between nations, a parent company exporting goods and services to a subsidiary in a high-tax nation (as compared with the taxes charged in the home country) could set a high transfer price. This has the effect of decreasing the profits of the foreign subsidiary and leading to lower taxes in the host country. In the same manner, if the subsidiary is located in a low-tax nation, an MNC could minimize taxes by charging a low transfer price. However, if import tariffs are present, the MNC will consider both taxes and tariffs in formulating the transfer pricing policy. This is because a high transfer price means a high value for the goods and services sold. Similarly, a low transfer price means a low value for the goods and services sold. Because import tariffs are imposed on the declared value of imports, this leads to a higher or lower tariff cost as the case may be. Thus, an MNC should measure the tax benefit of a higher or lower transfer price against the resulting higher or lower tariff cost. A high transfer price will be charged if the savings on the host country's taxes are greater than the additional tariff costs. A low transfer price will be used if the savings on tariffs are greater than the additional taxes.

Foreign exchange controls prevent repatriation of funds by MNCs. To circumvent such controls, an MNC can charge high transfer prices to its subsidiaries, thus repatriating profits from those host countries that impose foreign exchange controls.

Other circumstances in which an MNC may use transfer pricing to minimize its costs occur when taxes are imposed on dividends or when a host country's currency is rapidly depreciating. Because dividend taxes, in essence, tax the MNC's profit two times, the MNC can transfer funds using a high transfer price instead of repatriating dividends. If a host country's currency is rapidly depreciating, that is, its value is falling as compared with other currencies, the MNC can protect itself by adopting a high-transfer pricing policy. This allows the MNC to exchange the depreciating currency to stronger currencies, thus minimizing the exchange losses that may result from the weaker currency.

To modify the impact of transfer pricing practices by MNCs, many host country governments have tried to intervene in the negotiations on agreements for technology payments. In the United States, the government is given the right to reallocate gross income, deductions, credits, or allowances between the parent company and the subsidiaries if arbitrary pricing or allocation of expenses may have taken place to avoid taxes. If the taxpaying company is not happy with the government reallocation procedure, it has to prove that the reallocation was not warranted and a refund is in order. An example of the tax implication of transfer pricing is seen in the case of Eli Lilly & Company in the 1950s. In this case, the IRS ended up collecting $4 million from the company. Although the company appealed the decision, it did not win the case. The tax court maintained that the company's pricing policy had resulted in "tax avoidance and does not clearly reflect the income of the related organizations."[12]

## TECHNOLOGICAL FORECASTING

New technologies are introduced every day, and the forecasting of technological change is an integral part of a firm's decision-making process. Such forecasting not only prepares a firm to deal with the question of obsolescence, but it also allows the firm to predict the number of workers and the kinds of workers that are needed for the production activities. This prepares the firm to plan for the recruitment and training of people with the needed skills, thereby enabling it to better compete in the marketplace.

There are three different approaches to technological forecasting: seeking expert opinions, extrapolating from statistical trends, and forecasting with the aid of models.

The first and the easiest approach is to simply bring scientific experts together and ask their opinion about the future with regard to a given technology. Unfortunately, however, such predictions, even by highly respected scientists, may result in large errors. For example, Ernest Rutherford, the Nobel Prize-winning nuclear scientist, predicted that the use of nuclear energy on a large scale was not probable. However, as we know today, he was proven to be wrong.

The second approach is based on the extrapolation of statistical trends. This means plotting the historical data regarding the rate of improvement of a given product or process and examining the trend as it develops over time. For example, if the trend is positive, that is, if the rate of improvement is rising over time, we might assume that it would continue to rise. The shortcoming of this approach is that the variables that have caused a trend in the past might change in the future. As a result, the forecasting might turn out to be completely wrong.

The third approach is based on the use of forecasting models.* This is a scientific approach that tries to relate different aspects of technological change to a set of quantifiable variables. With improvements in statistical techniques and advances in computer applications in recent years, the reliability of this approach has significantly increased over the years.[13]

---

*A *model* is a means for explaining the relationship between different variables. Models can be presented in three different forms: tables, graphs, and equations. An example of a simple model is the demand-supply model. This model could be presented in tables, showing the quantity demanded, the quantity supplied, and the prices of a given good. It could also be presented graphically as a demand curve and a supply curve, or mathematically as a demand equation and a supply equation.

## TECHNOLOGY AND CULTURE

Because a technological innovation requires advances in scientific knowledge and demands exploitation of human and nonhuman resources, it interacts with the culture within which it is introduced. Such an interaction leads to changes in the many variables that affect and are affected by the introduction of a new technology. These variables are the economic systems, the value systems, the religious systems, the political systems, the social organization systems, and the educational systems (see Figure 11.1).[14]

### Technology and Economic Systems

The impact of a new technology on an economic system stems from the increase in efficiency that is caused by the introduction of that technology. Efficiency in this context can be defined in three different ways: (1) an increase in output with the same amount of input, (2) the production of the same output with a smaller amount of input, and (3) an improvement in the quality of products produced.

Given the above definitions, the increase in efficiency of an economic system leads to changes in factor proportions; that is, it leads to changes in the

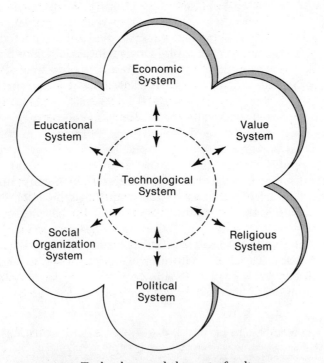

**Figure 11.1** Technology and the rest of culture

*Source:* Adapted from Thomas Neil Gladwin, "Technology and Material Culture," in Vern Terpstra and Kenneth David, eds., *The Cultural Environment of International Business* (Cincinnati, Oh.: South-Western, 1985), p. 182.

relative amount of resources that are used in producing a unit of a given commodity or service. Additionally, improvement in efficiency causes the system either to produce more goods and services with the same amount of resources or to produce better products that command higher prices in the national or the international market. In other words, the increase in efficiency introduced by a new technology causes the GNP of a country to increase, changing the economic picture of that country. In fact, transfer of new technology is one of the major factors that has contributed to the development process in the LDCs, and this is why some LDCs count on the MNCs to facilitate this technology transfer to them.

Several studies have attempted to measure the impact of a nation's rate of technological change on its rate of economic growth. For example, a study by Robert Solow, an economist, concluded that about 40 percent of the total increase in national income per person employed in the United States from 1929 to 1957 can be attributed to technological change.[15] As a more recent example, a study by Edward Denison, also an economist, reported that about 55 percent of the total increase in national income per person employed in the United States from 1929 to 1982 is attributed to technological improvements.[16] Although such studies are useful in highlighting the importance of technology for a nation's economic growth, their conclusions are very inexact. This is because it is extremely difficult to take into account the myriad of factors that affect an economic system. Nevertheless, it is certain that technology has a significant impact on a nation's economy.

In addition to raising economic efficiency and contributing to economic development, technology plays a significant role in the international trade of a nation. According to the technological gap theory and the product life cycle theory discussed in Chapter 2, technology is considered to be the most important element in explaining the pattern of international trade.

## Technology and Value Systems

The cultural values, that is, the attitudes and beliefs of a society regarding what is right and wrong, play a significant role in determining the technologies that are developed and used in that society. For example, the development and the wide use of smoke detector alarms in the United States in recent years could be viewed as a response to an increasing regard for safety among many Americans. Other examples of technologies that reflect cultural values in the United States include technological improvements in pollution control devices, diet foods, exercise equipment, contraceptive devices, and fast foods.

## Technology and Religious Systems

Because a society's value system is affected by its religious beliefs, religion has a significant impact on a society's view of change and technological improvement. For example, conservative Amish and Mennonite sects in the United States oppose the introduction of any new technology into their societies on the grounds that it will lead to the sociological ills that accompany all modern societies. Thus, they continue to ride in their horse and buggies, arguing that the use of the automobile is just a first step in a series of steps leading toward modernization and its resultant social problems, such as teenage pregnancy, drunk driving, and drug addiction.

As another example, Mahatma Gandhi, who was opposed to India's dependence on England, used the Hindu concept of "Nirvana" or "wantlessness" to oppose technological industrialization. He advised his followers to beware of infatuation with machinery, arguing that by working with machines people will become like machines, losing all sense of art and craftsmanship.[17]

## Technology and Political Systems

The political system (that is, the governing institutions of a country) is affected by technology. The political system also affects the nature of the technology and its development and future direction.

Technology can be advanced because of certain goals that have been set by the political system. For example, U.S. plans regarding the "Star Wars" weapons system have set in motion research and development that is pushing forward the frontiers of technology concerned with laser beams and electronics. As another example, the U.S. space program has resulted in numerous advances in satellite technology, which have greatly improved communications.

Advancements in technology can disturb the tranquility of a political system and create resistance toward change. For example, labor union leaders have resisted technology on the grounds that it would create "technological unemployment"; that is, they feel technology would replace humans with machines. Advances in technology have also resulted in toxic waste, environmental pollution, and urban decay, giving rise to the emergence of environmentalist groups whose activities have resulted in the enactment of laws that are aimed at the protection of the environment. Ironically, the environmental problems caused by technology have resulted in the development of still more technology that is used to clean up the environment.

## Technology and Social Organization Systems

Social organization, that is, the order or the norm by which individuals or groups in a society relate to each other, is affected by technology, and the social organization also affects technology.

Japanese technological advancement in recent years provides a good example of the impact of social organization on technology. Many observers believe that one of the main reasons for Japanese technological progress is related to their social organization, that is, their feudalistic social order that recognizes a definite hierarchy and specifies individual responsibilities.

Technology can affect the social order by encouraging the migration of laborers to the technologically advanced areas. This is especially true in LDCs, when industrialization brought about by technology causes the movement of workers from the agricultural sector to the industrial sector where wages are higher. Such a migration goes against the social order in the agricultural sector, which is based on the extended family that works together on the same farm.

## Technology and Educational Systems

Educational systems, both formal and informal, affect technology and are also affected by technology.

In the formal educational setting, universities and the research and development (R&D) departments of corporations provide the primary source for the development of technologies through their continuous scientific endeavors, conducted by groups of scientists. In the informal educational setting, different technologies are developed by individuals every day. Some of these technologies have had an enormous impact on our lives. Examples of this include the Wright brothers' invention of the airplane and Alexander Graham Bell's invention of the telephone.

Technology has a significant impact on the educational systems by providing them with new methods of research and development and instruction. For example, today microcomputers are used to teach preschool children to learn mathematics, to draw pictures, and to learn the alphabet. The invention of the video cassette recorder (VCR) has contributed significantly to education by simplifying the recording and playing of educational programs.

In summary, technology is significantly affected by the different aspects of a culture. Because MNCs are sought by many LDCs as the primary source of technology transfer, the success of their operation in such LDCs depends on their ability to introduce and implement modern technologies. The introduction and implementation of modern technology, in turn, require an understanding of the elements that shape a culture and demand a comprehension of their interaction with technology. This is an especially sensitive issue in LDCs, where MNCs have to tackle the question of which technology is the appropriate one in different cultural environments.

# TECHNOLOGY AND ECONOMIC DEVELOPMENT

One of the most significant factors that contributes to the process of economic development in LDCs is technology. To emphasize the importance of this factor in the course of development, economists have referred to technology as the "prime mover" and the "vital growth component."[18]

Throughout history, technologies have been developed and advanced in modern nations at such a fast pace that a technological gap has been created between the advanced nations and the LDCs. To bridge this gap, many LDCs have turned to the international market as a channel for the transfer of modern technology. This view is clearly stated by the Organization for Economic Cooperation and Development:

The efficient exploitation of advanced technologies calls for both technological resources beyond national boundaries and access to markets that are international in scope.[19]

The concern of the LDCs with the subject of technology has led economists to investigate more rigorously the process of technology transfer. This has resulted in the creditability of technology as a vital element of economic development. Because the belief that technology is vital to economic development shapes the thought processes of policymakers in most of the LDCs, the understanding of technology's role in development is important for the managers of an MNC. As managers of MNCs, we would like to know what theories concerning technology are advocated in a particular LDC. This knowledge will enable us to use strategies of technology transfer that best suit the views of technology which are held in the LDC in question.

Among the existing theories, there are three major theories that have elaborated on the role of technology in the process of economic development. They are the classical theory of economic stagnation, Rostow's theory of the stages of economic growth, and Hagen's theory of the stages of industrialization.

## The Classical Theory of Economic Stagnation

The classical economists of the late eighteenth and early nineteenth centuries assumed that technological progress was taking place at a steady rate. As long as sufficient capital was forthcoming to permit the exploitation of resources, technological change was assured. The rate of capital accumulation, in turn, depended on profits. As the population grew, however, according to the classical economists, technological progress would be incapable of overcoming the process of diminishing returns in agriculture.* As a result, food prices would rise. Because the cost of food is the major component of wage costs, the classical economists assumed that this would lead to higher wages in the industrial sector. The higher wages in industry would, in turn, lead to lower profits. The lower profits would lead to a decline in investment and retard technological progress. Thus, the continuous growth of population would lead to economic stagnation. At this so-called stationary state there would exist low income for the masses and the population growth would be checked by poverty.

The classical economists, however, did not generally appreciate the role that could be played by the entrepreneur in the process of technological change. The appreciation of the role of the entrepreneur was recognized by many writers who followed the classical economists. For example, Schumpeter referred to the entrepreneur as the innovator who operates in a capitalist

---

*Assuming that technology stays constant, the addition of a variable factor of production (for example, labor) to some fixed factors of production (for example, land) may initially lead to increasing amounts of extra output per unit of the variable factor added. However, a point will be reached beyond which each additional unit of the variable factor will yield diminishing amounts of extra output. This is the point of the diminishing returns.

environment of monopolistic competition. He distinguished between profits and the entrepreneur. With a banking system in place, Schumpeter explained, the entrepreneur could use people's savings to finance the introduction of technological change. The motivating force behind the entrepreneur's quest for technological innovation was still profit. These innovations allowed the entrepreneur to introduce a new idea or a new product that allowed him or her to enjoy monopolistic profit for some time.

Today the significance of the individual entrepreneur as an innovator and contributor to the process of economic development is emphasized by many economists. The work of Everett Hagen, which characterizes the individual entrepreneur as the prime mover of development for today's LDCs, will be discussed in this section.

## Rostow's Stages of Economic Growth

In analyzing the process of economic development, W. W. Rostow, a prominent economist, studied the history of economic growth in industrialized nations. His study showed that, based on the experience of the advanced nations, growth can be divided into the five following stages:[20]

**1.** The Traditional Stage. A predominantly agricultural society that is based on "pre-Newtonian science and technology." The level of productivity is limited by the unavailability of modern science and technology.

**2.** The Preconditions for Takeoff. A transitional stage that is marked by the application of modern science to production activities in both agriculture and industry. New entrepreneurs emerge, in the private and public sectors, who would engage in risk taking in the pursuit of profit. Finally, major changes occur in both the economy and the balance of social values.

**3.** The Takeoff. During this stage, resistances to growth are subdued and factors contributing to economic growth expand. The rate of investment and savings increases rapidly and there is a rapid growth in new industries, stimulating the economic system. New technologies are introduced in agriculture and in industry. The agricultural sector is commercialized and goes through "prerevolutionary" changes. The changes occurring in this stage during a decade or two lead to a sustained and steady rate of growth.

**4.** The Drive to Maturity. During this stage, an era of about 60 years after the inception of takeoff, modern technology expands to include the whole range of economic activities. As technologies improve, the new industries expand, the economic structure changes, and international trade accelerates. Industry comes to use more complex technologies. The application of these complex technologies to a wide range of resources allows the production of anything that the society desires, given the market conditions and any constraints on resources.

**5.** The Age of Mass Consumption. The leading sectors of the economy shift toward durable consumer goods and services. During this stage, the percentage of the population in urban areas increases, and the percentage of the population employed in offices and in skilled factory jobs soars. As a result, the composition of the working class changes, and the real income per capita increases, enabling the population to attain a higher standard of living.

Rostow's stage theory has been subject to many criticisms. One of the major criticisms is that these stages are arbitrarily established and hence it is not possible to clearly distinguish one stage from another. Another criticism points out that it is not necessary for a nation to go through all these stages of development. For example, history shows that England, Germany, and Sweden did not go through the takeoff stage. Rather, these countries experienced a steady growth that extended over a long period of time.

In spite of these criticisms, Rostow's theory has gained some popularity because it seems to provide some simple answers to the questions that are raised regarding economic development. Rostow's theory emphasizes the significance of saving, investment, and technology in the process of economic development. It also teaches us that economic development is a time-consuming process that demands that certain changes must occur before a country can depart from the traditional stage and realize some degree of economic growth.

## Hagen's Stages of Economic Industrialization

Everett Hagen's stages of economic industrialization are similar to Rostow's stages in the sense of being based on historical observations. However, unlike Rostow's stages, which are based on data from the advanced countries of the West, Hagen's stages are formed from his observations of Japan and the LDCs in Latin America.[21]

Hagen's stages of economic industrialization describe how an industrialized system is likely to be developed by domestic entrepreneurs who are equipped with the knowledge of technologies that are employed in other nations. He divides the process of industrialization into the following six stages:

**1.** The Emergence of the Self-Contained Factory Processes. This is a stage during which some of the entrepreneurs who are engaged in small manufacturing shops feel secure enough in their ventures to contemplate a change. This change is achieved by the adoption of simple machinery and techniques that are used abroad in the production of familiar goods, such as footwear, matches, rice, soaps, sugar, textiles, and wheat flour. These are goods that have already been produced indigenously by traditional methods and are well known to the home country residents. The new method of production introduced in this stage is a "straight line, self-contained" process that does not require a large number of suppliers and components from other sectors. In this stage, workers are organized into teams, foremanship is developed, and there is an increase in the delegation of authority.

**2.** The Development of Initial Interrelationships. Further advances in technology that occur during this stage lead to the use of more capital-intensive methods of production. Growth in the volume of production allows for the specialization of production in some products, such as paper specially produced for packing, bottles made to contain beer, and coal mined for steam engines. "Forward" linkages also occur; that is, some plants that are producing a given product extend their operations to include further processing of that product. For example, sugar refineries engage in the production of alcohol and sugar syrup as well. The expansion of industrial activities leads to the local production of simple tools and machinery that were formerly imported.

**3. The Expansion of Light Engineering.** In this stage, light engineering begins to expand at a faster rate than industry in general. Consequently, products that do not require too exact specifications are produced domestically. Examples of such products include refrigerators, bicycles, and commercial air-conditioning systems.

**4. The Improving Control of Quality and Industrial Tolerances.** In this phase, the country is capable of employing more complicated technologies than the technologies that were used in the previous stages. This allows advancements in metallurgy and chemicals. There is improved quality control and the size tolerances in the metal-working industries become more exact. This stage can be marked by an increase in management's ability to manage more complex industrial establishments.

**5. The Elaboration of the Industrial Complex.** In this stage further advances in technical capability ultimately lead to heavy metal working processes, and an advanced electronics industry may develop.

**6. The Stage of Industrial Complexity.** In this stage, there is a continuous increase in specialization. The supply interrelationships increase to the extent that no productive establishment can operate independently. Thus these establishments become part of a productive complex that can produce any product within some area of specialization.

The stages of economic industrialization show that economic development is a timely process that involves a progressive evolution of the industrial structure. One implication is that a technology that is used in an advanced country may not be appropriate for an LDC that is in a given stage of economic development. This raises the issue of "appropriate technology" that we discussed earlier in the chapter. Another implication of Hagen's stages is that the foreign firms play a significant role in supplying technology to LDCs. According to Hagen, those firms do not play a role in the process of economic development until an LDC has reached stage four of its economic industrialization.

In closing this chapter, we may note that the controversies surrounding the issues that are raised by the question of technology are going to be with us for a long time. At the national level, environmentalists and consumer advocates have continued to raise questions regarding the environmental effects and the safety aspects of technologies that are being introduced. At the international level, LDCs have passionately pressed MNCs for the transfer of "appropriate" technology to their countries. What seems to be needed in the midst of such controversies is more cooperation among home countries, host countries, and

MNCs. To this end, numerous observers have recommended an international code of conduct that governs international technology transfers. Such a code should take into account the legitimate rights of the parties involved.

## SUMMARY

1. Technology can be defined as the method or technique for converting inputs to outputs in accomplishing a specific task.
2. The variables that affect the choice of technology are the cost of capital and of labor, the availability of technological alternatives, the size and the potential growth of the market, and the obsolescence of the existing technology.
3. Technology transfer is a complex, time-consuming, and costly process that is composed of many stages. This process ranges from research and development to product planning and design. It includes labor training, quality control, management practices, marketing skills, and service support.
4. The successful transfer of technology requires close cooperation between the parties involved. In practice, however, both home countries and host countries have raised questions regarding the potential benefits or drawbacks of technology transfers to their nations.
5. Home countries have argued that the establishment of production facilities abroad decreases their export potential and increases their imports. These lead to the loss of jobs and a decrease in the GNP in the home country.
6. Suspicion of MNCs, fueled by the fear of technological dependency, has caused the residents of many host countries, especially laborers, to persuade their governments to enact regulations that control the activities of these corporations.
7. Technology transfers to the LDCs have met with more criticism in the LDCs than in the advanced countries. Two major criticisms that are raised by LDCs regarding technology transfers are (a) that the MNCs are monopolistic in nature and (b) that the type of technology that is transferred by the MNCs is inappropriate for LDCs.
8. It is argued that the technology that is transmitted through an MNC is not "appropriate" to the conditions that exist in LDCs. To avoid this problem, it is necessary for an MNC to adapt its technology to the requirements of the LDCs.
9. It has been argued that as long as a technology is flowing from the donor country to the recipient country in a perfectly competitive market, free from government intervention, then both countries would benefit.
10. Modes of technology transfer include exporting, licensing, setting up turnkey operations, establishing management contracts, franchising, setting up joint ventures, and creating wholly owned subsidiaries.
11. The factors that determine the mode of technology transfer that is chosen by an MNC are (a) the sophistication of the technology, (b) the national environment of the home and the host countries, (c) the characteristics of the domestic firms in both countries and (d) the characteristics of the MNC.
12. Given the complexity of international technology transfer and the lack of a standard model for negotiation, the success of the MNC's manager in dealing with a nonaffiliated foreign buyer of technology depends on his or her negotiating skills and bargaining powers.
13. Transfer pricing refers to the pricing of goods and services that pass between a parent company and its subsidiaries or between the subsidiaries themselves.

14. Because transfer prices are set by the corporate family when they are dealing with each other, the prices may not reflect the true market prices. Often a market price may not even exist for a particular good or service.

15. An MNC may use transfer pricing to minimize taxes or to overcome foreign exchange controls that prohibit repatriation of funds.

16. The three different approaches that are used in technological forecasting are (a) seeking expert opinion, (b) extrapolating trends from statistical data, and (c) using forecasting models.

17. The interaction of technology and culture produces variables that affect and are affected by the introduction of a new technology. These variables include (a) the economic systems, (b) the value systems, (c) the religious systems, (d) the political systems, (e) the social organization systems, and (f) educational systems.

18. According to the classical economists, continuous growth of the population would lead to economic stagnation. At this so-called stationary state there would exist low income for masses and the population growth would be checked by poverty.

19. According to Rostow, the process of economic growth can be divided into five stages: (a) the traditional stage, (b) the preconditions for takeoff, (c) the takeoff, (d) the drive to maturity, and (e) the age of mass consumption.

20. According to Hagen, the process of economic industrialization can be divided into six stages: (a) the emergence of self-contained factory processes, (b) the development of initial interrelationship, (c) the expansion of light engineering, (d) the improving control of quality and tolerances, (e) the elaboration of the industrial complex, and (f) the stage of industrial complexity.

## QUESTIONS

11.1 Explain the home countries' and the host countries' reactions to the issue of technology. Why is technology transfer a source of conflict between host and home countries? Are both host countries and home countries correct in their opposing views of technology? Explain.

11.2 What are the major differences and similarities between Hagen's stages of economic industrialization and Rostow's stages of economic growth? What can we learn from these theories?

11.3 To maintain its competitive position in the world market and protect jobs, the U.S. government should ban the transfer of U.S. technology to any other country. Do you agree with the above statement? Discuss.

11.4 To alleviate some of the problems that are raised in the international transfer of technology, it is believed that a code of conduct is needed that should govern such transfers. Whose rights do you think should be incorporated into such a code? What do you think the major objectives of such a code should be?

11.5 You are the manager of an MNC that is planning to install a new plant in India (a labor-abundant country) to manufacture prefabricated housing units. You have been advised by the production manager that the production process can range from a very labor-intensive to a very capital-intensive technology. How do you choose the correct technology. Why is your choice the correct one? Would your answer to these questions change if the plant were to be built in an advanced country, say, for example, Canada? What would happen if you were dealing with a different type of industry?

11.6 How can an MNC minimize its costs by means of transfer pricing? What are the reactions of the governments of host countries to transfer pricing?

11.7 As the manager of an MNC that enjoys a technological edge in the domestic market, what factors would you consider in selecting your strategy for expansion into the international market?

## NOTES

1. Bela Gold, "Changing Perspectives on Size, Scale, and Returns: An Interpretive Survey," *Journal of Economic Liturature* 19 (March 1981): 5–33.
2. Daniel B. Suits, "Agriculture," in Adams Walter, ed., *The Structure of American Industry,* 7th ed. (New York: Macmillan, 1987).
3. Anita M. Benvignati, "International Technology Transfer Patterns in a Traditional Industry," *Journal of International Business Studies* (Winter 1983): pp. 63–75.
4. Mehdi Samii, "The Role of Foreign Private Investment in Iran's Economic Development," *Bank Markazi Iran, Bulletin* (January/February 1971), p. 531.
5. "American Auto Makers Using More Mexico Assembly Lines," *The New York Times,* 25 July 1982, p. 1.
6. "Sioux City Still Suffers After Its Top Employer Moves Business Abroad," *The Wall Street Journal,* 5 April 1979, p. 1.
7. Raymond Vernon, *The Multinational Spread of the U.S. Enterprise* (New York: Basic Books, 1971).
8. R. S. Eckaus, "Technological Change in the Less Developed Countries" in Stephen Spiegelglas and Charles J. Welsch, eds., *Economic Development: Challenge and Promise* (Englewood Cliffs, N.J.: Prentice-Hall, 1970), also see, chap. 2, pp. 18–23 for a summary of other empirical studies in the area of technology transfer.
9. Roy B. Helfgott, "Multinational Corporations and Manpower Utilization in Developing Nations," *Journal of Developing Areas* 7 (January 1973): 225–246.
10. Doug Hellinger and Steve Hellinger, "The Job Crisis in Latin America: A Role for Multinational Corporations in Introducing More Labor-Intensive Technologies," *World Development* 3 (June 1975): 399–410.
11. Samuel A. Morely and Gordon W. Smith, "Limited Search and Technology Choices of Multinational Firms in Brazil," *Quarterly Journal of Economics* 31 (May 1977): 263–287.
12. U.S. Tax Cases, Vol. 67-1, 1967 (Chicago: Commerce Clearing House, Inc., 1967).
13. Edwin Mansfield, *The Economics of Technological Change* (New York: Norton, 1968).
14. Thomas Neil Gladwin, "Technology and Material Culture," in Vern Terpstra and Kenneth David, eds., *The Cultural Environment of International Business* (Cincinnati, OH: South-Western, 1978), chap. 6.
15. Edwin Mansfield, *The Economics of Technological Change,* pp. 4–5.
16. Edward Denison, *Trends in American Economic Growth: 1929–1982* (Washington, D.C.: Brookings Institution, 1985), p. 30.
17. D. P. Mukergi, "Mahatma Gandhi's Views on Machines and Technology," *International Science Bulletin,* vol. 6, no. 3 (1954), p. 441.
18. Charles P. Kindleberger, *Economic Development* (New York: McGraw-Hill, 1958);

James B. Quinn, "Scientific and Technical Strategy of the National and Major Enterprise Level," *The Role of Science and Technology in Economic Development* (Paris: UNESCO, 1970), chap. 4.

19. Organization for Economic Cooperation and Development, *Gaps in Technology, General Report* (Paris: Organization for Economic Cooperation and Development, 1968), p. 41.
20. W. W. Rostow, *The Stages of Economic Growth: A Non-Communist Manifesto* (Forge Village, Mass.: Murray, 1960), chap. 2.
21. Everett E. Hagen, *The Economics of Development,* 3rd ed. (Homewood, Ill.: Irwin, 1980), chap. 6.

## SUGGESTED READINGS

Asheghian, Parviz. "Technology Transfer by Foreign Firms to Iran." *Middle Eastern Studies* 21 (January 1985): 72–79.

———. "The R&D Activities of Foreign Firms in a Less Developed Country: An Iranian Case Study." *Journal of Business and Economic Perspectives* 10 (Spring 1984): 19–28.

———. "The Comparative Capital Intensities of Joint Venture Firms and Local Firms in Iran." *Journal of Economic Development* 7 (December 1982): 77–86.

Baranson, Jack. *Technology and the Multinationals: Corporate Strategies in a Changing World Economy.* Lexington, Mass.: Lexington Books, D.C. Heath, 1978.

Benvignati, Anita M. "International Technology Transfer Patterns in a Traditional Industry." *Journal of International Business Studies* 16 (Winter 1983): 63–75.

Daniels, John P., and Fernando Robles. "The Choice of Technology and Export Commitment: The Peruvian Textile Industry." *Journal of International Business Studies* 13 (Spring/Summer 1982): 67–87.

Davidson, W. H. "Key Characteristics in the Choice of International Technology Transfer Mode." *Journal of International Business Studies* 16 (Summer 1985): 5–21.

Donaldson, Loraine. *Economic Development: Policy and Analysis.* New York: West, 1984. Chap. 5.

Dunning, John H. *International Production and the Multinational Enterprise.* London: Allen & Unwin, 1981. Chap. 12.

———. "Technology, United States Investment and European Economic Growth." In Charles P. Kindleberger, ed., *The International Corporation: A Symposium.* Cambridge, Mass.: Massachusetts Institute of Technology Press, 1970.

Eckaus, Richard. "The Factor Proportions Problems in Underdeveloped Areas." *American Economic Review* 45 (1955): 539–565.

Kujawa, Dune. "Technology Strategy and Industrial Relations: Case Studies of Japanese Multinationals in the United States." *Journal of International Business Studies* 16 (Winter 1983): 9–22.

Magee, Stephen P. "Multinational Corporations, the Industry Technology Cycle and Development." *Journal of World Trade Law* 11 (1977): 297–321.

Mansfield, Edwin. *The Economics of Technological Change.* New York: Norton, 1968.

Mason, Hal H. "The Multinational Firm and the Cost of Technology to Developing Countries." *California Management Review* 15 (Summer 1973): 5–13.

————. "Some Aspects of Technology Transfer: A Case Study Comparing U.S. Subsidiaries and Local Counterparts in the Philippines." *The Philippine Economic Journal* 9 (September 1970): 83–108.

Morley, Samuel A., and Gordon Smith. "Limited Search and the Technology Choices of Multinational Firms in Brazil." *Quarterly Journal of Economics* 91 (1977): 263–287.

Pavitt, Keith. "The Multinational Enterprise and the Transfer of Technology." In John H. Dunning, ed., *The Multinational Enterprise.* London: Allen & Unwin, 1971.

Peck, Morton J. "Technology." In Hugh Patrick and Henry Rosovsky, eds., *Asia's New Giant: How the Japanese Economy Works.* Washington, D.C.: Brookings Institution, 1978, Chap. 8.

Pickett, James D., J. C. Forsyth, and N. S. McBain. "The Choice of Technology, Economic Efficiency and Employment in Developing Countries." *World Development* 2 (1974): 47–54.

Steward, Frances. "Choice of Technique in Developing Countries." *Journal of Development Studies* 9 (October 1972): 99–122.

————. *Technology and Underdevelopment.* Boulder, Colo.: Westview Press, 1977.

Teece, David J. *The Multinational Corporation and the Resource Cost of International Technology Transfer.* Cambridge, Mass.: Ballinger, 1976.

Vernon, Raymond. *The Technology Factor in International Trade.* New York: National Bureau of Economic Research, 1970.

# Patterns of International Involvement

Multinational corporations conduct their overseas operations in a variety of ways. An MNC with a full global orientation usually makes use of many patterns of involvement with regard to their operations. The choice of different patterns of involvement depends on their specific product and service lines, the foreign environment in question, and the firm's operating characteristics.

MNCs initiate their presence in other countries either by exporting to that country, by entering contract agreements with other companies in the country, by creating or purchasing a local firm, or by various combinations of these actions.

In this chapter, we first discuss pre-export activity as an initial step in internationalization. Second, we explain exporting. Third, we elaborate on other patterns of international involvement. Finally, we cover countertrade.

## FOREIGN MARKET ENTRY

As our previous discussion of the product life cycle theory in Chapter 2 implied, the ways of entering overseas markets can be classified into two major categories. Exporting is usually the first category and stage of the international operations of an enterprise. If exporting is successful, it may lead to other forms of international operations, such as licensing, franchising, owning foreign enterprises (joint ventures or wholly owned subsidiaries), negotiating management contracts, and building turnkey operations.

This progression of involvement, however, does not imply that this is the only path to foreign market entry. Environmental conditions and business characteristics may necessitate the building of complete manufacturing operations as the initial form of entry for some MNCs into new foreign markets. MNCs may use all of these methods and patterns of foreign involvement simultaneously to serve their global markets. In the following sections we discuss these patterns of involvement in overseas markets.

## PRE-EXPORT ACTIVITY: THE FIRST STEP IN INTERNATIONALIZATION

Before going international, a firm usually engages in some pre-export activities.[1] A study of 75 small Australian, domestically owned and operated manufacturing firms has shown that pre-export activities of the firms played an important role in explaining the internationalization process. Figure 12.1 portrays the model that was developed by this study.

According to this study, three major factors explain pre-export activities and the final internationalization process. The first factor is the *decision maker* of the company. It is shown that the international orientation of the decision maker leads to higher pre-export activity, which may lead to actual exports. The second factor is the *domestic environment* and the *location* of a firm. Firms that are located in urban areas that include a large number of businesses with international activities and substantial contact with parties from other countries are more likely to engage in pre-export activities. The third explanatory factor in the model is *characteristics of the firm.* These characteristics include (1) the goals of the firm, (2) the product line, and (3) the history of the firm and its extraregional expansion. It is found that firms with unstable sales performance are more likely to find other sources of sales and growth in order to isolate themselves from potential domestic sales disturbances. Therefore, increased sales stability and growth are major goals for firms that initiate pre-export activity. In addition, firms with a product line with little dependence on service or software provided by the seller have a greater chance of being exposed to export stimuli. Finally, firms that have a history of extraregional expansion in

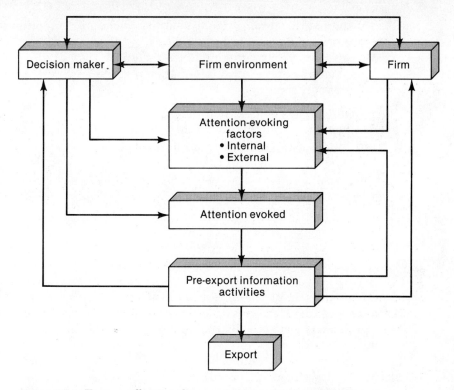

**Figure 12.1** Factors affecting the pre-export activities of the firm

*Source:* F. Wiedersheim-Paul, H. C. Olson, and L. S. Welch, "Pre-Export Activity: The First Step in Internationalization," *Journal of International Business Studies,* vol. 9, no. 1 (Spring/Summer 1978), p. 48.

their domestic market, that is, companies that have expanded in more than one local market, are more likely to pay attention to export opportunities. This process of extraregional expansion is called **domestic internationalization.**

Although these three factors play an important role in pre-export activities, other factors, called "attention-evoking factors," provide real input into the process. **Attention-evokers** are those factors that cause a firm to consider exporting as a possible strategy. In other words, they are the "triggering cues" that, if properly perceived by the decision maker, can lead to the initiation of pre-export activities.

There are two types of attention-evokers, namely, internal and external. The first internal attention-evoker is the possession of a unique competence by the firm. For example, a firm that offers a new product or has a superior product is a good candidate for pre-export activity. The second internal attention-evoker is excess capacity in the management, the marketing, the production, or the financial resources of the company. The external attention evokers include the following:

1. Fortuitous orders from foreign customers.
2. Recognition of market opportunities abroad.

3. Competition among domestic firms abroad or competition in the domestic markets from foreign firms.
4. Government export stimulation measures, such as direct financial assistance or provision of information regarding market opportunities in a foreign country.

In summary, it is evident that the pre-export activities of a firm are important factors in explaining the start of an internationalization process. In addition to more "traditional" factors, such as decision-maker characteristics and product line, other factors such as the environment of the firm and the history of the firm play important roles. A very important aspect of a firm's history is the experience it has gained from extraregional expansion—a process that may be called "domestic internationalization."

## EXPORTING

**Exporting** is the most traditional mode of entry into international markets. Since ancient times, people have traded goods produced in one country for those produced in another. By trading, people have been able to gain access to a wider variety of goods at a lower cost than if those goods were produced at home. Exporting and trading have been the subject of different theories of international trade, as was discussed in Chapter 2.

Exporting is still the most important entry strategy for many companies. The majority of international marketing is carried out by firms that sell domestically produced goods in foreign markets. Through exporting, Japanese automobiles, American agricultural products, Russian furs, Persian rugs, French wine, Australian meat, and numerous other products are sold worldwide.

Exporting is favored by small and large companies as an initial entry strategy or as the most effective means of continuously serving foreign markets.

In addition to manufactured goods, exports can include services, information, and raw materials. Exporting is also an excellent way for companies to get a feel for international business and foreign involvement without a great deal of resource commitment. Exporting is more flexible than many other patterns of international involvement.

There are a number of motives behind exporting domestic production. Among these motives are the following:

1. The desire to utilize excess production capacity at home. For example, small-scale steel mills in the United States export excess supply to overseas markets. This is because they do not want to sell off excess inventory at depressed prices in home markets, for doing so might depress the domestic market even further.
2. The desire to overcome problems of domestic market saturation.
3. The desire to explore new avenues for growth.
4. The desire to gain from the effects of economies of scale and from

experience curve through increased sales, thereby realizing cost competitive advantages, both domestically and internationally.*

5. The desire to get a feel for further international involvement.

Many firms lack the resources to acquire factories in foreign countries, or they fear the problems and risks associated with production abroad. As a result, these companies find some way to serve foreign markets with the products they produce in their domestic factories. Exporting takes advantage of operating leverage from domestic operations because fixed costs may already have been covered by domestic operations. Exporting also helps a firm to become experienced in foreign markets. Such experience may help further expansion through other patterns of involvement.

Exporting can take two different forms: indirect and direct.

## Indirect Exporting

**Indirect exporting** is the selling of domestically produced products in foreign markets without any special activity for this purpose being carried out within the firm. This means that activities related to exporting are delegated to outside agents and firms. This is the easiest of the two exporting options. There is no special expertise or heavy cash outlay required. The firm just follows the instructions of an agent or firm that already carries out marketing activities overseas. Among the channels available for indirect exporting are the following:

1. Domestic firms that buy another firm's products for foreign sales. These domestic companies are known as "**buyers for exports.**"

2. Domestic MNCs that use a firm's products as components in their production facilities abroad.

3. Foreign buyers in the domestic market. Some foreign companies have buying and procurement offices in a firm's country. These foreign firms may be retailers or wholesalers seeking to buy products from small and sophisticated companies for resale overseas. For example, large U.S. retailers, such as Sears and Macy's, have foreign buying offices in other countries, which purchase foreign products for resale in the United States. Other examples include foreign firms from a manufacturing or extractive industry that are looking for supplies and equipment instead of items for resale.

4. **Manufacturers' export agents**. These agents sell products overseas for the domestic manufacturers. For example, a firm that produces plumbing fixtures contracts with an independent export company to act as its export department.

5. **Export commission agents**. These agents buy from manufacturers for their overseas customers.

---

*Experience curve affect refers to the lowering of unit cost of operation that results as accumulated sales volume increases. We will discuss this phenomenom in detail in Chapter 18.

**6. Export merchants.** These firms buy domestic products and sell them overseas for their own account.

**7. International trading companies (ITCs).** International traders have purchasing offices in many countries. These firms are usually the major suppliers of foreign goods to the home markets in which they operate. The largest of these ITCs are Japanese *sogo shosha* (general trading companies), such as Mitsubishi, Mitsui, and Sony. These firms account for half of the Japanese imports. For example, some of the American manufacturers of home appliances sell their products in Japan through these Japanese trading companies. Such is the case for Whirlpool Corporation, which uses Sony Trading Company to export its cooking appliances to Japan.[2] Another leading trading company, the United Africa Company, a subsidiary of Unilever, is the largest importer into many African nations. The large trading companies operate in many different countries and carry a wide range of consumer and industrial goods.

**8. Export management companies (EMCs).** An EMC manages exports for other firms. It has no production of its own and acts only as an international marketing agent. EMCs serve as the export department of many manufacturers. They can provide instant knowledge of overseas markets and international marketing expertise. EMCs usually handle several complementary lines of products, which provide for economies of scale in shipping and marketing to foreign markets. EMCs charge the producers a commission based on the volume of products they handle.

EMCs play a very important role in encouraging exports to foreign countries. For example, as we will explain shortly, in its efforts to correct the U.S. trade deficit the U.S. government modified the Webb–Pomerene Act in 1982 to encourage the growth of U.S. EMCs.

In addition, in order to promote the use of EMCs by small manufacturers, the U.S. Department of Commerce publishes a pamphlet entitled "The EMC—Your Export Department." This pamphlet lists the major international marketing activities of EMCs. These activities include issuing credit and arranging overseas travel and shipping. The pamphlet discusses each EMC and the specific activities it conducts.

EMCs act as important agents or middlemen for firms with relatively small international volume or for those companies who do not want to involve their own personnel in international marketing. An EMC usually provides personalized service with minimum investment on the part of the manufacturer. In addition to small firms, many large manufacturers also use EMCs. They are useful to firms, regardless of size, by helping them to market a product more efficiently, more effectively, or at a lower cost.[3]

**9. Webb-Pomerene export associations.** In Chapter 9 we mentioned the Webb-Pomerene Act of 1918. This law allows U.S. companies that compete domestically to cooperate internationally. In 1982, the U.S. Congress modified the Webb-Pomerene Act to further encourage the growth of U.S. EMCs as a means to correct the U.S. trade deficit. This enables smaller U.S. firms to gain market leverage against monopolistic foreign buyers and manufacturers. The American firms in a Webb-Pomerene export association take advantage of monopolistic powers, avoid competition and duplication of effort among themselves, and benefit from economies of scale. Today, even large U.S. firms form such associations. The Rubber Export Association is an example of joint efforts by Goodyear and Firestone to cooperate internationally. Other examples include the American Peanut Export Corporation, the California Rice Export Corporation, the Motion Picture Export Association of America, the Texas Produce Export Association, and U.S. Poultry Export, Inc.

Webb-Pomerene associations may perform a number of functions. Among their major functions are the following: (a) To export in the name of the association. (b) To promote freight consolidation, rate negotiation, and ship chartering. (c) To conduct market research. (d) To act as selling agents in the United States or abroad. (e) To set prices. (f) To establish uniform contracts and terms of sale. (g) To encourage cooperative bids or sales negotiation.[4]

**10. Piggyback exporting.** In this case, a domestic firm with excess exporting and international marketing capacity finds complementary products produced by other domestic firms to carry and sell overseas. This not only benefits its own operations through synergy and economies of scale, but also improves the profitability and efficiency of other domestic firms that lack exporting capabilities. For example, piggyback operations account for over 15 percent of the exports and sales of Borg-Warner, a major piggybacker. As a second example, Singer, in addition to its sewing machines, sells fabrics, patterns, and other related items produced by other firms. This operation is designed to provide customer convenience as well as to increase company sales. Piggyback exporting is also used by firms with seasonal sales in order to maintain foreign operations and distribution channels at full capacity throughout the year.

## Direct Exporting

Many domestic manufacturers prefer to do their own export marketing by entering foreign markets directly. In other words, in **direct exporting** the firm performs the export task rather than delegating the job to others. Some of the export tasks carried out by a direct exporter include analyzing the potential markets, selecting the foreign markets to enter, and choosing the distribution channels or agents to represent it in these markets. A direct exporter also establishes a working relationship, motivates, and controls the distributors. A direct exporter may select, modify, or design product lines for the target markets. Some of the tasks may include setting prices, formulating promotional strategies, handling international insurance, arranging for shipping, and getting finance. It may also prepare export documentation and do the accounting.

Initially, domestic employees may handle many of the tasks including billing, arranging credit, and shipping. If the export business expands, then a separate export department is formed. We will discuss the evolution of MNC organizational structure in Chapter 15.

Normally, direct exporting is more involved, more expensive, and riskier than indirect exporting. However, many firms choose direct exporting because it may result in higher sales than indirect exporting. Whether or not direct exporting leads to greater profits depends on whether or not the increase in sales is greater than the increase in costs that result from running an in-house export operation.

For many companies, direct exporting evolves from indirect exporting. As knowledge about overseas marketing and about the sales made by an indirect exporter grows, the firm may decide to do its own exporting. It may first choose to sell to the wholesalers in their foreign markets, support services being provided by home-office personnel or sales representatives in the foreign country. For example, Toro Manufacturing Company, a U.S. manufacturer of power tools and engines, including lawn mowers, exports its products to Europe through its own network of distributors. The company provides sales conferences for its European distributors on site. These conferences, which are provided by Toro's U.S. personnel, help Toro to get better insights into the marketing problems of each country.

When the sales reach a point that warrants a complete market affiliate, the company moves in that direction by establishing a sales company. Such sales companies may grow to large establishments with extensive sales. They may even serve as regional sales affiliates. Repair facilities, assembly plants, and component production facilities may follow. This gradual evolution may end in full production facilities, which transforms a pure exporter to a foreign manufacturer. However, this evolutionary path from indirect exporting to direct exporting and then to full foreign production does not need to be followed sequentially. One or more of the steps may be skipped by a firm because of a conscious choice or because of the nature of the business.

Exporting is sometimes used in combination with other patterns of involvement in international trade. In addition, many MNCs export domestically produced products and components to their own foreign subsidiaries. The integration of domestic and foreign operations can assure supply, reduce costs, and increase production coordination. For example, Volkswagen used to export engines and other parts of its cars from Germany for assembly in its American plant before its closing in 1988.

In 1988, a new form of exporting started in the United States. Japanese auto manufacturers with plants in the United States began exporting their U.S.–produced automobiles to Japan for sale in that country. This has occurred because the devaluation of the U.S. dollar against the Japanese yen has reduced the price of the U.S.–manufactured automobiles to Japanese consumers. It is estimated that a U.S.–manufactured car on the average cost about $2,000 less in 1988 than it did in 1985. Toyota, Honda, and Nissan are examples of Japanese firms with plants in the United States that are engaged in this practice.

# OTHER FORMS OF INTERNATIONAL INVOLVEMENT

Most firms prefer to export their domestically produced products to their overseas markets rather than producing their products in some foreign countries. There are economic and political reasons for this preference. Foreign production requires greater capital investment and carries higher risks. Among these risks, the most important one, as we discussed in Chapter 9, is the potential for expropriation or nationalization of the company's facilities by a foreign government. Conflicts between home and host governments can create operational problems for the firm with facilities in a foreign nation. These conflicts will be discussed in Chapter 20. In addition, environmental differences, especially in the sociocultural environment, can pose new problems and challenges that have never been encountered at home. The cost of operating in an unfamiliar foreign environment can also be higher. As a result, most MNCs are reluctant to have foreign production, or they limit their production facilities to selected nations that produce for regional markets.

To offset these problems, there are many benefits associated with foreign manufacturing. High transportation costs, insurance, and special packaging needs to withstand rough handling of the product during air, sea, and land shipping can make the domestically produced products too expensive for export and overseas sales. In addition, import duties and quotas, as well as outright bans on certain imports, may prompt the MNC to produce abroad. Lower labor costs, production costs, and incentives and preferential treatment provided by a host government can make foreign production appealing. Finally, creating goodwill by providing local employment may play a great role in establishing foreign manufacturing operations. Usually, the MNC wants to take advantage of a number of these benefits. For example, Bata Shoe Company, the world's largest shoe company, produces its shoes in more than 100 countries. As another example, to prevent potential problems that may result when the European Community (EC) integrates in 1992, some non-European MNCs have opened production facilities in Europe. Sony and Texas Instruments are among these MNCs.

If a company chooses to produce abroad for foreign markets, then it has a number of alternative patterns of involvement from which to choose.

## Licensing

Although a firm may need to manufacture its product abroad, this does not mean that it has to carry out the production activities itself. Foreign production can be performed by a firm in a host country through a licensing agreement. In other words, **licensing** is the process of entering a foreign market by selling technology to an independent foreign firm. This is in contrast to foreign direct investment, which takes place by the "internalization" of technology, that is, using the technology in the company-owned affiliates. Through licensing, a firm provides a combination of technology, brand name use, the right to use certain patents or copyrights, and management services to another firm that produces the product in a foreign country. The supplier is called the **licensor**. The firm receiving the know-how and the right to manufacture in the host country is called the **licensee**.

By engaging in licensing a firm avoids investing in production facilities, as well as the other headaches of producing and marketing in a foreign environment. Therefore, the licensor will be only minimally involved internationally. In return for its minimal involvement, the licensor receives a modest return, perhaps 2 to 5 percent from the licensee. For example, Disney receives a 5 percent royalty on its licensed amusement park in Japan. Usually, the licensing agreement stipulates the responsibilities of each party, the markets to be served, the rights granted, the control specifications, and the provisions for royalty payments.

An MNC may have licensing agreements with firms producing a variety of products that use its technology. Licensing does not usually prohibit the licensor from using the technology in its own foreign manufacturing operations. The existence of licensing agreements with firms in a host country does not prevent company-owned production or other forms of involvement for the licensor in that country, unless exclusive rights have been granted to the licensee. Usually licensing royalties is not the main source of income for a firm. However, licensing may be the cheapest, easiest, and quickest way to foreign production and the marketing of a firm's product. Licensing is an arm's length approach to international business.

The licensing agreement is usually made for a certain period of time with an option for renewal. The licensor receives royalties, but does not share in the licensee's profits over this time period. Because of this modest return, many licensors have reservations about giving up the firm's valuable know-how. They may also fear that they might establish a competitor through licensing. If the technology is not protected by patents, the foreign manufacturer may still continue to produce the product using the licensor's technology it has mastered after the licensing agreement has run out. This is a legal and competitive issue that the licensor has to address before entering a licensing agreement. It has been shown that the weakening of patent systems in some LDCs may result in diminishing international licensing in these countries. MNCs are afraid of losing their patent's rights to technology that they have developed. This has lead many of these companies to "internalize" such technology by establishing wholly owned subsidiaries. Some other firms may decide to stay away altogether from countries with weak patent systems.[5] Licensing has been an easy route for producers from LDCs as well as some advanced nations, such as Japan, in establishing themselves as new global competitors by accessing technology from foreign MNCs. For example, after World War II, the Japanese government restricted domestic industries to local participants. As a result, exporting and the licensing of technology to Japanese firms became the only two alternatives to enter the Japanese market for foreign producers. Japanese companies thereby gained access to otherwise unavailable and valuable technologies that helped the industrialization of that country after World War II.

Licensing agreements provide for a varying amount of control by a firm. At times, the agreement may call for the purchase of components or intermediate products from the licensor by the licensee. The agreement may also call for adherence to its quality standards, for a limitation of marketing territory, or for other forms of control. The agreement is drawn under the local law of the host nation and thus is under its jurisdiction.

Licensing may be used as a first step in a sequential strategy for entering a new market. After gaining knowledge in a new market through a licensing agreement, a firm may establish its own foreign plant and service facilities. Many MNCs have used this kind of arrangement. For example, in the 1950s IBM entered the Japanese market through licensing arrangements with Japanese companies. As we mentioned earlier, at that time the Japanese government prohibited foreign direct investment in that nation. After the removal of this restriction, IBM established its own operations in Japan and became one of the most successful foreign firms in that country.

A survey conducted by the U.S. Department of Commerce in 1977 reported that the number of independent licensees by U.S. firms exceeded that of the number of American-owned affiliates. If we also consider the licensing arrangements in which the subsidiaries of American MNCs in foreign countries are engaged, and include combinations of joint ventures and licensing, the importance of licensing arrangements becomes more evident.[6]

In summary, licensing is an arm's length pattern of international involvement that plays an important role in international business. The choice of licensing versus FDI is influenced by country environmental factors, industry conditions, and company preferences. Usually, licensing decreases in relative importance as a host country's per capita GNP and industrialization rises. In countries with restrictions on FDI, such as post–World War II Japan, licensing becomes more important. On the other hand, in the presence of incentives for FDI, licensing becomes a strategy that is less and less pursued. Licensing also requires the presence of certain indigenous technical capabilities in the host country. Licensing is used more often when a firm's technology is less research-intensive and when it can be codified, patented, and transferred.[7]

## Franchising

**Franchising** is a form of licensing. This is the fastest-growing segment of international licensing. Franchises involve giving the permission to produce a product, and to use the name, trademark, or copyright. In producing the product, the **franchisee**, that is the receiver of the rights, is usually required to use a specific set of procedures and methods and follow a set of quality guidelines. In return, the **franchiser**, that is the supplier of rights, receives a franchise right fee and royalties. The franchisee, that is, the local (host country) partner, provides the capital and knowledge of the local environment. The local partner also operates the business using operational and marketing strategies provided by the franchiser.

In addition to the right to use its name, the franchiser generally sells the franchisee some array of products and services. For example, one can make a franchisee contract with Hilton Hotels to buy its supplies, to receive its training, and to connect up with its reservation system. Hilton maintains the right to control the quality of services provided by the franchisee. This right is maintained so that the franchisee cannot tarnish the company's image. In return for using the Hilton name and for these services, the franchisee pays the franchiser a fee based on the volume of sales. The technology that is transferred includes a well-known name, an established reputation, a management system, some marketing skills, and certain supplies.

Today, franchise operations in retailing and in the restaurant business are popping up all over the world. You can see familiar McDonald's and Kentucky Fried Chicken restaurants next to Hilton Hotels in countries such as Japan, England, Canada, Malaysia, and Mexico.

## MNC-Owned Foreign Enterprise

If an MNC needs or chooses to have its production and marketing facilities in certain countries, then it creates an entity under the local law of the host country. The production facilities may be in the form of assembly lines or complete manufacturing plants.

Assembly line production requires less capital investment, and it is less expensive and less complicated to operate. It is also preferable to full production because it provides for more control by the MNC of the operations, and it also benefits the home country by keeping jobs and the **value-added** at home.* Because most of the vital elements of the MNC's technologies stay out of the host nations, assembly plants are less likely to be nationalized by a host government. This type of foreign involvement may be preferred for satisfying a host government's requirements, or it may be used as a strategy to improve goodwill or prevent the hostile actions of host nations.

Complete foreign production, however, reduces the cost of the transportation of parts and reduces the cost of import duties and tariffs. It can also improve marketing by providing better adaptation of a firm's products and services to the host nation's local market conditions.

Company-owned foreign manufacturing may be 100 percent company owned, that is, **wholly owned**, or it may be a **joint venture** with another firm. The firm with which an MNC enters a joint venture agreement may be a local firm or a firm from another country.

In Chapter 1, we discussed the differences between foreign direct investment (FDI) and portfolio investment. Portfolio investment is investing in foreign operations for capital gain without the exertion of control over operations. FDI was defined as sufficient investment in production facilities in a foreign

---

*Value-added is the increase in the value of a product contributed by each producer or distributor as the product progresses through the stages of production and distribution. Value-added may also be defined as the value of the product (sales price) of a firm minus the cost of its input purchased from other firms.

country to give the investor effective control of the operations. Technically, any FDI involving 10 to 50 percent ownership is a **minority-owned joint venture** or affiliate. An equity ownership of 50 to 90 percent of the voting shares of stock implies a **joint venture**. If an MNC owns 100 percent of qualified voting stock, then the operation is considered a **wholly owned subsidiary or branch**.

There are advantages and disadvantages for wholly owned and joint venture operations. We now turn to a discussion of each option and their characteristics.

## Joint Ventures

**Joint ventures** are corporate entities or partnerships created under a host country's law between an MNC and other parties. If the joint venture parties are local, then it is called a foreign-local joint venture. If all the parties involved are foreign to the host country, then the joint venture is called foreigners' joint venture. For example, General Motors of the United States and Isuzu of Japan have a foreigners' joint venture to produce automobiles in Egypt. In order to entice the two companies to operate in that country, Egypt has offered a number of incentives. This includes an extension of the usual five year income tax holiday to eight years.[8] A joint venture may also be a cooperative, limited-duration project between two or more firms.

Formation of a joint venture with local partners may be required by a host government. A joint venture may also be desirable to improve local goodwill and to reduce the chance of possible hostile actions from the local customers, the local government, or local labor. For instance, when faced with the threat of a protectionist move from the U.S. Congress and the so-called Buy American campaign, the Japanese automobile makers voluntarily limited their auto exports to the United States and sought joint venture partners among U.S. automakers. For example, Toyota entered a joint venture agreement with General Motors to produce cars in the United States.

Joint ventures are also used to fade out foreign ownership over a period of time. Instead of demanding an immediate sale of a foreign MNC's affiliate to locals, a number of LDCs are requiring the sale of 51 percent or more of the ownership to locals over a period of ten to 20 years. For example, such a policy is followed by India (60 percent local ownership), Mexico (51 percent local ownership), and Nigeria (40 or 60 percent local ownership, depending on the industry). These fading-out policies are considered partial nationalization of the industry in question, since the intent of the LDC is to pass ownership and control away from a foreign MNC to local investors.[9]

Increased nationalistic sentiments in some LDCs have encouraged many MNCs to hide their identity by seeking joint ventures with local partners. In such cases, the local partner simultaneously publicizes local ownership and a foreign technology link. The foreign technology used in the production may be indicative of superior product quality to the local customers.

Joint ventures are usually less expensive. An MNC may provide technology and management, and the joint venture partner may raise the necessary capital. Joint ventures can make entry into new markets easier and quicker than wholly owned subsidiaries. Using a local partner with its knowledge of the local environment and with local business contacts may be advantageous for the MNC. The local partner may know of existing product facilities and distribution capabilities that will reduce the time and effort spent by the MNC. The local partner can serve as a potential cushion against mishap and help the MNC to avoid mistakes. It may make the MNC's presence less visible and troublesome. Lower overall investment risks make the joint venture an appealing option to some MNCs. For example, Pepsico has a joint venture bottling plant in Minatitlan, Mexico.

On the negative side, joint ventures mean less control and flexibility for the MNC. Control is at best shared, especially if the MNC's interest is less than 50 percent. However, minority involvement by foreign MNCs may be required by local law. The MNC and its partners may have differing objectives. The global objectives of an MNC mean organizing operations and getting returns on an international basis. Such objectives may be meaningless to a local partner who is interested in its own objectives and interests.

Joint ventures may mean revealing the exclusive technology of an MNC to other firms. These firms may use the technology in the future to compete with the MNC. Such technology disclosure may prove expensive to the MNC. Thus, many MNCs are reluctant to enter into joint venture agreements. For example, Coca-Cola decided to pull out of India rather than share its long-kept secret syrup formula with the Indian government through a required joint venture.

The methods and philosophies of the MNC and the local partner may be different enough to lead to conflicts over the way the affiliate is run. Product lines and marketing approaches may not transfer to the host country. This may cause difficulties in teaching the partners the methods preferred by the MNC. Further product choices may be limited because of such difficulties.

Another disadvantage of the joint venture is the sharing of profits with a partner. Profits are shared in proportion to the ownership. An MNC that needs to show a large profit from a risky venture may find this a problem. Joint ventures tend to be unstable. One obvious reason is the conflict between partners. Another less obvious, but more frequent reason, is the shifting of the interests and priorities of an MNC. MNCs by virtue of their global orientation must balance product and market diversification against concentration on the local area. This may lead to shifts in priorities among production facilities, product choices, market coverages, and market concentrations. Such shifts may require pulling out of a joint venture contract.

## Wholly Owned Subsidiary

This is the preferred type of foreign production ownership because it provides the MNC with greater control and flexibility. Under this arrangement, coordination among multinational operations can prove to be easier, and conflicts with joint venture partners are nonexistent. At the same time, 100 percent ownership means more investment and greater commitment by the MNC. It also increases the risks associated with greater involvement in a host nation that may have a different and potentially hostile environment.

Some international markets may be closed if the MNC insists on complete ownership of a subsidiary. For instance, IBM was forced to leave India when IBM insisted on full ownership. The strong attachments to full ownership may need modification in order to open certain markets to MNCs. The advantages and disadvantages of the wholly owned subsidiary form of foreign involvement are the opposite of the advantages and disadvantages of the joint venture form of involvement, as discussed in the previous section.

Figure 12.2 depicts some of the determinants of ownership strategy.

## Management Contract

**A management contract** is an arrangement by which a company provides managerial assistance to another company in return for a fee. Such managerial help can be provided for other independent companies, joint venture partners, or MNCs' wholly owned subsidiaries in foreign nations. In providing help to a wholly owned subsidiary under a management contract, the MNC is trying to extract a larger proportion of its subsidiary's profits out of a host country. This can be a strategy to combat limitations set on the repatriation of profits out of a host nation. We will discuss this situation in Chapter 17.

Contracts to manage can also be used in nationalized or expropriated operations. In addition to the normal compensation, an MNC receives fees for providing vital expertise needed in operations. Such contracts may be for a specific time period or on an ongoing basis. Management contracts can also be used in combination with turnkey contracts. An example of a management contract is the operation of many American hotel chains in foreign countries.

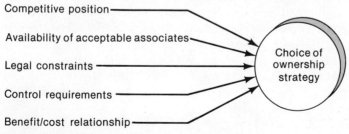

**Theoretical Determination of Ownership Strategy**

Competitive position

Availability of acceptable associates

Legal constraints

Control requirements

Benefit/cost relationship

Choice of ownership strategy

**Figure 12.2** Determinants of ownership strategy

*Source:* Figure from *Internationalization of Business: An Introduction,* by Richard D. Robinson, copyright © by The Dryden Press, reprinted by permission of the publisher.

Under a management contract arrangement, these hotel companies agree to operate, for a fee, hotels owned by foreign investors or governments. A management contract can also be used in combination with a franchise agreement. A franchisee can arrange for a third party to manage the franchised operation.

## Turnkey Operations

A **turnkey operation** is an arrangement by which an MNC agrees to construct an entire facility or plant, prepare it for operation, and then turn the key of the plant over to the new owners. The essence of turnkey is the construction and equipping of the facility rather than the future use of its technology and operations, as is the case in licensing agreements. Typical turnkey projects include large-scale construction projects, such as dams, nuclear power plants, or airports. The operation of such projects is less complex than the initial construction. Operation of the project may also require expertise that an MNC lacks. In a licensing agreement the purpose is the use of technology in operations. In contrast, a turnkey operation consists of the construction of facilities that can be turned over to another firm for operation. For example, many telecommunications firms, such as Siemens of West Germany, NEC of Japan, and AT & T, construct telephone installations in foreign countries that are then turned over to local operators.

If an MNC has the expertise for operating such projects, and if the local firm or government chooses, then a management contract can be arranged. If a management contract is agreed upon with the turnkey project, the MNC would provide the expertise to enable the project to be operational when construction is completed. The MNC provides training and instruction for local individuals to make the local firm self-sufficient. The MNC will receive additional monies for providing management assistance and training services.

Turnkey operations fit the plans of some countries, such as the Soviet Union, the People's Republic of China, India, Iran, and Turkey. These countries speed up their development process by contracting with foreign firms that then build the much-needed projects for these countries. For example, in 1980 the Soviet Union contracted with firms from Germany, France, Britain, and Italy to build its $4 billion natural gas pipeline. The contract also arranged for a payback to the four Western European countries in the form of natural gas. In other words, a turnkey operation was combined with a buyback counter trade agreement, which we will discuss later in this chapter. Other examples of turn key operations include the building of steel mills by the Soviet Union in Iran and the building of fertilizer and chemical plants by the Japanese in Iraq and Iran.

Table 12.1 presents the costs and benefits associated with licensing, foreign-local joint venture, foreigners' joint venture, and wholly owned subsidiary. It should be pointed out that none of these arrangements is always the most desirable.

Table 12.1   COSTS AND BENEFITS FROM VIEWPOINT OF A FOREIGN PARENT
ENTERPRISE, RANKED ACCORDING TO FORM OF LOCAL LINK

|  | Licensing arrangement | Foreign-local joint venture | Foreigners' joint venture | Wholly owned subsidiary |
|---|---|---|---|---|
| *Costs* | | | | |
| 1. Cost of capital commitment | 1 | 2 | 3 | 4 |
| 2. Cost of management commitment | 1 | 2 | 3 | 4 |
| 3. Restraint on strategic and operational flexibility of rest of multinational firm | 4 | 3 | 2 | 1 |
| *Benefits* | | | | |
| 1. Amount of payment to parent | ? | ? | ? | ? |
| 2. Stability of payment to parent | 4 | ? | ? | ? |
| 3. Political security for parent | 4 | 3 | 2 | 1 |
| 4. Contribution to parent's store of knowledge | 1 | 2 | 3 | 4 |
| 5. Contribution to value of parent's trademark and trade name | 1 | 2 | 3 | 4 |
| 6. Future availability of local outlet to parent | 1 | 2 | 3 | 4 |

*Note:* 1 is the lowest and 4 the highest cost or benefit.

*Source:* Vernon/Wells, MANAGER IN THE INTERNATIONAL ECONOMY, 4/E, © 1981, p. 25. Reprinted by permission of Prentice-Hall, Inc., Englewood Cliffs, NJ.

## COUNTERTRADE

**Countertrade** is a process by which an importing nation imposes conditions that link the imports with exports and, as a result, minimizes the net outflow of foreign exchange from its economy. Countertrade is usually practiced by those nations that have small reserves of foreign currencies or have tightly controlled economies. This is the case in many LDCs and in the Eastern bloc nations.[10]

Countertrade is characterized by a significant substitution of payment in kind for payment in a foreign currency. For both parties to want to countertrade there need to be compatible economic incentives to forego ordinary market alternatives.

Countertrade can take the following forms:

**1.** In a **simple barter,** imported goods are traded for commodities of equal value produced domestically. Simple barter is the oldest form of countertrade and is practiced when foreign exchange reserves or credit is not available for one or both of the trading nations. Sometimes trading partners prefer barter arrangements to boost trade between the respective countries. For example, the government of Iran on numerous occasions has engaged in the barter of oil for the importation of light industrial equipment, such as power generators from Yugoslavia. As another example, the Russian government has arranged to swap vodka for Pepsi syrup and bottling equipment from the American firm Pepsico. As a third example, Volkswagen (of West Germany) sells compact automobiles to East Germany in return for canned hams. As a result, East Germany receives cars-plus-marketing services for hams. From the countertrader's (East Germany's) point of view, imported cars and marketing service for the sale of excess ham are more cheaply obtained when bundled together.

2. **Buy-back** or **compensation trading** is probably the most prevalent form of countertrade. It usually consists of the export of a technology package, the construction of an entire project, or the provision of services by a firm. The buyer in return pays back the supplier by delivering a share of the output of the project in the future. For example, recently Volkswagen (VW) constructed an engine production plant in East Germany. Based on a buy-back agreement, VW receives every year, during a certain period of time, a fixed number of the engines that are produced in that plant. Buy-back countertrade is a substitute for foreign direct investment by an MNC, especially in those countries in which the political environment is not receptive to FDI.

3. In a **counterpurchase** agreement or **parallel barter**, a seller is paid partially in terms of credits that must be used for purchase of products from a prespecified list. Such a purchase is subject to time and availability constraints. In addition, part of the payment may be made in hard currencies. For example, a country with increasing use of counterpurchase is Iran. In order to keep abreast of its need for certain imported essentials, such as food, pharmaceuticals, and certain machinery, Iran has entered into counterpurchase agreements with many other nations. Accordingly, Iran pays for the purchases through a list of products, including oil.

Although the trade credits provided under a counterpurchase agreement are sometimes negotiable, nonfulfillment of such a commitment usually invokes penalties in the form of reductions in the trade credits. The main characteristic of this kind of trade is the exchange of products that are delivered now for goods to be delivered in the future. Counterpurchase is, therefore, a more complicated form of simple barter. Counterpurchase is also a more uncertain form of trade because some of the products on the shopping list may not be available.

Counterpurchase can also be viewed as a form of exchange control because it mandates the making of payments in terms of credits instead of hard currencies. In addition, countertrade can be viewed as a form of forward purchase of the MNC's marketing skills by the local countertrader, normally in the Eastern bloc countries.

4. **Switch trading** uses at least three parties to complete the countertrade transaction. A switch trade is used when the products received from the importer are not of any use to the exporter or cannot be converted to cash. The original exporter may then barter the products received in trade for other products that

may be sold for cash. This chain of transactions may be repeated a number of times. As a result, this greatly expands the amount of goods that can be purchased and sold. It becomes extremely useful to a country with unique requirements or products. Switch trading can open untapped markets for these types of products. For example, ContriTrade recently exported Brazilian corn to East Germany and received various products in return; the German products were then sold for hard currency. This is just one example of how switch trading can expand markets.

**5. Offset trading** is contingent on the procurement of a portion of the raw materials or components used in the products from local sources. In order to facilitate offset trading, the MNC may establish or help the local firms to build manufacturing or assembly plants in the importing nation. Offset trading can be made through coproduction, subcontracting, joint ventures, licensing, or turnkey arrangements. The offset arrangement is most popular in the defense industry and with other expensive items such as aircraft and ships. The principal reason for this kind of countertrading is to offset the negative effects of such large purchases on the balance of payments of the importing country. For example, a country purchasing equipment from the American firm LTV may require that certain parts of the equipment be produced or assembled locally.

**6. Evidence accounts** are the agreements between an exporter and one or more foreign trade organizations (FTOs) from the importing nation. Based on this agreement the exporter sells a prearranged amount of goods or services to the FTO and in return buys local products from the same or other FTOs to balance the account. The importing country's bank of foreign trade and a bank in the exporter's country simultaneously maintain an evidence account in order to ensure the transaction balance. This arrangement fits well with the central economic-planning systems of the Eastern bloc countries.

In summary, countertrade is increasing in popularity. Countertrade is usually a cost-saving arrangement, and sometimes it improves the efficiency of trade. Contrary to common belief, countertrade is not detrimental to the growth of international business. Countertrade is generally a national response to environmental constraints and market imperfections. Therefore, it does not necessarily represent inefficient economic exchange.

We may conclude this chapter by stating that deciding which pattern of foreign involvement for an MNC to choose is not easy. Each form of involvement has its own strengths and weaknesses, its own costs and financial benefits. There are no magic formulas or easy rules to follow. The choice depends on the national environment, the MNC's conditions and preferences, the nature of the business, and the characteristics of particular patterns of involvement.

## SUMMARY

1. In this chapter we discussed the different patterns of foreign involvement for MNCs ranging from indirect exporting to the establishment of a wholly owned subsidiary in a foreign country.

2. There are two broad options for entering foreign markets. These are (a) exporting to a foreign market and (b) establishing other forms of involvement, which include licensing, franchising, owning foreign enterprises (joint ventures or wholly owned subsidiaries), establishing management contracts, and building turnkey operations.

3. Before going international, a firm usually engages in some pre-export activity. Three major factors explain pre-export activities and the final internationalization process; these are the decision maker, the domestic environment, and the characteristics of the firm.

4. Exporting involves making the product at home and selling it abroad. Exporting is accomplished either indirectly or directly.

5. Indirect exporting can be accomplished by (a) selling to domestic firms for resale abroad, (b) selling to domestic MNCs for use in their production overseas, (c) selling to foreign buyers in the domestic market, (d) selling through manufacturers' export agents, (e) selling to export commission merchants, (f) selling to export merchants, (g) selling to international trading companies, (h) selling through export management companies, (i) joining a Webb-Pomerene export association, and (j) selling through piggyback exporters.

6. Direct exporting consists of undertaking the complete task of export marketing by creating an export department, a foreign sales office, or a wholly owned export subsidiary.

7. Other forms of foreign involvement require more capital and carry higher risks.

8. Manufacturing can take place in a foreign country by signing a licensing agreement with a proxy firm that obtains the right to produce and sell the product in return for a modest fee.

9. Franchising involves granting permission to a foreign business to produce a product and to use the name, trademark, or copyright, based on a contract, in return for a fee and royalties.

10. An MNC may have part ownership (a joint venture) or complete ownership (a wholly owned subsidiary) of its foreign production and marketing operations.

11. In a management contract, a company provides managerial assistance to another company in return for a fee.

12. A turnkey arrangement is when an MNC agrees for a fee to construct an entire facility or plant, ready it for operation, and then turn the key over to the new foreign owners.

13. Countertrade is a process by which an importing nation imposes conditions that link the imports with exports, and, as a result, minimizes the net outflow of foreign exchange from its economy.

14. Countertrade can take the following forms: (a) simple barter, (b) buy-back or compensation trading, (c) counterpurchase or parallel barter, (d) switch trading, (e) offset trading, and (f) evidence accounts.

## QUESTIONS

12.1 What is meant by the patterns of foreign involvement? Discuss.

12.2 What is IPLC? Discuss its stages. What are the implications of IPLC for an MNC?

12.3 Choose a product and explore the different ways that this product can be exported to a foreign country.

12.4 What are the advantages and disadvantages of exporting as compared with foreign production?

**12.5** Compare and contrast management contracts and turnkey arrangements. Can these two be combined? How? Give new examples.

**12.6** Pick a domestic MNC and follow the evolution of its pattern of foreign involvement. Have all the patterns discussed in this chapter been used?

**12.7** Discuss the concept of pre-export activity as the first step in internationalization. Can you identify the activities of domestic firms with which you are familiar that may lead to their eventual internationalization?

**12.8** Discuss the concept of countertrade. Provide new examples of countertrade.

**12.9** Choose three MNCs and trace their path to internationalization. Identify the different patterns of involvement that they have utilized in their foreign operations.

**12.10** Give examples of some "attention-evokers" in pre-export activity.

## NOTES

1. F. Wiedersheim-Paul, H. C. Olson, and L. S. Welch, "Pre-Export Activity: The First Step in Internationalization," *Journal of International Business Studies,* vol. 9, no. 1 (Spring/Summer 1978), pp. 47–58.

2. "Interest Heightens on Exports of U.S. Products for Japan Sales," *Merchandising Week,* 12 November 1973, p. 3.

3. John J. Grasch, "Export Management Companies," *Journal of International Business Studies,* vol. 9, no. 1 (Spring/Summer 1978), pp. 59–72.

4. "Webb-Pomerene Association: Ten Years Later," *Federal Trade Commission* (November 1978), p. 12.

5. Farok J. Contractor, "Choosing Between Direct Investment and Licensing: Theoretical Considerations and Empirical Tests," *Journal of International Business Studies,* vol. 15, no. 3 (Winter 1984), pp. 167–188.

6. Ibid., p. 167.

7. Ibid., p. 167.

8. IL&T Egypt. *Business International Corporation* (October 1986), p. 4.

9. Robert Grosse and Duane Kujawa, *International Business: Theory and Managerial Applications* (Homewood, Ill.: Irwin, 1988), pp. 612–613.

10. For a discussion of countertrade the reader is referred to Rolf Mirus and Bernard Yeung, "Economic Incentives for Countertrade," *Journal of International Business Studies,* vol. 17, no. 3 (Fall 1986), pp. 27–40; Bahman Ebrahimi and Bill Bowman, "ABCs of Countertrade: A Vehicle for Successful Exporting," *InfoTrade Report* (September–October 1988), pp. 4–5; Louis Kraar, "How to Sell to Cashless Buyers," *Fortune* (7 November 1988), pp. 147, 150, 154; and Leo G.B. Welt, *Countertrade: Business Practices for Today's World Market* (New York: American Management Association, 1982).

## SUGGESTED READINGS

Alexandrides, C. G., and B. L. Bowers. *Countertrade.* New York: Wiley, 1987.

Ebrahimi, Bahman, and William Bowman, "ABCs of Countertrade: A Vehicle for Successful Exporting," *InfoTrade Report* (September–October 1988), pp. 4–5.

*Export Marketing for Smaller Firms,* 2nd ed. Washington, D.C.: U.S. Small Business Administration, 1979. Chaps. 6 and 7.

Kahler, Ruel, and Ronald L. Kramer. *International Marketing,* 5th ed. Cincinnati: South-Western, 1983, Chap. 10.

Mirus, Rolf, and Bernard Yeung. "Economic Incentives for Countertrade." *Journal of International Business Studies,* vol. 17, no. 3 (Fall 1986), pp. 27–40.

Terpstra, Vern. *International Dimensions of Marketing,* 2nd ed. Boston: Kent, 1988, Chap. 6.

Tsurumi, Yoshi. *Multinational Management: Business Strategy and Government Policy,* 2nd ed. Cambridge, Mass.: Ballinger, 1984, Chaps. 9 and 12.

Vernon, Raymond, and Louis T. Wells, Jr. *Manager in the International Economy,* 5th ed. Englewood Cliffs, N.J.: Prentice-Hall, 1986, Chap. 2.

Wiedersheim-Paul, F., H. C. Olson, and L. S. Welch. "Pre-export Activity: The First Step in Internationalization." *Journal of International Business Studies,* vol. 9, no. 1 (Spring/Summer 1978), pp. 47–58.

# Dolefil*

## INTRODUCTION

Dole Philippines, Inc., which operates under the name Dolefil, is a subsidiary of Castle & Cooke, Inc., which has its headquarters in Hawaii. Castle & Cooke, Inc., is the world's largest producer of pineapples.[1] The Dolefil subsidiary is wholly owned by Castle & Cooke, and is located on the island of Mindanao, the largest of the 7,000 Philippine islands.

The Philippines, like many Third World countries, has welcomed foreign corporations. American companies, in particular, have always found favorable conditions in the Philippines, even as far back as the colonial days.

> The colonial relationship with the United States and the so-called free-trade policy tended to concentrate Philippine trade with the United States. By the late inter-war period the Philippines was sending three-quarters of its exports (by value) to the United States. . . .[2]

Tariff policy is one of the critical determinants in the success of the Philippine export industries. U.S. tariff policy permits Philippine products to have special access to the U.S. marketplace.[3]

## OPERATIONS

The operation of Dolefil is located mainly in Polomolok municipality, but there are some fields in Tupi and General Santos. This region is comparatively under-developed.

The operation commenced in 1963 on a 6,000 hectare plantation. It is now one of the largest plantations and processing operations in the world, with 10,000 hectares of land under its control. Out of these 10,000 hectares, 8,000 are leased from the National Development Corporation, which is a government agency. The lease is for a 25-year period, subject to renegotiation for renewal. Rent is based on production, with a minimum guarantee that is reviewed

---

*This case was originally written by Ayda Kimemia of St. Lawrence University as a term project; it was subsequently revised by Professor Asheghian for inclusion in this textbook.

periodically. The remaining 2,000 hectares have individual owners and are obtained through Farm Management Arrangement contracts. Dolefil can use this land for ten years with a renewal option. Individual owners receive a set annual rent per hectare plus a premium based on production.[4] Production is based on a three-year cycle. The first crop is ready for picking between 14 and 17 months after planting. The maturation of pineapples is chemically controlled so as to maintain the cycle. A year later a second crop is produced. After knocking down the plants, the land is left fallow for two to three months before it is tilled and then replanted. Waste from the cannery is incorporated back into the soil to increase its organic content and fertility. The degree of labor-intensive production varies with the scheme used. Planting and harvesting are labor-intensive, whereas the rest of the agricultural operations is more mechanized, using bulldozers, tractors, and spraying mechanisms for pest control.[5]

In addition to plantations, Dolefil owns a highly mechanized cannery, which is considered to be the best in the world. Every part of the pineapple is used, including the shell, which is used for cattle feed and field emulsion.[6] The company participates in comprehensive training programs in an effort to educate Filipino employees, thus enabling them to move upward in the company organization.[7]

Initially, the entire output was shipped to the United States; now it is shipped mainly to Japan and the United States. Some of the product also goes to the rest of the world.[8]

The company also has its own support services, which provide it with electrical generation, repair services, maintenance, and engineering facilities. Water used in the area is treated at the company's water treatment plant. Paper cartons that are used for packing are built by Dolefil at its plant at Calumpang Wharfin. In addition to building and maintaining hundreds of kilometers of dirt roads throughout the plantation, Dolefil also maintains many of the provincial roads that run through the plantation. Finally, it owns the warehouse, which is fully equipped for storage at the shipping dock. Transportation to and from the field is provided by the company. Workers are picked up from specific locations in uncovered cargo trucks, which have no provisions for rain or sun.[9]

## EMPLOYMENT PRACTICES

The company employs 9,000 workers. Half are in agricultural operations; a third in industrial operations; and the rest in administrative and general service activities. Of the 9,000, less than ten are permanent non-Filipino executive staff; all ten are in top management. Between 1963 and 1980 there has been a large increase in the Polomolok population. In 1963, the population was only 15,000. It reached 59,200 in 1980, a 294.6 percent increase. This increase is largely due to Dolefil's creation of jobs that were made available not only to local residents but also to immigrants from the northern part of the Philippines. Well-established unionization of labor exists, but the effectiveness of unions is questionable due to internal squabbles. Furthermore, martial law has been in effect since

1972, banning strikes in "vital industries." These industries include companies engaged in foreign exports, such as Dolefil. The workday consists of 10- to 12-hour shifts, and there is compulsory work on Sundays during peak seasons.[10]

Housing in Polomolok and the cannery area is scarce and overcrowded. Dolefil has underway two housing development schemes that occupy two 12-hectare areas. The scheme is controlled through a real estate agency, and plots may be purchased by employees of the company. Dolefil has subsidized the loans needed for the completion of the project, thereby exerting control over the quality of the structures constructed. Workers who cannot be accommodated by the subsidized housing scheme must seek housing from local residents. This generally means exorbitant rents, with no electricity and a limited water supply. However, the mid-level managers are provided with housing at the residential compound near the cannery site. This compound has several sports and recreational facilities, which are subsidized by Dolefil. About five kilometers north of the cannery on a mountain slope is Kalsangi, the housing area for top management. It is an exclusive housing complex with suburban-style homes. Invitation is required for entrance. The area has 55 executive homes. It also has its own school (the elementary grades through high school), a well-maintained golf course, a swimming pool, tennis courts, and a clubhouse that is used as a center for community activities. A small number of people own their own homes, but they must pay rent for the land.[11]

As with any MNC, Dolefil has its own interests to serve, namely, to make a profit. In the pineapple business in the Philippines, where Dolefil faces stiff competition from another MNC, Del Monte, the question that is often raised is whether or not it is possible to simultaneously serve the interests of the local community and also to continue to make a profit and prosper as a business?

## COMMUNITY RELATIONS

Dolefil has taken a number of steps in the overall development of the local community of Polomolok. It provides a 99-bed hospital, serviced by eight doctors and one dentist. In an emergency situation, up to 120 beds may be accommodated by taking advantage of all available space. The company has also improved water availability, health, sanitation, and educational and recreational facilities. Total aid to the community from 1973 to 1979 amounted to $754,666. Dolefil's extensive training programs in management, mechanics, and engineering have enabled Filipinos to start their own businesses or find employment elsewhere. Agricultural workers are paid approximately 40 percent more and industrial workers approximately 55 percent more than the required minimum wage. They also receive fringe benefits, such as hospital care and the use of recreational facilities. The average annual wage in 1980 was 10,170 pesos (about $1,375). This is inadequate to provide the average family with the necessities of life. The average wages are also far less than the average wages at the company's operation in Hawaii. With regard to the land, Dolefil has made some attempts to combat soil erosion by contour plowing of fields across rather than down the slopes of hills. Dolefil has also reorganized and reshaped dry creeks, and it has extensively planted, ipil-ipil trees on the creek banks. Contours are placed at regular distances and at a given slope to carry away surplus water through natural waterways across the plantation.[12]

In Polomolok, the host of this highly mechanized and modern industrial plant, there are no paved roads, no street lights, inadequate health care, and a very poor garbage and waste disposal system. Although taxes from the corporation have contributed millions of pesos to the local government, the government administration does not use these funds for community development. Furthermore, the use of numerous chemical additives in the soil in an effort to increase its fertility is causing the gradual deterioration of the land. If Dolefil were to pull out, the soil would be unproductive and thus useless to local farmers. The presence of Dolefil and Del Monte has discouraged local entrepreneurs from trying to penetrate the pineapple market. They accuse both of these corporations of dumping, and thus monopolizing, the market. Finally, constitutional questions have been raised concerning Dolefil's sublease agreement with the government-owned National Development Corporation for Dolefil's use of the land in Mindanao. The constitution imposes a 1,024 hectare limitation on foreign corporate land holdings.[13]

## QUESTIONS

1. Does Dolefil fit the pattern of criticisms that are aimed at MNCs? Explain.
2. Do you think Dolefil has been beneficial to the Philippines? Discuss.
3. What can the government of the Philippines do to enhance the potential benefit of FDI in that country?
4. What mistakes do you think have been made by Dolefil? Could Dolefil have prevented its mistakes in the Philippines?

## NOTES

1. Lee A. Tavis, *Multinational Managers and Poverty in the Third World* (Notre Dame, Ind.: University of Notre Dame Press, 1982), p. 199.
2. Ibid., pp. 194–195.
3. Ibid., p. 195.
4. Ibid.
5. Frank H. Golay, *The Philippines: Public Policy and National Economic Development* (Ithaca, N.Y.: Cornell University Press, 1961), p. 47.
6. Tavis, *Multinational Managers*, p. 195.
7. Ibid., pp. 199–203.
8. Ibid., pp. 201–202, 204.
9. Ibid., pp. 205–206.
10. Ibid., pp. 195, 209–216.
11. Ibid., pp. 215–217.

12. Ibid., pp. 195, 209.
13. Ibid., pp. 215–217.

## SUGGESTED READINGS

Frank, Isaiah. *Foreign Enterprise in Developing Countries.* Baltimore, Md.: Johns Hopkins University Press, 1979.

Golay, Frank H. *The Philippines: Public Policy and National Economic Development.* Ithaca, N.Y.: Cornell University Press, 1961.

*Moody's Industrial Manual.* Moody's Investors Service, 1986. p. 2673.

Nafziger, Wayne P. *The Economics of Developing Countries.* Belmont, Calif.: Wadsworth, 1984. Ch. 16.

Steinberg, David Joel. *The Philippines, a Singular and a Plural Place.* Boulder, Colo.: Westview Press, 1982.

Tavis, Lee A. *Multinational Managers and Poverty in the Third World.* Notre Dame, Ind.: University of Notre Dame Press, 1982.

# Aluminum Industry of Jamaica and Reynolds Metals Company*

## INTRODUCTION

There exists an ongoing conflict who's center is in Jamaica. The nature of the conflict is not to be described as open warfare; yet there are many battles. The gains and losses are not measured by body counts, but in dollars and cents. The struggle is between the government of Jamaica and the North American aluminum companies, and the battles are played out in the halls of government and the boardrooms of the aluminum producers. Gains and losses are measured by the level of governmental revenues, taxes, and royalties in the case of the Jamaican government, and by the level of net income or loss in the case of the aluminum producers.

## THE ALUMINUM INDUSTRY IN JAMAICA

Jamaica is a nation in the West Indies. It is the third largest island in the Caribbean (after Cuba and Hispaniola), with a population of approximately 2.2 million. Jamaica covers an area of 4,244 square miles. This country has vast reserves of bauxite.[1]

Bauxite is the natural ore from which aluminum is extracted. In 1980, 11.4 million tons of bauxite were mined in Jamaica, making that country the third largest source of bauxite after Australia and Guinea.[2] Four aluminum companies dominate bauxite mining in Jamaica. All are North American metals and mining companies that are classified as MNCs. The combined total revenues of these companies were $13,784 million in 1980. Table II:2.1 illustrates the relative performance of these companies.

In addition to mining, all of these companies have operations in Jamaica for the conversion of bauxite into alumina. Alumina is the intermediary product

---

*This case was originally written by Robert Nichols as a term project; it was subsequently revised by Professor Asheghian for inclusion in this textbook.

Table II:2.1    THE RELATIVE PERFORMANCE OF THE FOUR MAJOR ALUMINUM
COMPANIES IN JAMAICA

|  | Alcoa | Alcan | Reynolds | Kaiser |
|---|---|---|---|---|
| Primary aluminium production ('000 tonnes) | 1,863 | 1,302 | 974 | 992 |
| Total revenues (US$mn) | 5,196 | 5,264 | 3,738 | 3,351 |
| Net income (US$mn) | 470 | 542 | 180 | 248 |

Source: Michael Kaufman, Jamaica Under Manley: Dilemmas of Socialism and Democracy (London: Zed Books, 1985), p. 26.

in the production process whose end product is aluminum. Alcan Aluminum, the most important of the MNCs in Jamaica, provides an example of the size and the extent of the operation of these corporations. In 1980, Alcan "had $5.3 billion in sales and revenues (or almost two and a half times the entire Gross Domestic Product of Jamaica) and employed almost 64,000 people in its operations in 35 countries and sales outlets in another 100."[3]

The importance of the aluminum industry to Jamaica is well known and acknowledged. In its 1982 report on Latin America, the Inter-American Development Bank states that "the aluminum industry is critical to the economic growth, foreign exchange earnings, and government revenues in Jamaica."[4] Bauxite and alumina led the country's list of export products and contributed an average of $300 million per year to merchandise export earnings during the period from 1978 to 1982. Exports fell 20 percent to $240 million in 1982, reflecting the severe effects of the 1982 recession on the aluminum industry.[5]

## THE JAMAICAN BUSINESS ENVIRONMENT

The relationship that has existed between the industry and the government of Jamaica since the industry's first presence in the 1940s has been tested many times, but never more so than in the 1970s. The confrontation is between a sovereign nation and MNCs over the control, the price, and the distribution of the nation's raw materials.

In 1972, Michael Manley, a U.S.–educated leftist leader was swept into office as Jamaica's Prime Minister. He had promised to free the former British Colony from colonialism and create a new economic order. In 1980, a journalist vividly described what happened next:

> He promptly installed his aggressive brand of democratic socialism, expropriating private farms, taxing business heavily, abolishing private education, and spending huge sums of mostly borrowed money on social programs. Abroad he nuzzled up to the Soviet bloc nations and railed against Western imperialism in fiery eloquent speeches from Moscow, Baghdad, and Havana. The results for Jamaica were disastrous. If a country could be declared bankrupt, it would be among the first to go.[6]

If Manley's efforts alone were not sufficient to cripple the economy, most certainly the effects of the OPEC oil price hikes would. Oil prices began rising in 1972. "OPEC's quadrupling of oil prices in 1973–74 was an expensive shock: it pushed Jamaica's oil bill up from $73 million (11% of its imports) in 1973 to $195 million (21%) in 1974."[7] Unfortunately for Jamaica, the nation imports almost 100 percent of its energy needs. The Inter-American Development Bank observes that "The oil crisis dealt a severe blow to Jamaica's industrialization strategy and helped reduce its imports capacity sharply through the second half of the decade [1970s]."[8]

To finance the trade deficits, the government of Jamaica borrowed heavily from anyone who would lend. In addition to international commercial banks (that have long considered Jamaica a poor risk), the government relied on supranational institutions and the International Monetary Fund. In 1982, it was observed that "on a per capita basis, Jamaica's foreign debt of $2.1 billion is nearly as large as Mexico's and debt service of $300 million will swell its total payments deficit to an estimated $500 million."[9]

Looking elsewhere for hard currency revenues, two traditional sources held little potential. The agricultural sector was badly managed and disorganized; and tourism revenues were poor because of the threat of economic chaos and political violence.

Mr. Manley turned his attention to the bauxite and alumina industry, upon whose shoulders he felt the government of Jamaica could ride out of the storm. It was in 1974, after the initial oil price hikes, that the government sought a different relationship with the industry. Manley raised a "7.5% levy on aluminum prices. The levy increased total government revenues by over 60% in a single year." This first step by Manley seemed as if it would help Jamaica. But the five MNCs in Jamaica decreased the volume of their production. As a result, the volume of bauxite and aluminum production decreased by 38 percent during the 1974–1976 period.[10]

In addition, the government of Jamaica acquired nearly all the land that the companies had owned and 50 percent of their assets, which the government then leased back to the companies. Instead of cash, the companies were given promissory notes to be repaid over 10 years—presumably out of the proceeds of the new levies. The Jamaican government was also instrumental in organizing the International Bauxite Association (IBA), a cartel of 11 bauxite-producing nations which sought to set minimum prices and production quotas for the ore.[11]

The attempts of the International Bauxite Association to develop a unified pricing and levy structure throughout its membership have proven unsuccessful for a number of reasons. First, there has been no essential unanimity among its members concerning the pricing and levy structure. This problem is aggravated by Australia's competitive edge in the production and exports of bauxite and alumina.[12] Australia was the leading bauxite producer by a wide margin (27.8 million tons in 1980) and its actions had a great impact on the cartel's influence.[13] Second, the IBA has tried to operate during a period of economic recession without realistic flexibility. Third, the association did not take into account the already occurring shift of production from member countries to nonmember countries prior to the development of the levy structure. Finally, and most important, historically speaking cartels have had relatively short lives. When dealing with entities operating in a competitive environment, the attempt to maintain unanimity within a cartel seems doomed to failure.[14]

## REYNOLDS METAL COMPANY

At the level of the individual firm, Reynolds Metals Co. suffered significantly as a result of its heavy investment in Jamaica. It was fortunate, however, that the years from 1975 to 1986 were years of strong demand for aluminum with the growth of new markets—particularly in the beverage can market industry. This helped offset the drain of the bauxite levy on Reynolds resources.

Since the imposition of the levy, Reynolds has undertaken substantial negotiation efforts to reduce the magnitude of the tax. As first imposed, the levy was 7.5 percent of the average realized price of a ton of primary aluminum. In terms of a ton of bauxite, the cost of production doubled.[15]

It is important to note the reasons that Reynolds had not chosen to sell, or abandon, its operation in Jamaica. Chief among these reasons were: (1) the large write-off of capital investment that would have been necessary, (2) the problem of raw materials replacement to supplant the Jamaican bauxite ore at a reasonable cost, and (3) the high capital cost of building replacement facilities.

From the introduction of the levy, Reynolds management has had a desire to lower this tax burden. An agreement was signed in 1975 between the Jamaican government and Reynolds that outlined levy relief covering bauxite mining operations, subject to finalization in formal agreements. This formal agreement was signed in 1977. It was a plan of lower taxation coupled with joint venture participation.[16]

The agreement of 1977 had not yet become effective in late 1978 so Reynolds stepped up its efforts to obtain levy relief. Meetings between the government of Jamaica and a Reynolds representative occurred to outline the severe problem that Reynolds was facing and its need to reduce the production levy in order to make the Jamaican operations more competitive. Reynolds arguments for lower production levies did not insist upon immediate action, but only upon agreements on steps that would bring Jamaican bauxite cost to competitive levels within a reasonable time period. Reynolds added, however, that immediate levy relief was essential to eliminate the disparity between the levy costs and the costs of other procedures, both in Jamaica and in other countries.

Many more meetings were held with the government of Jamaica. During 1979 a new levy compromise was reached, placing a levy of about 7 percent on the primary aluminum ingot price. Additional concessions, for using lower grade bauxite and for increasing production, were later added, as well as a cap on the primary ingot prices. Each year brings additional negotiations based primarily upon industry market conditions.

The battles referred to here do not promise to abate soon, nor is it to be expected that they should. The executives of Reynolds have planned a continued geographical diversification program that promises to add additional clout to their arguments for lower taxes.

## QUESTIONS

1. Why are aluminum companies investing in Jamaica? Why did the Jamaican government allow these firms to invest there? Explain.

2. What is an international cartel? Who benefits from a cartel? Is it the firms or the countries in which the cartel is operating? Explain, using the Jamaican case as an example.

3. To curve its foreign debt the host country should impose heavy taxes on the subsidiaries of MNCs that are operating in that country. Do you agree with this statement? Discuss.

4. Given the levy of 7.5 percent in Jamaica on aluminum production, do you think that Reynolds should have abandoned its operation in that country? Discuss.

## NOTES

1. *The New Encyclopaedia Britannica,* 15th ed. vol. 6 (Chicago: Encyclopaedia Britannica, Inc., 1985), p. 478.
2. Michael Kaufman, *Jamaica Under Manley: Dilemmas of Socialism and Democracy* (London: Zed Books, 1985), p. 25.
3. Ibid., p. 27.
4. Inter-American Development Bank, *Economic and Social Progress in Latin America: The External Sector,* 1982 Report (Washington, D.C.: Inter-American Development Bank, 1982), p. 278.
5. Ibid., p. 184.
6. "For Socialist Jamaica, Big Capital Infusion May Be Only Salvation," *The Wall Street Journal,* 25 February 1980, p. 1.
7. "Jamaica: Island in the Soup," *Economist* (21 June 1980) p. 51.
8. Inter-American Development Bank, *Economic and Social Progress in Latin America,* p. 278.
9. "Why Jamaica's Economy May Run Aground," *Business Week,* 18 October 1982, p. 162.
10. "Jamaica: Island in the Soup," p. 51.
11. "Bauxite Producers to Meet," *The New York Times,* 14 February 1974, p. 62; "International Bauxite Association," *Yearbook of International Organizations 1983/1984,* Union of International Associations, ed. Vol. 1, 20th ed. (New York: K. G. Sam Müchen, 1983), p. C4625.
12. "Australia Exploits Edge in Aluminum," *The New York Times,* 20 February 1979, p. D1.
13. Kaufman, *Jamaica Under Manley,* p. 25.
14. Ibid., pp. 83–85.

15. Ibid., pp. 8–9.
16. "Reynolds Unit in Pact on Jamaica Bauxite," *The New York Times,* 1 April 1977, p. D12.


## SUGGESTED READINGS

"Australia Exploits Edge in Aluminum." *The New York Times,* 20 February 1979, p. D1.

"Bauxite Producers to Meet." *The New York Times,* 14 February 1974, p. 62.

"For Socialist Jamaica, Big Capital Infusion May Be Only Salvation." *The Wall Street Journal,* 25 February 1980, p. 1.

Hurwitz, Samuel J. *Jamaica: A Historical Portrait.* New York: Praeger, 1971.

Inter-American Development Bank, *Economic and Social Progress In Latin America: The External Sector.* Washington, D. C., Inter-American Developmental Bank, 1982.

"Jamaica: Island in the Soup." *Economist,* 21 June 1980, pp. 51–53.

Kaufman, Michael. *Jamaica Under Manley: Dilemmas of Socialism and Democracy.* London: Zed Books, 1985.

*The New Encyclopaedia Britannica,* 15th ed., vol. 6. Chicago: Encyclopaedia Britannica, Inc., 1985. pp. 478–479.

"Reynolds Unit in Pact on Jamaican Bauxite." *The New York Times,* 1 April 1977, p. D12.

"Why Jamaica's Economy May Run Aground." *Business Week,* 18 October 1982, pp. 162–163.

# Case II:3

# *The Sony Corporation**

## INTRODUCTION

When Akio Morita was browsing in a Tokyo antiques shop one day shortly after World War II, he saw a customer pick up an ivory figurine and proceed to buy it for a huge sum of money. "I learned," Morita said, "that if a thing has quality, and people know its value, they will be willing to pay the price for it."[1] Morita then took this valuable lesson and used it to help him build Sony, the highly successful multinational corporation.

Whether it be a Trinitron, a Betamax, a Walkman, a word processor, or even life insurance or spaghetti, Sony's got it, but why the name *Sony?* Looking through several dictionaries in 1958, Mr. Morita and his partner, Masaru Ibuka, came up with two terms. Sonus, a Latin word meaning sound, and sonny boy, meaning a young boy. These founders of the company decided that since they were a couple of sonny boys in the sound business, they would call their business "Sony." It was just what they were looking for: a short name that was international and sounded the same all over the world.[2]

In 1946, Morita started his business with $528 and seven employees in a small, boarded-up room in a Tokyo department store. Sony is now a huge multinational corporation, boasting an annual sales level of more than $10 billion, owning 16 plants worldwide, and providing jobs for over 45,000 employees.[3]

It is hard to say that it has been smooth sailing for Sony throughout its existence. Sony has had setbacks, some major and some minor. Sony's management has always been optimistic in a crisis situation, and although Sony may have occasionally stumbled, it has never fallen.

### Company History

Akio Morita, founder and now chairman of Sony, was working in a business with his father in 1945 when he read in a newspaper about a small telecommunications laboratory that had recently opened up. Morita wrote to Masaru Ibuka,

---

*This case was originally written by Glen Sundin of St. Lawrence University as a term project; it was subsequently revised by Professor Asheghian for inclusion in this textbook.

an old friend of his, who was founder of the newly opened Tokyo Telecommunications Laboratory. A few days later, Morita received a letter from Ibuka asking Morita to join him, and they started working together.[4]

In 1946, they decided to incorporate and became Tokyo Telecommunications Company, making communications equipment for the Japanese telephone and telegraph companies and also for the national railroads.[5]

They started research for the production of consumer goods in 1947, and they put their first tape recorder on the market in 1950. They started doing research on their first transistor radio in 1953 and subsequently marketed it in 1955. In 1957 they made their first big impact in the world market by marketing their first export product, the world's first pocket radio, which was very successful in the United States and other advanced countries. In the beginning of 1958 they adopted their present name of *Sony,* because they needed a shorter, more universal name for international business. At the end of 1959, after much research, Sony introduced the world's first all-transistorized television, and was very successful in doing so.[6]

In 1960, Sony Corporation of America in New York and Sony Overseas S.A. in Switzerland were established. In 1965, Sony formed a joint venture with Tektronix, Incorporated, to produce electronic measuring devices in Japan. In 1968, Sony established a subsidiary in the United Kingdom called Sony (U.K.) Ltd. In 1970, Sony formed a fifty-fifty joint venture with Columbia Broadcasting System in Japan to make, sell, and promote musical equipment. This new company was originally named CBS/Sony Records Corporation but is now called CBS/Sony Group Incorporated. In 1970, Sony established a subsidiary in West Germany called Sony GmbH. This subsidiary's name was changed in 1980 to Sony Deutschland GmbH.[7]

In 1972, Sony established the Sony Trading Company, a wholly owned subsidiary that takes products that were made in the United States and Europe and then markets them in Japan.[8]

In August 1972, Sony opened up a manufacturing facility in San Diego, California. This television assembly plant was its first manufacturing facility outside the Orient. In fall of 1972, Sony changed its management characteristics by appointing Harvey L. Schein, an American, president of Sony Corporation of America.[9]

In 1973, Sony established a subsidiary in France (Sony France S.A.). In 1975, Sony formed a joint venture with Union Carbide Corporation and called it Sony Eveready Incorporated. This fifty-fifty joint venture enabled the import and eventual sale of Union Carbide's high performance dry cell batteries to Japan. This was done under the trademark Sony-Eveready.[10]

Also in 1975, Sony had to lower its inventories by cutting production; they therefore gave one-half of its labor force five extra holidays for the year.[11]

In 1978, there were some problems with communications between the parent company and its U.S. subsidiary. Sony made some shifts in management to speed decision making. Harvey Schein resigned after five years with Sony. Akio Morita, president of the parent company, replaced him.[12]

In 1979, Sony formed a joint venture with Prudential Life Insurance

Company of America Ltd. This enabled Sony to start selling group and individual life insurance in Japan. Prudential owns 50 percent plus one share of Sony Prudential Life Insurance Company Ltd.[13]

In 1979, Sony formed a joint venture with PepsiCo Incorporated to produce Wilson Sporting Goods products in Japan.[14]

In May 1982, Sony started manufacturing Betamax VCRs in West Germany.[15]

In December 1982, Sony had to remove its VCRs from France because of import restrictions on VCRs that had been imposed by France.[16]

In April 1984, Sony bought hard disc technology from Apple Computer Incorporated so that it could produce hard disks in Japan and market them in the United States.[17]

In October 1985, Sony bought out Columbia Broadcasting System's half interest in the joint venture that had been set up in 1970. This move gave Sony a wholly owned subsidiary that would manufacture compact disks in Indiana. The disks had previously been produced in Japan and imported into the United States.[18]

In November 1985, Sony raised its prices on electronic products by 5 percent to 12 percent. This price increase was due to the strengthening of the yen.[19]

In March 1986, Sony's U.S. subsidiary formed a medical data firm to make products that analyze and display medical products.[20]

## Industry Description

Sony is classified as a Japanese diversified company. In this industry, Sony's sales are only 7.6 percent of the industry's total sales, but this figure is misleading because Sony's sales are mainly in consumer electronics. Sony's main competitor in the consumer electronics business is Matsushita Electronic Industrial Corporation. Matsushita ranks first in the business in sales of consumer electronics, with Sony ranking second. As Table II:3.1 shows, Matsushita clearly outperformed Sony in sales in 1987.

Table II:3.1 COMPARATIVE SALES OF SONY AND ITS COMPETITION (MILLIONS OF DOLLARS) IN 1987

| Sony | | Matsushita | |
|---|---|---|---|
| Sales | $ 11,450 | Sales | $ 38,552 |
| Net Profit | $ 293.9 | Net Profit | $ 1,302.7 |
| Net Profit Margin | 2.6 % | Net Profit Margin | 3.4 % |

*Source: The Value Line: Investment Survey,* 10 (November 25, 1988), pp. 1564 and 1567.

## Company Description

Sony is a leading producer of consumer electronics, but it is concentrating more and more on broadcasting equipment, office equipment, and computer chips. Sony has a total of 16 plants worldwide, nine of which are in Japan, three in the United States, and four in Europe. Foreign sales represent 74 percent of its total sales. Sony spends 18 percent of its sales on labor, and 9.2 percent on research and development. In 1985, Sony had a little over 52,000 shareholders who owned over 231 billion shares. Thirty-seven percent of Sony is owned by foreign investors.[21]

In addition to its factories, Sony owns a research center, an audio/video technology center, the Sony Development Center, and their headquarters, all of which are located in Japan. Sony's management is made up of a seven-man executive board, with nine managing directors, 14 directors, and four statutory auditors. Sony and all of its subsidiaries use the accounting principles that are generally accepted in the host countries (for example, Sony Corporation of America uses accounting principles that are generally accepted in the United States). At year-end, Sony sums up all of the asset and liability accounts and expresses these figures in terms of Japanese yen at the appropriate year-end current rates.[22]

## Sony Goes Multinational

Sony had always been a corporation that depended on its exports, but in 1972 it decided to start producing its products in the United States. In 1973, Sony made some management changes and appointed an American to be in charge of its U.S. subsidiary. These key moves made Sony a true multinational corporation.

Sony management felt that they were better off going multinational because of two upward revaluations of the Japanese yen and because the world market was flooded by Japanese products.

Sony began planning to go multinational in 1971, after President Nixon put economic controls into effect. The president had imposed a price freeze and a surcharge on all imports. Nixon also put an end to the conversion of the U.S. dollar into gold.[23] Sony was plagued by a similar problem in France in 1982, when the French put up custom barriers against Japanese makers of VCRs because of their opposition to Japanese exports.[24]

When Sony analyzed Nixon's policies, it realized that it could not continue to make its products in Japan but had to start manufacturing them in the different countries where markets for its goods existed. Sony also had to start thinking multinationally, and it began hiring foreign nationals to manage its foreign subsidiaries.[25] Sony responded to France's custom barriers in 1982 by cutting its shipments to France.[26]

Another reason why Sony went multinational is because the United States was moving more toward protectionism. Sony came to the conclusion that it would not cost more to manufacture its products in the United States and other advanced countries. Sony came to this conclusion by taking into account the higher costs of labor in the United States, the upward revaluation of the yen, and the newly increased shipping charges and custom duties.

Although it seems that Sony became multinational solely to cut costs, the company claims that it went multinational in order to change its management philosophy. Sony did not want anything, such as trade barriers or currency problems, to get in the way of its production.

Sony prices were raised by about 5 percent after the dollar was devalued in February 1973. This brought Sony's price increases to an average of 10 percent to 12 percent following the first revaluation of yen in December 1971.

Sony insisted that its problem in the United States has always been a shortage of merchandise rather than price competition from other companies. It contended that, even though it had announced the price increases, there had been no order cancellations and that, in fact, orders had been backlogged since the end of February 1973.[27]

## Quality

Sony could easily have taken advantage of cheap labor by opening up manufacturing subsidiaries in LDCs instead of in the United States. An LDC such as Mexico would be inclined to invite a company like Sony to open up a factory and create both employment and income. But Sony is, and always has been, turned off to the idea of manufacturing in LDCs.

Sony would still have to contend with the trade barriers and currency problems by producing in an LDC, and Sony has always taken pride in the quality of its products, its innovations, and its progress in the industry. If Sony moved to a less-developed country, the factor of quality in its products might be greatly reduced.

Sony has always been a pioneer in its industry, having spent a large percentage of its revenues on research and development. At one time, Akio Morita stated that "we don't market products that have already been developed. Rather, we develop markets for products we make."[28] Such a philosophy has led Sony to plan way in advance in developing its products. An example of this attitude is shown in Sony's research for Betamax, which began in 1960, 16 years before the product was introduced in the United States.[29]

Sony's innovation and research had always paid off because it had always had a monopoly of its products for two or three years. But in the late 1970s and early 1980s, Sony's competitors started closing the technological gap. Sony could no longer charge a high price for its quality products. Other manufacturers have started producing products of comparable quality at a much lower price. In October 1982, Sony introduced its first compact laser disk player. It had taken Sony six years and $25 million to develop this product. This move paid off at first, but only ten months later Sony's major competitors, Matsushita and Hitachi, were selling disk players of the same quality at a price that was as much as 35 percent lower.[30]

## Lifetime Employment System

Why are competitors catching up to Sony so quickly? It may be, in part, because Japan's lifetime employment system has put quite a burden on Sony. During slow years, instead of laying off workers, Sony has been committed to putting its employees into meaningless positions where they do nothing but busy work, but where they still receive the same wages. Former computer chip makers might be transferred to work in the company's cafeteria. Some 2,100 employees, who had previously been working on the production lines in a Betamax factory, spent their time putting together suggestions to improve productivity. These workers were efficient, putting together 8,000 ideas (close to their target of 12,000). But many feel that these maneuvers were not good for Sony. One competitor, Sharp Incorporated, had cut production of their calculators, and, instead of laying off people, Sharp had sent almost half of its production people out to sell overstocked calculators that had accumulated when the calculator market collapsed in 1972.[31]

Is Sony spending too much on labor? Looking at the 1987 statistics in Table II:3.2, it is clear that compared with its competitors, Sony is making the least amount of sales per employee.

## Diversification

Since Sony had been facing a lot of competition in its consumer electronics business, it has decided to concentrate on other market targets, such as nonconsumer electronics and other businesses, some of which are related to the electronics business. Sony wanted to concentrate on the tape and disk business

Table II:3.2  COMPARATIVE SALES PER
EMPLOYEE OF MAJOR
JAPANESE CORPORATIONS
IN 1987

| Company | Sales Per Employee |
| --- | --- |
| Pioneer Electric | $195,119 |
| Hitachi | $248,896 |
| Matsushita | $248,640 |
| Sony | $189,256 |

Source: Adapted from The Value Line: Investment Survey, 10 (November 25, 1988), pp. 1562–1567.

because of the high profit margin (50 percent) and because people will keep buying tapes and disks even after they buy their VCRs, tape recorders, and disk players. Morita uses the example of Kodak, which is making much more money from selling film than from selling its cameras.[32]

Sony surprised a lot of people in the late 1970s when, instead of getting into promising electronics markets, it opened up some unrelated businesses, selling such products as cosmetics, sporting goods, life insurance, and even spaghetti. Morita stated, "If we have enough money and know-how to create new businesses around our main business, it has to improve our long term outlook."[33]

Another example of this diversification came in 1972 when Sony, having a reputation as an exporter, decided to get into the import business. Sony opened up 8,000 of its retail outlets to imported products. This gave manufacturers with products that were suitable to Sony the opportunity to deal with the final retailer in Japan, instead of a merchandising house. Sony gained on this deal by getting a commission and increasing the variety in its outlets. This also went against the worldwide belief that Japan was exporting too much and not importing enough. This move may have encouraged other nations to cut back on their trade restrictions against Japan as it began some importing.[34]

## Looking into the Future

Sony has always been known as a firm that concentrated on the consumer electronics business, but according to Sony's management times are changing. Sony has started to shift, and wants to continue shifting, from the consumer electronics market to the communications industry. This communications company would concentrate on such products as computers, telecommunications, air navigation equipment, and broadcasting equipment.

Why this change in philosophy? Sony was plagued by a profit slump that started in 1980 and continued until 1983. For the first time in Sony's history, it had to go against the lifetime employment philosophy by offering incentives for workers to quit. Sony had to change its thinking.

Sony now sells 80 percent of its products to consumers. By 1990, executives at Sony want more than 50 percent of its products to be sold to businesses because these sales represent bigger profits and more faithful customers.[35]

The product that Sony has its eye on the most is digital videotape equipment for businesses. This product would record pictures by using a computer code. This is a high-priced item, and it would be sold mostly to broadcasters. Sony also feels that the computer-data storage business will be profitable since the U.S. Army wants to store its data on hard disks in order to facilitate training.[36]

Looking even further into the future, Morita feels that Sony will be selling different types of equipment that use its Trinitron tube to display information that is transmitted by computers. He foresees airplane pilots and car drivers looking at computer screens instead of reading dials.[37]

## QUESTIONS

1. What factors should be considered when an MNC chooses a name? Explain.

2. What motivates a firm to go international? Explain. What motivated Sony?

3. Why does an MNC diversify its business? Explain. Why did Sony?

4. Since labor is cheaper in LDCs than in advanced countries, it always pays off for an MNC to locate its production facilities in those countries. Do you agree with this statement? Explain. Do you think that Sony's decision not to operate in LDCs is correct? Explain.

5. What is the impact of revaluation of the home country's currency on an MNC? How did Sony deal with yen's revaluation? Explain.

6. What are the major reasons behind Sony's success? Explain.

7. A policy of lifetime employment by a company breeds a sense of loyalty in employees, causing them to work harder. As a result, in such companies efficiency rises and profits increase. Do you agree with this statement? Explain.

8. What are the major elements of Sony's global strategy? Explain.

## NOTES

1. "Akio Morita of Sony Corp.," *Nation's Business,* December 1973, p. 45.
2. Ibid., p. 48.
3. *Moody's Industrial Manual,* 1986, vol. 2, pp. 4401–4404.
4. "Akio Morita of Sony Corp.," p. 45.
5. Ibid., p. 46.
6. *Moody's Industrial Manual,* p. 4401.
7. Ibid.
8. "Sony Marketing Subsidiary Attacks U.S. Applications," *The New York Times,* 4 July 1972, p. 25.
9. Gerd Wilke, "The Americanization of Sony," *The New York Times,* 18 March 1973, sec. III, p. 1.
10. *Moody's Industrial Manual,* p. 4401.
11. "Sony Adds 5 Holidays to Reduce Production," *The New York Times,* 11 January 1975, p. 41.
12. "Sony's U.S. Operation Goes in for Repairs," *Business Week,* 13 March 1978, p. 31.
13. "Prudential and Sony in Insurance Accord," *The New York Times,* 14 August 1979, sec. IV, p. 4.
14. "Sony: An Incongruous Search for Greener Pastures," *Business Week,* 11 February 1980, p. 105.
15. "Sony to Manufacture VTRs at German Plant," *The Wall Street Journal,* 1 April 1982, p. 31.
16. "Japanese Makers of VTRs Cut Shipments to France as Customs Barriers Take Hold," *The Wall Street Journal,* 2 December 1982, p. 32.
17. "Apple Sets Accord to Sell Hard-Disk Technology to Sony," *The Wall Street Journal,* 6 April 1984, p. 12.
18. Laura Landro, "Sony Set to Buy CBS Inc.'s Stake in Disk Venture," *The Wall Street Journal,* 17 October 1985, p. 8.

19. "Sony's U.S. Affiliate Plans a Price Boost of 5% to 12% for Electronic Products," *The Wall Street Journal*, 6 November 1985, p. 5.
20. "Sony U.S. Unit Forms Medical Data Firm: Pollack Is President," *The Wall Street Journal*, 21 March 1986, p. 34.
21. *Value-Line Ratings and Reports*, 1985, p. 1568.
22. *Moody's Industrial Manual*, pp. 4401–4404.
23. Wilke, "The Americanization of Sony," p. 1.
24. "Japanese Makers of VTRs Cut Shipments to France," p. 32.
25. Wilke, "The Americanization of Sony," p. 1.
26. "Japanese Makers of VTRs Cut Shipments to France," p. 32.
27. Wilke, "The Americanization of Sony," p. 9.
28. "The Surge in Sony," *Financial World*, 1 October 1980, p. 43.
29. Ibid., pp. 42–44.
30. Michael Cieply, "Sony's Profitless Prosperity," *Forbes*, 24 October 1983, pp. 129–130.
31. Ibid., p. 133.
32. "Sony, A Diversification Plan Tuned to the People Factor," *Business Week*, 9 February 1981, p. 88.
33. Ibid.
34. "Sony'll Sell for You," *The Economist*, 21 October 1972, pp. 86–89.
35. E. S. Browning, "Japan's Sony, Famous for Consumer Electronics, Decides that the Future Lies in Sales to Business," *The Wall Street Journal*, 9 October 1984, p. 33.
36. Ibid.
37. Ibid.

## SUGGESTED READINGS

"Akio Morita of Sony Corp." *Nation's Business*, December 1973, pp. 45–48.

Browning, E. S. "Japan's Sony, Famous for Consumer Electronics, Decides that the Future Lies in Sales to Business." *The Wall Street Journal*, 9 October 1984, p. 33.

"Chinese–Hong Kong Venture to Produce Sony VTR's in China." *The Wall Street Journal*, 6 April 1984, p. 12.

Cieply, Michael. "Sony's Profitless Prosperity." *Forbes*, 24 October 1983, pp. 129–130, 133.

Landro, Laura. "Sony Set to Buy CBS Inc.'s Stake in Disk Venture." *The Wall Street Journal*, 17 October 1985, p. 8.

*Moody's Industrial Manual*, 1986. vol. 2, pp. 4401–4404.

"Sony Marketing Subsidiary Attacks U.S. Subsidiary Application." *The New York Times*, 4 July 1972, p. 25.

"Sony Adds 5 Holidays to Reduce Production." *The New York Times*, 11 January 1975, p. 41.

"Prudential and Sony in Insurance Accord." *The New York Times*, 14 August 1979, sec. IV, p. 4.

"Sony, a Diversification Plan Tuned to the People Factor." *Business Week*, 9 February 1981, p. 88.

"Sony: An Incongruous Search for Greener Pastures." *Business Week*, 11 February 1980, p. 105.

"Sony U.S. Unit Forms Medical Data Firms: Pollack Is President." *The Wall Street Journal*, 21 March 1986, p. 34.

"Sony U.S. Operation Goes in for Repairs." *Business Week*, 13 March 1978, p. 31.

"Sony'll Sell for You." *The Economist*, 21 October 1972, pp. 86–89.

"The Surge in Sony." *Financial World*, 1 October 1980, pp. 42–44.

"Sony to Manufacture VTRs at German Plant." *The Wall Street Journal*, 1 April 1982, p. 31.

"Japanese Makers of VTRs Cut Shipments to France as Custom Barriers Take Hold." *The Wall Street Journal*, 2 December 1982, p. 32.

"Sony's U.S. Affiliate Plans a Price Boost of 5% to 12% for Electronic Products." *The Wall Street Journal*, 6 November 1985, p. 5.

Wilke, Gerd. "The Americanization of Sony." *The New York Times*, 18 March 1973, sec. III, pp. 1, 9.

# U.S.-Japan Trade War:
# The Case of Semiconductors*

## INTRODUCTION

On July 31, 1986, the United States and Japan signed a semiconductor trade accord. According to this agreement, all foreign market dumping of semiconductors by Japanese firms was to be stopped. Also Japan was to allow U.S. microchip manufacturers to gain a larger share of the Japanese semiconductor market. Tokyo promised to facilitate an increase of the U.S. market share in Japan from 8.5 percent in 1986 to 20 percent in 1991.[1]

The United States claims that Japan has failed to live up to this agreement, and that Japan has continued to dump semiconductors into foreign countries. Dumping is selling a commodity in a foreign market at a price that is cheaper than the domestic market price. The United States also says Japan is not keeping its promise to allow the United States a larger share of its home market. In fact, market share of the United States in Japan has actually slipped slightly to 8.4 percent by March 1987.[2]

In retaliation for Tokyo's failure to comply with the agreement, in 1987 the United States imposed a 100 percent tariff on certain Japanese electronics imports.

## ADVISORS RECOMMEND TARIFFS

During March 1987, President Reagan's advisors recommended that the United States impose steep tariffs on Japan for not living up to the semiconductor accord. According to a congressional strategist, "Everyone was complaining that the administration had been too soft on Japan."[3] The United States and Japan have had several trade disputes in the last ten years. But in 1987, the United States finally got frustrated and decided to retaliate.

---

*This case was written by Yolanda Sparks of University of North Texas as a term project; it was subsequently revised by Professor Ebrahimi for inclusion in this textbook. Copyright © 1989 by Bahman Ebrahimi.

## EUROPEANS TAKE ACTION

The United States was not the only one angry with Japan. The European Community had also reached its maximum frustration point. "After years of pleading with Japan to sell less and buy more, Europe has decided tariffs speak louder than words."[4] In 1987, the EC imposed a 20 percent antidumping duty on most Japanese copying machines. With the imposition of this duty the European producers felt they would be able to capture more of the European market. Japan had already captured 80 percent of the European market. Common Market investigators said that the Japanese were selling too cheaply. As James Moorhouse, a Briton who serves on the European Parliament's subcommittee on Japanese trade, put it, "While we may practice free trade at this end, they don't have any intention of doing so."[5]

The European Community (EC) officials contend that in 1986 Japan dumped dynamic random access memories (DRAMs) in Europe at half their production costs. It is interesting to note that an American manufacturer, Texas Instruments (TI), was also accused of dumping DRAMs, made at its Japanese plant, in Europe. Therefore, the EC's policy is to take a firm stand on semiconductor chips manufactured in Japan. By April or May of 1989, the EC was supposed to implement a mechanism for calculating floor prices for semiconductor chips. Many industry analysts, however, believe the EC must be careful not to hurt European companies that use in their products these semiconductor chips made in Japan and the United States.[6] They also are pushing all foreign manufacturers, especially Japanese and South Korean manufacturers, to conduct more advanced chip making in Europe. The EC also requires all Asian electronic products to have 40 percent European content. These measures have provided an opportunity for some U.S. companies. For instance, TI is building a $250 million chip plant in Italy; this new plant should keep TI out of trouble and give it an edge against Japanese competitors. In 1988, TI was neck-and-neck with Toshiba Corporation for first place in the European DRAM market. European industry sales were $933 million in 1988.[7]

## THE U.S. STRATEGY

The U.S. strategy was to concentrate on the dumping issue. The Reagan administration wanted to separate the semiconductor issue from other trade issues. This would stop Japan from trying to drop the semiconductor issue by bargaining for other trade concessions. The U.S. plan involved placing tariffs on consumer electronics products that use microchips. This was considered better than trying to limit semiconductor imports, because limiting the importation of semiconductors would also hurt U.S. manufacturers who use imported Japanese microchips in making their products. The tariffs were to take effect on April 17, 1987.[8]

The penalties against Japan would result in 100 percent tariffs on some

$300 million worth of Japanese imports. These imported products either contained Japanese-made semiconductors or were manufactured by the same Japanese firms that made the microchips that were dumped.

The list of products to be burdened with tariffs appeared to be crafted to avoid hitting U.S. consumers very hard. For example, the advisors refrained from targeting hi-fi stereo equipment, microwave ovens, and other popular consumer items. Some of the items targeted by the tariffs included small electric motors, hard disc drives, central processing units for computers, communication satellites and satellite parts, electric measuring devices, power hand tools, tape players, phonographs, window air conditioners, 18- and 19-inch color television sets, smaller color TVs, and black-and-white television sets.

The strategy changed a little over time. Those products in which the Japanese had a dominant U.S. market share were deleted from the list. These included video tape players and compact disc players. They also targeted only finished microcomputers, not their parts or supplies for other use.[9]

## Victims

The products chosen were tailored to inflict severe penalties against six Japanese electronic firms that the United States alleges breached the semiconductor accord. The six companies were Mitsubishi Electric Corp., Toshiba Corp., Hitachi Ltd., NEC Corp., Fujitsu Ltd., and Matsushita Electric Industrial Co.

The 100 percent tariffs were designed to effectively double the price of affected goods if they were passed on to consumers. "The previous tariffs were 3.9% for small computers, 5% for color TV sets, and 2.2% for power tools."[10] The idea behind the tariffs was to keep these Japanese products out of the U.S. market.

Some victims of the tariffs, however, are innocent bystanders. According to a U.S. trade official, the government cannot single out individual companies when setting a tariff.[11] At least five Japanese companies that made personal computers but did not even make the chips had to pay the 100 percent tariffs. Several U.S. companies that sold Japanese-made personal computers in the United States under their own labels may also be victims.

Although some experts indicate that U.S. consumers are not likely to be significantly affected by this trade battle, many think otherwise. They estimate that the sanctions increase retail prices by as much as 30 percent and more. It seems that the ultimate victims are the consumers who have to pay higher prices for the products they purchase.[12]

## Political Importance

The tariffs imposed on Japanese imports were more important politically than economically. The president decided the tariffs would send a strong message to other countries. It would show these countries that the United States would not tolerate infractions of trade agreements. At the same time, it would show the Congress that President Reagan could get tough on trading partners.[13]

"Some international trade and chip industry executives and analysts say the measures are more symbolic than punitive."[14] The dollar amount of products involved is really small. The tariffs totaled less than 1 percent of 1986's $112.3 billion two-way trade between the United States and Japan.[15] Although the Japanese "lap top" personal computer inventories may have been in trouble, the effect on other supplies of computers was expected to be minimal. This is because many retailers stocked up on their inventories before the tariff sanctions came into effect. In fact, it seems that the United States did not want a trade war.

Many U.S. executives doubted that tariffs would remain in place very long. Several people estimated a few months. As a result of the sanctions, Japan cut microchip production. President Reagan indicated that if compliance by the Japanese continued for an uncertain period of time, he would withdraw the sanctions.

## The Nation's Reaction

Some people felt that the tariffs were good, but others disagreed. F. Thomas Dunlap, general counsel and secretary of Intel Corp., and George Scalise of Advanced Micro Devices were industry officials who agreed with the imposition of tariffs on Japanese products. But companies outside the industry were also affected.[16] Some felt the sanctions are regrettable, but necessary. A spokeswoman for IBM in New York said that the company hoped sanctions would not be necessary. Henry Nau, a former Reagan administration national security aide, saw the tariffs as having a real potential for future misunderstandings. Interestingly enough, National Security Advisor Frank Carlucci and Secretary of State George Shultz opposed the sanctions.

According to *The Wall Street Journal* and the NBC news poll, 69 percent of Americans favored new tariffs on Japanese items sold to the United States.[17]

## Considerations Were Made

The decision to impose tariffs was not easy for the president and his advisors. The U.S. officials were aware that Japan had begun taking steps to enforce the semiconductor accord. On March 23, 1987, the Japanese Ministry of International Trade and Industry (MITI) ordered the Japanese chip makers to cut their production by 11 percent during the next quarter. This was done to reduce some of the excess inventories that prompted dumping of the chips in the United States. But U.S. officials felt that this move would not provide relief soon enough. The officials felt that Japan had a snail's pace response time to U.S. trade complaints. A senior U.S. trade official said, "the Japanese have been nickel and diming us for years."[18]

The political impact on Japanese Prime Minister Yasuhiro Nakasone was also a consideration. The tariff issue could cause difficulty for him politically and eventually cause him to resign.[19] The issue could hurt him because he had built his reputation on managing relations with the United States. There was strong concern for Nakasone's future because he was probably America's biggest friend in the Japanese government. But top officials were frustrated, and the administration was facing the possibility of losing leverage with the U.S. Congress. Thus, the tariffs were levied on April 17, 1987.

## WAS JAPAN GUILTY?

In most respects, Japan claimed that it had lived up to the 1986 accord. MITI denied that Japanese companies were dumping semiconductors in Southeast Asia and Europe. But the United States claimed that MITI had not been closely monitoring Japanese sales in Asia and Europe.[20] Another source reported that Tokyo admitted that Japanese chip makers had been dumping in foreign markets, but the report said that MITI had been unable to stop the practice.[21] The dispute was complicated by the fact that the two governments did not agree on a common method for calculating the extent to which Japanese semiconductors were being dumped in foreign markets.[22]

The Electronics Industries Association of Japan pointed out that "The U.S. was premature and even irrational to attempt an assessment of the impact of the agreement and our efforts to comply with it only six months after concluding the agreement."[23] Some people wondered whether a quick termination of dumping was possible in the first place.

## SOME TARIFFS LIFTED

During the 1987 Economic Summit, Mr. Reagan told Mr. Nakasone he would remove the tariffs on 17 percent, or $51 million worth, of the Japanese imports. The administration removed 20-inch color television sets from the 100 percent tariff list. The White House said the Japanese were still dumping in Third World countries, but to a lesser degree.[24]

The partial removal of the tariff sanctions was considered to be a political reward to Mr. Nakasone. The president said Mr. Nakasone had worked hard. Japanese companies were still dumping chips, but now with an average price of 85 percent of the fair market value instead of an average price of only 59 percent of the fair market value, as was the case when the tariffs were first imposed.

Nakasone felt all sanctions should have been removed. The Japanese delegation issued a statement calling for "an early and total lifting of the sanctions." Japan's minister of International Trade and Industry said, "I appreciate to some extent the U.S. decision."[25]

Reagan said the Japanese had given assurances that the dumping would be further reduced; however, no new trade-offs were promised. Future decisions were to be made after more time had passed and more results seen.

Commerce Secretary Malcolm Baldrige said, "If the Japanese are selling chips at full market value by year end, then punitive duties could be removed from an estimated $84 million more of the Japanese goods covered by the sanctions."[26] This figure would not affect the remaining sanctions of the $165 million because that figure is tied to Japan's failure to allow U.S. chip makers into the Japanese market.[27]

On November 5, 1987, President Reagan ordered another partial lifting of the sanctions left in place since the Economic Summit.[28] The president lifted the tariffs on $84.4 million of annual imports of certain Japanese products such as computers, color television sets, and power tools. This lifting became effective on November 10, 1987.[29]

The remaining sanctions will stay in place, with time as the only determinant of Japan's compliance in allowing U.S. chip makers into the Japanese market. Further decisions will be made after more time passes, and more results are seen.

## NEW DEVELOPMENTS

In the second quarter of 1988, the Japanese imported 12.5 percent of their chips from the United States;[30] that is up from the previous quarter share of 11.7 percent.[31]

On Friday, June 3, 1988, the talks on foreign access to Japan's chip market collapsed. The main reason for the derailment of talks between U.S. and Japanese chip manufacturers was their disagreement on how to measure foreign access to the Japanese market. The U.S. Semiconductor Industry Association wanted to measure the access by market share. The Japanese, however, refused to acknowledge that increased market share should be the goal of foreign access. The Japanese indicated that market share is a result of effort and not a goal to be established ahead of time.[32] The controversy continued.

In 1988 the U.S. semiconductor industry faced a shortage of chips. The shortage was attributed to several factors, including the increase in demand, the 1986 trade agreement with Japan, and the industry's transition to denser, harder-to-make, one-megabit memory chips.[33] Some analysts think one of the reasons is that the Japanese manufacturers are manipulating supplies to gain an advantage over U.S. companies.[34]

The shortage led to the doubling of prices between the fall of 1987 and the summer of 1988. The increase in prices led American firms, including TI, to increase their production; Japanese and South Koreans followed suit. As a result, the shortage eased and prices started falling toward the end of 1988.[35]

Although estimates vary, many industry analysts and executives predict moderate growth.[36] Worldwide, $43.6 billion worth of semiconductors were sold. Estimates of 1989 sales range from $43.7 billion to $49 billion.[37]

Meanwhile, the Semiconductor Industry Association wants the U.S. government to use the Semiconductor Trade Agreement as leverage to force the Japanese to increase the design-in of American-made semiconductors in their high-definition television (HDTV) equipment.[38]

In 1987 Japan's price cutting and dumping forced many American chip makers out of the market. As a result, the United States imposed sanctions against that country. Some analysts see history repeating itself. As the Korean semiconductor industry builds up its capacity, and with the prospects of a slowdown in demand, one gets a sense of déjà vu. Chances are that the South Koreans will not sit there empty, and may price below cost to keep capacity at optimal levels. Many of the Korean chip makers, such as Samsung, Hyundai, Goldstar, and Korea Electronics, are conglomerates that could afford to subsidize hefty losses in semiconductors.[39]

## QUESTIONS

1. Was Japan dumping semiconductors? If so, why?
2. Should the United States have imposed tariffs?
3. What were some alternative solutions to the imposition of tariffs?
4. What effect will this issue have on future U.S. trade with Japan?
5. How will this issue affect trading with other countries?
6. What were Japan's options?
7. Should President Reagan have partially removed the tariffs?
8. How do you see the future of the semiconductor industry?

## NOTES

1. Art Pine, "Chips Fight: Reagan's Tariff Move May Be Turning Point in Japanese Relations," *The Wall Street Journal,* 30 March 1987, pp. 1, 8.
2. Ibid., p. 8.
3. Ibid.
4. John Marcom, Jr., "Europeans Take Similar Action on Japan Trade," *The Wall Street Journal,* 30 March 1987, p. 10.
5. Ibid.
6. "The EC Just Says No to Japan's Cheap Chips," *Business Week,* 30 January 1989, pp. 46–47.
7. Ibid.
8. Pine, "Chips Fight," p. 8.
9. Peter Waldman, "Import Tax Is More Important Politically than Economically, U.S. Executives Say," *The Wall Street Journal,* 20 April 1987, p. 9.
10. Ibid., p. 10.
11. Ibid.
12. Mitchell Schnurman, "Experts Say Tariff Won't Hurt Consumers—Much," *Dallas Times Herald,* 18 April 1987, pp. A–1 and A–11.
13. Eduardo Lachica and Ellen Hume, "Trade Sanctions Expected to Last at Least to June," *The Wall Street Journal,* 20 April 1987, p. 3.
14. Brenton R. Schlender, "Tariffs Please U.S. Chip Concerns; Others See Them as Necessary Evil," *The Wall Street Journal,* 30 March 1987, p. 10.
15. Waldman, "Import Tax," p. 3.

16. Schlender, "Tariffs Please U.S. Chip Concerns," p. 10.
17. Washington Wire, "Trade Tensions Between the U.S. and Japan Will Get Even Tenser," *The Wall Street Journal*, 17 April 1987, p. 1.
18. Pine, "Chips Fight," p. 8.
19. Marcom, "Europeans Take Similar Action on Japan Trade," p. 10.
20. Damon Darlin and Karl Schoenberger, "Tokyo Reacts Cautiously; Some Firms Are Defensive," *The Wall Street Journal*, 30 March 1987, p. 10.
21. Art Pine, "Reagan Top Advisors Recommend Steep Tariffs on Some Japanese Consumer Electronics Products," *The Wall Street Journal*, 27 March 1987, p. 3.
22. Lachica and Hume, "Trade Sanctions," p. 3.
23. Marcom, "Europeans Take Similar Action on Japan Trade," p. 10.
24. Walter S. Mossberg, Ellen Hume, and Phillip Revzin, "U.S. Lifts Punitive Tariffs on Some Goods from Japan, but Nakasone Isn't Satisfied," *The Wall Street Journal*, 9 June 1987, p. 3.
25. Ibid.
26. Walter S. Mossberg, "Baldrige Sees Drop in Japan's Dumping of Chips, But No Progress in Its Imports," *The Wall Street Journal*, 17 August 1987, p. 40.
27. Ibid.
28. Eduardo Lachica, "President Eases Trade Sanctions Against Japan," *The Wall Street Journal*, 5 November 1987, p. 2.
29. "U.S. Remains Unhappy with Chip Market Share," *The Japan Economic Journal*, 14 November 1987, p. 11.
30. Stephen K. Yoder, "Plan to Aid Sales of U.S. Chips in Japan Is Announced by Industry Group There," *The Wall Street Journal*, 21 September 1988, p. 10.
31. "Japanese Imports of Chips From U.S. Rose in Quarter," *The Wall Street Journal*, 4 August 1988, p. 17.
32. "Pressure Builds to Seek More Sanctions Against Japan After Chip Talks Collapse," *The Wall Street Journal*, 6 June 1988, p. 3.
33. Brenton R. Schlender, "Chip Prices Fall; Easing of Shortage Seen," *The Wall Street Journal*, 18 July 1988, p. 2.
34. Eduardo Lachica, "U.S. Is Asking for Japanese Assurances About Supplies of Computer Memories," *The Wall Street Journal*, 22 April 1988, p. 5.
35. Schlender, ibid., p. 2.
36. "Will Computers Take a Dive?" *Business Week*, 17 October 1988, pp. 26–27.
37. "Outlook '89: Predict Moderate Growth Ahead," *Electronic News*, 2 January 1989, pp. 1, 6.
38. Joanne Connelly, "SIA: Press Japan Use of U.S. ICs in HDTV," *Electronic News*, 6 February 1989, pp. 1, 7.
39. Stephen K. Yoder, "Looming Chip Slump Threatens Korean Makers," *The Wall Street Journal*, 9 December 1988, p. B4.

## SUGGESTED READINGS

Darlin, Damon, and Karl Schoenberger. "Tokyo Reacts Cautiously; Some Firms Are Defensive." *The Wall Street Journal*, 30 March 1987, p. 10.

Lachica, Eduardo, and Ellen Hume. "Trade Sanctions Expected to Last at Least to June." *The Wall Street Journal*, 20 April 1987, p. 3.

Letter to the Editor. "U.S. Policies Victimized Japan," *The Wall Street Journal,* 10 April 1987, p. 19.

Marcom, John, Jr. "Europeans Take Similar Action on Japan Trade." *The Wall Street Journal,* 30 March 1987, p. 10.

Mossberg, Walter S., Ellen Hume, and Phillip Revzin. "U.S. Lifts Punitive Tariffs on Some Goods from Japan, But Nakasone Isn't Satisfied." *The Wall Street Journal,* 9 June 1987, pp. 3, 10.

Pine, Art. "Chips Fight: Reagan's Tariff Move May Be Turning Point in Japanese Relations." *The Wall Street Journal,* 30 March 1987, pp. 1, 8.

———. "Reagan Top Advisors Recommend Steep Tariffs on Some Japanese Consumer Electronics Products." *The Wall Street Journal,* 27 March 1987, p. 3.

Review and Outlook. "Hold Your Pen, Mr. President." *The Wall Street Journal,* 17 April 1987, p. 10.

Schlender, Brenton R. "Tariffs Please U.S. Chip Concerns, Others See Them as Necessary Evil." *The Wall Street Journal,* 30 March 1987, p. 10.

Waldman, Peter. "Import Tax Is More Important Politically than Economically, U.S. Executives Say." *The Wall Street Journal,* 20 April 1987, pp. 3, 9.

Washington Wire. "Trade Tensions Between the U.S. and Japan Will Get Even Tenser." *The Wall Street Journal,* 17 April 1987, p. 1.

# Texas Instruments and the Semiconductor Industry*

## INTRODUCTION

The imposition of tariffs on Japanese exports by the United States is a result of the increasing U.S. trade deficit in the high-tech electronics industry. Specifically, semiconductor manufacturers, which produce wafer-thin microchips that execute a computer's software commands and provide its memory, have suffered greatly as a result of this deficit.[1] Texas Instruments (TI) is among these manufacturers threatened by the Japanese semiconductor industry.

Texas Instruments is a multinational, technology-based company with over 50 manufacturing plants in 18 countries.[2] Four of these manufacturing plants are located in cities throughout Japan, including Tokyo, Hiji, Miho, and Oyama.[3] Texas Instruments' subsidiary in Japan is called TI Japan. Consequently, TI made a tough decision when it joined the industry in seeking protection against low-priced Japanese chip imports. Microchip producers face the threatening reality of tough Japanese competition. These producers must formulate strategies in order to successfully compete in the Japanese market as well as in the U.S. market.

## COMPANY HISTORY

Texas Instruments was founded in 1930 under the corporate name "Geophysical Service." In the same year the firm introduced the reflection seismograph, which revolutionized the petroleum exploration industry. Within the next 20 years, TI received its first U.S. Navy contract for technology that would detect enemy radar. It also began electronic systems manufacturing and delivered the first airborne radar system.[4]

In 1952, TI adopted its present name and entered the transistor business.

---

*This case was written by Karen English and Rhonda Ivy of University of North Texas as a term project; it was subsequently revised by Professor Ebrahimi for inclusion in this textbook. Copyright © 1989 by Bahman Ebrahimi.

This began a new era of dynamic growth, and, as a result, in 1953 the company was first listed on the New York Stock Exchange. The company announced in 1958 their invention of the integrated circuit, which has provided the basis for all modern developments in electronics. With this new invention, TI introduced the first antiradar missile.[5]

Another milestone in TI's history was their 1967 invention of the world's first hand-held calculator. The impact of this creation is apparent today. In 1968, TI opened their first Japanese semiconductor manufacturing plant in Oyama, Japan. This business decision, plus the company's strong patent position in the 1970s, prompted the Japanese to try to catch up with TI's technology.[6]

Dallas-based TI had little reason to worry about quality in 1973. The company commanded most of Japan's market for chips and had few Japanese competitors. But TI was left behind as Japanese chip makers improved quality.[7] In 1980, the defect rate for TI Japan's chips was so incredibly high that several major customers threatened to order elsewhere. Five years later, after a major program in quality control was implemented, the TI Japan factory became the first foreign-owned plant in Japan to win the Deming prize, which is Japan's most prestigious award for industrial quality. Because of this quality control program, the average defect rate fell from 5,000 parts per million in 1980 to 20 parts per million in 1985.[8]

In the 1980s, TI continued to introduce new products which have an impact on the general public as well as on the computer industry. In 1982, TI introduced their signal-processing microcomputer chip, and in 1983 they introduced the TI Professional Computer (PC). The TI PC has had an incredible impact on the business world in terms of diverse end-user computing. And in 1984, TI introduced the Explorer System, which is a symbolic processor computer for artificial intelligence. This will be the information processing system of the future.[9]

In 1986, TI, the largest U.S. chip maker, began shifting its chip production to a subsidiary based in Miho, Japan. This is one of the factors that led to TI's growing position in the world market. As a result, TI is considered the only American supplier that can seriously compete with the Japanese.

## INDUSTRY DESCRIPTION

The semiconductor industry has grown rapidly along with the growth of the high-tech environment throughout the world. For the past few years, however, the industry has been in a slump, with record losses and massive production overcapacity. Currently, the American semiconductor manufacturers dominate their own domestic market by a small margin, but they command more than a 50 percent share in every other major market. However, U.S. chip makers have less than 9 percent of Japan's $8.9 billion chip market. Furthermore, Japanese manufacturers not only dominate their domestic market, but they have 15 percent of the American market and their share is growing.[10]

American microchip manufacturers attribute Japan's dominance in the market to unfair trade practices. These practices include Japan's failure to end dumping of semiconductors in world markets outside the United States.[11] As a result of Japan's trade practices, on March 27, 1987, President Reagan announced a new 100 percent import tariff on certain Japanese products. The new tariff was effective on April 17, 1987.[12] Figure II: 5.1 provides a description of the resulting cost of the tariffs on the Japanese semiconductor products.

By January 1988, there was a serious shortage of memory chips due to the tariff sanctions. However, the trade agreement between the United States and Japan was not the main problem. The biggest threat to the chip industry was the failure of "Silicon Valley" in California to put out a large capacity of dynamic random access memory (DRAM) chips. Since Japan has been producing these chips, many U.S. companies have been forced out of business. As of April 1988, only Texas Instruments and Micron Technology sold DRAMs in the United States and these were sold at an inflated price. This means the computer industry has been affected as a whole since companies cannot get enough chips to make their computers.[13]

Since the tariff went into effect, Japan has slowed down its production of microchips and reduced its inventory. The strong yen has also hampered Japanese expansion of their export of chips. This gave the United States a chance to get a bigger slice of the pie in Japan's home market, since the Tokyo government was planning to lift the U.S. share of the market to 20 percent. U.S. firms are also making headway on the chip-making technology by pooling resources among different companies. All of these factors will help the chip market to stabilize in the United States.[14]

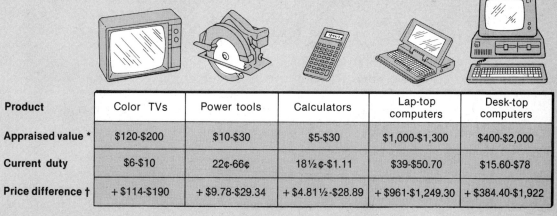

| Product | Color TVs | Power tools | Calculators | Lap-top computers | Desk-top computers |
|---|---|---|---|---|---|
| **Appraised value** * | $120-$200 | $10-$30 | $5-$30 | $1,000-$1,300 | $400-$2,000 |
| **Current duty** | $6-$10 | 22¢-66¢ | 18½¢-$1.11 | $39-$50.70 | $15.60-$78 |
| **Price difference** † | + $114-$190 | + $9.78-$29.34 | + $4.81½-$28.89 | + $961-$1,249.30 | + $384.40-$1,922 |

\* Appraised values represent typical wholesale price ranges for many of the goods. Retail prices are usually 50 to 100 percent higher.

† With new 100 percent tariff.

**Figure II:5.1**  What tariffs on Japanese imports will cost

*Source:* Mitchell Schnurman, "Experts Say Tariffs Won't Hurt Consumers—Much," *Dallas Times Herald* (18 April 1987), p. 1.

The Japanese market is difficult to penetrate for several reasons. First, a majority of the business done in Japan is based on customer loyalty. American companies find it difficult to gain the trust and loyalty of potential Japanese buyers.[15] Another penetration barrier is based on quality control; Japanese engineers have found it easy to reject U.S.-manufactured chips that do not meet their quality tests. Also, Japanese companies regard U.S. microchip manufacturers as only minor suppliers. U.S. companies complain that it is impossible to establish the genuine supplier-customer relationship that is necessary for successful operations in Japan.[16]

Another factor affecting the potential for growth in the Japanese chip market is the Japanese tendency to buy U.S. products only if those products are not produced by a Japanese firm. Revenues for U.S. producers decrease dramatically whenever integrated circuits are produced locally in Japan. As a result of these market barriers, selling to the Japanese home market requires a considerable investment in time and money.[17]

The Japanese microchip industry also has many strengths. One of these is the lower cost of borrowing money. Japanese companies can obtain funds more cheaply than American companies. Also, the major Japanese electric companies are conglomerates that are virtually integrated. Given these factors, the Japanese can absorb losses and establish strong alliances that no U.S. chip maker can even consider doing.[18] Furthermore, because of their integrated structure and their long-standing links to Japanese banking groups, most semiconductor operations in Japan do not necessarily need to make a profit.[19]

As a result of the increasingly tough competition in the integrated circuit market, microchip manufacturers around the world are forming joint ventures, acquiring smaller operations, and integrating vertically. These actions by chip makers are the result of their attempts to increase their size and leverage in the market.[20] Furthermore, companies are moving toward diversified product lines that accommodate specific customer needs. One such company is a Dallas-based chip maker, Dallas Semiconductor. Dallas Semiconductor manufactures specialized components, called silicon solutions, that can be used by a wide range of customers. The company believes that by marketing a diversified array of products, it is less vulnerable to failures in a few product lines. Due to their diversified product lines, Dallas Semiconductor is also less susceptible to increased competition at home and overseas and to shifts in demand.[21]

U.S. chip manufacturers in Japan are using three basic marketing approaches to build on their combined 1984 Japanese sales of $600 million.[22] The first approach involves competing in mass products. This entails producing microchips in mass quantities. Texas Instruments Japan is doing this with its Japanese production facilities. The second approach is to capitalize on patented technology. Companies such as Nippon Motorola and Intel Japan are utilizing this option with their microprocessors and other products. On November 22, 1989, Texas Instruments was awarded a major patent covering all integrated circuits made or used in Japan. The third approach involves targeting specialized "niche" markets. For instance, Monolithic Memories has a patented programmable-array-logic circuit, and National Semiconductor Japan produces programmable-logic and hard-disc, chip-set products.[23]

Since most U.S. companies have not chosen to make the sizable investments necessary to produce in Japan, the third approach is the most popular one among these U.S. producers.[24] Niche-seeking is a continuing trend, which involves the production of application-specific integrated circuits. These circuits include standard-cell or full-custom products. These products continue to show strong growth worldwide. Therefore, chip producers that want to hold their present technological edge in these application-specific products will find their production increasingly attractive.[25] For instance, Signetics, a worldwide supplier of digital chips, produces Dolby noise reduction integrated circuits, which at one time composed 60 percent of its business. Now, however, Signetics is pursuing another niche—programming-logic—in which it has been a leading developer.[26]

The semiconductor industry is a worldwide business with several major competitors. The five biggest U.S. chip makers are Texas Instruments, Motorola, Intel, National Semiconductor, and Advanced Micro Devices.[27] Among the major worldwide producers are Hitachi, NEC, and Fujitsu.[28] Another major worldwide microchip supplier is Signetics. A number of U.S. companies either produce in Japan, or have superior technology that the Japanese cannot yet match. These are TI, Intel, and Motorola.[29]

Motorola's Nippon Motorola subsidiary operates one chip plant in Japan. It posted $90 million in sales in 1985. Texas Instruments' subsidiary, TI Japan, posted sales of $365 million in 1985 and expects to increase its sales to nearly $500 million in 1990.[30]

In January of 1986, National Corporation joined forces with Japan's NMB Semiconductor, which produces National's chips for local sale. National is also adding about 30 people to its Japanese staff of 130. National is taking these steps in hopes of boosting its revenue from the $38 million earned in 1985 to $100 million by 1990.[31]

The leading Japanese chip makers have annual revenues between $1.6 billion and $18 billion. They are all vertically integrated. Chips account for 5 percent to 22 percent of their corporate sales. The top five U.S. firms have annual sales of $900 million to $5.7 billion. Over half of their revenues, on average, are from chips. Overall, the Japanese can better afford to subsidize money-losing chip operations.[32]

## COMPANY DESCRIPTION

Texas Instruments produces a wide range of high-tech products including industrial controls, data systems, geophysical service equipment, defense systems, metallurgical materials, semiconductors, and consumer products. Typical consumer products include calculators and electronic learning aids. In addition, TI is considered a leader in the designing, manufacturing, and servicing of digital equipment for businesses and corporations worldwide. Professional and advanced computers for the development of artificial intelligence applications are typical digital products. Examples of defense systems include missile guidance systems, radar systems, and precision guided weapons.[33]

## Organization

TI's headquarters is based in Dallas, Texas. The company employs more than 80,000 people in 50 plants in 41 cities located in 18 countries. TI is a vertically integrated company.

The vertical structure was chosen to manage people and resources in a way that is most productive for the company and its customers. The major business areas of the company include groups or divisions, each with its own president. More specifically, in terms of the semiconductor group, the company recently created a unit which had the responsibility for developing new markets for the semiconductor business in the Far East.[34]

## Japanese Operations

One of TI's most strategically important markets in the Far East is Japan. TI Japan has four plants and more than 5,000 employees. Bipolar, MOS memory, and MOS logic products are developed in these Japanese plants. About 80 percent of these products are sold in Japan. The sales results in 1984 were very impressive. Analysts estimate that TI Japan's sales alone were $320 million, plus $80 million in export sales out of Japan. For the past 17 years, TI Japan has achieved 21 percent annual growth. As can be clearly seen, management's decision to establish plants in Japan was a key factor in its mass market production.[35]

## Finance

In April 1987, TI's stock split three shares to one. This was the first stock split since 1973. TI stocks soared from $100 to $200 per share in April of 1987. Sales increased 11 percent for the first three months of 1987, with profits climbing even more. For the first three-month period in 1987, TI's sales totaled $1.27 billion with a net income of $83.8 million (see Table II: 5.1 for more details). The earnings were increased by a $108 million settlement in favor of TI of a patent infringement suit involving six Japanese semiconductor companies. In addition, the first quarter of 1987 sales of semiconductors had increased over the fourth quarter of 1986, and had reported a profit. This compared with a loss for the same period in 1985. TI's president, Jerry Junkins, projected that the worldwide demand for all semiconductors will increase 15 percent in 1987 to about $10 billion. The improved forecast is based on the assumptions that (1) capital spending will increase in the second half of 1987 and (2) electronics growth, along with the company chip shipments, will remain moderate.[36]

Table II:5.1 TEXAS INSTRUMENTS
Year-end Performance (in Millions of Dollars, Except per Share Figure)

|  | 1987 | 1986 |
|---|---|---|
| Net sales | $ 5,594,500 | $ 4,974,000 |
| Operating income | $ 597,500 | $ 528,100 |
| Other income | $ 218,000 | $ 20,900 |
| Net income | $ 256,900 | $ 39,900 |
| Net income per share | $ 2.96 | $ 1.14 |
| Total assets | $ 4,256,300 | $ 3,336,700 |
| Long-term debt | $ 486,500 | $ 191,400 |
| Common shares outstanding | 78,700 | 25,700 |

Source: Standard & Poor's, March 24, 1988, vol. 49, no. 6, pp. 1940–1941; and Texas Instruments, Annual Report, 1987.

## Research and Development

The firm's corporate research and development is responsible for assuring the availability of future technology. Texas Instruments' research and development department is divided into three divisions. These include the Central Research Laboratories, the Semiconductor Process and Design Center, and the Corporate Engineering Center. The Central Research Laboratory is responsible for projects dealing with major technology thrusts for the next decade. The Semiconductor Process and Design Center develops VLSI (Very Large-Scale Integration) devices. In addition, the Corporate Engineering Center focuses on developing new products based on emerging technologies.[37]

In summary, Texas Instruments is involved in a wide range of technical innovations. By being a product innovator, TI has had a major impact on consumer, industrial, and government markets throughout its history.

## CONCLUSION

Texas Instruments is a diversified, vertically integrated, multinational company, with a history spanning more than 50 years. TI is one of the world's leading suppliers of semiconductor components and materials. In addition to plants in the United States, TI has plants in many parts of the world, including four plants located in Japan.

In order to maintain its market share and technological leadership, Texas Instruments must formulate strategies to successfully compete in the semiconductor industry. These strategies must address such issues as maintaining or increasing market share, maintaining a technological edge, and maintaining goodwill with host countries.

The semiconductor industry is suffering from the effects of mass production and dumping by the Japanese manufacturers. The survival of chip manufacturers, including TI, depends on their ability to diversify into specialized markets and to devise an effective marketing strategy. As a result of the company's financial strength and product diversification, TI's potential to achieve these goals seems to be great.

## QUESTIONS

1. Why has TI been so successful in the electronics industry?
2. How do you characterize the semiconductor industry?
3. What is the strategy of the Japanese chip makers?
4. What was the effect of U.S. tariffs on the industry? On U.S. chip makers? On the Japanese manufacturers?
5. What is the best strategy for U.S. companies to pursue? Why?

## NOTES

1. "Silicon Valley Pleads for Protection, But That Is the Wrong Rx for High Tech," *Time,* 7 October 1985, p. 33.
2. "A Brief History of Texas Instruments," *TI Brochure,* 1986, p. 1.
3. "Experience Texas Instruments," *TI Brochure,* 1985, p. 21.
4. Ibid., p. 5
5. Ibid.
6. Michael Berger, "Can U.S. Chip Makers Succeed in the Japanese Market?" *Electronics,* 15 July 1985, p. 32.
7. Stephen Kreider Yoder, "Texas Instruments Now Has Japan's Praise," *The Wall Street Journal,* 3 October 1986, p. 32
8. Ibid.
9. "Experience Texas Instruments," p. 6.
10. Michael Berger and John W. Wilson, "Now Japan Is Where It's at for U.S. Chipmakers," *Business Week,* 24 November 1986, p. 108
11. "Silicon Valley," p. 33.
12. "Groups Seek Exemptions from Tariff," *Dallas Times Herald,* 14 April 1987, pp. D-1.
13. "How the Chip Shortages Made Foes into Bedfellows," *Business Week,* 11 April 1988, p. 118.
14. "The Peaks and Valleys Are Leveling Out," *Business Week,* 11 January 1988, p. 114.
15. Berger, "Can U.S. Chip Makers Succeed," p. 30.
16. Ibid.
17. Ibid., p. 32.
18. Ibid., p. 30.
19. Ibid., p. 22.
20. Mitchell Schnurman, "Chipmaker Relies on Diversity," *Dallas Times Herald,* 12 April 1987, p. H-1.

21. Ibid.
22. Berger, "U.S. Chip Makers Succeed," p. 32.
23. Ibid.
24. Ibid.
25. Ibid.
26. Ibid., p. 33.
27. Bro Uttal, "Who Will Survive the Microchip Shakeout?" *Fortune*, 6 January 1986, pp. 82–85
28. John W. Wilson, Michael Berger, Peter Hann, and Otis Port, "Is It Too Late to Save the U.S. Semiconductor Industry?" *Business Week*, 18 August 1986, p. 63.
29. Berger, "Can U.S. Chip Makers Succeed," p. 32.
30. Berger and Wilson, "Now Japan Is Where It's at for U.S. Chipmakers," p. 108.
31. Ibid.
32. Uttal, "Who Will Survive," p. 84.
33. "Experience Texas Instruments," p. 5
34. "Mitchell Appointed Executive VP at TI," *Dallas Morning News*, 22 April 1987, p. 6-D.
35. Berger, "Can U.S. Chip Makers Succeed," p. 32.
36. Mitchell Schnurman, "TI Posts Another Quarterly Profit," *Dallas Times Herald*, 17 April 1987, p. C-3.
37. "Experience Texas Instruments," p. 18.

## SUGGESTED READINGS

"A Brief History of Texas Instruments." *TI Brochure*, 1986, p. 1.

Berger, Michael. "Can U.S. Chip Makers Succeed in the Japanese Market?" *Electronics*, 15 July 1985, pp. 30–33.

———, and John W. Wilson. "Now Japan Is Where It's at for U.S. Chipmakers." *Business Week*, 24 November 1986, p. 108.

"Experience Texas Instruments." *TI Brochure*, 1985, pp. 5–6, 18–19.

"Groups Seek Exemptions from Tariff." *Dallas Times Herald*, 14 April 1987, p. A-1, D-1.

Guteral, Fred V. "Another Blow to U.S. Chipmakers." *Dunn's Business Monthly*, July 1985, pp. 38–39.

"How the Chip Shortages Made Foes into Bedfellows." *Business Week*, 11 April 1988, p. 118.

"Mitchell Appointed Executive VP at TI." *The Dallas Morning News*, 22 April 1987, p. 6-D.

"Reagan Slaps Tariffs on Japanese Goods." *Dallas Times Herald*, 18 April 1987, pp. A-1, A-11.

Schnurman, Mitchell. "Chipmaker Relies on Diversity." *Dallas Times Herald*, 12 April 1987, p. H-1.

———. "Experts Say Tariff Won't Hurt Consumers Much." *Dallas Times Herald*, 18 April 1987, p. A-1, A-11.

———. "TI Posts Another Quarterly Profit." *Dallas Times Herald.* 17 April 1987, p. C-1, C-7.

"Silicon Valley Pleads for Protection, But That Is the Wrong Rx for High Tech." *Time,* 7 October 1985, p. 33.

"The Peaks and Valleys Are Leveling Out." *Business Week,* 11 January 1988, p. 114.

Uttal, Bro. "Who Will Survive the Microchip Shakeout?" *Fortune,* 6 January 1986, pp. 82–85.

Wilson, John W., Michael Berger, and Peter Hann. "The Chip Market Goes Haywire: Buyers and Sellers Alike Are Jittery over a U.S.–Japan Trade Pact." *Business Week,* 1 September 1986, pp. 24–25.

———, Michael Berger, Peter Hann, and Otis Port. "Is It Too Late to Save the U.S. Semiconductor Industry?" *Business Week,* 18 August 1986, pp. 62–67.

Yoder, Stephen Kreider. "Texas Instruments Now Has Japan's Praise." *The Wall Street Journal,* 3 October 1986, p. 32.

Zipzer, Andy, Stephen Kreider Yoder, and Jacob M. Schlesinger. "U.S. Chip Firms Expect Little Fallout from Texas Instruments Patent Award." *The Wall Street Journal,* November 24, 1989, p. A3.

# Overseas Troubles*

## INTRODUCTION

Sam Jones is an experienced sales preparation manager and auctioneer. He has been employed by Pure Profit Auctioneers International, Inc. (PPAI) for seven years. Up until 1982, Sam had only traveled on the North American continent for PPAI. Pure Profit Auctioneers International, Inc., is a multinational company that specializes in sales and auctions of oil field equipment, construction equipment, and pipeline equipment. They also sell and auction entire plants and companies. The main headquarters is located in Dallas, Texas, but the company conducts sales and auctions all over the North American continent.

In early 1982, John Smith, chief executive officer of Pure Profit Auctioneers International, called Sam into his office and told him that they had booked a sale in Saudi Arabia. They wanted him to go there and manage the sale and auction of the heavy equipment of several companies in Saudi Arabia. The company told Sam that they needed him to head this sale because he had such a good reputation for handling large and potentially troublesome sales. Also, he was the most experienced sales manager they had. Sam had only two weeks to get ready before he was due to leave. Sam was not at all happy about going overseas because his wife was seven and one-half months pregnant with their first child. In addition, he had no idea what Saudi Arabia would be like, and it seemed that Pure Profit Auctioneers did not know very much about the country either.

## THE COMPANY

Pure Profit Auctioneers International, Inc., is in the business of selling and auctioning heavy equipment. They also auction entire plants and companies. The company has been in business for 15 years. Most of their sales and auctions

---

*This fictional case was written by Mary Dyer of the University of North Texas and subsequently revised by Professor Ebrahimi for inclusion in this text. Any similarity with any actual situation, firm, or person is absolutely coincidental. The choice of Saudi Arabia as the background country is for illustrative purposes only. Copyright © 1989 by Bahman Ebrahimi.

have been in Canada, Mexico, and the United States. The sale in Saudi Arabia was the first overseas job that the company had booked. Pure Profit Auctioneers had contracted with ARAMCO (Arabian American Oil Company) to auction several plants and surplus equipment. They were to hold several sales in different cities in Saudi Arabia. Pure Profit Auctioneers were to hold a large auction every three to six months in a joint effort with ARAMCO. The large auction was to be held at a permanent yard maintained by both companies. Pure Profit's job was to get the equipment ready for sale and to do the advertising. The company would set up the yard and would make sure the equipment was delivered on time and was in running order. The company would also handle the sale from the beginning to end. It was Sam's job to set up the office, bring in the buyers, sell the equipment, handle the money, transfer the title, and ship the equipment if necessary. Each one of the sales was to last from one to three days and involve as much as $50 million. PPAI was to keep three employees permanently assigned to the yard.

## THE ASSIGNMENT

Sam Jones was to be the manager of the entire operation. He felt very confident because this was something for which he was well trained. He had been doing this job domestically for seven years. Sam left the United States with Cliff Smith, Pure Profit Auctioneers' CPA and financial advisor. Cliff had already been to Saudi Arabia to set up the financial connections. He had only stayed a week and would be staying only a week this time. He tried to fill Sam in on all he had learned about the country. He really did not know much, having spent most of the time with bankers. They left New York and flew into London's Gatwick airport, where they took a helicopter to Heathrow airport. There they boarded a plane to Dahran, Saudi Arabia, where they landed in the middle of the night. As the plane taxied down the runway after landing Sam could see F-15 and F-16 fighters, which were equipped with missiles and bombs and were sitting under floodlights. They got off the plane on the airport apron, and as Sam and Cliff walked toward the airport buildings they were nudged along by a very young man carrying a fully automatic weapon. They were told to line up for inspection, and then an inspector checked all of their papers and passports. The inspector also went through all of their luggage.

The trip from the airport to the hotel was like an Indy car race. There seemed to be no speed limits, and cars would dart in and out of the traffic lanes on the roadway. Sam wondered what it would be like to drive between the industrial yard and the different towns where some of his company's plants were for sale.

On his first morning Sam was awakened by someone screaming into a microphone. He immediately called the front desk to see what was happening. He was informed, amid laughter, that it was the call to prayer. As Sam hung up the phone he wondered what he had gotten himself into.

Later that morning Sam and Cliff went to the yard site and met with

ARAMCO representatives. These were the men Sam would be working with while he was in Saudi Arabia. Sam immediately started making plans and asking questions. He was surprised when one of the Arabs, Al-Shafi, told Sam that they would not discuss business before tea, so they all sat down to tea. During this tea break nothing but pleasantries were exchanged. Finally, they got down to business and made arrangements so that Sam could obtain a driver's license and the necessary passes to enter the plants and look at the equipment. Sam also had to get a resident's visa, which would be good for three months. After this they all toured the site where the industrial yard was going to be built. Everything seemed to be going smoothly and Sam felt confident about this assignment. At the end of the day Sam and several of the oilfield workers went to sample the food and see a little of the area. Sam had seen a lot and had tried some very different food. At night, as he fell asleep, he wondered what tomorrow would bring.

Sam's second day was spent trying to obtain a temporary international driver's license. It took him all day; it seemed the paperwork was never ending, even though he had all of his papers in order and he had a passport. Since the company already had a sponsor who was a Saudi national, Sam thought the paperwork would not take so long.

The company's sponsor's name was Sheik Ali Mahmoud. He had introduced the company, and without his backing, Pure Profit Auctioneers would never have been allowed to enter Saudi Arabia.

When Sam finally got his license, he took the company car and a map and went in search of the closest plant where there was equipment for sale. As he drove down the highway, he noticed how different the driving was compared with American driving habits. There seemed to be no speed limit, and he could not understand why there were junk cars on each side of the road.

When Sam arrived at the plant, he got out and started looking around the yard. He was stopped by a security guard, who went through his papers. Once he was cleared to go inside, it was tea time again. Sam was beginning to learn that tea came before anything. After tea everyone went outside, and Sam began to take an inventory of the equipment that was to be in the sale. Sam went to his car for the camera, so he could take pictures of the equipment for the sale brochure. As he was going to take the first pictures, he was stopped. The plant manager told him he needed special passes in order to take pictures, and then he could only take pictures of certain things that the authorities would allow. This meant that all he could do today was to take inventory and to list what equipment needed repairs. Sam went ahead and wrote a description of each piece for the sale brochure. This development also meant that another day would be wasted getting the proper passes just to photograph the equipment. He knew this would delay the printing of the brochure and its mailing to prospective buyers.

Sam wondered what else he would need a pass for, so he thought he had better talk to Haj Ahmed Ben Abdollah, the representative of ARAMCO. After two days of waiting, he finally got the proper passes and was able to take pictures of the equipment and get the sales brochures printed. He then told the plant managers which pieces of equipment needed repairs and which pieces would need major work done on them before the sale. All of the major repairs were to be made on the equipment before shipment to the sale yard. Once the equipment reached the yard, it would be cleaned and painted. Sam would then arrange each piece in the yard according to its order of sale.

Once Sam had located all the equipment and it had been written up and photographed, he returned to Alkohbar, the site of the sale yard. Sam met with his co-workers from ARAMCO and began to get ready to set up the yard for the sale. Setting up the yard entailed a great deal of cooperation on everybody's part. Offices had to be constructed and telephones installed. Sam found that it could take up to three months for this to get done. The area had to be graded and the loading ramps had to be installed. Sam was beginning to see that it was going to take a lot longer to set up this sale yard than his company had originally scheduled. He sent a telex to headquarters informing the company that due to many factors the sale would have to be delayed for several months. In response, Pure Profit Auctioneers telexed back, asking what the problems were. Sam responded, explaining some of the major problems—prayer breaks, tea breaks, and the general attitude of the workers. He explained that life moved a lot slower in Saudi Arabia than in the United States. Pure Profit gave the go ahead. Sam began to make arrangements to spend a longer time in Saudi Arabia. He moved from his hotel to the Hilton Inn Apartments, which would cost the company less. He found the move to be the best thing he had done so far. Here he had two houseboys to clean and do his laundry. This enthusiasm lasted only a short time; he found out that they starched everything—including his under-wear. Sam was learning that most of the workers, that is, the laborers, were from other Third World countries. Not only was he having to learn about his host country, but also he needed to learn about other cultures as well. It was going to take a while to learn all this, and then he needed to keep it all straight in his mind. Sam felt he needed to understand how these people felt and what they knew in order to get the most efficient production out of them.

## THE AUCTION SALE

There are a number of steps that must be taken before an auction sale can happen. After the sale yard had been set up, Sam's next task was to get the needed passes and visas for all the prospective buyers who would be coming to look at and to inspect the equipment. Sam also needed to make sure that all the buyers' lines of credit and all their papers were in order before they could enter the country. Sam also had to do all of the title work necessary to sell the equipment. In the meanwhile, Sam had gotten the sales brochures printed and mailed them out to the prospective buyers. Included in each brochure were pictures of each piece of equipment at the yard, pictures of the equipment at the plant for sale, and a map of the area. The map was included in the brochure to show the location of the sale yard and the location of the town in which the plant for sale was located. This part of the job was going smoothly, which was nice for a change, since the work at the plant, the transporting of the equipment, and the work on the sale yard were all at a virtual standstill.

It seemed that only part of the equipment at the plants had been repaired. The pieces of equipment for sale at the yard were either at the yard, just sitting there, or they were en route. Sam had learned that when it was prayer time not only did some workers stop for prayer, but also it shut the entire operation down. After the prayer break it always took some time before the workers went back to work. Sam figured out that because of this and other breaks, almost a fourth of each day was wasted. He had to speed up the job because he knew he could not delay the auction sale any longer. As the equipment began to pile up, Sam knew he needed more workers. He was able to hire temporary workers through ARAMCO. He needed the extra workers because once the equipment arrived at the sale yard, it had to be cleaned and painted. Finally, the equipment was arranged by the order of sale as indicated in the brochure and assigned a lot number. The most used items, such as small equipment that all contractors can use, were arranged first. The next items were the larger and more expensive pieces of equipment. The last items were the plunder (junk) items.

Sam had been trying to get the equipment in place for a week now, especially a large crane that was very hard to move. He had finally gotten the crane halfway to its sale place in the yard when everyone was called to prayer. Sam was so close to completing this job that he did not want to stop. He ordered the operator to stay in the cab and not to get out until he had finished moving the crane. The worker did as he was told. Later that day the Matawa, the religious police, came to the yard to see Sam. The worker had reported Sam to the religious police. The Matawa told Sam that it was the religious custom of all in Saudi Arabia to stop and pray five times a day. They stressed to him that everything stopped at prayer time. They told him that this would be the only warning he would receive. Sam was upset because of the lost time, but he knew that he must comply with the religious customs of the country. He would have to work the prayer breaks into the work schedule, just as he had figured tea time into his own schedule. Sam had found that before any new business could be conducted, or whenever anyone new came to see you, you must stop and have tea before doing anything else.

During all this, Sam was also in contact with the prospective buyers. It was part of Sam's job to handle all communications with the buyers. He had to arrange for all of their visas and special passes. The special passes were needed in order for the buyers to enter some of the plants where the larger equipment was on display and ready for sale. The day of the auction was nearing and Sam was ready. All of the pieces of equipment at the plant were repaired and in running order. The smaller pieces were already on the sale yard, where they had been made ready for sale. Most of the pieces were cleaned and there were only two more pieces left to paint when the day of the sale arrived. These pieces were hurriedly finished just as the sale started. Sam now had his hands full with the buyers. He had to be in a hundred places at once, and Sam only had one assistant the day of the sale. Sam had already checked each of the buyers' credentials and lines of credit so he didn't have to worry about the monetary aspects until the end of the sale. As he walked from buyer to buyer he noticed that some buyers had brought cash. There were open paper sacks of money just sitting on the hoods of their automobiles. No one seemed concerned. There were no guards. Sam thought to himself, "What strange business practices go on in this part of the world." The sale went off without a hitch.

Because there had been no major problems, later that day Sam began to wind things down. He met with all of the buyers and had tea. Then he began to collect the money from each sale. As Sam did this he would transfer the title over to the new owner. It was also part of Sam's job to arrange for shipping, if the buyer needed that service. If not, Sam just had to make sure the customer was happy and that he had received the piece of equipment he had bought. At the end of the day everyone got together to celebrate. The sale had gone smoothly, and they had all made money. After four months Sam was finally getting used to some of the Saudi customs. He was also getting used to the food and the very strong Turkish coffee. Sam was ready to end the auction and go home to see his wife and son. He had only seen his son once, during the week off that they had given him when his son was born. All that Sam needed to do now was stay long enough in Saudi Arabia to make sure that each piece of equipment was shipped either now or later to the proper place. He had to pay the employees their final check and finish paying the company's bills, then he could catch a flight home.

As Sam was closing out the books the next day, several officials came to the office. Sam greeted them with tea and polite conversation, but he was shocked when they told him that he had used the wrong map in the sales brochure. The brochure map showed the gulf between Saudi Arabia and Iran as the "Persian Gulf," which is the customary name used in Iran and western countries, instead of the "Arabian Gulf," which is the name used in most Arab countries. He was told to change the map if the company wanted to conduct another auction. This new problem was going to delay his trip home. Sam immediately telexed the home office with the news. They responded with instructions on what steps needed to be taken on Sam's part. They would advise Sam when their attorney would be arriving in Saudi Arabia.

Pure Profit Auctioneers also informed Sam that the company had booked another sale at the yard location in six months. Sam was to start preparations immediately for this sale, and the company would be sending details in a few days. The company also informed Sam that he could not have any time off for about six weeks. This would give him enough time to get everything started for the new sale. Sam was beginning to wonder whether this job was worth all of the problems he had encountered so far. Not only had he experienced problems with the culture of Saudi Arabia, but also he was thousands of miles away from his family. He had learned a lot, but if they were going to continue to conduct many auctions and sales in this country, he realized he would have to learn what was acceptable and what would not be acceptable. Up until now most of the Saudis had been very cooperative, but Sam knew that the reason for their kindness was because he was so inexperienced. Now that he had one sale under his belt, he would be expected to know the laws and customs of the Saudi Arabian people.

## CONCLUSION

Sam knew that the next sale that Pure Profit Auctioneers had booked was during the summer months. He had learned enough to know that the Saudi Arabians were to hold two religious holidays during the summer of this year, Ramadan and Zel Hadjah. Ramadan was the fasting month and ZelHadjah was the month when many people made a pilgrimage to Mecca. These holidays last one month each. Sam knew that everything closed down during the day in Ramadan. He knew his company had made a mistake in booking the sale during the summer months of this year. It was so hot during the summer that nobody did much work outdoors. Sam sat in his office, wondering what to do next.

## QUESTIONS

1. Discuss the different options Sam has available to him to solve his problems. Which one would you choose if you were in his place? Why?

2. What could Pure Profit Auctioneers have done to make Sam's job easier? How could they have helped him to be more efficient?

3. If Sam decides to stay for the next sale, what can he do differently to increase efficiency and productivity?

# Polaroid: The Instant Image and the Sun City*

## INTRODUCTION

Polaroid Corporation, a Delaware-based company founded in 1937, and its 23 subsidiaries are a worldwide enterprise with annual sales of $1.27 billion. The company designs, manufactures, and markets a variety of products primarily in the "instant" photography field. These products include "instant" photograph cameras and their films, light polarizing filters and lenses, and other diversified chemicals and optical products.

For the past half a century, Polaroid has continually dominated its niche in the photography market. Initially, the concept of "instant" photography, in which the film is developed quickly inside the camera, was difficult for consumers to understand. Today, the "instant" photograph camera is used in millions of households around the world.

Polaroid uses a highly specialized marketing and business strategy for each country. A heated controversy that occurred between South Africa and Polaroid several years ago shows the corporation's stylish attack in conquering the marketing problem, thus enabling them to remain the dominant pioneer of their industry.

## THE PROBLEM

In the fall of 1970, the Polaroid Corporation was stuck with a thorn in their side that would bother them for the next seven and a half years. Upon arrival at his Cambridge, Massachusetts, office on October 7, Dr. Edwin Land, founder, chief executive officer, and president of Polaroid discovered leaflets tacked to numerous company bulletin boards proclaiming: "Polaroid Imprisons Black People in 60 Seconds."[1] Taking a closer look into the matter, Land found that the memos

---

*This case was originally written by H. Winston Holt IV of St. Lawrence University as a term project; it was subsequently revised by Professor Asheghian for inclusion in this text book.

were distributed by the Polaroid Revolutionary Workers Movement (PRWM; Land had never heard of such a group), who claimed that the corporation was guilty of "grave moral offenses for its involvement—through the sale of identification equipment and other polaroid products—with the white supremacist regime of South Africa."[2]

Naturally, this development was quite a shock to the entire company. The following day, another memo was distributed throughout the offices, only this time the assistant secretary of the corporation was doing the handing out. His note stated that Polaroid did not sell any film, cameras, or identification equipment to the government of South Africa. He did point out that the company's identification equipment had been sold to its distributor in the country, Frank and Hirsch, Ltd., but that to their knowledge none of the identification equipment had been resold to the South African government. His last point in his note stated that their distributor in South Africa had, in fact, taken a strong public stand against apartheid.

The next day there was a protest rally staged outside the Polaroid building in Cambridge. The Polaroid Revolutionary Workers Movement, led by activist Kenneth Williams, made clear-cut demands of Polaroid. They insisted on an immediate halt to all sales in South Africa, a severing of all Polaroid's ties with that nation, and the turning over of all profits earned there to groups combatting the racist system of apartheid.[3]

In most MNCs, this problem would be seen as mundane. But with Dr. Land and his company, this situation was treated quite differently from the start. Land had run Polaroid as an extension of his own beliefs. He believed in smooth operations with no surprises and no tricks. This was one of the reasons for Polaroid's total success. Land was always by the corporation's side to lead it through any problem it might encounter. Other multinational companies might have just passed the problem to someone else to worry about it. But this was not one of those wheeler-dealer corporations with no personal involvement—this was Polaroid!

Why was there so much protest against Polaroid? The entire problem evolved around South Africa's Pass Laws, which had been revised in 1952. Under these laws, all "nonwhite" citizens in the country were forced at all times to carry a "passport" bearing their photograph and showing where the bearer lived and worked. Although it was initially unaware of it, Polaroid discovered that its film was being used to make many of the negatives, for these "passport" photographs.

Strangely enough, it was necessary to try to understand how a country such as South Africa, whose contribution to Polaroid's total income was less than 1 percent, could have had such a major effect on a large corporation.[4] The problem was that unlike their other dealings in foreign nations, where Polaroid had set up profitable subsidiaries, the company in South Africa was selling to a distributor, Frank and Hirsch. But at first glance, it did not seem as though this distributor was selling directly to the government of South Africa. If Polaroid wanted to really make a profit, they probably would have sold to the ruling white class, but they had chosen not to do so.

The tension in Cambridge grew over the weeks, but still no solutions were forthcoming. It was a very delicate matter, and although both the corporation and the protesters abhorred apartheid, there was no unanimity as to what to do about it.

## THE SOLUTION

Positive momentum on the issue was achieved in late October when an ad hoc committee, consisting of seven black and seven white employees was set up by executive vice-president William McCune.[5] Through weeks of meetings, the committee discussed the idea of completely boycotting South Africa. But would this actually accomplish anything? It was felt by the committee, as well as by Dr. Land himself, that his company was being watched by many other multinational firms that had a much greater stake in South Africa. Polaroid was pulled out of a basket of hundreds of corporations to be used as an example of the "unprecedented position" of many American businesses in South Africa.[6]

Finally, a decision was reached. It was concluded that a fact-finding team, consisting of four Polaroid employees, should be sent to South Africa. This group was to consult experts in economics, African history, and other related areas to try and determine the possible outcomes of the many options that the company could pursue in South Africa.

While this was taking place, other uproars, as expected, began to erupt all over the United States. After Polaroid, many other large corporations found themselves in the same boat. Only this time, church groups were telling the other firms to boycott South Africa, and the influence of these groups caused boycott campaigns at IBM, at a few airline companies, and at several automobile factories in Detroit.[7]

On November 25, 1970, in *The Boston Globe*, Polaroid ran an ad trying to explain why they were doing business with South Africa in the first place. The advertisement asked the question, "Why was Polaroid chosen to be the first company to face pressure (handbills, pickets, a boycott) about business in South Africa?"[8] The answer stated, "Perhaps because the revolutionaries thought we [Polaroid] would take the subject seriously. They were right. We do."[9] The gist of the ad was that the company was dealing with the ethical questions of its involvement in South Africa, and that Polaroid would make a sound decision on what it felt would be right for the future.

During their ten-day stay in South Africa, the Polaroid inquiry group interviewed close to 150 individuals involved with Frank and Hirsch. They found that nonwhite workers for the company were paid considerably less wages than their white co-workers in the same level jobs. But most nonwhite workers felt that Polaroid could do more to upgrade their socioeconomic conditions by staying in South Africa than by boycotting the country.[10] Upon returning, the inquiry group submitted their suggestion to Polaroid. All four members of the group unanimously agreed that the company should stay and take specific steps to upgrade the working situation not only at Frank and Hirsch, but also in the rest of the country as well. A few weeks later, on January 13, 1971, Polaroid Corporation ran an ad that appeared in *The Boston Globe, The Wall Street Journal, The Washington Post, The Chicago Tribune, The Los Angeles Times, The Christian Science Monitor,* and *The New York Times.* The ad stated the company's decision about South Africa. The advertisement was a page in length and was entitled, "An Experiment in South Africa." The company declared that they would continue their business relationship with South Africa, except for sales to the government, which their distributor would discontinue, but only under an experimental basis for the next year. If things were running smoothly in 1972, then the company would continue its business with the country. There were three major reforms that the company hoped to successfully accomplish within the next year in South Africa. They were as follows:

1. Polaroid would drastically improve the benefits and salaries of its non-white employees.
2. Polaroid would require their South African distributor and suppliers to initiate a program to train a significant number of nonwhite employees for the more responsible jobs within the company.
3. Polaroid would make a commitment toward the education of non-whites at all levels, with a grant to underwrite the educational expenses for about 500 nonwhites. Also included would be a donation to assist all teachers of various levels.[11]

Land's program, known as the "South African Experiment," gained support from a wide range of respected institutions and leaders. Among them was Ulric Haynes, a former African affairs specialist with the State Department. In a *New York Times* article, Haynes pointed out that South Africa had an abundant shortage of skilled labor and that "conscious attempts" to upgrade the capabilities of nonwhite workers would have eventually enabled these peoples to assume more responsible positions in the industry. Haynes said that "attacking apartheid by shoring up the weaknesses in the South African economy is both beneficial to nonwhites and the most effective way of highlighting the senseless contradictions of apartheid and ultimately destroying it."[12]

Polaroid's lead was eventually followed by other top multinational firms. Several of these companies were influenced by Polaroid's breakthrough in management technique. After Polaroid's experience, there was a new willingness for employers to utilize nonwhites in jobs that were previously reserved for white workers only. Other companies found that increased training and preparation for any particular job brought the nonwhite worker up to the same level as his or her fellow white worker.[13] Although nonwhites were forbidden by law to supervise whites in South Africa, there was a much greater respect for the senior nonwhites among many of the junior white employees. Only in the sales department were nonwhites not able to rise in rank, and this was because white customers refused to deal with nonwhite salesmen.

In December of 1971, the entire program was evaluated. Because it seemed as though the experiment was an important factor in creating new awareness of the oppressed situation of nonwhites in South Africa, Polaroid agreed to continue with its monumental reforms. These reforms continued for six more years, until they were overshadowed by a dark cloud.

## RECURRENCE OF THE PROBLEM

*The Boston Globe* printed an article in November 1977 claiming that Polaroid's distributor, Frank and Hirsch, had violated the 1971 agreement with the parent company and were selling company products to the South African government. The *Globe* reporter claimed that the Polaroid products were being delivered in unmarked boxes to various military stations around the country. When a Polaroid representative was sent from Cambridge to investigate the situation, he found the unfortunate truth. Hans Jensen found concrete evidence showing that Polaroid products were, in fact, being used to promote apartheid. With no other alternatives available, Dr. Land and his Board of Directors decided to withdraw their business from South Africa. Polaroid had been the first U.S. company to remain in South Africa for ideological reasons, and they became the first to vacate for ideological reasons.[14]

## QUESTIONS

1. What is Dr. Land's management philosophy? Explain.
2. Do you think that Dr. Land's decision to implement the "South African Experiment" program was a good choice? Explain.
3. Overall, do you think Polaroid's strategy in dealing with South Africa was a success? Explain.
4. Is there anything that the company could have done to prevent its eventual downfall in South Africa? Explain.
5. Do you think that Polaroid acted in a socially responsible way in the case of South Africa? Explain.

## NOTES

1. Mark Olshacker, *The Instant Image* (New York: Stein and Day, 1978), p. 147.
2. Ibid.
3. Murray Illson, "Polaroid, Under Attack, Plans to Aid Some South African Blacks," *The New York Times*, 13 January 1971, p. 9.
4. Olshacker, *The Instant Image*, p. 149.
5. Ibid., p. 152.
6. Ibid., p. 153.
7. Kathy Tetsch, "Wide Drive Against U.S. Trade with South Africa Is Expected," *The New York Times*, 7 February 1971, p. 2.
8. "What Is Polaroid Doing in South Africa?" *The Boston Globe*, 25 November 1970, p. 15.

9. Ibid.

10. Olshacker, *The Instant Image,* p. 156.

11. Illson, "Polaroid Under Attack," p. 9.

12. Ulric Haynes, "Church Action Plan Ill-Conceived," *The New York Times,* 28 March 1971, Sec. 3, p. 14.

13. Olshacker, *The Instant Image,* p. 161.

14. Ibid., p. 162.

## SUGGESTED READINGS

Illson, Murray. "Polaroid, Under Attack, Plans to Aid Some South African Blacks." *The New York Times,* 13 January 1971, p. 9.

Keegan, Warren J. *Multinational Marketing Management.* Englewood Cliffs, N.J.: Prentice-Hall, 1974.

Madden, Carl. *The Case for the Multinational Corporation.* New York: Praeger, 1977.

Olshacker, Mark. *The Polaroid Story.* New York: Stein and Day, 1978.

Rodwin, William. "Polaroid Outlook." *The Boston Globe,* 25 November 1970, p. 17.

Tetsch, Kathy. "Wide Drive Against U.S. Trade with South Africa Is Expected." *The New York Times,* 7 February 1971, p. 2.

# *THREE*

# *Operational and Strategic Aspects of International Business*

**B**eing equipped with a knowledge of the economic framework and of the broad environmental issues of international business, we now take up topics that deal specifically with the strategies that are used in the management of international business. We focus our attention on MNCs with manufacturing or service operations abroad and discuss various strategies that could be used by these firms to engage in international business activities. Some of the main questions that are raised in this part are the following:

1. What organizational framework should a firm choose for engaging in international business?
2. How should a firm devise and implement its global strategies?

3. How should a firm develop and market its product or service on the international level?
4. Where should a firm locate its plants?
5. How should a firm go about its capital budgeting?
6. How can a firm manage its foreign exchange exposure?
7. How can a firm finance its foreign operations?
8. How should a firm formulate its remittance strategy?
9. What are the advantages of going international?

Part Three, therefore, is devoted to a detailed explanation of the strategies that can be used by a firm that is operating on an international level.

# A Framework for Global Strategic Management

*B*ecause no one knows what tomorrow holds, it is very difficult for any business to plan its future course of action. No matter how good our forecasts are, and no matter how carefully we lay our plans, many factors remain that we are unable to predict. Nevertheless, because the continued existence of an organization deeply concerns managers, they use all available strategies to foresee the future of their organizational environment.

Planning is an important part of all organizational activities. Forecasting future conditions; formulating objectives and strategies; mobilizing capital, personnel, and materials to achieve objectives are at the heart of a manager's job in all organizations.

Because executives cannot avoid making assumptions about the future, the question is not if they should plan, but how well they should plan for the future. Business activity can be harmful if it does not lead toward objectives that contribute to the long-term profitability, effectiveness, and success of an organization. In the words of Theodore Levitt, "If you don't know where you are going, any road will take you there."[1] All executives spend time thinking about where their company is going in the future. Still, many executives give insufficient thought to the future. Occasionally some executives look at the future through rose-colored glasses, or they watch it with fearful pessimism. But then they return to daily issues, such as focusing on this year's performance and profits.

The purpose of this chapter is to provide us with a conceptual framework for global strategic management. First, we define new terms that are necessary to explain the conceptual framework. Second, we elaborate on the importance of global strategic management to an MNC. Third, we cover the process of strategic management and strategic thinking. Fourth, we discuss the differences between domestic and global strategic management. Fifth, we explain the differences between strategic and operational decisions. Sixth, we discuss the determinants of the time horizon—or what is called the strategic period— for strategic management. Seventh, we elaborate on the key decisions about strategy that are considered at different organizational levels of an MNC. Finally, we briefly discuss the different steps involved in the global strategic management process, and thus establish the groundwork for a more in-depth coverage of the process in Chapter 14.

## DEFINITIONS

A **global strategy** is a statement of the fundamental means an MNC will use, subject to a set of environmental constraints and its own resource capabilities, to achieve its objectives. A global strategy is a unified plan, tying all the parts of an MNC together. It is comprehensive and covers all major aspects of an MNC. Finally, it is an integrated plan; all parts of a global strategy should be compatible with each other and fit well together.

**Global strategic management** is a process through which objectives for an MNC are formed, a global strategy is formulated for the achievement of these objectives, and plans for implementation of this global strategy are drawn. Strategic management accepts that there is no certainty about tomorrow's results, let alone next year's or the results of the year after that. Nevertheless, it systematically considers likely future events in relation to every decision made in the organization. Strategic management is a way of operating a business instead of a particular technique of operating. Under strategic management, the future implications of every decision are evaluated in advance of their implementation. Standards of performance are established beyond annual budgets. Using this method, an MNC can clearly define what the entire corporation and its subsidiaries are striving to achieve.

Global strategic management is an extension of planning globally. It includes the implementation, the evaluation, and the control of a global strategy.

Global strategic management considers the total global environmental conditions and the MNC's internal capabilities. Global strategic management is a new stage of planning, which succeeds the long-range planning and strategic planning stages prevalent during the 1960s and 1970s. This new stage is marked by top managers such as Lee Iacocca at Chrysler Corporation, John Akers of International Business Machines Corporation (IBM), and John Harvey-Jones at IC Industries. The impact of this new stage is the establishment of "lean" planning units and an emphasis on integration and implementation.[2]

Formulation of a global strategy begins by conceptualizing how to use the resources of an MNC most effectively in the ever-changing global environment. It is similar to the idea in sports of a "game plan." Before starting a game, coaches examine their opponent's past plans, plays, strengths, and weaknesses. They also look at their own strengths and weaknesses. The objective is to win the game with a minimum number of injuries, without humiliating the opponents, and without exhausting all of their best plays (thereby saving some for future games). So with these things in mind they devise a game plan.

There are differences between a game plan and a global strategy. A game plan is formulated for only one game. A global strategy is a long-term plan for an MNC. Only one competitor is involved in a game plan. An MNC has to deal with many competitors in its global environment. It not only has to deal with many competitors, but also with many governments, many markets, many customers, many suppliers, many labor markets, and so forth.

A global strategy tries to answer many questions: What is (are) our business (businesses)? What should it (they) be? What are our products and services? Where are our markets? What objectives should our company strive to achieve? What can our company do to accomplish its objectives? These are not exactly the questions that the Chicago Bears' coach asks. But they are questions that are raised by major corporations such as IBM, Nestlé, and Matsushita.

For successful performance, a global strategy (like a coach's game plan) needs effective implementation. Thus, a global strategy includes operational concerns. The probability of success is enhanced when good strategic formulation is combined with effective strategic implementation. Either good global strategy with poor implementation or poor global strategy and effective strategic implementation usually leads to problems.

A **strategic business unit** (SBU) is an operating division of an MNC that serves a distinct product or market segment, a specific country or geographical area, or a specific set of customers. Each SBU has the authority to make its own strategic decisions within an MNC's guidelines as long as its decisions fit the global strategy of the MNC and help to meet the MNC's global objectives.

**Strategists** are the people who are responsible for the formulation of global objectives and for the development of a global strategy for an MNC. Of course, making strategic decisions is a function and a responsibility of managers at all levels of an MNC. Included in the strategist group are the executives of the divisions, the regional offices, and the national subsidiaries. In addition, the MNC's Board of Directors (in the United States), or Management Board (in Europe), and its consultants are involved in the strategic management process.

The role of the "Board" in the strategic management process varies with different MNCs. At a minimum, the Board has the responsibility to approve or to disapprove the objectives and strategies formulated by top management. Occasionally, MNCs use in-house corporate planners or external consultants to build a strategic management system, to carry out environmental assessment, or to provide advice on new strategies. Regardless of the use of other strategists, the final responsibility for global strategic management rests with the MNC's top management at the headquarters.

## THE IMPORTANCE OF GLOBAL STRATEGIC MANAGEMENT

Formulating a global strategy means that an MNC's strategists consider world markets and world resource locations, instead of simply the markets or resources of one country alone. A global strategy is an attempt to maximize performance and results on a multinational basis, rather than treat international operations as a portfolio of diverse and separate national subsidiaries. Development of a global strategy requires that an MNC engage in a formal process of strategic management. Without a global strategy, the MNC runs the risk of going in so many directions that it will miss the advantages of being a multinational company.

Global strategic management provides an MNC with (1) a tool for coordinating and integrating national operations that are diverse and geographically distant, (2) a way of anticipating and preparing for environmental change, (3) a means of involving national subsidiaries in global concerns, and (4) a way of establishing a critical linkage between the formulation and the implementation of a global strategy.

However, the main justification for strategic management lies in its contribution toward increasing profits and toward the long-term effectiveness of the MNC. Strategic management contributes to profits in the following ways:

1. Strategic management is a communication process. It helps the communication between the MNC and its environment, and among the organizational units and members of the MNC. Strategic management improves coordination among different organizational parts. Coordination and cooperation are acute problems in all companies, especially in large MNCs.

2. Strategic management motivates by involving managers down the line, while clarifying expectations and developing a clear-cut sense of purpose by establishing a specific objective. Strategic management also stimulates a cooperative approach to tackling problems.

3. Strategic management leads to better strategic and operational decisions by bringing more relevant factors, alternatives, and implications into consideration.

4. Strategic management generates an acceptance of change and improves the attitude toward change. Nothing stays unchanged in an MNC's environment.

The forward-looking MNC sees opportunities in the new environmental patterns, and, by enacting innovative measures, it adapts and takes advantage of these changes. Strategic management makes an MNC an effective forward-looking, forward-thinking organization.

**5.** Strategic management creates a new central process. It provides a realistic model of future results and makes it possible to adjust global strategies to keep an MNC on target. Strategic management makes sure that the resources are allocated properly, are not wasted, and become available as needed. However, strategic management cannot help an MNC reach unrealistic, badly thought out, or wishful objectives.

**6.** Strategic management helps to integrate the behavior of individuals and units in an MNC.

## STRATEGIC ACTIVITIES AND DECISIONS

We can view global strategic management as a series of activities. Based on this view, strategic management can be broken down into eight sequential phases. These phases are parts of a global strategic management process, which can be presented in a model.

Figure 13.1 depicts a global strategic management process model. The eight phases of the strategic management process (in the order of their appearance in the model) are: (1) the definition of the MNC's purpose and mission, (2) the global environmental assessment, (3) the MNC's organizational analysis, (4) the global objective formulation, (5) the generation of alternative global strategies, (6) the choice of a global strategy, (7) the implementation of the global strategy, and (8) the evaluation and control. The model and these eight phases will be discussed at the end of this chapter and more fully in Chapter 14.

The activities included in the model are part of a single strategic management process. Each phase is closely related to and dependent on the other phases. In other words, none of the phases is completed until the entire process is finished. The mutual interdependence of these phases is further increased by the need to control the MNC's operations in conformity with the global strategy. The interdependence is also increased because the strategists must review and control the global strategy in light of changing internal and external environmental conditions. To control the global strategy, management must receive feedback information on operations. A strategic review may call for a new environmental or organizational assessment, a revision of objectives, or an adjustment in the strategy or its components. Finally, strategists must periodically extend the current strategic period further into the future because of the passage of time. At times, strategic management needs to address specific issues. The methods employed vary among different MNCs. It is also most crucial to receive and use feedback from all phases of the process.

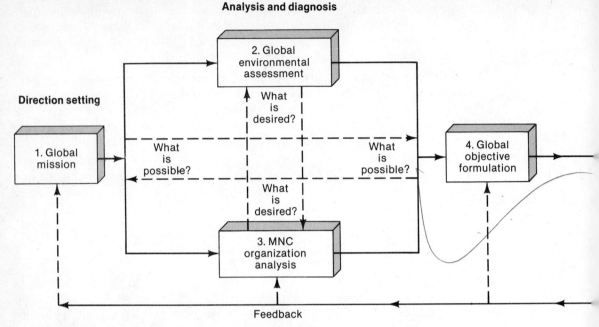

**Figure 13.1** Global strategic management process model

## THE ART OF STRATEGIC THINKING

Strategic management is a process that requires creative thinking.* Although strategists often use statistical and analytical techniques, they cannot avoid the need to make subjective estimates and judgments about the consequences of their actions and the likelihood of future events.

The most creative step in strategic decision making is recognizing that all or many alternative courses of action may reach the desired objective. Global strategic management offers the MNC's executive a chance to consider new and better ways to interact with global environmental conditions. It appeals to the imagination. This is why conventional minds are a drag on strategic management. They cling to the old ways with which they feel comfortable and safe.

Developing a planning document does not mean that the company is, in fact, planning. The process of planning is more important than the written plans themselves. Strategic management is not a scientific, mechanical, and rigid activity. It is creative, continuous, and flexible. In other words, strategic management is an art that requires strategic thinking.

---

*The interested reader is referred to Kenichi Ohmae, *The Mind of the Strategist: Business Planning for a Corporate Advantage,* 2nd ed. (New York: Penguin Books, 1986) and Jeff Mason, "Developing Strategic Thinking," *Long Range Planning,* vol. 19, no. 3 (June 1986), pp. 72–80. For a discussion of creative techniques the reader should also consult Angelo M. Bioni, ed., *Have an Affair with Your Mind* (Buffalo, N.Y.: The Creative Education Foundation, 1974).

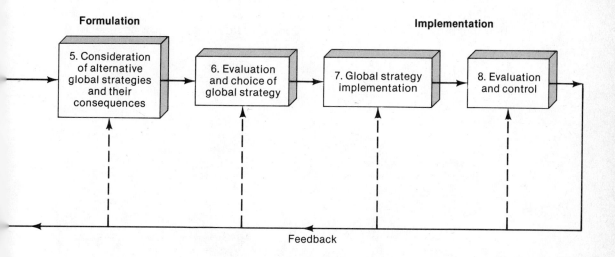

Global strategy must answer questions on how to gain a competitive advantage and on how to create and to exploit change. For example, global strategy needs to create new technology that may provide a competitive advantage or to anticipate the implications of competitors' strategies. As we mentioned earlier the process of developing a global strategy needs to be de-bureaucratized, and directed toward strategic thinking. Global strategy should also be responsive to changes in a rapidly changing and turbulent environment. It is vital that the MNC's objectives and strategies remain creative and responsive to rapid changes in the global environment. Global strategic management is an evolutionary process.

The global strategic management is also dependent on corporate culture and the values and knowledge of the corporate strategists. The role of the corporate planner as a strategist has become more active as a valuable assistant. He or she has become a thinker as well as a doer. The task is to invest in the future and to avoid the pitfalls of the past.

## ENVIRONMENTAL TURBULENCE

Global strategic management has never been more necessary, or more difficult and frustrating, than it is today. MNC executives should be aware that new kinds of global competition, as well as government interference and politically motivated actions, have emerged as critical forces in international business. For example, developments in the negotiations of social agreements between host governments and MNCs have resulted in demands for indigenization, nationalization, national planning, and the global distribution of power and wealth. These developments are powerful forces, creating turbulence in the environment of international business. Successful management of the global strategies of MNCs must be increasingly environmental, strategic, and political in orientation. Nothing less than the MNC's survival and existence are at stake.

**Table 13.1   CHANGES IN THE MULTINATIONAL CORPORATION'S ENVIRONMENT**

| Parameters | Third Quarter Century (World War II–Early 1970s) | Fourth Quarter Century (Early 1970s) |
|---|---|---|
| Geopolitics | 1. General political stability | 1. Breakdown of old alliances, nationalism, new conflicts |
| | 2. Ideologically based Cold War | 2. Resource-based "economic war" |
| | 3. U.S. dominance in international political economy | 3. Erosion of U.S. pre-eminence and superiority |
| | 4. North–South gap | 4. Food, population, Fourth World† Problems, Interdependence with shifting locus of power |
| Resources | 5. Ready availability of low-cost energy | 5. Uncertain availability but high cost |
| | 6. Ready access to raw materials | 6. Resource nationalism and cartels |
| | 7. MDC-controlled* exploration, exploitation | 7. LDC and resource-rich controlled production |
| Economics | 8. Reconstruction in Europe and Japan | 8. Preventing Malthusian prophesies of doom |
| | 9. Economic growth objectives | 9. Socio-ecological balances |
| | 10. Closing international gaps | 10. Problematique: Multivariant, Interactive, Global |
| | 11. "Limits to growth" unknown | 11. Conserving resources |
| | 12. GATT: promising free international trade | 12. Bilateralism, regionalism, and barter |
| | 13. IMS: offering monetary stability | 13. Breakdown of Bretton Woods system |
| Institutional framework | 14. International communications and transportation | 14. Improved communications and transportation |
| | 15. International banking and financial markets | 15. More prudent and controlled developments |
| | 16. Eurodollars, Eurobonds, Eurocurrencies | 16. Currency cocktails, shifting currency strength |
| | 17. EEC, EFTA, LAFTA, COMECON, ANCOM | 17. OPEC, IBA-type political-economic organization |
| Foreign Investments | 18. Long tradition of portfolio investments | 18. Foreign dominance or influence resisted |
| | 19. Open host environments welcoming direct investment as means to close gaps | 19. Restrictive host environments scrutinizing existing and new foreign investments |
| | 20. Home country tolerance for export of capital, technology, and management | 20. Home country concern with export of jobs and loss of national economic welfare |
| | 21. Emphasis on short-term benefits, discounting long-term costs | 21. Perception that costs exceed benefits and that MNC is a threat to sovereignty |
| | 22. Direct investments a means to national ends | 22. Important gaps are closed and direct investments have served primary purpose |
| | 23. Minor government involvement or interference | 23. Extensive government involvement in national planning and management of economic affairs |

*MDC: More-developed countries.

†Fourth world: Underdeveloped countries.

*Source:* Ringbakk, KJell-Arne, "Strategic Planning in a Turbulent International Environment," *Journal of Long-Range Planning* (June 1976) pp. 2–11.

Table 13.1 shows some of the changes that contribute to the ever-increasing turbulence in the environment of an MNC. These changes are organized under five categories: (1) geopolitics, (2) resources, (3) economics, (4) institutional framework, and (5) foreign investments.

## DOMESTIC VERSUS GLOBAL STRATEGIC MANAGEMENT

The strategic management process is similar for both domestic companies and multinational companies, but the issues confronted are not. As we discussed in Chapter 8, an MNC deals with the challenges from three different environments: domestic, foreign, and international. The sheer number of factors and the interaction among these three environments lead to complexities. Some of the main differences between domestic and international planning are highlighted in Table 13.2.

Table 13.2 DOMESTIC VERSUS INTERNATIONAL PLANNING

| Domestic planning | International planning |
|---|---|
| 1. Single language and nationality | 1. Multilingual/multinational/multicultural factors |
| 2. Relatively homogeneous market | 2. Fragmented and diverse markets |
| 3. Data available, usually accurate and collection easy | 3. Data collection a formidable task, requiring significantly higher budgets and personnel allocation |
| 4. Political factors relatively unimportant | 4. Political factors frequently vital |
| 5. Relative freedom from government interference | 5. Involvement in national economic plans; government influences business decisions |
| 6. Individual corporation has little effect on environment | 6. "Gravitational" distortion by large companies |
| 7. Chauvinism helps | 7. Chauvinism hinders |
| 8. Relatively stable business environment | 8. Multiple environments, many of which are highly unstable (but may be highly profitable) |
| 9. Uniform financial climate | 9. Variety of financial climates ranging from overly conservative to wildly inflationary |
| 10. Single currency | 10. Currencies differing in stability and real value |
| 11. Business "rules of the game" mature and understood | 11. Rules diverse, changeable, and unclear |
| 12. Management generally accustomed to sharing responsibilities and using financial controls | 12. Management frequently autonomous and unfamiliar with budgets and controls |

*Source:* William W. Cain, "International Planning: Mission Impossible?" *Columbia Journal of World Business* (July/August 1970), p. 58.

Global strategic management is used by MNC executives to answer such questions as: In what regions or countries should the company expand its international commitment of capital, technology, management, and other resources? Should it enter a new market(s)? What pattern of involvement should be used? What are the opportunities and risks in different countries? What are the opportunities and risks with different patterns of involvement? What products should the MNC introduce in different markets? To what extent should it change its marketing strategy and product mix in different nations? How should it hedge against the exchange risk? What should it do about political risk and governmental interventions? Should it phase out or divest its businesses in any region or country? Where should it raise the necessary capital for its operations?

The diversity of these questions is an indication of the importance and complexity of global strategic management. It also shows some of the differences between strategic management for an MNC and planning for a domestic business. These differences stem from the complexity of undertaking business in foreign countries with different economic, legal/political, technological, competitive, and sociocultural environments.

## STRATEGIC VERSUS OPERATIONAL DECISIONS

MNCs, like their domestic counterparts, engage in two types of decision making; these are: (1) strategic or long-term and (2) operational or tactical. The terms strategy and tactics were first used in the military. *Strategy*, in military parlance, involves the overall approach used to combat the enemy in war. Examples include decisions regarding the defense of enclaves or countryside, or the deployment of special air, sea, and land forces to attack the enemy. *Tactics* are the specific means of carrying out a strategy: how to defend enclaves or the countryside; how to carry out a specific attack; how many planes, ships, tanks, or personnel to deploy. A tactic is the battle plan for each skirmish or battle period.

General George Patton said that it is virtually impossible to win a war using the wrong strategy, even if your tactics are the correct ones. On the other hand, if the correct overall strategy is used, then tactical errors may not lose the war. In a similar way, the MNC that tries to market the wrong mix of products in a market will not succeed, even though the marketing plan for each product and market is properly carried out. On the other hand, the MNC with the proper product mix may be successful, even if some of its marketing plans are in error.

A strategic decision is one that significantly affects what an organization does and how it does it. For the MNC, a strategic decision may involve one or many of the following: its basic concept, its roles in various societies, its choice of nations and markets within each nation, its product or service mix, its competitive positioning in each market, its formulation of long-term objectives, its allocation of resources among units in various countries to achieve the established objectives.

Operational or tactical decisions deal with the ongoing day-to-day operations of the MNC. They cover the production and marketing of goods and services and the management of the personnel and operations. Operational decisions are aimed at the efficient delivery of an MNC's goods and services to the marketplace. They deal with "doing things right." Personnel management, supervisory skills, management information systems, plant operations, organization charts, sales meetings, advertising campaigns, and so forth are all examples of operational or tactical activities.

An example may clarify the differences between the strategic and the tactical decisions of the MNC. Matsushita Electric Industrial Company is the biggest Japanese electronics manufacturer. Matsushita had developed a three-year corporate strategy for the years 1983 to 1986. The major thrust of this strategy was a "metamorphosis from a manufacturer of home-appliance products to a manufacturer of consumer and industrial electronics."[3] The reason for this shift in the strategy was the slow rate of growth in the home-appliance industry. If Matsushita had continued as a manufacturer of home-appliance products after 1986, they might have had less than 5 percent average sales growth per year.

Matsushita's strategic shift to consumer and industrial electronics is based on their belief that electronics and related technologies will be key to their survival and growth through the year 2000. According to a forecast by the Japanese Association for Electronics Industries Development, the average annual growth rate for the whole industry will be 12.6 percent. This is an example of a strategic decision on the part of Matsushita. In order to implement this strategic decision, Matsushita established a semiconductor laboratory in the summer of 1985. The establishment of this laboratory is an example of a tactical or operational decision by this firm. Operational and tactical moves are necessary ingredients in the proper implementation of a strategy.[4]

Operational decision making involves highly detailed plans, procedures, and budgets for the MNC and its subsidiaries. These decisions are made for a period of one or two years. These operational plans are used as a framework for day-to-day operations. They are also used as a basis for monitoring and controlling operations.

Strategic decisions are less obvious in the operating systems and procedures. Nevertheless, strategic decisions are linked to operations because they are designed to capitalize on the organization's distinctive competencies (competitive advantages) in order to take advantage of environmental opportunities or to face its threats. To achieve these goals, the whole organization and its parts must operate effectively and must "do the right things" as well as efficiently "do things right."

Here, the term **effectiveness** means that the MNC is producing goods and services that its markets want. On the other hand, **efficiency** means that the company and its affiliates are producing their goods and services at a minimum cost. For example, how good is it to be an efficient producer of slide rules? Since calculators came to market, not much. How critical is efficiency when the MNC has a monopoly on a product? On the other hand, in some markets or stages of the product life cycle, efficiency may prove crucial to the strategy of being lowest-cost producer. For example, the Yugoslavian manufacturer of Yugo automobiles enjoys very low manufacturing costs that provide for a strategy based on price competitive advantages over other auto manufacturers in the United States.

Usually the top management at the headquarters or the executives of divisions, regional offices, and national subsidiaries are involved in making strategic decisions for an MNC. For operational decisions, not only the top but also the middle-level executives and the functional staff of country affiliates, regional offices, and divisions of an MNC participate in the process. The operational plans and policies of all subsidiaries and units of the MNC need to be integrated and made consistent with the firm's global strategy. In addition, the major operational decisions have to be approved by the top management at the headquarters.

In summary, the primary determinant of the success or failure of the MNC in fulfilling its mission and attaining its objectives is the global strategy. The choice of a global strategy is based on the firm's distinctive competences (its strengths). Global strategic management also provides a framework for the effective and efficient tactics and operations necessary to implement the global strategy. The MNC cannot afford to neglect either the strategic or the tactical aspects of its operations. In this chapter, and the following chapter, we focus on the strategic aspects of international business. Operational considerations will be covered in subsequent chapters.

## STRATEGIC PERIOD

For most MNCs the **strategic period** (the time horizon) runs from two to five years. The time period for which objectives are established and strategies are enacted depends on the characteristics of the company and the industry. The strategic period should be long enough to project the future effects of decisions made in accordance with the overall global strategy. For example, as was explained earlier, Matsushita Electric Industrial Company develops three-year strategic plans.[5]

The difference between a long-term strategy and a short-term tactic or plan is a matter of degree. Both are needed in a strategic management process. The short-term plan or tactic is a means for implementing the long-term strategy. Without action, there is little reason to formulate a strategy.

Short-term plans are formulated for a period of one or two years. They are linked to the implementation of the long-term strategy and with the budgetary control process. The meaning of "long term" is relative, ranging from two to five years. Each MNC must decide how long its strategic period needs to be. It is important that the period be sufficiently long for the strategy to be developed. For example, because many years must pass before planted trees can be harvested fully, an MNC involved in forestry must think ahead for decades. Similarly major capital investments in a petroleum plant may take years to complete. Major oil companies such as Exxon need to have very long-term strategies of ten to 20 years.

The strategic period should be long enough so that a realistic picture of its effect can emerge. The strategic period should take into account any normal cycle of events important to the industry and the MNC's operations. For example, natural resource companies (such as energy, mining, and paper companies) need a strategic period of 20 to 25 years. Certain petroleum companies may forecast supply and demand curves for oil for two decades or longer into the future as a part of their planning. Some other MNCs may have very long-term strategies of 15 to 20 years. These strategies may be designed to stay on the top of their future markets by conducting research to develop new high-technology products. For example, in 1985 Kawasaki Steel Corporation of Japan developed a strategy they call "A Fifteen-year Vision for 2000." A major theme of this strategy is to change from a steel manufacturer to a manufacturer of raw materials. There are two components to this very long-term strategy: (1) the strengthening of the company's competitive position in the international steel industry and (2) the aggressive development of new high-tech–related businesses. Kawasaki's strategic (main) objective is to increase the sales dependence on nonsteel (that is, engineering and chemicals) businesses from 10 percent in 1985 to 20 percent, 30 percent, and 40 percent in the years of 1990, 1995, and 2000, respectively.[6] The time horizon in some industries such as toys, foods, clothing, and consumer products may be as short as one year or one season. For example, a survey of 420 companies by the National Planning Commission in the United States revealed the following differences in their strategic periods:

Table 13.3　STRATEGIC PERIOD
　　　　　　 FOR U.S.
　　　　　　 COMPANIES

| | |
|---|---|
| 5 years only | 53% |
| 10 years only | 11% |
| More than 10 years | 6% |

*Source:* Darryl J. Ellis and Peter P. Pekar, Jr., *Planning Basics for Managers* (New York: AMACOM, A Division of American Management Association, 1980), p. 28.

It should be pointed out that the shorter the strategic period, the more accurate the forecast of future events will be. An MNC should choose a period that fits its businesses. For instance, Culligan and SKF, Swedish firms, both have a three-year strategic period, whereas the Ciba-Geigy and Burroughs firms follow a five-year strategic period.

A five-year strategic plan does not mean that the global strategy is formulated for only five-year intervals. Nor does it mean that the MNC should limit its forecasts of trends to five years into the future. The strategic period is continuously extended to cover the time horizon chosen by an MNC. The strategies may be revised and updated at least once every year. Because an additional year is added at every revision there is always a strategy for the length of the chosen strategic period. Strategic management is a flexible process. As the environment changes, strategies should change to act upon or to react to environmental conditions.

Developing a planning document does not mean that the company is, in fact, planning. The process of planning is more important than the written plans themselves. Strategic management is not a mechanical and rigid activity. It is creative, continuous, and flexible.

## LEVELS OF STRATEGIC MANAGEMENT

In large, diversified companies, strategic management involves a hierarchy of objectives and strategies. At the lower level, strategic management addresses segments of the environment, which are considered as discrete business units. At a higher level, strategic management takes a broader view, ultimately encompassing all units at the corporate level.

In domestic firms, the distinguishing factors separating one strategic business unit from another are the differences in customers, products, service lines, technologies, and other characteristics. In MNCs, geographic distinctions are also introduced. In many cases, geographic boundaries may, in fact, be the national boundaries that represent different legal and political jurisdictions. Today, as in the past, these national boundaries have acted to distinguish national business operations or SBUs. These national boundaries are also the relevant geographical distinctions that define an MNC's environmental units. However, in some situations other territorial distinctions, such as climatic conditions or religious and ethnic differences, would prove more effective than national boundaries for distinguishing areas of business operations.

Achievement of objectives is the main aim of global strategy. A combination of objectives, global strategies, and policies form a "grand design" or master strategy for an MNC. There are four levels of objectives and strategies in an MNC: (1) the enterprise level, (2) the corporate level, (3) the business level, and (4) the functional level. Each level of strategy deals with a different type of "integration." Table 13.4 indicates these relationships.

### Enterprise Level

Enterprise strategy attempts to integrate the MNC with its external environments (domestic, foreign, and international). This integration is a way of establishing an MNC's overall role. As an important institution of the societies in which it operates, an MNC should fulfill its role in the everyday affairs of each society as well as the global community.

The increasing interdependencies of MNCs and governments have led to a closer evaluation of their legitimacy. MNCs are reexamining their societal

Table 13.4  LEVELS OF OBJECTIVES AND STRATEGIES

| Level of objectives and strategies | Integrates |
| --- | --- |
| Enterprise | Total MNC with the world society and national societies |
| Corporate | Businesses, SBUs, regional or national affiliates, with portfolio of businesses and regional or national markets |
| Business, SBU, regional or national affiliates | Functions with business, SBU, regional or national affiliates |
| Functional | Units and subunits with functions |

roles and are considering whether their decisions and operations can be insular. Questions concerning the governance and the roles of the MNC, and the way in which it will be allowed to exist, are raised today. These questions are forcing a reexamination of enterprise strategy and the overall mission of the MNC. In the future, there will be more explicit attention to the broader legitimacy considerations of the strategies of multinational corporations.

## Corporate Level

Corporate strategy addresses these questions: "What business(es) are we in?" "What business(es) should we be in?" "In which markets do we operate?" "In which markets should we operate?" It also focuses on how the different businesses and markets in which an MNC competes may be integrated into an effective portfolio.

Corporate strategy deals with how environmental factors influence the future prospects of an industry, a market, and the MNC's operations.

Corporate-level decisions are more value oriented, conceptually based, and less concrete than strategic decisions made at the lower organizational levels. They carry greater risks and costs, but they also can mean greater potential profit. They are longer term and require greater flexibility and injection of more resources. These consequences are the result of the innovative, futuristic, far-reaching, and pervasive nature of these decisions. The choice of the businesses and markets in which to compete, the dividend policies, the priorities for expansion, and the methods of long-term capital generation are examples of MNC corporate-level strategic decisions.

Recall the example given earlier of the Kawasaki Steel Corporation. In 1985, this MNC formulated a 15-year corporate objective and corporate strategy, called "A Fifteen-year Vision for 2000." Its objective was to incrementally increase its sales dependence on nonsteel (that is, engineering and chemical) products from 10 percent in 1985 to 40 percent in year 2000. To implement this corporate objective, Kawasaki is aggressively redirecting its business portfolio. As a result, the company's dependence on the steel business is expected to decline from 75 percent in 1985 to 50 percent in 1995. Their 25 percent dependence on the shipbuilding and engineering businesses is expected to remain the same during this period. On the other hand, they are adding new advanced technology businesses to their current portfolio. They aim at increasing the contribution of their new advanced technology businesses to 25 percent of total sales by the year 1995.[7]

Kawasaki's new corporate strategy necessitates certain changes. For example, on the domestic front, it formed Kawasaki Techno Research in June 1984. In the international arena, the company entered into the semiconductor business in 1985 by establishing a joint venture with SLI Logic, an American semiconductor manufacturer. The newly formed joint venture is named Nippon Semiconductor. In order to strengthen its new joint venture Kawasaki also acquired NBK, an American manufacturer of wafers.[8]

### Business (SBU) Level

In small businesses, or in businesses that market one product or service line (a group of similar products or services), in one country, the business level of strategy is not distinguishable from the corporate-level strategy described earlier. This so-called corporate level strategy is implemented in this case at the next lower level by functional policies. Figure 13.2 illustrates this.

In domestic conglomerates, domestic multiple industry companies, and MNCs, there is usually another level of organization between the corporate level and the functional level. In some companies, these mid-level units are called "operating divisions" or strategic business units (SBUs). A strategic business unit for an MNC may also take the form of a regional or national affiliate that has a certain degree of autonomy.

For example, Pepsi-Cola USA, Pepsi-Cola Bottling Group, Pepsi-Cola Inter-

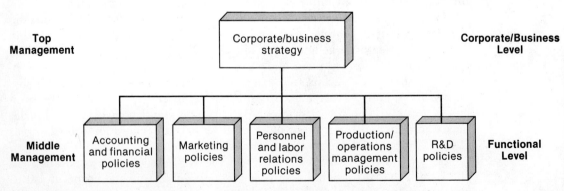

**Figure 13.2** Relationship of corporate strategy and functional policies for a domestic single SBU company

national, Pepsi-Cola Bottling International, PepsiCo Wines and Spirits International, Frito-Lay, PepsiCo Foods International, Pizza Hut, Taco Bell, La Petite Boulangerie, Pepsico Food Service International, North American Van Lines, Lee Way Motor Freight, and Wilson Sporting Goods are the principal divisions and subsidiaries of Pepsico, Incorporated. It should be pointed out that some of these SBU groupings are based on product and service lines, whereas some other SBUs are geographically based.[9]

Identification of an MNC's SBUs is based on the significant differences (significant for purposes of global strategy) that distinguish each part of the MNC from another part. Because of the diverse geographical and national makeup of an MNC, location plays a major role in defining an SBU's boundaries within the company. Therefore, an MNC conducting one type of business in Hong Kong considers and operates that business separately and distinctly from similar operations in Venezuela, France, or the United States. For example, World Trade Europe/Middle East/Africa Corporation, a subsidiary of International Business Machines Corporation, is responsible for operations in 85 countries. While, IBM World Trade Americas/Far East Corporation, with a territory extending across four continents, is responsible for IBM's operations in 46 countries, including Australia, Brazil, Canada, China, and Japan.[10]

Table 13.5 is an illustration of SBUs within an MNC. The vertical axis is the representation of diverse product and service lines, while the horizontal axis shows the geographical location. Of course, similar to domestic firms, differences in customers or technology can also be used as distinguishing factors to separate various SBUs within the MNC.

The strategies of the SBUs may differ from one another, but they are all guided by the overall corporate strategy. This relationship is shown in Figure 13.3.

Table 13.5   STRATEGIC BUSINESS UNITS (SBUS) DEFINED BY PRODUCT/SERVICE LINE AND GEOGRAPHIC LOCATION

| Country / P/S Line | Country 1 | Country 2 | Country 3 | Country 4 |
|---|---|---|---|---|
| P/S Line A | SBU A1 | SBU A2 | SBU A3/4 | |
| P/S Line B | SBU B1 | SBU B2 | SBU B3 | SBU B4 |
| P/S Line C | SBU C1 | SBU C2/3 | | SBU C4 |
| P/S Line D | SBU D1 | SBU D2 | SBU D3 | SBU D4 |

*Source:* Reprinted by permission of the publisher from MULTINATIONAL CORPORATE STRATEGY by James C. Leontiades (Lexington, Mass.: Lexington Books, D. C. Heath and Company, Copyright 1985, D. C. Heath and Company), p. 42.

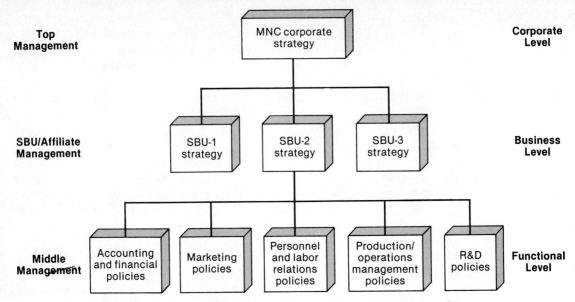

**Figure 13.3** Relationship among strategies and policies in multi-SBU/multinational companies

In MNCs with an SBU structure, each SBU sets its own business strategies. Each SBU strategy is formulated to make the best use of the SBU's resources and its strategic advantages, given its unique environmental conditions. The overall corporate global strategy sets the long-term objectives of the MNC and the broad constraints and resources within which each SBU must operate. The corporate level (global strategy) helps the SBU define its scope of operations. It limits or expands the SBU's operations and performance through the resources it allocates to the SBU.

At the MNC corporate level, the strategy focuses on the "portfolio" of SBUs and the markets the firm wishes to put together to accomplish its objectives. Business-level strategy deals with the question, "How should the MNC's SBU compete in a given business?" In other words, business strategy defines how each individual business (SBU or affiliate) should position itself among its rivals to reach its objectives, and thereby contribute to implementing corporate global strategy and to achieving corporate global objectives. At this business level, each SBU decides how it can allocate its resources to achieve a competitive advantage over its rivals. For example, Kawasaki's new SBUs (Nippon Semiconductor and NBK) are responsible for strengthening the position of this MNC in the global semiconductor and advance technology industries.[11]

In addition to answering the question of how to compete, business strategy integrates the various functional areas, such as accounting and finance, management, marketing that make up an SBU.

Business-level strategic decisions bridge the corporate-level and the functional-level decisions. Business-level decisions involve costs, risks, and profit potentials that are less than those found at the corporate level but more than those characteristic of the functional level. Examples of SBU decisions include deciding on such issues as the location of plants, the segmentation of markets, the coverage of geographical areas, and the selection of distribution channels.

## Functional Level

Functional strategies or policies focus on supporting the corporate and business strategies. Functional strategies address two issues. First, they integrate the various subfunctional departments and activities in the SBU. Second, they relate the various functional area policies to changes in the functional area environments. For instance, through marketing strategy, the various advertising, pricing, and packaging policies and activities are integrated. The resulting marketing program should not only be internally consistent, but also consistent with other functional areas of the SBU, and it should fit the perceptions and responses of the market.

For example, Navistar (formerly International Harvester), the American manufacturer of trucks and heavy machinery, has implemented production and marketing strategies aimed at combating the changes in its competitive environment. In the 1970s and 1980s Navistar had been facing severe competition from manufacturers from other countries, such as Japan. According to a Navistar company official, "the truck you make in Japan and ship to the United States will arrive here at a cost 25 percent lower than our manufacturing costs. And that includes the tariffs and taxes." This stiff competition had led to heavy losses that put Navistar at the verge of bankruptcy. After reorganization and a name change from International Harvester to Navistar, this giant MNC took drastic actions to cut costs and become more competitive. At the corporate level, Navistar changed its portfolio structure by disposing of its money-losing agricultural equipment business. At the functional level, Navistar attacked costs by improving its productivity levels. In 1979, it built 6.1 trucks per manufacturing employee per year. In 1985, its productivity had more than doubled to 12.6 trucks per employee per year. Although Navistar is silent about specific future figures, they state that the new production strategies are aimed at further improvements in the productivity levels.[12]

Corporate-level and business-level strategists center their attention on "doing the right things." Functional-level executives focus on "doing things right." Functional-level managers are concerned with the efficiency and the effectiveness of production and marketing systems, and they deal with the quality and the extent of customer service, hoping to increase their area market shares through successful products and services. Thus, their decisions are action-oriented and center on operational issues. These decisions are relatively short-range, low-risk, and less-costly, and they rely upon available resources. Functional-level strategies are designed to be highly adaptable to ongoing activities, and these strategies need little cooperation from other parts of the organization. Functional-level strategies are formulated to help the implementation of corporate- and business-level strategies.

Functional-level decisions are relatively concrete and quantified. For example, decisions concerning inventory levels, package design, pricing, the use of generic or brand name labels, the use of general or specific purpose production equipment, the use of basic or applied R&D, and the use of advertising media are all functional-level decisions.

In summary, there is a hierarchical relationship among objectives and strategies in different levels of the MNC. As we move through different levels of strategic management, from the enterprise level to the functional level, we not only move down the MNC's organizational hierarchy, but also downward in terms of constraints. Each level of strategy constrains every other level, particularly those levels below it.

## PHILOSOPHIES OF CENTRALIZATION

A successful multinational corporation organizes itself in ways that position its system of products and/or services, marketing, and production in order to obtain the maximum potential leverage from economies of scale and experience, lower prices, barriers to entry, standardization of components and products, patterns of involvement, and so on to compete effectively. This type of global strategy is similar to the creation of a portfolio of products and markets that are highly interdependent and need to be balanced to achieve optimum performance.

In formulating global strategies, MNC executives usually consider the global marketplace as a group of interacting markets with the possibility of being mutually supportive. This multiplicity of markets requires a multistrategic business unit (SBU) organization. Furthermore, as a result of this multilevel nature of an MNC, different objectives and strategies exist for each level. Therefore, in addition to planning and control at the subsidiary level, a broad supplementary system of planning and control is needed at the global level. In order to coordinate these interacting but separate systems, an MNC needs to decide how much decision making, strategy formulation, and control should be centralized.

With a highly centralized structure, decisions are made and controlled by the MNC headquarters with little autonomy given to the regional and national subsidiaries. On the other extreme, some companies choose to decentralize decisions and provide autonomy for the regional, national, and even local managers of their foreign operations. Still other companies centralize decision making in some areas and decentralize it in others. To this end, we may find three philosophies of control of foreign operations. These are: ethnocentric, polycentric, and geocentric.[13]

### Ethnocentric Philosophy

Ethnocentricity is a very strong orientation toward the home country. The basic assumption underlying this philosophy is that the home country's management practices, products, and so on are superior to those of other countries. As a result, this philosophy necessitates the exertion of central control from headquarters over all operations in foreign subsidiaries. For example, as we will discuss in Chapter 16, the product, distribution, pricing, and promotional strategies in foreign subsidiaries are controlled by headquarters. A multinational corporation that advocates an **ethnocentric philosophy** pursues a narrow strategy of selling the products that are successful at home in foreign countries. Usually the home plants are used for the production of standardized products that require little or no modification for export in order to gain some marginal business.

American automobile manufacturers "big car syndrome," is a reflection of what could be called Detroit's ethnocentricity. For example, General Motors used to consider its foreign subsidiaries' automobiles as "foreign." The situation has changed in recent years and internationalism is replacing nationalism at GM.

An MNC that is ethnocentrically oriented exerts centralized control over financial, marketing, personnel, manufacturing, and other aspects of its foreign subsidiaries.

## Polycentric Philosophy

The opposite of ethnocentricity, a **polycentric philosophy** advocates a strong orientation toward the host country. This philosophy places emphasis on differences in local conditions, including culture, politics and laws, consumers, competition, and so forth. The assumption is that each subsidiary's environment is unique and consequently difficult for outsiders to understand. Therefore, host country managers are employed and given a great deal of autonomy in making decisions. It is felt that these managers, because of their closeness to the local markets and environments, are most capable of making decisions that are suitable to the conditions of foreign subsidiaries.

The polycentric philosophy results in geographic decentralization of all operations in foreign subsidiaries. A multinational corporation that utilizes this strategy decentralizes all its decision making. The MNC acts as a holding company. The corporate role is limited to the business portfolio analysis of different and isolated SBUs. For example, a polycentric product strategy has the advantage of increased response to local conditions and reduces risks to the MNC by marketing a narrow product line in a geographically decentralized fashion. Under this philosophy, managers at foreign subsidiaries are given almost complete autonomy to conduct financing, manufacturing, and marketing activities independently of other subsidiaries and the headquarters. Therefore, if one foreign subsidiary is having difficulty, the remaining subsidiaries may continue to function.

Companies that advocate a polycentric philosophy include Alcoa, General Foods, Honeywell, and Procter and Gamble (P & G). Only in the late 1980s did P & G change its philosophy from ethnocentricity to polycentricity. For many years, P & G acted as an "ugly" American. The company was taking products developed for the U.S. market and trying to push them into foreign markets by using American style marketing and advertising. This process of standardization of worldwide marketing techniques was even labeled "global marketing" in the early 1980s. Through some hard lessons and big losses, Proctor and Gamble learned that the trick to going global is to act like a local. In the words of an American marketing executive in Japan, "P & G had a very hard time accepting that Japan was not going to be like the U. S." As a result of the change in attitudes, things have turned around dramatically. For example, to help achieve its goal of being the number one consumer products company in Japan, P & G took some drastic actions. The company has hired more Japanese staff and attuned its ways to local styles. A Japanese analyst says about P & G, "It's more Japanese than some Japanese companies." As a result, sales in Japan grew 40 percent, to $1 billion in fiscal year ended on 30 June 1989. Globally P & G is introducing new products more rapidly partially because it has built strong local operations that are closer to the market. The commitment to international operations has already been dramatically increased. One sign of this increased commitment is the fact that there are talks about Edwin L. Artzt, vice-chairman in charge of international operations, becoming P & G's next chief executive officer.[14]

Disadvantages of polycentric philosophy include duplication of effort among various subsidiaries and an absence of cost savings due to the effects of the experience curve. In other words, similarities among countries might well permit the development of efficient procedures and effective common strategies that are forgone by advocating polycentricity.

## Geocentric (Global) Philosophy

**Geocentric philosophy** is a compromise between the two extremes and is an attempt to provide balanced centralization. This philosophy is probably the most effective for the global market of today. Geocentric philosophy considers the whole world rather than any particular country as the target market. A geocentric firm may be thought of as denationalized, supernational, or truly transnational and global. Based on this attitude, international or foreign departments, subsidiaries, or markets do not exist. This is because the firm does not designate anything international or foreign about a market. Resource allocation decisions are made without regard to national boundaries. The company does not hesitate to make direct investment (as opposed to foreign direct investment) wherever it is warranted. Talented managers are recruited and deployed regardless of their nationality. Most likely, a truly global MNC does not identify itself with a particular country except through the location of its headquarters and its corporate registration. Examples of global companies include Caterpillar, Citizen, General Electric, Komatsu, Mitsubishi, Siemens, and Timex.

An MNC that advocates a geocentric philosophy realizes that while countries may differ, these differences can be understood and managed. In the process of controlling and coordinating the global functional activities such as marketing, financing, production, and so forth, the company adapts its programs to meet local needs within the broader framework of its global strategy. In other words, a firm that is a proponent of this philosophy realizes that some operations are better centralized to take advantage of the effects of experience and economies of scale, while others should be decentralized to provide flexibility and adaptability to local conditions. For example, marketing activities may be decentralized, while most financial activities may be centralized at the headquarters.

The global philosophy is based on an integrated view of foreign subsidiaries. As we pointed out earlier, because of advances in communication, information processing, and transportation the world is shrinking to become a "global village." Today, a global marketplace exists and it should be treated as such. The global philosophy acknowledges this fact, and, therefore, fits all strategies of various subsidiaries and SBUs into a single comprehensive long-term strategy that we have been calling global strategy. The country subsidiaries, therefore, are considered as a portfolio of interdependent entities.

The global strategy philosophy assumes that worldwide distribution of the product is possible on the basis of the effects of experience curve. This strategy assumes that many products will be customized to local conditions after they cross national borders. Producing products that are readily modifiable reduces lead time and logistics costs. For example, today, many automobile manufacturers use a global marketing strategy by building a base model. Appropriate modifiers are built in the base model so it may then be changed to fit the local conditions. For example, although Mercedes-Benz sold its standard bus in Brazil, the firm added other products and services to the package to meet the needs of Brazil.

In summary, regardless of philosophy used, the environment of each country needs to be analyzed carefully and the firm's approach needs to be tailored to satisfy local needs. The global or transnational corporation looks at the whole world as one market. It manufactures, conducts research, raises capital, and purchases supplies wherever it is best. It keeps up with the technology, innovations, and market trends all around the globe. To a global corporation, national boundaries and government regulation tend to be irrelevant, or a mere hindrance. Corporate headquarters might be located anywhere in the world. "For many companies, going global is a matter of survival, and it means radically changing the way they work."[15]

## THE GLOBAL STRATEGIC MANAGEMENT PROCESS

As we pointed out earlier, one way to view global strategic management is to consider it as a set of decision-making activities. There are eight distinct, but interrelated, decision-making processes. Figure 13.1 is a visual presentation of the global strategic management process model. The total process determines whether an MNC excels, survives, or dies. The job of the strategists is to make the best use of an MNC's resources in a changing and turbulent international environment. The global strategic management process results in the formulation and implementation of global strategies designed to achieve the objectives of an MNC. While it is convenient to order the eight decision-making processes sequentially, these activities are interactive, cyclical, continuously repetitive, and do not move forward in a neat sequence as described subsequently and as depicted in Figure 13.1.

## Defining the MNC's Purpose and Mission

The starting point in setting a direction for an MNC is developing an internal concept of the organization's scope and makeup. In this phase, we can raise the following fundamental questions: Where are we now and where are we going? What businesses and activities should we engage in? What products or services should we provide? What uses and applications of our products do we want to provide? Where are our markets? What type of technologies do we want to use? Who are our customers and why do they buy our products and services? Is there anything that we can do better or different from our competitors? What are our distinctive competencies or competitive advantages? The answers to these questions mold the organization's identity, character, makeup, image, and scope of activities. They form the MNC's purpose and mission.

## Global Environmental Assessment

Because the MNC cannot control (but may influence) its environment, it must assess its current conditions and make forecasts, not choices, about the environmental conditions it expects to encounter in the future. Such forecasts or assumptions about the future are an important part of the strategy formulation aspect of strategic management.

In addition to the difficulty of accurately forecasting the future influences of particular environmental factors, a major problem in environmental assessment is knowing what factors to examine in the first place. It may be a more serious error to overlook a factor than to inaccurately forecast it. For example, completely ignoring the effect of a technological advancement in a product may prove deadly to a firm in the personal computer industry because its products may become obsolete. But inaccurately forecasting a new technological development will probably prove damaging, but not fatal to the firm. As the rate of environmental change and turbulence increases, this forecasting problem becomes more critical. Environmental assessment provides necessary input into the strategy formulation phase. It may also provide clues about major events and discontinuities in the environment that will necessitate major changes in the strategy. In such situations, a major proportion of resources may have to be allocated to build flexibility and breadth of capabilities to survive environmental shocks.

During the global environmental assessment process, the MNC evaluates its domestic environment, foreign environments, and international environment. This evaluation involves information gathering (environmental scanning), the evaluation of the information, environmental forecasting, the recognition of present and future threats and opportunities, and finally, the development of a summary of key environmental threats and opportunities. This summary is called an environmental threat and opportunity profile (ETOP).

## MNC Organizational Analysis

A parallel process to the global environmental assessment is the organizational analysis. Organizational analysis recognizes the values and expectations of stakeholders (those with an interest in the MNC's operations and performance), the objectives and aspirations of the MNC's top management, and the resource and capability assessment. It also includes an assessment of the competitive advantages (both the strengths and the weaknesses) of both the MNC and its subsidiaries. Organizational analysis is similar to environmental assessment. The only major difference is that the focus of the analysis in the organizational mode shifts to the internal rather than the external environment. At the conclusion of organizational analysis the MNC strategists develop a strategic advantage profile (SAP), which contains the firm's relative strengths and weaknesses.

## Global Objective Formulation

While the ultimate strategic objective of any firm is to survive, survival, as such, is only a minimal objective. Most firms want to grow and receive, at least, a reasonable return on their investments (ROI).

The MNC must first formulate long-term objectives and then translate them into short-term annual objectives. The most important and number one long-term priority of an MNC is called the global **strategic objective**. In addition to the global strategic objective, an MNC needs to establish other long-term priorities, called the long-term objectives, for the entire corporation and its subsidiaries.

## Generation of Alternative Global Strategies

In generating alternative strategies for the achievement of global objectives, the primary concern is to take advantage of the environmental opportunities and to face environmental threats by using a firm's internal capabilities and strengths.

## Choice of a Global Strategy

Evaluation of the different alternative global strategies that have been generated and choosing the best one comprise the next phase. At the end of this phase

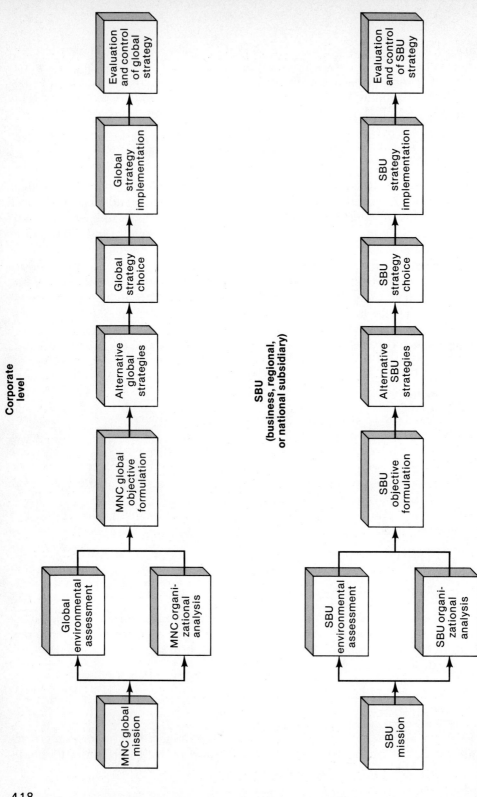

**Figure 13.4** Corporate-level and SBU-level strategic management process models for an MNC

a global strategy and various business-level strategies have been formulated. This is the end of the strategic thought or strategy formulation process.

## Implementation

Implementation means putting the selected strategy into action. This step requires building an organization structure to support the strategy, staffing the organization, and formulating functional strategies and policies to make the strategy work. Rallying the needed resources and allocating them among national affiliates or SBUs and functional departments are also key requirements in the implementation phase.

## Evaluation and Control

Evaluation and control are accomplished through feedback and by determining whether or not the strategy is working. Steps to make it work, if results are proving unsatisfactory, may now be taken.

As mentioned earlier, the phases in the global strategic management process are interrelated. Although it is convenient to present them sequentially, in practice, each phase affects all the other phases. While the strategists are analyzing the environments and organizational conditions, they should consider the choice made in the implementation of past strategies.

Figure 13.4 is a modification of Figure 13.1. Another point worth noting is that Figure 13.1 is drawn up for an MNC that is using first-generation planning. Many MNCs use second-generation or contingency planning. Figure 13.5 shows the choice and implementation phases for a second-generation planning system. Under a second-generation planning system, the strategists consider several scenarios of future environment and the resulting internal strengths and weaknesses of each scenario. They then formulate several strategies and implementation guidelines for each strategy. In the future, the strategy and implementation scheme closest to meeting the actual environmental conditions, as characterized in each scenario and strategy, will be put into effect. The other contingency plans will be kept and implemented if needed. Whenever contingency planning is used, Figure 13.5 should be considered.

We conclude this chapter by reemphasizing the fact that global strategic management is a continual process. The parts of the process are interrelated and interacting. For clear presentation, we can separate them, but, in practice, we cannot.

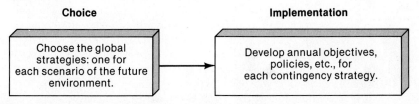

**Choice**  **Implementation**

Choose the global strategies: one for each scenario of the future environment. → Develop annual objectives, policies, etc., for each contingency strategy.

**Figure 13.5** Global strategic management process for second-generation planning

## SUMMARY

1. Planning is an important part of all organizational activities. Forecasting future conditions, formulating objectives and strategies, and mobilizing capital, personnel, and materials to achieve objectives are at the heart of a manager's job in all organizations.

2. A global strategy is a statement of the fundamental means that an MNC will use, subject to environmental constraints and its own resource capabilities, to achieve its objectives. A global strategy is a unified plan, tying all the parts of the MNC together.

3. Global strategic management is a process through which objectives for the MNC are formed, a global strategy is formulated for the achievement of these objectives, and plans for implementation of global strategy are drawn.

4. A strategic business unit (SBU) is an operating division of an MNC that serves a distinct product or market segment, a specific country or geographical area, or a specific set of customers. Each SBU has the authority to make its own strategic decisions within an MNC's guidelines, as long as the SBU's activities fit the global strategy of the MNC and help to meet the MNC's global objectives.

5. Strategists are the people who are responsible for the formulation of global objectives and for the development of a global strategy for an MNC.

6. The main justification for strategic management is its contribution to increasing profits and to planning for the long-term effectiveness of the MNC.

7. We can view global strategic management as a series of activities. Based on this view, strategic management can be presented in a model that contains eight phases. The eight phases in the strategic management process, in the order of their appearance in the model, are: a) defining the MNC's purpose and mission, b) global environmental assessment, c) MNC organizational analysis, d) global objective formulation, e) generation of alternative global strategies, f) choice of a global strategy, g) implementation of the global strategy, and h) evaluation and control.

8. Strategic management is a process that requires creative thinking, and it can be seen as an art that requires what can be called "strategic thinking."

9. Global strategic management has never been more necessary, or more difficult and frustrating, than it is today. Recent developments have created powerful forces for turbulence in the environment of international business. Successful MNC global strategic management must be increasingly environmental, strategic, and political in its orientation. Nothing less than the MNC's survival and existence are at stake.

10. The strategic management process is similar for both domestic companies and MNCs, but the MNC deals with the challenges from three different environments: domestic, foreign, and international. The many factors, and their interaction, in these three environments lead to complexities in strategic management for the MNC that the domestic firms do not have to face.

11. MNCs, like their domestic counterparts, engage in two types of decision making: a) strategic or long term and b) tactical or operational. Strategic decisions deal with "doing the right things." Operational decisions deal with "doing things right."

12. For most MNCs the strategic period (time horizon) runs from two to five years. The length of time period for which objectives are established and strategies are enacted depends on the characteristics of the company and the industry.

13. In large, diversified companies, strategic management involves a hierarchy of objectives and strategies. At the lower level, strategic management addresses segments of the environment, which are considered as discrete business units. At a higher level, strategic management takes a broader view, ultimately encompassing all units

at the corporate level. There are four levels of strategic management, these are: a) enterprise, b) corporate, c) business, and d) functional.

14. Enterprise strategy attempts to integrate the MNC with its external environments (domestic, foreign, and international). This integration is a way of establishing the MNC's overall role. As an important institution of the societies in which it operates, the MNC should fulfill its role in the everyday affairs of each society in which it participates as well as in the global community.

15. Corporate strategy addresses these questions: "What business(es) are we in?" "What business(es) should we be in?" "In which markets do we operate?" "In which markets should we operate?" Corporate strategy also focuses on how the different businesses and markets in which the MNC competes may be integrated into an effective portfolio.

16. Business-level strategy (also called SBU, national, or regional-level strategy) deals with the question, "How should the MNC's strategic business unit compete in a given business?" In other words, business-level strategy defines how each individual business (SBU or affiliate) should position itself among its rivals to reach its objectives, and thereby contribute to implementing corporate global strategy and achieving corporate global objectives.

17. Functional-level strategies or policies focus on supporting the corporate and business strategies. Functional strategies address two issues. First, they integrate the various subfunctional activities of departments and units within the function. Secondly, they relate the various functional area policies to changes in the functional area environments.

18. Corporate- and business-level strategists center their attention on "doing the right things." They are concerned with the effectiveness of the entire MNC and its SBUs. Functional-level executives focus on "doing things right." They are concerned with the efficiency and effectiveness of production, marketing, and other operating systems.

## QUESTIONS

13.1 What is meant by global strategy and global strategic management? What role does strategic thinking play in global strategic management?

13.2 What are the key features of global strategy?

13.3 How does global strategic management contribute to the survival and performance of an MNC? Discuss.

13.4 Go to your school library and find an MNC that utilizes formal strategic management. Develop a model for the strategic management process that this company uses. What are the differences between their process and the process discussed in this chapter?

## NOTES

1. Theodore Levitt, *Innovation in Marketing* (New York: McGraw-Hill, 1962), p. 11.
2. Bernard Taylor, "Corporate Planning for the 1990s: The New Frontiers," *Long Range Planning*, vol. 19, no. 6 (December 1986) pp. 3–12.

3. Gen-Ichi Nakamura, "Strategic Management in Major Japanese High-tech Companies," *Long Range Planning,* vol. 19, no. 6 (December 1986), pp. 82–91.
4. Ibid.
5. Ibid.
6. Ibid., p. 86.
7. Ibid.
8. Ibid., pp. 86–87.
9. Pepsico, Inc., *Annual Report,* 1983, p. 48.
10. International Business Machines Corp., *Annual Report,* 1985, p. 48.
11. Nakamura, "Strategic Management," p. 87.
12. Navistar, *First Quarter Report,* 1985, pp. 17–18.
13. For an in-depth discussion, refer to Thomas Hunt, Michael Porter, and Eileen Rudden, "How Global Companies Win Out," *Harvard Business Review,* vol. 60 (Sept.–Oct. 1982), pp. 98-108.
14. Zachary Schiller, and Ted Holden. "P & G Goes Global By Acting Like a Local," *Business Week* (28 August 1989), p. 58.
15. Jeremy Main. "How to Go Global—and Why," *Fortune* (28 August 1989), p. 70.

## SUGGESTED READINGS

Abt, Clark, et al. "A Scenario Generating Methodology." In James R. Bright, and Milton Schoeman, eds., *A Guide to Practical Technological Forecasting.* Englewood Cliffs, N.J.: Prentice-Hall, 1973.

Aguilar, Francis J. *Scanning the Business Environment.* New York: Macmillan, 1967.

Aharoni, Y. *The Foreign Investment Decision Process.* Boston: Division of Research, Graduate School of Business Administration, Harvard University, 1966.

Bates, Donald L., and David L. Eldredge. *Strategy and Policy: Analysis, Formulation, and Implementation,* 2nd ed. Dubuque, Iowa: Brown, 1984.

Biondi, Angelo M., ed. *Have an Affair with Your Mind.* Buffalo, N.Y.: The Creative Education Foundation, 1974.

Brooks, Michael, and H. Lee Remmens. *International Management and Business Policy.* Boston: Houghton Mifflin, 1978, Chap. 5.

Cain, W. W. "International Planning: Mission Impossible?" *Columbia Journal of World Business,* vol. 5, no. 4 (July/August 1970), pp. 53–60.

Chambers, John C., S. K. Mullick, and D. D. Smith. "How to Choose the Right Forecasting Technique." *Harvard Business Review,* vol. 49, no. 4 (July/August 1971), pp. 45–74.

David, Fred R. *Strategic Management,* 2nd ed. Columbus, Oh.: Merrill, 1989.

Delbecq, André L., A. H. Van de Ven, and D. H. Gustafson. *Group Techniques for Program Planning: A Guide to Nominal Group and Delphi Processes.* Glenview, Ill.: Scott, Foresman, 1975.

Digman, Lester A. *Strategic Management: Concepts, Decisions, Cases.* Plano: Tex.: Business Publications, 1986.

Doz, Yves L. "Strategic Management in Multinational Companies." In H. V. Wortzel and L. H. Wortzel, *Strategic Management of Multinational Corporations: The Essentials,* 2nd ed. New York: Wiley, 1990.

Dymsza, William A. *Multinational Business Strategy.* New York: McGraw-Hill, 1972.

Ellis, Darryl J., and Peter P. Pekar, Jr. *Planning Basics for Managers.* New York: AMA-COM, A Division of American Management Association, 1980.

Emery, F. E., and E. L. Trist. "The Causal Texture of Organizational Environments." *Human Relations,* vol. 18, no. 1 (February 1965), pp. 21–32.

Fahey, Liam, and William R. King. "Environmental Scanning for Corporate Planning." *Business Horizons,* vol. 20, no. 4 (August 1977), pp. 61–71.

Fannin, W. R., and C. B. Gilmore. "Developing a Strategy for International Business." *Long Range Planning,* vol. 19, no. 3 (June 1986), pp. 84–88.

Fannin, W. R. and A. F. Rodrigues. "National or Global?—Control vs Flexibility." *Long Range Planning,* vol. 19, no. 3 (October 1986), pp. 84–88.

Galbraith, Jay R., and Robert K. Kazangian. *Strategy Implementation: Structure, Systems and Process,* 2nd ed. St. Paul, Minn.: West, 1986.

Garland, John, and Richard N. Farmer. *International Dimensions of Business Policy and Strategy.* Boston: Kent, 1986.

Gates, S. R., and W. G. Egelhoff. "Centralization in Headquarters-Subsidiary Relationships." *Journal of International Business Studies,* vol. 17, no. 2 (Summer 1986), pp. 71–92.

Ghoshal, Sumantra. "Global Strategy: An Organizing Framework," *Strategic Management Journal,* vol. 8, no. 5 (September/October 1987), pp. 425–440.

Glueck, William F. *Strategic Management and Business Policy.* New York: McGraw-Hill, 1980.

Jauch, Lawrence R., and William F. Glueck. *Business Policy and Strategic Management,* 5th ed. New York: McGraw-Hill, 1988.

Gordon, William J. *Synetics: The Development of Creative Capacity.* New York: Collier Books, 1968.

Gup, Benton E. *Guide to Strategic Planning.* New York: McGraw-Hill, 1980.

Hamel, Gary, and C. K. Prahalad. "Managing Strategic Responsibility in the MNC." *Strategic Management Journal,* vol. 4 (1983), pp. 341–351.

Hanna, Nagy. "Strategic Planning and the Management of Change." *Finance and Development,* vol. 27, no. 1 (March 1987), pp. 30–33.

Henderson, Bruce D. "The Experience Curve . . ." Boston Consulting Group, 1974.

Higgins, James M. *Organizational Policy and Strategic Management: Text and Cases,* 2nd ed. Chicago: Dryden Press, 1983.

Hofer, Charles W. "Toward a Contingency Theory of Business Strategy." *Academy of Management Journal,* vol. 18, no. 4 (December 1975), pp. 784–810.

———. "Research on Strategic Planning: A Survey of Past Studies and Suggestions for Future Efforts." *Journal of Economics and Business,* vol. 28 (Spring/Summer 1976), pp. 261–286.

———. *Strategic Management.* St. Paul, Minn.: West, 1984.

Hussey, D. E. *Introducing Corporate Planning,* 2nd ed. Oxford: Pergamon Press, 1983.

Keegan, Warren J. "Multinational Scanning: A Study of Information Sources Utilized by Headquarters Executives in Multinational Companies." *Administrative Science Quarterly,* vol. 19, no. 3 (September 1974), pp. 411–421.

Kefalas, Asterios, and Peter P. Schoderbek. "Scanning the Business Environment: Some Empirical Results." *Decision Sciences,* vol 4, no. 1 (January 1973), pp. 63–74.

Kiechel, Walter, III. "Corporate Strategy for the 1990s." *Fortune,* 29 February 1988, pp. 34–42.

Kirkland, Richard, Jr. "Entering a New Age of Boundless Competition." *Fortune,* 14 March 1988, pp. 40–48.

Klein, Harold E., and Robert E. Linneman. "Adoption of Multiple Scenario Analysis in Corporate Long Range Planning Processes: An Empirical Study." *Working paper,* Temple University, 1978.

Klein, Harold E. "Incorporating Environmental Examination into the Corporate Strategic Planning Process." Ph.D. diss. Columbia University, New York, 1973.

Kupfer, Andrew. "How to Be a Global Manager." *Fortune,* 14 March 1988, pp. 52–58.

Lawrence, Paul R., and Jay W. Lorsch. *Organization and Environment: Managing Differentiation and Integration.* Boston: Division of Research, Graduate School of Business Administration, Harvard University, 1967.

Leontiades, James C. *Multinational Corporate Strategy: Planning for World Markets.* Lexington, Mass.: Lexington Books, 1985.

Linneman, Robert, and Harold E. Klein. "The Use of Multiple Scenarios by U.S. Industrial Corporations." *Long Range Planning,* vol. 12, no. 1 (February 1979), pp. 83–91.

Lorange, Peter. "A Framework for Strategic Planning in Multinational Corporations." *Long Range Planning,* vol. 9, no. 3 (June 1976), pp. 30–37.

———, and Richard F. Vancil, ed. *Strategic Planning Systems.* Englewood Cliffs, N.J.: Prentice-Hall, 1977.

Main, Jeremy. "How to Go Global—and Why." *Fortune,* 28 August 1989, pp. 70–76.

Martino, J. *Technological Forecasting for Decision-Making,* 2nd ed. New York: Elsevier North-Holland, 1983.

Mason, R. H., and M. B. Goudzwaard. "Performance of Conglomerate Firms: Portfolio Approach." *Journal of Finance,* vol. 31, no. 1 (March 1976), pp. 39–48.

McHale, John, and Magda C. McHale. "An Assessment of Futures Studies Worldwide." *Futures,* vol. 8, no. 2 (April 1976), pp. 135–145.

Metzner, H. E., J. L. Wall, and W. F. Glueck. "Product Life Cycle and Stages of Growth: An Empirical Analysis." *Academy of Management Proceedings,* 1975.

Miles, Raymond E., Charles C. Snow, and Jeffrey Pfeiffer. "Organization-Environment: Concepts and Issues." *Industrial Relations,* vol. 13, no. 3 (October 1974), pp. 244–264.

Mintzberg, Henry, D. Raisinghani, and A. Theoret. "The Structure of 'Unstructured' Decision Processes." *Administrative Science Quarterly,* vol. 21, no. 2 (June 1976), pp. 246–274.

Nakamura, Gen-Ichi. "Strategic Management in Major Japanese High-tech Companies." *Long Range Planning,* vol. 19, no. 6 (December 1986), pp. 82–91.

Negandhi, A., and B. S. Prasad. *The Frightening Angels: A Study of Multinationals in Developing Nations.* Kent, Oh.: Kent State University Press, 1975.

Newman, William H., James P. Logan, and W. Harvey Hegarty. *Strategy: A Multilevel Integrative Approach,* 10th ed. Cincinnati, Oh.: South-Western, 1989.

Omahae, Kenichi. *The Mind of Strategist: Business Planning for Corporate Advantage.* 2nd ed. New York: Penguin Books, 1986.

Padbury, Peter, and Diana Wilkins. *The Future: A Bibliography of Issues and Forecasting Techniques.* Monticello, Ill.: Council of Planning Librarians, 1972.

Pearce, John A., II, and Richard B. Robinson, Jr. *Strategic Management: Strategy Formulation and Implementation,* 3rd ed. Homewood, Ill.: Irwin, 1988.

———, and Richard B. Robinson. *Formulation and Implementation of Competitive Strategy.* 3rd ed. Homewood, Ill.: Irwin, 1988.

Porter, Michael E. *Competitive Strategy: Techniques for Analyzing Industries and Businesses.* Free Press, 1980.

Prahalad, C. K. "The Strategic Process in a Multinational Corporation." Ph.D. diss., Harvard University, Cambridge, Mass., 1975.

Prasad, Benjamin S. *Policy, Strategy, and Implementation: Text and Cases with a Global View.* New York: Random House, 1983.

Ringbakk, K. J-Arne. "Strategic Planning in a Turbulent International Environment." *Long Range Planning,* vol. 9, no. 3 (June 1976), pp. 2–11.

Rumelt, Richard P. *Strategy, Structure and Economic Performance.* Boston: Division of Research, Graduate School of Business Administration, Harvard University, 1974.

Sackman, Harold. *Delphi Critique: Expert Opinion Forecasting and Group Process.* Lexington, Mass.: Lexington Books, 1975.

Schendel, Dan E., and Charles H. Hofer, ed. *Strategic Management: A New View of Business Policy and Planning.* Boston: Little, Brown, 1979.

Schoeffler, Sidney. *PIMS Newsletters, Nos. 1 and 2.* Cambridge, Mass.: Strategic Planning Institute, 1977.

———, Robert D. Buzzell, and Donald F. Heany. "Impact of Strategic Planning on Profit Performance." *Harvard Business Review,* vol. 52, no. 2 (March/April 1974), pp. 137–145.

Sharplin, Arthur. *Strategic Management.* New York: McGraw-Hill, 1985.

Smith, J. "The Management of Social Responsibility in Multinational Companies and Its Effect on Corporate Planning." Manchester, England: M.B.A. diss., Manchester Business School, 1977.

———. *SPI Guide to Portfolio Analysis.* Cambridge, Mass.: Strategic Planning Institute, 1977.

Starbuck, William H. "Organizations and Their Environments." In M. D. Dunnette, ed. *Handbook of Industrial and Organizational Psychology.* Chicago, Ill.: Rand McNally, 1976.

Steiner, George A. *Multinational Corporate Planning.* New York: Macmillan, 1966.

———, John B. Miner, and Edmund R. Gray. *Management Policy and Strategy: Text, Readings, and Cases,* 3rd ed. New York: Macmillan, 1986.

Taylor, Bernard. "Corporate Planning for the 1990s: The New Frontiers." *Long Range Planning,* vol. 19, no. 6 (December 1986), pp. 13–18.

Terpstra, Vern. *International Marketing,* 4th ed. Chicago Ill.: Dryden Press, 1987.

Thompson, Arthur A., Jr., and A. J. Strickland III. *Strategic Management: Concepts and Cases,* 4th ed. Plano, Tex.: Business Publications, 1987.

Utterback, James M., and James W. Brown. "Monitoring for Technological Opportunities." *Business Horizons,* vol. 15, no. 5 (October 1972), pp. 5–15.

Vancil, Richard F. "Strategy Formulation in Complex Organizations." *Sloan Management Review,* vol. 17, no. 2 (Winter 1976), pp. 1–18.

Vernon-Wortzel, Heidi, and Lawrence H. Wortzel. "Globalizing Strategies for Multinationals from Developing Countries." *Columbia Journal of World Business,* vol. 23, no. 1 (Spring 1988), pp. 27–35.

Walter, Ingo, and Tracy Murray. *Handbook of International Business,* 2nd ed. New York: Wiley, 1988, section 40.

Wheelwright, Steven C., and Spyros Madradakis. *Forecasting Methods for Management,* 5th ed. New York: Wiley, 1989.

Wilson, Ian H. "Socio-Political Forecasting: A New Dimension to Strategic Planning." In Edmund R. Gray, ed., *Business Policy and Strategy: Selected Readings.* Austin, Tex.: Lone Star, 1979, chap. 11.

Zaleznik, A., and M. R. R. Kets de Vries. *Power and the Corporate Mind.* Boston: Houghton Mifflin, 1975.

# Chapter
## *14*

# *Application of Global Strategic Management Process*

*I*n Chapter 13 we laid out the framework and introduced a model for global strategic management. As we explained, the model starts with the establishment of the MNC's mission, then moves to an assessment of its environmental conditions, and then to an analysis of the internal strengths and weaknesses of all the SBUs and the total corporation. After these two diagnostic phases are completed, the MNC strategists formulate objectives and global strategies for the entire corporation, its subsidiaries, and its functional areas. In addition, contingency plans are developed to deal with changing and unexpected developments. After the formulation of global strategies, plans will be devised to help in the implementation of these global strategies. Periodically, frequently on an annual basis, the firm evaluates and recycles its strategies in order to adapt to changes that have taken place. This step was called the evaluation and control phase. Figure 14.1 shows the global strategic management process we presented in Chapter 13. In this chapter we provide an in-depth discussion of the steps described in the global strategic management process model.

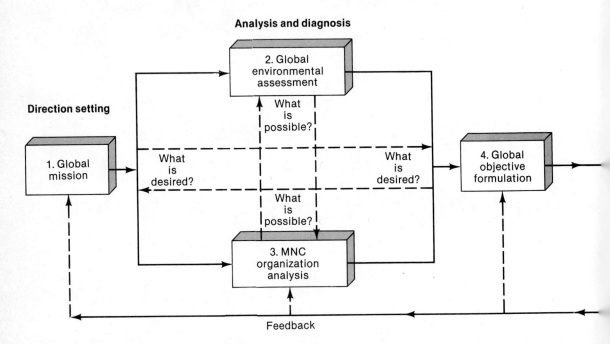

**Figure 14.1** Global strategic management process model

1. To determine the mission of the MNC, including broad statements about its purpose, philosophy, social roles and responsibilities, and goals.

2. To search the global environment and examine the impact of significant remote and task factors in the domestic, foreign, and international environments. To recognize environmental opportunities and threats and develop a global environmental threat and opportunity profile (ETOP).

3. To examine and distinguish competitive advantages (relative strengths and weaknesses). Development of MNC's profile reflecting its internal conditions, capabilities, and strategic advantages, that is, the strategic advantage profile (SAP).

4. To establish a global strategic objective and other specific long-term objectives for the overall MNC, its affiliates, and SBUs.

## MNC PHILOSOPHY, MISSION, CHARTER, AND CREED

The MNC's mission is the basis upon which critical quantitative and qualitative objectives for the national affiliates, the SBUs, the divisions, and the entire organization are formulated. The examination and reexamination of the MNC's

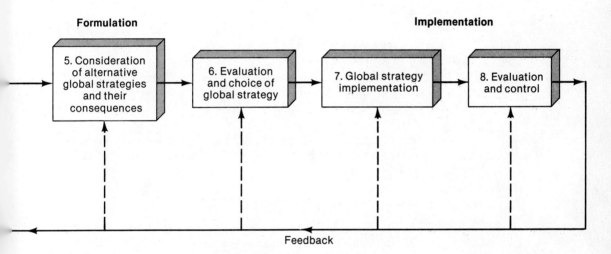

**Formulation**

5. Consideration of alternative global strategies and their consequences

6. Evaluation and choice of global strategy

**Implementation**

7. Global strategy implementation

8. Evaluation and control

Feedback

5. To generate alternative solutions and ways to achieve global objectives and to make an interactive opportunity analysis by matching the ETOP with SAP.

6. To ensure that the most appropriate global strategy for the achievement of objectives is chosen.

7. To put the strategy into action by allocating resources, developing proper organization, utilizing proper leadership, and formulating short-term objectives and functional policies that fit and support the selected global strategy.

8. To review the success of the strategic process, to serve as a basis for control (to ensure that global strategy and its implementation achieve objectives), and for future decision making.

basic philosophy and mission are the cornerstone of the global strategic management process. The statement of mission is equivalent to the enterprise level strategy that we discussed in Chapter 13.

The MNC's **business philosophy** establishes its inherent nature, its guiding principles, and its underlying conception of itself. It establishes the functions and services an MNC performs globally. It also sets up the long-term basic directions and goals and the profit motivation of the MNC. The business philosophy and mission of an MNC should stress its international business focus. The following is an extract from the business philosophy maintained by the Sony Corporation:

Sony is a pioneer, always a seeker of the unknown.

Sony never intends to follow others, and in blazing the path into new fields where no one has ventured, Sony hopes to find its own way of progress. Through progress, Sony wants to serve mankind.

The trail of a pioneer is strewn with difficulties. But in spite of many hardships, people of Sony work in harmonious unity, because they find joy in participating creatively and pride in contributing their own unique talents to each pioneering effort.

Sony has the principle of respecting and encouraging each one's abilities—the right person in the right post—and always tries to bring out the best in the person. Sony believes in each one and constantly allows the individual to develop his or her abilities.

This is the vital force of Sony.[1]

The **mission** of an organization defines its role in the society and the economy. The MNC's mission defines why it exists and why it competes in some selected industries, markets, regions, and nations, and not in others. The MNC's mission is a general, enduring statement of the intentions of enterprise. The statement of an MNC's mission embodies its business philosophy, the image it seeks to project, and its self-concept. This statement forms an identity for the MNC that distinguishes it from its worldwide competitors. This self-knowledge and identity can dynamically and aggressively help to pinpoint global markets, products, technological areas for emphasis, and resources.

Establishment of a well-defined corporate mission is a prerequisite for the formulation of a corporate strategy. But first a firm needs to have a realistic view of its particular skills so it can objectively establish its mission. Defining the particular skills of a company is not an easy matter. Generalizations, such as "we are a communications company" or "we serve the market for leisure-time activities" do not work. A company needs to be specific. For example, according to the Marriott Corporation's chief executive officer, J. Willard (Bill) Marriott, Jr., it took the company over a decade to figure out that it had special expertise in running hospitality and food-service operations, building lodgings, and financially packaging real estate for sale to investors. As a result of this realization, Marriott got out of its business involving cruise ships, travel agencies, and theme parks.[2]

The written statement of a mission is sometimes called a **charter.** The charter defines not only the range of products, customers, and markets, but also the international nature of an MNC. It also designates profit centers and formulates the relationships among headquarters, divisions, major SBUs, and national affiliates.

Some MNCs write **creeds,** showing the broad ethical tone and the social responsibilities of the enterprise. The statements of philosophy, mission (charter), and creed are interrelated.

The following is a list of elements that need to be present in an MNC's statement of mission:

1. The basic product(s) or service(s) offered
2. The customers whose needs are served
3. National or regional markets covered
4. The technology(ies) used in the production or delivery of product(s) or service(s)
5. The fundamental concerns for survival of the MNC through growth and profitability
6. The managerial philosophy (including the basic beliefs, values, aspirations, and philosophical priorities) and the corporate creed
7. The MNC's desired public image
8. The concept that the people affiliated with the MNC should have about the firm
9. The recognition and acknowledgment of the legitimate claims of the stakeholders
10. The social responsibility of the MNC

The MNC's mission should address these issues, and through a mission statement cover the scope of its operations, methods, and intentions.[3]

As we mentioned earlier, the statement of mission is an enduring statement of purpose and intent. However, at the beginning of each strategic period, the MNC strategists have an opportunity to redefine the mission statement. In defining or redefining the mission, strategists must recognize and acknowledge the legitimate claims of the MNC's stakeholders. The **stakeholders** are individuals, groups, or parties who have an interest or claim on the MNC. Such stakeholder groups consist of employees and investors, as well as those outsiders who are affected by the MNC's actions and operations.

Table 14.1 provides us with a list of stakeholders. To this list we can add the top management in the home and host offices. It must be kept in mind that this

**Table 14.1  STAKEHOLDERS**

**A claimant view of company responsibility**

| Claimant to the business firm | General nature of the claim |
|---|---|
| Stockholders | Participate in distribution of profits, additional stock offerings, assets on liquidation; vote of stock, inspection of company books, transfer of stock, election of board of directors, and such additional rights as established in the contract with corporation. |
| Creditors | Participate in legal proportion of interest payments due and return of principal from the investment. Security of pledged assets; relative priority in event of liquidation. Participate in certain management and owner prerogatives if certain conditions exist within the company (such as default of interest payments). |
| Employees | Economic, social, and psychological satisfaction in the place of employment. Freedom from arbitrary and capricious behavior on the part of company officials. Share in the fringe benefits, freedom to join a union and participate in collective bargaining, individual freedom in offering up their services through an employment contract. Adequate working conditions. |
| Customers | Service provided with the product; technical data to use the product; suitable warranties; spare parts to support the product during customer use; R & D leading to product improvement; facilitation of consumer credit. |
| Suppliers | Continuing source of business; timely consummation of trade credit obligations; professional relationship in contracting for, purchasing, and receiving goods and services. |
| Governments | Taxes (income, property, etc.), fair competition, and adherence to the letter and intent of public policy dealing with the requirements of fair and free competition. Legal obligation for businessmen (and business organizations) and obey antitrust laws. |
| Unions | Recognition as the negotiating agent for the employees. Opportunity to perpetuate the union as a participant in the business organization. |
| Competitors | Norms established by society and the industry for competitive conduct. Business statesmanship on the part of contemporaries. |
| Local communities | Place of productive and healthful employment in the local community. Participation of the company officials in community affairs, regular employment, fair play, local purchase of a reasonable portion of the products of the local community, interest in and support of local government, support of cultural and charity projects. |
| The general public | Participation in and contribution to the governmental and business units designed for reciprocal understanding; bear fair proportion of the burden of government and society. Fair price for products and advancement of the state of the art in the technology that the product line offers. |

*Source:* William R. King and David J. Cleland, *Strategic Planning and Policy* (New York: Van Nostrand Reinhold, 1978), p. 153.

list was designed for a domestic company. An MNC's list includes more groups of stakeholders in different nations all around the world.

## GLOBAL ENVIRONMENTAL ASSESSMENT

Global environmental assessment is a process through which an MNC evaluates the actual (present) and potential (future) conditions that it may face in the domestic, foreign, and international environments. Scanning and assessing the turbulent global environment present a complex task. It can be achieved by building a **management information system** (MIS), which supplies information about trends in the economy, in governmental interference, in social development, in market conditions, and in other environmental conditions in all the nations in which the MNC operates. One major difficulty is translating the positive and negative effects of these trends. Strategists need to determine when and how they will feel these effects.

Global environmental assessment involves the collection and evaluation of information from the relevant remote and task factors in the domestic, foreign, and international environments of an MNC. Using this information, the MNC should also forecast the future conditions of these factors. The environmental aspects of international business, their importance, and the need for their assessment were discussed in depth in Chapter 8.

Examples of key environmental factors include changes in consumer purchasing power, the entry or exit of a major competitor in a certain product or service line or country market, changes in legal systems, increases in the political vulnerability in a host country, increases in the cost of raw materials, economic downturns, and changes in the consumption habits of a customer segment. It should be noted that not all the environmental changes are detrimental to an MNC. Environmental changes may lead to improvements in the operations of an MNC. Positive actual or positive potential environmental conditions are considered *opportunities,* whereas negative changes that impact an MNC are labeled *threats.*

An important component of an MNC's environment is the competition that it faces in its major markets. **Competitive assessment** evaluates the actual (present) and potential (future) competition that an MNC and its subsidiaries face in their markets and the effects of these conditions on the MNC's operations. The competitive assessment should deal with companies that are producing products or providing services that are close substitutes for an MNC's products and services. Many MNCs try to predict the strategies of their major competitors in product and service and in country markets in order to better respond to the challenges of their competitors. For example, a major diversified electronics MNC conducts a competitive assessment of its major competitors in many key product lines and country markets. The firm uses this information to simulate strategic plans for its major competitors in the same manner as it makes strategic plans for its own enterprise. These simulated competitors' strategies enable this electronics firm to deal with existing and emerging competition in specific markets.[4] (See Chapter 8 for in-depth coverage of competitive analysis.)

## Sources of Information

Data for environmental analysis can be obtained from internal or external sources. Sources can be oral or from published documents. Documented environmental information is published by the company's own MIS and by competitors, suppliers, trade associations, banks, customers, governments, international organizations, special research organizations, magazines, newspapers, embassies, and other groups. Studies of environmental scanning practices in business have shown that most corporations base their decisions on internally generated facts and that for external information oral (human) sources are preferred. These sources and their reliability can be tested. Appendix I in Chapter 8 contains a partial list of Selected Sources of International Business Data.

MNC corporate planners (strategists) frequently construct a human intelligence network. Through such a network, questions can be answered by phone, resulting in tremendous cost savings in both time and money. Of course, possible biases and prejudices can weaken the information obtained from these sources. For example, relying on local officials to gain information on local markets or labor availability may lead to inaccurate and misleading information.

Some MNCs employ globe-trotters in order to glean knowledge at its source. An example of such a company is Pall Corporation, which is a leading manufacturer of filters for many substances ranging from airplane fuel to wine. Pall employs a special group of Ph.D.s to gather useful information from customers and feed it back to researchers. This process has proved helpful on a number of occasions. In one instance, makers of magnetic tape could not figure out how to lay down a smooth layer of magnetic particles without filtering the slurry over and over again, at great cost. With the help of this information-gathering gang, Pall's scientific and laboratory services unit called on manufacturers and users of tape in Japan, West Germany, the Netherlands, and the United States in search of an answer. As a result, Pall devised a simple two-step procedure that led to great cost savings.[5]

## Environmental Forecasting

The major responsibility of MNC strategists is to ensure the survival of the firm by anticipating change and adapting to environmental change in ways that provide the opportunity for profitability and growth. To achieve this task, strategists need to develop skills in forecasting and in predicting environmental changes. The following steps can be taken when searching for future opportunities and threats:

1. Select the key factors in the environment critical to the firm.
2. Select the major sources of environmental information and collect necessary data.*
3. Develop forecasting techniques and forecast future environmental conditions.
4. Integrate the forecasted results into the global strategic management process.
5. Monitor the accuracy of these forecasts.

The selection of key environmental factors by an MNC depends upon its international experience, the amount of its global involvement, the nature of its businesses and industries, its product and service lines, and its customers and markets. The selection of these factors also depends upon the types of business and the patterns of involvement an MNC has or plans to undertake.

Surprisingly, an MNC's ability to assess single future trends and changes is quite accurate and complete. Forecasting methods are increasing in number, and the number of predictions of specific events and trends is growing even faster. These forecasting techniques are also gaining popularity among policy-makers in all industrial sectors and countries. Despite this, the usefulness of forecasting techniques is severely limited in practice. This is because predicting the impacts of events and trends on a firm is much more difficult than forecasting the primary changes themselves. Additionally, forecasts are rarely free of the values and biases of the forecasters. Many forecasts are meant to be self-fulfilling, guiding efforts and resources toward the achievement of certain goals.

Some forecasts involve a rich and diverse collection of data with little attempt to order them in a systematic way. Other forecasts involve elaborate manipulation of narrow and subjective data. Sophisticated model building is no substitute for poor data gathering or misuse of the forecasted results. It must be kept in mind that no firm can entirely manipulate its environment, nor can it completely predict outside changes and events.

## Forecasting Techniques

Many approaches and methods have been developed to predict the nature and direction of environmental changes and their impacts on MNCs. We discussed legal and political risk forecasting in Chapter 9 and technological forecasting in Chapter 11. In this section we will provide only a brief summary of forecasting methods.†

**Qualitative techniques** are used when data are scarce, such as prior to or during product introduction or initial market entry. These forecasts are based

---

*See Chapter 8, Appendix I, "Selected Sources of International Business Data," for a collection of documented sources.

†The reader interested in a detailed coverage of forecasting techniques is referred to the Suggested Readings list at the end of Chapter 13.

on judgment, opinion, personal experience, or intuition. They usually represent the opinions or advice of some person or some group knowledgeable in the area. There is no test to prove or disprove the accuracy of these forecasts. Faith in these forecasts depends on the reputation or track record of the forecaster. Visionary historical analogy and panel consensus approaches are also called qualitative methods. Often, qualitative techniques are used in addition to quantitative approaches to interpret the results of more formal methods.

**Quantification of expert opinions** is based on questions about the probability of the occurrence of a given event. In Chapter 9 we discussed "Delphi" techniques, in which questions are asked of an anonymous panel of experts. After receiving feedback on the distribution of the panel's estimates and on an individual's reasons for an extreme position, each expert is given a number of opportunities to revise his or her estimate. Revisions are made until a consensus of opinions emerges. Of course, computers can be used to increase the interaction and feedback among the panelists. Two other opinion quantification techniques are the Nominal Group Technique (NGT) and marketing research. Generally, these methods use rating schemes to turn qualitative information into quantitative estimates.

**Quantitative techniques** are also used for forecasting. **Extrapolation of trends** is one of these forecasting methods. Various equations, based on both theoretical and empirical results, can be used to derive projections from available historical data. These traditional forecasting techniques try to project the past and present into the future in different ways. Statistical techniques such as regression analysis, time-series analysis, and projection are examples of the extrapolation of trends method. Other approaches include moving averages, exponential smoothing, seasonal adjustments, trend projections, and the Box-Jenkins techniques. All of these methods use quantitative data and are best used for forecasting quantifiable events. Other more sophisticated techniques, such as *simulation,* the *cause and effect methods* (including econometric models), and *scenario building* can also be used.

## Environmental Threat and Opportunity Profile

The aim of environmental assessment is to help MNC strategists to better understand the complexities and constraints involved in formulating the strategies that optimize an MNC's opportunities and minimize its threats in the highly competitive markets in which it operates. This type of global strategic management allows strategists time to anticipate key opportunities and to plan optional and optimal responses to these opportunities. In addition, environmental assessment functions as an early warning system. This system helps to prevent key threats and to develop strategies that reduce their impact. Or it may possibly turn these threats into the firm's advantage.

For example, a diversified MNC requires its country and product managers to focus on two or three critical strategic environmental issues in order to establish more realistic goals within the context of the broad corporate objectives in profit growth. The same MNC also fosters confrontation and debate on strategic issues by line and staff managers from headquarters and subsidiaries.[6]

An important aspect of environmental assessment is to assess the difference between the future environment and the present environment. The strategists seek to state the problem, either a positive opportunity or a negative threat, that the environment is offering. If first-generation strategy formulation is used, the assessment is based on the most probable future. If second-generation planning is used, several assessments of the future are drafted with best-case, most-probable case, and worst-case scenarios. Then several sets of statements about the future environmental threats and opportunities are made. Strategists formulate contingency strategies to deal with each separate scenario of future environment.

A systematic approach is needed in order to effectively bring the impact of key threats and opportunities to management's attention. One such approach is called an environmental threat and opportunity profile (ETOP).[7] ETOP is a document that summarizes the key opportunities and threats and their impact on an MNC.

In Chapter 8, we discussed the broad environmental factors facing an MNC. Remember that the MNC's environment consists of a number of environmental units. One component is the domestic environment. It is also possible that the MNC has a number of SBUs in its domestic market. For example, as you will recall from Chapter 13, Pepsico, in addition to its international SBUs, owns companies such as Frito-Lay in the U.S. market. As another example, Coca-Cola Corporation owns Columbia Pictures, Minute Maid, and a number of other subsidiaries in its home country, the United States. The foreign environment consists of separate but interactive regional and national environments also, that is, SBUs in foreign countries. The final component is the international environment, which includes the unique concerns involved in operating across national borders. The international environment consists of regional and national regulations and organizations that govern international business activities. In other words, the MNC has to operate in a number of environments. As a result, for the MNC, environmental assessment consists of a number of distinct and related steps that involve assessing separate environments as well as assessing their interaction.

In summary, for a diversified MNC a number of ETOPs should be developed, one for the entire corporation and one for each distinct SBU.

## MNC ORGANIZATIONAL ANALYSIS

With a strategic profile of the MNC's environment complete (a compilation of different SBU environments), the analytical spotlight should be turned on the firm's internal conditions. In this phase, we look at those factors that strategists need to analyze and examine to determine the MNC's (and its SBU's) relative internal strengths and weaknesses. These strengths and weaknesses are used to face the opportunities and threats from the environment.

An MNC should be able to determine the competitive advantages (relative strengths) that it has over competitors in specific markets and countries. The firm should lead with these relative strengths in the implementation of its strategies. For example, an MNC that has one or more competitive advantages in proprietary product lines, product design, brand names, advertising, distribution, or production costs in different markets and nations should emphasize these strengths in determining its global strategy. This is because it is usually more important to lead with strengths than to allocate resources to overcome weaknesses.[8]

The primary issues in organizational analysis at the business (SBU) level include the following:

1. Identification and evaluation of each SBU's relative internal strengths and weaknesses.
2. Assessment of each SBU's competitive market position, that is, whether or not it is gaining or losing ground, and why.
3. Appraisal of how well the present business-level and functional-level strategies are working, and why.
4. Recognition of any special strategic issues and problems that are unique to the MNC and the SBUs under consideration.

These factors determine what business strategy has the best "goodness-of-fit" with the firm's overall situation, that is, what business strategy best fits its internal and external conditions. The box on page 439 is a checklist of functional area factors to be used in organizational analysis of SBUs and the entire MNC.

## Sources of Internal Information

The management information system (MIS) is used as the internal information source. Such information can be cross-examined. This information originates from the domestic and foreign subsidiaries and from MNC employees. Financial data, market information (such as figures on sales and market share), production figures (including plant and equipment utilization and delays), labor quality and turnover data, and training and development requirements can be obtained through internal sources.

As we explained earlier, organizational analysis is parallel and similar to environmental assessment. The main difference is that in organizational analysis the focus is on relative internal strengths and weaknesses rather than on external opportunities and threats. The strategist's aim is to seek a statement of competitive advantages—relative strengths and weaknesses—of each SBU and the entire MNC. One systematic approach to the development of such a statement is called the strategic advantage profile (SAP).[9] The SAP is a document that contains key relative strengths and weaknesses for an MNC.

# Example of Organizational Analysis for Overseas Subsidiaries and the Entire MNC

**A. Analysis of Profitability**

1. Past trends in profits, rate of return on invested capital, growth in profits, and earnings per share.

2. Evaluation of profitability in terms of objectives established and in terms of companywide standards.

3. Reasons for differences in profitability among various units.

**B. Marketing**

1. Achievement of past sales and market penetration objectives.

2. If there were no past objectives, how has company done in terms of growth of sales and share of market in major products in relation to growth of national and regional markets?

3. Effectiveness in developing markets, in marketing new products, and in adapting product mix to national and regional markets.

4. Effectiveness of distribution, selling, advertising, and pricing strategies.

5. Evaluation of strengths and weaknesses of marketing organization and its strategies.

6. Recommendations for improvement.

**C. Accounting/Finance**

1. Effectiveness of company in long-term and short-term budgeting.

2. Effectiveness in balancing capital investment requirements from internal sources (including earnings from parent company and from local sources), considering priorities of investments and costs of funds in the home country and in foreign countries.

3. Return on investments in relation to cost of capital.

4. Effectiveness in protection of capital, considering exchange risk fluctuations, inflation, and other problems.

5. Evaluation of strengths and weaknesses of financial management.

6. Recommendations for improvement.

**D. Production/Operations Management**

1. Effectiveness in supplying markets from plants located in the home country and in other countries.

2. Evaluation of production efficiency on the basis of costs, productivity, scale of operation, and products handled at all plants.

3. Effectiveness of management in cost reductions and quality control.

4. Evaluation of inventory levels and inventory policies to supply various national and regional markets.

5. Recommendations for improvement.

**E. Personnel, Executive Development, and Labor Relations**
1. Effectiveness of management development, especially training of nationals of country for positions of high responsibility.

2. Effectiveness of training and recruitment of engineers, technicians and other personnel, especially nationals of country.

3. Effectiveness of labor relations, especially of adapting to dealings with unions in various countries.

4. Recommendations for improvement.

**F. Evaluation of Overall Effectiveness of Management**
1. Overall evaluation of company's past strategies and policies.

2. Effectiveness of management in carrying out past policies, strategies, and major programs.

3. Evaluation of organizational structure and recommendations for changes.

4. Recommendations for changes in strategies and policies.

5. Ways of strengthening company management throughout the enterprise.

**G. Research and Development (R&D)**
1. The nature and depth of the company's R&D activities.

2. The return on investment from R&D activities.

3. Significant new products or improvements in products or in manufacturing processes that have resulted from R&D activities.

**H. Past Objectives and Strategies**
1. Effectiveness in the formulation and achievement of major objectives.

2. Effectiveness in the formulation and implementation of past strategies.

**I. Overall Corporate Factors**
1. Corporate reputation, image, and relationship with its stakeholders (customers, communities, creditors, governments, stockholders, etc.).

# GLOBAL OBJECTIVE FORMULATION

The formulation of specific objectives for an MNC starts after the completion of the environmental assessment and the organizational analysis. As a result of the previous steps in the global strategic management process, the MNC strategists possess a clear understanding of the present and the probable future conditions in the environment. Strategic objectives should reflect the competitive strengths and weaknesses of the MNC. Specific objectives are not established in a vacuum. They cannot precede the strategic assessment process. Strategic objectives grow out of the thinking and the analysis that MNC strategists put into the strategy formulation process.

## Objective Formulation Process

Objectives are formulated for each level—corporate, SBU, and functional—of an MNC by the strategic decision makers at that level. The choices of objectives are affected by a number of factors, which are discussed subsequently.

**The Forces in the Environment**   The first factor influencing the formulation of objectives involves the realities of the external environment and the external power relationships. The realities of the environment manifest themselves in the environmental assessment process. External power relationships refer to the demands, claims, and expectations of external stakeholders. These realities and external power relationships act as constraints on objectives.

For example, the maximization of a sales objective may need modification because of government antitrust regulations or laws against excess profits, and so on. Another reason for modification may be due to high wage contracts with labor unions, leading to higher costs and resulting in higher prices and lower sales. Usually, executives do not consider all stakeholder claims simultaneously. For example, if some minimum level of profit is met to satisfy the shareholder claims, then the strategists move on to the claims of the next group of stakeholders.

**Competitor Actions**   The anticipated and the actual behavior of competitors in global markets are key considerations in formulating strategic objectives. Strategic objectives must be achieved in light of counterstrategies by competitive firms. Indeed, competition lies at the very heart of all business strategies. Effective global strategic management, however, seeks to initiate action and to minimize the need to make unexpected adjustments and reactions to the actions of competitors.

**The Realities of MNC Resources and Power Relationships**   It is clear that the financially stronger and more profitable MNCs can command more resources than smaller and poorer companies. And firms with stronger resource positions are more capable of facing environmental threats and of taking advantage of opportunities.

Another influential factor in objective formulation is the nature of the internal power relationships. For example, if there is a difference of opinion on the choice of an objective or on the trade-offs among different objectives, power relationships help to settle the difference. When a person or a coalition of people has a dominant power position, its opinions emerge from the process as the dominant ones. If a balanced power relationship exists, then a compromise solution may evolve and no opinion will be dominant.

**The Value Systems and Goals of the Top Management and the MNC Strategists** Personal value systems and individual goals are formed from one's cultural background, education, past experiences, and insights gained on the job. These values and goals are a set of philosophies about what is desirable and good, or what is undesirable and bad. These values influence the perceived advantages and disadvantages of certain strategic actions and the choice of objectives. An MNC strategic group consists of people from many cultures with varying value systems and goals. As a result, the effect of these individual factors is stronger on the objective formulation process, and on the choice of corporate and SBU objectives, in a large, diversified MNC. An example of the influence of personal values and attitude took place at Toyota Motor Corporation, the leading Japanese automobile manufacturer. Because of their spectacular performance, Toyota's top management was rather reluctant to develop aggressive strategies in three essential areas: internationalization, advanced technology development, and diversification. However, in the mid-1980s the managers intelligently changed their attitudes toward risk regarding the trade-off between the cost of entry and the opportunity cost of nonentry. It seems that they gained an awareness that, in today's turbulent global environment, staying in the traditional product markets will be much riskier than entry into new product markets. As a result, Toyota's top management seems to be increasingly entrepreneurial in their strategic thinking.[10]

**Past Objectives, Strategies, and the Development Track of the MNC** Objective formulation does not start from scratch. Most objectives are based on past objectives and the experience gained in attaining—or failing to attain—them. Completely new objectives are seldom formulated. Instead, strategists consider incremental changes from the present set of objectives, given the current and forecasted environment and the current claims of conflicting groups. Unless a major change or crisis occurs, past objectives will not be altered drastically. As with a large ship that requires time to change course, it takes time to make major changes in the direction of a large MNC. Therefore, objectives and strategies to accomplish these changes are influenced by past objectives and how well they were attained.

In summary, the formulation of the corporate and other objectives, and of the corresponding global and other strategies, is influenced by a number of factors. Environmental conditions, competitor actions, the stakeholders' power relationships, and the MNC's past performances shape the objectives that the MNC pursues. A firm's top management tends to bargain with different outside coalitions and forms objectives that can minimally satisfy their conflicting demands. What an MNC can do and attempts to achieve are also influenced by its internal resource capabilities and the power relationships among potential coalitions inside the firm, as well as by the personal values and aspirations of the decision makers. Finally, the choice of present strategies is greatly influenced by past objectives, strategies, and the track record of the MNC. Usually, objectives evolve incrementally to reflect all these factors.

## Types and Characteristics of Objectives

The terms "goal" and "objective" are sometimes used synonymously. We consider **goals** to be more fundamental, of longer term, and more open-ended than objectives. **Objectives** are long-term targets that are necessary, but not sufficient, for the achievement of goals. By virtue of this distinction, goals are not fully achievable because they are unbounded. The profit maximization goal is never completely possible because more profitable alternatives probably exist that have not been known and pursued. The survival goal can never be achieved because an end comes to all things—bankruptcy and total failure are always possibilities. Objectives are achievable within a predesignated time period. In other words, objectives are milestones in the never-ending pursuit of goals.

An objective should have four components: (1) the goal sought, (2) a yardstick for measuring progress, (3) a target to be achieved, (4) a time frame to reach the target. Table 14.2 shows some typical business objectives. Notice that they all possess these four components.

To be useful, objectives and their components should be stated as specifically and precisely as possible. Components should be selected thoughtfully. For example, to eliminate the impact of inflation, the MNC might measure growth in constant dollars or units, rather than current dollars. Objectives are usually stated as a simple sentence establishing a single, clear, unambiguous, quantifiable, and time-phased future target. For example:

Increase share of the world market to 5 percent within three years.

Increase sales to $1 billion in five years.

Achieve a net profit of 10 percent within two years.

Achieve a 10 percent return on investment within four years.

The MNC should formulate objectives on corporate, SBU, and functional levels. In a well-run MNC, the subsidiary-level objectives should conform to the corporate objectives. Functional-level objectives should also be consistent with those of the corresponding business-level objectives. SBU executives are expected to translate broad corporate objectives into more narrow business-level

Table 14.2  SOME TYPICAL BUSINESS OBJECTIVES

| Possible Attributes | Possible Indices | Targets and Time Frame | | |
|---|---|---|---|---|
| | | Year One | Year Two | Year Three |
| Growth | $ Sales | $100 mil | 120 mil | 140 mil |
| | Unit sales | X units | 1.10 X units | 1.20 X units |
| Efficiency | $ Profits | 10 mil | 12 mil | 15 mil |
| | Profits/sales | .10 | .10 | .11 |
| Utilization | ROI | .15 | .15 | .16 |
| of resources | ROE | .25 | .26 | .27 |
| Contribution to | Dividends | $1.00/share | $1.10/share | $1.30/share |
| owners | Eps | $2.00/share | $2.40/share | $2.80/share |
| Contribution to | Price | Equal or better | Equal or better | Equal or better |
| customers | Quality | than competition | than competition | than competition |
| | Reliability | | | |
| Contributions to | Wage rate | $3.50/hour | $3.75/hour | $4.00/hour |
| employees | Employment stability | <5% turnover | <4% turnover | <4% turnover |
| Contributions to | Taxes paid | $10 mil | $12 mil | $16 mil |
| society | Scholarships | $100,000 | $120,000 | $120,000 |
| | awarded etc. | | | |

*Source:* Adapted from C. W. Hofer, "A Conceptual Scheme for Formulating a Total Business Strategy" (Dover, Mass.: Lord Publishing Company, BP 0041), p. 2. Copyright © 1976 by Charles W. Hofer. Used by permission.

objectives. The same is true of functional area managers. Lower-level objectives should always agree with higher-level objectives.

When individual corporate objectives are decided on, MNC executives should complete the following steps:

1. Check whether the selected objectives are consistent with each other. Can they be achieved simultaneously as well as individually? If simultaneous achievement is not possible, objectives need to be modified so they can be achieved simultaneously.
2. Rank the objectives to establish priorities.
3. Break each objective down into subobjectives applicable to different SBUs.
4. Check each set of internally consistent objectives and priorities against current corporate and business strategies, environmental conditions, and organizational capabilities to see whether or not they are indeed achievable and realistic. If they seem unachievable, either new strategies must be formulated or the objectives need modification.

This process should be repeated at all levels of the organization. This results in a hierarchy of objectives called the *MNC goal structure.*

## Strategic Objective

By now, it is apparent that at each level of the MNC (corporate, SBU, and functional) a set of objectives is formulated and pursued. To be useful, however, these objectives need to be ranked to establish priorities at each level. The objective ranked number one at each organizational level is called the **strategic objective**. Therefore, the strategic objective at each level is the number one priority pursued at that organizational level. The global strategic objective is the number one priority for the overall MNC. The strategic objective for a specific SBU is the most important target for that strategic business unit.

Strategic objectives at different levels are normally established in terms of profit, sales, return on investment (or equity), market share efficiency and productivity, employee relations, and social responsibility. Market share is pursued as an overall goal only if the MNC is in one business and is not diversified into a number of different businesses. If a firm is in different businesses, market share cannot be aggregated to form a meaningful target. The selection of one objective as strategic is not intended to suggest that the other objectives are unimportant. The purpose of selecting one strategic objective for each organizational level is to identify the objective that is most important. As we mentioned in the previous section, the process of ranking objectives at all levels of an MNC leads to a hierarchy of objectives that is called the MNC goal structure.

# GLOBAL STRATEGY: ALTERNATIVE GENERATION AND CHOICE

**Global strategy** is a statement of the fundamental means an MNC will use, subject to a set of environmental constraints and its resource capabilities, to achieve its objectives. The formulation of a global strategy and its components assures the MNC's effectiveness and efficiency. In a manner similar to the objective formulation process, the MNC should formulate strategies for the achievement of objectives at different organizational levels, that is, at the corporate, the SBU, and the functional levels. In this section we will discuss the process of generating alternative strategies at the corporate and SBU levels. The process of formulating functional-level strategies will be discussed later in this chapter, in the section Global Strategy Implemtation.

When the assessment of environmental factors relevant to each SBU is combined with the corresponding organizational analysis, the MNC can generally pinpoint SBUs with the most promising future. However, many diversified MNCs use sophisticated portfolio approaches to determine priorities for the allocation of resources among alternative businesses and SBUs at the corporate level. As was discussed in Chapter 13, global corporate strategy focuses on how different businesses and markets in which an MNC competes may be integrated into an effective portfolio.* Corporate-level strategists in diversified MNCs must consider a number of questions: What businesses and markets are we

---

*A portfolio is the collection of businesses and SBUs that an MNC owns.

involved in? Should we allocate additional resources to businesses and markets with high future growth potential? Is there enough cash flow generated by our present businesses and markets to meet our future investment opportunities? What additional businesses and markets should we seek? Are we overcommitted to a specific business or market? Are we too involved in nations with high political and financial risk? Should we reduce our allocated resources or withdraw from these businesses, countries, or markets?

*MNC global portfolio strategy* deals with resource allocations that can change to assure a balance of risk and business characteristics across SBUs considered collectively. Considering various SBUs collectively, rather than as isolated units, opens up new opportunities. For example, an acquisition or entry into a new market may seem too risky when considered separately, but the same risky strategic move may be desirable when balanced against the MNC's other conservatively positioned businesses. As another example, a new high-debt venture may be reasonable for a low-debt MNC.

Global portfolio strategy is practiced by most large, diversified MNCs at the corporate level. One such company is Nestlé, the Swiss-based MNC. Nestlé identifies its various products in 17 categories, such as cosmetics, soups, and pharmaceuticals. These diverse products are sold in over 55 different national territories.

An easy way to visualize corporate portfolio strategy is the use of a so-called **portfolio matrix**. Corporate strategists utilize a number of different portfolio matrices. **The Boston Consulting Group (BCG) matrix** is the simplest of these matrices.* Figure 14.2 depicts a typical BCG matrix.

As shown in Figure 14.2, each SBU is placed in the BCG matrix according to the growth rate of the industry in which it competes and its relative competitive position, as measured by the SBU's market share in that industry. Each SBU is shown by a circle. The size of the circle is proportional to the size of the business involved, as measured by total industry sales.

"Stars" are located in the upper left quadrant of the matrix. These represent businesses that are rapidly growing and are more or less self-sufficient regarding cash flow. They represent the best profit and growth potential for an MNC.

The lower left quadrant represents **"cash cows."** They are characterized by low growth and high market share. They are usually entrenched, having superior market position and low costs because they have high sales volume and require low amounts of investment funds. In other words, they are established businesses that generate profits beyond their own investment requirements. The surplus cash flow from these SBUs can be reinvested elsewhere, in those SBUs with high investment needs, that is, in the "stars" or "question marks."

Businesses plotted in the lower right quadrant are called **"dogs."** They are

---

*The interested reader is referred to B. Hedley, "Strategy and the Business Portfolio," *Long Range Planning,* vol. 10 (February 1977), pp. 9–15; C. W. Hofer and D. E. Schendel, *Strategy Formulation: Analytical Concepts.* St. Paul, Minn.: West Publishing, 1978; and J. C. Leontiades, *Multinational Corporate Strategy: Planning for World Markets.* Lexington, Mass.: Lexington Books, 1985.

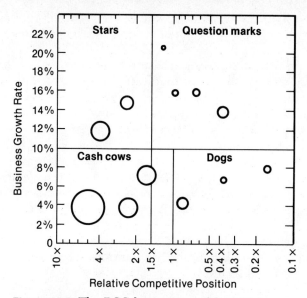

**Figure 14.2** The BCG business portfolio matrix

*Source:* Reprinted with permission from *Journal of Long-Range Planning,* B. Hedley, "Strategy and the 'Business Portfolio'," p. 12, copyright 1977, Pergamon Press.

not very profitable because of the relatively high cost and weak competitive position. At times, "dogs" may not even generate enough cash to keep their existing weak positions. Companies should sell such businesses. MNCs, however, may decide to keep these businesses for a number of reasons. For example, a "dog" may complement the other businesses a firm is in, or it may represent a vital link in the vertical integration of the company's operations. "Dogs" may be essential to maintain goodwill, or they may have potential for a turnaround and fixing, or they may be used as tax write-offs.

"**Question marks,**" "wild cats," or "problem children" are located in the upper right quadrant. They are companies that need the most attention, have high cash needs because of the low cash generation, and have high investment requirements because of the rapid growth. Thus, they are usually in the worst cash flow position of all four business types. There are two possibilities for "question marks"—either to become a star or to become a divested dog.

As mentioned earlier, after an MNC's current portfolio position is depicted on a grid, such as the BCG matrix, the future position should be projected on a new matrix. Combining these two matrices—present and projected—helps to describe the scope and the competitive advantage components of global strategy, as well as identifying some of the major strategic issues an MNC faces. In addition, some of the basic characteristics of each SBU's strategy are isolated by using the matrices.

If the decision is made to change the balance of a firm's portfolio, a redistribution of corporate resources among the SBUs is required. This can involve both divesting present businesses and adding new ones. Of course, there are good reasons for the present location of different SBUs. Realities concerning each SBU situation should be realized. There are careers, historical connections, and traditions, and other less easily transferable resources attached to each business. Larger scale investments or divestitures require careful examination. Time is also needed for engaging or disengaging from a national location. Nevertheless, certain locational changes can be desirable in order to take advantage of new opportunities or to face increasing threats.

It should be kept in mind that corporate-level portfolio decisions are complex by nature. These decisions should not be based solely on market and competitive factors. Each business in the portfolio is affected by a host of other environmental factors, especially those factors in the remote environment. National characteristics in the economic conditions, in the legal and political climate, in the sociocultural makeup, and in other factors should influence the MNC's portfolio decisions. Many firms, therefore, use multiple portfolio approaches that are based on different SBU attributes in order to formulate a global corporate portfolio strategy.

## Global Versus National Competitive Strategies

A successful MNC strategy is built upon competitive advantages that are not easily duplicated by other competitors. Today, the competition for goods, services, and ideas pays no heed to national borders or the old geopolitical divisions of North and South, or East and West.[11]

As industries become more global, strategists are faced with two quite different orientations toward competitive strategy, national or global.* **National (SBU) strategies** are those that are aimed at the development of competitive advantages that are based on a firm's existence and operations in a certain national environment. In addition, the MNC's competitive performance is measured on a nation-by-nation basis. For example, market share is measured on a national basis.[12]

**Global competitive strategies** are based on an international perception of the company's environment and capabilities. The MNC that adopts a global strategic approach seeks to develop international competitive strengths that are not available to purely domestic firms or other MNCs with only a national orientation. The MNC that pursues a global strategy perceives its key opportunities and threats on a worldwide basis. Such an MNC mobilizes its resources internationally toward these globally defined opportunities and threats, though this may involve only a limited number of countries. We need to point out that an MNC may pursue a global strategy in some parts of their

---

*Adapted from James Leontiades, "Going Global—Global Strategies vs. National Strategies," *Long Range Planning*, vol. 19, no. 6 (December 1986), pp. 96–104; and by the same author, *Multinational Corporate Strategy: Planning for World Markets* (Lexington, Mass.: Lexington Books, 1985), pp. 51–67.

operations and may adopt a more national competitive strategy in other parts of the world.

Figure 14.3 specifies four generic international competitive strategies, which are classified according to geographic scope and the MNC's market share objective. It can be seen that there are two types of global strategies: global high share strategies and global niche strategies. There are also two types of national strategies: national high share strategies and national niche strategies.[13] We will cover these generic strategies in the following sections.

## Global Competitive Strategies

There are two types of global competitive strategies that the MNC can pursue: (1) global high share strategies and (2) global niche strategies.

**Global High Share Strategies**   Many giant MNCs follow a global high share strategy, for example, IBM, SKF, Dow Chemical, Citicorp, and Sony. These MNCs consider themselves as part of a global industry, and, as a result, their strategic approach reflects this global interpretation. The MNC that pursues a global high share strategy identifies high-volume segments in its global mar-

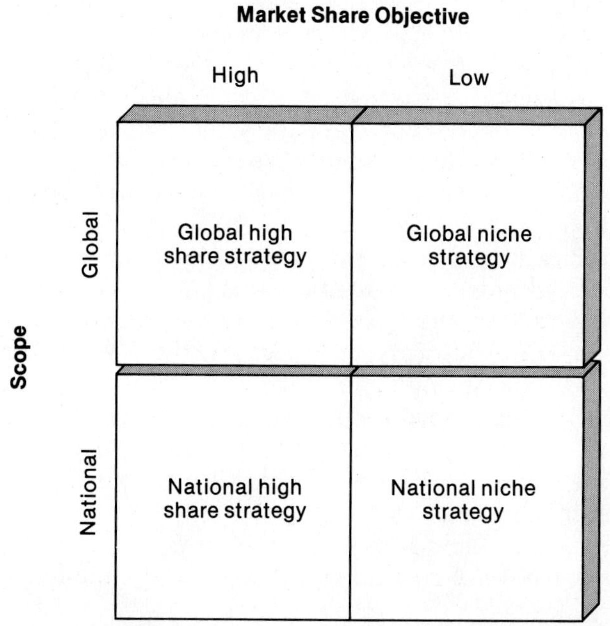

**Market Share Objective**

|  | High | Low |
|---|---|---|
| **Global** | Global high share strategy | Global niche strategy |
| **National** | National high share strategy | National niche strategy |

Scope

**Figure 14.3** Four generic international competitive strategies

*Source:* Reprinted by permission of the publisher from MULTINATIONAL CORPORATE STRATEGY by James C. Leontiades (Lexington, Mass.: Lexington Books, D. C. Heath and Company, copyright 1985, D. C. Heath and Company).

ket. Product, pricing, promotion, distribution, and other elements of the marketing strategy are geared toward these high-volume global market segments. Although research and development (R & D) expenditures are high in absolute terms, they are often low in terms of the percentage of sales as compared with industry standards. For example, IBM spends over $2 billion annually on R & D. However, this is only about 6 percent of IBM's global sales volumes, which is well below the industry average spent on R & D.

The basic philosophy of global strategies is the worldwide coordination of an MNC's resources behind its global objectives. As a result of this global orientation, the MNC may gain several competitive advantages: (1) the attainment of lower costs, which result from economies of scale and from experience, due to their high worldwide production volume; (2) the provision of a global service to their customers, for example, banks such as Citicorp, through their network of branches, can provide worldwide services to their clients; (3) the ability to have international sourcing, providing for the worldwide acquisition of inexpensive raw materials and labor; (4) the ability to transfer experience across national borders; (5) the ability to project an international worldwide corporate image, for example, IBM's worldwide reputation and name recognition; (6) the ability to focus on global resources; and (7) the maintenance of a global portfolio of SBUs.

**Global Niche Strategies**   Not all MNCs have the resources to pursue a global high share strategy. For many companies, especially small ones, the motive for going international is to gain one or more of the global competitive advantages we just discussed through specialization. As a result of specialization, a firm avoids head-on competition with companies that pursue global high share strategies. Global specialization is usually through a product or service. Specialization may also be based on a technology, a stage of the product life cycle, a market segment, a stage of production, or other particular activities.

An example of a firm that pursues a global niche strategy is Wartsila, a Finnish ship-building company. At the time that larger European and Japanese ship builders competed in the high-volume dry cargo ships and oil tankers, Wartsila had been successfully serving a market niche in building luxury cruise ships and ice breakers. Enjoying smaller size flexibility, Wartsila adapts quickly to customer needs in this specialized segment, which has been unattractive to larger MNCs.

Other firms pursuing a niche in the global market include Ferranti, an electronics firm that produces gate-array integrated circuits; BMW, which competes in a global segment of the motorcycle market; and Schlumberger, which provides a variety of specialized services to the oil and computer industries.

Another example is AT & T. AT & T, in its attempt to go global, is pursuing a number of global niches with the formation of alliances with foreign companies, such as the Italian firm Olivetti.

## National Competitive Strategies

There are two types of national competitive strategies that an MNC can pursue: (1) national high share strategies and (2) national niche strategies.

**National High Share Strategies**   MNCs that pursue national high share strategies target high national market share through the use of nationally based competitive advantages. These firms' marketing and production strategies are designed to achieve high volume and low cost relative to other national competitors. The major disadvantage of a national high share strategy is its vulnerability with regard to the greater economies of scale and volume that characterize global strategies.

A firm pursuing a national high share strategy usually depends on national entry "barriers" to counter global competitors. As we discussed in Chapter 4, a "barrier" is anything that obstructs the freedom of an MNC to transfer and coordinate resources across national borders. Tariffs, quotas, subsidies, and other preferential laws that favor national competitors (both domestic and foreign owned) are examples of such barriers. Other barriers may include transportation and communication impediments and institutional and taste preferences in the host countries that would deter foreign MNCs.

For example, ICL, a British computer firm, was able to effectively use national barriers, such as direct government assistance and preferential treatment, to obtain British government contracts. These barriers provided competitive advantages against other global competitors such as IBM. Later, as a result of diminishing barriers and rapid technological change, ICL had to abandon its national high share strategy and shift to a global niche strategy by forming alliances with Fujitsu, Mitel, and other foreign computer manufacturers. The result was a move into the specialized and the small end of the computer product business.

**National Niche Strategies**   Firms that pursue national niche strategies capitalize on the advantages of specialization on a national basis to help defend their market against both national and global competitors. The size of the target market for a firm pursuing this kind of strategy is below the threshold size that is usually attractive to larger companies. In this type of strategy, as is similar in the national high market share strategies, national entry barriers are used to defend against global competitors.

Examples of companies that pursue a national niche strategy can be found in industries dominated by unique national taste preferences for certain products. Food, clothing, and small-scale handicrafts are among these industries.

As we pointed out earlier, large MNCs may use a combination of these generic strategies. In addition, as a firm increases its international involvement, it may have to pursue a variety of these strategies. The evolution of American Express is a case in point. American Express began as a national freight company. In its path toward going international, American Express developed a niche in specialized financial services based on its travelers' checks. Since then, American Express has implemented a series of global niche strategies in credit cards, in travel agencies, and in investment banking.

## Business-level Strategy

As we explained in Chapter 13, at the business level or SBU level, strategy focuses on how to compete in a particular industry, product or service line, or geographic location. Therefore, the most important components of business strategy are the SBU's distinctive competencies and competitive advantages. Business strategy also emphasizes the integration of different functional areas within the SBU.*

**Strategic Choice at the SBU or Business Level**   Strategic choice at the SBU level is the decision process that selects from among the alternative strategies the strategy that will meet the SBU objectives best and, in the process, will contribute the most to the MNC's global objectives. This process consists of selecting criteria, evaluating all the alternatives against these criteria, and making the final choice. After the choice is made, it needs to be submitted to the MNC corporate headquarters for approval and authorization.

**Factors Influencing Strategic Choice**   There are five factors that influence the strategic choice decisions:

1. Perceptions of the degree of the MNC's dependence on its environment;
2. Strategists' attitudes toward risk, values, and decision-making styles;
3. The past strategies of the MNC and its SBUs;
4. The MNC's internal power relationships and culture, organizational structure, and resource capabilities;
5. The lower-level managers' cooperation and attitudes.

Lower-level managers play an important role in global strategic management. Global strategic management is not a top to bottom process; that is, decisions are not made by top management alone. Rather, it is both a bottom to top and top to bottom process; that is, information is obtained from the lower echelons of the organization, and strategic decisions are made at top. Strategic decisions are then communicated and delegated to lower-level managers for implementation. Some companies involve their middle managers in the strategy formulation process. Information obtained by the strategists goes through a filtering process by lower-level managers. Some information may never reach top management. In addition to this filtering process, in some countries (such

---

*For a more extended discussion of this topic, see Michael E. Porter, "How Competitive Forces Shape Strategy," *Harvard Business Review,* vol. 59, no. 2 (March/April 1979) pp. 137–145; and Michael E. Porter, *Competitive Strategy: Techniques for Analyzing Industries and Businesses* (New York: Free Press, 1980), Chaps. 1, 3, 8, 13, and App. B.

as some European countries), workers' councils may influence the strategic choice. For example, at Volvo, the Swedish automaker, the decision to open a plant in the United States was influenced by its workers' demands. The workers' council demanded that no plants be closed in Sweden. As a result, Volvo did not open a new plant in the United States. Similarly, Volkswagen's strategic choices in the redistribution of its resources have usually been influenced by German workers' councils.

The choice of a strategy is not a routine or easy decision. Like other decisions, it is made in the context of the decision situation and is influenced by the decision makers themselves.

## GLOBAL STRATEGY IMPLEMENTATION

At the end of the strategic choice phase, the MNC knows how it wants to achieve its objectives. Now it is time to implement the strategies and translate strategic thought into strategic action. The first step in the implementation phase is the formulation of the short-term, that is, the annual or the semiannual, objectives. In addition, functional-area strategies and policies need to be formulated to achieve these objectives and to guide the operational decision making. The second step includes the allocation of the MNC's resources, that is, its capital, human resources, technology, and so forth among the different SBUs and functions. The third step is the designing of an organizational structure that is suitable for the implementation of the global strategy that the MNC has selected. The final step is the assignment of key leaders and managers to direct the implementation of the strategy; this process is called human resource management. We proceed with a brief discussion of these implementation steps.

### Short-term Objectives

Short-term objectives are specific targets established for each functional area, department, and unit within each SBU. The process of short-term objective formulation is similar to the process of the objective formulation we discussed earlier. As we explained in Chapter 13, short-term objectives have shorter time horizons and are more specific and more limited in scope than long-term objectives. They are designed to improve the efficiency of operations and are action oriented. One important difference between long-term and short-term objectives is the measurement characteristic of each. While both types of objectives are quantifiable, long-term objectives are measurable in broad, relative terms; for example, a long-term objective might be to achieve a 20 percent market share within three years. Short-term or annual objectives are established in absolute terms, and are directly traceable to the performance of the organization subunit to which they correspond. For example, a short-term or annual objective might be to increase the proportion of total sales through direct distribution or retail stores to 90 percent of sales within one year.

## Functional-level Strategies and Policies

Strategies and policies should be formulated and implemented in the functional areas of accounting and finance, marketing, personnel, production and operations, R & D, and so forth. These functional area strategies should be consistent with the business-level objectives and strategies.

Functional-level strategies are also called policies. **Policies** operationalize business strategy by organizing and activating specific methods for the implementation of the business strategy in daily business activities. They translate strategic thought, that is, business strategy, into action. These policies identify and coordinate actions to be taken in different areas that support the SBU's strategies and improve the likelihood of achieving the MNC's objectives. Policies are guidelines to action that bridge business strategy with the implementation process.

Figure 14.4 depicts the importance of functional policies in operationalizing corporate-level and business-level strategy for the General Cinema Corporation. It can be seen that General Cinema's corporate strategy defines the company's general posture in the broad economy. The business strategy establishes the competitive positioning of the movie theaters in the U.S. domestic market. More specific functional strategies are formulated to successfully implement and operationalize business strategy. These functional strategies provide specific, short-term guidance to the operating executives of the firm.

In addition to the functional areas illustrated in Figure 14.4, other policies in other functional areas, such as personnel, are needed. Figure 14.4 shows the differences among the levels of strategy, and it also shows the logical flow from corporate strategy to functional strategy.

## Resource Allocation

MNCs have three kinds of resources available to them: people, money, and fixed assets. Streamlined strategy implementation is achieved when these resources are allocated without any superfluity or waste. For example, allocation of excessive cash over and beyond what competent managers can intelligently use leads to wasted resources. On the other hand, when too many managers are allocated with less than sufficient funds, they will engage in exhausting and time-wasting maneuvers over the allocation of limited funds.

Of the three resources, management talents should be allocated first on the basis of available fixed assets (plant, machinery, technology, process and product know-how, and so forth). These talented people can then develop creative ideas, business-level and functional-level strategies to take advantage of their environment. Money should then be allocated to these specific ideas, projects, and strategies that have been formulated by individual managers.

Balance should exist not only among these three types of resources, but also among the different ideas, projects, SBUs, and functional areas within each SBU. Remember that only good strategists can generate good ideas and only good managers can execute good strategies. Thus, each organizational unit is in need of good people for proper strategy formulation and implemen-

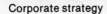

## Corporate strategy

15-20 percent annual growth through existing businesses and carefully selected diversification into leisure-oriented, consumer-oriented product/service businesses to absorb increasing cash flow from theater and soft-drink bottling operations

Business strategy

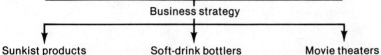

| Sunkist products | Soft-drink bottlers | Movie theaters |

## Concentration and market development selective

Maintain and selectively expand leading nationwide position in the movie exhibition industry to provide positive cash flow for corporate diversification opportunities

## Functional strategies: Marketing

Seek only first-run films by outbidding competition in each local market; provide primarily family-oriented movies and maintain an admission price only slightly above local competition

Offer concurrent movies of varying rating (P,PG, R) at multiscreen locations to attract different audiences at the same location

## Functional strategies: Operations

Use multiscreen facilities with minimal maintenance requirements and a joint service area to serve each minitheater

Locate in popular regional shopping centers; selectively dominate theater locations in local markets to allow flexibility across areas in bidding for first-run films

## Functional strategies: Financial

Use lease or sales and leaseback arrangements of each theater to maximize cash flow for corporate expansion; seek profitability through volume not higher ticket prices

Selectively underwrite the production of quality films to insure an adequate supply of first-run movies

**Figure 14.4** Role of functiional strategies at General Cinema Corporation

*Source:* John A. Pearce II and Richard B. Robinson. *Formulation and Implementation of Competitive Strategy.* 3rd ed. (Homewood, Ill.: Irwin, 1988), p. 335.

tation. Other resources are also vital in the implementation of the generated strategies. MNCs allocate and shift critical resources among SBUs over a long time horizon with particular corporate objectives in mind. This process was discussed as being part of the global portfolio strategy approach. On the SBU level, these SBU-level companies use different approaches to allocate resources among their different functional areas, units, ideas, and projects. At this SBU level, allocation of funds is usually in the form of a budgeting process. The question is how much resources should be allocated to each functional area, department, unit, idea, and project? Should the SBU increase its production capacity or invest more in the improvement of the management techniques and staff training? With limited resources, SBUs may not be in a position to do both. Increases across the board may not be possible or desirable. This dilemma calls for a resource allocation decision. SBU management should use the guidelines from the MNC executives to decide which function or operation has the highest priority in terms of the allocation of assets, funds, and people.

Figure 14.5 shows a visual analogy of the resource allocation process. Consider an invisible storage tank suspended above one SBU. The company's strategists must decide how to allocate, say, the $215 million content of this tank. They should decide which stopcocks to open and how far to open them in order to provide the greatest contribution to the SBU, and thus to the overall corporation.

In practice, a large company with huge investment funds tends to be bureaucratic in its allocation decisions, without regard to the overall balance of a company's business portfolio. Once every five to 10 years, however, the question of resource allocation, that is, the amount of money to devote to each area, is reexamined closely. This thorough reevaluation of the distribution of resources, without clinging to the past criteria used for such allocations, is similar to the so-called *zero-based budgeting* process at the SBU and functional levels. Past inadequacies and bottlenecks should be recognized on a total company basis, as should the potential contributions to the long-term effectiveness, efficiency, profit, and growth of the MNC.

## Organizational Structure

Accomplishment of strategic objectives and purposes requires organization. The important consideration in strategy implementation is the formulation of a planned organizational structure. Activities, responsibilities, and interrelationships consistent with the needs of strategy should be deliberately organized. The unplanned evolution of an organizational structure prevents the essential coordination between structure and strategy from developing. This lack of coordination is likely to lead to inefficiencies, misdirections, miscommunications, and fragmented efforts.

Structure is a means to an end, not an end in itself. It is a tool for managing the size and the diversity of operations to enhance the success of strategies. The

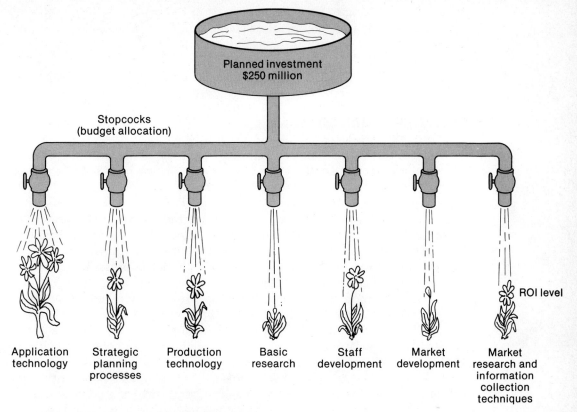

**Figure 14.5** Overall view of funds allocation

*Source:* Kenichi Ohmae, *The Mind of the Strategist: Business Planning for Competitive Advantage* (New York: Penguin Books, 1982), p. 178.

question of how to structure the MNC so it can effectively implement its strategy is a strategic concern that will be discussed in Chapter 15.

## Human Resource Management—Assignment of Key Leaders and Executives

Individuals, groups, and units are the mechanisms of organizational action. The effectiveness of their action determines the success of the strategy implementation. Effective leadership is essential in motivating and directing individual and group efforts toward successful strategy implementation and the achievement of the objectives. The following three dimensions of leadership are vital for proper implementation:

1. The support and involvement of the chief executive officer (CEO)
2. The assignment of key executives and personnel

3. The matching of the leadership style of the managers to the requirements of the selected strategy

The leadership and human resource management aspects of the strategy
implementation will be further discussed in Chapter 15.

## STRATEGY EVALUATION AND CONTROL

The evaluation and the control of strategy form the process through which
MNC strategists determine if the right global strategy was chosen and whether
or not the strategy as implemented is meeting its strategic objectives.

Strategic management is similar to the process involved in treating ill-
nesses. The long-term well-being of a patient is the objective of a physician;
the survival of the firm is the objective of the strategist. When the patient is
suffering from an illness, the physician looks at the symptoms and makes a
diagnosis. From this probable diagnosis, the physician prescribes the best
treatment or medicine. When a firm is not performing well, the strategists
conduct an environmental and organizational evaluation, and then they
choose the best objectives and strategy to improve performance. When the
patient follows the prescription, he or she is implementing the physician's
choice. If the prescription is ineffective, the physician will change it. If this
still does not work, the physician may consider that the wrong diagnosis was
made—a wrong strategic choice. The doctor may then make another diagnosis. When a firm is still not performing well, strategists can choose another
strategy and different objectives. When, through feedback, they find out that
their strategy is not working, they should be ready with alternative choices,
that is, with contingency strategies.

A follow through on global strategy and implementation necessitates an
effective control system, a proper reward system, and an appropriate management information system (MIS). The control system is needed to monitor the
progress toward the achievement of objectives and to take corrective action if
deviations in the plan occur. The reward system is used to motivate people and
to tie rewards to the progress made toward achievement of the strategically
relevant objectives. A company's MIS provides the strategists with timely, accurate, and complete feedback, so that strategists can act upon data and take
corrective action if necessary.

Strategists should make decisions based upon control criteria most relevant
to their businesses. These criteria should be indicative of the progress made
toward the achievement of the strategic objectives. In evaluating strategy, the
MNC can use two types of criteria, quantitative and qualitative. *Quantitative
criteria* are hard data, such as figures on net profit, sales, growth in sales, market
share, return on investment or equity, stock prices, earnings per share, production costs and efficiency, marketing costs and efficiency, employee turnover,
absenteeism, and satisfaction indexes. Consistency, appropriateness, and workability are among *qualitative criteria* used for evaluation of a strategy. Consis-

tency criteria are used to see if the chosen global strategy is consistent with the global objectives, environmental assumptions, and organizational conditions of the MNC. Appropriateness criteria are used to test the appropriateness of the resource capabilities, the risk tendencies, and the time horizon that are attached to the chosen strategy. Finally, workability criteria test to see whether or not the strategy is feasible, stimulating, and workable.

We conclude this chapter by stating that many MNCs faced with rapid changes in their turbulent environments have responded by formulating and implementing global strategies. Global strategic management is the process through which these global strategies are devised and the guidelines for their implementation are established.

Although we presented a specific global strategic management process model in this and in the preceding chapter, we should point out that many variations exist in strategic management. Variations in planning practices occur not only across companies, but also across countries. For example, there are significant differences between American and Japanese firms with regard to their strategic management approach.

In the United States corporate strategies are used to integrate the strategies of divisions and to control the divisions. The strategic management process in the United States is usually from the bottom to the top rather than from the top to the bottom of the MNC hierarchy. In Japan, strategic management is used for improving the strategic decisions of top management, so the process is more centralized and interactive than in the United States.

To cope with uncertainty, American firms tend to update their strategies every year or even more often. In order to successfully update their strategies, they adopt contingency plans. Japanese firms, however, use two time horizons to cope with uncertainty. These are a long-term strategy and medium-range strategy.

There are also differences between America and Japan with regard to follow-up and implementation. American firms tend to follow-up more closely, and the strategies are used to evaluate division managers. Rewards are based on the quality of strategies and the accomplishment of objectives. Japanese firms, however, are less inclined to follow-up the strategy itself. They implement the strategy through the budget and the project plan. In Japan, project plans are quite frequently used.[14]

Regardless of variations, there is general agreement that the formulation and implementation of strategies through some form of process is vital to the long-term survival, the effectiveness, and the profitability of any firm. Global strategic management has become more realistic as MNCs drive to increase their profitability in the world market by concentrating on their more promising global product lines and by divesting product, market, and country operations that do not contribute to their objectives or do not fit their missions.

MNCs are increasingly utilizing sophisticated forecasting models, portfolio matrices in resource allocation, and rigorous competitive and environmental assessments. They are also developing global strategies aimed at productivity improvement, cost reduction, new product development, increased penetration in the global market, and management development.

## SUMMARY

1. The MNC's mission is the basis upon which critical quantitative and qualitative objectives for national affiliates, SBUs, divisions, and the entire organization are formulated. The examination and reexamination of the basic philosophy and the mission of the MNC form the cornerstone of the global strategic management process.

2. The MNC's business philosophy establishes its inherent nature, its guiding principles, and its underlying conception. It includes the functions and services an MNC performs globally. It also states the MNC's basic long-term directions, goals, and profit motivation. The business philosophy and the mission for an MNC should stress its international business focus.

3. The mission of an organization defines its role in the society and the economy. The MNC's mission defines why it exists and why it competes in selected industries, markets, regions, nations; and why it does not compete in others.

4. The written statement of a mission is sometimes called a "charter." The charter defines the MNC's range of products, customers, and markets, and it defines the international nature of an MNC.

5. Some MNCs write "creeds," describing the broad ethical tone and the social responsibilities of the enterprise. The statements of the philosophy, the mission (charter), and the creed are interrelated.

6. Global environmental assessment is a process through which an MNC evaluates the actual (present) and potential (future) conditions that it may face in domestic, foreign, and international environments. Global environmental assessment involves the collection and evaluation of information from the domestic, foreign, and international environments. It also involves the forecasting of future conditions in these environments.

7. Environmental assessment allows strategists time to anticipate key opportunities and to plan optional and optimal responses to these opportunities. In addition, environmental assessment functions as an early warning system. It anticipates key threats and develops strategies that can reduce their impact or possibly turn them into opportunities for the firm.

8. In the organizational analysis phase of global strategic management internal factors are examined. Those are factors that strategists need to analyze and to examine in order to determine the MNC's (and its SBUs') relative internal strengths and weaknesses. These internal strategic factors are used to face the opportunities and threats from the environment.

9. The MNC should be able to determine competitive advantages that it has over other competitors in specific markets and countries. The firm should lead from these relative strengths in formulating its strategies.

10. The formulation of specific objectives for the MNC starts after the completion of environmental assessment and organizational analysis. Strategic objectives should reflect the competitive strengths and weaknesses of an MNC.

11. Objectives are formulated for each level of an MNC by the strategic decision makers at that level. The choices of objectives are affected by a number of factors. These factors are the forces in the environment; the competitor actions; the realities of the

MNC's resources and power relationships; the value systems and goals of the top management and the MNC strategists; and the past objectives, strategies, and developmental track of the MNC.

12. The terms *goal* and *objective* are sometimes used synonymously. We consider *goals* to be more fundamental, longer-term, more open-ended than objectives. Objectives are long-term targets that are necessary, but not sufficient, for the achievement of goals. By virtue of this distinction, goals are not fully achievable because they are unbounded.

13. An objective should have four components: (a) the goal sought, (b) a yardstick for measuring progress, (c) a target to be achieved, and (d) a time frame within which to reach the target. To be useful, objectives and their components should be stated as specifically and as precisely as possible.

14. The objective ranked number one at each organizational level is called the strategic objective. Therefore, the strategic objective at each level is the number one priority pursued at that organizational level. The global strategic objective is the number one priority for the overall MNC.

15. There are four generic international competitive strategies: global high share strategy, global niche strategy, national high share strategy, and national niche strategy.

16. The MNC that pursues a global high share strategy identifies high volume segments in its global market and gears all its marketing efforts toward these segments.

17. The MNC that uses global niche strategy gains one or more global competitive advantages through specialization and avoids head-on competition with firms that pursue global high share strategies.

18. MNCs that pursue national high share strategies target high national market share through the use of nationally based competitive advantages.

19. Firms that pursue national niche strategies capitalize on the advantages of specialization on a national basis in order to defend their market against both national and global competitors. The size of the target market for a firm pursuing this kind of strategy is below the threshold size that is usually attractive to larger companies.

20. There are five factors that influence the strategic choice decisions: the perceptions of the degree of the MNC's dependence on its environment; the strategists' attitude toward risks, values, and decision-making styles; the past strategies of the MNC and its SBUs; and the MNC's internal power relationships, culture, organizational structure and resources; and lower-level managers' cooperation and attitudes.

21. Implementation translates strategic thought into strategic action. The first step in the implementation phase is the formulation of the short-term, that is, the annual or the semiannual, objectives. In addition, functional-area strategies and policies need to be formulated to achieve these objectives and to guide the operational decision making. The second step includes the allocation of the MNC's resources, that is, their capital, human resources, technology, and so forth among different SBUs and functional areas. The third step is the design of an organizational structure that is suitable for the implementation of the global strategy that the MNC has selected. The final step is the assignment of key leaders and managers to implement the strategy. This process is called human resource management.

22. Evaluation and control of strategy form the process through which MNC strategists determine if the right global strategy was chosen and whether or not the strategy, as implemented, is meeting its strategic objectives.

23. A control system is needed to monitor the progress of objective achievement and to take corrective action if deviations from the strategy occur.

24. In evaluating strategy, the MNC can use two types of criteria: quantitative and qualitative. Quantitative criteria are hard data such as figures on net profit, sales,

growth in sales, market share, return on investment or equity, stock prices, earnings per share, production costs and efficiency, marketing costs and efficiency, employee turnover, absenteeism, and satisfaction indexes. Consistency, appropriateness, and workability are among qualitative criteria used for evaluation.

## QUESTIONS

**14.1** How does global strategic management contribute to the survival and performance of an MNC?

**14.2** Go to your school library and find an MNC that utilizes formal strategic management. Develop a model for the strategic management process this company uses. What are the differences between their process and the process discussed in this and the previous chapter?

**14.3** Discuss the advantages and disadvantages of using a global strategy rather than utilizing national or local strategies.

**14.4** Provide a list of global strategies used by an MNC of your choice. Are they successful? Discuss.

**14.5** Provide a list of strategies used by MNCs that use national strategies.

## NOTES

1. Joe Thomas, "The Sony Corporation," in Lester A. Digman, *Strategic Management. Concepts, Decisions, Cases* (Plano, Tex.: Business Publications, 1986), p. 707.
2. Walter Kiechel III, "Corporate Strategy for the 1990s," *Fortune,* 29 February 1988, p. 38.
3. John A. Pearce II, and Richard B. Robinson, Jr., *Strategic Management: Strategy Formulation and Implementation,* 3rd ed. (Homewood, Ill.: Irwin, 1988), pp. 71–96.
4. William A. Dymsza, "Global Strategic Planning: A Model and Recent Developments," *Journal of International Business Studies* (Fall 1984), p. 173.
5. Andrew Kupfer, "How to Be a Global Manager," *Fortune,* 14 March 1988, p. 54.
6. Dymsza, "Global Strategic Planning," p. 176.
7. William F. Glueck, *Strategic Management and Business Policy* (New York: McGraw-Hill, 1980), Chap. 3.
8. Dymsza, "Global Strategic Planning," p. 173.
9. Glueck, *Strategic Management,* Chap. 4.
10. Gen-Ichi Nakamura, "Strategic Management in Major Japanese High-tech Companies," *Long Range Planning,* vol. 19, no. 6 (December 1986), p. 82.
11. Richard I. Kirkland, Jr., "Entering a New Age of Boundless Competition," *Fortune,* 14 March 1988, p. 40.
12. James C. Leontiades, *Multinational Corporate Strategy: Planning for World Markets* (Lexington, Mass.: Lexington Books, 1985), p. 51.

13. Ibid.
14. Toyohiro Kone, "Long-Range Planning-Japan-USA: A Comparative Study," *Long Range Planning,* vol. 9, no. 5 (October 1976), pp. 61–71.

## SUGGESTED READINGS

Please refer to the Suggested Readings list at the end of Chapter 13.

# Human Resource Management and Organizational Structure

$A$ s we pointed out in Chapters 13 and 14, the successful performance of an MNC requires the effective implementation of a global strategy. Therefore, good global strategy with poor implementation can lead to problems. Furthermore, we mentioned that there are four components to effective implementation:

1. Formulation of short-term (annual and semiannual) objectives and formulation of functional-area strategies (policies) to achieve these objectives and to guide operational decision making.
2. Allocation of corporate resources (people, money, and fixed assets) among different SBUs, functional areas, and organizational units in a strategically balanced fashion.

3. Selection, training, and assignment of key leaders with proper leadership styles who are committed to the global strategy and its implementation. This process is called human resource management.
4. Formation of a planned organizational structure that is in harmony with the requirements of the global strategy.

In the previous chapter we briefly discussed these aspects of strategy implementation. Two of the elements of strategy implementation require further explanation. These are human resource management (staffing) and the determinants and forms of a planned organizational structure in a global setting.

## HUMAN RESOURCE MANAGEMENT

Human resource management* and staffing at an MNC are more complex than the same activities are for a domestic firm. Some of the reasons for this complexity follow.

One of the major differences between a domestic company and an MNC is the nationality of its managers. A domestic company usually employs nationals of its own country in managerial positions, whereas an MNC has three different sources of management personnel: home country nationals, host country nationals, and third country nationals. In addition to managers, a firm also has other employees. For the MNC these other employees are usually natives of the host country. Thus, an MNC may bring together persons from a variety of cultural backgrounds to work together in one organization.

A possible reason for assigning home country or third country nationals to managerial positions in a foreign subsidiary may be the inadequacy of the managerial skills of host country nationals. A second reason may be the ethnocentric attitudes of the headquarters personnel, that is, their preference for people of their own culture in key positions in a foreign subsidiary. Table 15.1 summarizes the advantages and disadvantages of these three sources of management personnel.

Another difference between a domestic firm and an MNC is that the subsidiaries of an MNC are physically more dispersed and distant from their headquarters than are the subsidiaries of a domestic firm. As a result, MNC managers in foreign locations have to make quick on-site decisions without the benefit of consulting with headquarters executives. Here, the importance of effective functional policies as guides to action becomes more obvious. If the right people (executives) are provided with proper guidance (policies) from the headquarters, they will be better able to respond to the demands from the local environment through effective decision making.

Due to greater variations in environmental conditions and factors, MNC executives face a more complex set of problems than their domestic company

---

*The authors greatly appreciate the contributions of Dr. Ercan G. Nasif of University of North Texas-Pan American to this section.

Table 15.1 ADVANTAGES AND DISADVANTAGES OF THREE SOURCES OF MANAGEMENT PERSONNEL

| Advantages | Disadvantages |
|---|---|
| **Home Country Nationals** | |
| 1. Familiarity with headquarters philosophies, objectives, strategies, policies, and business practices. | 1. Complications in adapting to the host country's culture, language, legal/political environment, and business practices. |
| 2. Technical and/or managerial competence. | 2. Excessive selection, training, compensation, and maintenance costs for expatriates and their families. |
| 3. Effective communication and relationships with headquarters personnel. | 3. Increased pressure from host governments for localizing operations and utilizing their citizens in top positions in their countries. |
| 4. Better control over the subsidiary's operations. | 4. Family problems. |
| **Host Country Nationals** | |
| 1. Familiarity with the host country's culture, language, legal/political environment, and business practices. | 1. Unfamiliarity with headquarters philosophies, objectives, strategies, policies, and business practices. |
| 2. Less costly. | 2. Lack of opportunities for home country managers to gain international and crosscultural experience. |
| 3. Increased goodwill with the host country government demanding localization and employment of their citizens. | 3. Communication problems in dealing with the headquarters personnel. |
| 4. Increased advancement possibilities for host country nationals which may increase their commitment and motivation. | 4. Potential difficulties in exerting control over subsidiary's operation. |
| 5. Socially responsible act on part of an MNC in a host country. | |
| **Third Country Nationals** | |
| 1. Possible compromise in securing needed technical and/or managerial competence. | 1. Host country's sensitivity to the hiring of these managers especially if cultural or national animosities exist. |
| 2. Usually international business career managers. | 2. Less acceptable than home country managers in many LDCs. |
| 3. Less expensive than home country managers. | 3. Decrease potential for advancement for host country nationals. |

counterparts. These problems include their own unfamiliarity with the local culture and the changing economic and political relations between the home and the host countries.

## MNC Nationality Mix

The nationality mix of MNC executives in the field of international management is important because of the implications for the host country and the MNC. When we mix executives and employees from a variety of cultural and national backgrounds, then we must start questioning the effectiveness and the universality of management principles and theories. Some of the typical questions are the following: How should we plan, organize, and control the work that is done by people of different nationalities? How should we manage, motivate, communicate with, and lead the people in our organization? How should we select, train, and compensate our employees? How should we evaluate their performance? How should we practice our labor relations, unionization, and collective bargaining principles? These and many other questions arise when we cross national borders and mix together management personnel and employees from different cultural and national backgrounds.

In most MNCs, the nationality mix of managers varies at different levels of the organizational hierarchy. Figure 15.1 shows the variation in nationality mix, based on organizational level.

Usually the top-levels of the hierarchy in an MNC are staffed by home-country nationals, especially the chief executive officer (CEO) and the chief financial officer (CFO). The main reason behind this practice is the MNC's desire to control the operations of foreign subsidiaries more closely. This practice also makes it easier for the top executives of an MNC to communicate with and manage the executives of the subsidiary. At this point, the principles and theories of management are universal. We know how to manage these people, and the consequences of our behavior, that is, whether our managing and leadership styles are effective or not, are known.

The managers who are not host-country nationals are called **expatriates** (persons working in a country other than their own). Employment of expatriates causes many problems for the expatriated individual assigned to the job, such as the stresses of adapting to a foreign culture, stresses on family life, changes in the career plans, and so forth. This may lead to failure of the individual to do the assignment, but when the reasons for failures are overcome there are a number of benefits for the MNC in using expatriates. The reasons MNCs use expatriates are the following:

1. Control. The MNC needs to be represented, at least symbolically, in the subsidiary by home-nation expatriates.
2. Trust. The MNC may have more trust in a manager from the home nation because host-country nationals may have a conflict between their interests and the company's interests.
3. Staffing. The MNC may need to fill a position for which there is a shortage of local talent.

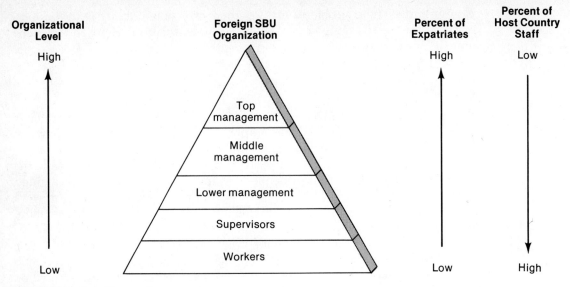

**Most likely nationality:**

CEO: Home country national (expatriate)
CFO: Home country national (expatriate)
COO: Home, third, or host country national
Personnel manager: Host country national
Other managers, supervisors: Third or host country nationals
Workers: Host country nationals

**Figure 15.1** MNC foreign subsidiary nationality mix based on organizational level

4. Management Development. By assigning home-country executives to foreign subsidiaries, the MNC provides a valuable international experience to these managers. Later the MNC can use these managers at the headquarters for managing the international operations.
5. Organization Development. Every MNC has an organizational culture independent of its home and host countries. By transferring managers around the world, an MNC socializes these managers into the company culture. These managers, with personal contacts around the world, can better enhance the organization's functioning and effectiveness.

The lower levels of the organizational hierarchy in the MNC's subsidiaries are usually staffed by the host-country nationals. Subsidiary executives, therefore, do not have the same luxury of managing in a familiar cultural environment as do the headquarters executives. The management of employees from different cultures is more difficult than the management of employees sharing a common background. In foreign cultures many of the familiar management practices may not apply. For example, an American manager in an LDC like India may find it difficult to get the lower-level and even middle-level managers involved in the managerial decisions, even though participative management is the desired style of most U.S. managers.

The first job of a nonnative subsidiary executive (the expatriate) is to study the sociocultural, political, legal, economic, business, and technological subenvironments of the host country. In managing the human resources of a subsidiary the first three—sociocultural, political, and legal subenvironments—are the most relevant. These factors greatly influence the human resource management strategies in the host country. The areas of human resource management that are most affected by these environmental conditions include recruitment, selection, placement, training and development, compensation, performance appraisal, and labor relations.

Because people of different cultures and nationalities are involved, managing human resources is one of the key differences between a domestic firm and an MNC. The management of expatriates is a key issue for the MNC's human resource management practices. The success of an MNC depends on its ability to recruit, select, develop, and deploy qualified managers for its foreign operations. In the next section we will discuss the issues related to the success or failure of expatriate managers in their foreign assignments.

## Expatriate Socialization Process

The process of selection and training of expatriates plays an important role in the overall success of expatriate managers when they arrive on the job in a foreign country. If expatriates are properly selected and trained for their assignments, the chances of their success will increase. On the other hand, improper selection and training, and improper assignment of expatriates may lead to their failure. For example, a study reported a 40 percent failure rate for expatriates on their assignments.[1] Seeing such a high failure rate, one wonders whether or not MNCs are approaching the problem in too narrow a fashion by selecting managers who are successful in their domestic operations, but then assigning them to foreign locations without regard to the complex issues involved in switching cultures.

The selecting, training, and assigning of expatriates must be considered as part of a broader concept of expatriate development and the expatriate socialization process. If MNCs use such an integrated approach, then the high failure rate of expatriates may decline.

Every single aspect and step of the expatriation process is important and is interrelated to all the other aspects and steps. To provide only predeparture training and to forget about overseas support, or to ignore preparation for repatriation (returning home), is a common fault in managing expatriates. An expatriation system should not use a "hit or miss," or "sink or swim" approach; instead, it should be a well balanced, carefully developed, and concisely planned and implemented program. Figure 15.2 presents a model of such a program, called the expatriate socialization process.

The process of adapting to a new culture is similar to the process of adapting to a new job. The expatriate socialization process model is based on the so-called model of organizational socialization.[2]

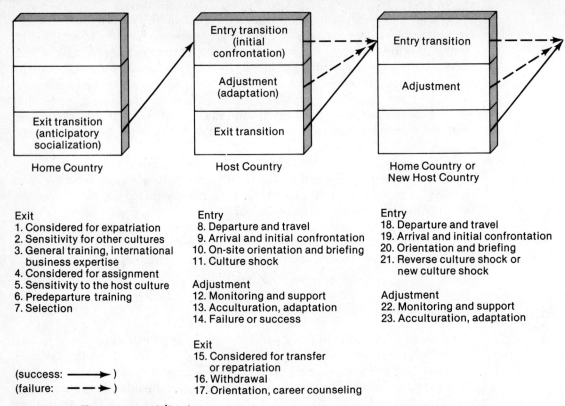

**Figure 15.2** Expatriate socialization process

This organizational process model of expatriate socialization has three basic stages: exit transition, entry transition, and adjustment.

Organizational socialization is the process by which a new employee learns to perform his or her job and to understand the larger context in which the job is embedded. It is also a process whereby the employees learn to participate in the social life of the new organization. The first major stage in this process is the **exit transition**, also called the anticipatory socialization. This process refers to the degree to which an individual is prepared, prior to entry, to occupy the new position. For example, when an individual is selected for an assignment, training in the culture and language of the host country provide for a better exit transition. The second major stage is the **entry transition**, also called the initial confrontation. This is the first encounter of the employee with the new organization. The person begins to master the task and also to define the interpersonal relationships. Earlier expectations of the employee are either confirmed or disconfirmed. In international assignments, **culture shock** happens at this stage. In repatriation, that is upon returning home, another shock, **reverse culture shock**, occurs (see Figure 15.2, Steps 11 and 21). **Adjustment** is the third step in expatriate socialization. This is the adaptation stage. The person has successfully socialized into the new situation. Repatriation should be treated as a new cycle in the process that includes all of the three basic stages explained previously.

There are two types of outcomes to successful organizational socialization: behavioral and attitudinal. Examples of **behavioral outcomes** are dependable job performance, assignment completion, innovation, and spontaneous cooperation. Examples of **attitudinal outcomes** are general satisfaction, internalized work motivation, and job involvement. All of these outcomes are the criteria for determining successful socialization, and these outcomes are also the characteristics of the fully adjusted and successful expatriate. The outcome of an unsuccessful socialization process will be the early withdrawal and the premature departure or failure of the expatriate.[3]

## Selection

Selection of an international manager should encompass the many dimensions involved in a successful expatriate socialization process. One major problem in the selection process is determining what criteria should be used to evaluate success. We do not clearly know what "success" is on an international managerial assignment. Like many other constructs (concepts) that we study in international management, effectiveness (success) is multidimensional and situation dependent. Thus, selection for these positions should consider as many of these dimensions as possible. In dealing with the expatriate assignments, management research has largely focused on identifying reasons for failure. It has generated lists of personal characteristics that might contribute to success, but it has not attacked the problem head-on by defining what expatriate success is. In selecting an international manager the following factors should be considered: failure, success, and training.

## Failure

Failure due to technical incompetence has been rare in international assignments because most selection decisions have been based on technical competence only. Most MNCs assume that if the person is technically and managerially competent he or she will do a good job both at home and abroad. The effect of the new environment on expatriate performance is usually ignored. Most frequently the reason for expatriate failure is related to behavior and adjustment. Besides job-related problems, the major causes of expatriate failure are adjustment-related problems, family-related problems, culture-related problems, and personality-related problems.

**Adjustment-Related Problems**   These problems stem from several factors. Some of these factors are the following:

1. Self-oriented. The expatriated manager should try to enjoy local entertainment and leisure-time activities. He or she should try to cope with stress and to build technical and managerial competence.

2. **Others-oriented.** The expatriated manager should develop local relationships and a local social network. He or she should be willing to communicate with the local people.
3. **Perceptual.** The expatriated manager should be able to see the real causes of local behavior and of his or her own behavior.
4. **Cultural toughness.** The expatriated manager should see the extent of the differences between the home and the host cultures.[4]

**Family-Related Problems**   The involvement of the expatriate's spouse is very important in all phases of the socialization process. Living abroad may bring the family together or pull it apart.[5] Both outcomes have significant effects on the expatriate's job performance. We should not forget that there may be more stress on the spouse and their children than on the expatriate. The expatriate has the support of fellow nationals at work. The family may feel isolated and depend totally on the expatriate for care and comfort.

**Culture-Related Problems**   Effective dealings on foreign assignments will not be possible until we understand the tenets of our own culture.[6] Only then can a person understand and cope with another culture. Culture shock and reverse culture shock are the main problems that expatriates face in the early days of their transfers and returns. Suggestions on how to cope with culture shock depend on the individual's situation and the degree to which the home and host cultures differ. Some suggestions for coping with culture shock include having a hobby or interest, having a local mentor, strengthening family relations, undertaking language training, and being open-minded. Other strategies to deal with cultural differences were discussed in Chapter 10.

**Personality-Related Problems**   These problems can be overcome by training the expatriate, but the effectiveness of such training may be limited. A better solution is to select an expatriate manager who has demonstrated sensitivity toward others. Some of the personality-related traits of a successful expatriate will be mentioned later.

## Success

The studies on expatriate success have generally focused on generating lists of personal characteristics that contribute to success. The list includes the following characteristics: technical and managerial skills, interpersonal skills, personality traits, cultural abilities, family considerations, language abilities, and the gender of the expatriate.

Recent studies, however, cast doubt on the importance of such characteristics. For example, previous studies have maintained that males are more successful as expatriates than females, but the validity of this finding is questionable. After all, data show that less than 3 percent of all expatriate managers have been females, and it has been suggested, therefore, that companies should reconsider their current reluctance to send women managers abroad.[7] However, care should be taken because there is a cultural bias against women as authority figures in certain cultural areas. The assignment of female managers to certain areas of the world may prove detrimental to their success. Such assignments may also jeopardize the MNC's projects that are overseen by these female managers. Careful consideration should be given to the cultural acceptance of women managers in each culture. This is particularly true in regard to the cultures of Japan and some countries in the Middle East.

It seems that measuring and defining expatriate failure (mainly by the premature return of the expatriate) are easier than defining expatriate success. Extreme levels of success or failure are also easier to measure than intermediate levels. Figure 15.3 shows a model of expatriate success.

**Expatriate success** is defined as a three-dimensional construct consisting of job performance, satisfaction about the job and life in general, and adjustment to the local culture. Three sets of factors contribute to expatriate success: the individual, the organization, and the environment.

Individual factors consist of personal characteristics, expectations about the job and life, and family considerations. Organizational factors that contribute to success include the type of orientation, training, and development provided by the firm; the task demands; and the organizational reward structure. Environmental factors such as local culture and conditions also play important roles in expatriate success.

## Training

As the expatriate socialization process model suggests, training the expatriate is important and necessary before, during, and after the deployment of the expatriate abroad. We can differentiate among three types of expatriate training programs: predeparture training, on-site orientation, and repatriation programs.

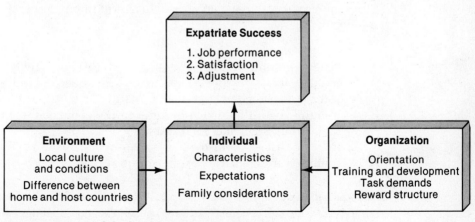

**Figure 15.3** A model of expatriate success

**Predeparture Training**  In preparing the expatriate for an assignment, MNCs range in their predeparture training from those having no programs (a "sink or swim" approach) to those having complete and extensive programs. For example, Japanese MNCs have more comprehensive expatriate training programs than American MNCs. Not surprisingly, they have fewer expatriate failures.[8] The expatriate's family should definitely be involved in all aspects of the predeparture training, as well as in all the steps and stages of the expatriation process. It has been suggested that a nonobligatory, one-week, expenses-paid visit to the country for the whole family be provided since there is no substitute for actual experience in a country.[9]

Predeparture expectations are important antecedents to adjustment after arrival. As knowledge about the new culture increases, the expatriate family experiences less and less culture shock. Thus, predeparture training programs are significant factors in expatriate success. Most predeparture training programs include technical and managerial training, cultural training, and language training. All predeparture programs should be planned to aid in an understanding of environmental differences between the home and host countries. In a survey, American business people were asked to rank in order of importance the training needs for expatriate managers. The following is their ranking:

1. human relations skills
2. understanding of other cultures
3. ability to adapt
4. technical competence
5. sensitivity training
6. politics
7. language ability
8. understanding of the mission
9. understanding of the American culture
10. orientation for the service.[10]

In summary, a well-developed predeparture training program should have the following elements:

1. formal language training
2. general cultural training (training in cultural sensitivity)
3. training about the specific country (its life, people, history, geography, culture, business, politics, and so forth)
4. training about the MNC's business in the country (technical, managerial, commercial, and legal training)
5. training that involves meetings with nationals of the country
6. training through a visit to the country.

**On-site Orientation**  This kind of support, both from MNC headquarters and from local mentors, is crucial to an expatriate's success. It is suggested that there be a few months of coaching from the manager who the expatriate will replace.[11]

**Repatriation Programs**   These programs are aimed at reducing reverse culture shock and in furthering the career plans of the expatriate. The return of the expatriate can be problematic both for the individual and for the organization that must find a new place for this person. Properly integrating returning expatriates will help retain capable managers and ensure qualified managers for positions abroad.[12] Many expatriate decisions and behaviors are affected by their expectations about their return home. Much of the burden in planning and implementing repatriation programs can be transferred from human resource departments to assigned mentors for each expatriate at the headquarters.

The above argument suggests that at least two mentors are needed: one in the host country to help in the adjustment process of the expatriate while he or she is overseas, and another mentor at home to help reduce the reverse culture shock and ease the repatriation process.

## Differences in Human Resource Management Practices

In Chapter 10 we explored the role of sociocultural variables in international business. Much has been written on the importance of sociocultural variables on management practices and effectiveness. Unfortunately, it is difficult to measure the specific impact that these variables have on the human resource management of MNCs. As a result, the applicability, transferability, and utility of management practices across nations and cultures remain unclear.

Much of the writing in this area is subjective, but there are a number of empirical studies that shed light on the topic of crosscultural and crossnational differences in management practices. The following list is a brief review of a few of the findings of these studies.

1. In companies in Southeast Asia (other than Japan), the degree of formal organization utilized by managers is less than in similar Western companies.[13]

2. In Southeast Asian companies, staffing is less programmed and involves less training than in similar Western companies.[14]

3. Southeast Asian managers use less objective data in their promotional decisions than their Western counterparts.[15]

4. Southeastern Asian executives use a less interpersonal and confrontational leadership style than managers in the Western countries.[16]

5. Southeastern Asian managers take into account the effects of their managerial decisions on the relative status of other people more so than do their Western counterparts.[17]

6. Companies in Southeast Asia use less formal planning systems and utilize fewer variables in their planning than similar Western companies.[18]

**7.** Control in Southeast Asian companies is less formal, uses less information, and is used over a shorter time span than the control measures used by Western companies.[19]

**8.** Managers from Southeast Asia display less precision and less urgency in timekeeping, in scheduling, and in the completion of programs than managers from Western countries.[20]

**9.** Managers from developed countries use salary increases to differentiate between poor and average performers. Managers from LDCs do not use salary increases to distinguish between poor and average workers.[21]

**10.** Indian managers prefer high risk and ideal outcomes in contrast to U.S. managers, who prefer moderate risk and moderate outcomes.[22]

**11.** American managers are "prodelegation," whereas Mexican executives are characterized as "antidelegation." Participative management is perceived as incompatible to the managers' role by the Mexican managers and is seen as a threat to their image and role as perceived by others.[23]

**12.** Employees in Brazil prefer the participative leadership style, whereas Japanese employees prefer more authoritarian leaders. In general, employees in about 45 countries prefer a consultative style of leadership.[24]

**13.** Cultural differences exist in supervisory preferences and styles. India appears to be a more authoritarian country compared to other countries.[25] In India morale and productivity were higher under an authoritarian leader than under a democratic leader. The opposite is true in the United States.[26]

**14.** A study of the "power distance" between superiors and subordinates in 40 countries has shown that the power distance between these two groups is greater in LDCs than in developed nations. Larger "power distance" is indicative of a more authoritative or autocratic leadership style.[27] Table 15.2 shows the "power distance" index values for the 40 countries in this study.

We conclude this section by stating that there is no single way of managing people. Managers in various countries and cultures may achieve the same given objectives through various approaches. There are differences in the applicability of leadership styles across cultures and countries. Overall, U.S. managers utilize a more democratic, participative style of management, while executives from France, West Germany, and most LDCs are more autocratic and authoritarian. Furthermore, it seems that more objective measures are utilized in the decision making of the managers from the developed nations. LDC managers, on the other hand, use more subjective judgment in their decision making. There are differences in the managerial styles around the world, and these differences are mainly attributed to cultural differences. As we have explained earlier in Chapter 10, sociocultural factors are considered as the most important of the influencing variables. There are also similarities in management styles around the world and these similarities can be explained in terms of the industrialization or the industrial subculture of nations. We now shift our focus to a discussion of the organizational structure of MNCs.

Table 15.2  POWER DISTANCE INDEX VALUES FOR
           SELECTED COUNTRIES

| Country | Power distance index* (actual) | Country | Power distance index* (actual) |
|---------|-------------------------------|---------|-------------------------------|
| Philippines | 94 | South Africa | 49 |
| Mexico | 81 | Argentina | 49 |
| Venezuela | 81 | USA | 40 |
| India | 77 | Canada | 39 |
| Singapore | 74 | Netherlands | 38 |
| Brazil | 69 | Australia | 36 |
| Hong Kong | 68 | West Germany | 35 |
| France | 68 | Great Britain | 35 |
| Colombia | 67 | Switzerland | 34 |
| Turkey | 66 | Finland | 33 |
| Belgium | 65 | Norway | 31 |
| Peru | 64 | Sweden | 31 |
| Thailand | 64 | Ireland | 28 |
| Chile | 63 | New Zealand | 22 |
| Portugal | 63 | Denmark | 18 |
| Greece | 60 | Israel | 13 |
| Iran | 58 | Austria | 11 |
| Taiwan | 58 | Mean of 39 countries | 51 |
| Spain | 57 | (multinational | |
| Pakistan | 55 | organization) | |
| Japan | 54 | Yugoslavia | 76 |
| Italy | 50 | (same industry) | |

*The higher the index number, the higher will be the power distance and autocratic relationship between the superordinates and the subordinates.

*Source:* Geert Hofstede, "Hierarchical Power Distance in Forty Countries," In C. T. Lammers and D. J. Hickson, eds., *Organizations Alike and Unlike,* (London: Routledge and Kegan Paul, 1979), p. 105.

## MNC ORGANIZATIONAL STRUCTURE

The implementation of the global strategy requires organization. Every organized activity, from simple to complex, needs a balance between two fundamental and opposing forces: the **division of labor** into various tasks, and the **coordination** of these tasks in order to perform the activity. The structure of an organization is defined as the ways by which it divides its labor into separate tasks, and then accomplishes coordination among these tasks.[28]

Other important considerations in organizational structure include control and communication. There are two sides to an organizational structure: a formal structure and an informal structure. The **formal structure** refers to the documented official relationships among the members and units of the organization. The **informal structure** is the result of unofficial relationships within the work groups.

The formal and informal structures are intertwined and usually indistinguishable from each other. The formal structure relies on formal authority relationships and direct supervision for the coordinating of different work groups in the organization. The formal structure side of the organization is where the principles of organization apply. These principles include: (1) unity of command, that is, each subordinate should have only one supervisor; (2) scalar chain, that is, a direct line of command from the top to the bottom of the organization; and (3) span of control, that is, a limit on the number of subordinates that may effectively report to one superior.

The **design** of organizational structure means deciding on how labor should be divided and which coordinating mechanism should be used. Such design decisions influence how an organization functions, that is, how materials, authority, information, and the decision processes flow through an organization. It has been suggested that an organization may use nine design parameters to divide and to coordinate their activities in order to establish a stable pattern of behavior.[29] Table 15.3 shows these nine design parameters, grouped into four areas and concepts related to each parameter.

As the figure suggests, organizational structures are fluid entities. Thus, an organization should be capable of changing its design to fit its unique requirements. Reorganization is costly and time consuming. It may be painful for the people involved, and therefore it may be resisted.

The question that may be raised at this point is what organizational structure is the best? The answer depends on many factors. These factors include the environmental conditions, the type of technology, the size of the organization, and the company's strategy. Specifically, the structural design ties together the key activities and resources of the firm and must be closely aligned with the needs and demands of the firm's strategy.

Many firms go through a sequence of organizational structures. For example, General Electric Company (GE) was following a simple divisional structure in the late 1950s. Then it chose a broad diversification strategy. In the 1960s, GE experienced tremendous sales growth. At the same time, however, GE experienced administrative difficulties in attempting to control its diversified operations and to improve the lack of a corresponding increase in profitability. In the early 1970s, GE redesigned its structure to accommodate the administrative needs of its strategy. It eventually selected the strategic business unit (SBU) structure. This resulted in improved profitability and better control over the implementation of the diversification strategy.

It can be concluded that: (1) all forms of organizational structure are not equally effective in implementing strategies and that (2) structures also have life cycles of their own, that is, they pass through a set of evolutionary stages. As a result, strategists do not immediately perceive a need for radical changes in organizational structure. Low organizational performance is usually required to provoke politically sensitive structural changes or the redistribution of organization power.

Table 15.3   ORGANIZATION DESIGN PARAMETERS

| Group | Design parameter | Related concepts |
|---|---|---|
| Design of positions | Job specialization | Basic division of labor |
| | Behavior formalization | Standardization of work content |
| | | System of regulated flows |
| | Training and indoctrination | Standardization of skills |
| Design of superstructure | Unit grouping | Direct supervision |
| | | Administrative division of labor |
| | | Systems of formal authority, regulated flows, informal communication, and work constellations |
| | | Organigram |
| | Unit size | System of informal communication |
| | | Direct supervision |
| | | Span of control |
| Design of lateral linkages | Planning and control systems | Standardization of outputs |
| | | System of regulated flows |
| | Liaison devices | Mutual adjustment |
| | | Systems of informal communication, work constellations, and ad hoc decision processes |
| Design of decision-making system | Vertical decentralization | Administrative division of labor |
| | | Systems of formal authority, regulated flows, work constellations, and ad hoc decision processes |
| | Horizontal decentralization | Administrative division of labor |
| | | Systems of informal communication, work constellations, and ad hoc decision processes |

*Source:* Henry Mintzberg, THE STRUCTURING OF ORGANIZATIONS: A Synthesis of Research, © 1979, p. 67. Reprinted by permission of Prentice-Hall, Inc., Englewood Cliffs, N.J.

As the firm's size, diversity, and competitive environment change, the firm moves through different stages of organizational evolution. To compete effectively, at each stage of evolution, a different organizational structure is needed. Table 15.4 shows a proposed evolution of the organizational structure as a firm changes its strategy and passes through the different patterns of international involvement discussed in Chapter 12.

Table 15.4  INTERNATIONAL ACTIVITY AND EVOLUTION OF ORGANIZATIONAL ARRANGEMENTS

| Activities of company | Organization responsible for international activities | Executive in charge |
|---|---|---|
| Exports directly and indirectly, but trade is minor | Export department | Export manager, reporting to domestic marketing executive |
| Exports become more important | Export division | Division manager |
| Company undertakes licensing and invests in production overseas | International division | Director of international operations, usually vice-president |
| International investments increase | Sometimes international headquarters company as wholly owned subsidiary | President, who is vice-president in parent company |
| International investments substantial and widespread, diversified international business activities | Global organizational structure by geographic areas, product lines, functions, or some combination. Also worldwide staff support | No single executive in charge of international business |

*Source:* William A. Dymsza, *Multinational Business Strategy* (New York: McGraw-Hill, 1972), p. 22.

We now turn to a discussion of different organizational structures that an MNC can use.

## Export Organizational Structure

Our discussion of the patterns of international involvement in Chapter 12 indicated that most companies start their foreign operation by exporting. In companies involved in indirect exporting, there is usually no need for incorporating the exporting function into the firm's organizational structure. Many small and medium companies use export management companies (EMCs) as a method of organizing their export trade. In companies involved in direct exporting, the export activities need to be incorporated in the firm's formal organizational structure. In domestic companies with functional structure, that is, organizations in which activities are grouped into functions such as marketing and finance, exporting is usually attached to the marketing department.

Figure 15.4 depicts a functional organization structure with an export unit attached to its marketing function.

However, some companies are organized under a divisionalized product structure, that is, structural boundaries are based on distinct product lines. In such companies, individual export units are attached to those product divisions that have exporting needs. As the volume of exports increases, the firm may decide to consolidate the different export departments into a single unit serving the entire company. Figure 15.5 represents a firm with an export department.

An example of the evolution of export function is seen in the Singer Company and its sewing machine operations. Singer started with exporting its products. As exports grew in importance as compared with the sales in the domestic market, the company established an international division, which was concerned only with exports. This international division operated on a par with the domestic divisions and had some influence over product design, supply, and pricing in foreign markets. Gradually, the international division gained increased power. From merely accepting products and production schedules, this international division gained influence over product allocation and production schedules. This increased influence by the international division was necessary for export success.[30]

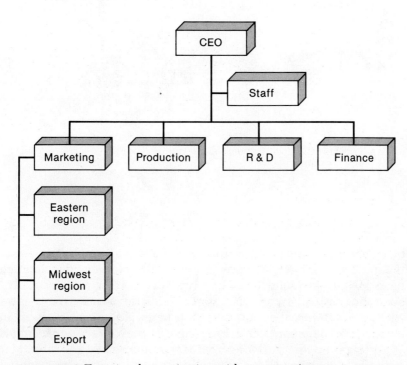

**Figure 15.4** Functional organization with export unit

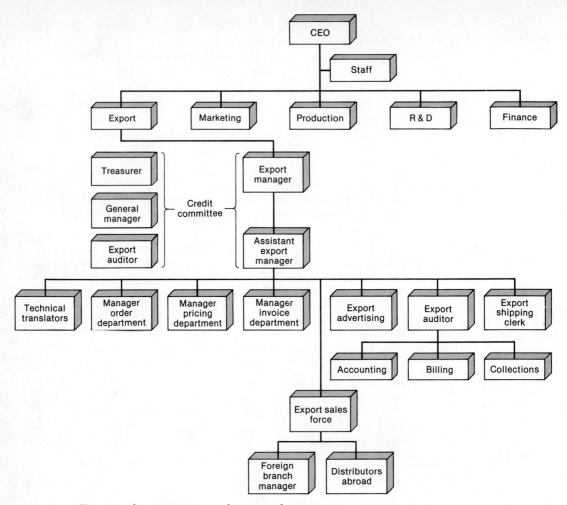

**Figure 15.5** Functional organization with export department

*Source:* Adapted from Ruel Kahler, *International Marketing,* 5th ed. (Cincinnati, Ohio: South-Western, 1983), p. 150.

## The National Subsidiary Structure

Many of the European MNCs tend to use a national subsidiary structure called the mother-daughter structure. A study of the stages of development of European MNCs has found that they typically start as a functionally organized domestic company. When they start subsidiaries abroad, they continue to deal with each subsidiary on an individual basis. No intermediate or intervening levels of management, such as international or divisional departments, are used. Reporting from foreign subsidiaries is done informally and directly to the CEO at the headquarters. Of course, the informal reporting, through visits to and from headquarters, is possible only because of the close physical proximity of the European countries and markets.[31] Figure 15.6 shows the mother-daughter organization structure.

The mother-daughter structure provides great autonomy for each of the national subsidiaries. In light of increased national sentiments, and because of the environmental differences among foreign environments, this high degree of autonomy is greatly welcomed by the national subsidiaries. It provides great flexibility in dealing with environmental demands unique to each country. Decentralized subsidiaries also create better training and development grounds for the expatriates in each SBU.

Deleting intermediate management layers, such as regional or divisional departments, makes it possible for the headquarters executives to be directly involved in the strategy formulation of each subsidiary. This increases coordination between corporate and SBU objectives and strategies. In a crisis situation, the mother-daughter structure is the most strategically responsive structure. Additionally, the deletion of the intermediate management layers provides for direct contact and enhances the communication between the headquarters and the individual subsidiaries.

The mother–daughter structure is most effective for a relatively small multinational holding company that controls a few subsidiaries that are located relatively nearby. As the organization expands its horizons both geographically and in terms of diversification, the limitations of the mother-daughter structure are realized. The coordination mechanisms of personal control and relationships through frequent visits to headquarters tend to be physically impossible when company operations become geographically widespread. The diversity of environmental conditions across many SBUs in numerous regions of the world also prevents the headquarters managers from becoming truly knowledgeable about, and involved in, the operations of each subsidiary.

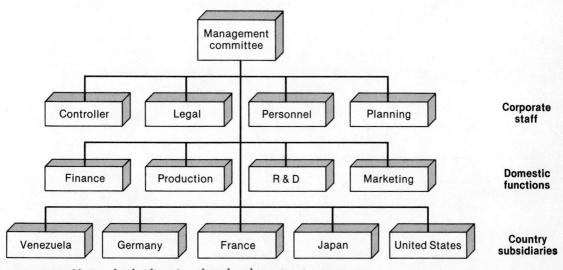

**Figure 15.6** National subsidiary/mother-daughter structure

The national subsidiary structure does not handle global issues well. When each subsidiary is seen in isolation by the headquarters, it is less likely for the company to be globally oriented and to stay responsive to global environmental changes. As a result of growth and the increased involvement in many countries, most MNCs have abandoned this mother-daughter structure for the more responsive multidivisional structure.

### The International Divisional Structure

The international divisional structure is used by many of the U.S. MNCs. The international division is a part of the domestic structure. The MNC groups all of its international activities, based on function, product, or geography, in one division. This format is a natural evolution for domestic companies that are already structured along divisional lines, which are based on functions, products, or domestic geographical divisions.

Figure 15.7 is a representation of the divisional structure. As the figure indicates, the international division has its own chief executive officer (CEO) and staff. Included in the international division are all those activities that deal with foreign operations. This means that all foreign subsidiaries are housed in the international division and report directly to its CEO, who in turn reports to headquarters. This results in the creation of an intermediate level of management between headquarters and the foreign subsidiaries.

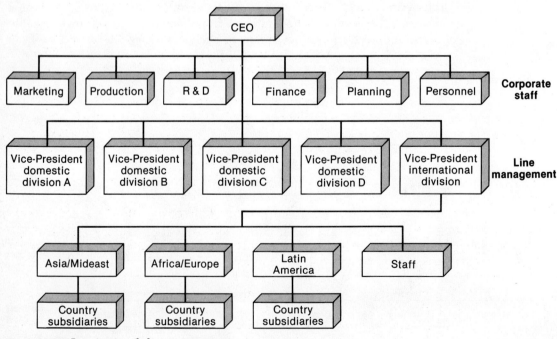

**Figure 15.7** International division structure

The creation of an international division provides a cohesive global orientation. It also concentrates resources for foreign operations under one roof, resulting in better resource allocation decisions. In addition, increases in cohesion and unity in foreign operations can be obtained. The international division structure promotes the formulation of a global strategy. This, in turn, increases the ability of an MNC to respond to global markets and to environmental opportunities and threats.

The divisional structure is more formal and lacks the personal control and personal touch of the national subsidiary organization. Coordination mechanisms are based on formal control; that is, reporting procedures are used as coordinating mechanisms in divisional organizations.

The creation of another layer of organization in international division structure may reduce the MNC's responsiveness to individual market needs. However, this organizational form can stay flexible by supplementing the existing organization with special project teams and committees to accommodate special market demands, while increasing international coordination.

On the negative side, the international division structure can create conflicts between the international division and the other divisions of an MNC. Because international operations are complex, relatively larger amounts of resources and management attention are channeled toward the international division than toward the domestic operations. Another source of conflict is the difference between the orientations of the internationally involved managers and the domestic executives. The first group sees the MNC globally and perceives its growth potential in the international markets, whereas the second group places greater emphasis on the firm's domestic operations. This creates a cultural split in the MNC's top management team. The conflict is further aggravated by the possible differences in the training and backgrounds of the two executive groups. The training and development of the international division executives takes place in the international division and in foreign countries, whereas that of the domestic managers takes place only in their home country.

In addition to these problems, the international division may actually prevent the crossnational experience of its managers. This is because it groups its activities according to individual national subsidiaries. Most managers spend a long time in one national SBU. Although rotations of executives across national subsidiaries can help solve this problem, these rotations cannot completely overcome it. Rotation of managers can broaden their vision by exposing them to several nations; however, this may make them less capable of coordinating several national operations simultaneously. Another disadvantage of international divisional structure is that the domestic subsidiaries, when combined together, may outweigh in influence the international division. This can lead to the creation of a disadvantaged international division, thereby reducing the MNC's international commitment.

To overcome this problem, companies have two remedies. First, some MNCs transform their international division into a wholly owned international headquarters company. The vice-president of the parent company acts as the president of the international headquarters company. The international headquarters company and the parent MNC also have an interlocking board of directors and joint executive officers. This provides more autonomy for the international division and greater emphasis on international operations, while maintaining coordination with headquarters and control by the parent company.

In other words, the international division can be organized as a separate corporation, as an SBU. The international vice-president of the parent company becomes the president of this international headquarters subsidiary. This SBU has its own board of directors. The international division's board of directors are represented on the board of directors of the parent company.

The second remedy to the problem is for the MNC to evolve into one of the more integrated global organizational structures. We will discuss such global structures in the next section.

Examples of companies that utilize an international division include International Business Machines, Coca-Cola, and Pepsico. The international divisions of these companies are IBM World Trade, Coca-Cola Export, and Pepsi-Cola International.

### Integrated Global Structures

Integrated global structures create a balance between international and domestic operations. They are created in response to increased product diversification, and in an attempt to optimize the benefits gained from both domestic and foreign operations. These structures are an evolutionary replacement for the international division structures.

Integrated global structures can take four different forms. We will discuss each briefly.

**Global Functional Structures**   In this type of structure, global functional divisions such as finance, marketing, and manufacturing are created. These divisions are responsible for worldwide operations in their own functional areas. This structure is suitable for MNCs with narrow and integrated product lines, such as those in the automobile industry. However, they are not appropriate for companies with highly diversified and distinct product and service lines. The global functional structure is depicted in Figure 15.8.

As the figure indicates, each function is responsible for all activities related

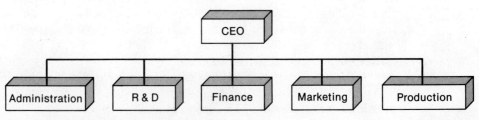

**Figure 15.8** Global functional structure

to its area on a global basis. Central control and centralized decision making are results of this structure. In this type of structure, duplication of effort is minimized and operations are streamlined. This allows for a lean organization, consisting of small numbers of top management, who are primarily responsible for high levels of profit and low costs.

Although in this type of organizational structure there is functional coordination, geographic or product coordination may prove difficult. Also, there is a lack of flexibility and responsiveness to local environmental conditions. In addition, the global functional structure restricts the transfer both of products and of technical expertise across organizational levels. Finally, due to their operationally oriented training and backgrounds, functional managers in this type of organizational structure tend to focus on operating concerns at the expense of strategic issues.

**Global Geographic Structure**   To overcome lack of regional coordination and environmental responsiveness, some MNCs design and utilize global geographic structures. In this form, geographic divisions headed by regional groups are created. Each division manages all the activities and operations within a specific geographic area. A regional manager heads such divisions, and he or she is responsible for its operations and performance. The regional manager directly reports to the headquarters' president. Figure 15.9 shows a global geographic structure.

The geographic division can better respond to regional, environmental, and market needs. In comparison to the global functional structure, the global geographical structure is more flexible in responding to local market needs and to government requirements. It is also a good structure for consolidating re-

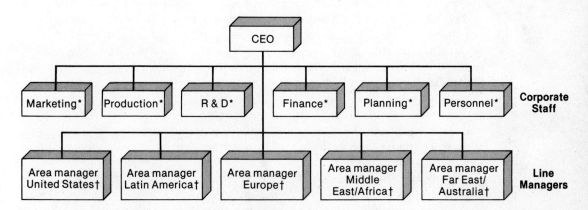

* Managers with total corporate and worldwide responsibilities. Corporate staff activities on a worldwide basis generally involve policy matters, strategic management, and basic product planning. The staff also gives functional guidance to the line geographic unit and coordinates activities between geographic units.

† Managers with line responsibility for all operations in a particular geographic area.

**Figure 15.9** Global geographic structure

gional expertise. Economies of scale within a region can be enhanced, but this is at the expense of product coordination. Functional efforts are also duplicated across different regions. Communication and coordination among different regions can prove difficult.

Global strategic management is conducted by the corporate headquarters' managers and a central staff, acting as a coordinating unit. This organizational structure is effective in marketing-oriented companies with narrow and integrated product lines.

MNCs that produce a range of products which can be marketed through similar or common channels of distribution to similar customers use a global geographic structure. Products marketed by these companies require adaptation to customer requirements. As a result, marketing, rather than production, becomes the critical function. MNCs such as food producers often possess these products and use this type of structure. Examples of companies that use the global geographic structure include Unilever, Nestlé, International Flavors and Fragrances, and Corn Products (CPC). All of these companies have broad consumer product lines. It should be pointed out that the pure geographic structure is usually ineffective for high-tech products. This is because it may be difficult to secure sales personnel and technical personnel who are well trained in all product lines. Another difficulty with these high-tech products is achieving a balanced sales effort for the total product line.[32]

**Global Product Structure**   Companies with global product structures are organized according to product divisions; that is, similar products are grouped into one division. Each product division is responsible for the production, sales, and profits related to its products. The global product structure is effective in MNCs with high product diversifications. The global product structure provides for greater product and marketing integration among diverse product lines and markets. Each product division is a complete organization with complete functional-level departments and staffs. The global product structure allows greater flexibility in product-related innovations. It is also more responsive to market conditions. This structure is useful for rapidly growing diversified companies. Figure 15.10 shows a global product organization structure.

As always, with any type of structure there are disadvantages. International expertise can become fragmented and dispersed among different product divisions. International or regional knowledge, coordination, and responsiveness also can be inadequate in the global product type of structure. Functional and regional coordination also tends to be difficult, if not impossible.

For example, in the early 1970s, Westinghouse, which has consistently lagged behind General Electric (GE) in foreign sales and profits, decided to close the gap and reorganized its structure. Westinghouse eliminated its international division in favor of four new global product divisions. This resulted in parity between foreign sales and domestic sales. The reorganization was also designed to take advantage of the international ubiquity of product technology.

This successful reorganization led to significant foreign sales growth and increases in product lines from 1971 to 1976. Encouraged by these results,

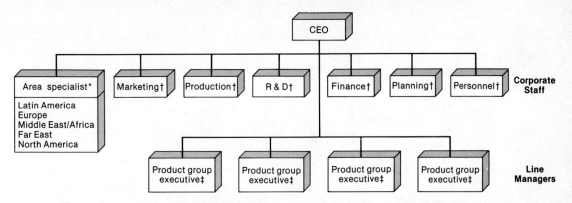

\* Managers with total corporate and worldwide responsibilities. Corporate staff activities on a worldwide basis involve policy matters, overall strategic management coordination between product groups, and the provision of specialized advice to product groups.

† Managers with staff responsibilities in a particular geographic area mainly to identify potential investment opportunities and to provide information to individual affiliates and corporate management.

‡ Managers with worldwide responsibility for product groups.

**Figure 15.10** Global product structure

Westinghouse reorganized again in 1976. It established 37 SBUs with global product-specific responsibilities. The results were unfortunate. Foreign sales fell from 31 percent to 24 percent of total sales during the 1976 to 1978 period. This decrease was attributed to rivalry between different product divisions in the same markets, to a lack of coordination across and a duplication of efforts in different product divisions, and finally, to an inability to put together project packages that cut across SBU lines.[33]

**Mixed Global Structures**  In order to overcome the problems and to benefit from the advantages of each global structure, some MNCs adopt mixed global structures. A combined or mixed global structure focuses on the interdependence among functions, geographical areas, and product groups.

Figure 15.11 provides an example of a mixed global structure. A global matrix structure is a variation of the mixed global structure. Because of its wide utilization in the industry, we will discuss the global matrix structure separately in the next section.

## Global Matrix Structures

A global matrix structure is a type of mixed global structure. It assigns equal authority to at least two of the three dimensions: functional area, geographic territory, and product group. This is an attempt to benefit from the advantages of the combined structures and to increase the coordination among the combined dimensions.

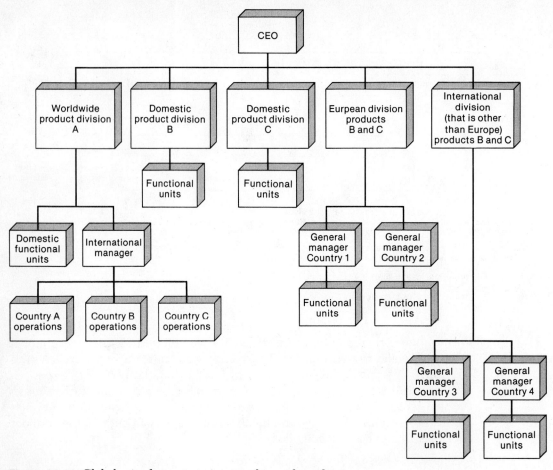

**Figure 15.11** Global mixed structure (geographic and product)

Matrix organizations based on function and product provide for coordination and integration along these two dimensions. Product and geographical area matrix structures coordinate product groups and geographical area activities. An example is provided in Figure 15.12.

This "new wave of the 1970s" structure has shortcomings of its own. Among the most important are the following:

1. Combining two or more dimensions leads to the creation of a multiple command system. This means that each person has to report to two or more supervisors (a functional manager, a regional manager, and a project or product manager).
2. Combining various dimensions necessitates a process of shared decision making among different managers from the dimensions that are combined.

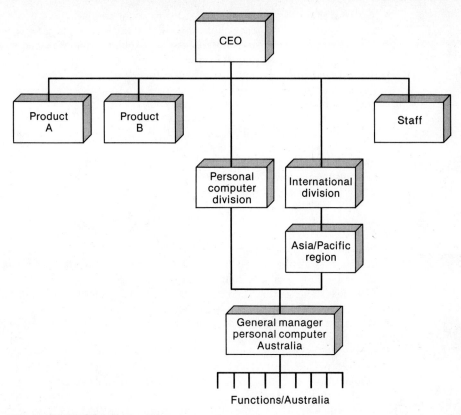

**Figure 15.12** Matrix structure

Despite problems associated with matrix organizations, many leading MNCs utilize them in a variety of ways in designing their global organization.

We conclude this chapter by stating that an MNC needs to pay close attention to the design of a proper organizational structure that fits the requirements of its global strategy. In addition, there is no best way for an MNC to organize. The best organization structure depends on the MNC's size, technology, environmental conditions, and strategic requirements. Furthermore, proper implementation of a global strategy requires the effective recruitment, selection, assignment, and training of human resources. Good managers and a suitable organizational structure are essential for the MNC's success and survival.

## SUMMARY

1. Two of the most important components to the effective implementation of a global strategy are the assignment of key leaders and managers and the formation of a planned organizational structure.

2. The staffing and managing are more complex in an MNC than in a domestic firm. This is because of the nationality mix of MNC managers, the physical disparity of MNC operations, and the complexity of the problems that are faced by MNC executives due to variations in environmental conditions and factors.

3. An expatriate is a nonnative subsidiary manager.

4. The success of an MNC depends on its ability to recruit, select, develop, and deploy qualified managers for its foreign operations.

5. The expatriate socialization process is a well-balanced, carefully developed, and concisely planned program of predeparture training, overseas support, and preparation for repatriation (the return home).

6. There is no single way of managing people. Managers in various countries and cultures may achieve given objectives through various approaches. There are differences in the applicability of leadership styles across cultures and countries.

7. Overall, U.S. managers utilize a more democratic, participative style of management, whereas executives from France, West Germany, and most LDCs are more autocratic and authoritarian.

8. It seems that more objective measures are utilized in the decision making of the managers from developed nations. LDC managers, on the other hand, use more subjective judgments in their decision making.

9. Evidence suggests that the organizational structure follows the growth strategy of a firm, and that there is no single best way to organize an MNC.

10. When the domestic company decides to test foreign markets, it usually starts exporting indirectly before entering the export market fully. The increase in export sales prompts the firm to establish an export department.

11. If the firm decides to commit itself to foreign direct investment (FDI), either it would follow a national subsidiary structure (a mother-daughter structure) or it would follow an international divisional structure.

12. International divisional structure is the initial structural response to the diversification of FDI.

13. As the amount and complexity of the diversification strategy increase, an MNC can utilize one of the integrated global structures. There are four types of integrated global structures: global functional, global geographic, global product, and mixed global.

14. One type of the mixed global structure is the global matrix organization. By using matrix structures MNCs attempt to benefit from a combination of two or more global structures.

## QUESTIONS

15.1 Why is MNC staffing more complex than domestic firm staffing? Discuss and provide examples.

15.2 What is meant by the expatriate socialization process? Discuss.

15.3 Assume you have been offered a foreign assignment in a company of your choice. Do you accept it? Why? Why not?

15.4 Suppose you have been offered a foreign assignment. How do you prepare your family and yourself to face culture shock?

15.5 How many structures can an MNC design and utilize in foreign operations? Briefly discuss the advantages and disadvantages of each organizational structure. Provide examples of each structure.

## NOTES

1. M. Mendenhall and G. Oddou, "The Dimensions of Expatriate Acculturation: A Review," *Academy of Management Review,* vol. 10, no. 1 (January 1985), pp. 39–47.
2. D. C. Feldman, "The Multiple Socialization of Organization Members," *Academy of Management Review,* vol. 6, no. 2 (April 1981), pp. 309–318.
3. Ibid.
4. Ibid.
5. I. Torbiorn, *Living Abroad* (New York: Wiley, 1982).
6. T. O. Wallin, "The International Executive's Baggage: Cultural Values of an American Frontier," *MSU Topics,* vol. 24, no. 2 (Spring 1976), pp. 49–58.
7. N. J. Adler, "Expecting International Success: Female Managers Overseas," *Columbia Journal of World Business,* vol. 18, no. 2 (1983), pp. 29–47; and N. J. Adler, "Women Do Not Want International Careers: Another Myth About International Management," *Organizational Dynamics,* vol. 13 (Autumn 1984), pp. 66–79.
8. R. L. Tung, *Key to Japan's Economic Strength: Human Power* (Lexington, Mass.: Lexington Books, 1984).
9. D. M. Noer, *Multinational People Management* (Washington, D.C.: The Bureau of National Affairs, 1975).
10. R. D. Robinson, *International Business Management* (Chicago: Dryden Press, 1978).
11. Y. Zeira, "The Role of the Training Director in Multinational Corporations," *Training and Development Journal,* vol. 33, no. 3 (March 1979), pp. 20–28.
12. C. G. Howard, "How Best to Integrate Expatriate Managers in the Domestic Organization," *Personnel Administrator,* vol. 27, no. 7 (July 1982), pp. 27–33.
13. S. G. Reading and T. A. Martyn-Johns, "Paradigm Differences and Their Relation to Management, With Reference to South-East Asia," in G. W. England, A. R. Negandhi, and B. Wilpert, eds., *Organizational Functioning in a Cross-Cultural Perspective* (Kent, Ohio: The Kent State University Press, Comparative Administration Research Institute, 1979), pp. 103–125. Excerpts appeared in A. R. Negandhi, *International Management* (Boston: Allyn and Bacon, 1987), pp. 322–323.
14. Ibid.
15. Ibid.
16. Ibid.
17. Ibid.
18. Ibid.
19. Ibid.
20. Ibid.
21. K. M. Thiagarajan and B. M. Bass, "Differential Preferences for Long vs. Short-term Payoffs in India and the United States," *Proceedings, XVIth International Congress of Applied Psychology* (Amsterdam: Swets & Zeitlinger, 1969), pp. 440–446. Excerpts reported in A. R. Negandhi, *International Management,* p. 321.
22. Ibid.
23. Eugene McCann, "Anglo-American and Mexican Management Philosophies," *MSU Business Topics,* vol. 18, no. 3 (1970), pp. 28–37.

24. R. D. Meade and J. D. Whittaker, "A Cross-cultural Study of Authoritarianism," *Journal of Social Psychology,* vol. 72 (1967), pp. 3–7.

25. R. D. Meade, "An Experimental Study of Leadership in India," *Journal of Social Psychology,* vol. 72 (1967), pp. 35–43.

26. G. V. Barrett and E. C. Ryterband, "Life Goals of United States and European Managers," *Proceedings, XVIth International Congress of Applied Psychology* (Amsterdam: Swets & Zeitlinger, 1969), pp. 413–418, in A. R. Negandhi, *International Management,* p. 321.

27. Geert Hofstede, "Hierarchical Power Distance in Forty Countries," in C. J. Lammers and D. J. Hickson, eds. *Organizations Alike and Unlike* (London: Routledge and Kegan Paul, 1979), pp. 97–119.

28. For a complete discussion of "The Essence of Structure," the reader is referred to Henry Mintzberg, *The Structuring of Organizations: A Synthesis of Research* (Englewood Cliffs, N.J.: Prentice-Hall, 1979), Chaps. 1 and 2.

29. Ibid.

30. Robert Grosse and Duane Kujawa, *International Business: Theory and Managerial Application* (Homewood, Ill.: Irwin, 1988), p. 335.

31. Lawrence G. Franko, *The European Multinationals* (Stamford, Conn.: Greylock, 1976).

32. Ruel Kahler, *International Marketing,* 5th ed. (Cincinnati, Ohio: South-Western, 1983), p. 159.

33. Hugh D. Menzies, "Westinghouse Takes Aim at the World," *Fortune,* 14 January 1980, pp. 48–53; "Westinghouse's Third Big Step Overseas," *Business Week,* 2 October 1971; and various Westinghouse Electric Corporation *Annual Reports,* as reported in Robert Grosse and Duane Kujawa, *International Business.*

## SUGGESTED READINGS

Baker, J. C. "Foreign Language and Predeparture Training in U.S. Multinational Firms." *Personnel Administration* (July 1984), pp. 68–72.

Dymsza, William A. *Multinational Business Strategy.* New York: McGraw-Hill, 1972, Chap. 2.

Feldman, D. C. "The Multiple Socialization of Organization Members." *Academy of Management Review,* vol. 6, no. 2 (April 1981), pp. 309–318.

Fontaine, Gary. *Managing International Assignments: The Strategy for Success.* Englewood Cliffs, N.J.: Prentice-Hall, 1989.

Galbraith, Jay R., and Robert K. Kazanjian. *Strategy Implementation: Structure, Systems and Process,* 2nd ed. St. Paul, Minn.: West, 1986, Chaps. 3 and 9.

Haner, F. T. *Multinational Management.* Columbus, Oh.: Merrill, 1973, Chap. 7.

Harris, P. R., and R. T. Moran. *Managing Cultural Differences,* 2nd ed. Houston, Tex.: Gulf, 1987.

Harvey, M. G. "The Other Side of Foreign Assignments: Dealing with the Repatriation Dilemma." *Columbia Journal of World Business,* vol. 17, no. 1 (Spring 1982), pp. 53–59.

Hill, R. "Coping with the Culture Shock of an Overseas Posting." *International Management,* vol. 38, no. 3 (March 1983), pp. 81–85.

Hofstede, G. "The Cultural Relativity of Organizational Practices and Theories." *Journal of International Business Studies,* vol. 14, no. 2 (1983), pp. 75–89.

Howard, C. G. "How Relocation Abroad Affects Expatriate's Family Life." *Personnel Administrator,* vol. 25, no. 11 (November 1980), pp. 71–78.

———. "How Best to Integrate Expatriate Managers in the Domestic Organization." *Personnel Administrator,* vol. 27, no. 7 (July 1982), pp. 27–33.

Lanier, A. R. "Selecting and Preparing Personnel for Overseas Transfers." *Personnel Journal,* vol. 58, no. 3 (March 1979), pp. 160–163.

Leontiades, James C. *Multinational Corporate Strategy: Planning for World Markets.* Lexington, Mass.: Lexington Books, 1985, Chap. 15.

Mendenhall, M., and G. Oddou, "The Dimensions of Expatriate Acculturation: A Review." *Academy of Management Review,* vol. 10, no. 1 (January 1985), pp. 39–47.

Mintzberg, Henry. *The Structuring of Organizations: A Synthesis of Research.* Englewood Cliffs, N.J.: Prentice-Hall, 1979.

Moran, R. T., and P. R. Harris. *Managing Cultural Synergy.* Houston, Tex.: Gulf, 1982.

Ondrack, D. "International Transfers of Managers in North American and European MNEs." *Journal of International Business Studies,* vol. 16, no. 3 (1985), pp. 1–19.

Rehfuss, J. "Management Development and the Selection of Overseas Executives." *Personnel Administrator,* vol. 27, no. 7 (July 1982), pp. 35–43.

Ronen, Simcha. *Comparative and Multinational Management.* New York: Wiley, 1986, Chaps. 8, 9, 10, and 12.

Torbiorn, I. *Living Abroad.* New York: Wiley, 1982.

Tung, R. L. "U.S. Multinationals: A Study of Their Selection and Training Procedures for Overseas Assignments." *Academy of Management Proceedings* (1979), pp. 298–301.

———. "Selection and Training of Personnel for Overseas Assignments." *Columbia Journal of World Business,* vol. 16, no. 1 (1981), pp. 68–78.

———. "Selection and Training Procedures of U.S., European, and Japanese Multinationals," *California Management Review,* vol. 25, no. 1 (1982), pp. 57–71.

Vernon, Raymond, and Louis T. Wells, Jr. *Manager in the International Economy,* 5th ed. Englewood Cliffs, N.J.: Prentice-Hall, 1986, Chap. 2.

Walter, Ingo, and Tracy Murray. *Handbook of International Business,* 2nd ed. New York: Wiley, 1988.

# Chapter 16

# International Marketing Management and Strategy

$M$arketing management is the process of formulating and implementing an integrated strategy aimed at serving a market and providing customer satisfaction. The marketing strategy contains decisions about the *product* or *service* offered, the *place* and *system* of distribution used, the *price* charged, and the *promotion*. These so-called *four Ps* of marketing form the marketing mix that influences customer behavior and competitor response. The four marketing mix variables, the four Ps, are controlled by the firm.

The multinational company serves both domestic and foreign markets by undertaking similar, but not necessarily identical, marketing activities in all areas based on its own marketing mix. Simply because of the unfamiliarity with a foreign environment, however, the activities in foreign marketing segments are more complex.

In this chapter we will discuss the major strategic and operational aspects of international marketing. We will elaborate on such macro-level issues as the assessment of potential markets in foreign countries, and we will address the micro-level considerations of marketing mix, that is, the combination of product, price, place, and promotion.

# MARKET ASSESSMENT

In Chapters 14 and 15 we discussed the importance of resource allocation in the implementation of a global strategy. Because the resources at an MNC's disposal are limited, allocation decisions must lead to the concentration of the limited resources in those countries and markets with the greatest potential for sales. Thus, an assessment of markets is vital in allocating the resources of an MNC among different countries.

Two factors must be considered in assessing markets for a given product: (1) the size and potential of existing markets and (2) the size and potential of possible future markets. An assessment of foreign markets requires that all aspects of the foreign environment be considered.

For the MNC already in a foreign market, information is required to monitor changes in the business environment and to decide on the best allocation of resources across different countries and product markets. In such instances, information relating to the product market and to company performance is needed. Because markets are dynamic and often change quite rapidly, they need to be reassessed periodically. Market reassessment may point to market changes that may necessitate a shift in the firm's marketing strategy.

When management contemplates foreign market entry, a process for screening potential markets is essential. A step-by-step screening procedure allows all markets to be evaluated with the same criteria. If the markets have been evaluated by similar criteria, selection of the best markets can be simplified. In the absence of such a process, the MNC would be aiming at the world market in general. In order to scan international markets, information is needed to determine what countries or markets to enter, and then how to enter those markets.

## Reallocation Decisions in Existing Markets

Occasionally MNCs must reallocate resources and efforts across national boundaries and product markets. This requires: (1) monitoring environmental conditions and (2) assessing the relative profitability available in different nations and product markets.

**Monitoring Environmental Conditions**   In Chapters 8 and 13 we discussed the turbulent nature of the international business environment. We further stated the importance of predicting and understanding environmental change through constant monitoring of environmental conditions. Accordingly, monitoring environmental conditions requires surveillance of two sets of key factors.

The first set, remote factors, shows the general health and growth of the country—its economic and societal conditions. The second set, task factors, monitors the specific product market and the operating conditions. The factors chosen as monitors must be tailored to the specific product, service, or product or service line that is being marketed.

**Assessing the Relative Profitability**    A periodic reassessment of the MNC's resource allocation among different SBUs and product markets requires an examination of the relative long-term profitability of each SBU and market. Reallocation may be necessary because of changes in the relative profitability due to shifts in environmental conditions (economic or noneconomic) that have adversely affected profitability. Reallocation may also be stimulated by the decision to enter new regions, countries, or product markets that have a greater long-term profitability potential. The following section will address new market entry strategy.

## The Elements of Market Entry Strategy for New Markets

A **market entry strategy** is a comprehensive plan that establishes the objectives, resources, and strategies that will guide an MNC's business over a period of time (strategic period) long enough to achieve a sustainable growth in a certain foreign market.

Planning foreign market entry is a process of deciding on the direction of a company's foreign business by combining reason with empirical knowledge. Planning requires managers to carefully examine all assumptions about foreign markets and the competition in those markets.

A foreign market entry plan is based on and is an integral part of the global strategy we discussed in Chapters 13 and 14. In the globally competitive world of today, a company must think systematically about where its international business should be in two to five years. Without a market entry strategy, a company is limited to short-run, ad hoc reactions to changing environmental conditions and competition. This "sales" approach to foreign markets can no longer be an effective form of conducting business in today's global market.

When entering a new market or introducing a new product, a unique entry strategy needs to be formulated. The company's overall market entry strategy is an aggregation of individual product and market strategies.

Environmental differences between foreign markets require unique market entry strategies for each different product and market. For example, the market entry strategy for a consumer product would be different from the strategy for a computer product. As another example, upon its entry into the Soviet Union's market, Pepsico had to pursue a different strategy than it had previously used in other markets, such as the United Kingdom, Thailand, or Argentina. Even markets that are apparently similar may require different strategies. Of course, if a clustering of similar national markets is possible, then the same market entry strategy can be utilized across all the markets in the cluster. Clustering can also be used within a single country market. In these instances, clustering results in the identification of market segments and is a technique employed by companies interested in target marketing.

The global market entry strategy addresses issues such as the following:

1. The identification of potential target markets and products (to be discussed in this chapter).
2. The formulation of the MNC's overall and specific objectives in each target market (discussed in Chapter 13).
3. The selection of the patterns of involvement and the means to penetrate the targeted foreign country markets (discussed in Chapter 12).
4. The formulation and the implementation of marketing strategy to penetrate targeted markets (to be discussed in this chapter).

These issues are interdependent. For example, the selection of the pattern of involvement depends on the targeted country and its environmental conditions. Formulating a marketing strategy may necessitate reevaluating the decision to enter a market or the selection of the pattern of involvement to be used. As we explained in Chapter 12, selection of a pattern of involvement limits the choices among alternative marketing strategies. At times, during operations, problems arise that may call into question different elements of market entry strategy and affect similar market entry decisions in the future.

As the preceding discussion shows, the MNC executive should consider the development of a market entry strategy as a complex and interdependent process. Marketing strategy decisions should be made in light of the global strategy decisions made for the overall corporation.

In the following section, we will discuss a step-by-step process for selecting markets to enter.

## The New Market Screening Process

The global market contains a large number of markets and market segments. Because a firm's resources are limited and can only be used effectively in selected markets, the choice of markets should be based on finding the markets that have the greatest potential for contributing to the firm's long-term performance and profitability.

The new market screening process described here enables management to screen a large number of markets without investing a great deal of time, money, and effort. As a result of this process, less attractive markets are eliminated. After a few selected markets with good potential are identified, each can be further examined before resources are committed. The new market screening process entails a series of steps that become increasingly more complex until the markets with the best potential are identified. These screening steps are called: (1) potential need screening, (2) need satisfaction screening, (3) economic screening, (4) legal and political screening, (5) sociocultural screening, (6) ranking and clustering of markets, and (7) field trip, market research, and testing in the selected markets.

**Step 1: Potential Need Screening**  Underlying the demand for a product or service is the existence of an unsatisfied basic need. Without need, marketing efforts will be useless.

Environmental conditions determine the basic need for many products. Selling heaters in a country such as Malaysia, where the temperature hardly falls below 70°F, would adversely affect a company's profit. A producer of an all terrain vehicle may find little need for that product in a small urban country such as Kuwait.

The need patterns for many consumer products are often similar across many countries, but exceptions do exist. A given product may serve different purposes in different countries. For example, a U.S. toothbrush manufacturer experienced an unexpected surge in sales volume in South Vietnam during the late 1960s. Years later, the company found that the toothbrushes were being used by the Vietcong to clean their weapons instead of their teeth.[1] In a country in which housewives have a tradition of making daily trips to the market to purchase fresh meat, fruits, and vegetables, refrigerators with a large freezer compartment may serve either as temporary food storage or as a status symbol. When the refrigerator is used as a status symbol, it may be kept in the living or guest room, where it would be immediately visible, indicating to visitors that the family has the means to buy luxury items.

Potential need usually stays constant over a period of time. In cases where the product is not sold in a country, a definite potential need pattern is difficult to determine. In these cases, an MNC manager must rely on whatever information he or she can gather from any source.

**Step 2: Need Satisfaction Screening**  The marketing manager must determine whether or not the need for the product has been satisfied. Needs may already be satisfied from local production or from foreign imports into the country. For products with existing sales, the marketing manager can examine the trade statistics that show the foreign imports of the product or the product line into a country. This method assumes that the greatest potential target markets are countries that already import substantial amounts of the product.

A currently high level of imports, however, does not guarantee a high future demand for the product. Such a statistic only indicates that a country has been buying a product from abroad. A country on the verge of initiating its own local production can lower or stop importation of a given product. The government may decide to protect the local infant industry through the imposition of quotas or tariffs. Changes in the political climate may also reduce or curtail the imports of a product into a foreign country. For example, the Sandanista revolution in Nicaragua completely blocked the importation of products from the United States into that country. As another example, the decrease in oil revenues for OPEC in the mid-1980s resulted in a decline in the attractiveness of these nations as potential markets.

**Step 3: Economic Screening** During this step, the reduced list of countries selected after the first two screening steps will be subjected to scrutiny on the basis of financial and economic factors. The MNC evaluates the market for its products and services using a number of national economic statistics. These statistics include data on GNP growth, per capita income, income distribution, demographics, exchange rate stability, level of economic development, inflation rates, levels of literacy, skill levels of labor, power and electricity consumption, road mileage and transportation, and the availability of credit and financing.

Given such statistics, one can decide whether or not a country has sufficient market potential to warrant a marketing effort. Furthermore, these data can be used to measure the size, intensity (richness), and growth of a market. Such statistical measures help the international manager select countries and regions with the fastest growing markets and the highest concentration of purchasing power. *Business International* publishes a set of 44 worldwide market indicators for 131 nations (see Table 16.1). Other techniques for measuring market potential include seeking expert opinion, making estimates by analogy (extending data from existing markets to new markets), using regression analysis, and using trend analysis, as discussed in the forecasting section in Chapter 13.

**Step 4: Legal and Political Screening** The previous step in the new market screening process generated a list of countries with a large market potential and with the purchasing power necessary to make marketing the firm's products or services economically feasible. Given this list, the international marketing manager must delete those countries that are legally and politically prohibitive or excessively risky for marketing purposes.

Obviously, the countries in which conducting business is prohibited should not have been included in the initial list of nations to be considered. For example, in the late 1980s the United States had an embargo on trade with Cuba, Nicaragua, Vietnam, and Libya. Such an embargo rules out these countries as prospective markets for U.S. companies.

Another major consideration is the political stability of a nation. Political stability is more important than the political system. Today, many Western-based multinationals conduct business in communist and socialist countries. However, many MNCs stay away from or minimize their business involvement in countries with political instability, regardless of the form of government. This is because political instability increases uncertainty and risks, thus causing difficulties in strategy formulation.

Consideration should also be given to the trade restrictions or the incentives to trade that are established by the governments in potential markets. The MNC should examine the repatriation of funds regulations (transfer of profits out of the host country), the ownership requirements, the tax laws, the price controls, and so forth. The interested reader should refer to Chapter 9 for a complete list of the legal and political factors.

Table 16.1   WORLD MARKET INTENSITY INDEX, 1976 AS COMPARED WITH 1981

| | Market Size (Percent of World Market) | | Market Intensity (World = 1.00) | | Five-Year Market Growth (Percent) | |
|---|---|---|---|---|---|---|
| | 1976 | 1981 | 1976 | 1981 | 1971–1976 | 1976–1981 |
| **Major regions** | | | | | | |
| Western Europe | 22.65 % | 22.29 % | 2.65 % | 2.79 % | 21.05% | 12.73% |
| EC | 16.94 | 16.44 | 3.07 | 3.26 | 18.23 | 9.89 |
| EFTA | 2.67 | 2.58 | 3.09 | 3.20 | 17.68 | 12.62 |
| Eastern Europe | 15.61 | 13.23 | 1.74 | 1.47 | 96.19 | 7.47 |
| Middle East | 1.84 | 1.94 | 0.62 | 0.64 | 75.18 | 42.47 |
| Africa | 3.56 | 3.90 | 0.29 | 0.30 | 57.11 | 40.26 |
| Asia (excluding Communist Asia) | 17.94 | 19.20 | 0.48 | 0.53 | 34.17 | 26.29 |
| China | 11.20 | 10.06 | 0.24 | 0.28 | 89.38 | 96.66 |
| Australasia | 1.23 | 1.07 | 3.63 | 3.34 | 21.55 | 2.13 |
| North America | 23.86 | 23.13 | 4.86 | 4.87 | 18.21 | 12.29 |
| Latin America | 6.67 | 7.51 | 0.87 | 0.97 | 53.25 | 35.04 |
| LAFTA | (5.91) | (6.77) | (0.92) | (1.04) | 53.90 | 37.85 |
| World (total or average) | 100.00 | 100.00 | 1.00 | 1.00 | 31.34 | 17.71 |
| **Major markets** | | | | | | |
| United States | 20.96 | 21.67 | 4.89 | 4.91 | 17.28 | 11.68 |
| USSR | 11.34 | 11.18 | 1.76 | 1.91 | 49.64 | 38.38 |
| China | 11.20 | 10.06 | 0.24 | 0.28 | 89.38 | 96.66 |
| Japan | 7.47 | 7.07 | 2.86 | 3.22 | 28.86 | 20.59 |
| India | 4.83 | 4.65 | 0.15 | 0.16 | 33.06 | 75.68 |
| West Germany | 4.28 | 4.52 | 3.59 | 3.78 | 16.33 | 10.87 |
| United Kingdom | 3.17 | 3.39 | 2.88 | 3.05 | 8.83 | −0.71 |
| France | 3.51 | 3.46 | 3.27 | 3.57 | 24.10 | 16.71 |
| Italy | 3.13 | 3.14 | 2.67 | 2.87 | 23.67 | 10.42 |
| Brazil | 2.75 | 2.37 | 0.93 | 1.05 | 71.89 | 46.06 |
| Canada | 2.17 | 2.19 | 4.57 | 4.51 | 27.64 | 17.45 |
| Spain | 1.83 | 1.75 | 2.22 | 2.45 | 47.75 | 40.73 |

*Source:* BI/DATA. Reprinted from page 7 of the January 6, 1984 issue of *Business International.*

**Step 5: Sociocultural Screening**   The remaining markets should be scrutinized with regard to sociocultural factors. Chapter 10 provides a checklist of sociocultural factors. The international marketing manager should be familiar with the buying habits and consumption patterns of the population based on sociocultural factors of the potential markets. For instance, a pork producer would delete Moslem dominated countries from its list of potential markets. A dried meat producer should consider deleting countries where a premium is placed on fresh meat.

**Step 6: Ranking and Clustering of Markets**   At this stage, the remaining countries should be ranked according to their market appeal. In addition, these nations should be examined for geographical clusters that may facilitate the formation of regional organizations and subsidiaries within the MNC. Such subsidiaries are essential for regional production facilities and market penetration. For instance, the countries in the European Community (EC) or the markets of the Latin American Free Trade Association (LAFTA) can be clustered together and served by the MNC from one or two member countries.

**Step 7: Field Trip, Market Research, and Testing**   As indicated earlier, the new market screening process enables a firm to scan a large number of potential markets inexpensively by using available published data. This will allow the marketing manager of an MNC to concentrate analysis on the most promising markets through field trips, market research, and testing.

In the final step of the new market screening process, an executive or a group of executives should visit selected countries. During the trip, besides validating the data collected during the other steps of the screening process, new firsthand information can be obtained and contacts can be made. The field trip should provide information on competitive activity, the suitability of the firm's product mix for that particular foreign market, and the availability of distribution channels and support services. Another reason for spending money and time visiting a country is to more accurately assess the potential needs of the market and to assess the infrastructure available for implementing marketing strategies.

New contacts should be made during the field trip. The home country embassy officials, trade mission personnel, and business associates can prove helpful in making new contacts in the potential host country. Visiting trade shows, the chamber of commerce, or the ministry of business and commerce can provide further information and opportunities for future contacts.

If information collected during the field trip reveals that the new market is drastically different from those markets previously served, then marketing research and testing may be essential in deciding on an entry strategy. In fact, in many countries the socioeconomic data that are usually relied upon during the screening process may be inadequate to forecast the market potential.

The worst strategic error in the screening process is a failure to determine prior to market entry if a market exists for the firm's products or services. Many MNCs have committed this mistake by blindly assuming that their products will have appeal in new markets. Although making such an assumption may lead to the "right" outcome, many firms have not been so fortunate. For example, a U.S. ketchup manufacturer decided to beat potential competitors by shipping a large quantity of its popular brand name product to Japan. The company never stopped to wonder why ketchup was not already marketed in Japan. A marketing test would have indicated that soy sauce was the preferred seasoning in Japan.[2]

Table 16.2 provides the topics of appraisal for the business environment in screening new national markets.

**Table 16-2  APPRAISING THE BUSINESS ENVIRONMENT IN NEW NATIONAL PRODUCT MARKETS**

| Topic of appraisal | Items to be considered |
|---|---|
| Product-market dimensions | How big is the product-market in terms of unit size and sales volume? |
| Major product-market "differences" | What are the major differences relative to the firm's experience elsewhere, in terms of customer profiles, price levels, national purchase patterns, and product technology? |
| | How will these differences affect the transferability and effectiveness of company capabilities to the new business environment? |
| Structural characteristics of the national product-market | What links and associations exist between potential customers and established national competitors currently supplying these customers? |
| | Identify the major channels of distribution (discount structure, ties to present producers, levels of distribution separating producers from final customers, links between wholesalers, links between wholesalers and retailers, finance, role of government). |
| | Identify links between established producers and their suppliers. |
| | Industry concentration and collusive agreements. |
| Competitor analysis | Major competitor characteristics (size, capacity utilization, strengths and weaknesses, technology, supply sources, preferential market arrangements, and relations with government). |
| | Competitor performance in terms of market share, sales growth, and profit margins. |
| Potential target markets | Characteristics of major product-market segments. |
| | Segments which are potential targets upon entry. |
| Relevant trends (historic and projected) | Changes in total size of product-market (short-, medium-, and long-term). |
| | Changes in competitor performance (market share, sales, and profits). |
| | Nature of competition (e.g., national and international). |
| | Changes in market structure. |

**Table 16-2** (*Continued*)

| Topic of appraisal | Items to be considered |
| --- | --- |
| Explanation of change | Why are some firms gaining and others losing? |
| | Are foreign firms already operating here gaining or losing? |
| | Is there some general explanation of observed change, for example product life cycle, change in overall business activity, and shift in nature of demand? |
| | What is the future outlook? |
| Success factors | What are the key factors behind success in this business environment, the pressure points which can shift market share from one company to another? |
| | How are these different from those we have experienced in other countries? |
| | How do these success factors relate to our company? |
| Strategic options | What elements emerge from the above analysis which point to possible strategies for this country? |
| | What additional information is required to identify our options more precisely? |

Reprinted by permission of the publisher from MULTINATIONAL CORPORATE STRATEGY by James C. Leontiades (Lexington, Mass.: Lexington Books, D.C. Heath and Company, Copyright 1985, D.C. Heath and Company), pp. 124–125.

## INTERNATIONAL MARKETING STRATEGY

Formulating and implementing a successful international marketing strategy are challenges that all MNCs face when they seek to expand sales and gain profits outside their home countries. The problem is not only deciding what marketing approach to use, but also deciding how to combine all market approaches into an integrated and unified strategy. The different elements of a unified strategy should reinforce each other so that there is a synergistic result. Synergism is realized when the whole (the integrated strategy) is greater than the sum of its parts (the different marketing approaches).

The development of a marketing strategy is the next logical step following the decision to enter a new market with potential demand. In this step, factors that affect the firm's capability to reach the market potential are analyzed.

Figure 16.1 depicts the elements of the marketing strategy formulation and implementation process. The process includes the following:

1. An examination of the new market conditions. As discussed previously, this includes a series of steps to select new markets and to estimate the

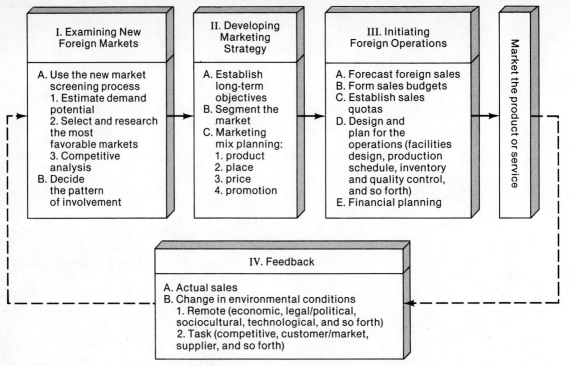

**Figure 16.1** Elements of marketing strategy formulation and implementation

*Source:* Adapted from Felix Turrel, "Go Global," U.S. Department of Commerce (n.d.).

demand, while analyzing the competition, assessing the general consumer behavior patterns, and deciding on the patterns of involvement for the MNC.

2. A formulation of long-term marketing objectives, while dividing the market into meaningful segments and deciding on the marketing mix variables of the four Ps.

3. An estimation of the resources (financial, management, personnel, material, production, and so forth) that will be required to implement the plan, while drawing implementation guidelines and policies.

4. A monitoring of the environmental conditions and the actual operating results, while comparing the actual results with the forecasted ones for the purpose of control.

## MARKET SEGMENTATION

Market segmentation is the process of breaking the market into sets of homogeneous customers. This process allows the marketing manager to adapt to the differences that exist among customers regarding their needs, wants, willingness, and ability to purchase a product. Different customers require different marketing approaches based on market segmentation. There are three approaches to market segmentation in international marketing: segmenting the world, segmenting foreign markets, and international market segmentation.[3]

## Segmenting the World or Segmenting Between Nations

Countries can be clustered using criteria such as language, religion, political and economic system, level of development, climate, and geographical location. For example, refrigerator and freezer manufacturers can segment nations based on their level of development. Expensive refrigerators with large freezer compartments may be marketed to the nations in the developed country cluster, whereas smaller refrigerators with small freezer compartments can be marketed in the developing countries. Another reason for marketing smaller refrigerators in LDCs is because of the different shopping habits in those countries. In LDCs, as well as in some European nations, consumers make frequent grocery shopping trips. Therefore, a large freezer compartment is unnecessary for consumers in those countries.

## Segmenting Foreign Markets

Markets within each country can be segmented on the basis of three criteria:

1. Traditional—geographic, demographic, and socioeconomic characteristics of the consumers in the market area.
2. Psychographic—lifestyle, personality, and attitude of the consumers in the market area.
3. Behavioral—benefits sought, usage background, brand loyalty, channel choice, and sensitivity to changes in price, product, quality, or promotion of the consumers in the market area.

For example, for many years the Japanese market was perceived to be a homogenous market that could not be segmented. The basis for this perception was that there is less ethnic, religious, and cultural diversity in Japan than in a nation of immigrants such as the United States. In addition, according to many polls, most Japanese consider themselves middle-class. The myth of the impenetrable Japanese market is being shattered daily, however. Many American market researchers see large differences in income levels and life-styles in Japan. These differences are being used by many U.S. firms as a base for segmenting that country's market.

In addition, niche marketing is rapidly increasing, mainly as a result of this knowledge. Marketing cigarettes in Japan provides a good example. Today, there are different brands for various market segments. For example, Lucky Strike is aimed at young men, and brands such as Kent are targeted at older men. Brands such as Capri and Virginia Slims are aimed at Japanese women. These market segmentation practices have led the Japanese to develop their own market segmentation. For example, Japan Tobacco sells a number of products aimed at various niches. These include a cigarette called Dean for young men and another one named Alex for young women.[4]

### International Market Segmentation

International market segmentation is a transnational or global concept. When consumers have similar tastes, products can be divided on the basis of those tastes instead of on the basis of other commonalities, such as religion or nationality. For example, certain types of people all over the world like caviar, fine perfume, scotch whiskey, designer watches, or English language newspapers. Similar marketing mix approaches can be utilized in the worldwide marketing of such products.

Industrial products can be segmented on the basis of usage. A supplier of gasoline engines, for example, can distinguish worldwide market segments among the manufacturers of automobile engines, of industrial equipment, and of agricultural machinery. Based on such an approach, an MNC that manufactures gasoline engines could formulate its marketing strategy by gearing it toward these three international market segments.

International customers can also be segmented by distinguishing among: (1) industrial users that import the product for their own use, including military and government organizations; (2) industrial users that buy through middlemen; and (3) individual consumers.

### Criteria for Selecting Market Segments

Regardless of the approach used in international marketing, the selection of market segments must satisfy a number of criteria, including the following:

1. **Measurability.** The MNC marketer should be able to measure the size and purchasing power of each segment.
2. **Accessibility.** The MNC should be able to reach each segment through available distribution channels and media.
3. **Reasonability of Size.** The identified market segments should be large enough to justify the change or modification of the marketing approach in order to reach them.

Creative market segmentation may prove vital in the development of new markets. Japanese MNCs appear to be particularly successful in gaining tremendous competitive advantages and in developing new markets through creative marketing. For example, the Japanese have adapted garden fillers for agricultural purposes in LDCs. As another example, Honda has modified small automobile engines for home power generation in LDCs.

## INTERNATIONAL MARKETING MIX MANAGEMENT

In order to successfully target its specific market segments, the MNC must develop an appropriate marketing mix. As mentioned earlier, marketing mix includes decisions about the product and service, the price, the place (the distribution), and the promotion—the four Ps. In this section we will elaborate on the four Ps as variables that relate to the selection of an international marketing mix strategy.

## Product Strategy

A **product** or **service** is something that people buy.* The people buying a product spend their money for the satisfactions received from the product. A product is defined as a collection of physical, service, and symbolic attributes that yield satisfaction or benefits to the people who buy or use it. **Product strategy** refers to the decisions concerning these attributes that influence the buyer's perception of the product. As all the other elements of the marketing mix must fit the product, the product is the most crucial element of the marketing mix. The choice of the product also determines the firm's customers and competitors, as well as all aspects of the company's operations.

In addition to the physical product, other aspects of the product, such as packaging, brand name, label, and presale and postsale services, alter the perceptions of the product. Such aspects and other marketing mix elements differentiate among similar products produced by competing firms in a market.

An option for a multinational firm is providing a service or intangible product, instead of a physical product. In Chapter 12 we discussed licensing, franchising, management contracts, and turnkey operations as representative methods of providing services in international markets. Except for the marketing mix decisions dealing with the physical characteristics of a product, the other material in this chapter also applies to marketing services as well as products.

An MNC usually markets a number of variations of a product or service in different countries. These variations, based on differences in function, price, quality, method of operation, and maintenance, are called a product line. For example, an auto manufacturer can produce a number of different vehicles for different types of consumers. A sports car may transport the young couple from a city apartment to a weekend resort. Later, a station wagon or van may transport that same couple plus their children to the beach. A truck may transport bricks for the building of their new suburban house after they outgrow their city apartment. The function of an automobile may include its use as a prestige symbol. A Ford Mustang is as efficient as a people carrier as a Lamborghini or a Rolls-Royce, but distinguished visitors to a foreign country are not transported in Ford Mustangs.

**Product Life Cycles**    The concepts of the product life cycle theory and international product life cycle (IPLC) were discussed in Chapters 2 and 12, respec-

---

*While we will use the terms product and service interchangeably, a service lacks the apparent physical characteristics of a product.

tively. Recall that the product life cycle theory states that every product goes through several stages during its life. There are five stages (introduction, growth, maturity, decline, demise) in a product life cycle. Some authors identify more stages, but most agree on at least five. One commonly identified stage, the shake-out, falls between growth and maturity in which the less efficient producers are shaken out or dropped out of a crowded marketplace.

In the global market, the same product may be in the growth stage in some less developed nations while in other countries it is in maturity or decline. Figure 16.2 and Table 16.3 illustrate this point.

In some instances it is possible to revitalize the product life cycle by pushing the product to a new stage of growth. This is possible through finding new uses for the product. A prime example is baking soda. After realizing that the sales of baking soda were declining, Arm and Hammer, a major producer of the product, started a promotional campaign aimed at making the customer aware of other uses for the product besides baking. The firm also started pro-

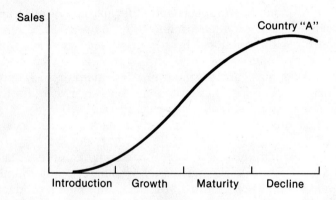

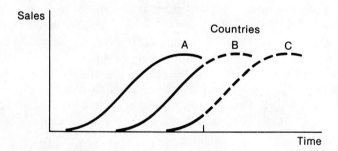

Note: Solid line = actual; dashed line = projected.

**Figure 16.2** Product life cycles in different countries

*Source:* Reprinted by permission of the publisher from MULTINATIONAL CORPORATE STRATEGY by James C. Leontiades (Lexington, Mass.: Lexington Books, D. C. Heath and Company. Copyright 1985 by D. C. Heath and Company), p. 74.

**Table 16.3  STAGES OF INTERNATIONAL PRODUCT MARKET DEVELOPMENT: WORLD AUTOMOBILE MARKETS**

| Stages / Variables | I Pre-market | II Less developed markets | III Take-off markets | IV Early mass markets | V Mature mass markets |
|---|---|---|---|---|---|
| Product Source | Occasional imports | Regular imports | Domestic assembly and partial manufacture imported parts | Domestic mass production | Domestic research design and mass production "New style" |
| Product Characteristics | Assorted types | Luxury products | Moderate size product designed for local production and broad appeal | Utility product designed for new mass market infrequent design changes | Specialized products, frequent model change, wide range, many options |
| Price | No discernable trend | High price category (Low volume) | Moderate price | Low price category (High volume) | Broad range of base prices directed at all market segments |
| Distribution | No company facilities | Single company appointed distributor | Multiple retail outlets serviced by local plant staff | Manufacturer sells to wholesale and retail outlets | Close co-ordination of factory and retail level electronic ordering |
| Service Facilities | No company facilities | Low volume personalized service by distributor | Local plants supply parts and training to outlets | Geared for high volume low cost service | Training and equipment for wide range of specialized products |
| Brand | Foreign brands | Foreign brands | Foreign brands produced domestically and identified with Host country | Domestic brands | "Families" of domestic product brands tied in with single company brand |
| Advertising and Promotion | None | Point of sale and personal contact | Wide use of printed mass media | Extensive use of all mass media (less emphasis on personal contact) | Research directed use of all mass media. Specialized campaigns for major market segments |

*Source:* James C. Leontiades, "Planning Strategy for World Markets," *Long Range Planning* (Elmsford, N.Y.: Pergamon, December 1970), p. 43.

ducing products, such as a carpet freshener, that use baking soda as the main ingredient.

As explained in Chapter 2, the stages in the international product life cycle were (1) domestic exports, (2) foreign production, (3) foreign competition in export markets, and (4) import competition in the domestic markets. The product life cycle concept applies to both domestic and international marketing. Figure 16.3 depicts the relationship between the stages of international product life cycle and the stages of product life cycle.

The IPLC is also used by many firms when they attempt to expand their sales and to prolong the growth and maturity stages of their products by seeking new markets in other nations.

**Product Strategy Alternatives**   There are five strategic alternatives available to an MNC that is seeking to extend its market base to other geographical areas. These strategies are based on the degree of standardization of the product and promotional strategies that are used in the home market and in foreign markets. On the one hand, a company can sell the same product and promote it in a similar manner at home and abroad. In other words, extend its domestic product and promotional message to other countries. On the other hand, a firm may have to change both its product and its promotional strategies or develop new ones to suit the conditions in foreign markets. These strategies can be categorized as: (1) product-promotional extensions, (2) product extension-promotional adaptation, (3) product adaptation-promotional extension, (4) dual adaptation, and (5) product invention.[5]

*Product-Promotional Extensions*   An extension of an existing product using an existing promotional campaign is the easiest, often the most profitable, and the most commonly used product strategy. The MNC pursuing this strategy sells what it already makes. The product is designed from its inception to fit conditions in more than one national market. The multinational corporation sells exactly the same product with the same advertising and promotional policy in every country in which it operates. Many soft drink producers, such as Pepsico, follow this strategy with great success.

But this strategy does not work for all products and markets. Many food producers face problems when they try to export prepared foods that do not suit local preferences. For example, General Foods, the American producer of Jello brand gelatin dessert, found difficulties in using this strategy in Great Britain. The American-style Jello package contained the powdered gelatin substance that American customers are so used to. Hot water is added, and the mix is chilled to form the dessert. The British were not interested. They were used to the jelled form of the product. To the British, the product was not food unless it jiggled and looked good. General Foods prevented a disaster by changing its product to conform to British customers' normal expectations.[6]

The product-promotional extension strategy is very appealing because it provides cost savings. The standardization of the product leads to an increase

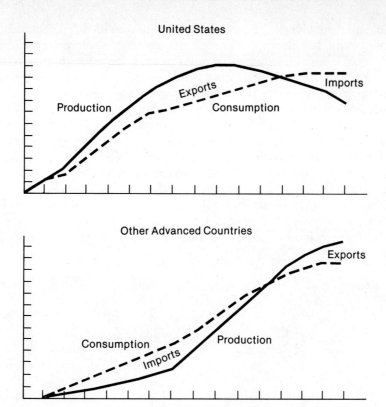

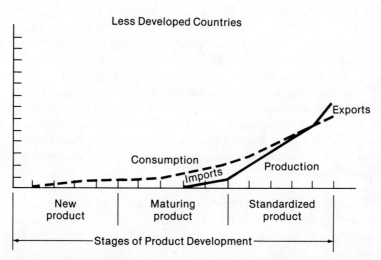

**Figure 16.3** Relationship between the stages of international product life cycle (IPLC) and the stages of product life cycle (PLC)

*Source:* Raymond Vernon, "International Investment and International Trade in the Product Life Cycle" (Cambridge, Mass.: Harvard University Press, May 1966), p. 99.

in the experience curve effects and to a reduction in R & D costs. Economies of scale are further increased through standardization of promotional activities.

Even in countries which are perceived to be very different from the United States, the extension of the same product and promotion is used by many American firms. For example, although many Japanese are convinced that what they receive is different, the Coca-Cola, Kellogg's Corn Flakes, Kodak color film, Listerine mouthwash, McDonald's hamburgers, and M&M candies, except for packaging, are basically the same as those sold in the United States.[7]

Although the cost savings may be enormous, the MNC executive must keep in mind that product-promotional adaptations may be necessary for proper positioning of the product in new national markets.* Product-promotional extension, with all its short-term cost savings appeal, may, nevertheless, have a disastrous long-term effect on sales and profits. The strategy of product promotional extensions is based on the ethnocentric philosophy discussed in Chapter 13.

*Product Extension-Promotional Adaptation*  The strategy of marketing an existing product in another market area using a different promotional message is effective when the old product satisfies a different need or performs a different function in the new area. This results in cost savings in manufacturing and in research and development that are associated with producing the same product instead of manufacturing a new product. However, some costs are increased due to the development of different strategies aimed at promoting the different usage or function in the foreign market. The MNC must identify different product functions and reformulate its marketing communications, including its advertising and its sales promotion, around this new function.

For example, many countries see bicycles and motor scooters as basic transportation. In the United States, these items are mainly used for recreation. Because of this functional difference, foreign producers, such as Honda of Japan, promote their products differently in the United States than they do in other foreign nations. Other examples include outboard motors and single engine airplanes, which are used in recreational vehicles in the United States, but in transportation vehicles in other countries. Another example is the introduction of Irish Spring Soap to Mexico. Colgate-Palmolive renamed its Mexican version "Nordiko" to project a fresh and cool "double protection" image to the Mexican consumers.

*Product Adaptation-Promotional Extension*  This third strategy is used when the product serves the same function, but must be adapted to different local conditions. Many products must be modified to function similarly under

---

*Product positioning indicates the market segment(s) toward which a proposed or existing product or service is targeted. In other words, product positioning is an indication of the relative location of a product compared with similar products. The location can be based on price, customer preferences, product characteristics, and so forth.

different environmental conditions. For years gasoline manufacturers such as Exxon (Esso) have adapted their formulas for different weather conditions in different markets. Still, Exxon has used the same promotional message of "Put a Tiger in Your Tank" throughout the world. Soap and detergent manufacturers have adapted their products to fit local water and equipment characteristics. For example, because laundry is done in Japan in hard water, detergents are formulated specifically for this condition.[8] Agricultural chemicals have been adjusted for different soil conditions and for different insect populations. As was discussed earlier, household appliances, such as refrigerators, are scaled to different sizes for different local usages in foreign markets.

***Dual Adaptation: Product Adaptation-Promotional Adaptation*** If market conditions give rise to differences in both the function and the environmental conditions regarding the use of the product, then the dual adaptation strategy will be used. Both the product and the communication strategies will be adjusted to fit the local environmental conditions and desired local function. While this is a reactive attitude to consumer needs, it does not mean that the MNC is forgoing the economies of standardization completely. However, some sacrifice is required to make dual adaptation possible.

This combination of strategies was followed when the military regime in Brazil began to heavily tax "superfluous" products such as scotch whiskey. At the time, Brazil was one of the leading importers of scotch. The local bottlers and foreign manufacturers of scotch whiskey developed a number of new products, which were bottled or even distilled in Brazil. These usually sweeter products were promoted as thirst-quenching, cooling drinks. A dual adaptation strategy may be based on the geocentric philosophy discussed in Chapter 13.

***Product Invention*** Sometimes the MNC wants to enter and penetrate markets in a country because of the country's size, its growth potential, its political stability, or for some other reason. The question of what can be sold in this country must then be asked. The answer may lead to the development of products that may or may not be related to the company's current product line.

This strategy of inventing something new to meet the special needs of a segment of foreign customers is the most risky of all market expansion strategies. The extension and adaptation strategies discussed earlier, are effective only when potential customers in other markets have the purchasing power and the desire to buy the product the firm makes. The three quarters of the world population that live in LDCs may not be able to afford the expensive products designed for more affluent societies. This necessitates product invention for those markets.

If the product development costs are not heavy, the product invention strategy may prove fruitful in penetrating the mass markets in LDCs. Still, the number of firms responding to foreign market needs through new inventions is small. Nevertheless, some firms have been successful in developing inexpensive products that can be used by these low-income nations. For example, an estimated 600 million people in LDCs still wash their clothes by hand because electricity is not readily available. Colgate-Palmolive has seen potential in this market segment and has responded by developing an inexpensive (under $10) hand-powered plastic washer with the tumbling action of an electric washing machine. Not only has the product sold well in Mexico, but Colgate-Palmolive expects this to lead to an increase in demand for its laundry detergent.

**Strategy Selection** Companies usually try to select a product strategy that optimizes their profits in the long run. There is no easy answer to the question of which strategy achieves the firm's objective of long-run profit optimization. The answer depends on the unique combination of the product, the market, the company, and the environment. Some major factors to be considered in selecting an optimum product strategy are the following:

**1.** The customer and the market. The MNC needs to properly assess the needs, usages, purposes, resources, and perceptions of the new customers. The more similar the new market is to the old market, the smaller the need for product and promotional adaptation.

**2.** Regulation. Legal and governmental regulation may be the main reason for product and promotional adaptation in foreign markets. Governments usually establish standards for the quality, safety, purity, content, testing, packaging, and labeling of the products imported or produced in their countries. If the MNC does not satisfy governmental requirements, it will not be permitted to produce and to market the product in a foreign country. Besides indirect governmental interference, foreign governments can directly prohibit the production of certain products for reasons of national security, for the protection of domestic firms, or for other reasons.

**3.** Economics. The economics of design, production, and marketing usually favor standardization of the product and the promotional strategies. As a result of standardization, certain costs, such as product design and development costs, are minimized.

**4.** Compatibility with the MNC's strategies and resources. The product strategy should be properly aligned with the overall objectives and strategies of the firm, including its production, marketing, research and development, and financial capabilities.

Table 16.4 depicts the product-promotional strategic alternatives.

Making a uniform product is cheaper, but it may result in the loss of business in countries where product preferences differ from the home country norm. An option is to get inputs of information from many markets and use

Table 16.4  PRODUCT-PROMOTIONAL STRATEGIC ALTERNATIVES

| Strategy | Product function or need satisfied | Conditions of product use | Ability to buy product | Recommended product strategy | Recommended communications strategy | Relative cost of adjustments | Product examples |
|---|---|---|---|---|---|---|---|
| 1 | Same | Same | Yes | Extension | Extension | 1 | Soft drinks |
| 2 | Different | Same | Yes | Extension | Adaptation | 2 | Bicycles, motor scooters |
| 3 | Same | Different | Yes | Adaptation | Extension | 3 | Gasoline, Detergents |
| 4 | Different | Different | Yes | Adaptation | Adaptation | 4 | Clothing, Greeting cards |
| 5 | Same | — | No | Invention | Develop new communications | 5 | Hand-powered washing machine |

*Source*: Adapted from Raymond Vernon, "International Investment and International Trade in the Product Life Cycle," *Quarterly Journal of Economics* (Cambridge, Mass.: Harvard University Press, May 1966), pp. 190–207.

this information to make a standard for the product and for the promotional strategies. An example will clarify this point. Boeing introduced its 737 model jet aircraft 20 years ago to compete with McDonnell Douglas's DC-9. Initially, the 737 won orders from several U.S. airlines. In the early 1970s, however, sales began to dwindle. The DC-9 was slightly faster and had a competitive advantage because it was introduced three years earlier than the Boeing 737. Boeing was about to halt production of the 737, but to give the aircraft a last chance, Boeing assigned an engineering team to search for new markets in the Middle East, Africa, and South America. The team decided that Boeing needed to adapt the plane to the idiosyncrasies of Third World aviation. In these countries the runways were usually too short to accommodate the jet, and they were also too soft, being made of asphalt, instead of concrete. Boeing's engineers redesigned the wings of the aircraft to allow for shorter landings. They also added thrust to the engines for quicker takeoffs. Another problem was the prevalence of hard landings, which would lead to brake failures and to jets running beyond the runways. Boeing redesigned the landing gear and installed low-pressure tires so that the aircraft would stick to the ground at touchdown.

These actions worked. Boeing started selling a couple of 737 jets at a time to LDCs, rather than the customary orders of 20 or 30 aircraft found in the United States. As a result, production rates remained at reasonable levels, and the Boeing 737 slowly built its reputation as a suitable aircraft for LDCs. As aviation activities in the LDCs grew, so did Boeing's sales to those countries. The 737 jet eventually became the best-selling commercial aircraft in history.[9]

## Promotional Strategy

**Promotional strategies** are the means by which consumers are informed about products. These strategies also persuade customers that they can derive advantages from the use of a firm's products and services. These strategies are forms of marketing communications that are designed to influence the behavior of customers in different markets.

**Elements of the Promotional Strategy**   A promotional strategy is composed of four elements: (1) advertising, (2) personal selling, (3) sales promotion, and (4) publicity. The Committee on Definitions of the American Marketing Association defines these elements as follows:

**1. Advertising** is "any paid form of nonpersonal presentation and promotion of ideas, goods, or services by an identified sponsor."[10] Usually advertising is achieved through the use of mass media, such as radio, television, newspapers, and magazines. It is characterized by a high degree of control by the sponsor.

**2. Personal selling** is defined as "the oral presentation in a conversation with one or more prospective purchasers for the purpose of making sales."[11] In developed nations, certain consumer goods and many industrial products are promoted in this manner.

**3. Sales promotion** refers to the "marketing activities, other than personal selling, advertising, and publicity, that stimulate consumer purchasing and dealer effectiveness, such as displays, shows and exhibitions, demonstrations, and various nonrecurrent selling efforts not in the ordinary routine."[12]

**4. Publicity** includes "nonpersonal stimulation of demand for a product, service, or business unit by planting commercially significant news about it in a published medium or obtaining favorable presentation of it upon radio, television, or stage that is not paid for by the sponsor."[13]

We can also add branding and packaging to the elements of promotional strategy because they also attract consumer attention and influence purchasing behavior. Brand names convey an image of quality, reliability, and service. Package presentation influences the consumer's perceptions of quality and convenience. Packages can also be used as containers.

**Formulating Promotional Objectives and Strategies**   **Promotional strategy** refers to alternative communication channels and techniques that the international marketing executive can use to interpret the value of products and services for the potential foreign customer. Too often the promotional components of an international marketing strategy are formulated without any real analysis of just what such promotional programs are intended to accomplish.

The major objective of a promotional strategy is to create and maintain a favorable image for the company in the industry and among the public. Another important objective of a promotional strategy is the creation of interest in the product and the stimulation of product sales.

Promotional strategies must be effective in communicating a favorable image and in increasing awareness and interest in the target market. As discussed earlier, products are usually at different stages of the product life cycle in different markets. Because of differences in environmental conditions in these markets, the effective promotional appeal for a product may vary from market to market.

As was discussed in the previous section on product strategy, the MNC marketing manager must decide whether or not to extend (use the same strategy), adapt, or invent a promotional strategy for each national market. The requirements for effective communication and persuasion are the same in all countries, but the specific message often needs modification from region to region or from country to country.

After the market segments are properly identified, they should be carefully analyzed to formulate an effective promotional strategy. The choice of such a promotional strategy depends on the type of the product, the nature of the market, the MNC management's beliefs about the efficiency of the various elements in a specific market, the host government's regulations in regards to the acceptability of various promotional techniques, and the availability and cost of alternative media in a given market.

### Pricing Strategy

Today's world markets are highly competitive. Although price is only one of the four elements of a multinational marketing mix, it may be the major determining factor in the MNC's ability to compete in a given market.

**Pricing strategy** can be defined as the basic philosophy of pricing a product in the context of the general marketing mix. The strategy may be to establish low profit margins to secure sales volume or to meet, or beat, the competitor's prices. On the other hand, the strategy may be to recover developmental expenses early in the product life cycle. Pricing strategy is different from pricing tactics in that pricing tactics are the means by which strategy is implemented. A specific price in terms of the local currency is an example of a pricing tactic.

Based on philosophies of centralization (discussed in Chapter 13), the MNC may choose among three alternative worldwide pricing strategies: the ethnocentric, the polycentric, and the geocentric.[14]

1.  The **ethnocentric pricing strategy.** This is the strategy that employs universal pricing in all markets in which the MNC operates. Using this strategy, variations in the conditions of different markets are not considered by the MNC.

2.  The **polycentric pricing strategy.** According to this strategy, each national or regional subsidiary independently pursues its own pricing strategy. This flexible strategy allows for the most responsiveness to the unique market conditions of each local market. This strategy, however, does not benefit from the experience and sophisticated techniques that are available from headquarters or from other subsidiaries.

3.  The **geocentric (global) pricing strategy.** This is a compromise strategy that is less rigid than the ethnocentric pricing but more rigid than the polycentric strategy. The local decision-making structure considers local conditions under the general strategic guidance of the parent company. In addition to the local market factors, this approach takes into account the necessity of pricing coordination with headquarters in effectively dealing with international accounts and product arbitrage. The geocentric approach also consciously attempts to benefit from the accumulated national pricing experience that has been gained in different national markets.

### Distribution Strategy

**Physical distribution** refers to the array of activities that is concerned with the efficient movement of the finished product from the end of the production line to the consumer. These activities include plant and warehouse site selection, order processing, freight transportation, warehousing, material handling, protective packaging, inventory control, and customer service.

The American Marketing Association defines a **channel of distribution** as "the structure of intercompany organization units and external company agents and dealers, wholesale and retail, through which a commodity, product, or service is marketed."[15] According to this definition, the MNC marketing executive must combine the internal company marketing organization with the external independent channels in order to properly distribute its products.

The channels of distribution add utility to the product or service by providing: (1) the place, or the availability of the product at a location that is convenient to the potential consumer; (2) the time, or the availability of the product at a time that satisfies customer needs and wants; (3) the information that answers questions about the product and communicates proper usage of the product; and (4) the services, including presale and postsale, needed to maintain the product. Distribution is an integral part of the total marketing strategy, and it must be tailored to specific product, promotional, and pricing strategies. The distribution channels available to an MNC are highly differentiated and complex. As a result, the formulation of a distribution strategy is one of the most challenging and difficult elements of an international marketing system. Smaller companies are frequently prevented from competitively exporting their products by their inability to establish effective channels of distribution.

The initial step in deciding on the most effective distribution strategy is the identification of the target market and the determination of the needs and preferences of the potential customers. Among the important characteristics of the customers are their numbers, incomes, shopping habits, information requirements, price sensitivities, service expectations, credit needs, and reactions to different selling and promotional strategies.

Other important criteria for the selection of a distribution strategy include the product's characteristics, such as its standardization, bulk, service requirements, unit price, and perishability. The availability and characteristics of the middlemen and the environmental constraints, including economic, sociocultural, and legal factors, are also important considerations.

We conclude this chapter by stating that marketing strategy consists of the identification and the selection of target markets and the determination of a marketing mix. The marketing mix variables of product, promotion, price, and distribution (place) are greatly controlled, influenced, and manipulated by the multinational marketing executive. To a large degree, the MNC can choose the characteristics of its product, the price it charges, the message and the media for the product's promotion, and the channels of distribution for the product.

The amount of control exercised on the elements of an MNC's marketing mix is limited by noncontrollable environmental variables such as sociocultural factors, political and legal factors, economic conditions, customer and market preferences, and the behavior of competitors. Table 16.5 shows the key marketing mix questions that are raised in each market or country chosen by an MNC.

Finally, the marketing strategy of a multinational firm should fit the overall global objectives and strategies that the firm has established earlier.

**Table 16.5  KEY MARKETING MIX QUESTIONS**

| Marketing mix elements | Questions |
| --- | --- |
| A. Product policies | 1. What products and product lines should the company sell, for example, how broad and deep should the product line be for this market? |
| | 2. To what extent should the company adapt and modify products to cultural, sociological, and national characteristics for this market? |
| | 3. What improvements of existing products should be undertaken, and should the firm introduce a new product or products in this market? |
| | 4. How should products be packaged and labeled in this market? (Includes a review of existing packaging and labeling laws.) |
| | 5. How much emphasis is there on brand names and trademarks? Does the firm wish to use the same brand names and trademarks used in the United States and/or elsewhere in this market? |
| | 6. What warranties and guarantees, if any, are desirable or must be offered and what other postsale service(s), such as repair service, is required in this market? |
| B. Advertising policies | 1. To what extent should advertising themes and campaigns be differentiated from other markets to accommodate cultural, sociological, and national characteristics in this market? (Is standardized advertising a recommended and appropriate alternative in this market?) |
| | 2. Should a local advertising agency, a branch, or subsidiary of the firm's international advertising agency be used in this market? |
| | 3. What media are available, and what are their costs and unusual requirements? How reliable are media circulation or audience data? |
| | 4. What is the availability and quality of media research organizations? |
| | 5. What are the regulations on media advertising that would affect the firm's strategy in this market? What are the regulations on point-of-purchase and in-store materials? |
| | 6. What roles do channel members play, and what advertising assistance, such as cooperative advertising, in-store promotion, and point-of-purchase materials, do channel members expect? |
| C. Distribution policies | 1. What is the typical retail and wholesale structure for comparable products in this market? |
| | 2. Should the firm use existing channels of distribution or attempt to alter the established distribution patterns in this market? |
| | 3. Does the firm wish to sell directly to the retailer or through intermediaries in this market? |
| | 4. Should the firm attempt to obtain wide distribution at the retail level or rely on exclusive dealerships or outlets in this market? |

**Table 16.5** (*Continued*)

| Marketing mix elements | Questions |
|---|---|
| | 5. How much channel control does the firm want in this market? |
| | 6. What discount structure and credit terms are competitive and appropriate for this market? |
| | 7. What is the quality of the available transportation, warehousing, and the firm's other physical distribution needs in this market? |
| | 8. How much channel advertising support is necessary and appropriate for this market? |
| D. Pricing policies | 1. What tariff and dumping laws are applicable in this market? |
| | 2. Should the firm establish (or attempt to establish) uniform base prices? |
| | 3. What specific pricing approach should be used in the market? (Examples are cost-oriented, competitor-oriented, and customer-oriented.) |
| | 4. What are the price regulations (that is, price fixing and cartel arrangements) in this market? |
| | 5. As an overall strategy, is penetration or skimming pricing preferable for new products in this market? |
| | 6. What pricing approach do competitors use in this market? |

*Source:* Adapted from R. T. Hise, P. L. Gillet, and J. K. Ryans, Jr., *Basic Marketing* (Cambridge, Mass.: Winthrop 1979), pp. 546–550.

# SUMMARY

1. Marketing is the process of formulating and implementing an integrated strategy aimed at serving a market and providing customer satisfaction. The formulation of marketing strategy contains decisions on the marketing mix elements of the product or service, the distribution (place), the price, and the promotion.
2. Since an MNC needs to concentrate its limited resources in the countries and markets with the greatest potential, it needs to assess the size and potential of its existing markets and the size and potential of possible future markets.
3. The allocation of resources across existing national and product markets requires: (a) monitoring environmental conditions and (b) assessing the relative profitability in different nations and product markets.
4. A market entry strategy is a comprehensive plan that establishes the objectives, plans, resources, and policies that will guide the MNC's business over a period of time (the strategic period). This time period should be long enough to achieve sustainable growth in a foreign market. This market entry strategy is an integral part of the MNC's global strategic management.
5. A market screening process is used to select new markets to enter. The steps in this screening process involve: (a) potential need screening; (b) need satisfaction screening; (c) economic screening; (d) legal and political screening; (e) sociocultural screening; (f) ranking and clustering of markets; and (g) field trip, market research, and testing.

6. A marketing strategy is a unified and integrated long-term plan.
7. Market segmentation is dividing the market into sets of homogeneous customers. The international marketer has three segmentation options: (a) segmenting the world, (b) segmenting individual foreign markets, and (c) segmenting international markets. A market segment should be measurable, accessible, and reasonable in size.
8. A product or service is something that people buy. A product can be in different stages of its product life cycle in different countries.
9. There are five strategic alternatives for geographic expansion into foreign markets: (a) product-promotional extensions, (b) product extension-promotional adaptation, (c) product adaptation-promotional extension, (d) dual adaptation, and (e) product invention. The selection of one of these strategies depends on the customer and the market, the legal and governmental regulations, the economics, and the compatibility of the selected strategy with the MNC's overall strategies and resources.
10. Promotional strategies are the means by which consumers are informed about products and services. The firm also needs to persuade customers that there are advantages in using its products and services. The four elements of a promotional strategy are advertising, personal selling, sales promotion, and publicity.
11. Price is the major determining factor in an MNC's ability to compete. There are three worldwide pricing strategies for an MNC: ethnocentric (universal pricing), polycentric (unique pricing for each subsidiary), and geocentric (local pricing under corporate guidance and coordination).
12. Physical distribution refers to the array of activities concerned with efficient movement of the finished product from the end of the production line to the consumer. Distribution includes the use of an internal company marketing organization along with the use of external independent channels for the proper distribution of products. An effective distribution strategy depends on the needs and preferences of the potential customer, the product's characteristics, the availability and the characteristics of the middlemen, and other environmental conditions.
13. The marketing strategy of an MNC should be tailored to the overall global objectives and strategies that the firm has established earlier.

## QUESTIONS

16.1 What is marketing and what is its role in international business?

16.2 How do the four elements of marketing mix relate to each other?

16.3 How are resources allocated in an MNC?

16.4 Choose a product or a service, and a country. How do you go about examining the potential market for your product or service in this country? Elaborate.

16.5 What are some of the criteria that you can use in segmenting the market you have just evaluated in Question 16.4?

16.6 Discuss the elements of product strategy.

16.7 Examine the product-promotional strategies of 10 multinational firms. Can you classify these companies according to the five product-promotional strategies discussed in this chapter?

16.8 Discuss the different approaches to a promotional strategy and give examples of how companies follow these strategies.

16.9 What are the determinants of an effective pricing strategy? An effective promotional strategy?

16.10 Can you devise a strategy for proper marketing of the product or service you chose in Question 16.4? Discuss.

## NOTES

1. David A. Ricks, *Big Business Blunders: Mistakes in Multinational Marketing* (Homewood, Ill.: Dow Jones-Irwin, 1983), p. 3.
2. Ibid., p. 128.
3. Walter Ingo and Tracy Murray, *Handbook of International Business* (New York: Wiley, 1982), part 5.
4. Damon Darlin, "Myth and Marketing in Japan," *The Wall Street Journal,* 6 April 1989, p. B1.
5. Warren J. Keegan, *International Marketing Management,* 2nd ed. (Englewood Cliffs, N.J.: Prentice-Hall, 1980), pp. 273–279.
6. Ricks, *Big Business Blunders,* p. 24.
7. Darlin, "Myth and Marketing in Japan," p. B1.
8. Ibid.
9. Andrew Kupfer, "How to Be a Global Manager," *Fortune,* 14 March 1988, p. 52.
10. Committee on Definitions, American Marketing Association, *Marketing Definitions, A Glossary of Marketing Terms* (Chicago, Ill.: American Marketing Association, 1960), p. 9.
11. Ibid., p. 18.
12. Ibid., p. 20.
13. Ibid., p. 19.
14. Keegan, *International Marketing Management,* p. 319.
15. Committee on Definitions, *Marketing Definitions,* p. 10.

## SUGGESTED READINGS

Business International. *201 Checklists: Decision Making in International Operations.* New York: Business International Corporation, 1980, pp. 103–133.

Committee on Definitions, American Marketing Association. *Marketing Definitions: A Glossary of Marketing Terms.* Chicago: American Marketing Association, 1960.

Darlin, Damon. "Myth and Marketing in Japan," *The Wall Street Journal,* 6 April 1989, p. B1.

Haner, F. T. *Multinational Management.* Columbus, Ohio: Merrill, 1973.

Jain, Subhash C. *International Marketing Management,* 2nd ed. Boston: Kent, 1987.

———. *Marketing Planning and Strategy.* Cincinnati, Ohio: South-Western, 1981.

———, and Lewis R. Tucker, Jr. *International Marketing: Managerial Perspectives,* 2nd ed. Boston: Kent, 1986.

Kahler, Ruel. *International Marketing,* 5th ed. Cincinnati, Ohio: South-Western, 1983.

———, Ruel, and Ronald L. Kramer. *International Marketing,* 4th ed. Cincinnati, Ohio: South-Western, 1977.

Keegan, Warren J. *International Marketing Management,* 2nd ed. Englewood Cliffs, N.J.: Prentice-Hall, 1980.

Kupfer, Andrew. "How to Be a Global Manager." *Fortune,* 14 March 1988, p. 52.

Leontiades, James C. *Multinational Corporate Strategy: Planning for World Markets.* Lexington, Mass.: Lexington Books, 1985.

Negandhi, Anant R. *International Management.* Boston: Allyn and Bacon, 1987.

Ricks, David A. *Big Business Blunders: Mistakes in Multinational Marketing.* Homewood, Ill.: Dow Jones-Irwin, 1983.

Root, Franklin R. *Strategic Planning for Export Marketing.* Scranton, Penn.: International Textbook, 1966.

Terpstra, Vern. *International Dimensions of Marketing,* 2nd ed. Boston: Kent, 1985.

# International Financial Management and Strategy

*F* inancial management and strategy play an important role in the managerial decision making of multinational corporations. A number of factors make the financial aspects of multinational corporate management more complex than the financial management of a purely domestic firm. One of these factors is the greater risk usually associated with operating on a global level. Other factors include currency exchange rate fluctuations and the variations in the general environmental conditions, as discussed in Chapter 8.

The greater risk that MNCs face results from: (1) the greater political and economic risks that exist in some host nations as compared with the home country and (2) the managerial risk that stems from operating in an unfamiliar environment, where an MNC is always considered an outsider.

The purpose of this chapter is to provide us with a basic understanding of financial management and strategy. We define the elements of financial strategy for an MNC, including the concepts of centralization and decentralization. Then, we discuss in detail each element of financial strategy.

## FINANCIAL STRATEGY

Financial strategy is concerned with four fundamental decisions:

1. Financing the foreign operations—deciding how to secure funds for financing global operations.
2. Capital budgeting or long-term resource allocation—deciding where these funds should be invested.
3. Remittance strategy—deciding on how to transfer interest, profits, and other returns (such as dividends and royalty fees), and capital back to the parent company.
4. Operational policies—deciding on how to run the financial operations, including the management of working capital, cash flow, accounts receivable, inventory, and foreign exchange.

Figure 17.1 highlights the relationship among these decisions.

Because an understanding of these elements requires a comprehension of centralization and decentralization, we provide an explanation of these concepts before elaborating on the elements of financial strategy.

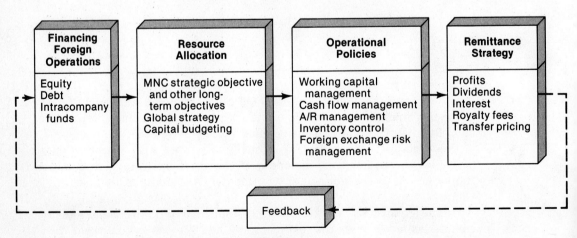

**Figure 17.1** Fundamental decisions in financial strategy

# THE CENTRALIZATION VERSUS DECENTRALIZATION DILEMMA

Our discussion on global strategic management in Chapters 13 and 14 revealed that a multinational firm is a multi–strategic business unit (SBU) organization; that is, it has many national or regional subsidiaries, with different layers of organization structure. Furthermore, as a result of the multilevel nature of an MNC, different levels of objectives and strategies exist for each level. Therefore, in addition to financial planning and control at the subsidiary level, a broad supplementary system of planning and control is needed at the global level. However, the creation of separate layers of organization, each with its own financial and nonfinancial strategic and control systems, results in additional costs and causes a dilemma (see Chapter 13).

The dilemma is concerned with how much decision making—both financial and nonfinancial—should be centralized. With highly centralized decision making, decisions are made and controlled by the MNC headquarters with little autonomy given to the regional and national subsidiaries. On the other extreme, some companies choose to decentralize decisions and provide autonomy for the regional, national, and even local managers of their foreign operations. Still other companies centralize decision making in some areas and decentralize it in other areas. Some financial matters, for instance, capital budgeting and controlling cash reserves, may be centralized, while the management of local accounts and working capital may be decentralized.

Three philosophies control the amount of centralization or decentralization in a business. These are: polycentric, ethnocentric, and geocentric.[1]

## Polycentric Philosophy

According to **polycentric philosophy**, decision making is decentralized to the subsidiaries with the MNC acting as a holding company. The corporate role is limited to the business portfolio analysis of different SBUs. The unit's performance is evaluated in comparison to similarly situated SBUs. Each subsidiary's financial statement is prepared according to both the home country's and host country's generally accepted accounting principles (GAAP). Except for decisions concerning new projects and financing, other decisions are also decentralized.

## Ethnocentric Philosophy

At the other extreme lies the **ethnocentric philosophy** that treats overseas operations as an extension of domestic operations. All strategic decision making and operational control (financial and nonfinancial) are integrated into a corporate system operated at the parent company. As a result, the overall corporate picture will be considered at all times. When detailed policies and guidelines are structured to guide all the decision making at the subsidiary and local levels, complete centralization will result.

All decisions are centralized with the purpose of minimizing costs and maximizing profits. Often local and subsidiary performance is sacrificed to achieve optimum profits at the corporate level. For instance, to minimize global taxes, the corporate headquarters may sell an intermediate product to a subsidiary at an inflated price. This manipulation of **transfer pricing** will result in lower subsidiary profits and taxes, but increased profits and taxes for the parent company. The manipulation is undertaken to transfer profits from high-tax countries to low-tax jurisdictions, reducing the overall corporate tax burden. Appendix 17.1 provides a numerical illustration of transfer pricing by an MNC.

Another common practice is to manipulate debt allocation and fund raising within different subsidiaries in order to achieve the lowest overall cost. Because of these manipulations, subsidiary financial statements are nearly meaningless. An actually profitable SBU may report huge losses because of an artificial allocation of debt and arbitrarily high transfer prices. Therefore, evaluation of actual subsidiary performance and objective planning and control with the aid of official financial statements become impossible.

To overcome this problem, ethnocentric MNCs prepare multiple sets of financial statements. A set is prepared to satisfy local reporting requirements, another for the consolidated financial statements, and a third "real one" for use in corporate decision making. Other sets of financial statements may also be prepared for tax reporting to the host country, the home country, and the minority stockholders in the foreign subsidiary. Obviously, preparing and keeping track of all the different prices, transactions, and financial statements is an enormous task. The task is even more complex as tax authorities request an examination of all these records. Of course, the MNC resists revealing these documents to tax authorities.

## Geocentric Philosophy

The **geocentric philosophy** is one solution to the problems found in the use of the other two philosophies. By an awareness of the implications of their decisions, the management of the true multinational firm recognizes the advantages of being a multinational, but still tries to prevent too much centralization. The management of such an MNC is aware that centralization limits flexibility and initiative.

The geocentric philosophy believes that the benefits of decentralization depend on the nature and location of the subsidiaries. If the local management in one nation is of high caliber and independent, decentralization is beneficial. In such a location, a holding company is formed and a polycentric philosophy is followed. Such is the case for the British MNCs operating in the United States. By the same token, the operations in many LDCs are centralized, being managed by the MNC's headquarters at home.

On the other hand, the MNC corporate executive knows that decentralization gains are dependent on the variations in competitive environments, financial systems, and tax rates. The gains are minimal in those developing nations where financial and economic systems are integrated and where bilateral tax treaties exist. Maximum centralization benefits are usually present in countries with less developed financial markets and divergent tax codes.

In summary, the MNC using a geocentric philosophy optimizes its benefits by decentralizing operations in some nations (usually developed countries) and centralizing operations in other nations (usually LDCs), based on local characteristics and variations in environmental conditions.

# FINANCING FOREIGN OPERATIONS

A multinational company needs funds for land, plants, equipment, and working capital to pay for inventory and operating expenses and to provide credit. Even a firm with only exporting activities needs funds for inventory, credit, and sales promotions.

Considering the need for the infusion of capital and the unusual risky environment of international operations, the MNC has a number of options and sources of financing. We will address these issues in this section.

## Equity Capital

**Equity** funds are those raised by an MNC that are not borrowed funds. Since no funds have been borrowed there is no diversion of cash flow into payments toward principal, interest, or other fees charged for the use of borrowed capital. The issuance of equity (capital stock) means that part of the ownership of the firm (or its subsidiary) has been sold. Money has not been borrowed. There is no loan to repay when stock has been sold. The stock buyer's return lies in the annual dividends the company pays and in stock price appreciation.

When the multinational company decides to raise capital through equity funding, it can list either its own stock or the stock in its subsidiary at one of the stock exchanges around the world. There are many stock exchanges (bourses) in the world.*

Usually, equity financing is provided for a subsidiary by the parent company. Such funds can originate from the parent company's retained earnings or from the sale of stock in the home stock markets. Other sources of equity for a foreign subsidiary can be from one or more other companies in the form of a joint venture or a consortium.

The subsidiary can also sell its own stock in the country in which it operates. The sale of stock can take place through a public offering, a stock exchange, or through a private sale. Because private sales of stock are not subject to govern-

---

*Examples of stock exchanges include: United States (the American, New York, and Over-the-Counter bourses); Europe (the London, Frankfurt, and Athens bourses); Far East (the Tokyo, Hong Kong, and Singapore bourses); South America (the Caracas and Bogota bourses); Australia (Sydney); South Africa (Johannesburg); Canada (Toronto); other parts of Asia (Tel Aviv, Bombay, and Teheran bourses). The amount and volume of transactions and the amount of local stock as compared with foreign stock traded vary from exchange to exchange.

mental regulation, this is frequently the preferred type of equity funding for a foreign subsidiary. Unless the private sale of stock is a widespread action, it is considered a joint venture between private individuals. Of course, the public sale of stock must conform to the local regulations for such sales.

### Debt Capital

**Debt** funds are funds raised by an MNC that must be repaid to a lender. Regular payments are made toward the principal, and toward the interest, and the other fees charged for the use of the borrowed capital. When debt securities (bonds) are issued, the money raised is borrowed and must be repaid.

Debt financing has a greater number of options than equity financing. The multinational company or its subsidiary can obtain debt capital at markets in the home country, in the host country, or in a third country, or from the Euromarkets. Debt capital can also be obtained from a variety of other sources, such as public markets, home or host country governmental agencies, commercial banks, international and regional agencies (such as development banks), and private parties and syndicates of private funds. Debt financing, unlike equity financing can be arranged either for short-term or long-term periods.

The many attractive sources of financing available from lenders and providers of funds in today's financial markets demand a creative search for the best option by the MNC. There are a number of factors to consider when choosing a source of funding: exchange rates, interest rates, qualification requirements and procedures, repayment periods, and the need for collateral.

*Business International Corporation* provides lists of individual sources of debt financing all over the world. This service, *Financing International Business,* organizes the information on interest rates and the other terms of loans on a country-by-country basis in a looseleaf binder.

Because each of these sources of financing differs with regard to the determination of interest rates and other fees, we provide here a brief explanation of the major institutions that can provide an MNC with different sources of financing.

### Sources of Financing

**Developmental Banks and Government Agencies in the Host Country**   Numerous developmental banks facilitate economic growth in less developed and developing nations. They will provide funding for appropriate projects that might otherwise lack funding from other sources. Such funds can be used for construction, equipment, working capital, or other needs paid for in local currency, such as the purchase of required goods and services from abroad. In addition, such funds may be needed to bring equity in line with cash flow estimates and the objectives of the MNC.

Various types of guarantees and low interest rates by government agencies also can be used as incentives to encourage MNCs to invest in the country. Usually, most managers of local sources of financing prefer the use of local goods and services, instead of imported ones. For this reason, the lender may restrict the way funds are used by the multinational firm to ensure the use of local goods and services.

The *Moraccoean Banque Nationale pour le Development Economique,* the *National Investment Bank for Industrial Development (NIBID)* in Greece, and trade promotional agencies in many nations are examples of developmental banks.

**Investment and Commercial Banks in Host Countries**  If the MNC cannot secure funds from other sources (the development banks, government agencies, and international money markets) or if the host government regulations on currency exchange conversions prevent borrowing from outside sources, investment and commercial banks in the host countries may be used. Normally the host country banks charge foreign companies high rates, thus making this source of capital expensive.

In some instances, the multinational firm must pay interest rates from 8 to 12 percent plus whatever is the current rate of inflation in the host country. When inflation rates are high, the cost of borrowed money can go as high as 30 percent. Of course, the estimated returns on the investment should justify the cost of debt, and the cash flow from the project should provide enough for the repayment of the loan.

The cost, duration, and terms of loans from host country investment and commercial banks vary greatly from country to country.

**Financial Markets**  The large investment and commercial banks offer funds at variable rates of interest in the financial markets around the world. For instance, the investment banking houses of Wall Street that arrange the sale of equity in foreign subsidiaries can also help secure intermediate-term and long-term loans. These banking houses identify pension funds, insurance companies, and other private sources that may be interested in the venture.

The investment banks of the United States and other countries are also good sources of financing for foreign projects. These sources require suitable guarantees for the repayment of the loans. The loans may have fixed rates or adjustable rates that float from 1.5 to 2.5 percent over the interbank interest rate. Sometimes, the rates can be lowered if the bank receives minority interest in the venture.

The multinational firm can shop in the national financial centers for the most suitable source of funds in terms of achieving its objectives at the lowest costs. These financial and capital markets are located in such cities as New York, London, Paris, Zurich, Bahrain, Singapore, Tokyo, and the Cayman Islands. Another option for MNCs is to shop in the international or Eurobond and Eurocurrency markets located in major cities throughout the world.

The Eurocurrency market, as we explained in Chapter 7, has become the dominant financial market in the world. Euromarkets have great depth and breadth. The *depth* of the market refers to the "placing power" or the ability of the market to provide large sums of money. The *breadth* is the ability of the market to serve a wide variety of needs for a variety of borrowers.

**Export Credit Agencies, Banks, and Financiers**   Since the day of mercantalists (see Chapter 2), every country has been attempting to increase its exports. In order to encourage exports and foreign trade activities, many nations provide long-term credit to companies by direct loans or loan guarantees through export banks. The cost of such money is usually reasonable and the repayment period can be extended as long as seven to 12 years. This results in a light cash flow burden for the foreign project. As a result, the MNC's subsidiary can gain a competitive advantage through this facilitating long-term credit arrangement.

The export bank of Washington, D.C., known as the Export-Import Bank in the United States, and firms such as CIT Financial Corporation and International Credit Corporation (outside the United States) are examples of this source of financial institution. A complete list is available through Business International Corporation, as mentioned earlier.

**International and Regional Development Agencies**   The scarcity of venture capital (either debt or equity) in developing nations is one of the main reasons that these countries have continuously lagged behind the industrial economies. In order to facilitate investment in their member countries, a number of international and regional organizations lend money in exchange for equity in the venture. Such a practice improves the debt-to-equity ratio and lessens the burden on cash outflow from the project.

Many regional political and economic development organizations have the capability to lend to selected private projects that will enhance the region's development. These organizations are scattered in Asia, Africa, Latin America, and Europe. These organizations are helpful when more than one member country of the region is involved.

As we explained in Chapter 5, the United Nations provides funds for developmental projects through several agencies. The International Bank for Reconstruction and Development, the World Bank, and others lend money to developing nations for specific projects. The International Finance Corporation (IFC), a subsidiary of the World Bank, lends money for worthy developmental projects to private and public companies, including multinational firms.

Similarly, the U.S. Agency for International Development (AID) lends directly to foreign governments, while the Overseas Private Investment Corporation (OPIC) provides loans, guarantees, and insurance against losses due to war, nationalization, and commercial activities to the American firms in developing nations.

Table 17.1 summarizes the main characteristics of selected major multinational financial sources.

**Table 17.1  MAJOR MULTINATIONAL FINANCIAL SOURCES**

| | World Bank Group | | | Inter-American Development Bank (IDB) | | Asian Development Bank (ADB) | |
|---|---|---|---|---|---|---|---|
| | International Bank for Reconstruction and Development (IBRD) | International Development Association (IDA) | International Finance Corporation (IFC) | Ordinary Capital Resources | Fund for Special Operations | Ordinary Capital Resources | Special Funds Resources |
| **Function** | Promote the economic development of member countries primarily by extending loans on conventional terms for specific high-priority projects. | Promote the economic development of less-developed member countries by making credits on concessionary terms, thereby lessening the burden on the recipient countries' respective balance of payments positions. | Encourage the growth of productive private enterprise in developing countries by extending loans and noncontrolling equity capital, providing underwriting and standby commitments, and attracting outside financing. | Contribute to the acceleration of the process of development of its member countries individually and collectively by providing loans on conventional and concessionary terms. | Contribute to the acceleration of the process of development of its member countries individually and collectively by providing loans on concessionary terms. | Finance loans on conventional terms and technical assistance for projects and programs to foster economic development in and among the developing countries of Asia and the Far East. | Provide loans on concessional terms for high priority development projects in developing member countries. |
| **Criteria and limitations** | Government guarantee required when borrower is a private entity; borrowing country must be credit-worthy; borrower must be unable to obtain funds from other sources on reasonable terms; loan decisions are made only on the basis of economic development considerations; loans must be for specific projects; funds may be spent only for purposes for which a loan was granted; project must have high economic priority; and recipient enterprise must have productive potential. | Government guarantee required when borrower is a private entity; borrowing country must be credit-worthy; borrower must be unable to obtain funds from other sources on reasonable terms; credit decisions are made only on the basis of economic considerations; credits must be only for specific projects; funds may be spent only for purposes for which loan was granted; project must have high economic priority; and recipient enterprise must have productive potential. Per capita income level of borrowing country should be below $250. | The corporation considers the degree of economic development of borrowing country; availability of sufficient capital from private sources on reasonable terms; prospects of profitability; evidence of sound planning; sponsorship from companies with proven industrial experience; extent of sponsor's share capital in enterprise; provision for local investor participation; and project's economic priority for the country. It will not lend where primary object is refunding, direct financing of trade, or land development. | The Bank must take into account the creditworthiness of the borrower, may finance only specific projects, must consider the ability of the borrower to get financing from private sources on reasonable terms, and may not finance a project on a member country's territory if the member objects. | The Bank must take into account the creditworthiness of the borrower, may finance only specific projects, must consider the ability of the borrower to get financing from private sources on reasonable terms, and may not finance a project on a member country's territory if the member objects. | Loans to be made in less-developed member countries of ADB. | Loans to be made in less-developed member countries of ADB. |

**Table 17.1** (*Continued*)

| | World Bank Group | | | Inter-American Development Bank (IDB) | | Asian Development Bank (ADB) | |
|---|---|---|---|---|---|---|---|
| | International Bank for Reconstruction and Development (IBRD) | International Development Association (IDA) | International Finance Corporation (IFC) | Ordinary Capital Resources | Fund for Special Operations | Ordinary Capital Resources | Special Funds Resources |
| Eligible borrowers | Member governments, their political subdivisions, and any public or private entities in their territories. | Member governments, their political subdivisions, any entities in their public or private territories, and public international or regional unit. | Private firms in developing member countries. | Member governments, private local firms or joint venture enterprises with local participation, and public or private relending agencies. | Member governments, private local firms or joint venture enterprises with local participation, and public or private relending agencies. | Any member government or any agency, instrumentality or political subdivision thereof, or any entity or enterprise operating in the territory of a member. | Governments of developing member countries. |
| Lending volume (FY 1975) | $4.3 billion. | $1.6 billion. | Total commitments of $212 million. | $1.1 billion. | $413 million. | $376 million. | $194 million. |
| Current interest rates and fees | 8.85% interest, commitment charge of ¾% accruing from a date 60 days after date of loan agreement. | No interest. Service charge of ¾% per annum to cover IDA administrative costs. | Interest rates are keyed to the IBRD rate. | 8% annual interest, including 1% commission allotted to special reserve; ¼% commitment fee on undisbursed balance. | 1–4% interest per annum; service charge of ¾%. | 8¾% interest per annum including 1% commission plus commitment charge of ¾ of 1% per annum on unused balances of loan. 9¼% interest for borrowers in countries with a per capita GNP of $850 or higher | Interest rates have ranged from 1½ to 3% per annum, including ¾ of 1% service charge. |
| Loan maturities | 15 to 30 years, including grace periods. Most are on 20 to 25 year terms. | 50 years, including 10-year grace period, following which 1% per annum of principal is repayable over second 10 years and 3% per year over next 30 years. | Loans are usually 7 to 12 years. Amortization is generally on a semiannual basis after a grace period. Equity capital sold to private investors where appropriate. | 15 to 20 years, including grace period. | 20 to 40 years, including grace periods. | 10 to 25 years with grace periods from 2 to 5 years. The average is 20. | From 16 to 50 years, including grace periods from 5 to 10 years; average maturity, 40 years. |
| Currency of repayment | Currency lent. | Currency lent or another convertible currency. | Generally currencies lent or invested, most commonly dollars. | Currency lent. | Mexico and Venezuela repay in currency lent; others may pay in their own currencies. Service charge payable in dollars. | Currency lent. | Currency lent. |
| Resources | $25.5 billion subscribed capital. Major sources of funds are sales of bonds on world capital markets. | About $3.2 billion in funds available for lending, of which about 70% is already committed. | Initial subscriptions and four replenishments plus transfers from IBRD. | $2.74 billion subscribed capital, of which $388 million paid-in. Major source of funds is sales of bond issues on world capital markets. | $2.33 billion in member contributions. | Subscribed capital, $3.2 billion; borrowings, equivalent to $451 million. |

*Source:* From *International Business Management: A Guide to Decision Making*, 3rd ed. by Richard D. Robinson, copyright © 1983 by The Dryden Press, reprinted by permission of the publisher.

## Leveraging

Leveraging is the maximum use of borrowed (debt) capital, in place of equity capital, in the expectation that the project will yield a higher return than the cost of the borrowed money. Leveraging allows either the lowering of equity capital in the project or an increase in the size of the venture, or both.

The amount and extension of leveraging is a function of the after-tax cash inflow generated by the project. The lender, which is the party at risk, carefully examines the proposal before granting a loan. The lender considers the reliability of the cash inflow estimates, the contingency plans included to allow for unexpected events, and the capacity of the annual cash inflow after taxes to make the yearly payments on the principal and interest. Each lender has specific criteria and safety factors that must be satisfied before lending.

The multinational executive would like to satisfy certain goals including the following:

1. As far as debt capital is concerned, the executive looks for the minimum cost of borrowing, the longest grace period before the first payment, and the most compatible repayment schedule with the after-taxes cash flow.
2. As far as equity capital is concerned, the executive seeks stockholders and investors with the same expectations and objectives as the MNC so as to prevent conflict and future complexities in problem solving.
3. The executive seeks a stable cash flow to ensure the payback of the loan and satisfactory investor returns.

The goal of finding the optimum leveraging situation is reached by obtaining the capital that results in the maximum estimated profit. Of course, there are variations in leveraging practices, depending upon the nation and the sources of the funds. The financial manager's task is to adjust the financial structure so that it results in the achievement of these three goals, subject to local conditions and the constraints of the lenders and investors.

Table 17.2 highlights the advantages and disadvantages for MNCs of different sources and methods of debt and equity financing.

## Risk Sharing

An investment is a major commitment, especially if it is substantially financed by equity capital. If the facilities are taken over or destroyed, the cost to the investor can be great. The potential risk can be lowered by using local sources through a joint venture or a highly leveraged situation. The providers of equity or the providers of debt capital in the host country can prove helpful allies in case of conflict with the local government.

The shifting of the risk to the investor can be further enhanced if the foreign subsidiary can obtain debt financing on its own merit and the parent

Table 17.2  ADVANTAGES AND DISADVANTAGES OF DIFFERENT SOURCES AND METHODS OF FINANCING FOR MNCs

| Sources/methods | Advantages | Disadvantages |
|---|---|---|
| Debt financing through host country sources | Low political risk<br>Tax deduction on interest paid<br>Elimination of foreign exchange exposure risks<br>Possibility of establishing good relationship with local businesses and other financial institutions | Availability of capital<br><br>Less control over subsidiary operations |
| Debt financing through home base sources (parent company, affiliates and home country) | Tax deductions on interest paid<br>Ease in remittance and repatriation<br>Access to low-cost funds | Higher foreign exchange exposure risks for subsidiaries |
| Equity financing through parent company sources | Possibility of enhancing debt capacity of overseas subsidiaries<br>Higher parental controls on subsidiary operations<br>Access to low-cost funds | Higher foreign exchange exposure risks<br><br>Higher risks for remittance of earnings and repatriation of invested capital<br>Higher risks for expropriation and nationalization |
| Equity financing through host country source | Less foreign exchange exposure risks<br>Stronger identity with host country and local interest groups | Less parental control on overseas operations |

*Source:* Adapted from William H. Davidson, *Global Strategic Management* (New York: Wiley, 1982), p. 233.

company is not the final obligor. However, if the parent company extends a loan or guarantees a loan that is provided to the foreign subsidiary by an outside source, then, generally, the investment risk is not shared because the debtor has recourse to the parent company. In order to minimize this recourse, the MNC may try to conceal the fact that loans extended to their subsidiary are guaranteed by the parent company. Another motive for hiding guarantees is the fear that the knowledge of such a guarantee might encourage a government to confiscate a subsidiary.

One approach in hiding such loan guarantees is to place a deposit with a bank. The bank then provides a loan to the subsidiary supposedly from the bank's own account. By using the bank as a "front," the true source of the loan is not revealed.

## CAPITAL BUDGETING AND LONG-TERM RESOURCE ALLOCATION

Investment of an MNC's capital for longer periods of time should be handled with care and sophistication. The management of long-term investment is called **capital budgeting** and includes the comparative assessment of alternative long-term projects. Capital budgeting involves the development of alternative investment proposals, the assessment of their cash flows, and the selection of investment projects based on certain criteria. The continuous reassessment of selected investment projects after their acceptance is essential. Appendix 17.2 provides a numerical illustration of multinational capital budgeting.

In our discussion of global strategic management in Chapters 13 and 14, we indicated that the main decision at the corporate level concerns the composition of a portfolio of businesses (related or unrelated). For a multinational corporation, such a portfolio decision includes (but is not limited to) the selection and operation of different projects in various national markets. The analysis that leads to the selection of such an investment portfolio is capital budgeting.

Capital budgeting should be a part of the global strategic management process. The multinational financial manager needs to work closely with other executives, especially the marketing manager, to screen markets and forecast returns from those markets. The financial manager can then estimate cash flows and select the new projects. Resources are then committed to the proposed projects. The new projects should then be evaluated periodically for possible reallocation of the resources.

Because the cash inflows from the project are either reinvested in the firm or paid to shareholders as dividends, the most important aspect of the capital-budgeting analysis is the estimation of the cash flow adjusted for various risks.

In a capital-budgeting decision, the anticipated receipts, including terminal or salvage value, should be evaluated against all the costs and risks of the project. Such receipts should be adjusted for inflation. The cost of capital and the estimated returns of different projects should be considered in a capital-budgeting analysis. The box on page 540 explains the basic tools of capital budgeting. For an in-depth coverage of capital budgeting, the reader is referred to any finance book in the Suggested Reading list.

Although capital budgeting is essentially the same for domestic and international projects, certain complications can arise in international environments because of the following:

1. The political risks involved
2. The variations in the sources of financing
3. The foreign exchange rate fluctuations
4. The restrictions on capital, exchange, and profit flows

# Basic Tools of Capital Budgeting

Two basic tools of capital budgeting are the *internal rate of return* and the *net present value*. The latter, NPV, is the most prevalent tool; if the two tools were to give conflicting recommendations between alternative projects, most analysts would recommend that the decision suggested by the NPV method should be followed. Therefore, this discussion focuses upon that method.

Both these basic capital-budgeting tools are based upon *discounted cash flows.* Future cash flows are reduced in value (that is, discounted) at a particular interest rate (the *discount rate*) for every year between the time of that cash flow and the present time. The result is the *present value* (that is, the value at the beginning period of a cash flow that is expected to be received or paid at some date(s) in the future).

If an amount equal to the present value is invested to earn interest at the same interest rate as that used for the discount rate and if the interest earned is reinvested each period, then the *future value* of the total earnings plus principal would exactly equal the *future cash flow(s)*. This process is called *compounding.*

Thus, another way of defining the present value is that amount which, if invested at the beginning of a period of time and with the earnings reinvested each period, would equal the future cash flow: discounting, or seeking the present value, is the opposite of compounding, or seeking the future value.

Within the field of capital budgeting the question of how to incorporate the problem of variable risks between alternative investments is very important. Risk differentials can either be incorporated into the discount rate (the greater the risk, the higher the discount rate) or into the anticipated cash flows (the greater the risk, the lower the cash flows, all else being equal). Most analysts of both domestic and international capital budgeting prefer the adjustment of cash flows so that the same discount rate is applied to each alternative investment. A major advantage to the use of the adjustment of cash flows is that it allows a finer degree of tuning of cash flows. If a higher discount rate is used, then the total present value of the cash flows in the more distant years would be very sharply reduced.

**Source:** Christopher M. Koroth, INTERNATIONAL BUSINESS: *Environment and Management,* 2nd ed. (Englewood Cliffs, N.J.: Prentice-Hall, 1985), p. 502. Reprinted by permission of Prentice-Hall, Inc.

5. The differences in tax systems between the home and host countries
6. The variation in the economic system and the economic conditions
7. The differences in inflation rates
8. The varying interest and discount rates
9. The uncertainty in the estimation of salvage value
10. The difficulty in choosing between the foreign project's or the parent company's point of view for the purpose of measuring rates of return

These complications result in complexities in calculating the net present value, because it is more difficult to estimate the future cash inflows and the appropriate discount rate.

The greater difficulty found in capital budgeting for international investments does not mean that overseas projects are less attractive. On the contrary, great opportunities exist in foreign markets for the firms with the proper attitude and decision-making capabilities. The increasing amount of foreign trade and investment is evidence of the existence and the desirability of such opportunities across the globe.

## REMITTANCE STRATEGY

A **remittance strategy** refers to a set of decisions and guidelines concerning payments from the foreign subsidiary to the parent company. Such payments may be for profits, dividends on equity capital, interest and principal payments on loans, fees for services (managerial, technical, entrepreneurial, distributive), contributions toward headquarters overhead (salaries, rent, and so forth), research and development, and royalties (on copyrights, patents, trademarks, and other technical knowledge).

Variations in tax and foreign exchange control systems and in remittance regulations impose different restraints in different nations. In some cases, conditions in a host country may lead a government to impose severe exchange and capital flow controls. These controls can lead to the prohibition of some forms of payments. If funds or payments are temporarily or permanently blocked, they cannot be *repatriated* or remitted to the parent company. Such restrictions will make the currency inconvertible. Such is the case in Brazil, where it is illegal for a local firm to pay fees and royalties to any foreign company which has 50 percent or more ownership in the local firm's equity. Some nations limit the remittance of dividends to a specific percentage of registered capital.[2]

The following factors need to be considered in formulating a remittance strategy:

1. The multinational firm's business goals and objectives
2. The reinvestment requirements and opportunities for growth in foreign nations
3. The availability of capital from local sources
4. The stability of currency exchange
5. The economic and political (environmental) conditions at home and abroad
6. The cost and ease or difficulty of converting foreign payments into domestic currency
7. The host government's restrictions on remittances
8. The tax systems at home and in the host nation
9. The impact of remittances on the subsidiary and the MNC's image in the host countries[3]

Avoiding controls in a remittance strategy is an important role for the international manager. Avoidance as opposed to evasion (an illegal or improper act) is the act of legally and properly dealing with the controls and effectively remitting the payments from the subsidiary to the parent company. Of course, there are variations in the legal systems and regulations, and in their interpretation, from country to country. Therefore, perfectly legal actions in one nation may be illegal in another and the multinational financial manager must be aware of these differences.

A number of guidelines in the formulation of a remittance strategy can be suggested:

1. In countries with high economic and political risk, an immediate payback policy is more desirable.
2. For a fast-growing subsidiary (a "star"), a slower payback cycle is preferred.
3. A subsidiary in a mature industry (a "cash cow") should remit larger payments.
4. In countries with high-tax structures, a slower payback cycle to reduce earned profits should be followed. This should be done if reinvested profits are not taxed.
5. Whenever possible, profits should be remitted through countries with low withholding taxes. One example of this strategy would be establishing a financial holding company in Bermuda,[4] which has low withholding taxes.

The effect of the host government controls and the public perceptions of remittances should be considered when designing a remittance strategy. In the following section, we will briefly discuss a number of specific remittance strategies.

### Transfer Pricing

As we explained in Chapter 11, the transfer price is the price charged for goods and services traded among different subsidiaries and branches of the same company. Because companies have extensive control over such pricing decisions, transfer pricing can play an important role as an antiblockage technique in the remittance of profits. In a country with blockage on the remittance of dividends, intracompany prices are adjusted so that the subsidiary or parent company that provides the supplies charges an artificially higher price. This results in the lowering of profits in the controlled subsidiary and the shifting of the profits to the subsidiary or the parent company that has been the supplier.

Transfer pricing can also be used to avoid high import duties by artificially lowering the prices of imported raw materials that are supplied by another subsidiary of the same company. This, of course, results in an increase in profits of the subsidiary with high import taxes. This is especially desirable if the local tax rates on profits are low. Of course, if local tax rates are high, the desirability of such action is reduced.

The use of transfer pricing to lower import duties, to lower income taxes, or to remit dividends to the parent company is possible if the local government is not aware of the normal price for raw materials and the components used in the process. Today, the governments have become aware of the use of transfer pricing as a system of tax avoidance and profit remittance. Therefore, many host governments are controlling and regulating its use. Appendix 17.1 provides a numerical illustration of transfer pricing by an MNC.

## Swaps

As we discussed in Chapter 7, host governments have a practice of allowing the repayment of international debts by foreign subsidiaries even if capital and profit remittances from those subsidiaries may be blocked. The MNCs usually channel loans to foreign subsidiaries in such countries through banks. The loan may be from a bank (with the parent company's guarantee) or an arrangement may be made for the bank to merely pass the parent company's funds to the subsidiary in the form of a loan. In a **credit swap**, the bank provides a loan to the subsidiary in the local currency in exchange for the parent company's deposit of similar funds in a safe country as collateral. At the end of the repayment period, the deposit is returned to the parent company. If the loan is not repaid, the bank seizes the deposit.

Two companies may also arrange a swap. The two companies can exchange currencies or extend loans to each other. Such a loan is called a *parallel* or *back-to-back* loan. For instance, two Canadian multinationals with operations in Brazil can engage in a swap. The subsidiary of one company extends a loan in Brazilian cruzeiros to the subsidiary of the other company. In return, the second company loans Canadian dollars to the first company in Canada. As a part of the swap, currencies will be exchanged back at a later date in order to prevent currency exchange losses. Therefore, the loan is considered a covered contract for the companies involved.

## Unbundling

Occasionally, when limitations have been placed on the repatriation of profits, the host country will make allowances for additional payments to the parent company. In such cases, the parent company itemizes charges to the subsidiary instead of bundling the charges in a lump sum. The process of breaking up the charges for headquarters' services to the subsidiary is called **unbundling**. Such unbundled charges may include direct headquarters' expenses associated with the services provided to and for the subsidiary, trademark fees, patent royalties, allocations for overhead, and allocations for research and development.

If there is severe blockage of profit and capital remittances, other procedures may be pursued. For instance, the funds can be used to make local purchases (in the host nation) for export to other subsidiaries. The company may also try to pay for as many expenses in the host nation as possible. For instance, all travel expenses associated with the region, whether by the parent company or by subsidiary, will be paid for in the country with severe controls.

The funds can also be used to purchase local appreciative assets such as real estate. Eventually, after the controls are lifted, the assets can be sold and the proceeds can be transferred to the parent company.

A host government that imposes remittance controls is usually harsher on MNCs with inconsistent remittance strategies or on those that attempt to change their strategy in reaction to imposed controls. Whenever a subsidiary has a consistent record of payments to its parent company, usually the practice can be continued even after restrictions are imposed. Therefore, the best remittance strategy for an MNC is to establish a consistent pattern of repatriation. Such a practice of consistency can prove helpful in case severe restrictions are imposed on the transfer of capital and profits to the parent company.

## OPERATIONAL POLICIES

In this section we will address some of the operational aspects of the multinational firm's financial management.

### Working Capital and Cash Flow Management

**Working-capital management** refers to management of the short-term liquid (current) assets and liabilities of a firm. The short-term assets include items such as cash, accounts receivable, notes receivable, and marketable securities. The short-term (current) liabilities include accounts payable and short-term notes payable. Ineffective management of working capital and cash flow may cause tremendous problems in operations and can lead to business failures. A firm usually needs about 8 percent of its annual capital outflow as working capital.

A firm usually needs money to pay for the labor, raw materials, components, and services in order to produce, distribute, and market its products and services before any payment is received from the customer. This lag between outflows and inflows requires working capital (an excess of liquid assets over liquid liabilities) and effective cash flow management.

A multinational firm needs cash to provide a cushion against unforeseen contingencies, to meet daily expenses, or to be ready when a better use for such funds becomes possible. For example, if the firm expects the price of assets to decrease, it may carry more cash than usual in order to purchase such assets when the price has bottomed out.

Of course, holding cash in a vault does not generate interest and it is costly to transfer. Therefore, the MNC tries to maintain an optimum balance between cash and interest-bearing short-term assets. Such a practice is called **cash flow management**.

Because debt requires payments toward the principal and interest of the borrowed money, it lowers the amount of working capital. Except for dividends, which are usually paid out of annual income, equity does not require regular payments. Therefore, high leveraging (a high debt-to-equity ratio) leads to a need for increased working capital. Thus, care should be taken when assessing the implications of debt financing on the management of working capital.

The effective management of working capital and cash is needed: (1) to improve the company's collection and disbursement of cash and to decrease the cost of transfers among the parent company and its subsidiaries and (2) to minimize the amount and level of cash balances needed to economically support proper operations. This increases the amount of funds available for investment. Some of the main factors that should be considered for effective management of working capital and cash are the government restrictions on the flow of funds, the complications of the tax system differences, the complications of multiple fluctuating currencies, and the costs and difficulties involved in transferring funds across national boundaries.

As was discussed in Chapter 7, multinational funds can be transferred either by mail or by cable. A cable transfer may carry a higher fee, but when costs associated with delays by mail are considered, the overall cost may be less. Cable money transfers are normally quicker, more efficient, and overall less expensive.

## Types of International Cash Flows

There are two types of international cash flows: (1) *intracompany* (within the company) transfers and (2) *intercompany* (between the company and outside parties) transfers.

**Intracompany Transfers**   Multinational companies are most concerned with the efficient transfer of funds among their different units and subsidiaries. There are four alternatives for intracompany transfers.

    ***Keeping the Liquid Cash in the Subsidiary Where It Has Been Earned***  With this method the parent company has less control over the available current assets and this may lead to inefficiencies in effective allocation and investment.

    ***Netting***   The transfer of funds is costly because of transfer and foreign exchange charges, and transfers carry exposure to exchange rate fluctuation risks and require expensive processing. Because the parties involved in intracompany transfers are both in the same company, the payments are flowing back and forth between the same units, and, as a result, multinational companies try to minimize the amount of actual transfers among their own units. To minimize the intracompany transfers, MNCs utilize a type of in-house clearing system of funds. **Netting** is the process of determining the amount of inflows and outflows among various units and then balancing the flows so as to "net-out" the final amounts before transfers are made. The net inflow and outflow for each unit is determined. The unit then pays only its net debt or receives its net credit. Actual transfers of funds are thereby minimized, costs are lowered, and risks are reduced.

*Pooling* Another technique to minimize intracompany transfers is pooling. **Pooling** refers to the accumulation or pooling of all liquid assets that exceed the current needs of each unit into a single, central "pool" or reserve. Such a pool may be located in the parent company or in a country that offers the best tax, security, and interest advantages. The advantages of centralizing liquid assets through pooling are increased control, improved allocation, and better investment of such funds.

*Leading and Lagging* The centralization of liquid assets enables the multinational company to use leading and lagging as a cash management technique. Under this technique, fund transfers are deliberately timed so as to delay (lag) some payments or to accelerate (lead) other payments. This technique helps in minimizing the adverse effects of inflation or exchange rate instability on the value of and returns from liquid assets.

Subsidiaries in nations with depreciating currencies or high inflation rates normally accelerate (lead) their payments. This prevents losses due to the erosion of the value of the cash holdings in those nations. On the other hand, if the local currency is appreciating in value or if the inflation rate is low, payments to other units (or even other companies) are delayed (lagged) to increase the value of the cash holding.

Intercompany Transfers Timing is of great importance in intercompany transfers. There is an opportunity cost (foregone interest) associated with overdue receivables. Cable transfers should be insisted upon for the payment for accounts receivable. This is especially true in the collection of large payments. In the case of small receivables, cable transfer costs may be prohibitive. For small payments (such as payments from credit card customers, payment of insurance premiums, or payments on small loans) the company may want to arrange for regional collection centers. Funds collected can then be wired (cabled) to the central "pool."

When difficulties exist in collecting the payments for accounts receivable a collection agency can be used. In the case of large amounts, legal proceedings may need to be pursued if payments are not made.

## Foreign Exchange Risk Exposure

**Foreign exchange risk exposure** is the risk that MNCs face when dealing with different currencies and because of currency exchange rate fluctuations. In other words, foreign exchange risk refers to the risks involved when different currencies are transferred physically or translated for accounting purposes. One of the most important branches of international finance is the management of foreign exchange and exchange rate risks. The nature of the exchange rate risks has been already addressed in earlier chapters. We can comfortably state that virtually all the decisions made by a multinational company are affected to some degree by exchange rate considerations. Among the decisions affected are those about capital budgeting and investment, the selection of market-entry strategies, working capital and cash flow management, and the remittance of profits and capital. Also, the net worth and profitability of an MNC are greatly affected by the relative value of the currencies used in evaluating its assets, liabilities, and profits. There are three types of foreign exchange risk exposure.

**Translation Exposure** *Translation exposure* is a measure of how exchange rate fluctuations affect the recording and reporting of a company's financial position in its financial statements. This is basically an *accounting exposure.* Based on accounting principles or national laws, the financial statements of a firm's different subsidiaries need to be consolidated into a single set of corporate statements. This requires restating (translating) the values of assets and liabilities, revenues, expenses, profits, and other items that are denominated in foreign currencies into the parent company's home currency. The translation takes place on the books only and is not an actual conversion. Therefore, the recorded gains or losses are unrealized and do not actually occur.

Usually national accounting principles dictate the translation procedure to be used. For example, *Accounting Standards Board (FASB) Statement No. 52* specifies the translation procedure to be used by U.S. MNCs. Under FASB Statement No. 52, a company must first identify the functional currency for each foreign subsidiary or affiliate. If the foreign subsidiary does not face high rates of inflation and conducts most of its business in terms of a local currency, this currency is usually accepted by the U.S. government as the functional currency of the subsidiary. In such cases, all accounts are translated using the current exchange rate. Translation losses or gains are not combined with other reported income, but are combined with the equity account. In host countries with hyperinflation, that is, inflation which is over 100 percent cumulative over a three-year period, or if the foreign subsidiary conducts its business in U.S. dollars, the U.S. dollar will be accepted as the functional currency. In such cases, foreign currency accounts are translated using a temporal method. This temporal method is outlined in FASB Statement No. 8. According to this standard, the translation losses and gains are included in reported income. FASB Statement No. 52 also requires that foreign currency accounts be restated so as to conform to U.S. generally accepted accounting principles before translation.[5]

**Transaction Exposure** *Transaction exposure* is the determination of actual losses or gains that occur due to fluctuations in exchange rates when making or receiving payments, when conducting intracompany transfers, or when remitting profits. This exposure is present in transferring funds across national boundaries.

**Economic Exposure** *Economic exposure* is related to the total impact of fluctuating exchange rates on an MNC's profitability. Economic exposure includes the potential impact of changes in exchange rates on all aspects of an MNC's operation. Economic exposure is much broader and more subjective in nature than either translation or transaction exposures. Economic exposure relates to the long-term profit performance and strategic effectiveness of the MNC.

### Managing the Foreign Exchange Exposure

There are a number of techniques that help reduce the risks associated with transaction and translation exposures. Among these, netting and leading and lagging were discussed in this chapter. Hedging and swaps are other widely used techniques, which were discussed in Chapter 7.

We conclude this chapter by stating that the financial aspects of an MNC are more complex than similar activities in a purely domestic firm. In order to operate effectively, the MNC management needs to develop a financial strategy. This strategy should deal with four fundamental areas: (1) the financing of the foreign operations, (2) the capital budgeting or the long-term resource allocation, (3) the remittance strategy, and (4) the operational policies.

## SUMMARY

1. Financial management is the process of managing cash flow and working capital so as to have on hand the necessary cash for the daily operations of a business.
2. Financial strategy concerns itself with the following:

   Financing the foreign operations—deciding how to secure funds for financing global operations.

   Capital budgeting or long-term resource allocation—deciding where these funds should be invested.

   Remittance strategy—deciding on how to transfer returns (such as dividends, interest, profits, and royalty fees) and capital back to the parent company.

   Operational policies—deciding on how to run the financial operations, including the management of working capital, cash flow, accounts receivable, inventory, and foreign exchange.

3. The policies of centralization or decentralization of an MNC concern the degree of control the parent company holds over the foreign subsidiary. Three philosophies control the amount of centralization or decentralization in a business: polycentric philosophy, ethnocentric philosophy, and geocentric philosophy.
4. Numerous options are available for financing international operations. A creative and careful search is necessary to meet the needs of the MNC for affordable capital.
5. Equity is that portion of an invested capital that does not require repayment. The issuing of equity (stocks or securities) means that part of the ownership of the firm has been sold. Stocks can be sold privately (as in a joint venture) or publicly (through a stock exchange).

6. Debt capital is invested capital that is borrowed and so it must be repaid by payments toward the principal borrowed, and toward the interest and other fees. Sources of debt capital (bonds) include developmental banks and agencies in the host country, investment and commercial banks, financial markets, export credit agencies, export banks and financiers, and international and regional development agencies.

7. Leveraging is the maximum use of borrowed (debt) capital, in place of equity capital, in the expectation that the project will yield a higher return than the cost of the borrowed money.

8. The risks of overseas ventures can be lowered by using local sources in a joint venture or by using high leveraging (large debt financing).

9. The management of long-term investments is called capital budgeting. Capital budgeting is part of the global strategic management process. The most important aspect of capital budgeting is the estimation of cash flows.

10. Capital budgeting entails some risks for the MNC that a domestic firm does not face, including political risks found in the host country and the effects of varying tax rates at home and abroad.

11. The remittance strategy refers to a multinational company's decisions and guidelines concerning payments from the foreign subsidiaries. These payments may be for profits, dividends, interest, fees, overhead, and royalties. Some host countries may temporarily or permanently block some forms of these payments, and, in that case, the payments cannot be repatriated or remitted to the parent company.

12. Important factors for consideration in the formulation of a remittance strategy include the goals and the objectives of the firm, the stability of the foreign economic and political environment, the nature of the subsidiary, and the nature of the tax structures in the countries where the MNC is operating.

13. Transfer pricing, swaps, and unbundling are remittance strategies followed by MNCs when repatriation of funds is blocked by the host nation. Blocking funds is not usually a problem for subsidiaries that have established a consistent payment record to the MNC.

14. The management of working capital refers to the management of short-term liquid assets and liabilities. A firm usually needs about 8 percent of its annual capital outflow as working capital.

15. Effective management of working capital and cash flow is needed to improve the collection and disbursement of cash and to minimize the amount and level of cash balances needed to economically support operations.

16. The two types of international cash flows are intracompany (within the company) and intercompany (between the company and outside parties). Transfers can be made by mail (which entails delays and the risks of loss or diversion) or cable (which means higher fees, but the immediate transmission of funds and no risks of loss or diversion).

17. Foreign exchange risk exposure is the risk that MNCs face when dealing with different currencies and because of currency exchange rate fluctuations. The risks involved when different currencies are involved include the translation exposure, the transaction exposure, and the economic exposure.

18. Managing the foreign exchange exposure refers to the techniques that help in reducing the risks associated with transaction and translation exposures. Included are the techniques of netting, leading and lagging, and hedging.

## QUESTIONS

**17.1** Why is the estimation of cash flow important in capital budgeting? Discuss.

**17.2** List the risks associated with capital budgeting in the global environment. Discuss any two of these risks.

**17.3** What is repatriation? Discuss the options that an MNC has if repatriation is temporarily or permanently blocked.

**17.4** What does an MNC use cash for? What are the disadvantages of having excess cash on hand?

**17.5** List and define the types of foreign exchange risk exposures. How can an MNC manage foreign exchange risk?

**17.6** Go to your library and research the ways an MNC of your choice manages its global financial concerns.

## APPENDIX 17.1: An Illustration of Transfer Pricing by an MNC*

The first device that can be used to repatriate blocked funds is transfer pricing, which refers to the prices set by the company on sales between two elements of the corporate system. Assume that the government of the island of Caribia places severe restrictions on the company's ability to repatriate capital and profits back to the parent. The Caribian subsidiary buys most of the subassemblies used in its production process from the parent in the United States, and ships all of its finished products to the parent's marketing subsidiary in Curacao for worldwide distribution. The cost of goods sold for the subassemblies in the United States is $100, and the normal markup is 25 percent, but the firm desires to set transfer prices between the United States and Caribia, and between Caribia and Curacao, to minimize the profits realized in Caribia.

Table 1 shows an example of this kind of transfer pricing strategy as compared to arm's length transfer prices. By setting the price at $150 instead of $125, an extra profit of $25 is realized in the United States. Also, the cost of goods sold in Caribia is elevated by the same $25. Then, an artificially low transfer price of $205, instead of the arm's length price of $250, is used to reduce Caribian profit to only $5 instead of $75. This low transfer price allows the Curacao marketing subsidiary to earn a profit of $105, a net increase of $45 over the arm's length profit. The world price of $310 at which Curacao sells the goods is determined by free market forces, so it is not subject to arbitrary manipulation. Note that in both cases, the total corporate profit is $160, but where the

---

*Reprinted with permission from Eugene Brigham and Louis C. Gapenski, *Financial Management: Theory and Practice*, 4th ed. (New York: Dryden Press, 1985), pp. 1049–1051.

profit is realized was changed via transfer pricing. In essence, $70 of profit has been brought out of Caribia in spite of restrictions on the repatriation of profits from that country.

Transfer pricing manipulation can also be valuable to the firm, even if repatriation of profits is not restricted. If the corporate tax rate in Caribia is higher than in the United States or Curacao, the scheme described in Table 1 could be used to shift the profits to lower tax areas. Thus, on an after-tax basis, the company increases its cash flow, and hence its value, by manipulating transfer prices. This is an important aspect of tax planning by the multinational firm.

The Minister of Commerce of Caribia also understands how transfer prices can be manipulated to the benefit of the multinational corporation. The minister's concerns are with the lost tax revenue and the reduction of capital for reinvestment locally caused by the company's actions. To the extent that the minister is able to determine fair arm's length prices for both the subassemblies and the finished goods, the minister will recast Table 1 as shown in the left column and base the corporation's taxes on the $75 figure. Also, this amount, less taxes and penalties for trying to circumvent local regulations, will be added to the equity accounts in the balance sheet. Transfer pricing strategies can be used as devices for removing value from a subsidiary in violation of local regulations, so they are watched very carefully by local authorities.

It is much easier to determine fair market prices for some goods than for others. In general, the closer the product is to a standardized commodity, the easier it is to estimate an arm's length price. Specialized intermediate goods involving new technology probably afford the company the greatest opportunity to exercise creativity in setting transfer prices. However, since this device is so well known and so carefully watched, most companies avoid abusing transfer prices, except, perhaps, in special circumstances where political risks are high. Such conditions are less likely to arise when corporate relations with the host government are cordial.

Table 1    USING TRANSFER PRICING TO CIRCUMVENT BLOCKED FUNDS

|  | Arm's length transfer prices | Manipulated transfer prices |
|---|---|---|
| U.S. cost of goods sold | $ 100 | $ 100 |
| U.S. selling price | 125 | 150 |
| U.S. profit | $ 25 | $ 50 |
| Caribian cost from the United States | $ 125 | $ 150 |
| Caribian local costs added | 50 | 50 |
| Caribian cost of goods sold | $ 175 | $ 200 |
| Caribian selling price | 250 | 205 |
| Caribian profit | $ 75 | $ 5 |
| Curacao's cost from Caribia | $ 250 | $ 205 |
| Curacao's selling price | 310 | 310 |
| Curacao's profit | $ 60 | $105 |
| Total corporate profit | $160 | $160 |

## APPENDIX 17.2:  An Illustration of Multinational Capital Budgeting*

The principles of capital budgeting in a multinational setting can be illustrated with data from International Electronics Corporation (IEC), which is analyzing a proposal to build a plant in Caribia to assemble electronic monitoring and testing equipment for sale worldwide through the company's marketing and distribution facility in Curacao. If the project is accepted, a new subsidiary, IEC Caribia, will be incorporated in Caribia. It will be financed only with common stock, all of which will be owned by the parent firm.

While the corporate income tax in Caribia is a low 20 percent compared with the 50 percent federal-plus-state rate that IEC pays in the United States, the government of Caribia places several restrictions on multinational corporations that will have an impact on the analysis. To preserve investment capital in Caribia, the government prohibits the removal of contributed equity until the investment is sold or otherwise liquidated. Thus, depreciation cash flows may not be repatriated until the end of project's life. Dividends are not subjected to a withholding tax, but they must come only from net income, and they are restricted to a maximum of 20 percent of the contributed equity in any year. At the end of the project's life, any reinvested earnings can be repatriated to the parent. The investment, to be made in January 1985, consists almost entirely of plant and equipment, and the cost will be $10 million or 50 million Caribian pesos (P50 million). Because of the nature of technological change in the electronics industry, IEC bases its analysis on a time horizon of five years. At the end of the five years (in December 1989), the company estimates that the book value of the facility, 25 million Caribian pesos, is the best estimate of its market value.

The Caribian government recognizes that IEC has developed and patented much of the technology employed in the operations, and is willing to compensate the company for its use. IEC and the Minister of Commerce have reached an agreement that establishes a royalty rate of 10 percent of gross revenues to be paid directly to the parent. Management fees, however, are prohibited by law in Caribia. Table 2 summarizes the projected income statements for the Caribian subsidiary.

The data in Table 2 are straightforward down to "Dividend repatriated." In the 1985 column, we see that net income, 8 million pesos, is less than 20 percent of the 50 million pesos of original equity (0.2 × 50 million = 10 million pesos, which is the maximum dividend in any year), so the entire 8 million pesos can be returned to the parent as a dividend. Dividends in subsequent years are limited to 10 million pesos. IEC reports its worldwide net income to the U.S. Internal Revenue Service, but it receives tax credits for taxes paid overseas, including a credit for taxes paid by its subsidiary to the Caribian tax authorities. The amount of the credit depends on the dividend payout ratio of the subsidiary. With a 100 percent payout, the parent would pay the difference between the U.S. tax rate of 50 percent and the Caribian tax rate of 20 percent. For example, in 1985, when the payout was 100 percent, the subsidiary earned 10 million pesos before Caribian tax and paid 2 million in tax (20 percent) to the Caribian govern-

---

*Reprinted with permission from Eugene Brigham and Louis C. Gapenski, *Financial Management: Theory and Practice,* 4th ed. (New York: Dryden Press, 1985), pp. 1060–1064.

Table 2 PROJECTED END-OF-YEAR FINANCIAL CASH FLOWS TO THE U.S. PARENT
(Millions of Caribian Pesos)

| | 1985 | 1986 | 1987 | 1988 | 1989 |
|---|---|---|---|---|---|
| Revenues | 50.0 | 55.0 | 60.0 | 65.0 | 70.0 |
| Operating costs | 30.0 | 30.0 | 35.0 | 35.0 | 40.0 |
| Depreciation | 5.0 | 5.0 | 5.0 | 5.0 | 5.0 |
| Royalties (10% of revenue) | 5.0 | 5.5 | 6.0 | 6.5 | 7.0 |
| Income before tax | 10.0 | 14.5 | 14.0 | 18.5 | 18.0 |
| Caribian tax (20%) | 2.0 | 2.9 | 2.8 | 3.7 | 3.6 |
| Net income | 8.0 | 11.6 | 11.2 | 14.8 | 14.4 |
| Dividend repatriated (10.0 maximum) | 8.0 | 10.0 | 10.0 | 10.0 | 10.0 |
| U.S. tax on dividend | 3.0 | 3.75 | 3.75 | 3.75 | 3.75 |
| After-tax dividend | 5.0 | 6.25 | 6.25 | 6.25 | 6.25 |
| Royalty (10% of gross revenues) | 5.0 | 5.50 | 6.00 | 6.50 | 7.00 |
| U.S. tax on royalty (50%) | 2.5 | 2.75 | 3.00 | 3.25 | 3.50 |
| After-tax royalty | 2.5 | 2.75 | 3.00 | 3.25 | 3.50 |
| After-tax cash flow | 7.5 | 9.00 | 9.25 | 9.50 | 9.75 |

ment, so an additional 30 percent tax, or 3 million pesos, must be paid to the U.S. government. The total tax paid on the dividend is limited to 5 million pesos, or 50 percent of taxable income; this is the same rate as would be paid if the subsidiary had been located in the United States, in which case, it would have paid a 50 percent tax on 10 million of net income.*

In 1986 through 1989, net income exceeds 10 million pesos, the maximum dividend payment allowed under Caribian law, so dividends are set at 10 million. To see what is involved, consider 1986. Theoretically, the United States could tax the 14.5 million peso pre-tax income, getting 14.5(0.5) = 7.25 million pesos, less a credit of 2.9 pesos, for a net tax bill of 4.35 million pesos, but this is not done. Alternatively, the United States could treat as taxable income only the dividends repatriated, which would produce a net tax bill of 10(0.5) − 2.9 = 2.1 million pesos, but this is not done either. Under U.S. law, taxes are collected on the portion of income that is actually repatriated. In the years 1986–1989, we proceed as follows: (1) We "gross up" the dividend payment to determine the before-tax net income which would be required to produce the actual dividend payment. This is equal to the dividend repatriated divided by (1.0 − Caribian tax rate), or 10/0.8 = 12.5 million pesos. Had IEC Caribia had 12.5 million pesos of income, it would have paid 20 percent, or 2.5 million pesos, in taxes and had 10 million left for the dividend which it actually paid. (2) We now

---

*If the foreign tax rate had been higher than the U.S. tax rate, the tax credit would be greater than the taxes owed to the U.S. government on equivalent before-tax earnings by a U.S. firm. This deficit could be used to offset U.S. taxes on income from other foreign subsidiaries in any part of the world. For a more detailed explanation of multinational taxation, see the U.S. Tax Reform Act of 1976, or Price Waterhouse, *U.S. Corporations Doing Business Abroad* (New York, 1976).

**Table 3  DEPRECIATION CASH FLOWS REPATRIATED**
(Millions of Caribian Pesos)

| Year of depreciation | Amount of depreciation | Future value interest factor at 8 percent | Terminal value in 1989 |
|---|---|---|---|
| 1985 | 5.0 | 1.3605 | 6.802 |
| 1986 | 5.0 | 1.2597 | 6.299 |
| 1987 | 5.0 | 1.1664 | 5.832 |
| 1988 | 5.0 | 1.0800 | 5.400 |
| 1989 | 5.0 | 1.0000 | 5.000 |
| | 25.0 | Total | 29.333 |
| | | Less depreciation | 25.000 |
| | | Taxable income | 4.333 |
| | | Caribian tax (20%) | 0.867 |
| | | After Caribian tax | 28.466 |
| | | U.S. tax | 1.300 |
| | | After U.S. tax | 27.166 |

multiply this 12.5 million before-tax equivalent amount by the difference between the tax rate in the United States and the Caribian rate, or 30 percent, getting 0.30(12.5) = 3.75 million pesos. This is the additional tax liability in the United States on the income repatriated.*

However, 3.75 million pesos is not the total U.S. tax liability. An additional source of taxable income to the parent is the royalties paid by IEC Caribia. Royalties are an operating expense to the subsidiary, so they are not subject to Caribian tax. To the parent, however, they are income, and the royalties are taxed at the full 50 percent tax rate. Total operating cash flow to the U.S. parent, then, is the sum of the after-tax dividend and the after-tax royalty. This is shown in the last line of Table 2.

Since cash flows from depreciation cannot be repatriated until the company is liquidated at the end of 1989, they must be reinvested locally. Assume that there are no other attractive real asset investments available, so the depreciation cash flows will be invested in Caribian government bonds which earn 8 percent annual interest, with interest not subject to tax until it is repatriated. The accumulated and interest-compounded depreciation cash flow at the termination of the project is shown in Table 3 to be 27.166 million pesos after adjusting for Caribian and U.S. taxes.

Operating profits that exceed the dividend repatriation restrictions are also assumed to be invested in 8 percent Caribian government bonds. As shown in Table 4, the U.S. tax adjustment is more complex than it was for the depreciation cash flows because Caribian tax is only due on the interest income, but U.S. tax is due on both

---

*Notice that the foreign subsidiary's payout ratio has a major effect on total corporate taxes paid—if no dividends are repatriated, no U.S. taxes are paid. This works as an incentive for multinational corporations to reinvest earnings overseas. It also explains why U.S. oil companies and other multinationals often have very low U.S. taxes in relation to their reported income.

Table 4    BLOCKED OPERATING PROFITS
              (Millions of Caribian Pesos)

| Year earned | Amount of blocked profits | Future value interest factor at 8 percent | Terminal value in 1989 |
|---|---|---|---|
| 1985 | 0.0 | 1.3605 | 0.000 |
| 1986 | 1.6 | 1.2597 | 2.015 |
| 1987 | 1.2 | 1.1664 | 1.399 |
| 1988 | 4.8 | 1.0800 | 5.184 |
| 1989 | 4.4 | 1.0000 | 4.400 |
|  | 12.0 | Total | 12.998 |
|  |  | Less investment | 12.000 |
|  |  | Taxable income | 0.998 |
|  |  | Caribian tax (20%) | 0.200 |
|  |  | After Caribian tax | 12.798 |
|  |  | U.S. tax[a] | 4.799 |
|  |  | After U.S. tax | 7.999 |

[a]Caribian taxes have already been paid on the blocked profits. The pre-tax income that gave rise to the 12.0 of blocked profits was $12.0 \div 0.8 = 15.0$. U.S. taxes at a rate of 30 percent must be paid on this income: $15.0(0.3) = 4.50$. In addition, a 30 percent U.S. tax must be paid on the 0.998 of interest income: $0.998(0.3) = 0.299$. Therefore, the total U.S. taxes payable upon repatriation of the interest-accumulated blocked profits are $4.50 + 0.299 = 4.799$ million pesos.

interest and "grossed up" operating profits. The total after-tax cash flow from blocked operating profits, approximately 8 million pesos, will be added to the 1989 end-of-project cash flow.

The next steps in the analysis are (1) to convert the annual cash flows as developed in Tables 2, 3, and 4, plus the terminal value (assumed to be equal to the ending book value), from pesos to dollars, and (2) to find the net present value of the project. We will assume that a 12 percent cost of capital is appropriate for this investment.* These steps are shown in Table 5. Column 5 gives the annual cash flows in pesos; the component parts of these cash flows are indicated in the four preceding columns. The estimated exchange rates are shown in Column 6. The current rate, 5 pesos to the dollar, is expected to hold during 1985, but the peso is expected to depreciate thereafter at a rate of 5 percent per year.

Dividing the cash flows in pesos (Column 5) by the exchange rates (Column 6) gives the expected cash flows in dollars (Column 7). The dollar cash flows are converted to a present value basis (Column 9), and the sum of the present values of the annual cash flows is $11.468 million. By subtracting the initial cost of the project, $10 million, from this sum, we obtain the project's NPV, $1,468,000. Since its NPV is positive, the project should be accepted.

---

*This hurdle rate is based on the cost of capital employed in the project, adjusted as appropriate for risks associated with the foreign environment and any diversification or other benefits that are applicable.

Table 5  PROJECT CASH FLOWS
(Millions of Dollars)

|  |  |  | | Cash flow (millions of pesos) | | | | | |
| Year | Operations (1) | Depreciation (2) | Profits blocked (3) | Terminal value (4) | Total cash flow (5) | Exchange rate (6) | Dollar cash flow (7) | PVIF at 12% (8) | PV of cash flow (9) |
|---|---|---|---|---|---|---|---|---|---|
| 1985 | 7.500 |  |  |  | 7.500 | 5.00 | $ 1.500 | 0.8929 | $ 1.339 |
| 1986 | 9.000 |  |  |  | 9.000 | 5.25 | 1.714 | 0.7972 | 1.366 |
| 1987 | 9.250 |  |  |  | 9.250 | 5.51 | 1.679 | 0.7118 | 1.195 |
| 1988 | 9.500 |  |  |  | 9.500 | 5.79 | 1.641 | 0.6355 | 1.043 |
| 1989 | 9.750 | 27.166 | 7.999 | 25.000 | 69.915 | 6.08 | 11.499 | 0.5674 | 6.525 |
|  |  |  |  |  |  |  |  |  | $ 11.468 |

Less investment of 50 million pesos at 5 pesos/$    10.000

NPV of project    $ 1.468

## NOTES

1. This section is adapted from Alan M. Rugman, et al., *International Business: Firm and Environment* (New York: McGraw-Hill, 1985), Chap. 18.
2. Richard D. Robinson, *International Business Management,* 2nd ed. (Hinsdale, Ill.: The Dryden Press, 1978), p. 448.
3. Donald J. Summa, "Remittance by U.S. Owned Foreign Corporations: Tax Considerations," *Columbia Journal of World Business,* vol. 10, no. 2 (Summer 1975), p. 40.
4. Anant R. Negandhi, *International Management* (Boston: Allyn and Bacon, 1987), p. 495.
5. William R. Folks, Jr., and Raj Aggarwal, *International Dimensions of Financial Management* (Boston: PWS-Kent, 1988), pp. 90–91.

## SUGGESTED READINGS

Brigham, Eugene, and Louis C. Gapenski, *Financial Management: Theory and Practice,* 4th ed. New York: Dryden Press, 1985.

Carlson, R. S., H.L. Remmers, C. R. Hekman, D. K. Eiteman, and A. I. Stonehill. *International Finance: Cases and Simulation.* Reading, Mass.: Addison-Wesley, 1980.

Davidson, William H. *Global Strategic Management.* New York: Wiley, 1982.

Eitman, David K., and Arthur I. Stonehill. *Multinational Business Finance,* 3rd ed. Reading, Mass.: Addison-Wesley, 1982.

Folks, William R., Jr., and Raj Aggarwal. *International Dimensions of Financial Management.* Boston: PWS-Kent, 1988.

Haner, F. T. *Multinational Management.* Columbus, Ohio: Merrill, 1973, Chap. 8.

Kahler, Ruel. *International Marketing* 5th ed. Cincinnati, Ohio: South-Western, 1983, Chap. 15.

———, and Ronald L. Kramer. *International Marketing,* 4th ed. Cincinnati, Ohio: South-Western, 1977, Chap. 15.

Madura, Jeff. *International Financial Management.* New York: West, 1986.

Melvin, Michael. *International Money and Finance.* New York: Harper & Row, 1985, Chaps. 3 and 4.

Negandhi, Anant R. *International Management.* Boston: Allyn and Bacon, 1987, Chap. 12.

Summa, Donald J. "Remittance by U.S. Owned Foreign Corporations: Tax Considerations." *Columbia Journal of World Business,* vol. 10, no. 2 (Summer 1975), pp. 40–45.

Versluysen, E. L. *The Political Economy of World Finance.* New York: St. Martins Press, 1981.

Weston, Fred J., and Bart W. Sorge. *Guide to International Financial Management.* New York: McGraw-Hill, 1977.

# Chapter 18

# International Operations Management and Strategy

$A$ multinational corporation undertakes foreign direct investment (FDI) to reduce production costs and to overcome operational problems. For example, a firm may decide to go international to take advantage of cheaper labor or less expensive raw materials abroad. We have explored the motives and reasons that lead to the establishment of facilities abroad in earlier chapters. In this chapter we will elaborate on some of the strategic issues and operational processes involved in managing foreign production and operations.

First, we define operations management. Second, we address the issue of productivity. Third, we elaborate on different types of operations systems. Fourth, we extend our coverage of operations management to the international area. Fifth, we discuss the issue of centralization of operations decisions. Sixth, we discuss different aspects of multinational operations strategy. Finally, we present the topic of international research and development (R & D).

## OPERATIONS MANAGEMENT

**Operations management** includes those activities of a firm that are related to the design, planning, and control of resources for the production of goods and the provision of services. The main objective of operations management is the most efficient use of the organization's scarce resources. These resources are financial, physical (materials and facilities), human (labor and management), and technological (know-how and information).

**Operations design** includes decisions on product development and design, through research and development and on product engineering. **Operations planning** is concerned with plant design and facilities layout, site selection, and the procurement of raw materials and components. Finally, **operations control** deals with the day-to-day operational activities of scheduling, inventory control, and quality control. In service sectors, inventory control, procurement, and sourcing are usually irrelevant because there are no raw materials, components, or finished goods to deal with. An exception to this may be an ad agency that depends on media and market research firms. We use the term operations management to include the production of goods as well as the provision of services. Today, it is increasingly apparent that many of the techniques and skills traditionally referred to as production management are applicable to the provision of services as well. For example, services rendered by Cooper and Lybrand (an international accounting firm) demand administration of a highly complex operations system. This system is, in many ways, similar to those utilized in the production of automobiles, VCRs, and watches. Although differences do exist between service organizations and manufacturing firms, similarities are being found with increasing frequency.

The above definition of operations management encompasses the complete product or service life cycle. The life cycle includes all activities, from the original conception and development of a product or service through its demise, when output is discontinued and facilities are written off or salvaged. For a firm, the life cycle may restart by the development and production of a new product, or the provision of a new service. Additionally, if the firm is diversified, a number of concurrent life cycles will exist for the variety of products and services it offers.

In summary, we define operations management as those activities that are related to the design, planning, and control of scarce resources necessary for the production of goods and the provision of services. Because the main objective of operations management is the most efficient use of scarce resources, the productivity of operations plays a major role in the discussion of this issue.

## PRODUCTIVITY

**Productivity** is a measure of the output of a production unit—a business, a university, a hospital, a government agency, or an entire nation—during a specific period of time. The productivity of a plant or factory can be measured as the ratio of total output to the hours of labor required to produce that output, given a constant quality of output. It should be noted that an improvement in the quality of the output is also considered an increase in productivity. However, because it is difficult to measure quality in a quantitative fashion, measurement of productivity resulting from an increase in quality is not commonly done.

Because it is not usually possible to count the number of units produced in a given period in service industries, measuring service industry productivity is more complex and subjective than measuring productivity in the manufacturing industries. In the United States, where seven out of ten people are employed in the service sector, it is becoming increasingly important to be able to measure service productivity.

It should be pointed out that productivity is influenced by more than just the efficiency of labor. For example, a study of 30 plants of an MNC in a dozen countries, over a seven-year period, indicates that the most important determinants of productivity are management and worker-related factors.[1] In general, productivity is a function of capital, management, technology, and labor. Figure 18.1 depicts the relationships between these factors and productivity.

Productivity plays a vital role in providing a competitive edge in the global market. This holds true not only for MNCs, but also for nations. For instance, today the United States is suffering from a trade imbalance, a budget deficit, and a loss of competitiveness in the world market. Many observers attribute these problems to a slowdown in the growth of U.S. productivity, and many people believe that the key to overcoming these ills is a surge in productivity.

Many experts consider the difficulties that the United States is experiencing (i.e., low productivity and lack of competitiveness) to be a direct result of failures in some aspect of the managerial process. For example, a study indicates that managerial motivation is at a lower level in the United States than in a

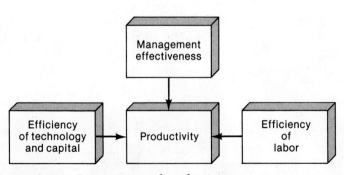

**Figure 18.1** Determinants of productivity

number of other countries.[2] As another example, a survey of nearly 4,000 *Harvard Business Review* readers indicates a belief that "America's competitiveness is declining—largely because of the performance of U.S. managers—and it is up to them to respond to the challenge."[3]

## THE OPERATIONS SYSTEM

A system is a set of relationships, interdependencies, and interacting functions that constitutes a purposeful means of achieving an objective. An **operations system** is a system composed of various inputs (resources), transformation processes (to create value); and outputs (products or services). Figure 18.2 provides a graphic representation of an operations system. Thus, an operations system is a process that attempts to transform inputs (capital, materials, and so forth) into outputs (goods and services).

### Types of Operations Systems

There are three types of operations systems:

**1.** The **job system**. In this system, an entire product or service is completed by a group of workers in one set of facilities. As a result, a variety of different products or services can be completed simultaneously. This is a general and versatile system. It is, however, the least efficient and most expensive system to operate. For example, large passenger ships, power plants, office buildings, and custom-built items are made through the job system. Examples of service industries following this system include custom butcher shops, small insurance brokers, and a la carte restaurants.

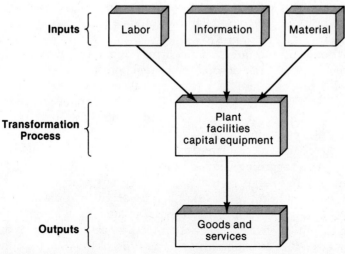

**Figure 18.2** A model of an operations system

**2.** The **batch system**. This is a system in which a number of products or services are processed in batches or lots. The batch system is designed to share some of the repeating fixed production steps among individual items in the batch. With this system, however, some of the versatility of the job system is sacrificed. Additionally, because of variations in production and consumption patterns, there may be a need for the storage or queuing of materials or customers at some stage within the system. Manufacturing industries that use the batch system include the machine tools, furniture, and glassware industries. The batch system is used in the service sector in the fast food, the health care, and the airline industries.

**3.** The **flow system**. This is a system where products or customers are processed continuously and are passed successively through the required sequence of facilities and stations. Such a sequencing requirement makes the flow system the least flexible and the least versatile of the three systems. The flow system requires standardization of products or services. Because of the inflexibility of this system, changes in the products or services can only be made infrequently. Continuity of demand is necessary so that the rate of production can match the rate of consumption. Industries that produce household items, automobiles, computers, and similar mass-produced products use the flow system. There are very few flow systems in the service sector. Self-service restaurants and banks are among the few usages of this system by service companies.

## INTERNATIONAL OPERATIONS MANAGEMENT

International operations management, like its domestic counterpart, is concerned with the efficient use of plant, equipment, technology, labor, and management in an effort to improve productivity and reduce costs. Such improvement in productivity and cost reduction usually enhances the firm's competitive positioning in the global marketplace and leads to better profit performance.

Both domestic and international firms need to invest in ongoing R & D (on both the process and the product) to bring about new products and services or improve existing ones and to increase operations efficiency. Domestic firms and MNCs are both involved in the planning and control of an operations system, but international operations management is complicated by the differences in environmental conditions, the magnitude of the opportunities and the alternatives available, and the constraints imposed on a multinational firm. Complications may arise regarding the use of factors of production. Cultural variations in values, working habits, and industrial relations practices, as well as in wage rates, literacy, and skill levels also play important complicating roles. Sources of financing and the various concerns of financial management, discussed in Chapter 17, influence the choices of projects for research and development and the amount of R & D expenditures. The type of technology in use influences the location and size of facilities and the decision to lease or to purchase.

**Table 18.1  ADVANTAGES OF INTERNATIONAL PRODUCTION OVER DOMESTIC PRODUCTION**

| Types of international production | Ownership advantages | Location advantages | Internalization advantages | Illustration of types of activity which favor MNEs |
|---|---|---|---|---|
| 1. Resource-based | Capital, technology, access to markets | Possession of resources | To ensure stability of supply at right price, control of markets | Oil, copper, tin, zinc, bauxite, bananas, pineapples, cocoa, tea |
| 2. Import substituting manufacturing | Capital, technology, management and organizational skills; surplus R&D and other capacity, economies of scale; trademarks | Material and labor costs, markets, government policy (with respect to barrier to imports, investment incentives, etc.) | Wish to exploit technology advantages; high transaction or information costs; buyer uncertainty, etc. | Computers, pharmaceuticals, motor vehicles, cigarettes |
| 3. Export platform manufacturing | As above, but also access to markets | Low labor costs incentives to local production by host governments. | The economies of vertical integration | Consumer electronics, textiles and clothing, cameras, etc. |
| 4. Trade and distribution | Products to distribute | Local markets. Need to be near customers; after-sales servicing. etc. | Need to ensure sales outlets & to protect company's name | A variety of goods—particularly those requiring close consumer contact |
| 5. Ancillary services | Access to markets (in the case of other foreign investors) | Markets | Broadly as for 2/4 | Insurance, banking, and consultancy services |
| 6. Miscellaneous | Variety—but include geographical diversification (airlines and hotels) | Markets | Various (see above) | Various kinds: (a) portfolio investment—properties. (b) where spatial linkages essential (airlines and hotels) |

*Source:* H. V. Wortzel and L. H. Wortzel. *Strategic Management of Multinational Corporations: The Essentials* (New York: Wiley, 1985), p. 320.

Host government regulations are other factors with which the MNC must wrestle. Governments may require the use of local R & D investment, the use of a certain type of technology, the use of specific labor relations practices, the use of local supplies and machinery, the use of local labor, and the training of local people for management positions.

On a positive note, however, a multinational firm's options and opportunities are much greater than those that are available to a domestic firm. Because of its broader horizon, the MNC may have access to better investment opportunities in R & D, plant facilities, and equipment. An MNC may also enjoy less expensive raw materials and labor, a variety of technological options, and other location-specific advantages.

Table 18.1 highlights some of the advantages of international production over those found in domestic production. This figure is based on John Dunning's eclectic theory of international production, which we discussed in Chapter 3.[4]

## CENTRALIZATION VERSUS DECENTRALIZATION

As we indicated in Chapter 13, a major strategic concern of an MNC is the question of centralization. The firm must decide the degree to which its facilities, operations, and R & D functions should be centralized. This decision has great implications for the firm's global strategic positioning, its cost competitiveness, and its ability and flexibility in serving specific market needs.

Usually decentralization leads to increased product adaptiveness, better order processing, and better scheduling. Decentralization, however, may mean sacrificing the cost savings available through the effects of the experience curve.

**The experience curve** refers to the inverse relationship between the accumulated volume of production and the unit manufacturing cost. Empirical findings have shown that, for many firms, unit cost of production falls when the volume of production increases. The increased efficiency or cost reduction can be attributed to the following factors:

1. *Economies of scale* realized through the increased size of the production unit and spreading of the fixed costs over a larger volume of production.
2. *Learning curve effect* due to greater learning of the manufacturing process and utilization of more efficient equipment and improved production techniques.
3. New *improvements* in design and processing.
4. Increased *control and bargaining power* over the costs of labor, raw materials, and capital associated with the larger size.

The phenomenon of the experience curve is not only evident in manufacturing firms but it can also be responsible for cost saving in marketing of manufactured products. That is, the unit cost of marketing a product decreases with increased sales volume.

The concept of the experience curve effect was originally derived from research on the relationship between manufacturing cost and accumulated productive volume. But we should point out that this phenomenon can also be seen in the service corporations. The centralization of operations in a service company may also lead to certain cost reductions because of shared overhead costs, improved learning from the exchange of ideas and expertise, and reduced waste stemming from the elimination of redundant efforts. In other words, larger service firms usually enjoy a lower per unit cost in providing their service to their customers. Benefits from these efficiencies, however, must be balanced against reduced customer and market responsiveness and increased travel costs.

Phillips, the Dutch multinational, provides us with an example of a company that lost its competitive edge to competitors with experience curve benefits. Phillips provided its subsidiary managers with significant autonomy and made intense efforts to localize their products and operations. But Phillips lost its competitive edge to the Japanese, who developed products for world markets and derived economies of scale and experience curve benefits.

In general, the decision on the degree of centralization of operations is a function of the gains from experience curve effects, the host government requirements for local production contents and employment, the competitive characteristics, the transportation costs of raw materials as compared with finished goods, the availability of labor, the skill and wage levels, and the company's objectives, strategies, and resources.

## MULTINATIONAL OPERATIONS STRATEGY

Multinational operations strategy is a set of decisions and guidelines that is formulated to encourage efficiency and the effective functioning of the MNC's operations system. MNC operations strategy is concerned with decisions about the following:

1. The location and size of facilities across the globe.
2. The choice of operating processes and systems.
3. The choice of appropriate technology (as discussed in Chapter 11).
4. The nature and location of R & D units.
5. The control of operations system.
6. The licensing of technology (as discussed in Chapters 11 and 12).

Multinational operations strategy is a functional-level strategy. As we indicated in Chapter 13, a functional strategy needs to fit the needs of the business-level strategy. In other words, to be effective, the operations strategy must support, through a consistent pattern of decisions and trade-offs, the competitive advantage being sought by the business strategy. For example, the decisions with regard to facilities, degree of automation, vertical integration and capacity levels, and so forth which constitute subparts of the operations functional strategy should be consistent with the needs of the business-level strategy. These operations decisions would be very different if the desired competitive advantage was high volume/low cost than if it was unique features/customer service.[5]

## Matching Operations Strategy with Product Strategy*

Some MNCs have been slow to realize that a change in product strategy necessitates altering the task of the operations system. John Deere, the agricultural equipment manufacturer, and Warwick Electronics, formerly the supplier of color TVs to Sears, Roebuck have both been in this situation.

Deere was slow in adapting its manufacturing strategy to match its new product strategy in Europe. The old manufacturing strategy was designed around products such as low horse power tractors that the company was selling in Europe in the 1950s and 1960s. As new products were introduced in Europe by the competitors in the 1970s, Deere was slow in adapting its manufacturing process to the needs of its European market. The slow adjustment cost Deere a valuable share of that market. Warwick lost its market position when it failed to redesign its manufacturing system to cope with changing technology and price competition in the electronics industry. As a result, Warwick lost its best customer: Sears, Roebuck. Eventually, Warwick was forced to sell its television business to Sanyo of Japan.

There are a number of tasks in an operations system that are closely related to the product strategy. These include manufacturing costs, flexibility in production design and volume, and product performance and consistency. These tasks determine which operations strategy should be used in a company. Once the product strategy has changed, these tasks need to be modified to match the needs of the new product strategy. In other words, the operations strategy needs to change when the product strategy changes.

We can identify a conceptual framework for matching operations strategies with product strategies. This framework is based on three strategic options: (1) technology-driven strategy, (2) marketing-intensive strategy, and (3) low-cost strategy.

**Technology-Driven Strategy**  This is a product strategy that involves serving high-income markets with a continuous flow of new, usually unique, high-performance and high-technology products. The product itself becomes the most important factor in competition, and the importance of production cost in competition is diminished. Due to rapid changes in the product, sales forecasts are difficult to make, and, therefore, flexibility in the volume of production is essential.

With this strategy, plants are built in the home country or in other devel-

---

*This section is adapted from Robert Stobaugh and Piero Telesio, "Match Manufacturing Policies and Product Strategy," *Harvard Business Review* (March/April 1983), pp. 113–120. The section has been modified to apply to the operations strategy for both products and services, instead of being applicable only to manufacturing, as was the thrust of the original article.

oped nations, and usually exports serve other markets until and unless sales growth justifies the building of foreign facilities. Because of difficulty in forecasting demand, such companies usually lower their risk by purchasing as many components as possible from other suppliers. Examples of industries that use this strategy include engineering plastics manufacturers, biogenetics firms, and computer manufacturers.

IBM provides us with an example of a company that employs the technology-driven strategy. This company has allowed market considerations to determine the order of establishing its foreign facilities. IBM established facilities in Germany in 1925, in Italy in 1935, and in Brazil in 1950. Also market considerations have determined the type of products that IBM has produced. As a result, technologically advanced products have been produced in larger, higher-income markets. In the mid-1970s, half of the facilities in West Germany, one quarter of the capacity in Italy, and none of the operations in Brazil were devoted to building central processing units (CPUs) for computers.

Normally, small markets are served through assembly plants by IBM. Large plants in advanced nations provide finished goods for worldwide markets and components for smaller plants. IBM's plants in the United States and Europe, for instance, are either full production facilities or make semifinished goods to take advantage of economies of scale. The company's plants that serve regional or local markets have small-capacity assembly operations.

**Marketing-Intensive Strategy**   In this strategy the concentration of the MNC is on the market, not the product. The firm relies on heavy advertising and marketing expenditures to differentiate its products or services from those of its competitors. Operations costs become a secondary consideration to marketing, yet operational considerations are still vital. At a minimum, an operations system should ensure the provision of the right mix of dependable quality output that the market requires. Examples of products for which the marketing-intensive strategy is used are detergents, foods, over-the-counter drugs, and soft drinks.

The establishment of local facilities increases the MNC's responsiveness to changes in the nature and volume of demand. One manufacturer of a canned soup, for instance, decentralizes its operations by building local plants. Then local ingredients are used and local taste preferences are incorporated in the preparation of the soup. For canned soup, the benefits of local production outweigh the loss of the minimal costs saving that a large centralized production facility would provide. The cost savings would have been minimal because most differentiated, brand-name items are priced well over manufacturing costs, and their sales are insensitive to price changes.

With the use of marketing-intensive strategy, the size and span of foreign plants grow along with the size of local markets. Limited local operations will evolve to a full-scale integrated operation. An example of this is the evolution of operations for Colgate-Palmolive (C-P) plants in more than 40 foreign countries. Most of the output of these plants is sold in the local market. Colgate-Palmolive usually builds a small, economically operated toothpaste manufacturing plant. Then the first operation is followed with the production of soap and then detergents. A completely integrated operations system will be the final phase of this evolutionary process.

**Low-Cost Strategy**  A product in the maturity stage of its life cycle is unsuitable for a marketing-intensive strategy. For mature products, the MNC must choose between divestment or low-cost production while it maintains product quality. The vehicles of a low-cost strategy include: (1) using large-scale plants to take advantage of the effects of experience curve, (2) relocating facilities to countries with low labor costs, (3) operating in locations with access to other critical inputs, such as cheap and abundant energy or raw materials. Table 18.2 shows the relationship between product strategy and operations strategy.

**Implications of Matching Operations with Product Strategy**  A strategy must work in a dynamic setting. For instance, a product that is based on a technology-driven strategy of innovation often matures and necessitates the use of a different strategy. Thus the MNC executives must be aware of the possibilities of change as they formulate manufacturing strategies. In practice, the multinational manager needs to do the following:

1. Formulate a product strategy.
2. Define the critical tasks of an operations system for the purpose of that product strategy.
3. Design, plan, control, and adapt this operations system so as to perform these tasks.
4. Periodically reevaluate the ability of this operations system to perform the required tasks.
5. Stay on top of the changes in product strategy so the operations strategy can be modified accordingly.

## The National Location Portfolio Matrix

In Chapters 13 and 14 we indicated that one of the major decisions at the corporate level is determining the types of businesses in which to engage. This decision leads to the composition of a business portfolio. For an MNC, the portfolio contains businesses in the forms of subsidiaries and affiliates in different regional and national locations.*

We further discussed some of the techniques a multi–strategic business unit (multi-SBU) firm can use in deciding the composition of its business portfolio. One such technique, which we discussed in Chapter 14, is the Boston Consulting Group (BCG) matrix. Another technique is the so-called General Electric (GE) portfolio matrix.

---

*In fact, an MNC can also engage in the operation of unrelated businesses, as does a domestic conglomerate firm. Some of an MNC's businesses can operate multinationally and some domestically. Our focus in this book has been on those businesses that cross national boundaries.

**Table 18.2   RELATIONSHIP BETWEEN PRODUCT STRATEGY AND OPERATIONS STRATEGY**

| | Technology-driven strategy | Marketing intensive strategy | Scale economies | Low-cost strategies | | Other low-cost |
|---|---|---|---|---|---|---|
| | | | | Low-cost labor | | |
| **PRODUCT STRATEGIES** | Key manufacturing task: To manufacture high technology products and be flexible enough to change products and processes quickly. | Key manufacturing task: To operate marketing programs with good product quality and prompt delivery. | Key manufacturing task: To operate large-scale plants so as to keep costs at a minimum. | Key manufacturing task: To minimize cost by using low-cost labor for labor-intensive mature products and components. | | Key manufacturing task: To keep costs low by using low-cost resources. |
| **OPERATIONS STRATEGIES** | | | | | | |
| **Establishing Facilities Abroad** | | | | | | |
| **Location** | Large market, high-income countries, but invest only when the company cannot serve a market by importing from another company plant. | Local markets to be able to respond to marketing needs. | Large national or large regional markets. | Countries with low-cost labor. | | Countries with low-cost inputs. |
| **Scale** | Small scale at first, then larger as markets grow. | Heterogeneous mix of sizes, depending on local market size. | Large-scale plants. | Small-scale plants. | | Depends on nature of key input. |
| **Choice of Process** | Little incentive to adapt technology to local factor costs. | Little incentive to adapt technology to local factor costs. | Little incentive to adapt technology to local labor costs. | Much incentive to adapt manufacturing technology to making use of low-cost labor. | | Much incentive to adapt manufacturing to the use of low-cost inputs and to ensure product quality. |

**Table 18.2** (*Continued*)

| | Technology-driven strategy | Marketing intensive strategy | Low-cost strategies | | |
| --- | --- | --- | --- | --- | --- |
| | | | Scale economies | Low-cost labor | Other low-cost |
| **Span** | First, assembly; then simple fabrication; finally, full-scale manufacture. | From contract manufacturing to fully integrated production. | Facilities specialized; limited number of components for which manufacturing scale economies are important. | Manufacturing of labor-intensive products or components. | Manufacturing limited to process steps using low-cost resources. |
| **Managing Technology** | | | | | |
| **Research and Development** | Establish facility to aid technology transfer and to adapt products to local market specifications and processes to local raw materials. | Establish facility to adapt products to local market's tastes and local raw materials. | R & D facility occasionally needed to improve process. | Little need for local R & D. | Little need for local R & D. |
| **Controlling the System** | Parent heavily influences major manufacturing decisions unless transshipment among subsidiaries is large. | Parent has little influence. | Parent has tight control. | Parent has tight control. | Parent has tight control if system is integrated; less need for tight control on operations otherwise. |
| **Licensing Technology** | Some technologies are suitable for licensing; in some industries, licensing for reciprocal access to technology of other innovators is also desirable. | Little incentive to license. | License if company is not a dominant producer. | Licensing unlikely. | Licensing likely for some technology. |

*Source:* R. Stobaugh and P. Telesio. "Match Manufacturing Policies and Product Strategy." *Harvard Business Review* (March/April 1983), pp. 116–117.

In the GE portfolio matrix, businesses are classified according to two factors: industry attractiveness and the firm's competitive position. The GE matrix can be extended as a tool for analyzing national location opportunities to determine if foreign direct investment is justified. This extended version is called the National Location Portfolio matrix.[6]

Similar to the GE matrix, the two dimensions used in the National Location Portfolio matrix are the national market attractiveness and the ability-to-compete. The **national market attractiveness dimension** is a measure of the general business potential in the specific country. It includes factors such as the total size of the product market (industry), the political stability of the country, the per capita income level, the economic development and growth of the country, the exchange rate stability, the policies on the repatriation of capital and profits, the general business climate, the industrial and labor relations conditions. Much of the data necessary for development of this dimension can be collected by using the new market screening process discussed in Chapter 16.

The **ability-to-compete dimension** measures a firm's relative strengths and weaknesses as compared with its competitors. This dimension indicates how effective an MNC will be when competing in the specific national product market (industry). The ability-to-compete dimension includes the following factors:

1. The degree of a competitor's capacity utilization—low utilization means that the competitor can increase production and rapidly intensify competition.
2. The competitor's technological advantages or disadvantages.
3. The degree of industry concentration—high concentrations make it more difficult for a firm to enter the market or find its own niche.
4. The competitors' market power and their links with each other and to the host government.
5. The number and concentration of customers—few buyers may mean more powerful buyers and closer ties with existing suppliers. At the same time, it is easier to identify a few customers and develop ties with them.

The number and type of factors to be included in the two dimensions of national attractiveness and the ability-to-compete depend on the industry characteristics, the national conditions, and the company's preferences and strategy. Figure 18.3 depicts the National Location Portfolio matrix.

According to this matrix, countries characterized by high attractiveness and high ability-to-compete are the best candidates for a major commitment of new foreign direct investment (FDI). Accordingly, manufacturing companies will invest in new plant and equipment, and service companies will establish local facilities in these countries to serve the regional or national market.

The countries in the middle regions of the matrix are suitable candidates for a lower degree of resource commitment. These national markets should be served through exporting or licensing. In the quadrant labeled "rethink," representing countries of high attractiveness but low competitiveness, ques-

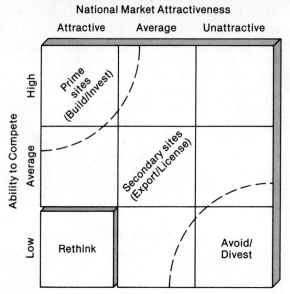

**Figure 18.3** The National Location Portfolio matrix

*Source:* Adapted from S. J. Q. Robinson and D. P. Wade, "The Directional Policy Matrix: Tool for Strategic Planning," *Long Range Planning* (Elmsford, N.Y.: Pergamon, June 1978), pp. 8–15

tions need to be asked and answered with the goal of improving the company's competitive position. Some of the questions that can be raised in this respect are: Is the firm adequately represented in the attractive market? What is hampering its ability-to-compete? Using this matrix, countries characterized in the "rethink" group will receive the attention they deserve.

As our discussion in other chapters indicates, portfolio decisions can also lead to the divestment of certain investment involvements. The National Location Portfolio matrix highlights areas for investment avoidance and areas for divestment in its lower right-hand segment. An MNC's decisions need to consider the long-term returns of a national market or the existence of better investment opportunities elsewhere, and, of course, there are situations in which the country's attractiveness or the company's ability-to-compete as indicated in the matrix is adverse so that a firm may consider investment avoidance or divestment.

The National Location Portfolio matrix can prove to be useful as one of the main analytical tools in deciding whether or not to establish foreign manufacturing or operations facility in a specific nation.

## Facilities Location

After the decision to establish facilities in a foreign country is made, a site for these facilities must be selected. An MNC and its subsidiaries must deal with changing business conditions. Properly locating facilities is a constant challenge. This demands that an MNC adjust to changes, among which are changes in the nature and volume of sales, changes in the market and competitive conditions, changes in government regulations, changes in labor conditions, and changes in energy and raw materials. A firm may also add new products and services to its existing line or integrate its facilities. All of these changes must be dealt with as the firm strives to reduce its costs and maintain or increase its market position. The following factors should be considered when deciding on locations for facilities:

**1.** Staff availability and cost. Facilities need to be staffed by managerial, technical, and labor (skilled manual, semiskilled, and unskilled). The availability, skill level, and cost of personnel play an important role in the selection process. The cost factors of labor should include social security charges and fringe benefits payed to employees in addition to wages and salaries.

**2.** Availability and cost of capital. The investment may not be feasible if the host government does not permit the investment, if local capital is expensive, or if difficult terms are demanded.

**3.** Proximity to markets and materials. Access to raw materials and markets is an important consideration in the site selection process. For example, perishable items should be located close to their markets in order to reduce spoilage and waste. As another example, beverage bottles should be manufactured close to bottling plants to avoid breakage in shipment. Other examples include locating consumer product outlets close to residential centers and placing lumber mills near forests.

**4.** Governmental restrictions on zoning and pollution. Governments restrict industrial expansion in some areas to control pollution or to prevent traffic problems.

**5.** Accessibility and cost of transportation. The accessibility and cost of transportation facilities play an important role in location decisions. MNCs need railroads, highways, docking facilities, and airlines for transportation of the needed raw materials, components, finished goods, equipment, and personnel.

**6.** Living conditions. Inadequate living conditions—such as substandard housing, schools, churches, shopping facilities, and entertainment—lead to employee dissatisfaction and a high turnover rate for personnel. This is especially true in the case of expatriate managers.

## Offshore Manufacturing and Maquiladoras*

**Offshore manufacturing** refers to the location of part of the manufacturing process of the products that are sold at home in another nation with lower labor costs than the home country. Until recently, offshore manufacturing was lim-

---

*The authors would like to express their appreciation to Professor Martin E. Rosenfeldt of University of North Texas for his input in this section.

ited to the assembly in a foreign location of components made at home. Today, however, offshore manufacturing covers a wide range of production activities. For many companies, offshore manufacturing has provided an alternative to losing the home-country market to low-cost foreign competitors.

Offshore manufacturing became popular in the late 1960s and 1970s. During that time many firms in the global electronics industry located production facilities in Far Eastern countries such as Taiwan and Singapore, where labor and raw materials were inexpensive. Today, offshore manufacturing is extended to many Asian and Latin American nations and other low-cost countries. Indonesia, Malaysia, South Korea, Thailand, Brazil, and Mexico are among the new wave of "low-cost" countries used in offshore manufacturing.

Through the use of **maquiladora**, or as it is formally known **in-bond export industry**, Mexico is rapidly becoming a desirable offshore center for U.S. companies. Under this concept, the components that are produced in the United States are shipped to Mexico duty-free. These components are then assembled by Mexican workers and shipped back to the United States for sale. Import duties in the United States are levied on that portion of the finished goods that is value added in Mexico. That is, only the value added that is contributed by Mexican workers is tariffed. Because of the very low cost of Mexican labor, this value added and the corresponding tariff are minimal. As a result, the maquiladora industry provides great opportunities for both Mexico and the United States. It allows U.S. manufacturers to produce their products more cheaply and provides employment opportunities for Mexican workers.

Some of the maquiladoras are joint ventures among U.S., Japanese, and Mexican partners. This is because many U.S. companies are trying to expand the economic interdependence among the United States, Mexico, and the Pacific rim countries including Japan and other southeast Asian nations.

The growth of maquiladoras has surpassed most experts' optimistic projections. The value added by the Mexican in-bond industry has risen from a mere $100 million in 1970 to $1,580 million in 1985. Estimates indicate the value added by this industry will increase to about $10 billion by the year 2000.[7] There are a number of reasons for the surge of international interest in the Mexican production-sharing activities through maquiladoras. Massive devaluations of the Mexican peso in 1982 and the subsequent sliding depreciation of this currency against the world's major currencies have made the cost of Mexican labor one of the most attractive of international labor rates. For example, the average manufacturing hourly wage (including fringe benefits) in the northern Mexico borderland has fallen from $1.45 in 1985 to $0.86 in 1987.[8]

In recent years, the Mexican government has aggressively promoted the in-bond industrialization program not only in that country's northern borderland, but also has opened the national territory for these types of industrial enterprises. The result of these efforts has led to a rapid expansion of the Border Industrialization Program (BIP) since 1984.[9] For example, in 1984, the in-bond industry employed over 230,000 people in 675 plants. In early 1988, the in-bond industry consisted of over 1,400 plants that employed over 350,000 Mexican workers.[10] The numbers had increased to 1,459 plants and 390,422 employees by April 12, 1989.[11] Most experts estimate that by the year 2000 the in-bond industry will employ about 1 million people.

Traditionally, the in-bond assembly plants were mostly "screwdriver" operations. Today, however, a major percentage of the maquiladoras in Mexico fabricate and assemble complicated products requiring considerable manufacturing technologies and industrial operations with capital-intensive production equipment and processes.[12]

## Facilities Design

Decisions regarding the design of facilities are directly related to the nature of technology that a firm has decided to use in a foreign location. We discussed the transfer and choice of appropriate technology in Chapter 11.

In capital-intensive industries and process-type manufacturing (such as in the manufacturing of petrochemicals, chemicals, and synthetic fibers) relatively similar technologies are used at home and abroad. New overseas plants may even use more advanced technology. Because of the similarities shared by the technologies used by an MNC at home and those used by its subsidiaries abroad, there will be little difference between locations with regard to facilities design and layout. In LDCs, major differences may exist in materials handling and in transportation. This is because local conditions in LDCs may necessitate more labor-intensive material handling and the use of less sophisticated transportation.

The downgrading of facilities design and layout usually takes place in the technologically labor-intensive industries located in LDCs. In such cases, MNCs usually build facilities that are comparable to those of local counterparts. These facilities are downgraded and outmoded in comparison with the facilities in the home country and in other developed nations.

## Facilities Integration

The integration of facilities is a matter of degree. It may be viewed as a continuum with 100 percent purchase on one end, and 100 percent production on the other end. Between these extremes lie all other combinations of purchase and production. A subsidiary may buy materials, components, finished goods, and services from its parent company or other subsidiaries. It may also make its purchases from entirely independent sources from home, host, or third nations.

Many companies in the United States have recently adopted global manufacturing integration programs. However, in order to benefit fully from these globally integrated manufacturing strategies, MNCs need to overcome the problem of coordinating operations where interdependence exists among subsidiaries.[13]

The process of coordinating integrated production facilities in different countries is very complex and may have long-run implications for an MNC. For example, political unrest and labor strikes in Korea in 1987 created production problems for U.S. assembly lines that were dependent on Korean parts.

The degree of integration—vertical or horizontal—may be regulated by host governments. The host government may impose a local content requirement. This means that a subsidiary must use a certain level of local resources in the product. For example, when Ford Motor Company decided to establish production facilities in Spain it was forced to abide by a 50 percent local content requirement.

Some other companies, such as Sears, Roebuck in Mexico, have tried to build themselves into the local economy. To this end, they have engaged in local integration by subcontracting all those processes and services to Mexican firms where the local skills have been adequate. Sears has even provided training, financing, and technical assistance to local subcontracting firms in Mexico.

Frequently there has been too much building of industrial plants in LDCs, resulting in overcapacity and idle plants. As a result, the excess capacity and idle plants have been used for subcontracting, which has been profitable.

The decision to purchase from local market or to import the needed materials and components (from the parent company, other subsidiaries, or independent foreign sources) is a function of the following factors:

1. The availability and cost of local supply.
2. The foreign exchange controls and regulations.
3. The availability and costs (the price, plus the costs of transportation, freight insurance, and tariffs) of imported supplies.
4. The existence of bias toward the use of foreign-made products and components.
5. The sensitivity of local organized labor toward loss of jobs.
6. The appeal of foreign goods to customers in the host country.
7. The government controls on local content in the product.

## INTERNATIONAL RESEARCH AND DEVELOPMENT

An MNC may have five different motives for engaging in international research and development:[14]

1. To take advantage of skills, expertise, and talents that are not available in a single country.

2. To establish technological intelligence posts and to draw benefits from differences in research philosophy and approaches that exist between the home country and other countries. When the MNC establishes national R & D centers, these centers are staffed by local scientists and researchers who keep up with the innovations and inventions being pursued by local competitors and local R & D.

**3.** To take advantage of the lower costs found in some countries for research personnel salaries, for laboratory equipment, and for research space.

**4.** To support overseas manufacturing and sales operations. Many MNCs have foreign markets that equal or even surpass the size of their domestic markets. Those companies find that it is increasingly important to build coordinated R & D programs in those markets. These programs help the firm adapt to local raw materials and labor and to develop new products for particular markets. This is why MNCs establish design, technical, service, and R & D departments in their major foreign plants.

**5.** To promote the development of host country economies. International R & D makes significant contributions toward the political, economic, competitive, and social environments of the countries in which it is conducted. The reasons for this are many. International R & D provides stimulating projects that provide opportunities for R & D personnel in different locations to exchange ideas with each other. This motivates important local scientists to stay in their own countries, increasing the incentives for additional local training, and generally enhancing the prestige and importance of the local scientific community.

These are all good reasons for establishing an international R & D network. Not all corporations, however, have succeeded in persuading a large international network of scientists to work closely and effectively with each other. Disappointments may occur. Some MNCs have even reduced the scope of their research efforts outside their home countries. The causes of these disappointing results may be attributed to: (1) an insufficient consideration of the real reasons why the firm needed international technology and what form that technology should take, (2) an insufficient assessment of the risks and limitations of international R & D, (3) an overestimation of the depth of local scientific talent in a particular field, and (4) an underestimation of the costs of running the R & D program from a distance.

The MNC needs to avoid making generalizations about the benefits of international R & D and to take a realistic attitude toward its benefits and costs. The MNC executive should remember that ideas can be generated anywhere in the world as long as the conditions are right.

We conclude this chapter by providing some insights into new trends in the world economy and their implications for MNC operations strategy. It has been stated that the dominate trend in the world economy over the next quarter of a century or longer will be the acceleration of an industrialization and innovation process. This will result in the creation of a *"new global industrial map."* Major economic and technological forces are leading to a migration of traditional industries from the advanced nations to the LDCs. In addition, these forces are triggering a reallocation of resources in the advanced nations from traditional capital-intensive manufacturing to emerging knowledge-based and service-based industries. The result of this radical transformation of the global industrial map is the emergence of several LDCs with leading roles in the world economy. Included in this group of nations will be India, the People's Republic of China, South Korea, Mexico, and Brazil.[15]

As a result of the narrowing of many technological gaps, the ease of access to capital, and the abundance of cheap and productive labor, many of these newly industrialized countries (NICs) are able to manufacture mature products at lower cost than the advanced nations. These NIC-produced products include textiles, shoes, steel, consumer electronics, light aircraft, and automobiles. The competition from these NICs is creating turmoil in the global marketplace.[16]

There are a number of inferences which can be drawn from the creation of this new global industrial map. First, the new economic and technological order will further the formation of global markets. As we discussed in Chapters 13 and 14, to survive in this global market, MNCs need to pursue global strategies that enable them to manufacture and market world-class products. These products need at least to match, in terms of cost and quality, those goods produced by leading competitors everywhere. In the global market, cost and quality are becoming the most important competitive factors.[17]

Second, the increasing displacement of national markets with global markets will add to the multifold influence of the environment on MNCs. As we pointed out in Chapters 8 and 13, the global environment is becoming more turbulent, complex, and "surprise-intensive." The result will be a greater emphasis on environmental scanning and assessment, the development of early warning systems, and the utilization of contingency plans to enhance proactive MNC strategy.[18]

Finally, these new developments will cause MNCs to pursue more long-term contractual arrangements with other firms than they have in the past. As a result MNCs will move away from "internalization" and toward "externalization." MNCs will be more willing to transfer nonstrategic technologies to other firms, especially in the LDCs. The increase in contractual arrangements will be supplemented with another type of cooperation, that is, the sharing of corporate resources among MNCs. These pooled resources may be used in joint ventures, in R & D, in new product development, and in manufacturing plants.[19]

The new global industrial system requires a new breed of MNC executives. This new breed will be more cosmopolitan, more person-oriented, and more flexible than the existing generation of international managers has been.[20]

## SUMMARY

1. Operations management includes those activities of a business that are related to the design, planning, and control of scarce resources for the production of goods and the provision of services.
2. Operations design involves decisions on product development and design through research and development and product engineering.
3. Operations planning is concerned with operations system planning (plant design

and facilities layout), site selection, and planning for the procurement of raw materials and components.

4. Operations control deals with the day-to-day operational activities of scheduling, inventory control, and quality control.

5. The term operations management is used to include the production of goods and the provision of services.

6. Productivity is a measure of the output of a production unit (either in manufacturing or in the service industry) during a specific period of time. It is measured as the ratio of total output to the hours of labor required to produce that output, given a constant quality of that output.

7. Productivity is a function of capital, management, technology, and labor.

8. An operations system is composed of various forms of input, transformation processes, and output.

9. The three types of operations systems are: (a) the job system, (b) the batch system, and (c) the flow system.

10. International operations management is similar to domestic operations management. The complexities in international operations management arise from the differences in environmental conditions found in the international setting, the magnitude of opportunities and alternatives available internationally, and the constraints imposed on the MNC by foreign environments.

11. Usually, decentralization of operations leads to an increased ability for product adaptiveness, better order processing, and better scheduling. But it may also mean sacrificing the cost savings that are possible due to the experience curve effect.

12. The experience curve refers to the inverse relationship between the accumulated volume of production and the unit manufacturing cost. Empirical findings have shown that, for many firms, the unit cost of production falls when the volume of production increases. The increased efficiency or cost reduction can be attributed to economies of scale, learning curve effect, improvements in design and processing, increased control and bargaining power over costs.

13. The experience curve effects are also evident in many service industries. In other words, larger service firms usually enjoy a lower per unit cost in providing their service to their customers.

14. Multinational operations strategy is a set of decisions and guidelines that are formulated to encourage the efficiency and the effective functioning of an MNC's operations system.

15. The operational strategy of an MNC must match its product strategy. We discussed three alternative strategies: (1) the technology-driven strategy, (2) the marketing-intensive strategy, and (3) the low-cost strategy.

16. The National Location Portfolio matrix is a useful analytical technique that is used for deciding whether or not to establish a manufacturing or operations facility in a specific foreign nation.

17. The following factors should be considered when deciding on facilities location: (1) staff availability and labor cost, (2) the availability and cost of capital, (3) the proximity of the proposed facility to markets and materials, (4) the local governmental regulations, (5) the accessibility to transportation and its cost, and (6) living conditions available for employees.

18. Offshore manufacturing refers to locating part of the manufacturing process of the products that are sold at home in another nation with lower labor costs than the home country.

19. Mexico, through the use of maquiladora or, as it is formally known, in-bond export

industry, is rapidly becoming a desirable offshore center for U.S. companies. Under this system, the components that are produced in the United States are shipped to Mexico duty-free. These components are then assembled by Mexican workers and shipped back to the United States for sale.

**20.** Decisions regarding the design of facilities are directly related to the nature of technology that a firm has contemplated using in a foreign location.

**21.** Regardless of the motives for establishing an international R & D program, the MNC needs to realistically weigh the costs and benefits expected from such a program.

## QUESTIONS

**18.1** What are the operational differences between the production of a tangible product and the rendering of a service? Explain. Give some examples that are not given in the text.

**18.2** Discuss the concept of productivity. What is productivity? What are its main determinants? Why is productivity so important?

**18.3** What are the different types of operations systems? Give some examples of these types of systems.

**18.4** How is international operations management different from domestic operations management? What effect does centralization have on international operations management.

**18.5** What are the main decisions that are made in the course of implementing an MNC's operations strategy? Discuss.

**18.6** How is the location for an MNC's facility decided upon on an international basis and in a specific country? Discuss.

**18.7** How can international R & D benefit an MNC? What are the precautions an MNC should take before starting international R & D. Research the way some MNCs conduct R & D.

**18.8** Visit a local production facility and a branch of a local bank. Can you identify their operational similarities and differences? Discuss.

## NOTES

1. Robert N. Mefford, "Determinants of Productivity Differences in International Manufacturing," *Journal of International Business Studies,* vol. 17, no. 1 (Spring 1986), pp. 63–82.
2. John B. Miner, Jeffry M. Wachtel, and Bahman Ebrahimi, "The Managerial Motivation of Potential Managers in the United States and Other Countries of the World: Implications for National Competitiveness and the Productivity Problem," *Advances in International Comparative Management,* vol. 4 (August 1989), pp. 147–170.
3. HBR Editors, "Competitiveness Survey: HBR Readers Respond," *Harvard Business Review,* vol. 65, no. 5 (1987), p. 8.
4. John H. Dunning, "Toward an Eclectic Theory of International Production: Some Empirical Tests," *Journal of International Business Studies,* vol. 11, no. 1 (Spring/Summer 1980), p. 13

5. Steven C. Wheelwright, "Manufacturing Strategy: Defining the Missing Link," *Strategic Management Journal,* vol. 5, no. 1 (1984), pp. 77–91.

6. S. J. Q. Robinson, and D. P. Wade, "The Directional Policy Matrix: Tool for Strategic Planning," *Long-Range Planning,* vol. 11, no. 3 (June 1978), pp. 8–15.

7. Martin E. Rosenfeldt, "Industrial Development in Texas-Mexico Borderland: Assessment of Current Tendencies." Working paper presented to the annual meeting of the North American Economic and Finance Association, Chicago, Ill., 30 December 1987, p. 5.

8. Ibid., p. 6.

9. Ibid., p. 8.

10. *1988 Directory of In-Bond Plant (Maquiladoras) in Mexico,* El Paso, Tex.: Mexico Communications, 1988.

11. Statistics provided by the *Secreteria de Fomento Industrial y Comercial, Gobierno del Estado de Nuevo Leon,* 12 April 1989.

12. Rosenfeldt, "Industrial Development," p. 8.

13. Briance Mascarenhas, "The Coordination of Manufacturing Interdependence in Multinational Companies," *Journal of International Business Studies,* vol. 15, no. 3 (Winter 1984), pp. 91–106.

14. David B. Hertz, "R & D as a Partner in World Enterprise," in Roland Mann, *The Art of Top Management: A McKinsey Anthology* (New York, N.Y.: McGraw-Hill, 1971), p. 320.

15. Franklin R. Root, "Some Trends in the World Economy and Their Implications for International Business," *Journal of International Business Strategy,* vol. 15, no. 3 (Winter 1984), p. 21.

16. Ibid., pp. 21–22.

17. Ibid.

18. Ibid.

19. Ibid.

20. Ibid.

## SUGGESTED READINGS

Boddewyn, J. J., M. B. Halbrich, and A. C. Perry. "Service Multinationals: Conceptualization, Measurement, and Theory." *Journal of International Business Studies,* vol. 17, no. 3 (Fall 1986), pp. 41–58.

Brooke, Michael Z., and H. Lee Remmers. *International Management and Business Policy.* Boston: Houghton Mifflin, 1978, Chap. 8.

Chase, Richard B., and Nicholas J. Aquilano. *Production and Operations Management: A Life Cycle Approach,* 5th ed. Homewood, Ill.: Irwin, 1989.

Ebrahimi, Bahman, and William Bowman. "ABCs of Countertrade: A Vehicle for Successful Exporting." *InfoTrade Report* (September–October 1988), pp. 4–5.

Globerman, Steven. *Fundamentals of International Business Management.* Englewood Cliffs, N.J.: Prentice-Hall, 1986, Chap. 13.

Leontiades, James C. *Multinational Corporate Strategy: Planning for World Markets.* Lexington, Mass.: Lexington Books, 1985, Chap. 9.

Mann, Roland, ed. *The Art of Top Management: A McKinsey Anthology.* New York: McGraw-Hill, 1971.

Mascarenhas, Briance. "The Coordination of Manufacturing Interdependence in Multinational Companies." *Journal of International Business Studies,* vol. 15, no. 3 (Winter 1984), pp. 91–106.

Mefford, Robert N. "Determinants of Productivity Differences in International Manufacturing." *Journal of International Business Studies,* vol. 17, no. 1 (Spring 1986), pp. 63–82.

Miner, John B., Jeffry M. Wachtel, and Bahman Ebrahimi. "The Managerial Motivation of Potential Managers in the United States and Other Countries of the World: Implications for National Competitiveness and the Productivity Problem." *Advances in International Comparative Management,* vol. 4 (August 1989), pp. 147–170.

Negandhi, Anant R. *International Management.* Boston: Allyn and Bacon, 1987, Chap. 9.

Robinson, S. J. Q., and D. P. Wade. "The Directional Policy Matrix—Tool for Strategic Planning." *Long-Range Planning,* vol. 11, no. 3 (June 1978), pp. 8–15.

Root, Franklin R. "Some Trends in the World Economy and Their Implications for International Business." *Journal of International Business Strategy,* vol. 15, no. 3 (Winter 1984), pp. 19–23.

Rosenfeldt, Martin E. "Industrial Development in Texas–Mexico Borderland: Assessment of Current Tendencies." Working paper presented to the annual meeting of the North American Economic and Finance Association, Chicago, Ill., 30 December 1987.

Sisk, Henry L. and J. Cliffton Williams. *Management and Organization,* 4th ed. Cincinnati, Ohio: Southwestern, 1981.

Stobaugh, Robert, and Piero Telesio. "Match Manufacturing Policies and Product Strategy." *Harvard Business Review,* vol. 61, no. 2 (March/April 1983), pp. 113–120.

Timms, Howard L., and Michael F. Pohler. *The Production Function in Business: Decision Systems for Production and Operations Management,* 3rd ed. Homewood, Ill.: Irwin, 1970.

Wheelwright, Steven C. "Manufacturing Strategy: Defining the Missing Link." *Strategic Management Journal,* vol. 5, no. 1 (January/March 1984), pp. 77–91.

# The Ingersoll-Rand Corporation*

## INTRODUCTION

The Ingersoll-Rand Corporation is analogous to a wise old grandfather who has learned certain lessons through experience. The first lesson learned was that a top-quality product at a premium price will sell well. The second lesson was that diversifying products will ensure substantial profits in good times and serve as a cushion in bad times. The third lesson was that making acquisitions instead of using profits to improve products with advanced technology meant larger profits. Consequently, this wise old grandfather of a company became very rich and powerful through the years, and Ingersoll-Rand kept to its staunch conservative beliefs because they were producing considerable profits. Eventually, the company was selling its products more than anyone else in the market. But then the competition began to catch up. New young blood entered the market, like Caterpillar Tractor, Clark Equipment, Gardner Dever, Dresser Industries, and Cooper Industries. These producers sold a product that was more technologically advanced than Ingersoll-Rand's old products. In addition, these new companies reinvested their profits back into their products in order to improve them and to increase efficiency. However, Ingersoll-Rand continued to invest in other companies so as not to put all of its eggs in one basket. As a result the new companies began to catch up, and eventually they surpassed Ingersoll-Rand which had kept its conservative views. That is the basic story of Ingersoll-Rand.

## HISTORY

This mass producer of industrial machinery was born on June 1, 1905, as a result of the consolidation of the Ingersoll-Sergeant Drill Company and the Rand Drill Company. From that point on, its history consists of the acquisitions of numerous other companies that all produce industrial machinery. These acquired

---

*This case was originally written by Carl Montante of St. Lawrence University as a term project; it was subsequently revised by Professor Asheghian for inclusion in this textbook.

companies became subsidiaries, and today, Ingersoll-Rand conducts its manufacturing and assembly operations in 44 plants in the United States and 29 plants outside the United States.[1]

Throughout most of its history, Ingersoll-Rand has been in the forefront of selling capital goods. In 1968, the company was called "the most profitable, best managed company, the closest thing to a blue chip in the industry."[2] Indeed, Ingersoll-Rand was the largest and most diversified of any of its competitors, and because of this it usually made most of the profits. However, this position was not always reflected in the stock market prices for the company.

Although Ingersoll-Rand has consistently topped the market for the production and sale of industrial machinery, its price per share in the stock market has usually fluctuated. For example, in 1968 its shares sold at $43.00 per share. This was 20 percent lower than the 1954 mark of $53.00. This also decreased the company's price-earning ratio over that time period from 27 to 11. Ingersoll-Rand reasoned that it had been the "victim of changing stock market fads."[3] In 1976, after the company announced that earnings would be off for the year, its stock dropped $9\frac{1}{4}$ points to $75\frac{3}{8}$ in one month. Moreover, the drop in the price of its stock carried many other machinery stocks, like Caterpillar Tractor, Clark Equipment, and Cooper Industries, down with it. Ingersoll-Rand's reason for decreased earnings was the "unanticipated slowdown in demand for capital goods and problems with its capital spending."[4] Finally, in 1983, Ingersoll-Rand's average return on equity decreased to 14.4 percent, well behind Dresser Industries' 17.9 percent, or Cooper Industries' 24.2 percent. Ingersoll-Rand expected a boom in capital spending that year, but it never happened. As a result, Ingersoll-Rand was burdened with overcapacity in production. Also, the wildly fluctuating dollar hurt Ingersoll-Rand, whose foreign sales amounted to 35 percent of total sales.[5]

Ingersoll-Rand still remains one of the largest manufacturers of industrial equipment to this date. However, according to a statement made in 1979 by William L. Wearly, chairman and chief executive officer of the company, since Ingersoll-Rand depends heavily on the lagging demand for capital goods, its earnings had been about 5 percent lower than what they could be. Moreover, Wearly thought this loss of profitability reflected a tremendous increase in competition. For example, portable compressors, which Ingersoll-Rand had made and sold successfully for years, were manufactured by only six companies in 1940. By 1960, however, there were 13 and by 1968 there were 18 companies manufacturing the product.[6]

## COMPANY DESCRIPTION

Portable compressors are just one of the many industrial products that Ingersoll-Rand manufactures. Through the years the company has supplemented its original business, which had mainly consisted of the manufacture and sale of rock-drilling equipment. Additional products had been developed internally, or through acquisitions, until three major production segments were created by the company.

The first segment is the standard machinery division. Products made in this division include air compressors, which are mainly used to supply pressurized air to chemical plants, industrial plants, and electrical utilities. Construction equipment is also manufactured within this division. This division also serves the construction and metal mining industries as well as well-drilling contractors. Mining machinery is the last group served by the standard machinery division. It serves the underground coal-mining industry by supplying coal haulers, crushers, and roof-stabling equipment.[7]

The second segment is the engineered equipment division. Three major products are made in this division. First, gas compressors, which are used in the oil, gas, and petrochemical industries, are manufactured. Turbo machinery is the second group of products made. These products include gas and steam turbines, positive-displacement compressors, and axial flow compressors. These are products used in the oil and gas production, refining and transmission, as well as in chemical and other processing industries. The third segment is the bearings, locks, and tools division. This consists of three broad production groups: bearings and their components, which are used primarily in the automotive and aerospace industries; professional tools, which are sold to the appliance, aircraft, construction, and automotive industries; and door hardware, which includes locks, electronic access systems, and exit devices, which are used in the commercial and residential construction industries.

Ingersoll-Rand's competition consists of companies that specialize in one of the many industries in which it does business. Hence, the company is like a large whale who must compete with many little fish for its food. In the process of eating so much food (profits), it devours (acquires) some of the smaller fish (other companies). In the long run, this whale realizes that it should not have eaten so many fish.

## INTERNATIONAL OPERATIONS

One cannot talk about Ingersoll-Rand's production and operations without discussing its international operations. The company originally went overseas in 1885 in order to serve the mining industry in Africa, South America, and Australia. However, as time went on, management realized that it was more profitable to manufacture most of its products in the United States and use foreign countries primarily as markets for its sales and service. Today, Ingersoll-Rand manufactures 70 percent of its products at home and only 30 percent abroad. Ingersoll-Rand's strategy regarding international marketing can be inferred from the statement made by William L. Wearly, the company's chairman: "In the export field, you have to have your service organization over there, and at least the standard products on the shelf."[8] In short, investing in foreign sales and service organizations helps support exports from the United States as well as production abroad. In 1978, Ingersoll-Rand exported $408 million worth of goods out of a total sales of $2.1 billion—a 20 percent export ratio that is relatively high for an American multinational.[9]

In the past, Ingersoll-Rand was managed by people who were supply oriented. That is, they were very conscious of manufacturing enough industrial products to supply the market. For example, in 1968 the company was concerned more with turning their profits into acquisitions than with turning out a better product. Wayne Hallstein, then-president of Ingersoll-Rand, exemplified this by saying: "Our people overseas tell us that their market shares are such that they can just about guarantee yearly increases no matter what the economy does—if they can get more product."[10] As a result, management had inventories increased substantially until, in 1978, Ingersoll-Rand's assets reached $723 million outside the United States, of which inventories and receivables accounted for $561 million, nearly 80 percent of the total.[11] Things were going well, and in 1981, Ingersoll-Rand reported record earnings of $9.71 per share, a 21 percent gain over 1980. President Holmes predicted a capital spending boom as a result. Inventories and stock prices began to increase considerably, until in 1983 inventory was up to a $1.1 billion high. Then things began to fall apart. The capital spending boom never came, and Ingersoll-Rand was stuck with huge inventories and, as a result, major losses. For the first time in 40 years, the directors cut the common dividend—from $0.85 to $0.65. Holmes was shocked at the collapse: "In the past, there was always some part of business going up when something else was going down."[12]

Since then Ingersoll-Rand has seen some growth potential. A new management has been formed called Hapton and Johnson, and they have begun to address the problems of overcapacity, overdiversification, and lack of efficiency. First, they have cut inventory costs, which is one of the biggest expenses for most manufacturing companies. They decreased the number of inventory warehouses from eight to two. To cut down on inefficiency, more than $100 million in unprofitable or unpromising businesses have been sold, using that money to pay off short-term debts. Thomas Holmes, president of Ingersoll-Rand in 1983, admitted the inefficiency with which the company had been run in the past.[13]

To deal with the lack of technology, the company began using its profits to address this problem. Today, for example, their entire pneumatic tool line has been redesigned. Also, their tools are now bioengineered for the world market. According to Gene Driscoll, president of the Ingersoll-Rand Tools Group, engineering has always been an important factor and the "majority in management have technical backgrounds."[14]

An intelligent step that has been taken by Ingersoll-Rand in order to catch up with its competitors is the development of Advanced Research Centers in Princeton and in Liberty Corners, New Jersey.[15] The sole purpose of the centers is research and development, having as its main objective the transformation of industrial machinery into high-tech products. One of the results of R & D is the X-Flow compressor. It is designed to increase efficiency by 5 percent, while decreasing installation and maintenance costs because it has fewer moving parts.[16]

## QUESTIONS

1. What are the implications for other MNCs of the lessons learned by the Ingersoll-Rand Corporation?
2. How critical is technology to the survival of an MNC? Explain.
3. Where did Ingersoll-Rand go wrong, and what can the company do to improve its sales in the future?
4. Is a "supply-oriented" strategy an efficient way of selling products to foreign markets? Explain.

## NOTES

1. "Ingersoll-Rand Company," *Moody's Industrial Manual,* vol. 1, New York: Moody's Investors Service, 1988, p. 436.
2. "We'll Be the Best of the Bad Guys," *Forbes,* 1 February 1968, p. 18.
3. Ibid.
4. "Guilt by Association," *Forbes,* 15 October 1976, p. 156.
5. John A. Byrne, ". . . And Then the Bottom Fell Out," *Forbes,* 14 February 1983, p. 142.
6. Jean A. Briggs, "Like Capital Goods? You'll Love Ingersoll-Rand," *Forbes,* 16 April 1979, p. 81.
7. "Ingersoll-Rand Company," p. 436.
8. "Ingersoll-Rand's Secret of Success," *Business Week,* 10 April 1978, p. 66.
9. Ibid.
10. "We'll Be the Best of the Bad Guys," p. 18.
11. "Ingersoll-Rand's Secret of Success," p. 66.
12. Byrne, ". . . And Then the Bottom Fell Out," p. 142.
13. Ibid.
14. Ernest Raia, "Litmus Test for 80's: Top Quality, Low Costs," *Purchasing,* 27 January 1983, p. 25.
15. "Supplier Profiles," *Automotive Industries,* June 1984, p. 145.
16. "New Turbo Compressor Called Major Advance," *Machine Design,* 8 August 1985, p. 2.

## SUGGESTED READINGS

Briggs, Jean A. "Like Capital Goods? You'll Love Ingersoll-Rand." *Forbes,* 16 April 1979, p. 81.

Byrne, John A. ". . . And Then the Bottom Fell Out." *Forbes,* 14 February 1983, p. 142.

"Guilt by Association." *Forbes,* 15 October 1976, p. 156.

"Ingersoll-Rand Company." *Moody's Industrial Manual,* vol. 1, New York: Moody's Investors Service, 1988, pp. 436–447.

"Ingersoll-Rand: Is Price Pressure Ending?" *Forbes,* 31 August 1981, p. 144.

"Ingersoll-Rand's Secret of Success." *Business Week,* 10 April 1978, p. 66.

"New Turbo Compressor Called Major Advance." *Machine Design,* 8 August 1985, p. 2.

Raia, Ernest. "Litmus Test for 80's: Top Quality, Low Costs." *Purchasing,* 27 January 1983, p. 25.

"Supplier Profiles." *Automotive Industries* (June 1984), p. 145.

"We'll Be the Best of the Bad Guys." *Forbes,* 1 February 1964, p. 18.

# Condition Liquid Soap*

## INTRODUCTION

Bob Richland, general manager of Blair Incorporated, sighed as he hung up the telephone. His conversation with Stefan Von Stropp, general manager of Hansel House, had left him troubled. Hansel House is responsible for the marketing of Condition Liquid Soap and other Blair products in Austria. Over the past three years, the parallel importing of Condition Liquid Soap into Austria has become an increasing threat.

Parallel importing, sometimes called "black importing," is a type of competition that poses quite a threat to Hansel House. Although it creates problems, it is not illegal. It simply means that a group of independent distributors are buying Condition Liquid Soap in the United States and taking it to Austria themselves, where it is then sold.

Stefan has asked Bob to recommend a strategy to fight back against the threat of this parallel importing. He asked that this strategy include, if necessary, a reduction of Blair's selling price for Condition Liquid Soap to Hansel House.

## BLAIR INCORPORATED

Blair Incorporated is the parent company of Hansel House. Blair feels that the quality of their products, their team of competent managers, and their ability to stay ahead of their competitors have been responsible for their success. Blair, on average, has enjoyed a 21 percent a year increase in earnings over the past eight years.

Blair is composed of the North American Division and the International Division, with subsidiaries in Italy, England, and Austria. Blair feels that this year the market in Europe will be responsible for much of the sales and profit that are projected for the company as a whole. Sales for Hansel House were up 22 percent in 1989 as compared with the year before.

---

*This fictional case was written by Professor Ebrahimi and Faith Moore of University of North Texas for the purpose of class discussion. Any resemblance to a real situation is completely coincidental.

### The Product

Condition Liquid Soap is a high-quality, all-purpose soap. It can be used on the hands as well as other parts of the body. In its advertising, the company stresses that Condition Liquid Soap is the "unmessy" way to stay clean, and, because it is concentrated, it takes only a small amount of soap for each washing. The company's advertising says that the soap leaves your hands and body feeling soft and smooth, and that the soap actually moisturizes as it cleans.

Over the years, Condition Liquid Soap has become popular in Austria. Because of this, parallel importers are easily able to sell Condition Liquid Soap that has been shipped directly from the United States to Austria, even though the directions on the bottle are in English. It is estimated that 120,000 bottles of Condition Liquid Soap were parallel imported into Austria this year as compared to 200,000 bottles sold by Hansel House, Blair Incorporated's subsidiary.

### Channels and Pricing

Condition Liquid Soap is manufactured in the United States and sold to independent wholesalers or large retail chains. In foreign countries with subsidiaries, Condition Liquid Soap is sold to the affiliated company and then resold to the wholesalers and retail stores. Blair Incorporated bills all of its foreign customers in U.S. dollars. However, the subsidiary is charged a standard manufacturing cost in the form of a transfer price.

Blair gives independent distributors in the United States a discount for cash purchases and a rebate for large purchases. Each month, promotions are also offered to encourage U.S. distributors to increase their volume.

### Parallel Imports

Parallel importing is the greatest problem facing Hansel House today. It is profitable for an Austrian distributor to send a buyer to the United States to purchase the product at a U.S. wholesale price and then ship it to Austria, to be resold to retail outlets there. Because of the monthly promotions to U.S. distributors it is cheaper for the Austrian distributors to purchase the goods in the United States at the promotion price.

The parallel importers do not have to pay for advertising because Hansel House advertises the product extensively. Therefore, this cost is eliminated for them.

The retail price of Condition Liquid Soap has not declined in the past few years even though parallel imports have increased. Therefore, with the consumer paying the same price, the parallel importers are enjoying higher profit margins than Hansel House.

Sales of Condition Liquid Soap have increased in Austria. This is partially due to the actions of the parallel importers, since greater brand recognition may be due to their higher market penetration. This actually benefits the parent company; however, Bob Richland cannot ignore the problem. It has caused low morale among Blair's Austrian salespeople because they receive commissions based on the units sold. As a result of parallel imports, the Austrian distributors at Hansel House have lost potential revenues. Therefore, they would like to cut the price so that they can better compete with the parallel importers.

## QUESTIONS

1. What alternatives should Bob Richland recommend to counter the parallel importing threat?

2. What alternative do you feel is the best? Why?

# Star-Style Barter*

Star-Style Furniture Company is not what most people would think of as a multinational enterprise. Star-Style is a small furniture manufacturing company owned by Bob Hanson. The company is located in El Paso, Texas, and employs about 40 workers. Each year the company sells about $3 million worth of custom-designed, made-to-order furniture to wealthy customers. The company's only link to international business is that it often imports exotic or elegant upholstery fabrics. A great deal of the imported fabrics come from nearby Mexico.

Bob Hanson often drives across the border into Mexico to personally inspect and select upholstery fabrics. On one such buying trip, Hanson called on Hector de la Garza, a sales representative for a Mexican weaving firm. Hector showed Bob samples of several unique fabrics, and Bob was eager to purchase a quantity of each. However, the transaction was delayed because Hector was not eager to quote a firm price. Hector reminded Bob of the recent serious drop in the value of the Mexican peso. Instead of the usual cash payment, Hector suggested a system of barter.

Hector's firm needed three new typewriters for its office. The value of the three typewriters would equal the value in U.S. dollars of the fabrics that Bob Hanson wanted. The brand of typewriters that Hector desired was not available in Mexico, but was readily available in Texas. There were no restrictions on bringing such typewriters into Mexico. Hector made the deal seem quite simple, and suggested that other such deals could be made in the future. Bob was uncertain because he knew nothing about barter systems.

## QUESTIONS

1. What should Bob Hanson do? Why?
2. What is barter trade? How can it lead to increased international trade and business activities?

---

*This fictional case was written by Professor Ebrahimi and Martha Grigsby of University of North Texas for the purpose of class discussion. Any resemblance to a real situation is completely coincidental.

3. What is the impact of this transaction on the balance of payments of the United States and Mexico, respectively?

## SUGGESTED READINGS

"Better Ball Bearings than Bad Debt?" *The Economist,* 15 December 1984, pp. 79–80.

Kassaye, W. Wossen. "Countertrade Prospects and Dilemma for Small Business." *Management Review,* vol. 74, no. 5 (1985), pp. 17–19.

Milmo, Sean. "Stage Set for Countertrade Boom in Europe." *Business Marketing,* vol. 71, no. 2 (1986), pp. 26–27.

Welt, Leo G. B. "Countertrade as a Competitive Tool." *Management Review,* vol. 75, no. 1 (1986), pp. 53–56.

# Case III:4

# A New Image*

Every man leaves a legacy. In John R. Wickfield's case, the legacy he left to his children was a multinational company and a bad reputation. John R. Wickfield was one of the greediest, most ruthless men in business history. His company, Wickfield International, consisted of 12 garment assembly plants scattered throughout Mexico and other parts of Latin America. His operations were notorious for low wages and dangerous working conditions. He often paid local goons to punish employees who dared to protest, and he was quick to squelch any union activity. But that's all over now.

For the past 10 years, John's children have run the company, and they have tried hard to undo the wrongs their father had committed. They changed the name of the company to ADA International and tried to project a new image in the business world. Their efforts have been very successful. The social consciousness and humanitarian efforts of ADA International have been the subject of many articles in professional business journals and newspapers. An American filmmaker has asked for permission to film a documentary about the new image of ADA International and its good deeds.

ADA International has recently moved some of its operations to the African nation of Zahuud. Zahuud is a small, poor nation, and its leaders are struggling to improve its economy and to care for its people. The Foreign Trade Minister of Zahuud is very proud of the new ADA plant in his country, and he hopes to encourage more foreign investment.

The new ADA plant in Zahuud is really something to be proud of, for it offers good working conditions and fair wages, along with benefits such as health care services for employees and their families. Because most of the employees are women, it also provides child care for small children and education for older children. ADA International is also training Zahuud managers in the United States so that they will be prepared for the day when ADA International sells the Zahuud plant to local owners. This sell-back arrangement was part of the original trade agreement with the Zahuud government.

The Zahuud plant produces moderately priced sportswear for export to

---

*This fictional case was written by Professor Ebrahimi and Martha Grigsby of University of North Texas for the purpose of class discussion. Any resemblance of names, characters, and conditions to a real situation is completely coincidental.

the United States. Jane Bitmore is the new marketing director for ADA International, and she is very interested in the Zahuud operation. She wanted it to do well and to serve as a model for other international companies. In her efforts to help the Zahuud operation, she looked for new markets for the Zahuud-made sportswear. Her research showed that Canada was a good market for the sportswear. She found a Canadian distributor, and soon the sportswear was for sale at several major outlets. The market forecast was for $4 million in sales the first year. The sportswear sold very well, and everything looked good for ADA International and its operation in Zahuud. No one expected the ghost of John R. Wickfield to show up in Canada.

The ghost was actually the memory of his bad reputation. A Canadian activist group called for a total boycott of all ADA International products and exposed the dreadful deeds of the old Wickfield International. The group was small and loosely organized, but it managed to get much attention from the local Canadian press. Sales dropped sharply. The Canadian distributor called Jane Bitmore and asked for help. Jane flew to Canada, where she was surprised to learn that the leader of the group was formerly employed by John R. Wickfield. It was obvious to Jane that the group was poorly informed. The directors of ADA International did not wish to press any legal charges against the group.

## QUESTIONS

1. What can Jane Bitmore do to inform the protest group and the public about the new image of ADA International?

2. Why should ADA International care about its public image in a foreign market?

3. What are the lessons to be learned by companies that engage in foreign production in LDCs?

# Case III:5

# *Citicorp* *

## INTRODUCTION

Citicorp is the largest multinational financial institution in the world. It operates approximately 3,100 offices and other facilities in 94 countries, employing over 88,000 people.[1] In 1986, it generated over $1,058 billion in earnings. Its home office, known as Citicorp Center, is located in New York City. It has a highly diversified offering of financial services, including commercial banking, investment banking, venture capital financing, insurance, brokerage houses, and industrial lending. Each of these services offers several lines of financial products. For example, Citicorp Industrial Credit—Citicorp's industrial lending subsidiary—offers the following product lines: Asset Based Lending, Corporate Asset Funding, Equipment Finance and Leasing, and Citicorp Business Loans. These specialized products have been developed so that clients can be easily identified, categorized, and serviced.†

## INTERNATIONAL OPERATIONS

In 1914, Citicorp became the first foreign bank in Buenos Aires, Argentina, and a year later purchased a private banking network, with offices in Shanghai, Yokohama, Hong Kong, Manila, Singapore, Calcutta, and London. Seventy years later, it had increased its multinational holdings to $128.3 billion in assets within 94 foreign countries.[2]

Citicorp's management philosophy has emphasized the grouping of assets and earnings by geography, currency, customer, and product. Its international hierarchy is contrived of five banking groups identified as North America (NA); Caribbean, Central, and South America (CCSA); Europe, Middle East, and Africa (EMEA); and Asia/Pacific (AP) and Other. In 1985, the North American banking group contributed $463 billion in earnings, which was 46 percent of

---

*This case was originally written by Tracy Gale of St. Lawrence University as a term project; it was subsequently revised by Professor Asheghian for inclusion in this textbook.

†For a summary of the important data on Citicorp, see Table III:5.1.

## Table III:5.1 CITICORP IN BRIEF

| (In Millions of Dollars Except Per Share Amounts*) | 1987 | 1986 | 1985 | 1984 | 1983 |
|---|---|---|---|---|---|
| **Results** | | | | | |
| Earnings (Loss) Per Share | $(4.26) | $ 3.57 | $ 3.56 | $ 3.22 | $ 3.24 |
| Net Income (Loss) | (1,138) | 1,058 | 998 | 890 | 860 |
| Return on Common Stockholders' Equity | (18.5)% | 13.8 % | 15.1 % | 15.0 % | 16.5 % |
| **Common Dividends** | | | | | |
| Cash Dividends Declared | $379 | $ 250 | $ 290 | $ 259 | $ 234 |
| Annual Dividend Rate Per Share at Year End | 1.35 | 1.23 | 1.13 | 1.03 | 0.94 |
| **Capital** | | | | | |
| Common Equity | $7,220 | $ 7,695 | $ 6,550 | $ 5,786 | $ 5,231 |
| Percentage of Total Assets | 3.55% | 3.92 % | 3.77 % | 3.84 % | 3.88 % |
| Total Stockholders' Equity | $8,810 | $ 9,060 | $ 7,765 | $ 6,426 | $ 5,771 |
| Percentage of Total Assets | 4.33% | 4.62 % | 4.47 % | 4.27 % | 4.29 % |
| Primary Capital | $16,771 | $ 13,490 | $ 10,892 | $ 8,872 | $ 6,588 |
| Percentage of Total Assets | 8.05% | 6.82 % | 6.23 % | 5.86 % | 4.86 % |
| Total Capital | $24,462 | $ 21,531 | $ 15,948 | $ 11,805 | $ 9,678 |
| Percentage of Total Assets | 11.75% | 10.88 % | 9.12 % | 7.79 % | 7.15 % |
| **Year-End Balances** | | | | | |
| Total Assets | $203,607 | $196,124 | $173,597 | $150,586 | $134,655 |
| Consumer Loans, Net of Unearned Discount | 78,959 | 68,243 | 55,518 | 42,661 | 28,995 |
| Commercial Loans, Net of Unearned Discount | 55,754 | 59,439 | 58,172 | 58,799 | 60,242 |
| Total Deposits | 119,561 | 114,689 | 104,959 | 90,349 | 79,794 |
| Common Stockholders' Equity Per Share | 22.83 | 27.96 | 25.32 | 22.91 | 21.00 |

*All per share amounts have been restated to reflect the Two-for-One stock split

| People | | Offices | |
|---|---|---|---|
| Common Stockholders | 50,000 | **United States** (in 40 States and the District of Columbia) | |
| | | Citibank, N.A., Branches | 306 |
| **Staff** | | Citibank, N.A., Subsidiaries | 59 |
| Domestic | 48,000 | Citibank (New York State) Branches | 44 |
| Overseas | 42,000 | Citibank (New York State) Subsidiaries | 34 |
| Total | 90,000 | Citicorp Savings | 293 |
| | | Other Citicorp Subsidiaries | 382 |
| | | Total Domestic | 1,118 |
| | | **Overseas** (in 90 Countries) | |
| | | Citibank Branches and Representative Offices | 284 |
| | | Banking Subsidiaries | 611 |
| | | Banking Affiliates | 105 |
| | | Other Financial Affiliates and Subsidiaries | 938 |
| | | Total Overseas | 1,938 |
| | | Total Domestic and Overseas | 3,056 |

Source: *Citicorp Annual Report,* 1987, p.19.

Citicorp's net income, while the EMEA banking group contributed $191 billion (19 percent), the CCSA contributed $245 billion (25 percent), and the AP contributed $99 billion (10 percent). The Other category contributed $340 billion and includes Citicorp's activities that are not grouped into geographic locations.[3] These activities are (1) general corporate expenses, (2) earnings and funding costs related to the investment securities portfolio, and (3) tax expenses.[4]

## LATIN AMERICAN OPERATIONS

Brazilian subsidiaries are responsible for almost half of the newly industrialized countries' (NICs') and the less developed countries' (LDCs') profit contributions to Citicorp, with earnings reported at $162 billion.[5] Citicorp in Brazil employs 6,000 people, which is almost 10 percent of the financial services workforce of the entire corporation.[6] Brazilian holdings include 11 branches and a 49.9 percent stake in Crefisul, a financial service holding company that is composed of an investment bank, a brokerage firm, a data processing company, and a credit card operation.[7]

Many U.S. banks in Brazil are failing. This is due to the state governors' liberal use of the banks to fund their election campaigns. Banks are failing also because of the country's weakening economy. Citicorp has managed to avoid these pitfalls by establishing strong relations with the Brazilian private sector and by designating its funds to them. The majority of profits were earned from investment banking, insurance brokerage, and fund management.[8]

Nearly 15 percent of the total U.S. bank exposure to the Latin American debt belongs to Citicorp.[9] They have taken advantage of these countries' nonrestricted financial worlds and have experienced large gains, as seen in the Brazilian reports, but they have also realized substantial losses in Mexico and in Argentina. Unfortunately, the losses outweigh the gains. Citicorp has not invested enough in Latin America so that these losses will not strongly affect its portfolio earnings. Because of this it will probably remain in Latin America as long as its financing operations continue to benefit its clients.

## UNITED KINGDOM'S OPERATIONS

In London, the financial center of the world, Citicorp is the fifth largest bank, outranked by a narrow margin by Midland (fourth largest) and Lloyd's (third largest). But Citicorp is still well behind the ancient British giants, Barclays and National Westminster. Since its entry into the United Kingdom in 1902, Citicorp's operations in London have grown to $10 billion in assets, with 2,500 people employed in 40 retail and 12 commercial branches within the United Kingdom.[10]

Citicorp has shied away from making large loans to governments and corporations in Europe and has, instead, concentrated on "going native" by lending in local currencies to consumers and small businesses.[11] The United Kingdom is no exception. Citibank Business Loans (CBLs), specializing in loans of between $1 million and $25 million, have been introduced into the British market and have successfully adapted to the market in a relatively short period of time. Most foreign banks within the United Kingdom support their own investors and usually with their own form of currency. Citicorp is not exclusive when choosing its clients, and in order to attract domestic (British) clients it simplifies the currency conversion procedure by converting from the dollar to the pound only once.[12]

Citicorp enjoys several advantages from its presence in the British market. London has seasoned and experienced financiers from whom young Citicorp employees can learn much. Minute by minute communications of currency valuations are at the bank's fingertips. Government restrictions are more relaxed than in the United States. The Bank of England has a liberal policy toward the banking and investment world in order to try to limit intrusive regulation, as it supports the freedom of the Euromarket businesses.[13]

By positioning itself in an atmosphere so conducive to growth, Citicorp has been given the opportunity to expand experimentally with new financial services, such as investment banking, stockbrokering, underwriting, life insurance, and other insurance selling. These activities are heavily regulated in the United States, but are possible in the United Kingdom. Citicorp has recently purchased the stocks of Scrimgeour Vickers, Seccombe, Marshall and Campion. These firms specialize in investment banking and venture capital. Market gains and the bank's domination of certain markets are expected in the future.[14]

Another strategic advantage enjoyed by Citicorp in this location is its aggressive and unpolished manner of doing business. The British traditional banking atmosphere is characterized by seasoned financiers making low-risk, high-cost decisions behind heavy oak desks. This way of doing business is being challenged by Citicorp. The market seems to be jumping right into their hands as Citicorp cuts costs and gets the deal signed, sealed, and delivered in half the time it has taken in the past. Not only does Citicorp benefit from this environment, but the British consumers also benefit from decreased borrowing costs due to this heightened competition between the old banks and Citicorp. As a result, Citicorp continues to penetrate the British banking system. For example, in January 1985, Citicorp became the first foreign bank in England to join the "circle of British clearing banks." In February of the same year, it became the first bank, British or foreign, to purchase a "discount house."[15]

## ADAPTATION

Because Citicorp is not a manufacturing firm, the marketing and advertising of Citicorp's service products are not so necessary for the creation of business as they would be for most manufacturing firms. After the initial notification to the consumer of Citicorp's service offerings, most prospective clients seek out Citicorp because they are in need of its services and there are few substitutes available due to the reasons described earlier. It is seldom that Citicorp participates in "cold call" campaigns to attract business. Thus, the entry of Citicorp into a foreign market has been made that much easier by the relative unavailability of substitutes for its services.

Banking, as is any service, is people oriented. Communication is essential for successful business. Often cultural barriers interfere with a multinational's endeavors. Two of these barriers are language and religion. Citicorp has been sensitive to this issue. Its West German-based subsidiary, KKB Bank in Dusseldorf, is operated entirely by Germans and German-speaking personnel so that it resembles a local bank.[16] To better facilitate the adaptation process, Citicorp has often taken over existing firms upon entering a country for the first time. By buying into a ready-made firm, usually one that is in a turnaround transition, Citicorp has acquired a trained workforce with knowledge not only of financial services but also of the host country's culture, which aids Citicorp in its relationships with employees and the public.

## QUESTIONS

1. Why does a bank go international? Why did Citicorp?
2. Given the debt crisis of some of its major clients in Latin America, how can Citicorp protect itself? Explain.
3. What are the differences between operating a subsidiary bank in an advanced country, like the United Kingdom, and operating in an LDC, like Brazil?
4. Describe Citicorp's management strategy with regard to international banking.
5. What are the differences between the operations of multinational manufacturing companies and the operations of multinational service companies?

## NOTES

1. *Moody's Bank and Finance Manual,* 1987, p. 142.
2. "Citibank's Pervasive Influence on International Lending," *Business Week,* 16 May 1983, p. 124.
3. *Moody's Bank and Finance Manual,* 1986, p. 131.
4. Citicorp, *Annual Report 1984,* (New York: Citicorp).
5. *Moody's Bank and Finance Manual,* 1987, p. 143.
6. "The Booty from Brazil," *The Economist,* 5 May 1984, pp. 89–91.
7. "Citibank's Pervasive Influence on International Lending," p. 126.
8. "The Booty from Brazil," pp. 89–91.
9. "Citibank's Pervasive Influence on International Lending," p. 126.
10. "What Are Britons Doing Patronizing a New York Bank?" *Christian Science Monitor,* 19 August 1985, p. 18.
11. "Citicorp's Gutsy Campaign to Conquer Europe," *Business Week,* 15 July 1985, p. 46.
12. "Citibank's Pervasive Influence on International Lending," p. 125.

13. Gunter Dufey and Ian H. Giddy, *The International Money Market* (Englewood Cliffs, N.J.: Prentice-Hall, 1978), p. 40.

14. "What Are Britons Doing Patronizing a New York Bank?" p. 18.

15. Ibid., pp. 18, 20.

16. "Citicorp's Gutsy Campaign to Conquer Europe," p. 47.

## SUGGESTED READINGS

"The Booty from Brazil." *The Economist,* 5 May 1984, pp. 89–90.

"Citibank's Pervasive Influence on International Lending." *Business Week,* 16 May 1983, pp. 124–127.

Citicorp. *Annual Report.* New York: Citicorp, 1984.

Dufey, Gunter, and Ian H. Giddy. *The International Money Market.* Englewood Cliffs, N.J.: Prentice-Hall, 1978.

Jensen, Michael C. *The Financiers.* New York: Weybright and Talley, 1976.

*Moody's Bank and Finance Manual,* 1984.

Sampson, Anthony. *The Money Lenders: Bankers and a World of Turmoil.* New York: Viking Press, 1982.

Wilson, Andrew B. "Citicorp's Gutsy Campaign to Conquer Europe." *Business Week,* 15 July 1985, pp. 46–47.

# Ford: "Quality Is Job One"*

## INTRODUCTION

As the first automaker in the world, Ford has been a leader in the automotive industry. Its history has been filled with accomplishments that pioneered the way for manufacturers throughout the rest of the world. Henry Ford's development of the assembly line radically changed the auto industry, but, more important, it changed the whole manufacturing process.

Unfortunately, Ford has been plagued by numerous liability suits in recent times. These suits have led to questions regarding Ford's goals and aspirations. Ford has pulled through these rough times and has since reorganized and changed its motto. Along with these changes, Ford has turned to its operations overseas for guidance. It will be only through cooperation, not only with its overseas subsidiaries but also with its competitors, that Ford will gain the knowledge and know-how that will keep it in the forefront of the automobile industry.

## THE HISTORY OF FORD

In 1903, the Ford Motor Company was incorporated into the business world in Michigan "to produce automobiles designed and engineered by Henry Ford."[1] Initially Ford was but a tiny operation located in a converted wagon factory in Detroit. Today, Ford is an MNC with a worldwide operation. It is one of the largest industrial enterprises with active manufacturing, assembly, and sales operations in 25 countries and on six continents. About 350,000 men and women work for Ford every day. The company's annual sales are greater than the gross national products of many industrialized countries.[2] Ford cars and trucks are manufactured and assembled by its subsidiaries in West Germany, Great Britain, Canada, Spain, Brazil, Australia, Argentina, and other countries. "At December 31, 1985, the company had approximately 13,240 dealers worldwide, including approximately 6,770 dealers in the United States."[3]

The principal business of Ford, accounting for 93% of total sales in 1985,

---

*This case was originally written by David Pivirotto and Margaret Boese of St. Lawrence University as a term project; it was subsequently revised by Professor Asheghian for inclusion in this textbook.

is manufacturing, assembly, and sales of cars, trucks, and related accessories. "Ford also assembles and sells farm and industrial tractors and markets related farm, industrial, and construction equipment."[4]

In its first year, the Ford Motor Company was a big success. Sales for the first three and one-half months totaled $132,482, and resulted in a net profit of $36,958.[5] A dividend of 2 percent was paid on October 1, 1903; a month later the dividend was 10 percent. In January, 1904, it was 20 percent, and six months later it was 68 percent.[6] In the first 15 months 1,700 cars—early Model As—were produced.[7] Between 1903 and 1908, Henry Ford, chief engineer and later president, used the first 19 letters of the alphabet to designate his cars, although some of the cars never reached the public.

The most successful Ford car was the Model N.[8] It was a small, light, four-cylinder luxury car which sold for $500.[9] The Model K was a six-cylinder luxury car for $2,500, but it sold poorly.[10] Because of the Model K's failure, Mr. Ford insisted that the company's future lay in the production of inexpensive cars for a mass market. This caused conflict between Mr. Ford and Alexander Malcomson, a Detroit coal dealer, who had helped finance the company. Because of these problems, Mr. Malcomson left the company, allowing Mr. Ford to acquire enough of his stock to become president in 1906. In 1908 the Model T was produced, and it became an immediate success because of improvements in its quality. Within 19 years, more than 15,000,000 Model Ts were sold, making Ford Motor Company a giant industrial corporation throughout the world.[11] Ford revolutionized manufacturing with wages of $5 a day—very high for that time.

By 1927, however, people were ready for a more stylish and powerful car. The Model T had been basically unchanged for two decades, and it was losing ground to its competitors. A vastly improved Model A was designed, and 4,500,000 of them were produced between 1927 and 1931.[12]

Eventually people again wanted a more luxurious and powerful car, so the Ford V-8 was designed in 1932. Ford was the first company in history to successfully cast a V-8 engine block in one piece, and it was many years before Ford's competitors learned how to mass-produce a reliable V-8 engine.[13]

In the post–World War II period, Ford experienced a definite decrease in the sales of its automobiles. Ford was losing money at a rate of several million dollars a month. Ford was in no position at that time to resume its role as a major competitor in the automobile industry. Henry Ford II reorganized the company, and an expansion plan was designed, restoring the company to prosperity.

Along with Ford's domestic growth, there was also foreign expansion. Ford Motor Company of Canada was formed by Gordon McGregor, who negotiated a contract with the Michigan company and Henry Ford on August 10, 1904.[14] According to this contract the Canadian corporation was to be established with the capital of $125,000, of which 51 percent was to be distributed pro rata to stockholders in the parent Ford Company. Thus, Ford could gain majority control of the Canadian branch.[15] A branch of Ford Motor Company was established in London in 1908. Since then, Ford has continued to expand, establishing subsidaries in a number of nations.[16] In 1988, Ford had "active manufacturing, assembly and sales operations in 25 countries on six continents."[17]

## LEGAL ACTIONS

The Ford Motor Company's slogan is "Quality Is Job One." Their customer research concludes that the quality of Ford's 1986 cars and trucks is more than 50 percent better than that of their 1980 models.[18] They claim Ford is the leader in quality among major domestic producers. For example, Louis Ross, executive vice president, stated that "Our goal of customer satisfaction dictates that quality is, and will remain, our number one priority. We are already the leader in quality among major North American manufacturers and our efforts now are aimed at being the best in the industry."[19]

The need for emphasis on quality had arisen from lawsuits against Ford over the quality of its products in recent years, particularly involving the Ford Pinto. In June of 1978, the Ford Motor Company recalled 1.9 million Pintos in order to improve the safety of the fuel tanks. This was done at the request of the government and because of public pressure.[20] The next year the company was brought to court to face three charges of reckless homicide in connection with the deaths of three young women in a fiery crash in August of 1978.[21] The prosecution claimed that Ford knew that the gasoline tanks of the subcompact Ford Pinto tended to explode when struck from behind. And the prosecution claimed that the company did nothing to correct this problem. Harley Copp, the chief witness for the prosecution, stated that "Ford knew about the problem, and that Ford failed to do anything about it because it would have cut into profits."[22] The prosecutor, Michael Cosentino, described the Pinto as being poorly designed and the only car that the government had ever asked an automaker to recall.[23]

Ford denied the charges against it, arguing that its vehicles were as safe as its competitors' vehicles. Ford was found not guilty on three charges of reckless homicide on March 13, 1980.[24] On Thursday, April 10, 1980, the case of the *State of Indiana* v. *Ford Motor Company* was officially closed after 19 months.[25] Ford had won, but the fact still remained that quality was not "job one" in the design of the Pinto.

Ford has been a defendant in various other actions for damages arising out of automobile accidents where injuries resulted from alleged deficiencies in the fuel systems. It has also been a defendant in cases involving defective automatic transmissions. In August 1981, owners of vehicles produced between the years 1976 and 1979 that were equipped with certain automatic transmissions claimed to have had property damage, personal injury, economic losses, or liability losses because of the tendency of the vehicles to slip from the parking gear into reverse.[26] Ford has also been a defendant in cases involving the failure to provide an air bag and in cases where injuries were alleged to have resulted from contact with certain Ford parts and other products containing asbestos.

In June 1986, Ford recalled 162,000 1985-model and 1986-model Ranger light trucks because the vapor emissions of these trucks were above federal standards. Tests indicated that vapor return lines may have been pinched during assembly.[27] Again, in February 1988, Ford announced that it would recall 103,000 1985-model through 1987-model Ford Ranger trucks for ". . . a defect that could cause them to exceed federal pollution guidelines."[28]

These documented cases seem to show the lack of social responsibility on Ford's part. But many improvements have been demonstrated since its major problems with the Ford Pinto during the late 1970s and the early 1980s. During this period of time Ford was the last U.S. automaker to adjust to the new demand for fuel-efficient cars. This resulted in decreased sales and a large loss of market share in the United States. Since the implementation of "Quality Is Job One," Ford's strategy had deviated from traditional ideas. It now looks to its European divisions for design and engineering ideas and management talent.[29] These changes have brought Ford success over recent years. Through the introduction of designs developed in Europe, Ford cars have taken on a new image. Ford is looking for greater fuel efficiency through improved aerodynamics, adapting a rounded, overtly aerodynamic appearance.

To make the Ford Bronco better, the company has installed robots, other automated equipment, and statistical controls. The Bronco's design has been improved and there are tougher inspection systems.[30] In Louisville, Kentucky, an employee involvement strategy has been implemented. The workers now have a voice in how the truck is put together. This is expected to increase morale, leading to better-quality automobiles. The Louisville assembly plant demonstrates that U.S. industry can achieve huge improvements in quality and productivity, but only when circumstances force labor and management to get together and work more intelligently.[31]

## FORD OVERSEAS OPERATIONS

Ford's operations span the world, but one must wonder why this U.S. automaker turned to foreign operations. Four main reasons seem to be the driving force for Ford's foreign direct investment abroad. First, car and truck sales in overseas markets are large, and although these markets can be served through exports, transportation costs are high. Additionally, servicing those exports would be difficult. The establishment of foreign facilities lowers the transportation costs and reduces the service of subsidiaries in those areas. Second, certain foreign governments do not allow participation in their markets without local investment. Third, some of these foreign markets have certain advantages economically over the U.S. market. For example, Korea and Mexico offer substantially lower costs to Ford since labor costs in those countries are relatively cheap. Thus, parts and even final products can be produced at a substantially lower unit cost in some foreign countries as compared with similar operations in the United States. Lastly, through diversification of investments, Ford has become less dependent on economic conditions in the United States. The idea of diversification definitely aided the company during the period from 1978 to 1982 when Ford in the United States began to take on heavy losses.

Ford's most important subsidiary has been its Ford of Europe division.

Until 1967, the foreign operations were independently owned and run.[32] They even made their own product lines of cars, which were different from the parent company's product lines.[33] In 1967, Henry Ford II brought these independent operations of Europe together to form Ford of Europe.[34]

It is interesting to note that Ford of Europe does not own any assets, nor does it directly run any of the plants. It acts as a high-level service center that coordinates and supervises all operations. The goal that Henry Ford II had behind this Ford of Europe concept was to foster competition between Ford in the United States and Ford of Europe.[35] How could this help? Europe is known for its preferences for high-performance, sporty cars. By learning and developing technology to suit the preferences of European consumers, Ford could gain this new technology and then transfer it to the United States. This would set up a network through which information and new developments could be shared between the Ford companies in Europe and Ford in the United States. This would then allow Ford to be producing products with the latest technology. Unfortunately, this strategy was not carried out to its full potential until 1981.

Prior to 1981, the parent company in the United States made all the decisions for Ford of Europe. Instead of sharing information, the parent company dictated the styles and product types for the European market. This was a big marketing flaw, because it did not take into consideration the different tastes and preferences of the Europeans. Because of this flaw, Ford, during the 1970s, did not perform very well. But in 1981, under the leadership of Robert Lutz, Ford of Europe broke away from previous policies and began manufacturing cars that would be competitive in the European market.[36] What is interesting to note is not only did Europe break from U.S. leadership, Ford's headquarters in the United States began looking to Europe for development of Ford's models for the world market.[37] In other words, "The parent is drawing on its subsidiary for design and engineering ideas and management talent."[38] Ford's European operations were saving the parent company from real difficulties and cash flow problems, which had left Ford in the United States with losses of $3.9 billion during the 1978–1982 period.[39] Coinciding with the losses, Ford was the slowest to react to the new demand for fuel-efficient, economical cars. This caused Ford's sales to drop to their lowest levels in two decades and lose 6.6 percent of its market share during the 1978–1982 period. Eventually Ford's market share was down to a mere 17 percent of the automobile market.[40]

During this period of slumping sales and large losses in the United States, Ford of Europe was doing very well. As the fifth largest automaker in 1981, Ford of Europe was one of only two automakers to turn a profit. Net profits generated in Europe from 1978 to 1982 came to over $2 billion for the parent company.[41] Also, Ford of Europe loaned the parent company an additional $1.2 billion to ease the losses in the U.S. market.[42] Thus, the European operations were not only breaking from tradition but also were aiding the company in avoiding financial disaster.

The major strategy that Ford of Europe undertook under the leadership of Robert Lutz was called the "After Japan" strategy.[43] The first priority that faced Ford of Europe was to gain back the market share which the Japanese had penetrated to the greatest extent, notably the markets in the Nordic countries and in Ireland.[44] Ford designed and manufactured cars that were specifically equipped to demonstrate to buyers that Ford cars were offering more value for their money.

To make such a statement, Ford had to be competitive with the Japanese in manufacturing efficiency. Lutz, through studying the Japanese automakers, began to reshape operations, and he copied some of the Japanese techniques. Many changes had to be made, but they seemed to have been implemented with few disruptions. The benefits of these changes have become very noticeable. Some statistics that prove the success of the "After Japan" strategy (the AJ strategy) are the following:

Body defects per 100 cars decreased from 835 in 1980 to 650 in 1982.

The average rate of growth of manufacturing productivity was 4.8 percent in 1981 and about 6.0 percent in 1982.

Reduction of the break-even point from 80 percent of capacity prior to the AJ program to 60 percent of capacity in 1982.[45]

These statistics demonstrated Ford's new commitment to producing quality built cars. They had abandoned some old ideas and replaced them with radically new ideas that were necessary to get Ford back on its feet again. The result of the AJ program paid off in 1984 when Ford became the number-one automaker in Europe.[46] But this distinction was not held for long. Competition in the European market has been heating up since 1984, locking its six major automakers in "a loss making battle for a larger share of stagnant sales." This has caused great increases in the amount of money spent on advertising, and these added costs have effectively reduced the profit levels in Europe. Once again Ford is faced with changing conditions in Europe. The reduction in profits has put pressure on top management. The predictions for the European market looked so bleak that in the early months of 1985, Ford of Europe began talks with Fiat of Italy on a possible merger. The possibilities of the linkup seemed endless. The merger would create a giant with a 25 percent share of the 10 million car market and would cause the other car makers to scramble. With a 25 percent share of the market, Ford could then specialize on its more profitable mid-sized models, while Fiat would pick up the small car market. With this type of specialization both companies would gain because they would be focusing on the models in which they have comparative advantages.

Unfortunately, the talks were curtailed toward the end of September 1985.[47] Reasons for the breakdown of talks were basically due to a power struggle. Neither company wished to surrender control to the other, but they did agree to merge their truck operations in Europe in March 1986. The hopes of another merger with the British government-owned BL and PLC car and truck divisions were struck down as a wave of anti-Americanism swept through Parliament.[48]

Because of these setbacks, Ford again changed its strategy. It would now focus its efforts on joint venture projects with other car manufacturers. Talks have shown possible areas of development in the manufacture of engines, transmissions, and other parts. There is even a possibility of joining with a European rival to design a car with common parts, keeping only the exterior styling of the car different.[49] Such plans are being suggested since plant closings could be difficult.

Plant closings, however, were one option that Ford used successfully in the United States. In 1978, Ford in the United States was selling roughly 2.8 million cars, but at a loss. From 1978 to 1983, Ford decreased the number of jobs and cut down on the volume of cars sold. The result was a substantial increase in profits. This strategy of reducing the amount of production and the number of jobs has many European workers nervous. Possible plant closing of Ford's Dagenham plant near London alone could place 2,000 out of work.[50] But while these fears are well warranted, Ford faces problems in initiating plant closings because it is dealing with a dozen different countries, each with its own unions and government policies, which in some cases would make plant closings almost impossible.[51]

Outside the U.S. and European markets, Ford is also making some adjustments. Decreasing sales in Argentina have caused Ford and Volkswagen to begin merger talks.[52] Similar to what Henry Ford II did in Europe, Ford management has restructured its operations in Brazil. Its 13 subsidiaries have joined together to form one single holding company. In so doing it is taking advantage of some tax breaks, and also it is able to increase efficiency. By centralizing operations, it will help solve some of the cash flow problems that have existed in the past. With interest rates at 20 percent, and inflation at 210 percent annually, the cash-poor divisions can now be aided by some of the more cash-rich divisions. Even under these adverse economic circumstances, and even with very complicated government restrictions, Ford sees a great potential for the development of vertically integrated operations in Brazil. Labor is cheap, and there is an abundant supply of energy and raw materials. And there is also a large potential market. But as of now, because of the restrictions placed on high-tech manufacturing areas by the nationalistic military government, it is difficult for Ford to integrate its operations in Brazil.[53]

In Japan, Ford has acquired 25 percent of the Mazda Motor Corporation.[54] Mazda will be working with Ford's affiliates in the Asian-Pacific region to develop with Ford a minicar that will be built by Kia of South Korea.[55] Here again is an example of Ford's strategy of using joint ventures with some of its leading competitors as a way of keeping abreast of the latest developments in technology. In return, Ford agreed to purchase a significant portion of the production from Mazda's new assembly plant that was being built in Flat Rock, Michigan.[56]

Overall, Ford is searching for ways to ensure that the vehicles that they produce meet customer requirements and are competitive in cost and in quality. And it is through the new strategy of sharing information and technology with competitors and among its divisions that Ford will continue to be a forerunner in the auto industry.

There are now indications that Ford's strategy is paying off. As Table III:6.1 shows Ford's share of the car market and its share of the truck market

Table III:6.1  FORD'S SHARE OF CAR MARKET AND TRUCK MARKET

| | Cars | | | | Trucks | | | |
| --- | --- | --- | --- | --- | --- | --- | --- | --- |
| | 1987 | | 1986 | | 1987 | | 1986 | |
| | Industry unit sales | Ford market share | Industry unit sales | Ford market share | Industry unit sales | Ford market share | Industry unit sales | Ford market share |
| United States | 10,191,686 | 20.2% | 11,405,235 | 18.2% | 5,000,737 | 29.1% | 4,921,213 | 28.1% |
| Canada | 1,064,713 | 18.1 | 1,095,676 | 17.2 | 463,671 | 30.7 | 419,458 | 29.7 |
| Mexico | 154,365 | 10.7 | 160,664 | 12.1 | 93,705 | 18.6 | 98,425 | 21.4 |
| Germany | 2,807,318 | 10.4 | 2,734,735 | 10.6 | 262,277 | 8.2 | 238,029 | 7.6 |
| United Kingdom | 2,004,015 | 28.9 | 1,875,234 | 27.5 | 320,419 | 28.2 | 296,307 | 25.9 |
| Other European Markets* | 7,289,834 | 8.1 | 6,792,973 | 8.0 | 1,150,339 | 6.4 | 1,043,527 | 5.4 |
| Brazil | 420,753 | 20.6 | 661,603 | 19.6 | 164,263 | 21.7 | 193,104 | 24.4 |
| Argentina | 156,199 | 12.3 | 137,016 | 14.2 | 34,733 | 39.8 | 32,730 | 39.3 |
| Other Latin American Markets* | 310,898 | 6.5 | 333,129 | 10.1 | 140,144 | 16.2 | 166,378 | 12.7 |
| Australia | 358,755 | 31.1 | 392,862 | 30.8 | 93,110 | 18.7 | 137,389 | 16.3 |
| All Other Markets* | 5,103,694 | 2.9 | 4,753,042 | 2.3 | 3,764,222 | 1.2 | 3,482,705 | 1.1 |
| Worldwide Total* | 29,862,230 | 13.8% | 30,342,169 | 13.4% | 11,487,620 | 16.8% | 11,029,265 | 16.5% |

Source: Ford Motor Company Annual Report, 1987, p. 39.

*1987 data estimated.

have risen both in the United States and in some other countries in recent years.

"In 1987, Ford Motor Company had record profits of $4.6 billion. It is ranked number three on the Fortune 500 list of the largest U.S. industrial corporations, based on sales, and is the second-largest manufacturing company in the United States. Ford's worldwide 1987 sales totaled a record $71.6 billion."[57]

A new challenge that is facing Ford is how to increase its relative share (23.5 percent in 1989) of the market as compared to GM (35.8 percent in 1989).[58] As the author of an article puts it, "Ford Motor is riding high, but success poses problems that are sometimes tougher than the problems of adversity."[59]

## QUESTIONS

1. What was Henry Ford's marketing strategy? Explain.

2. How do you perceive the Ford strategy during World War II? Explain.

3. Ford claims that "Quality Is Job One." Has it lived up to its promise? Explain.

4. Is the pursuit of short-run profit the only purpose of a business firm? Has Ford acted in a socially responsible manner throughout its history? Discuss.

5. Why does a firm engage in foreign direct investment? What are Ford's major reasons for doing so? Explain.

6. What degree of centralization has Ford utilized in controlling its foreign operation during its history? Explain. What have been the implications of Ford's centralization philosophy on its overseas operations?

7. Why does an MNC engage in a joint venture arrangement? Discuss the pros and cons of joint ventures, using Ford as an example.

## NOTES

1. *Ford Motor Company Annual Report on Form 10-K for the Year Ended December 31, 1985* (Dearborn, Mich.; 1985), p. 1.

2. *News from the World of Ford: An American Legend* (Dearborn, Mich.: Corporate News Department, March 1988), p. 1.

3. *Ford Motor Company Annual Report on Form 10-K for the Year Ended December 31, 1985* (Dearborn, Mich.; 1985), p. 2.

4. Ibid., p. 1.

5. Lawrence Seltzer, *A Financial History of the American Automobile Industry* (Boston: Houghton Mifflin, 1928), p. 91.

6. Ibid.

7. *News from the World of Ford: An American Legend* (Dearborn, Mich.: Corporate News Department, 1988), p. 2.

8. Ibid.

9. Ibid.

10. Ibid.

11. Ibid., p. 3.

12. Ibid., p. 4.

13. Ibid.

14. A. Nevins, *Ford: The Times, The Man, The Company* (New York: Scribner, 1954), p. 357.

15. Ibid.

16. Ibid., p. 362.

17. *News from the World of Ford: An American Legend* (Dearborn, Mich.: Corporate News Department, 1988), p. 1.

18. *Ford Motor Company Annual Report 1985* (Dearborn, Mich.: Corporate News Department, 1985).

19. Ibid.

20. "Ford Motor Company Cleared in Three Deaths," *The New York Times,* 14 March 1980, p. A1.

21. Ibid.

22. Lee Patrick Strobel, *Reckless Homicide? Ford's Pinto Trial* (South Bend, Ind.: And Books, 1980), p. 177.

23. Ibid., p. 157.

24. "Ford Auto Company Cleared in Three Deaths," p. D12.

25. Strobel, *Reckless Homicide?* p. 272.

26. *Ford Motor Company Annual Report on Form 10-K for the Year Ended December 31, 1985* (Dearborn, Mich., 1985), p. 22.

27. "Ford Announces Recall of 162,000 Ranger Trucks," *The Wall Street Journal,* 23 June 1986, p. 2.

28. "Ford Motor to Recall 103,000 Ranger Trucks," *The Wall Street Journal,* 10 February 1988, p. 4.

29. "Ford Is on a Roll in Europe," *Fortune,* 18 October 1982, p. 182.

30. "Ford's Drive for Quality," *Fortune,* 18 April 1983, p. 62.

31. Ibid.

32. "Ford Is on a Roll in Europe," p. 182.

33. Ibid.

34. Ibid., p. 191.

35. Ibid.

36. Ibid. p. 182.

37. Ibid.

38. Ibid.

39. Ibid.

40. Ibid.

41. Ibid.

42. Ibid.

43. Ibid., p. 184.

44. Ibid.

45. Ibid., p. 185.

46. "Ford Rolls Out the Profits," *Business Week,* 4 March 1985, p. 40.

47. "Ford–Fiat: How Their Contest of Wills Prevented a 'Perfect Marriage' in Europe," *The Wall Street Journal,* 21 November 1985, p. 34.

48. "Yanks, Go Home: Furor over Selling BL," *Business Week,* 24 March 1986, p. 50.

49. "Ford Moderates European Strategy with New Focus on Profitability," *The Wall Street Journal*, 27 March 1986, p. 37.

50. "Brits Out, Mexicans In," *The Economist*, 14 January 1984, p. 60.

51. "Ford Moderates European Strategy with New Focus on Profitability," p. 37.

52. "Ford–VW Talks," *The New York Times*, 27 August 1986, p. D3.

53. "Ford Revamps for an Export Push," *Business Week*, 27 February 1984, pp. 47–50.

54. *Ford Motor Company Annual Report*, 1985, p. 5.

55. Ibid.

56. *Ford Motor Company Annual Report 1985* (Dearborn, Mich., 1985).

57. *News from the World of Ford, p. 6.*

58. "Ford Offers New Incentives to Spur Sales," *The Wall Street Journal*, 30 March 1989, p. B1.

59. "The Ford Dilemma: Go for Glory?" *Forbes*, 28 December 1987, p. 35.

## SUGGESTED READINGS

"Either We're Crazy or They're Crazy." *Forbes*, 29 July 1985, pp. 64–66.

"Ford Announces Recall of 162,000 Ranger Trucks," *The Wall Street Journal*, 23 June 1986.

"Ford Auto Company Cleared in Three Deaths," *The New York Times*, 14 March 1980, p. A1.

"Ford's Drive for Quality." *Fortune*, 18 April 1983, p. 62.

"Will Fiat and Ford of Europe Tie the Knot?" *Business Week*, 29 April 1985, p. 44.

"Ford–Fiat: How Their Contest of Wills Prevented a 'Perfect Marriage' in Europe." *The Wall Street Journal*, 21 November 1985, p. 34.

"Ford Is on a Roll in Europe." *Fortune*, 18 October 1982, pp. 182–191.

"Ford Moderates Europe Strategy with New Focus on Profitability." *The Wall Street Journal*, 27 March 1986, p. 37.

*Ford Motor Company Annual Report.* Dearborn, Mich., 1985.

*Ford Motor Company Annual Report on Form 10-K for the Year Ended December 31, 1985.* Dearborn, Mich., 1985.

"Ford Motor Names Benton to Head International Lines." *The Wall Street Journal*, 18 March 1986, p. 14.

"Ford Revamps for an Export Push." *Business Week*, 27 February 1984, pp. 47–50.

"Ford Rolls Out the Profits." *Business Week*, 4 March 1985, p. 40.

"Ford–VW Talks." *The New York Times*, 27 August 1986, p. 3.

"A Japanese Beat for the Motown Sound." *The Economist*, 14 January 1984, pp. 59–60.

Marsden, D., T. Morris, P. Willman, and S. Wood. *The Motor Industry*. London: Hertford and Harlow, Simpson Shand, 1956.

Maxcy, D., T. Morris, P. Willman, and S. Wood. *The Car Industry*. London and New York: Tavistock, 1955.

Nevins, A. *Ford: The Times, The Man, The Company,* New York: Scribner, 1957.

*News from the World of Ford: An American Legend.* Dearborn, Mich.: Corporate News Department, April 1986.

Seltzer, L. *A Financial History of the American Automobile Industry.* Boston: Houghton Mifflin, 1928.

Strobel, Lee Patrick. *Reckless Homicide? Ford's Pinto Trial.* South Bend, Ind.: And Books, 1980.

"What's Good for Ford." *New Statesman,* 1 February 1985.

"Yanks, Go Home: The Furor over Selling BL." *Business Week,* 24 March 1986.

# Case III:7

# Imperial Power–Spain*

Late in 1978 Imperial Power Company (IPC) management was considering expansion of the firm's involvement in international business. IPC was a Chicago manufacturer of a variety of electric motors for use in automobiles, household goods, and industrial equipment. All of the company's sales were to other manufacturers, primarily in the automobile industry. IPC's worldwide market was supplied from subsidiaries in France, Germany, Brazil, and the Philippines as well as the United States. The company's success in Europe, which was based primarily on its technical expertise and prompt delivery of equipment meeting a variety of industrial needs, led top management to believe an expansion of IPC's European capacity was needed.

The French and German subsidiaries of IPC distributed, assembled, and performed a limited amount of manufacturing when special adaptations were required. With the maturing of European markets, particularly that for automobiles, an expansion of capacity to produce standard, five-horsepower motors was required. The French subsidiary's management had urged IPC (U.S.) to expand facilities in France. However, Spain had much lower labor costs and certain government incentives that were not available in France, so IPC's president had asked the treasurer's staff to prepare a financial evaluation of a possible investment in Barcelona, Spain.

The proposed Spanish subsidiary of IPC would be a wholly owned venture producing electric motors for the Spanish domestic market as well as for export to other European countries. The initial parent-supplied equity investment would be $1,500,000, equivalent to pesetas (Ptas.) 105,000,000 at the current exchange rate of 70 pesetas to the U.S. dollar. An additional $600,000 would be raised by borrowing $600,000 from Banque de la Société Financiére Européenne, a Paris-based consortium bank. Interest of 10 percent would be payable annually, and the entire principal would be due in 10 years. How-

*This case was written by Professor Ian Giddy of the Columbia University Graduate School of Business, and revised by David K. Eiteman with the permission of the author. The revised case was printed in Robert S. Carlson, H. Lee Remmers, Christine R. Hekman, David K. Eiteman, and Arthur I. Stonehill, eds., *International Finance: Cases and Simulation* (Reading, Mass.: Addison-Wesley, 1980), pp. 114–116.

ever, IPC-Spain did not anticipate any difficulty in renewing the loan indefinitely. The combined capital of $2,100,000 would be sufficient to purchase equipment of $1,000,000 and finance working capital requirements. No new working capital would be needed in the foreseeable future, and 10-year straight line depreciation would be applied to the original cost of the equipment.

The project was regarded as an ongoing operation, and therefore should, in principle, be evaluated for an indefinite time horizon. However, because of the difficulty of forecasting demand beyond a few years, the procedure used by IPC was to make cash flow forecasts only four years into the future and to treat the value of the subsidiary at the end of the fourth year as the present value of a constant annual cash inflow equal to that forecasted for the fourth year.

(If, for example, the cash inflow forecasted for year 4 were $150,000, then that amount was assumed to be the inflow for years 5, 6, and so forth. The net present value of this annual inflow can be found from the formula for the present value of a constant annuity:

$$\text{NPV} = \frac{\text{annual cash inflow}}{\text{discount rate}}$$

Assuming a 10 percent discount rate, the net present value at the end of the fourth year in this instance would be $150,000/0.10 = $1,500,000.)

The firm's overall marginal after tax weighted-average cost of capital was about 12 percent. However, because of the higher risks associated with a Spanish venture, IPC decided that a 16 percent discount rate would be applied to the project.

The initial sales price of an electric motor was to be Ptas. 1,300 in Spain. Because of Spain's high tariffs on competing imports, this price would enable the Spanish operation to sell 50,000 units domestically and 150,000 in the export market. Spanish inflation would probably force the company to raise its sales price by 15 percent per annum, which would not affect domestic demand but might reduce forecasted export sales unless the inflation were offset by a depreciation of the peseta. Discussions with the manager of the French subsidiary suggested that the price elasticity of demand in Europe was about 1.5; that is, for each 1 percent increase in the relative price of IPC's electric motors over the immediately prior year, demand would fall by 1.5 percent. Inflation in all Europe (except Spain) and in the United States was expected to run at a 5 percent annual rate.

For convenience, start-of-year prices and exchange rates would be used to calculate demand, sales prices, and operating costs for each year. However, interest (to the consortium bank) and royalty fees (to the parent) would be paid on December 31 at the year-end exchange rate.

In the absence of any price change or exchange rate change, sales for the first four years were forecasted as follows:

| Year | Price (Pesetas) | Price (French Francs) (16.67 Ptas./FF) | Domestic sales (units) | Export sales (units) |
|------|-----------------|----------------------------------------|------------------------|----------------------|
| 1979 | Ptas. 1,300 | FF 77.98 | 50,000 | 150,000 |
| 1980 | 1,300 | 77.98 | 60,000 | 165,000 |
| 1981 | 1,300 | 77.98 | 65,000 | 181,500 |
| 1982 | 1,300 | 77.98 | 70,000 | 199,650 |

The capacity of the Spanish plant would be 350,000 units per year.

Variable cost per unit was estimated to be Ptas. 840. Of this, 20 percent was for materials imported from the United States, 40 percent for domestic materials, and the remainder for labor. Domestic costs could be expected to rise at the forecasted inflation rate of 15 percent per annum. Annual fixed costs consisted of manufacturing overhead of Ptas. 75,000,000, depreciation of the equipment over 10 years with no salvage value, and royalty fees to the parent of $30,000 per year.

Spanish taxes consist of a 30 percent corporate income tax and a 10 percent withholding tax on dividends. No carry forward of losses is allowed. The U.S. income tax rate is 50 percent, with a credit allowed for foreign income and withholding taxes paid. Although the company expected that some of the subsidiary's earnings might be reinvested, for the purpose of evaluation, all profits were to be treated as if repatriated at the end of the year.

The project evaluation team at IPC was asked to evaluate the project on the basis of the above information, together with the following exchange rate forecasts received from the company's bank:

**CURRENCY FORECASTS, 1978–1982**
(Units of Foreign Currency Per U.S. Dollar)

| December 31 | Spanish Pesetas/$ | French Francs/$ |
|-------------|-------------------|-----------------|
| 1978 | 70.0 | 4.20 |
| 1979 | 70.0 | 4.00 |
| 1980 | 85.0 | 3.50 |
| 1981 | 95.0 | 3.50 |
| 1982 | 110.0 | 3.50 |

# QUESTION

1. What would be your recommendation and why?

# Social Responsibility and the Future of International Business

**W**ith the increasing importance of international business to the world economy, questions are being raised about the fundamental roles that MNCs are expected to perform in society. MNCs have created the most controversy in LDCs with regard to their roles in those societies. Such controversies have added to the uncertainty of the future events with which MNCs must deal. This, in turn, has contributed to the growing significance of forecasting methods in the decision-making processes of MNCs.

The purpose of Part Four is to discuss the question of social responsibility and examine the controversial issues that are surrounding MNCs. Because MNCs must make decisions on the basis of what they expect to occur in the future, we close this part with a chapter that is devoted to future issues. Some of the main questions that are raised in this part are the following:

1. What are the social responsibilities and ethical considerations that an MNC should deal with?
2. What are arguments for and against social responsibility?
3. How can one evaluate the social performance of an MNC?
4. What are the guidelines for social responsibility and ethical behavior of MNCs?
5. What are the major criticisms of MNCs?
6. What are the sources of conflict between MNCs, host countries, and home countries?
7. What are some of the policies that are used by host countries to alleviate the effects of FDI on their economic systems?
8. What are the major factors that affect the future of international business?
9. What are the future trends in the world economy?
10. What are the roles of advanced countries and LDCs in international business in the future?

Part Four, therefore, is designed to provide a thorough explanation of the social responsibility issues that are faced by an MNC, while trying to shed some light on future trends.

# Chapter 19

# Social Responsibility and Ethical Issues Facing MNCs

*N*ever before in the history of humankind have the interrelationships between business and society been so complex, dynamic, and important to the future of both business and society. For the first time, questions are being raised about the fundamental roles that MNCs are expected to perform in society. Essential changes in social values are just now being reflected in business. Today, businesses are increasingly expected to act for the benefit of society. The purpose of this chapter is to shed some light on social value changes, the MNC's social responsibilities, and the ethical considerations of doing business internationally.

## ENVIRONMENTAL HOSTILITY

In recent years, there has been an increase in the amount and the scope of criticism and hostility toward MNCs. Much of this criticism stems from the conflicts between home and host nations. We will discuss home and host country conflicts in Chapter 20. Our focus in this chapter is on the criticism and the hostility toward MNCs that are the direct results of MNCs' influences on social values.

This increased hostility toward MNCs is based on both hard facts and pure fantasies. There is historical evidence that the actions undertaken by some MNCs have in the past led to undesirable, often disastrous, outcomes for the societies in which these MNCs have operated. The following examples are cases in point:

**1.** Some MNCs have formed alliances with corrupt Third World elites. This has led many observers to believe that MNCs, whether they know it or not, are siding with the elites and promoting inequalities in these societies.[1]

**2.** MNCs' excessive interference in the political conditions of host countries in the Third World is a sore issue that has been documented on many occasions. The well-publicized alleged role of ITT in the 1973 coup d'etat against Salvador Allende's regime in Chile is a prime example. Another example is Gulf Oil's political involvement in Angola.[2]

**3.** The increase in African infant mortality that resulted from the introduction of Western-style baby formula into that continent by Nestlé and a number of other MNCs is seen as an example of their irresponsibility.[3]

**4.** The excessive use of transfer pricing, tax havens, and the manipulation of currency fluctuations by some MNCs exemplify the abuse of both home and host country laws. Examples of these abuses include the Hoffman-LaRoche use of transfer pricing and Lonrho's use of tax havens.[4]

**5.** The MNCs are also seen as disregarding the impact of their actions on consumer safety and environmental conditions. This is especially true when host government regulations to protect the consumer or the environment are absent. These activities can take different forms, such as the dumping of industrial wastes and pollutants, the use of harmful pesticides, and the sale of unsafe products. A well-publicized example is the leakage of a deadly gas at Union Carbide's chemical plant in Bhopal, India, in 1984. The accident caused the death of approximately 2,500 people, exposed 200,000 people to the gas, and made about 50,000 people sick. It killed thousands of animals and destroyed vegetation.[5] Another example is the case of a U.S. children's wear manufacturer. The sale of its sleep wear that was treated with a particular carcinogenic fire retardant has been banned in the United States, but the company continues to sell the banned product in other countries.[6]

**6.** There have been unfair labor practices by some MNCs in some host countries. For example, Kodak, Nestlé, and IBM have been associated with abuses in trade union recognition.[7]

**7.** Reports of illegal payments, bribery, and other corrupt practices by MNCs have been frequently written about in the press. Aircraft manufacturers and oil companies have been implicated in these illegal dealings. For example, Lockheed has been accused of trying to influence the Japanese government military purchases through multimillion dollar "commissions." Overall, the company has been accused of giving $25 million in bribes to government officials in different countries in order to win orders for its new aircraft. Similarly, Exxon was accused of making payoffs of $28 million in the form of political contributions. United Brands was accused of attempting to alter a tax law in Honduras by making a $1.25 million payoff in political contributions to influential individuals. And there have been bribery convictions against Imperial Chemical Industries of the United Kingdom and Marubeni Trading Company of Japan.[8]

The above examples illustrate why MNCs, which use the most sophisticated public relations services in the world, have gained such dubious reputations.

In response to these charges, there are those who argue in favor of the role that MNCs play in the world in general and in LDCs in particular. They argue that MNCs provide economic opportunities through their knowledge, technology, and vision. They focus resources to create projects in places where nothing existed before. To these supporters, there is no substitute for the experience offered by MNCs.[9]

There is little doubt that MNCs have been major contributors to the enhanced global productivity that had taken place during the past 25 years. These powerful companies channel the factors of production across the world. In the process of global production and marketing, MNCs tie sovereign nations not only to the firm but also to other nations. Often these linkages are made in ways that governments both resent and resist. MNC managers tend to make decisions based on the MNC's profit-oriented objectives. On the other hand, host government officials pursue their own set of social and economic objectives. Actions taken by one group often impact the other group, and when the objectives of the two are not congruent, conflict will result. We will discuss the nature of these conflicts in Chapter 20.

## SOCIAL RESPONSIBILITIES OF MNCS

In recent years, the concept of social responsibility of business has become popular in the United States and elsewhere. With all of its recent popularity, however, the underlying ideas are probably as old as the existence of business organizations themselves. The concept of **social responsibility** rests on the idea that, since the business firm is a creation of society, it has a responsibility to help in the accomplishment of societal goals.

In the United States, the concept of social responsibility has evolved through three distinct phases: (1) profit maximizing management, (2) trustship management, and (3) "quality of life" management.[10]

## Phase I—Profit Maximizing Management

This phase of social responsibility in business was based on the belief that business managers have only one objective—to maximize their company's profit. The pursuit of this single objective is limited only by the legal framework in which the firm must operate. The origin of this opinion can be traced back to Adam Smith's *Wealth of Nations.* Smith believed that individuals (and businesses), in pursuing their own self-interest, would be guided by an "invisible hand" to promote the good of the society. In other words, the drive for profit maximization would result in the greatest wealth for the nation, and hence society as a whole would be better off. It is this "invisible hand," found in perfect competition, that protects society. The movements of the "invisible hand" result in economic growth, more jobs, better products, and more wealth for everyone.

The personal values of Phase I managers reflect their profit maximization way of thinking: "What's good for me is good for my society." This sums up such a manager's way of thinking. Efficiency and profit maximization are the prime goals of the Phase I manager.

## Phase II—Trustship Management

During the 1920s and 1930s, the "trustship" concept emerged as the cornerstone of business-society relationships. According to this concept, the manager is viewed as a "trustee" of various contributing groups of the firm. As a result, the corporate managers are responsible not just for maximizing the stockholders' wealth, but also for maintaining an equitable balance between the often conflicting claims of the firm's stakeholders. As we discussed in Chapter 13, these stakeholders include customers, employees, creditors, suppliers, and society in general.

Two contributing factors to the development of the "trustship" management philosophy were: (1) the increase in the number of people who owned stock in American corporations and (2) the emergence of a pluralistic society.

The Phase II managers realize their own self-interest, while recognizing the interest of their company's stakeholders. They believe that "What is good for my company is good for my society." Their values are based on making a profit and satisfying the people. The trustship managers spend whatever is required to prevent potential harm to the society. They prevent air and water pollution. According to this view, a business should not create social problems by paying low wages, setting inflationary prices, producing unsafe products, or discriminating against minorities.

## Phase III—"Quality of Life" Management

In recent years, a new concept of social responsibility called "quality of life" has emerged. This concept of social responsibility goes beyond mere trustship and accountability. According to this view, business is a partner with government, education, and other social institutions in solving society's problems and creating a better quality of life for everyone.

The development of this new ideology can be attributed to the emergence of the so-called affluent society in the United States and other advanced nations. Because the scarcity of basic goods and services is no longer a major problem in these societies, the importance of other social problems has increased. As a result, a new set of societal priorities has emerged.

Based on these priorities, society demands that business should accept broader responsibilities. These socially imposed responsibilities are much broader than the traditional profit maximization quest of the Phase I concept. They are also broader than the act of balancing competing stakeholders' demands, as in the Phase II concept. In Phase III, the socially responsible business becomes deeply involved in solving society's major problems.

The "quality of life" managers believe in *enlightened self-interest.* To these managers, selfishness and group interest are important, but they also seriously consider society's interests when they make decisions. "What's good for society is good for my company" is the essence of their values.

A firm managed by "quality of life" ethics strives to fulfill many responsibilities. The MNC may strive to do the following:

1. To produce and to distribute sufficient quantities of quality products and services, as well as providing information needed by the customers.
2. To recognize the dignity of each employee.
3. To be accountable to the owners and to the contributors to the business.
4. To be responsible to society in general.

"Enlightened self-interest" is the driving force behind the Phase III firm. It can be described as the socially responsible actions of the firm that cannot be justified on the basis of economic costs and revenues alone. These actions are taken because they are in the best long-term interest of the firm. Table 19.1 provides a comparison of the managerial values of the three phases of social responsibility.

## Arguments for Social Responsibility

There are several arguments that support the necessity of social responsibility as a policy for the modern firm:[11]

1. Because business firms have sufficient resources to deal with social problems, they should take responsibility when all other institutions have failed to solve these problems.

2. It is generally accepted that the business sector is more efficient than the public sector. Therefore, it is a better means for resolving social problems. Of course, there are limitations to the efficiencies and capabilities of the business

**Table 19.1   COMPARISON OF MANAGERIAL VALUES OF THREE PHASES OF SOCIAL RESPONSIBILITY**

| Phase I<br>Profit maximizing<br>management | Phase II<br>Trusteeship<br>management | Phase III<br>"Quality of life"<br>management |
|---|---|---|
| *Economic Values* | | |
| 1) Raw self-interest | 1) Self-interest<br>2) Contributor's interests | 1) Enlightened self-interest<br>2) Contributor's interests<br>3) Society's interests |
| "What's good for me is good for my country." | "What's good for my company is good for our country." | "What's good for society is good for our company." |
| Profit maximizer | Profit satisfier | Profit is necessary, but . . . |
| Money and wealth are most important. | Money is important but so are people. | People are more important than money. |
| "Let the buyer beware."<br>*(caveat emptor)* | "Let's not cheat the customer." | "Let the seller beware."<br>*(caveat venditor)* |
| "Labor is a commodity to be bought and sold." | "Labor has certain rights which must be recognized." | "Employee dignity must be satisfied." |
| Accountability of management is to the owners. | Accountability of management is to the owners *and* customers, employees, suppliers, and other contributors. | Accountability of management is to the owners, contributors, and society. |
| *Technological Values* | | |
| Technology is very important. | Technology is important but so are people. | People are more important than technology. |
| *Social Values* | | |
| "Employee personal problems must be left at home." | "We recognize that employees have needs beyond their economic needs." | "We hire the whole person." |
| "I'm a rugged individualist, and I'll manage the business as I please." | "I am an individualist, but I recognize the value of group participation." | "Group participation is fundamental to our success." |
| "Minority groups are inferior. They must be treated accordingly." | "Minority groups have their place in society but their place is inferior to mine." | "Minority groups are people like you and I are." |
| *Environmental Values* | | |
| "The natural environment controls one's destiny." | "One can control and manipulate one's environment." | "One must preserve the environment." |

Table 19.1 (*Continued*)

| Phase I<br>Profit maximizing<br>management | Phase II<br>Trusteeship<br>management | Phase III<br>"Quality of life"<br>management |
|---|---|---|
| *Political Values* | | |
| "That government is best which governs least." | "Government is a necessary evil." | "Business and government must cooperate to solve society's problems." |
| *Aesthetic Values* | | |
| "Aesthetic values? What are they?" | "Aesthetic values are okay, but not for us." | "We must preserve our aesthetic values and we'll do our part." |

*Source:* R. D. Hay, and E. R. Gray, eds., *Business and Society: Cases and Text* (Cincinnati, Ohio: South-Western, 1981), pp. 10–11.

sector. Thus, one should recognize that it cannot solve all of the world's problems. However, it may be a major contributor to solving many social problems.

**3.** Traditionally, the business sector has been innovative. If this sector applies its innovative ability toward resolving social issues, it can handle many problems. Of course, not all problems can be solved by business. Furthermore, because business is motivated by profit, it may be more effective in resolving those social issues that may generate some profit.

**4.** Social programs, when publicized, tend to improve the public image of business. Such improvements in the public image of a firm will result in economic benefits to the firm in several ways. Investment in social programs is a form of advertising that may lead to increased name recognition and also enhanced public image of the firm. This, in turn, may improve the firm's long-term sales potential and earnings. It may also be that a firm with a well-known social responsibility program may attract a greater number of talented young employees who want to contribute to social welfare. In addition, the employees of socially responsible MNCs may have a greater sense of pride in their company. This may enhance morale and increase efficiency at the firm.

**5.** Governments may provide incentives to support investments in socially responsible programs. Such incentives may include tax relief, low interest loans, and the partial or complete reimbursement of certain costs.

**6.** Investment in social programs by business will prevent unnecessary and costly government regulation. Many people attribute the ever-increasing governmental interference in the private sector to the lack of voluntary action by business firms themselves to solve social problems.

**7.** Social responsibility is the moral obligation of the business sector. Business is sanctioned and supported by society for the good of all of its members. Thus, it is morally correct that business should be responsive to societal needs.

**8.** Participation in drafting new rules for business conduct is in the best interest of the business. Without this participation, these rules will be formulated by a small group of business critics who may not understand business and its requirements.

**9.** Acceptance of a larger role in social responsibility is good business as well as good citizenship. Healthy communities provide a better climate for business and lead to more profits than disintegrating communities.

**10.** Preventing social problems is better than attempting to cure them. If the business sector continues to resist dealing with social issues, it may find itself constantly under fire from critics. This may lead to a crisis severe enough to demand a disproportionate amount of attention and resources. Thus, it is better to prevent problems before they occur than to spend time and resources to cure them when they become critical.

## Arguments Against Social Responsibility

There have also been arguments against the involvement of business in social problems and issues. These arguments against business social responsibility are the following:

**1.** People such as Milton Friedman argue that the most socially responsible role of business is to make a profit, to use resources efficiently, and to obey the law.

**2.** A socially responsible manager is using funds for society without the direct consent or the input of the owners of those funds. Therefore, such social action may only be serving management's own interests. This may mean sacrificing the interests of the owners and the customers, whose interests management is supposed to serve in a free enterprise system.

**3.** There is no consensus about what some of the basic social problems are or how to resolve them, so business involvement in social issues may be inappropriate.

**4.** There are apparent conflicts of interest in some of the social issues faced by MNCs. The satisfaction of national interests in a world in which there is an obvious need for improved welfare is a difficult problem. An MNC is faced with the following dilemma: Should it give priority to the social problems at home? Or should it give priority to world problems such as the management of food, energy, diminishing resources, ecology, and the exploitation of space and the oceans?

**5.** Business is not the appropriate vehicle for generalizing the social priorities of its owners, managers, and employees, and this is what a firm is forced to do if it is required to use its resources in support of social programs.

**6.** Business is big enough as it is. Engaging business in social programs increases its power and broadens its voice in all facets of our modern world.

**7.** The efficiency of business and the subsequent benefits to society lie in pursuing the limited business objectives of making a profit. The pursuit of social goals contradicts the traditional objectives of efficiency, competitiveness, and profit. These traditional contributions alone justify the place of business in society.

**8.** Businesses lack the skills and the vision needed to assume responsibility for the achievement of social goals.

**9.** There is no broad-based support for the involvement of business in social issues. The lack of support may result in conflict among different groups in the society. This may reduce the capability of business to carry on a social role effectively.

Having discussed the arguments for and against business social responsibility, there nevertheless seems to be increasing public support for the greater social responsibility of business. This social responsibility must be carried out in the light of various limitations and constraints. No business can lose sight of its main objectives when pursuing socially responsible programs. Unless the public is willing to assume some of the costs and risks involved, business will not be able to fulfill its new role of helping to solve social problems.

Social responsibility is only one of the goals of a business. Our discussion on global strategy in Chapter 13 clarified this multiplicity of objectives. Overall, the objectives of MNCs are survival, profitability, growth in terms of market share and sales, efficiency and productivity, good employee relations, and social responsibility.

The economic objectives of sales, market share, productivity, and, above all, profitability are essential for the survival of a firm. The attainment of these goals is also vital for providing the resources needed for undertaking socially responsible activities.

The question is not whether or not MNCs should assume social responsibility; the major issue is to determine at what point the firm is assured of its survival and growth so that its social objectives can take top priority.

## THE CURRENT STATE OF AFFAIRS

The three phases of social responsibility we just described represent the evolution of the concept of business and social responsibility in the Western world in general, and in the United States in particular. However, the emergence of each new phase has not resulted in the disappearance of an old phase.

Phase I, profit maximization, is far from dead today, but it has fewer advocates. Virtually everyone recognizes the flaws that exist in Phase I. The socially irresponsible actions of some businesses, as we discussed earlier, are evidence of the presence of some socially irresponsible managers. Today, a great number of business managers follow a Phase II concept of social responsibility. These people understand the pluralistic nature of our present society. They are normally committed to an equitable treatment of various groups of stakeholders. Making profits is emphasized along with fair treatment of everyone. These managers try to compensate for past abuses and to enhance their corporate social responsiveness. In fact, substantial investment has been made in pursuing this goal. For example, Dow Chemical invested $20 million in pollution control equipment in only one year. Interestingly, $6 million of this investment was recovered through the reduction of corrosion in cooling towers and through the recycling of waste material—both benefits of the pollution control equipment.[12]

An increasing number of business executives and a larger number of academicians, however, are ascribing to the Phase III concept of social responsibility. A number of larger corporations, including some MNCs, are becoming involved in major social programs.

The types of corporate social programs vary greatly. MNCs are providing scholarships for deserving students, contributing to educational institutions, funding research, sponsoring minority businesses, and supporting athletic programs. Some MNCs also promote education, provide training, revitalize agriculture, construct housing, and engage in other socially responsible programs in their host countries.

In a survey of over 180 U.S. managers, more than half stated that business should be helpful in solving social problems regardless of who or what created these problems.[13] Because the survey did not report the personality characteristics of the surveyed managers, we can only hypothesize on the differences between managers who favor social responsibility in business and those who are against it. Possibly managers of those companies who have little difficulty meeting economic expectations would be more willing to take on social causes. Examples of such companies are IBM, Xerox, Eli Lilly, Coca-Cola, and Chase Manhattan Bank. Furthermore, managers who have difficulty in meeting minimum economic requirements for their companies may not worry about the social consequences of their actions. Thus, they may not invest in social programs. Examples of companies in this situation are U.S. steel manufacturers and oil companies during industry recessions.

Naturally, business managers will not go overboard in assuming social responsibilities. Thus, we should be cautious about accelerating social expectations that push business too far and too fast in accepting social responsibilities.

In summary, many people believe in incorporating the major elements of the three phases. To these people, not only should business have a deep commitment to social problems, but it should also be responsible to its major contributors and stakeholders. Above all, business should realistically understand the need for profits as an essential element of a high level of social responsibility.

## EVALUATING SOCIAL PERFORMANCE

A major problem in deciding the social role of business is the lack of clear criteria for judging social performance. This leads to difficulties in allocating limited resources between economic and social programs.

An approach to developing criteria for evaluating the social performance of business is to establish specific social responsibility objectives. These objectives can then be used to measure the firm's social performance.[14] The box that follows presents some typical areas of social concern for a business. Specific objectives should be derived from these broad areas.

## Social Audit

Similar to an accounting audit, a **social audit** measures a firm's social performance.[15] The social audit is an attempt to evaluate the degree of a firm's social involvement and to evaluate the effectiveness and efficiency of social programs supported by the firm.

The process of developing a social audit will be expedited if the firm has already established a set of specific social objectives. Three approaches are available for the development of a social audit. These approaches are: (1) the descriptive audit, (2) the cost-benefit analysis, and (3) the social responsibility accounting.

**The Descriptive Audit**  This is a verbal or written description of the degree of a firm's social performance. It describes the resources used and results gained from the firm's social programs. In other words, the descriptive audit is a structured description of a company's existing social policies and programs. A descriptive audit is of little help in the allocation of the firm's resources. However, it may be helpful in identifying areas of concern where decisions may be required or desirable.

---

## Categories of Social Responsibility Issues

a) Product line (e.g. dangerous products)

b) Marketing practices (e.g. misleading advertising)

c) Employee education and training

d) Corporate philanthropy

e) Environmental control

f) External relations (including community development, government relations, disclosure of information, and international operations)

g) Employee relations, benefits, and satisfaction with work

h) Minority and women employment and advancement

i) Employee safety and health

**Source:** Terry W. McAdam, "How to Put Corporate Responsibility into Practice," *Business and Society Review* (Summer 1973), pp. 11–13.

**The Cost-Benefit Analysis**   This approach is the systematic process of quantifying the associated costs and the benefits derived from each social program. Once quantified, programs may then be evaluated on the basis of the most benefit for the cost. A cost-benefit analysis can supplement the descriptive audit. It can provide structure and facilitate the decision-making process. Of course, there are difficulties in quantifying costs and benefits associated with social programs. However, problems notwithstanding, cost-benefit analysis can be a valuable tool for the measurement and control of a firm's social performance.

**The Social Accounting**   A number of people have been advocating the use of accounting procedures for measuring and reporting the social performance of business. However, the conceptual and the technical problems surrounding this approach have not yet been resolved. Consequently, the measurement of social performance in financial and semifinancial terms is still not feasible.

## ETHICS

Business ethics is a broad-based concept that applies to many aspects of the business-society relationship. There is no unequivocal moral answer to our social and economic problems. Similarly, there is no agreement as to what business ethics is and what constitutes ethical behavior in business. Thus, what is ethically moral or immoral in business depends on personal interpretation.

The disagreement on the meaning of ethics in business is apparent when one examines the definition of the term as given in different sources. For instance, *Webster's New World Dictionary of the American Language* defines ethics as "the study of standards of conduct and moral judgement; moral philosophy, and the system or code of morals of a particular philosopher, religion, group, profession, etc."[16] Another author gives this definition:

> Ethics is not the study of morals . . . ethics is not even identical with religious morality or moral theology. . . . Ethics is the science of judging specifically human ends and the relationship of means to those ends. In some way it is also the art of controlling means so that they will serve specifically human ends. . . . business ethics is concerned primarily with the relationship of business goals and techniques to specifically human ends.[17]

We define **ethics** as a standard of morality that guides individuals and organizations in following certain norms of conduct when dealing with each other. Furthermore, **international business ethics** is defined as the business conduct or morals of MNCs in their relationships to all individuals and entities with whom they come into contact.

The current debate over business ethics stems partially from the fact that a firm is a social system and thus should reflect social values. As we discussed earlier, society imposes responsibility on businesses to act ethically and to meet moral standards. Unfortunately, there is no social consensus on what these ethical and moral standards for business should be. Although there is consensus on many abstract values, these abstract values are not sufficient by themselves to resolve the specific business problems and social responsibility problems a manager may face.

Frequently a choice that a manager must make is not between right or wrong, good or bad, black or white. Rather, the choice becomes one of distinguishing among different shades of gray. The following are examples of questions which have no clear-cut answers:

Is it ethical for you to hire a competitor's employee? What if your competitor has made an important discovery that may jeopardize your profit?

Is a corporate raider acting ethically when taking over a company against the will of its present management? What if the existing management is kept after the takeover? What if it is replaced?

If you are an executive in a company earning $50,000 a year, would it be ethical to inflate your expense account by $2,000 a year? What if almost all executives in your firm are engaged in the same practice? What if all your superiors are aware of this practice?

Is it ethical for an MNC to get information about a new regulation from a host country's government employee before it is made public? From a home country's government employee? From a competitor's employee? What if this information is obtained with no payoff money? What if a payoff is made?

Another difficulty arises when a manager thinks actions taken by his company are ethical, but observers do not. For instance, many managers are highly supportive of the free enterprise system and believe in the spirit of competition. At the same time, in pursuit of their corporate objectives, they may seek mergers and acquisitions that may result in a reduction or in the elimination of competition. Those managers may not see any ethical conflict in this situation, but many observers may not share this view. They may see ethical conflict between the managers' beliefs and their actions.

## Ethics and MNCs

Today, the problem of ethics in business is more complex than it was just a few years ago. This is attributed to a number of factors:

1. Increased impact of business on society.
2. Weakened religious beliefs, which in the past determined standards of morality and guided business behavior.
3. Increased awareness of ethical issues by managers.

Furthermore, the ethical questions faced by an MNC with international dimensions are more complex than those faced by a domestic firm. This is due to the following factors:

1. The larger size and greater power of MNCs.
2. The greater potential for conflict between the objectives of MNCs and

the objectives of host governments, home governments, and the multiple societies in which an MNC must operate.

3. The increased complexity of balancing the claims and expectations of stakeholders, that is, owners, creditors, consumers, employees, suppliers, governments, and societies.

The ethical questions facing an MNC can take different forms. For instance, an MNC may locate its facilities in an LDC because of the cheaper labor there. But is it ethical to exploit foreign workers by paying them low wages or by providing poor working conditions for them. A socially conscious MNC may want to correct this problem by paying relatively higher wages to its foreign workers. This, however, may lead to other problems. The higher wages paid to MNC workers in the industrial sector may lure farmers from the agricultural sector in the LDC. This may lead to a decline in the production of food and raw materials that could severely harm the LDC's economic development in the long run.

Another undesirable consequence of the higher wages paid by an MNC in a severely poverty stricken area may be the creation of a small group of higher-income workers. The local merchants may perceive the higher purchasing power of this small group as an indication of the total community's purchasing capability. As a result, the merchants may raise prices, which will damage the poorer majority's ability to buy goods. This, in turn, may lead to social conflicts.

If the main reason for going international is to expand the MNC's market, an ethical question will arise. What are the social and cultural consequences of introducing the MNC's products or services in another country? For instance, to expand its market in infant formula, Nestlé launched an aggressive promotional campaign in a number of LDCs. Nestlé promoted its product—Similac— as a replacement for breastfeeding. Free samples of the baby formula were handed out without proper instructions for using the product. Massive numbers of infant deaths resulted. These deaths were attributed to the following factors:

1. The alleged sale of inferior or contaminated formula.
2. The lack of proper instructions for preparing the formula.
3. The mothers were not informed of the need for sterilizing water to mix with the formula and the need for sterilizing the bottles.
4. The dilution of the baby formula with excessive amounts of water resulted when the mother could no longer afford to buy the necessary amount of formula powder or concentrate.
5. The inability of the poverty stricken mothers to purchase more formula after the free samples were exhausted and after their own breastmilk had ceased flowing.

A seven-year boycott of Nestlé's baby products and a United Nations code for selling baby formula in the LDCs pressured Nestlé to change its marketing strategy in 1981. It took a massive promotional modification by Nestlé and more than two years to correct the problem.[18]

Is the use of tax havens to avoid the payment of taxes to the home country ethical? Some people question the ethics of funneling funds to places like the Bahamas in order to avoid taxes.

Some MNCs locate facilities overseas to avoid rigid environmental controls at home. This leads to abuses of the natural environment of the host nation. Is this ethical? We have addressed the problem of bribery in Chapter 10. One should distinguish between large-scale bribery used to corrupt top government officials and the small gifts or "grease" payments used to move the wheels of the bureaucratic systems in these countries. As we discussed in Chapter 9, the U.S. Foreign Corrupt Practices Act distinguishes between these two types of payments.

The MNC manager should consider the cultural differences, local customs, and differences in moral standards before trying to make a distinction between payments and gifts. In some cultures, gift giving is a common practice. On special occasions people of society's lower echelons make offerings to their superiors. Superiors in turn provide bonuses, cash payments, gifts, or return favors in some other fashion. In other cultures, when people visit their friends, they are expected to give them presents. One should understand the nature of these offerings and not treat them as bribes, and it should be noted in these situations that customary gift giving is a routine practice and is never asked for by the receiver.

Further ethical questions arise when MNCs in LDCs are involved in the selling of obsolete equipment, the promoting of unnecessary and luxury items, and the selling of products and services that may be disruptive to the cultural traditions of the host country's society.

## Sources of Business Ethics

An MNC manager's ethical choices are greatly influenced by his or her values. These values are interrelated and have their origins in various value systems. These value systems are rooted in a number of sources, including religion, philosophy, culture, profession, and legal system.[19]

**Religion**   In Chapter 10, we discussed some of the major religions of the world. Our discussion revealed many similarities among these religions. To put it simply, all religions consider a well-ordered social system as a prerequisite for achieving human dignity and welfare. We may say that all religions consider a person as socially responsible when he or she contributes to the well-being of society, or, at least, does not harm it in any way. The so-called golden rule of "Do unto others as you would have them do unto you" can be found in many religions.

However, there are many people who believe religious ethics are overly strict or irrelevant to business situations.

**Philosophy**   Great philosophers of the world have also established "golden rules" of their own for ethical behavior. For centuries, Eastern and Western philosophers have been debating over these rules of conduct. As a result, many standards of ethics have been formulated.

**Culture**   The ethical and social responsibilities of MNCs are also greatly influenced by the cultural experiences of their managers. What one regards as ethical or unethical is determined largely by one's own culture.

**Profession**   A source of guidelines for business ethics must include a variety of corporate and professional codes. Many corporations develop their own codes of ethics. Most of these documents are for the use of the public. Company creeds, as they are widely known, may be included in the MNC's statement of its mission or purpose. They are highly abstract and widely distributed. Other companies may have more specific and operational codes of conduct. For example, IBM publishes an 84-page booklet titled "Business Conduct Guidelines." Each manager must review this code of conduct annually and certify that he or she understands it. In addition, failure to comply with these guidelines can lead to dismissal.

Most professional organizations, industry trade associations, and chambers of commerce have also laid down codes of conduct and rules for ethical behavior.

**Legal System**   Legal systems in home and host countries provide guidelines for viewing what is right and wrong. The U.S. Foreign Corrupt Practices Act is just one example of a legal code of ethics. In addition, attempts are under way to articulate standards of conduct for both MNCs and governments. The U.N. Commission on Transnational Corporations and other international organizations have started efforts to devise such standards. In 1982, the United Nations devised a "Code of Conduct for Transnational Corporations."

The Organization for Economic Cooperation and Development (OECD) has established a broad-based code of ethics for MNCs. In this formulation, there are 29 rules of ethics classified into seven main areas. The OECD code of ethics states that MNCs should: (1) avoid politics, including any form of bribery, (2) provide full disclosure of corporate information, (3) avoid predatory behavior toward competitors, including participation in cartels, (4) pay their fair share of taxes, and (5) respect the rights of labor.[20]

## GUIDELINES FOR MNC SOCIAL RESPONSIBILITY AND ETHICS

The issue of social responsibility is receiving increased attention from MNCs and from the public. The emergence of important social problems involving ecology, consumerism, equality, poverty, education, and hunger has focused attention on the social responsibility role of MNCs. Social forces have forced business managers to reconsider their social obligations and to reshape their corporate strategy in fulfilling a new role of social responsibility.[21]

We conclude this chapter by providing the following guidelines for social values:

1. The MNC should protect the consumers.
2. The MNC should be honest in its dealings with its multiple publics.
3. MNCs should actively strive to reduce and eliminate inequalities.
4. MNCs should help individuals reach their full potential.
5. MNCs should not profit from human misery—from poor working conditions, poverty, famine, or war.
6. MNCs should formulate a situation-specific ethics code.
7. The MNC should protect the physical environment.
8. MNCs should take a stand on human rights.
9. The MNC should stay out of host country politics.

## SUMMARY

1. Interrelationships between society and business have become so complex that society demands that business take on a socially responsible role.
2. Society has become increasingly hostile and critical of business because of the often disastrous outcomes of the policies that some businesses have followed. In response to such criticism, some argue that MNCs provide economic opportunities that no one else can provide.
3. The evolution of social responsibility in business has followed three phases in the United States. Phase I, profit-maximizing management, believes that "what's good for me is good for my society." Phase II, trustship management, believes that "what is good for my company is good for my society." Phase III, "quality of life" management, believes that "what's good for society is good for my company."
4. The arguments that encourage business to take an increased role in socially responsible programs state that business is more efficient, innovative, and resourceful than the public sector and can solve social problems better. Also, business will help itself by attracting young, socially conscious employees, thereby improving its public image. In addition, social responsibility may lead to long-term profits.
5. Arguments against business social responsibility include the belief that business is a profit-making enterprise that must operate within the law but that business is not equipped to decide or to implement social policy.
6. Businesses, as a whole, are moving toward increased social responsibility, integrating their need for profits with the need for a high level of social responsibility.
7. Approaches for evaluating social performance include social audits of three kinds: the descriptive audit, the cost-benefit analysis, and the social accounting.
8. Ethics is a broad area of philosophy that applies to many aspects of the business-society relationship. Ethical guidelines help managers solve complicated problems when no one solution can be all right or all wrong.
9. Ethics is defined as a standard of morality that guides individuals and organizations in following certain norms of conduct when dealing with each other.
10. International business ethics is defined as the business conduct or morals of individuals and MNCs in their relationships to all individuals and entities with whom they come into contact.
11. Ethical value systems are rooted in many sources: religion, philosophy, culture, profession, and legal system.
12. The Organization for Economic Cooperation and Development (OECD) has established a broad-based code of ethics for MNCs.

## QUESTIONS

**19.1** Why is society beginning to demand that business act for the benefit of society? Do you agree with this demand for social responsibility from businesses? Discuss.

**19.2** Why is society becoming increasingly hostile toward big business. List some examples of inappropriate business behavior not found in the text. Discuss.

**19.3** Which one of the three phases of social responsibility do you believe in? Why?

**19.4** How does the concept of social responsibility fit into the major objectives of an MNC?

**19.5** Should business have a commitment to social responsibility? Discuss your answer.

**19.6** Define and discuss the concept of ethics.

**19.7** List and discuss some examples of ethical problems that you may face as a manager. How would you handle these problems?

## NOTES

1. L. M. Turner, "There's No Love Lost Between Multinational Companies and the Third World," *Business and Society Review,* vol. 11, no. 2 (Autumn 1974), pp. 75–78.
2. Michael Z. Brooke, and H. Lee Remmers, *International Management and Business Policy* (Boston: Houghton Mifflin, 1978), p. 311.
3. Ibid., p. 310.
4. Ibid., p. 311.
5. *The New York Times,* 6 December 1984, p. 1.
6. James Brady, "An Export Trade in Death," *Advertising Age,* vol. 49, part 2, 15 May 1978, p. 99.
7. Brooke and Remmers, *International Management,* p. 311.
8. Anant Negandhi, *International Management* (Boston: Allyn and Bacon, 1987) p. 55.
9. Orville L. Freeman, "The Underdeveloped Nations: Victor—and Victors—of Commodity Price Increases," *Conference Report* (Chicago: World Trade Conference, 1975), p. 39.
10. This classification and the corresponding discussion are adapted from Robert D. Hay and Edmund R. Gray, "Social Responsibilities of Business Managers," *Academy of Management Journal,* vol. 17, no. 1 (March 1974), pp. 135–143; and Robert D. Hay and Edmund R. Gray, eds., *Business and Society: Cases and Text* (Cincinnati, Ohio: South-Western, 1981), pp. 4–16.
11. For complete coverage of the arguments for and against social responsibility, the reader is referred to Keith Davis, "The Case for and Against Business Assumption of Social Responsibilities," *Academy of Management Journal,* vol. 16, no. 2 (June 1973), pp. 312–322.
12. L. Henry Sisk and J. Clifton Williams, *Management and Organization,* 4th ed. (Cincinnati, Ohio: South-Western, 1981), p. 45.
13. Sandra L. Holmes, "Executive Perceptions of Corporate Social Responsibility," *Business Horizons,* vol. 19, no. 3 (June 1976), p. 36.
14. Fred Luthans, et al., *Social Issues in Business,* 3rd ed. (New York: Macmillan, 1980), pp. 393–400.
15. Melvin Anshen, *Corporate Strategies for Social Performance* (New York: Macmillan, 1980), pp. 96–119.

16. *Webster's New World Dictionary. College ed.* (Cleveland, Ohio: World Publishing Co., 1966).

17. Thomas M. Garrett and Richard J. Klonoski, *Business Ethics,* 2nd ed. (Englewood Cliffs, N.J.: Prentice-Hall, 1986), pp. 1–2.

18. Douglas Clement, "Nestlé's Latest Killing in Bottle Baby Market," *Business and Society Review,* no. 26 (Summer 1978), pp. 60–64; "A Boycott Over Infant Formula," *Business Week,* 23 April 1979, pp. 137–140; "Killer in a Bottle," *The Economist,* vol. 279, no. 7184, 9 May 1981, p. 50; "World Health Organization Drafts Restrictive Ad Code," *World Health Organization,* 11 April 1981, p. 8; Robert F. Harley, *Marketing Mistakes,* 3rd ed. (New York: Wiley, 1986), Chap. 4.

19. George A. Steiner, *Business and Society* (New York: Random House, 1971), pp. 228–234.

20. "The 29 Commandments," *Time,* 7 June 1976, pp. 66–67.

21. Larry D. Alexander and William F. Mathews, "The Ten Commandments of Corporate Social Responsibility," *Business and Society Review,* no. 48 (Summer 1984), pp. 62–66.

# SUGGESTED READINGS

Alexander, Larry D., and William F. Mathews. "The Ten Commandments of Corporate Social Responsibility." *Business and Society Review,* no. 48 (Summer 1984), pp. 62–66.

Anshen, Melvin. *Corporate Strategies for Social Performance.* New York: Macmillan, 1980.

Barnet, Richard J., and Ronald E. Muller. *Global Reach: The Power of the Multinational Corporations.* New York: Simon & Schuster, 1974.

Brooke, Michael Z., and H. Lee Remmers. *International Management and Business Policy.* Boston: Houghton Mifflin, 1978, Chap. 17.

Davis, Keith. "The Case for and Against Business Assumption of Social Responsibilities." *Academy of Management Journal,* vol. 16, no. 2 (June 1973), pp. 312–322.

Freeman, Orville L. *The Multinational Company.* New York: Praeger, 1981.

Garrett, Thomas M., and Richard J. Klonoski. *Business Ethics,* 2nd ed. Englewood Cliffs, N.J.: Prentice-Hall, 1986.

Hawkins, Robert G., ed. *The Economic Effects of Multinational Corporations.* Greenwich, Conn.: JAI Press, 1979.

Hay, Robert D., and Edmund R. Gray. "Social Responsibilities of Business Managers." *Academy of Management Journal,* vol. 17, no. 1 (March 1974), pp. 135–143.

———, eds. *Business and Society: Cases and Text.* Cincinnati, Ohio: South-Western, 1981, pp. 4–16.

Hosmer, LaRue Tone. *The Ethics of Management.* Homewood, Ill.: Irwin, 1987.

Luthans, F., R. M. Hodgetts, and K. R. Thompson. *Social Issues in Business,* 3rd ed. New York: Macmillan, 1980.

Miles, Robert H. *Managing the Corporate Social Environment: A Grounded Theory.* Englewood Cliffs, N.J.: Prentice-Hall, 1987.

Negandhi, Anant. *International Management.* Boston: Allyn and Bacon, 1987.

Nicholson, E. A., R. J. Litschert, and W. P. Anthony. *Business Responsibility and Social Issues.* Columbus, Ohio: Merrill, 1974, Chap. 9.

Robinson, Richard D. *International Business Management,* 2nd ed. New York: Dryden Press, 1978, Chap. 9.

———. *Internationalization of Business: An Introduction.* New York: Dryden Press, 1984, Chap. 10.

Rothgeb, John M., Jr. "The Contribution of Foreign Investment to Growth in Third World States." *Studies in Comparative International Development,* vol. 19, no. 21 (Winter 1984–1985), pp. 3–37.

Sherwin, Douglas S. "The Ethical Roots of Business Systems." *Harvard Business Review,* vol. 61, no 6 (November/December 1983), pp. 183–192.

Sisk, Henry L., and J. Clifton Williams. *Management and Organization,* 4th ed. Cincinnati, Ohio: South-Western, 1981.

Steiner, George A. *Business and Society.* New York: Random House, 1971. Chaps. 1, 4, 5, 9, 12, 21.

Thomas, Aitkan. *The Multinational Man: The Role of the Manager Abroad.* New York: Wiley, 1973.

Travis, Lee A., and Crum, Roy L. "Performance-Based Strategies for MNC Portfolio Balancing." *Columbia Journal of World Business,* vol. 19, no. 2 (Summer 1984), pp. 85–94.

Vernon, Raymond. *Storm Over the Multinationals: The Real Issues.* Boston: Harvard University Press, 1977.

# Chapter
# 20

# Conflicts Between Home Countries and Host Countries

*T*he rapid growth of MNCs in recent years has given rise to heated debates regarding the usefulness of these corporations for both host countries and home countries. Nations differ in their attitudes toward the presence of foreign corporations, and they display different degrees of tension about this situation. In general MNCs have met with more resistance in LDCs than in advanced countries.

Some writers in advanced industrial nations have considered MNCs as the chief instrument in abrogating poverty in LDCs. Other writers in LDCs, however, have referred to MNCs as the main device of the advanced nations for achieving "economic imperialism." These writings have fueled tensions and have contributed to the imposition of the governmental policies that restrict the activities of MNCs.

Although objection to the presence of MNCs has an economic tone, political or nationalistic considerations have played a significant role in shaping conflicting views toward MNCs. Xenophobia and the fear of economic dependence have lured some politicians to suggest the economic confinement of foreign interests and the reserving of certain sectors exclusively for exploitation by local entrepreneurs.[1]

The purpose of this chapter is to provide us with a general understanding of the major opposing views of the activities of MNCs in host countries. First, we list the major criticisms of MNCs. Second, we study the sources of conflict. Third, we elaborate on host countries' reactions to MNCs. Finally, we raise the question as to who is right—MNCs or the countries in which the MNCs do business.

## MAJOR CRITICISMS OF MNCS

The subject of MNCs is imbued with a variety of complaints that are raised by host countries against these corporations. The criticisms of MNCs with regard to technology transfer and social issues were discussed in Chapters 11 and 19. Some other major criticisms that are aimed at MNCs are the following:

1. MNCs raise their needed capital locally, contributing to the rise in interest rates in those countries.
2. The majority (sometimes even 100 percent) of the stock of a subsidiary of an MNC is owned by the parent company. Consequently, the host country's residents do not have much control over the operations of these corporations within their borders.
3. MNCs reserve the key managerial and technical positions for expatriates. As a result, they do not contribute to the "learning-by-doing" process in the host countries.
4. MNCs do not provide training for their host countries' workers.
5. MNCs do not adapt their technology to the conditions that exist in host countries.
6. MNCs concentrate their research and development activities in their home countries. As a result, they restrict the transfer of modern technology and know-how to the host countries.
7. MNCs give rise to the demand for luxury goods in host countries at the expense of essential consumer goods.
8. MNCs start their foreign operations by the purchase of existing firms, rather than by developing a new productive facility from scratch in the host country.
9. MNCs do not contribute to the exports of their host countries.
10. MNCs worsen the income distribution of their host countries.
11. MNCs do not observe the objectives of the national plans for development in host countries.

12. MNCs earn excessively high profits and fees, due to their monopoly power in host countries.
13. MNCs dominate major industrial sectors.
14. MNCs are not accountable to their host nations, but only respond to their home country's government.
15. MNCs contribute to inflation by stimulating demand for scarce resources.
16. MNCs recruit the best personnel and the best managers from the host country at the expense of local entrepreneurs.

To understand the elements that give rise to these criticisms, one should look at the sources of conflicts.

## SOURCES OF CONFLICTS

Conflicts arise from a clash of goals between constituencies. A firm must satisfy different groups of people, each group with its own specific goals. Employees, customers, stockholders, and the governments of home and host countries have different objectives that may not be compatible. Employees strive for a higher compensation package and better working conditions. Customers expect high quality goods at a lower price. Stockholders would like higher rates of return on their investment. Governments, in both host and home countries, may want higher exports or strive for the achievement of certain social goals.

Thus, the incompatibility of objectives of the parties involved in international business may set the stage for confrontation among them.

### MNCs' Objectives

The main objective of an MNC is to maximize its profit. The pursuit of this goal leads the MNC (1) to choose the type of operation—exporting, foreign direct investment, licensing, franchising, management contract, or turnkey operations,—that best suits its objective; (2) to improve efficiency by allocating its resources within the corporate family; and (3) to retain as much of its profit as possible.

Because MNCs operate in different host countries, each with its own governmental jurisdiction, they are not accountable to these nations concerning most aspects of their operations. Each nation controls only that part of the MNC's activities that fall within its borders. This gives MNCs more power vis-à-vis local firms, when dealing with the host country's demands. MNCs can counter the pressure of any given host country by simply threatening to curtail their activities or to shut down their operations in that country. This unique characteristic of MNCs goes against a host country's goal of achieving certain economic and social objectives. For example, a host government might be interested in export promotion; however, the MNC may find exporting unprofitable and hence does not cooperate with the host government in achieving this goal. This situation may lead to a conflict of interests and can raise tensions between the MNC and the host country's government.

## Home Countries' Objectives

Conflicts between MNCs and home countries can arise both from economic goals and noneconomic goals.

**Economic Goals**   Economically speaking, there is often not much conflict between the goals of MNCs and the objectives of home countries. In its striving for profit maximization, an MNC generates earnings for (1) its stockholders in terms of dividends and capital appreciation; (2) its employees in the form of wages and salaries; and (3) its home government through the payment of corporate profit taxes. Because increases in the earnings of their residents is an economic objective that host countries try to achieve, there seems to be no conflicts of interest between these countries and MNCs on that score.

Because most managers and owners of an MNC are residents of the MNC's home country, they have a tendency to identify their interests with those of their home country. As a result, they may try to fuse the corporate interest with the home country's interest. For example, an MNC may try to buy most of its resources at home, as long as it is compatible with its profit maximization objectives.

However, in spite of this tendency, an MNC cannot ignore the world economic conditions when allocating its resources. Thus, if labor costs are high at home, or if the home country's economy is not strong, the MNC may close its factories at home and invest its capital abroad, helping increase employment in a foreign country rather than at home. Such an action leads to higher unemployment at home and may cause depression in areas where the MNC's factories have been closed. For example, when General Electric (GE) moved its plant from Ashland, Massachusetts, to Singapore, it caused the loss of 1,100 jobs in Ashland. As another example, 4,000 jobs were lost at home when RCA closed its Memphis, Tennessee, facilities and moved to Taiwan.[2]

Such incidents lead to tension between the unemployed workers and the MNCs. This might cause the home country government to step in and restrict the activities of MNCs abroad. For example, U.S. labor's opposition to MNCs contributed to the passage of the Trade and Investment Act of 1972, known as the "Burke-Hartke Bill" after its original cosponsors. This bill introduced certain measures that have restricted both U.S. imports and foreign direct investment by U.S. corporations. According to the bill, the president of the United States has the right to forbid any person within U.S. jurisdiction from making transfers of capital to or within any foreign nation, if in the president's judgment the transfer would lead to a net increase in unemployment in the United States.

**Noneconomic Goals**   Conflicts between MNCs and governments can also stem from noneconomic goals that are set by the home or host country's government.

Chief among these goals is national defense. A home country government might impose restrictions on: (1) the exportation of certain products, such as computer hardware and electronic devices, that might be strategically significant to hostile nations; (2) the licensing and the technology that are needed to produce such goods; and (3) the investment in facilities in host countries needed to produce these goods. While these restrictions might be necessary from the home country's national security standpoint, they may prove to be detrimental to the profit maximization process of the MNC.

Another noneconomic goal that might lead to conflict between an MNC and a home or host country's government is the government's objective of environmental protection. A host government may desire an environment which is free from water pollution, air pollution, and toxic wastes. Yet MNCs might not take these issues seriously because of the high cost of alleviating these problems. This may cause the government to step in and force the MNCs to take responsibility for cleaning up the environment.

## Host Countries' Objectives

The subject of MNCs is a more touchy issue in host countries than it is in home countries. While home countries perceive MNCs as an integral part of their economic systems, host countries may view them as foreign agents whose benefits are not worth their costs. Such a negative attitude toward MNCs is especially strong in LDCs. The notion that these large MNCs somehow undermine the independence of LDCs raises nationalistic fever in these countries and invites emotional reaction against MNCs. Nevertheless, the host countries' responses vary, depending on (1) the relative dominance of MNCs in their economy, (2) their perceived degree of dependence from the MNCs, and (3) the extent to which MNCs' activities are subsidized by the host government.

The sources of conflict between MNCs and host countries can be traced not only to the economic goals of the host countries, but to their noneconomic goals as well. A new area of conflict between host countries and MNCs is the so-called transborder data flow (TDF) problem. Given the increasing importance of this issue, with its economic and noneconomic implications, a separate discussion of this topic is also included in this section.

**Economic Goals**   The economic objectives of a host country in allowing MNCs to operate in their country can be stated as three separate goals: (1) the economic growth goal, (2) the distributive and allocative goal, and (3) the balance of payments goal.

*The Economic Growth Goal*   The increase in the rate of economic growth is the primary reason for a country to open its doors to MNCs. It is hoped that foreign investment will augment national resources, contributing to the growth of GNP. It is also hoped that MNCs will transfer their technology and provide training for the local workers. This is critical to a country's economic growth because it allows the nation to become technologically independent in the long run, achieving its economic growth goals without foreign help. However, because MNCs have obtained their superior knowledge and technology through their investment in research and development, they do not have any incentive to transfer completely their technology and know-how to the host countries. Such a transfer would cause these corporations to lose their competitive edge over local firms. The unwillingness of MNCs to transfer their technology to host countries leads to a technological dependence of these nations on MNCs, setting the stage for future conflicts.

***The Distributive and Allocative Goal***   The second economic goal of host countries is related to: (1) the distribution of profits earned by the MNCs and (2) control over the allocation of resources by these corporations.

The objective of host countries is to maximize the benefits that accrue to them from the MNCs' activities in their countries. To achieve this goal, they believe that they should have control over the allocation of resources flowing across their borders. This belief is based on the contention that the profits of MNCs in host countries arise from the employment of local resources and from access to domestic markets. MNCs, however, challenge this view. They maintain that their profits in host countries stem from the efficient utilization and allocation of their firm-specific advantages. Because MNCs have property rights over these advantages, they argue, the profits generated by their operations should accrue to them alone. Additionally, they should have the right to control their own scarce resources.

The controversy over the control of resources and distribution of profit is a major issue that has not yet been resolved, and it continues to intensify the tension between MNCs and their host countries.

***The Balance of Payments Goal***   The third economic goal of a host country in allowing MNCs to operate within its borders is to improve its balance of payments. Because foreign exchange is a scarce resource, especially in LDCs, many countries look to MNCs as a source of financing their foreign currency needs.

The impact of an MNC on the balance of payments of a host country changes with the passage of time. Initially, an MNC may bring in capital to a host country and contributes to the balance of payments position. This is because payment for this capital is usually made in a foreign currency, strengthening the country's holding of international reserve assets. However, if a well-developed capital market exists in the host country, an MNC might raise the demand for capital in the local market, causing the home country's interest rates to rise. If this happens, then the MNC's initial investment is not helpful to the balance of payments. For this reason, most countries, especially the LDCs, insist that MNCs pay for the initial cost of their new investment with foreign currencies that have been raised outside their national borders.

After the initial investment is made and the plant becomes operational, there is a second impact on the balance of payments. If the plant produces goods that can effectively compete with commodities that are imported from foreign countries, there would be a decrease in payments for imports. This results in a decline in the outflow of foreign currencies, causing improvement in the balance of payments. Additionally, if the plant produces goods that can be exported, there would be an increase in the inflow of foreign exchange, leading to further improvement in the balance of payments.

There is also a third impact on the balance of payments that results from the initial investment by an MNC in a host country. If the investment is profitable, then the foreign owners may wish to repatriate their capital in the form of royalties, licensing fees, and eventually dividends. This results in an outflow of foreign currencies from the host country worsening the balance of payments. Aware of this negative outcome on their balance of payments, as we explained in Chapter 17, many countries have passed ceilings on the amount of profits, licensing fees, and royalties that can be repatriated by the MNCs. Unfortunately, however, this has caused some MNCs to engage in deceptive policies, such as transfer pricing, to circumvent restrictions imposed by their host governments on the repatriation of their capital. Other MNCs have preferred to plow their earnings into future investment and further growth. This, in turn, has caused additional complaints by the host countries, who relate the size of MNCs in their countries to the degree of foreign domination that is imposed upon them.

A major way in which MNCs can contribute to the balance of payments position of their host countries is through the export of goods and services. However, many MNCs feel that the conditions which exist in LDCs are not conducive to exports from those countries. This is because production in many of these countries is supported by protectionist policies such as import tariffs. As a result, the products that are produced by these nations are relatively expensive and hence incapable of competing with the cheaper and better quality goods abroad.

**Noneconomic Goals**   The main noneconomic goal of a host country in dealing with MNCs is to maintain its independence. Another noneconomic goal is the maintenance of a social, political, and cultural atmosphere that is free from friction.

Many LDCs view MNCs with suspicion, and they fear that their interaction with these corporate giants will lead to a loss of control over their political, cultural, and economic lives. They feel that in dealing with MNCs they will become subservient, providing raw materials and cheap labor to these corporations, but never playing a crucial role in a production process that is based on advanced technology controlled by the MNCs. These nations feel that the intention of MNCs in investing in their countries is to serve the local market exclusively. They charge that MNCs reserve the exporting functions only for their parent companies or for some of their advanced subsidiaries. Such a view is a very gloomy picture of the role of MNCs in LDCs. This view, in turn, causes some of these countries to eventually pursue policies that are aimed at the curtailment of MNCs' activities within their borders.

Even in an advanced country such as the United States, MNCs cannot escape resistance. For example, in 1987 when a Japanese company gave in to pressure from the U.S. government and abandoned its bid to take over a semiconductor company, an American politician stated that "We have won one for America's national security."[3] Worried about the ever-increasing size of foreign investment in the United States, another politician was wondering if Americans would lose ". . . control over our economic destiny."[4] Yet such views are not shared by many economists, who believe the inflow of FDI to the United States will provide the country with know-how and capital. The restriction of FDI is detrimental, it is argued, to a nation that has assumed a new role as the world's largest debtor, requiring roughly $150 billion a year from overseas to finance its growth.[5]

Such pessimistic attitudes toward MNCs stem, to a large extent, from (1) the experience of LDCs with colonialism and (2) the income distribution effect of MNCs' investment.

*Colonialism*   In the past, colonialism in many LDCs crippled their efforts to industrialize. Colonies were forced by the mother countries, who made the resource allocation decisions, to specialize in the production of primary and intermediate goods. As a result, colonies did not develop an industrial base conducive to their economic independence. Today, some of the LDCs see a close resemblance between the former mother countries of colonialism and present-day MNCs. They believe that if the resource allocation decisions are made at the MNC's headquarters, the subsidiaries in the LDCs will end up producing goods that will not make any significant contribution toward the economic development of the host countries.

*The Income Distribution Effect of MNCs*   The activities of an MNC may disturb the income distribution in a host country, leading to social and political unrest. Investment by an MNC may cause the emergence of new entrepreneurs, whose fortunes may increase at the expense of those in power. The reverse may also be true, that is, an MNC may further intensify the strength of the group already in power. It is also possible that an MNC may pay higher wages than the wages paid by local firms. Any of these scenarios would cause one group to gain wealth and power at the expense of another group, at least in the short run. This may cause those who benefit from the operations of an MNC to lobby their government in support of such corporations. Those who lose from the activities of the MNCs, however, may demand that their government restrict the activities of these corporations. The power of those who lose from the activities of MNCs may be enhanced by those who feel a sense of subservience, weakness, and inferiority in dealing with these corporate giants. These feelings may stem from a suspicion that they may not be able to invent, produce, or market a product on their own without the help of MNCs. Whatever the reasons, this situation leads to social and political unrest and sets the stage for governmental intervention that leads to more restrictive policies toward MNCs.

**Transborder Data Flow**   Transborder data flow (TDF) refers to the flow of electronically transmitted information across national boundaries. The immense growth in the computer and telecommunication industries in the 1970s has tremendously facilitated the storing and transmission of massive amounts of information across national boundaries. This has enabled MNCs to collect information in different host countries and transmit it to their home country for use in their worldwide operations. For example, an MNC with its headquarters in New York can build a computerized marketing data file in Europe and transfer this information electronically to its headquarters in New York.

Information collected by MNCs in host countries covers a wide range of subjects. This information includes data on production, distribution, research and development, finance, marketing, personnel, and payroll. Europe is the end point for the transmission of information by many MNCs. Information is transmitted from Europe for storing and processing in the United States, and the results are then transmitted back to Europe for many MNCs.

Given the large volume of information collected by MNCs and the significance of this information in shaping today's global markets, host countries, both advanced countries and LDCs, have come to realize the impact of TDF on their countries' economic and noneconomic goals.

Economically speaking, information is an economic resource, and as such it is a marketable, transferable, and exportable commodity. The ability of one country to store and process information may give that country technological advantage over other countries. A case in point is the United States, which has derived immense benefits not only by processing and storing data in U.S.-based computer systems but also by exporting sophisticated computer equipment.

From a noneconomic standpoint, host countries are worried that the collection and storing of certain types of data may give the home countries a political advantage and may jeopardize their national sovereignty. Indeed, it has been argued that in times of war or national emergencies, host countries might not be able to gain access to vital information stored in hostile home countries.

Given the economic and noneconomic implications of TDF, European countries have decided to deal with the problem through a new form of privacy protection legislation. In addition, due to the diversity of laws in different countries and the importance of this issue globally, the Organization of Economic Cooperation and Development (OECD) devised guidelines on TDF in 1980. These voluntary guidelines were adopted by Canada in 1984. The purpose of these guidelines is to encourage the cooperation of member nations with regard to the exchange of information. Adherence to these guidelines means that the OECD member countries will consider the OECD guidelines equivalent to their own privacy laws. This may result in the relaxation or removal of barriers to the free flow of information between OECD members and the United States. The OECD hopes to publish a document by the late 1980s that outlines concrete steps regarding TDF.

The legislation regarding TDF can be considered as a form of nontariff trade barriers. The effects of these trade barriers can be viewed from two perspectives: international and domestic. Internationally, the decrease in the flow of information increases the uncertainty felt by potential importers and exporters. As a result, the volume of international trade in goods and services decreases. Service sector industries that are heavily dependent on TDF, such as the airlines, banking, financial services, and tourism, are especially affected by barriers against TDF. Domestically, as the flow of information into a country diminishes, the prices charged by the data-processing industries rise. Also, as the cost-cutting technological information of foreign origin is denied to the domestic producers their production costs rise. Thus, the legislation of TDF, like tariff barriers, may result in losses for business on both the national and international levels. We must stress that the abuse of TDF is a serious problem that would be best resolved by international cooperation rather than by protectionist barriers that retard the free flow of international trade.

## HOST COUNTRIES' REACTION TO MNCS

Given the conflicting goals of MNCs vis-à-vis the goals of host countries, the reaction of different nations to these corporations varies considerably. The factors that determine the intensity of these reactions are (1) the perceived degree of foreign domination and control and (2) the extent to which the activities of the MNCs are subsidized by the government of the host countries.

Suspicions concerning the presence of some foreigners have led some countries to go so far as to confiscate foreign enterprises in their country. For example, after the downfall of the shah in Iran, the new Islamic Republic government of that country confiscated all American companies. Some other countries, however, have been indecisive about the presence of MNCs and have gone from one extreme to another. For example, the French government has shifted its policies regarding FDI three times within a five-year period.

Some countries have developed different policy measures that have the intention of lessening the effects of FDI on their economic systems without banning FDI altogether. It is hoped that such policies would provide them with the benefits of FDI—technology, managerial know-how, labor training, the needed capital, and access to foreign markets—without forcing them to yield completely to foreign ownership and control.

Some of the major policies employed by host countries in dealing with MNCs are: requiring joint venture arrangements; controlling entries and takeovers; excluding foreigners from specific activities; controlling the local content and local employment; export requirements; controlling the local capital market; debt equity requirements; taking the foreign investment package apart; requiring disinvestment; and controlling remittances, rates, and fees.

## Joint Venture Arrangements

A joint venture arrangement calls for the partnership of an MNC with either the private entrepreneurs or the government of a host country. There are two advantages of engaging in a joint venture arrangement (rather than having a wholly owned subsidiary) for an MNC. First, by making a host country's residents part owners of the operation, it minimizes the control measures that are used by that country's government against the foreign operation. Second, by placing indigenous partners on the board of directors, it better equips an MNC to deal with the cultural elements that exist in a host country. For example, American Telephone and Telegraph (AT & T), the world's largest communication company, began to expand into the European market. After spending millions of dollars to figure out a strategy for Europe, the company decided to try local partnership. This decision was based on the realization that the European market was crowded, the governments were hostile, and the trade barriers were formidable. In 1983, AT & T began to form joint ventures with different European companies with the intention of gaining local expertise, political power in Europe's protected market, and faster growth. Accordingly, joint ventures were arranged with Phillips for producing communication gear, Olivetti for producing computers, and Cia. Telefonica Nacionale de Espara for producing microchips. There are signs that AT & T's strategy has paid off, and the company plans to form more partnerships with other European countries.[6]

The advantages of joint venture arrangements for host countries' residents are: (1) their ability, as partial owners, to decide about the operations of the firm and (2) their ability to share in the profits that result from the activities of the firm in their country.

Unfortunately, however, joint venture arrangements, like any other kind of partnership, are not without problems. First, a joint venture is composed of partners with different cultural backgrounds and different objectives. This can lead to disagreements between the partners regarding different aspects of the firm's day-to-day operations. For example, foreign partners are more likely to opt for plowing back their earnings into the company, whereas local partners might prefer higher dividends. The time may also come when the corporation needs to build up its capital, but the local partners are unwilling to contribute their share. As another example, a host government might desire a more equitable income distribution. However, an MNC might have entered into partnership with the wealthy class of the host country. If such a partnership is successful, then the high profit earned by the joint venture would further increase power and wealth of the wealthy class, thereby worsening the income distribution in the country as a whole.

Given the nature of problems associated with joint ventures, some MNCs have gone so far as to shut down their existing operations rather than engage in such arrangements. For example, in response to India's demand that IBM and Coca-Cola sell 60 percent of the equity of their Indian subsidiaries to domestic interests, both companies pulled out of that country.[7]

Today, joint venture arrangements are still popular in some countries, such as Japan and South Korea. Such arrangements have enabled these host countries to have access to the advanced technology of the West, without yielding complete ownership and control to foreign interests. Unfortunately, however, cultural gaps between partners have diminished the potential benefits of joint venture arrangements. For example, in a move to acquire aerospace technology, a group of Japanese companies negotiated a joint venture with Boeing, the American aerospace company. From the beginning of negotiations there were signs of disagreements between the two sides. For instance, the Japanese complained that "... Boeing assigns to the project too many young executives who don't understand Japanese business practice."[8] Americans complained about "... the Japanese negotiator's lack of technical knowledge."[9]

Joint venture arrangements are not only popular in market economies, but they are also encouraged in Eastern Europe, the People's Republic of China, and even in the USSR. However, due to difficulties that have afflicted Western joint venture projects in Eastern Europe and in China, Western entrepreneurs have remained reluctant to expand their investment into nonmarket economies, especially into the Soviet Union.[10]

## Controlling Entries and Takeovers

In most LDCs and in some advanced countries, the entry of foreign firms to their country is controlled. Such firms are required to obtain approval for a new investment venture or for the takeover of an existing firm. In Canada, for example, the Foreign Investment Review Agency (FIRA) is in charge of screening foreign direct investment. In India, a Foreign Investment Board is given the responsibility of reviewing foreign direct investment.

Although different countries have different requirements for approving foreign direct investment, most nations demand a detailed description of the applicant's operations and financial position. Additionally, they require the potential investor to explain the way in which the investment project would contribute to national objectives. The approval process puts the reviewing board of the country in the driver's seat, so to speak, enabling the board to approve only those projects that are potentially beneficial to the country.

There is a tendency by many countries to prohibit the purchase of existing plants, requiring that a foreign investment project start from scratch. This tendency arises from the argument against monopoly. It is felt that the takeover of an existing firm by an MNC keeps the number of firms in an industry constant and does not contribute to the market competition. Thus, for example, if an industry is composed of 10 firms, a takeover of an existing firm by an MNC leaves the total number at 10. A new entry, however, raises the number to 11, increasing the degree of competitiveness in the industry.

Although the above argument is theoretically strong, practically speaking it loses its appeal when an industry is already competitive and when the government feels, for no good reason, that a new investment is somehow preferable to a takeover of an existing one. Suppose an ailing domestic firm is operating in a relatively competitive situation and its operators are not capable of running it efficiently. In this situation, the plant and equipment are worth more to the foreign entrepreneurs who wish to invest in that country than the domestic entrepreneurs who are sustaining losses. Thus, both parties would gain from the takeover by the foreign entrepreneurs. In this situation, a policy of forcing the foreign entrepreneurs to start from scratch and causing the domestic entrepreneurs to scrap their plants seems to be unproductive.

Today, countries that are open to foreign investment gladly hand over the control of their troubled companies in the hope of acquiring as much foreign investment and technology as they can. For example, in pursuing its new policy of openness to foreign investment in 1986, Spain allowed four takeovers of domestic firms by foreign firms: SEAT group was taken over by Volkswagen AG of West Germany, a locally known maker of natural cosmetics was taken over by Gillette, a local meat packer was taken over by Unilever, and a canner was taken over by Pillsbury.[11]

## Excluding Foreigners from Specific Activities

According to this policy, a host country reserves certain business fields for domestic entrepreneurs only, prohibiting foreign involvement in those areas. The business activities that are usually prohibited to foreigners by host countries are banking, insurance, public utilities, communications and the media, and the exploitation of certain natural resources.

Banking, insurance, and other financial institutions in general are prohibited as investments for foreigners because of the fear by some host countries, such as Canada and Mexico, that these institutions have the potential for providing foreigners with influence and control over their economic system. Such control, it is argued, may be in conflict with the economic policies of the host country.[12]

Public utilities are prohibited as investments for foreigners by many host governments because such businesses are considered to be an inseparable part of national development.

The operation of communications and the media—radio, television, and newspapers—is usually restricted by host governments to the local entrepreneurs or to the host country government itself. It is argued that they represent a vital national interest that should not be entrusted to foreign hands.

Involvement of foreigners in the exploitation of certain natural resources in many host countries, such as Brazil, Finland, Mexico, and Morocco, is very limited, because these resources are considered a gift of nature that should be exploited only for public use, rather than for private gain. Many other LDCs have limited foreign involvement and investment in their mineral deposits, oil reserves, and forestry resources to purchases of concessions by foreigners. Such concessions have provided foreign firms with the exclusive rights to explore a given resource, but only for a limited time period. In return for these rights the host governments have received royalties on the extracted resource and income taxes on the net profits of the foreign firms.

### Controlling the Local Content and Local Employment

To ensure that the operations of foreign firms are conducive to the industrialization process and that they increase the employment in host countries, many LDCs have demanded foreign firms continually increase the amount of locally produced goods that are used as contents of their final products. Additionally, they have required that a certain percentage of the foreign firm's total employees be citizens of the host country. The local contents policies have been widely used by Latin American countries where MNCs are engaged in automobile manufacturing. Mexico has gone so far as to require foreign firms to employ a labor force that is 90 percent Mexican.

Nations that impose the local contents requirements in a new industry hope to improve their economy not only through that industry, but also via that industry's linkages with the suppliers of component parts and materials. Unfortunately, however, the local contents requirement may prove unproductive. This happens if the local market is not large enough to allow economies of scale in the production of the related component parts and materials.

### Export Requirements

Foreign exchange is scarce in many countries, especially LDCs. It provides these countries with the needed funds for the importation of items that they need in the process of their industrialization. Exports are the surest way of acquiring the necessary foreign exchange, and foreign investments projects are often evaluated on the basis of their potential contribution to the country's exports.

Many nations have learned that the overall strategies of MNCs may not permit or inspire their new subsidiaries to compete against the old subsidiaries in securing markets for their exports. This has led host countries to be skeptical of the MNCs' role in enhancing their exports. As a result, some countries have considered the ability of a subsidiary to freely export a prerequisite for its approval as a foreign investment.

Unfortunately, however, many LDCs' markets are protected with high tariffs and quotas. If a foreign firm's subsidiary is forced to operate in a protected industry, its high production cost will erode its competitiveness in the world market. Thus, the ability of the subsidiary to freely export should be weighed against the government's desire to engage in protectionist policies.

### Controlling the Local Capital Market

Because most LDCs lack the needed capital and technology for their own development process, they look upon MNCs as a major source of financing. However, the foreign exchange authorities of these countries often fear that an MNC might raise all or some of its capital in the host country, further draining capital out of the country. To ensure against this possibility, many LDCs exclude foreigners from their local capital market, requiring that all capital funds be raised outside their national boundaries. The impact of this requirement is to increase the inflow of foreign exchange into the host country, improving its balance of payments at the time of investment.

The policy of forcing foreign investors to bring in their own money, without furnishing any local capital, must be exercised with caution. Such a policy may discourage some prospective investors who might potentially be a significant source of technology transfer to the LDC.

## Debt Equity Requirements

Some countries provide guidelines on debt equity ratios. The purpose of such guidelines is to ensure that the investing firm has sufficient financial resources to minimize the possibility of bankruptcy. For example, a regulation by the People's Republic of China requires that: (1) for joint ventures with an investment of $3 million or less, there can be no debt; (2) for investments of $3 million to $10 million, the amount of debt cannot be greater that the equity investment; (3) for investments of $10 million to $30 million, the amount of debt cannot be greater than two times the equity; and (4) for investments greater than $30 million, the debt cannot exceed triple the equity investment. The problem with this requirement is that it might discourage some potential small investors from entering the marketplace. In the case of China, it is predicted that many people who had hoped to set up electronics assembly plants in China may now be forced out of business in China.[13]

## Taking the Foreign Investment Package Apart

One way for host countries to resist foreign investment, yet enjoy foreign capital and foreign technology, is by "taking the foreign investment package apart." This means buying the needed technology, management, and capital separately, rather than acquiring them in one package in the form of an MNC's investment.

Although this is a sound strategy, and it has been successfully implemented in Japan, its application in other countries is questionable. This is because many countries, especially LDCs, do not have the Japanese skill of imitating foreign technology and of adapting it to their national requirements. Additionally, many corporations are reluctant to break their package apart and leave control of their technology in foreign hands. As a result, for most LDCs the opportunity to pursue such a strategy is relatively limited. Nevertheless, it pays off for a host country to explore the possibility of purchasing only those parts of an investment package that are needed. For example, South Korea has attempted to follow Japan's lead by importing technology from Europe and the United States. To explain such a strategy, the South Korean head of technology transfer stated that "We're very weak in designing technology. We're very weak in process technology, so we import what we can't create."[14]

Although South Korea's strategy with regard to technology transfer has been relatively successful, it has met with some problems. For example, South

Korea has been unable to transfer robot technology from Japanese robot makers. The Japanese have refused to provide South Korea with the software that controls robot operation, stating that South Koreans are not ready for such technology.[15]

A more recent example involved the People's Republic of China and Chrysler Corporation. According to a contract, the Chrysler Corporation had agreed to the transfer of engine equipment to China's First Automotive Works. However, it remains to be seen if Chrysler can overcome the market pitfalls that other Western investors have experienced in China.[16]

### Requiring Disinvestment

According to this policy, the host government requires the potential foreign investor to disinvest over a period of time. This is achieved by transferring the corporation's ownership to the host country at a specified time for a predetermined price.

The problem with this strategy is the determination of a price that both parties can agree upon, given the uncertainty associated with the future course of events. Even if an agreement is reached, it may still lead to a distortion of incentives by the foreign firms and the host country. Assume that an MNC invests in a host country and agrees to surrender its ownership to that country at a predetermined price of $1 billion at the end of a 10-year period. Under the agreement, the MNC has the incentive to devise strategies to ensure that it will not have more than $1 billion worth of assets in its investment at the end of the 10-year period. However, at the same time, the host country tries to ensure that the value of the corporation's asset does not fall below $1 billion. Thus the stage is set for a conflict between the MNC and the host country. As a result, the company might follow strategies in the next 10 years that may not be helpful to its future, when its ownership is reverted to the host country.

### Controlling Remittances, Rates, and Fees

Some of the policies that can be used by host countries to improve their balance of payments, to fulfill their national domestic policies, or to prevent MNCs from reaping excess profits involves the restriction of remittances, the imposition of ceiling rates on royalties, and the imposition of limits on fees paid for technology. However, the problem with these policies is that an MNC may be in a position to circumvent these restrictions through extra charges for training, research and development, machinery, advice, use of overhead facilities, corporate overhead, interest, and other services. An MNC also has the power to circumvent the system by altering its transfer prices for raw materials, component parts, and final products. All these actions have the effect of increasing the flow of funds from the host country to the corporation's headquarters in the home country, thus dampening the effort of the host country's government to diminish the foreign exchange outflow.

## Other Policies

Other policies used by host countries in securing some of the benefits of MNC investment are requiring foreign firms to engage in labor training, requiring that certain key managerial positions be held by nationals, prohibiting foreign firms from engaging in technologically stagnant industries, and demanding that foreign firms engage in research and development in the host country.

The host countries hope that these measures will contribute to the internalization of the firm's technological and managerial know-how within the nation, thereby improving the country's balance of payments. Empirical studies suggest that host countries have been at least partially successful in implementing such measures. These studies show that MNCs usually engage in the training of the local labor. Studies also show that MNCs' training budgets might be greater than the training budgets of domestic firms.[17] However, the research and development activities carried out by MNCs in LDCs seem to be of an elementary nature, and these efforts usually do not lead to the adaptation of technology by these corporations. Additionally, there seems to be no significant difference between the amount of research rendered by foreign firms as compared with domestic firms.[18]

## WHO IS RIGHT?

Our prior discussion suggests that all the activities of MNCs do not have the same impact on either host countries or home countries. Additionally, it is difficult to measure these effects and to reach a general conclusion that can be applied to all countries and all MNCs. In fact, much of the literature in the area of FDI is composed of studies that deal with the isolated problems of individual countries. As a result, any generalization about the conclusions reached by these studies is questionable.

One thing is clear: many host countries believe that there are gains to be made from the operations of MNCs within their borders, and they continue to receive these corporations with open arms. This is especially true for countries with market economies. For example, Brazil offers a number of incentives to attract foreign investment. These include tax rebates for MNCs that reinvest corporate earnings into the economy, convertibility of earnings into the dollar, fiscal incentives, and the free repatriation of corporate earnings up to 12 percent of the invested capital. But even in the case of nonmarket economies, the most unlikely countries, such as the People's Republic of China and Nicaragua, are not reluctant to seek foreign investment. China has gone so far in receiving FDI that it even offers incentives to MNCs to engage in the exploration of one of its most precious resources, oil.[19] The Marxist government of Nicaragua continues to host about 60 MNCs, which contribute about 13 percent to its GNP.

Much of the conflict between MNCs and nation-states seems to be political. The sheer size of MNCs is indicative of their power. For example, data show that the sales of General Motors and Exxon are greater than the GNPs of Switzerland and Saudi Arabia.[20] As a result, these corporations can negotiate business contracts that may have a greater impact on the negotiating countries than many treaties would have.

There is considerable concern that MNCs can be used as a means by which home countries could impose their political wills on host countries. For example, the U.S. government has forbidden the affiliates of U.S. MNCs from selling to certain communist nations. This goes against the laws of France and Canada, which require that the sales be made. Enforcement of this law could thus be considered an intrusion by the United States into the sovereignty of France and Canada. A more recent example is the case of South Africa. The foreign affiliates of some of the U.S. MNCs, such as IBM and GM, under pressure at home, have reluctantly pulled out of this country because of its racial policies.[21] Some observers doubt that such a political move is significant in changing the South African racial policies. So far, the move has resulted in economic hardship on many South Africans, who have had to face the loss of jobs and fringe benefits that were associated with the operations of these companies.[22]

As the above example indicates, the curtailment of MNCs' operations does not seem to resolve political problems. A useful means for reaching agreements might be a forum for discussing controversial issues that have given rise to conflicting views between parties involved in international business.

## SUMMARY

1. MNCs have been criticized by host countries for many reasons.
2. An MNC must satisfy different groups. These groups include employees, customers, stockholders, and the governments of the home and host countries. Because the objective of these different groups are not necessarily compatible with each other, conflicts among these groups involved in international business are bound to arise.
3. The pursuit of the profit maximization goal leads an MNC (a) to choose that mode of operation that best suits its objective, (b) to improve efficiency by allocating its resources within the corporate family, and (c) to retain as much of its profit as possible.
4. Economically speaking, there are few conflicts between the goals of MNCs and the objectives of home countries. Conflicts do arise, however, if an MNC closes its factory at home and invests money abroad, leading to higher unemployment at home.
5. The conflicts between the MNC and its home country can also stem from noneconomic goals that are set by the government in the home country. Conflicts may arise over exports and over the licensing and production of certain products in certain host countries. Conflicts may also arise over environmental issues.
6. The objectives of a host country in allowing MNCs to operate within its borders can be divided into economic goals and noneconomic goals.
7. The economic goals of a host country in receiving MNC investment are: (a) to achieve economic growth, (b) to achieve better distribution and allocation of resources, and (c) to improve the balance of payments of the host nation.

8. The main noneconomic goal of a host country is independence. Other noneconomic goals are the maintenance of a social, political, and cultural atmosphere that is free from friction.

9. TDF refers to the flow of electronically transmitted information across national boundaries. TDF is an economic resource and, as such, is a marketable, transferable, and exportable commodity. The legislation regarding TDF may be considered as a form of nontariff trade barrier. The effect of this trade barrier may be viewed from two prospectives: international and domestic.

10. The factors that determine the intensity of reactions of a host country to an MNC are (a) the perceived degree of foreign domination and control and (b) the extent to which the activities of MNCs are subsidized by the government of the host country.

11. Some of the major policies that can be adapted by host countries to enjoy FDI without yielding to complete foreign ownership and control are requiring joint venture arrangements, controlling entries and takeovers, excluding foreigners from specific activities, controlling the local content and local employment, export requirements, controlling the local capital market, debt equity requirements, taking the foreign investment package apart, requiring disinvestment, and controlling remittances, rates and fees.

12. A joint venture arrangement calls for a partnership of an MNC with either the private entrepreneurs or the government of a host country.

13. Controlling market entries and takeovers of foreign firms is achieved by requiring these firms to have approval for a new investment venture or for the takeover of an existing firm. In most countries the purchase of an existing firm is not allowed.

14. Excluding foreigners from certain business activities is usually achieved by prohibiting their engagement in banking, insurance, public utilities, communications and the media, and in the exploitation of certain natural resources.

15. To control the local content of products and local employment, host countries can require foreign firms to continually increase the amount of the locally produced contents of their products. Additionally, they can require that a certain percentage of the foreign firm's employees be citizens of the host country.

16. According to the policy of export requirement, the approval of a potential investment project by an MNC is contingent upon its contribution to the host country's export.

17. The policy of controlling the local capital market calls for the exclusion of foreigners from the host country's local capital market.

18. The control of debt equity by a host government provides guidelines on the debt equity ratio of the potential investment project by the MNC in the host country.

19. "Taking the foreign investment package apart" means that a host country buys the needed technology, management, and capital in separate business deals, rather than acquiring all these ingredients in one package in the form of an MNC investment.

20. A policy of disinvestment calls upon the investing MNC to disinvest over a period of time. This is achieved by transferring the corporation's ownership to the host country at a specified time for a predetermined price.

21. The policies of controlling remittances, rates, and fees are used by host countries to improve their balance of payments position, to fulfill national domestic policies, and to prevent MNCs from reaping excess profits.

22. Other policies used by host countries in securing some of the benefits of MNCs investment are requiring foreign firms to engage in labor training, requiring certain key positions to be held by nationals of the host countries, prohibiting foreign firms

from engaging in technologically stagnant industries, and demanding that foreign firms engage in research and development in the host countries.

## QUESTIONS

20.1 In order to dampen the effect of foreign ownership and control, some host LDCs have forced MNCs to share their ownership with the host country nationals. Such policies have reduced the amount of capital inflow that MNCs can transfer to the host countries. Given the scarcity of capital in LDCs, why do you think that they continue to press for joint foreign-local ownership?

20.2 Some countries prohibit the purchase of an existing firm by an MNC, requiring a foreign investment project to start from scratch. What theoretical justification is given for such a prohibition? Explain. Does this theoretical justification hold true in practice? Explain.

20.3 Given the conflicts between MNCs and home and host countries, who do you think is correct—MNCs, home countries, or host countries? Explain. What is one possible way of alleviating the conflicts? Explain.

20.4 Suppose you are responsible for attracting foreign direct investment to your country. Which incentives do you use to attract FDI to your country, and why? How do you deal with the possible resistance to FDI in your country? Under what conditions do you prevent foreign firms from acquiring domestic firms in your country?

20.5 Choose an advanced country (AC) and an LDC and undertake a research project to determine:

The restrictions that are imposed by the LDC and the AC governments on foreign ownership.

The incentives offered to attract FDI by the LDC and the AC.

Compare your chosen LDC and AC. Which one seems to be pro-foreign investment, and why?

20.6 Some host countries have objected to the presence of MNCs inside their borders on the grounds that MNCs impinge upon their national independence. What factors have contributed to the existence of such an attitude? Explain.

20.7 Given the presence of hostility on the part of some LDCs toward the United States, do you think that the U.S. government should take any action against LDCs that expropriate the investments of the U.S. MNCs? Discuss.

## NOTES

1. Thomas W. Allen, "Industrial Development Strategies and Foreign Investment Policies of Southern Asia and South Pacific Developing Countries," in R. Hal Mason, ed., *International Business in the Pacific Basin* (Lexington, Mass.: Lexington Books, D.C. Heath, 1978), pp. 51–92.
2. California Newsreel, *Controlling Interest: The World of Multinational Corporation* (San Francisco: California Newsreel, 1978), video tape.

3. "U.S. Efforts to Deter Foreign Investor Vie with Need for Capital," *The Wall Street Journal,* 5 August 1987, p.1.

4. Ibid., p. 13.

5. Ibid., pp. 1, 13.

6. "AT & T Finding Success in Europe Elusive, So It Tries Local Partners New Strategies," *The Wall Street Journal,* 19 December 1985, p. 33.

7. "IBM Shuts Down Operations in India," *The New York Times,* 2 June 1978, p. D5; "India Demands 'Know-How' and 60% Share of Coca-Cola Operation," *The New York Times,* 9 August 1977, p. 45.

8. "Venture with Boeing Is Likely to Give Japan Big Boost in Aerospace," *The Wall Street Journal,* 14 January 1986, p. 22.

9. Ibid.

10. "Capitalists Wary of Moscow's Hard Sell to Invest in Joint-Venture Enterprises," *The Wall Street Journal,* 6 April 1987, p. 25.

11. "Spain's New Openness to Foreign Investment Is a Boon to Consumers," *The Wall Street Journal,* 29 July 1987, p. 1.

12. "Foreign Ownership and Structure of Canadian Industry," *Report of the Task Force on the Structure of Canadian Industry* (Ottawa: Queen's Printer, 1968), p. 389.

13. "China Sets Equity Requirement for Its Partners in Joint Ventures," *The Wall Street Journal,* 19 December 1985, p. 33.

14. "Weak in Technology, South Korea Seeks Help from Overseas," *The Wall Street Journal,* 7 January 1986, p. 1.

15. Ibid., pp. 1, 14.

16. "Chrysler Corp. to Enter Chinese Market with Major Sale of Engine Equipment," *The Wall Street Journal,* 21 July 1987, p. 12.

17. Parviz Asheghian, "Joint Venture Firms and Labour Training in Iran," *Management Research News,* no. 3 (1983):16–19

18. Parviz Asheghian, "The R & D Activities of Foreign Firms in a Less Developed Country: An Iranian Case Study," *Journal of Business and Economic Perspectives* (Spring 1984):19–28.

19. "China to Give Foreign Companies Better Terms in Oil Exploration," *The Wall Street Journal,* 3 December 1985, p. 34; "Multinational Corporations Continue to Be Crucial to Nicaraguan Economy," *The Wall Street Journal,* 14 November 1986, p. 34.

20. John Heim, "The Top 100 Economies," *Across the Board* (May 1980), pp. 8–11. This study uses data for 1978.

21. "GM, IBM, and Others Departing South Africa Are Faulted for Plans to Continue Sales There," *The Wall Street Journal,* 24 October 1986.

22. "South Africans Face Pain in Life Without U.S. Firms," *The Wall Street Journal,* 24 October 1986, p. 24; "U.S. Exodus Touches Many South Africans," *The Wall Street Journal,* 6 November 1986, p. 36.

## SUGGESTED READINGS

Agmon, Tamir, and Seev Hirsch. "Multinational Corporations and the Developing Economies: Potential Gains in a World of Imperfect Market and Uncertainty." *Oxford Bulletin of Economics and Statistics,* 41 (November 1979):333–344.

Asheghian, Parviz. "Comparative Efficiencies of Foreign Firms and Local Firms in Iran." *Journal of International Business Studies,* 13 (Winter 1982):113–120.

————. "Joint Venture Firms and Labour Training in Iran." *Management Research News,* no. 3 (1983):16–19.

————, and William G. Foote. "X-Inefficiencies and Interfirm Comparison of U.S. and Canadian Manufacturing Firms in Canada." *Quarterly Journal of Business and Economics,* 24 (Autumn 1985): 3–12; the abstract is printed in the *Journal of Economic Literature,* 24 (June 1986), p. 1085.

————, and William G. Foote. "The Productivities of U.S. Multinationals in the Industrial Sector of the Canadian Economy." *Eastern Economic Journal,* 11 (April/June 1983):123–133.

————, and William G. Foote. "Capital Efficiency, Capital Intensity and Debt-Equity: A Comparison of U.S.–Owned and Canadian-Owned Firms in Canada." *Midwestern Journal of Business and Economics,* 2 (Fall 1986):39–48.

Behrman, Jack N. *National Interests and the Multinational Enterprise: Tensions Among the North Atlantic Countries.* Englewood Cliffs, N.J.: Prentice-Hall, 1970.

Bergstan, C. F., and T. Moran. *American Multinationals and American Interests.* Washington, D.C.: Brookings Institution, 1978.

Brash, D. T. *American Investment in Austrian Industry.* Cambridge, Mass.: Ballinger, 1976.

Buss, Martin D. J. "Legislative Threat to Transborder Data Flow." *Harvard Business Review,* 62 (May/June 1984):111–118.

Casson, Mark. *Alternatives to the Multinational Enterprise.* London: Macmillan, 1979.

Dunning, John H. *American Investment in British Manufacturing Industry.* London: Allen & Unwin, 1958.

————. "Multinational Enterprises and Nation States." In A. Kapoor and Philip D. Grulb, eds. *The Multinational Enterprise in Transition.* Princeton, N.J.: Darwin Press, 1972, Chap. 28.

Forsyth, David J. C. *U.S. Investment in Scotland.* New York: Praeger, 1972.

Globerman, Stephen. "Technological Diffusion in the Canadian Tool and Die Industry." *Review of Economic Statistics,* 57 (November 1975):428–434.

————. "Foreign Direct Investment and Spillover Efficiency Benefits in Canadian Manufacturing Industries." *Canadian Journal of Economics,* 12 (February 1979): 42–56.

Johnson, Harry G. "The Efficiency and Welfare Implications of the International Corporation." In Charles P. Kindleberger, ed. *The International Corporation.* Cambridge, Mass.: Massachusetts Institute of Technology Press, 1970.

Kindleberger, Charles P. *American Business Abroad.* New Haven, Conn.: Yale University Press, 1969.

Lafalce, John J. "TDF Barriers to Service Trade." *International Data Report,* 8, no. 4 (1985): 190–193.

Lall, Sanjaya. "Performance of Transnational Corporations in Less Developed Countries." *Journal of International Business Studies* (Spring 1983):13–33.

Mansfield, Edwin, J. Teece, and S. Wagner. "Overseas Research and Development by U.S.–Based Firms." *Review of Economics and Statistics,* 46 (May 1979):187–196.

Rugman, Alan M. *Multinationals in Canada: Theory, Performance and Economic Impact.* Boston: Martinus Nijhoff, 1980.

Safarian, A. E. *The Performance of Foreign Owned Firms in Canada.* Washington, D.C.: Canadian-American Committee, National Planning Association, 1969.

———. *Storm over the Multinationals.* Cambridge, Mass.: Harvard University Press, 1977.

Streeten, Paul. "Costs and Benefits of Multinational Enterprises in Less Developed Countries." In John H. Dunning, ed. *The Multinational Enterprise.* London: Allen & Unwin, 1971, Chap. 9.

Tsanacas, Demetri. "The Transborder Data Flow in the New World Information Order: Privacy or Control." *Review of Social Economy,* 43 (December 1985): 357–370.

Vaistos, Constantine V. "Income Distribution and Welfare Considerations." In John H. Dunning, ed. *Economic Analysis and the Multinational Enterprise.* New York: Praeger, 1974, Chap. 12.

Vernon, Raymond. *Sovereignty at Bay: The Multinational Spread of U.S. Enterprise.* New York: Basic Books, 1971.

# Chapter 21

# Looking into the Future

$T$he innate human desire to look into the future is nothing new. Palmists, astrologers, mystics, and seers have tried to forecast the future for ages. What is new in recent decades, however, is the emergence of scientific forecasting methods, which use forecasting models and employ statistical techniques in predicting the future.

Today, even with all the improvements in forecasting techniques, there are still many forecasts that fall apart. Nevertheless, in an uncertain world, where international managers have to make numerous decisions, forecasting has become an integral part of any decision-making process.

The major forecasting techniques that are used today were introduced in Chapters 9, 11, and 14. In this chapter we first discuss the major factors that affect the future. Second, we review future trends in the world economy and elaborate on their implications for international business. Third, we study the international environment as it relates to the future. Fourth, we discuss the role of the advanced countries and the LDCs in international business in the future. Finally, we elaborate on the role of the international managers in meeting the challenges of the future.

## MAJOR FACTORS AFFECTING THE FUTURE

International business is affected by many factors. Chief among these factors are (1) the availability and the growth of human and nonhuman resources, (2) the efficiency of the production process through which these resources are employed, and (3) the means by which producers and consumers are brought together. The first variable calls for the study of population, natural resources, food, and capital. The second variable necessitates an understanding of technology. The third variable requires a knowledge of communications and transportation.

### Population

The study of population rests on different theories that each provide a basis for predicting the future. One of the best-known theories is the Malthusian theory of population. Because this theory laid the foundation for the later developments in the subject, we proceed with the discussion of population by first explaining this theory, and then we discuss other projections of population trends in the future.

**Malthusian Theory of Population**   The systematic study of population dates back to the late eighteenth century, when Thomas R. Malthus, an English economist, published his book *The Essay on Principle of Population* in 1798. Although Malthus had many precursors, his ability to systematically combine many strands of thought made his work stand out and gain much greater recognition. He presented his pessimistic view on the growth of population by stating that population tends to grow faster than food supply. That is, population unchecked would increase according to a geometric progression (1,2,4,8,16,32, . . .), while food supply would increase according to an arithmetic progression (1,2,3,4,5,6, . . .). Malthus illustrated the two progressions as shown in Table 21.1.

According to Table 21.1, population, when unchecked, would have in-

Table 21.1   THE MALTHUSIAN POPULATION GROWTH

| Year | 1 | 25 | 50 | 75 | 100 | 125 | 150 | 175 | 200 | 225 |
|------|---|----|----|----|-----|-----|-----|-----|-----|-----|
| Population | 1 | 2 | 4 | 8 | 16 | 32 | 64 | 128 | 256 | 512 |
| Food supply | 1 | 2 | 3 | 4 | 5 | 6 | 7 | 8 | 9 | 10 |

creased 512 times after 225 years. However, the food supply would have increased only 10 times after the same amount of time. Malthus's theory is based on the law of diminishing returns. According to this law, with a given state of technology, a growing population and a fixed amount of land would eventually lead to diminishing returns for agricultural workers. That is, each additional worker would add smaller amounts to output. This simply means that at a certain point in time the world would run out of food supply, and hence humanity would be doomed to misery and poverty unless the rate of population growth is somehow checked. This may be achieved, according to Malthus, either by positive checks, such as famine, disease, and war, or, by preventive checks, such as late marriage and the restraining of sexual desires.

Malthus's theory was criticized on many grounds. The major criticism of Malthus's theory was its inability to predict the miracle of technological progress that has drastically changed food production in the world.

Today, Malthus's name has become symbolic of the alarming growth of population in certain underdeveloped areas of the world, such as in Africa, Asia, and South America, where there is not enough food for the growing population.

**Population Projections**   The population growth, and its projection to the year 2000, are shown in Table 21.2. According to this table, the human population of the Earth reached the level of 4,602 million in 1985 (4,209 + 393). As the table indicates, although the rate of growth of the population is expected to slow down in the future, the annual population figures keep on increasing every year. If this trend continues, it is estimated that the world population would reach 6,530 million by the year 2000.[1] As Table 21.2 shows, the most striking feature of the forecast is that most of the population growth would occur in LDCs. More specifically, it is estimated that the number of people between the ages 20 and 40 will increase by about 2 to 6 percent a year until the year 2000 in the LDCs, which is approximately ten times faster than in the advanced countries. It is also expected that the total of the working age population in China and in India will be 150 percent larger than this total for industrialized countries by the year 2000. Thus demographic change is expected to increase the economic disparities between the LDCs and the advanced countries.[2]

Along with the population growth, urbanization is also expected to increase. It is anticipated that 50 percent of the world's population will be living in urban areas by the year 2000, up from 36 percent in 1970.[3]

Some conservative thinkers anticipate that population in the West will drop, resulting in economic problems for these countries. For the United States they predict that by the year 2025 the population will have leveled off and that it will then begin to gradually decline. They fear that such a decline will have serious economic consequences for the United States and other Western countries, such as West Germany and Denmark, which are already losing population. They believe that the depopulation of the West means a gradual decline in demand and a shrinking market. This will cause the loss of world influence for the United States and democratic allies. Fortunately, most economists and demographers dismiss such predictions as "alarmist hyperbole."

Table 21.2  POPULATION GROWTH, 1965–1985, AND PROJECTED TO 2000

| Country group | 1985 population (millions) | Average annual growth (percent) | | | | |
|---|---|---|---|---|---|---|
| | | 1965–1973 | 1973–1980 | 1980–1985 | 1985–1990 | 1990–2000 |
| Developing countries | 3,451 | 2.5 | 2.1 | 2.0 | 2.0 | 1.8 |
| Low-income countries | 2,305 | 2.6 | 2.0 | 1.9 | 1.8 | 1.7 |
| Asia | 2,071 | 2.5 | 1.9 | 1.8 | 1.7 | 1.5 |
| India | 765 | 2.3 | 2.3 | 2.2 | 2.0 | 1.7 |
| China | 1,041 | 2.7 | 1.5 | 1.2 | 1.3 | 1.2 |
| Africa | 234 | 2.8 | 2.9 | 3.0 | 3.2 | 3.1 |
| Middle-income countries | 1,146 | 2.5 | 2.4 | 2.3 | 2.3 | 2.0 |
| Oil exporters | 502 | 2.5 | 2.6 | 2.6 | 2.6 | 2.3 |
| Oil importers | 643 | 2.4 | 2.2 | 2.1 | 2.0 | 1.8 |
| Major exporters of manufactured products | 420 | 2.4 | 2.1 | 1.9 | 1.8 | 1.6 |
| High-income exporters | 20 | 4.6 | 5.4 | 4.3 | 3.9 | 3.3 |
| Industrial market economies | 737 | 0.9 | 0.7 | 0.6 | 0.5 | 0.4 |
| World, excluding nonmarket industrial economies | 4,209 | 2.2 | 1.9 | 1.8 | 1.7 | 1.6 |
| Nonmarket industrial economies | 393 | 0.8 | 0.8 | 0.8 | 0.7 | 0.6 |

*Source:* From THE WORLD DEVELOPMENT REPORT 1988. Copyright © 1988 by The International Bank for Reconstruction and Development/The World Bank. Reprinted by permission of Oxford University Press, Inc.

Some economists even believe that the fertility rates in the West will soon turn upward. But even if the conservative thinkers are correct, and the population in the West levels off or declines, many experts argue that this does not necessarily mean the loss of economic power for these countries. These experts argue that the engine of economic growth is education, technology, and capital, not the sheer size of the population. Additionally, if necessary, a shortage of population can be alleviated by more liberal immigration policies.[4] In any event, one thing is clear: The rate of population growth for LDCs is expected to be much faster than for advanced countries.

The implications of the above population projections for MNCs is that their market compositions, sizes, and locations will shift. The future MNCs, therefore, will be dealing with a relatively higher population in the LDCs as compared with the advanced countries. This population will also have a higher proportion of people between the ages of 20 and 40, and this population will mainly be concentrated in large urban areas.

## Natural Resources

With all the technological advances that have been made to date, the problem that was raised by Malthus is still before us. Can the fixed supply of natural resources keep up with the growing population? Unfortunately, there is no consensus among forecasters regarding the answer to this question. Different studies reach different conclusions. For example, a study by the Club of Rome concludes that shortages of raw materials will severely limit the future of the world growth.[5] As another example, the Global 2000 study reports that (1) the world's finite fuel resources are adequate; however, they are not evenly distributed; (2) nonfuel mineral resources seem to be sufficient, but to maintain their reserves it is necessary to enhance their discoveries and investments in them; and (3) severe water shortages are expected and it is anticipated that the world's forests will continue to decline in the next several decades.

Although most future studies give us a relatively gloomy picture of the future, there are great unknowns, such as (1) the future of space technology, which might provide us with additional resources from other planets; (2) the availability of resources from the ocean; and (3) an unexpected breakthrough in technology that might drastically change the world's need for natural resources. Given these unknowns, one might hope for a more prosperous future than is predicted by different forecasts.

## Food

As it was noticed by Malthus, one of the main problems associated with population growth is the inadequacy of food production. Today, this problem represents an international concern in a world in which some of the LDCs struggle to feed their hungry masses. According to a report by the World Bank, it is expected that malnourished people in the LDCs will increase to 1.3 billion by the year 2000, up from 400 million to 600 million in the mid-1970s.[6] Yet it is also estimated that if the Earth's resources are used efficiently it will be possible to feed the growing world population through the year 2000. Thus, although no one disagrees that there are definite limits to the world's capacity to produce food, world hunger can be diminished by the optimum use of the Earth's resources. In fact, the Food and Agriculture Organization of the United Nations (FAO) has concluded that with improved policies and with adequate investment the world food production can significantly increase. This is true even for Africa, where food production grows at 2 percent a year as compared with a 3 percent a year increase in the population.[7]

## Capital

Capital is a key factor of production, and it is mostly concentrated in the advanced industrialized nations. The relatively high per capita GNP in these countries has enabled them to save the necessary funds that are needed to generate a high level of investment. The data show that in 1984, of the total amount of investment in the world, about 77 percent was undertaken by the advanced industrial nations, as compared with only 23 percent undertaken by the LDCs.[8]

Economists have considered the lack of capital as the key element in preventing economic growth and development. Consequently, many LDCs have turned to the advanced nations to supply them with the needed capital for their economic development. In fact, as we discussed before, a major plea by these countries is that the MNCs should provide them with badly needed investment funds.

Unfortunately, the future does not seem to be very promising for LDCs. The external debt of LDCs, which has been accumulating over time, passed the level of $800 billion in the late 1980s and it continues to grow. Over half of this debt is owed to international commercial banks and other creditors. The largest portion of this debt is held by Latin American countries, such as Mexico and Venezuela, which have been devastated by the loss of revenue that has resulted from the decline in the world price of oil. This situation has forced the lenders and borrowers to undertake multilateral negotiations through the International Monetary Fund (IMF). These negotiations have resulted in debt restructuring or the roll over of debt. Under the restructuring arrangements, the IMF has imposed severe measures on debtor nations. Some of these measures call on the debtor nations to decrease government expenditures, to reduce inflation, to cut down on imports, and to employ more efficient monetary restraints.[9]

The debt problem of LDCs has had a significant impact on the MNCs. To cut down on their imports, the debtor nations have imposed new trade restrictions and have held back on licensing and other contractual arrangements. This has resulted in a decline in MNCs' exports to these nations. Additionally, some of the nations have followed policies of exchange control that have restricted the outflow of funds from these countries to MNCs. Furthermore, the uncertainty created by the debt crisis in the LDCs has had a deleterious effect on the investment climate, increasing the risk of foreign investment.

To date, there is no consensus among financial experts with regard to the future of the external debt of the LDCs and its impact on the world. Some observers believe that the problem can be resolved only by sustained economic growth in the advanced industrial nations, resulting in higher imports from LDCs. Other observers believe that major commercial creditors have to decrease their interest rates and increase time to maturity of their loans. Certain financial experts present a very pessimistic view. They maintain that the debt crisis of the LDCs might lead to a major breakdown of the IMF and a severely damaged world economic system. This in turn would have serious consequences for MNCs.[10]

While no one is certain of the future, one thing is clear: Both the advanced countries and the LDCs have a great deal at stake in this problem. This calls for international cooperation between the LDCs and advanced countries in resolving the debt crisis.

## Technology

As our discussion of technology in Chapter 11 indicated, technology affects every aspect of a culture. Thus, no forecasting of the future is complete without some discussion of technology. Futurists generally agree that technological progress will continue to accelerate and that it will be adequate to support long-run economic growth. Problems that are expected to accompany this technological development in the future are difficulties in adjusting to the speed of technological change; difficulties with increasing environmental problems; and difficulties with a widening gap between advanced countries and LDCs in the per capita consumption of essential materials whose relative scarcities continue to grow.

Thus, technology per se is not expected to block future growth. The impediment to the future progress, if any, might stem from the interaction of technology with other variables. Future technological development has to be more sensitive to the views of environmentalists, who demand a clean environment that is free from air and water pollution. This means that, in the future, MNCs have to assign a higher priority to R & D expenditures that lead to the development of technologies that are more conducive to environmental objectives, even at the expense of higher production efficiency. Thus, in the development of an airplane, for example, the objectives of fuel efficiency, lower production cost, and higher speed may have to give way to the new goal of a cleaner environment.

As our preceding discussion of natural resources indicated, the futurists warn us about the shortages of natural resources in the future. This means in the future we should expect higher prices for natural resources. Given these predictions, MNCs may have to shift somewhat away from capital-intensive technology to natural resource–saving technology.

Future technological development emphasizes four areas of innovation: (1) electronics, (2) ocean resources, (3) energy, and (4) biotechnology.[11]

In the area of electronics, it is expected that by 1990 we will have a greater ability to handle information that is needed in different pursuits, such as production, distribution, marketing, finance, accounting, education, banking, law, and medicine. This will enable us to perform different tasks with much greater speed and over a wider geographical area than was previously possible. Advancements in microcomputers, lasers, and robotics have already changed many industrial processes. In the last few years we have seen tremendous increases in the demand for robots in the industrial sector, and it is expected that this trend will continue. Even now, there is talk about robot prison guards that could watch over society's most dangerous criminals.[12] It is anticipated that there will be 35,000 robots of various types installed in the United States alone by 1990, up from 3,500 in 1980.[13]

Another area that will experience fast technological growth is the security systems industry. According to International Resource Development (IRD), a Norwalk, Connecticut, market research firm, "Never has concern with physical security been so great as it is now." The factors that contribute to this concern are terrorism and AIDS (Acquired Immune Deficiency Syndrome). These concerns are stimulating markets for high-tech identification of individuals by fingerprints, hand shapes, retinal patterns, or speech patterns.[14]

In the area of energy, the research on superconductors is expected to offer an array of potential energy applications. Superconductors are extremely efficient means of transmission of electricity. In comparison to the ordinarily used copper wire, which loses the majority of electricity that passes through it (due to dissipated heat), superconductors transmit electricity directly and without resistance. As a result, superconductors would substantially decrease electricity losses, leading to less pollution and less depletion of natural resources. Superconductors are expected to lead to higher efficiency and improvement in electric vehicles, high-speed trains, and nuclear fusion, just to name a few examples. The potential applications of superconductors are vast, and they are expected to play a major role in future global energy.[16]

The technological advancement in exploiting ocean resources seems to be very promising in the future. Not only are these resources expected to be utilized in the agriculture and cosmetic industries, but also in medicine. Undersea organisms have already provided us with a number of compounds that are hoped to aid in the fight against life-threatening diseases, such as cancer.[15]

In the field of biotechnology, it is expected that technological advancements will affect areas such as agriculture, energy use, chemistry, and pharmacy. The utilization of certain microorganisms will allow the emergence of new products that will partly or wholly replace some existing processes. For example, oil spills in the ocean can now be cleaned up by microorganisms that were developed in the laboratory.[17]

To be able to reap the benefits of technological progress in the future, MNCs need to modify the structures and the patterns of their activities to incorporate new technologies into their operations. This will require the restructuring of their budgets for research and development and for labor and management training.

## Transportation and Communication

The tremendous improvements in transportation and communication that characterize the twentieth century have drastically changed the nature of business. For instance, it is now possible for a business in Washington State to operate and control a plant in South Korea or Taiwan as easily as one in New York. Today, changes are taking place, especially in satellite and computer-related technologies, that are revolutionizing communication. In the 1960s, satellite telephone communication connected the world. Today, telecommunication technology is entering the competitive world of international business. This technology, which is already in place, allows, for example, a bank to put computer terminals on the desks of its financial officers in Europe for the purpose of transferring funds directly to the United States. It is expected that the use of telecommunications will grow in different areas of business, such as production, marketing, the provision of services, human resource management, technological development, and procurement.[18]

In our homes, cable and satellite television hookups will provide us with two-way communications and allow us to shop, to pay our bills, and to bank without leaving our home. It is also expected that computer terminals and telephones will allow us to do our office work at home, creating a new balance between our jobs and our personal lives.[19]

In the area of transportation, we have already witnessed the development of express delivery systems. With the growing number of cars, which are clogging bridges and tunnels in large cities like New York, it is expected that cities will increase their use of water ports. A new and faster ferry operation will be needed to get passengers to their destinations.[20] Smaller, lighter airplanes have been developed by companies such as ARV Aviation in England that make the dream of having an airplane in your garage a reality.[21] It is anticipated that vessels used for transportation will be larger. For example, it is estimated that by the year 2000, 50 percent of the oil tankers in service will be so large that they will not pass through the Panama Canal.[22]

## ECONOMIC TRENDS AND THE FUTURE

During the period from 1980 to 1982, the world experienced its deepest recession since the Great Depression of the 1930s. The year 1983 can be marked as the year in which the world economic recovery began. As Table 21.3 shows, the rate of growth of world output, which was 3.3 percent in 1979, fell to the level of 0.5 percent in 1982. This rate rose to 2.6 percent in 1983, and 4.4 percent in 1984. In 1985, however, the growth slowed down and fell to 2.9 percent. In 1986, this rate started to accelerate again.

Given the developments of the 1980s in the world economy, that is, the decline in oil prices, in real interest rates, and in inflation, what will the future look like? Will the relatively sustained growth of recent years continue or are we heading for another recession? We answer these questions by studying the world economic trends in the intermediate run (the next decade) and in the long run (the next quarter century).

### The Intermediate Run

Given the recent decline in the oil prices, it is expected that those oil-producing nations, such as Mexico, that are heavily dependent on oil will experience financial problems in the next few years. It is also expected that many other LDCs will face difficulty in supporting that level of investment and imports which is needed to sustain their growth and to serve their external debt. Because the lower level of the investment and imports will reduce the number of jobs in these countries, social and political tensions in these countries will probably increase.

What is the overall rate of growth of output for industrialized countries and LDCs in the next decade? In answering this question, the World Bank provides us with two scenarios regarding the international economy for the years 1987 to 1997. Each of these scenarios are based on certain assumptions regarding the policies of the industrial countries, and each scenario provides us with a specific picture of the world economy in the future.

Table 21.3 CHANGES IN WORLD OUTPUT, 1968 TO 1987[a]
(in Percent)

| | Average 1968–77[b] | 1978 | 1979 | 1980 | 1981 | 1982 | 1983 | 1984 | 1985 | 1986 | 1987 |
|---|---|---|---|---|---|---|---|---|---|---|---|
| World | 4.5 | 4.5 | 3.3 | 2.0 | 1.6 | 0.5 | 2.6 | 4.4 | 2.9 | 3.1 | 3.3 |
| Industrial countries | 3.5 | 4.2 | 3.3 | 1.2 | 1.4 | −0.4 | 2.6 | 4.7 | 2.8 | 3.0 | 3.2 |
| Developing countries | 6.2 | 5.1 | 4.3 | 3.5 | 2.2 | 1.6 | 1.3 | 4.1 | 3.2 | 3.0 | 3.4 |
| Fuel exporters | 8.4 | 2.7 | 3.7 | 1.1 | 0.9 | −0.1 | −1.8 | 1.2 | −0.1 | −0.6 | 0.3 |
| Nonfuel exporters | 5.4 | 6.1 | 4.6 | 4.6 | 2.7 | 2.5 | 3.0 | 5.5 | 4.8 | 4.6 | 4.8 |
| Other countries[c] | 6.2 | 4.8 | 2.1 | 3.0 | 1.9 | 2.8 | 4.3 | 3.4 | 3.0 | 3.8 | … |

[a]Real GDP (or GXP) for industrial and developing countries and real net material product (NMP) for other countries. Composites for the country groups are averages of percentage changes for individual countries weighted by the average U.S. dollar value of their respective GDPs (GXPs or NMPs where applicable) over the preceding three years. Because of the uncertainty surrounding the valuation of the composite NMP of the other countries, they have been assigned—somewhat arbitrarily—a weight of 15 percent in the calculation of the growth of world output. Excluding China prior to 1978.

[b]Compound annual rate of change.

[c]The U.S.S.R. and other countries of Eastern Europe that are not members of the Fund.

Source: International Monetary Fund, World Economic Outlook (Washington D.C.: International Monetary Fund, 1986), p.4.

**The High-Case Scenario**   In this scenario it is assumed that the industrial countries would follow policies that would capitalize on the stimulus that is generated by recent developments in the world economy. Such policies call for (1) reducing price distortions, (2) employing stable monetary and fiscal policies, (3) introducing more flexibility into the world market, and (4) reducing trade restrictions. If these policies are followed, it is speculated that the real gross domestic product (GDP) of the industrial countries would grow by an average annual rate of 4.3 percent. For LDCs the same rate is expected to be 5.9 percent.

**The Low-Case Scenario**   In the low-case scenario, it is assumed that the industrialized countries would follow policies that would dissipate the stimulus that is generated by recent developments in the world economy. In this case, it is predicted that the real GDP of the industrial countries would grow by an annual average rate of 2.5 percent. For LDCs the same rate would be expected to be 4.0 percent.[23]

## The Long Run

It is anticipated that the speed of the industrialization and innovation process in the world will accelerate in the next quarter of a century. This process is expected to entirely change the global industrial picture, as traditional industries move from advanced countries to China and to LDCs, such as Brazil, India, Mexico, and South Korea.

   Today, the availability of cheap labor, the accessibility of capital, and the narrowing of the technological gap between the advanced countries and LDCs have enabled several LDCs to produce goods more cheaply than the advanced countries. The emergence of LDCs in industries such as automobile manufacturing, consumer electronic assembling, light aircraft manufacturing, and steel production has already changed the nature of competition in the world, and this trend is expected to continue. It is forecast that LDCs will account for 25 percent of the world's industrial value added by the year 2000, as compared with only 12.5 percent in 1970. In the meantime, it is predicted that the share of advanced countries will fall from 66 percent to 33 percent in this time period. It is expected that the advanced countries' leading industries will be composed of a new "electronics complex," which will be global from the beginning. Unlike the old industries that are resource intensive, these new industries will be knowledge and service intensive. Such a characteristic will make these industries extremely dependent upon technological innovation, changing the nature of competition in the international market.[24]

## INTERNATIONAL COOPERATION AND THE FUTURE

Given the controversial nature of MNCs, an international mechanism is needed to resolve problems arising from the operation of these corporations. As of the late 1980s, some of these problems have been referred to existing international organizations, such as the World Health Organization, the United Nations Conference on Trade and Development (UNCTAD), and General Agreement on Tariffs and Trade (GATT). However, because these organizations deal with very specific issues that fall within their special jurisdiction, an overall treatment of MNC-related problems has not been possible. In recognition of such a deficiency in 1975, the United Nations set up a commission on transnational corporations and a center on transnational corporations. Together, the commission and the center became active in collecting information, in encouraging research on MNCs, and, as we explained in Chapter 19, in preparing a code of conduct for MNCs. The future of these organizations depends on close cooperation between different nations.[25] Fortunately, beginning in 1985, there have been signs of international cooperation in resolving the world economic problems.

An important event in 1985 was the meeting of the five largest industrial countries (Canada, England, West Germany, Japan, and the United States) in New York to pursue policies aimed at combating protectionism, reducing exchange rate misalignment, and promoting convergence of policies. Their actions are indicative of their attempts to increase mutual understanding and policy interaction aimed at internationally consistent policies.

Another major development in international cooperation in recent years is the so-called debt initiative introduced by the secretary of the U.S. Treasury in October 1985. This initiative emphasized the significance of cooperation between indebted countries, multilateral development banks, commercial banks, industrialized countries, and the IMF in resolving the debt crisis of the LDCs.[26]

Given all these developments, one can hope for a more promising future with regard to international cooperation.

## INTERNATIONAL MANAGEMENT AND THE FUTURE

The manager of an MNC in the future will have to deal with an organizational structure that is more complex than the organizational structure of today. Some of the major factors that contribute to this complexity are the following:

1. The increasing scarcity of natural resources, causing higher costs for materials and for energy.
2. The increasing competition between MNCs from the United States, Western Europe, Japan, and the Third World.
3. The growing demand by the LDCs for technology transfer, labor training, management know-how, and capital.
4. The growing skepticism of host and home countries about the benefits of MNCs from a societal point of view.
5. The quest for individual participation in the decision-making process requiring MNC managers to share their power with others, while maintaining effective control of these corporations.
6. The increasing pressure from different special interest groups, such as

labor unions, environmentalists, host and home governments, consumers, social interest groups, and others.

7. The growing public pressure on MNCs for more social responsibility, more disclosure of information, and more accountability to the societies in which they operate.

8. The growing interdependence of the global economy and the growing vulnerability of MNCs to economic and political instability.

9. The increasing rate of technological change and the increasing widespread use of computers in different business activities, producing constant change in the nature of production, employment, and competition in the world.

10. The changing patterns of age distribution in the world, that is, the increasing numbers of young people in the LDCs as compared with the advanced nations.

Given the above factors, new and greater demands will be placed on MNCs' managers. To deal with the increasing scarcity of natural resources in the next few decades, the manager of an MNC needs: (1) to move toward cheaper and more readily available raw materials, (2) to use those technologies that economize on the exploitation of scarce resources, (3) to enhance efforts in discovering new raw materials, (4) to find new sources of old materials, (5) to increase the recycling of used materials, and (6) to expand the development of by-products.

With increasing competition in the world, and the awareness in many LDCs of the consequences of MNC investment in their countries, the external affairs responsibilities of MNC managers continue to grow. This requires that managers develop skills for potential diplomatic, political, and technical negotiations. It will also necessitate a greater understanding of the cultural elements that shape each specific host country. This is especially important because it is expected that the number of joint venture firms will increase in the future.

A significant issue that the future U.S. manager will continue to grapple with is the question of productivity. In the late 1980s the United States has been suffering from a budget deficit, a trade imbalance, and the loss of competitiveness in the world market. Many observers believe that the solution to these problems is a surge in productivity. This, in turn, will depend on new investments in plants, equipment, technology, and education.[27]

It is believed by some that U.S. manufacturing companies should become more aggressive in the export market and spend a higher percentage of their budget on research that leads to newer and more sophisticated products. West Germany is cited as a good example of a country that has been successful in utilizing existing technology to support its basic industry. West Germany's commitment to quality and technology, manifest in its new products and new production techniques, has given it a competitive edge in the world market. Three companies that are cited as examples of West Germany's success in heavy industry are Bayer, for its emphasis on research; VW, for its robotics; and Kuerschner, for its commitment to the export market.[28]

On a positive note, there are now signs that some of the major U.S. manufacturers are aware of their problems and are regaining sales from foreign rivals by raising quality, cutting costs, and improving labor relations.[29]

## CORPORATE SOCIAL RESPONSIBILITY AND THE FUTURE

Corporate social responsibility is the expectation that stems from the transactions between a corporation and society. It represents a significant factor that affects the successful operation of a business. Although economically speaking the principal objective of a business is to maximize profit, such a practice is constrained by different social values, such as the desire for safer products and a cleaner environment. Any disregard or negligence for such values would have a significant negative impact on the company's reputation and may lead to expensive law-suits. An example of such a negative impact is seen in the 1984 Union Carbide accident in Bhopal, India, which was discussed in Chapter 19. Later, in 1985, a similar chemical leak from a Union Carbide plant in West Virginia hospitalized 135 workers. These incidents have outraged the world and have seriously damaged Union Carbide's reputation. It has also subjected the firm to costly lawsuits and a fine imposed by the U.S. Occupational Safety and Health Administration.[30]

In a more recent example, Chrysler Corporation was indicted in June 1987 by the U.S. government for selling as new 60,000 cars and trucks that had really been driven, in some cases up to 400 miles, with their odometers disconnected. To regain consumers' confidence, the company decided to extend the warranty on those cars and replace those that were damaged during testing, but were sold as new. Although Chrysler has not commented on the cost of this program it has admitted that the practice was "just dumb" and has promised that it would not happen again.[31]

In addition to its ideological and psychological benefit, corporate social responsibility is today considered good business practice because it represents good public relations. Many MNCs, such as GM, are well aware of this fact, and they have begun representing themselves as public service institutions that are as interested in public service as in profit.

In addition to labor unions, environmentalists, and consumer advocates, some academicians have also blamed corporations for seeking profit while ignoring their social responsibilities. *Corporate Violence: Injury and Death for Profit* presents the public controversy and outrage over the actual harms and injuries that have resulted from business misconduct. Among the examples cited in this book of faulty products and practices are the Ford Pinto, the Dalkon Shield, various unapproved drugs, and the existence of hazardous working conditions in coal mines, cotton mills, and chemical plants. The editor discusses the concept of "corporate violence" as being less present, but just as significant, in the public mind as common street crime.[32]

If our corporations remain in the future as powerful as they are today, one can expect a greater confrontation between MNCs and society in the future.

One can also expect that the intensity of these confrontations will increase as more people will be affected by endeavors of MNCs to spread out, to employ new technology, to enhance production, and to diversify their operations into new areas such as the agrobusiness.

To minimize social confrontation in the future, the manager of an MNC should be more sensitive to social issues, develop products that are safer, and attend to the public demand for a cleaner environment. This means that the future manager should allocate a relatively higher portion of the corporate budget to research and development and to technological innovations that will protect the environment and lead to safer products. The difficult problem for managers in the future will be finding a reasonable trade-off between producing a good at a reasonable cost and fulfilling the MNC's social responsibilities. For example, the addition of air bags to automobiles will make them safer, but it will also increase production costs. Placing electrical generating plants away from urban areas make them safer, while adding to the cost of electric transformation. Finding the right trade-off between cost and environmental protection and consumer safety is an issue that must be settled in the context of MNC cost constraints and the necessity for corporate social responsibility.

## SUMMARY

1. The major factors that affect international business are (a) the availability and the growth of human and nonhuman resources, (b) the efficiency by which these resources are employed in the production process, and (c) the means by which producers and consumers are brought together.
2. According to the Malthusian theory, unchecked population growth would increase at a geometric ratio, while food supply would increase at an arithmetic ratio. Thus, unchecked population growth would have increased 512 times after 225 years, but the food supply would have increased only 10 times during this same period. There are positive checks and preventive checks to population growth.
3. It is estimated that the world population will reach 6,530 million by the year 2000. Most of the population growth will occur in LDCs rather than in the advanced industrialized countries. Along with population growth, urbanization is also expected to continue, especially in the LDCs.
4. Market sizes, compositions, and locations will shift for MNCs as a result of future population trends.
5. Most of the studies on natural resources warn us of possible shortages in the future; however, these shortages may be ameliorated by (a) the future of space technology, (b) the availability of resources from the ocean, and (c) an unexpected breakthrough in technology.
6. Although no one disagrees that there are definite limits to the Earth's capacity to produce food, world hunger can be diminished by the optimum use of the Earth's resources.
7. Capital is a key factor of production that is mainly concentrated in advanced countries. Many LDCs have turned to the advanced countries and their MNCs to provide them with badly needed capital.
8. The external debt problem of the LDCs, which has been worsening over time,

amounts to about $800 billion in the late 1980s. This problem has had significant impact on MNCs.

9. Problems are expected to accompany technological progress in the future. They will involve (a) the adjustment of social systems to the speed of technological change, (b) the increase in environmental pollution, and (c) the increase in the gap between advanced countries and LDCs in per capita consumption.

10. Future technological development will see innovation in four areas: (a) electronics, (b) ocean resources, (c) energy, and (d) biotechnology.

11. The most recent developments in the world economy have been the decline of oil prices, the decline of real interest rates, and the curbing of inflation.

12. In the intermediate run (the next decade) it is predicted that those oil-producing nations that are heavily dependent on oil exports will experience financial problems. LDCs will face difficulties that hinder their economic development.

13. In predicting the future of the economy in the next decade, the World Bank provides us with two scenarios: the high-case scenario and the low-case scenario.

14. In the high-case scenario, it is assumed that industrial countries will follow policies that call for (a) reducing price distortions, (b) employing stable monetary and financial policies, (c) introducing more flexibility into the world market, and (d) reducing trade restrictions.

15. The low-case scenario predicts a higher rate of growth (4 percent) for the GDPs of the LDCs, as compared with advanced countries, which will have a lower rate of GDP growth (2.5 percent).

16. In the long run, it is expected that the global industrial picture will change, as traditional industries move from advanced countries to LDCs. It is expected that the advanced countries' leading industries will be composed of a new "electronic complex," which will be global from its beginning.

17. Since 1985 two important events have signaled the increase in international cooperation in resolving world economic problems: (a) the meeting of the five largest industrial countries in New York and (b) the debt initiative aimed at reducing LDC debt introduced by the U.S. secretary of the Treasury.

18. As listed in this chapter, there are a number of factors that will contribute to the complexity of the management of MNCs in the future. These factors place new and greater demands on the managers of MNCs.

19. To deal with the scarcity of natural resources in the future, the manager of an MNC will need to (a) move toward cheaper and more readily available raw materials, (b) use those technologies that economize on the employment of scarce resources, (c) enhance efforts in discovering new materials, (d) increase the recycling of used materials, and (e) expand the development of by-products.

20. If our MNCs remain as powerful as they are today, one should expect a greater confrontation between these corporations and society in the future.

21. To minimize confrontations with society in the future the manager of an MNC should be more sensitive to environmental issues and develop products that are safer and are more conducive to a clean environment.

## QUESTIONS

21.1 Discuss the future of natural resources. What is the consensus regarding the availability of these resources in the future? What are the great unknowns regarding these resources? Given answers to the previous two questions, what does the manager of an MNC need to do? Explain.

**21.2** Discuss the future of capital in the world. Where is most of the capital expected to concentrate? What major problem will the LDCs continue to experience in the future regarding capital, and what is being done about it? What will be the impact of this problem on an MNC? Is there any consensus among financial experts regarding this problem? Explain.

**21.3** How can an MNC's manager cope with the increasing complexity of managerial tasks in the future? Explain.

**21.4** Discuss the social responsibility of an MNC as it relates to the future. What major groups have put pressure on MNCs to be socially responsible? Why does an MNC's manager have to be concerned about the social responsibility issue? What should a manager of an MNC do in order to minimize social confrontation in the future?

**21.5** Given the abundance of labor in LDCs, what major factors do you think will contribute to further expansion of the MNCs into these countries?

**21.6** What major demands do you think will be placed upon future managers of MNCs?

**21.7** As the future population projections indicate, it is estimated that most of the population growth will occur in LDCs. What do you think are the implications of these projections for the advanced countries and the MNCs? What do you think an advanced country like the United States should do in order to ease the burden of a shrinking labor force in the future?

## NOTES

1. The World Bank, *The World Development Report 1984* (New York: Oxford University Press, 1984), Table 1, pp. 192–193.
2. Ibid., p. 100.
3. Alfred Sauvy, *Zero Growth* (Oxford: Basil Blackwell & Mott, 1975), p. 98.
4. "British Dearth: Some Thinkers Expect Population to Drop and Trouble to Result," *The Wall Street Journal,* 18 June 1987, p. 1.
5. D. Meadow, et al. *The Limits to Growth* (New York: Universe Books, 1972).
6. Council on Environmental Quality and the Department of State, *The Global 2000 Report to the President: Entering the Twenty-First Century,* 3 vols. (Washington, D.C.: U.S. Government Printing Office, 1980), Chap. 13.
7. George McGovern, ed., *Food and Population: The World in Crisis* (New York: Arno Press, 1975), p. 146.
8. As calculated by the authors from the statistical tables provided by The World Bank, *World Development Report 1986* (New York: Oxford University Press, 1986), pp. 154–157.
9. William A. Dymsza, "Trends in Multinational Business and Global Environments: A Perspective," *Journal of International Business Studies,* 15 (Winter 1984): 25–46.
10. Ibid.
11. Organization for Economic Cooperation and Development, *Interfuture* (Paris: 1979), p. 113.
12. *The Futurist,* 20 (November/December 1986): 60.
13. "Technology and the Changing World of Work," *The Futurist,* 18 (April 1984): 61–66.
14. "Technology," *The Futurist,* 20 (July/August 1986): 36.

15. "Search for New Drugs Focuses on Organism Under the Sea," *The Wall Street Journal,* 24 July 1987, p. 19.

16. World Resources Institute and the International Institute for Environment and Development in collaboration with the United Nations Environment Programme, *World Resources 1988-89* (New York: Basic Books, 1988), pp. 124–125.

17. "Technology," *The Futurist,* 20 (July/August 1986): 36.

18. Eric K. Clemons and F. Warren McFarlen, "Telecom: Hook Up or Lose Out," *Harvard Business Review,* 64 (July/August 1986): 91–97.

19. "Technology and the Changing World of Work," *The Futurist* 18 (April 1984): 61–66.

20. "World Trends and Forecasts: Transportation," *The Futurist* 20 (November/December 1986): 40.

21. "An Airplane You Can Keep in Your Garage," *The Futurist* 20 (January/February 1986): 45–46.

22. Atlantic-Pacific Interoceanic Commission, "Interoceanic Canal Studies 1970" (Washington, D.C., 1970), pp. 4–7.

23. The World Bank, *World Development Report 1986,* Chap. 1.

24. Franklin P. Root, "Some Trends in the World Economy and Their Implications for International Business," *Journal of International Business Studies* (Winter 1984): 19–23.

25. John H. Dunning, *International Production and the Multinational Enterprise* (London: Allen & Unwin, 1981), Chap. 15.

26. International Monetary Fund, *World Economic Outlook* (Washington, D.C.: International Monetary Fund, April 1986), pp. 17–18.

27. Mobil Corporation, "Toward a More Competitive America," Mobil Corporation, 1987.

28. Ibid., pp. 1, 22.

29. "U.S. Auto Makers Get Chance to Regain Sales from Foreign Rivals," *The Wall Street Journal,* 23 April 1987, pp. 1, 12.

30. "Union Carbide Faces Fine of $1.4 Million on Safety Violations," *The New York Times,* 2 April 1986, pp. A-1, A-15.

31. "Lee Iacocca Calls Odometers Policy 'Dumb'," *The Wall Street Journal,* 2 July 1987, p. 2.

32. Stuart L. Hill, ed., *Corporate Violence: Death and Injury for Profit.* Totowa, N.J.: Rowman and Littlefield, 1987.

## SUGGESTED READINGS

Amara, C., and Andrew J. Lipinski. *Business Planning for an Uncertain Future: Scenarios and Strategies.* New York: Pergamon Press, 1982.

Council on Environmental Quality and the Department of State. *The Global 2000 Report to the President: Entering the Twenty-first Century,* 3 vols. Washington, D.C.: U.S. Government Printing Office, 1980.

Drucker, Peter. *Managing in Turbulent Times.* New York: Harper & Row, 1980.

Dunning, John H. *International Production and the Multinational Enterprise.* London: Allen & Unwin, 1981, Chap. 15.

Dymsza, William A. "The Education and Development of Managers for the Future Decades." *Journal of International Business Studies,* 13 (Winter 1982): 9–18.

————. "Trends in Multinational Business and Global Environments: A Perspective." *Journal of International Business Studies,* 15 (Winter 1984): 25–46.

*The Futurist.* Bethesda, Md.: World Future Society (the most recent issue).

Gluck, Frederick. "Global Competition in 1980s." *Journal of Business Strategy,* 3 (Spring 1983): 22–27.

Hills, Stuart L., ed. *Corporate Violence: Injury and Death for Profit.* Totowa, N.J.: Rowman and Littlefield, 1987.

International Monetary Fund, *World Economic Outlook.* Washington, D.C.: International Monetary Fund (the most recent issue).

Kerr, Clark. *The Future of Industrial Societies.* Cambridge, Mass.: Harvard University Press, 1983.

Leontief, Wassily W. "The World Economy of the Year 2000." *Scientific American* (September 1980): 207–231.

McGovern, George, ed. *Food and Population: The World in Crisis.* New York: Arno Press, 1975.

Meadow, D., et al. *The Limits to Growth.* New York: Universe Books, 1972.

Ricks, David S. "International Business Research: Past, Present and Future." *Journal of International Business Studies,* 16 (Summer 1985): 1–3.

Root, Franklin R. "Some Trends in the World Economy and Their Implications for International Business." *Journal of International Business Studies* (Winter 1984): 19–23.

Sauvy, Alfred. *Zero Growth.* Oxford: Basil Blackwell & Mott, 1975.

Starchild, Adam, ed. *Business in 1990: A Look to the Future.* Seattle, Wash.: University Press of the Pacific, 1979.

The World Bank. *The World Development Report.* Washington, D.C.: International Monetary Fund (the most recent issue).

# Case IV:1

# Union Carbide and
# the Bhopal Accident*

## INTRODUCTION

Union Carbide is a long-established MNC that has many subsidiaries across the globe. It produces a diverse range of materials, from batteries to plastic bags, with the emphasis on the production of plastics and chemicals. This wide range of products has made this large organization a very stable company in the international market. Since 1984, however, there has been a change in Union Carbide's stability. This is mostly due to a severe chemical accident that occurred in Bhopal, India, in early December of 1984.

## HISTORY

The corporation's history has been one of consistent increases in production and in rapid diversification. Union Carbide Corporation was incorporated in 1917 with the name Union Carbide and Carbon Corporation.[1] Management soon realized its growth potential, and decided to go abroad to get needed materials and technology. Gradually Union Carbide became established in almost every area of the world. Today, the corporation has over 99,000 employees, working in 700 factories, mills, and labs in over 35 countries.[2]

Beginning in the late 1970s business started to slow down for the large corporation. In an effort to restore profit levels to where they had been in the early 1970s, Union Carbide tried to diversify its operation (like many other large chemical corporations had done), but this time it did not work.[3] It then decided to decrease diversification and to emphasize the production of chemicals, plastics, and gas—the products which had been most profitable.[4] In 1980 it sold two of its subsidiaries, Jaques Seeds Company and Amchem Products, Inc.[5] It also sold a water treatment business and a metals business.[6] The sale of

*This case was initially written by Julie Green of University of North Texas and Tom Charland of St. Lawrence University as term projects under the supervision of Professors Ebrahimi and Asheghian, who have subsequently revised it for inclusion in this textbook. Copyright © 1989 by Bahman Ebrahimi.

some businesses did not increase profits either, so, in 1984, Union Carbide put emphasis on the sale of patented technology and formed a group to help in the maintenance and the operations of its chemical plants.[7] In December 1984, as we will explain later, a disastrous chemical leak accident occurred at the Union Carbide India, Ltd. subsidiary in Bhopal, India. This incident has damaged the financial stability and public image of the corporation since that date.

## OPERATIONS

Union Carbide organization includes five industry units: petrochemicals; industrial gases; metals and carbon products; consumer products; and technology, services, and specialty products.[8] Chemicals and plastics are the products with which the company has been most competitive, but in the late 1980s those industry segments have not been doing so well.

The major competitors of Union Carbide are the big chemical producers. One of these is Rhom and Hass Company, which has 39 chemical plants worldwide. Chevron Chemical, Olin Corporation, Shell Oil, and Dow Chemical are some other major chemical producers that compete against Union Carbide.[9] Another chemical firm that has been in competition with Union Carbide is GAF. GAF is a small but aggressive company. It was going to buy out Union Carbide, sell all of its assets, and start another business with the cash. Union Carbide defended itself by selling its automotive and home products division to First Boston Corporation. It also sold the battery products division to Ralston Purina. The two sales generated over $800 million. This made Union Carbide too expensive for GAF to buy.[10] Although Union Carbide survived the GAF takeover bid, the Bhopal accident still lingers as a problem for the company.

### Union Carbide in India

In 1961 the Indian government wanted to eliminate chronic food shortages, and they felt the production of pesticides and fertilizers would provide more efficient farming.[11] That led to a joint venture between Union Carbide and Union Carbide India Ltd. According to Indian law, Union Carbide was required to engineer, design, build, and operate the Bhopal plant by using local Indian labor, materials, equipment, and staff. Union Carbide India was not controlled by the parent company. There was no monitoring or control of plant safety or of environmental protection measures. The plant was built under India's 1973 Foreign Exchange Regulation Act, which generally limits foreign investors to a 40 percent equity stake in operations in India.[12] At a later date, Union Carbide persuaded the Indian government to let the parent company have a larger stake (50.9% ownership) in the plant because of Union Carbide's large export volume and the technological expertise needed for the operation of the plant. Relations between the town of Bhopal and Union Carbide had always been good since the large corporation had brought jobs, wealth, and many more people to that area of India.

# THE BHOPAL ACCIDENT

## The Problem

During the night of December 3, 1984, methyl-isocyanate (MIC) gas leaked out of the Union Carbide India subsidiary pesticide plant in Bhopal, India. The toxic gas leak initially killed approximately 1,600 people, and as many as 700 more died of aftereffects.[13] Some of the medical problems include lung problems, shortness of breath, depression, eye irritation, and stomach pains. Iswar Dass, the state official in charge of relief efforts, stated that the death toll continues to rise due to the lingering effects of the gas.[14]

The suffering that the Indian people endured caused them to file lawsuits against the American-based Union Carbide Corporation. The major questions to be settled by the lawsuits were the following: (1) Was a Union Carbide engineer responsible for the design of the ill-fated Bhopal subsidiary plant? (2) Did Union Carbide officials know that safety equipment at the plant was not up to par? If so, were steps taken to remedy the problem?[15] The answers to these questions would determine the extent of the liability of Union Carbide in the Bhopal tragedy.

## The Company's Reaction

The immediate problems faced by company executives of Union Carbide as a result of the Bhopal accident required management decisions. Led by Chairman Warren M. Anderson, management had to decide how to help the survivors of Bhopal, how to ensure that this type of accident could never happen again, how to keep up employee morale, how to keep investors' attitudes positive about Union Carbide's financial stability, and how to protect the corporation from undue legal liability.[16] Chairman Anderson and management set a precedent in their handling of the Bhopal incident. As a journalist put it, "How Chairman Anderson and his team deal with the aftereffects will influence managers elsewhere who are imagining the unimaginable happening to them."[17]

On the morning of December 3, 1984, Van Den Ameele, Union Carbide's manager of press relations, and William Lutz, chairman of Union Carbide Eastern, gathered the other senior executives together to give India the quick response it needed to deal with the crisis situation.

The committee decided to immediately send food, shelter, and medical aid to help the survivors. Union Carbide also sent a doctor to India with knowledge of the effects of methyl-isocyanate (MIC) gas. A team of technical advisors was sent to inspect the Bhopal plant and make recommendations. Shortly thereafter, Chairman Warren Anderson flew to Bhopal to see what he could do. He was arrested upon arrival in Bhopal and was then asked to leave the country. Anderson offered the Indian government $1 million in cash for immediate aid, as well as use of the company's guesthouse to house orphans of the tragedy. India refused both gestures.[18] The total immediate relief offered by Union

Carbide to India was about $8 million. India accepted $1 million, but declined the rest because it felt there were too many strings attached to the use of the money. In return for the money, Union Carbide wanted records kept on what the money was used for and who it helped.[19]

While Union Carbide was desperately seeking to deal with the tragic gas leak in Bhopal, back in the United States, the worldwide publicity was taking its toll on Union Carbide as a corporation. Union Carbide stock fell sharply below $33 per share. This made Union Carbide a takeover target. As a result of the stock price fall and the Bhopal accident, Union Carbide reorganized, eliminating 4,500 staff positions. Union Carbide maintains that no one was directly fired as a result of the Bhopal accident.[20]

## Bhopal's Reaction

Union Carbide maintains that there were no U.S. jobs eliminated as a result of the Bhopal accident, but India claims that the world's largest industrial accident touched all but a few lives in Bhopal and has rendered almost the entire population of the city unable to work. There are still many dying from the aftereffects of the gas leak, and at least 60,000 people cannot work a full day because they are disabled.[21]

As to the questions to be settled in the lawsuit, India maintained that a Union Carbide engineer was responsible for the design of the Bhopal plant. The question that must be answered is whether the engineer, L. J. Couvaras, a Union Carbide employee, was under the Indian subsidiary's jurisdiction or whether he was under the jurisdiction of Union Carbide U.S.A.[22]

## The Carbide Strategy of Containment

Union Carbide, faced with a disaster of truly historic proportions which seems to have been caused by its own negligence, adopted a carefully orchestrated strategy of containment. "The objectives of the strategy are clear: downplay the seriousness of the situation, to minimize the adverse impacts, especially on health, and seek to implicate others."[23] It seems that the goal of such strategy was to protect the assets of the company at whatever cost. "It also appears to be a typical, if not standard, industry response to situations in which industry actions have inflicted great personal injury, suffering, and even death on their own workers, users of their products, and residents of communities nearby their industrial installations."[24]

"Life is cheap in India. That, at least, was the foundation of Union Carbide's legal strategy. . . ."[25] If the accident had happened in the United States, the cost of settling lawsuits on behalf of the more than 3,300 who died and the tens of thousands who were injured as a result of this incident might have run into billions of dollars. Such large settlement would have almost surely sent the Connecticut-based multinational company into bankruptcy court.[26]

In India, however, the value of life established by courts is a fraction of the amounts set by the juries in the U.S. courts. That is the main reason for Carbide attempting to move the suits to the Indian courts.

## Settlement Talks

There have been more than 130 lawsuits filed in the United States, and over 2,700 lawsuits filed in India, in connection with the Bhopal tragedy. The United States has tried to consolidate most of the U.S. lawsuits into the court system of New York. India has rejected Union Carbide's offer of $30 million to be paid out over a 30-year period.[27]

One of the main issues has been whether the lawsuits should be be tried in Indian courts or whether they should be tried in American courts. Bud Holman, the chief attorney for Union Carbide, has demanded that the trials be conducted in India because he feels it will be easier to see firsthand the results of the tragic gas leak, to interview witnesses, to inspect documents, and so forth. However, Michael Ciresi, a Minneapolis lawyer hired by the Indian government, has requested that the trials be kept in the United States because U.S. courts offer "the most expeditious hearings."[28]

A brief filed by Union Carbide before Judge Keenan implied that the preferred forum for the trial was the Indian Courts; however, Union Carbide found the Indian courts undesirable as well. Interestingly, Union Carbide could not hope to be clear of the case simply because no court could be found as a suitable forum for the trial. And yet, legal experts believed Union Carbide may have implied just that fact. "Union Carbide, it would appear, finds no court suitable, arguing in fact that it is beyond the law."[29] Ultimately, Judge John Keenan would rule that the United States District Court did not have jurisdiction over the case. The Bhopal accident trial would be moved directly into India's Supreme Court.

After three years to reflect on the problem, Union Carbide has thoroughly investigated the Bhopal accident. It has concluded that a large amount of water was added to the tank which contained the methyl-isocyanate (MIC) gas. It believes that a disgruntled employee deliberately added water to the tank, resulting in the chemical reaction that caused the disaster. Union Carbide will continue to investigate the alleged sabotage, and it has shared the information with the Indian government.[30]

Indian officials have rejected the company's claims of sabotage.[31] The Indian government continues to attack Union Carbide's negligence, wishing to "save face" and not wanting to appear to be "selling out." Both sides have seriously negotiated for an out-of-court settlement. Neither side wishes to endure a lengthy Indian trial, and both sides are afraid of damaging information that the trial would bring out. An out-of-court settlement has been difficult to reach because both sides feel the need to "save face."[32]

## India Settles Lawsuit

On February 14, 1989, the Indian government reached its historical settlement with the Danbury, Connecticut, based Union Carbide. According to the terms of this settlement, which outraged many people, the Indian Supreme Court ordered Union Carbide to pay $470 million in damages to the Indian government on behalf of victims of the Bhopal toxic gas tragedy. As a part of the settlement, all criminal charges and civil suits in India against Union Carbide and Warren Anderson the company's chairman at the time of the accident would be dropped.[33] When the Indian Federal Minister for Industries presented the settlement to the Parliament, opposition members, shouting "Shame, Shame," walked out of the house in protest.[34]

The Indian Supreme Court did not address the issue of whether Union Carbide or the Indian government was to blame for the accident.[35] However, the court did agree to determine how the $470 million settlement would be distributed to the victims. According to the court, Union Carbide is to pay the compensation award to the Indian government. Government officials indicated that the court will decide on the distribution of the award.[36] Many experts, however, believe that the Bhopal victims will get very little of the money. In the past, the Indian government has been accused of corruption and mismanagement of the funds that had been set to aid the victims. Kenneth Ditkowsky, a former Carbide lawyer indicated, "Most of the money will end up in the pockets of Indian government officials."[37]

Many members of the Parliament who belong to the minority Janata Party and the Communist Party and activists on behalf of Bhopal victims believe that the final judgement is an outrage and "ludicrously low."[38] Activists in Bhopal denounced the settlement as the betrayal of the 20,000 victims who still suffer from exposure to the deadly gas.[39]

On February 23, 1989, India's Supreme Court agreed to hear petitions from the activist group, the Association for Socio-Legal Literacy, demanding $600 million in civil liability. Currently, there is confusion as to whether the group wants either an additional $600 million in liability or $130 million added to the current monetary agreement. An Indian Supreme Court lawyer, however, warned the petitioners that the court has issued its order which legally binds all the parties involved and concludes the lawsuit.[40]

Since February of 1989, several other victims' groups and public-interest lawyers also have argued that the settlement is unconstitutional. Surprisingly, the Indian Supreme Court has taken these claims seriously enough to hear their arguments. In July of 1989, the court is expected to rule on these challenges to the settlement. If any of these challenges are considered valid, the settlement may become null and the case open once again.[41]

If the settlement would hold, the financial effects would be minimal on Union Carbide. Of the $470 million, $250 million will be paid by Carbide's insurance company; another $200 million will be paid by a reserve fund which is already established by Union Carbide. Therefore, Union Carbide has to pay the balance of $20 million out of its 1989 revenues. For a company with revenues of just over $8 billion in 1988, this is a very minimal amount.[42]

Many analysts believe that the settlement is psychologically good and financially reasonable for Union Carbide. On February 15, 1989, just one day after the settlement was announced, Carbide stock rose $2 to $31⅛ and was the New York Stock Exchange's most active issue. However, a few analysts think that the settlement could increase Union Carbide's attractiveness as a takeover target.[43]

## CONCLUSION

There is no agreement on the effects and the implications of the settlement to the worst industrial incident in the history. Legal experts cannot agree whether this hybrid settlement actually represents a successful conclusion to the unprecedented tragedy. Unlike earlier attempts to settle this international dispute, which were based on direct U.S.-style payments to the victims, it is not clear who will finally receive the money. The direct payment of damages to the Indian government raises concern over whether the money will reach the victims or whether it will be wasted in the inefficient and sometimes corrupt government bureaucracy.[44]

More fundamentally, it seems that the strategy of containment pursued by Union Carbide as described earlier had worked. The strategy was to value human life based on a Third World rather than a Western standard. The result was to pay about $10,000 per victim of the disastrous methyl isocyanide gas leak.[45] The settlement based on the Third World standard of human life is not even close to tragedies of lesser severity in the Western World. For example, Manville Corp. paid $3 billion to its asbestos victims, and $2.38 billion was paid by A.H. Robins to its Dalkon Shield users.[46] Generally, industry observers and legal experts praise the company's handling of the case. They believe that Robert D. Kennedy, who replaced Anderson as Carbide's chairman, effectively contained the damage from the accident.[47]

A number of analysts consider this case as a test of multinational corporations' social responsibilities in host nations and in industrial disasters. Again there is no agreement on this issue either. A trial lawyer indicated that this accident forced many companies to increase quality control in their foreign plants. He stated that, "Prior to Bhopal, few people thought American parents had to assume the liability for the problems of their subsidiaries. If Bhopal had gone the full route, it would have been interesting to see how that issue would have played out."[48] Another lawyer retained by the Indian government stated that, "This outcome sends a message to the world that these companies are responsible."[49]

Opponents, however, consider the settlement a victory for Union Carbide, and state that the Indian government had "surrendered before the multinational."[50] In the words of David Dembo, of the Bhopal Action Resource Center in New York, "We thought that enough pressure had been mounted in India itself against an inadequate settlement. I guess we were wrong."[51]

Professor Thomas Gladwin of New York University sees the effect of the Bhopal tragedy as relatively fewer plant investments in developing nations and a trend in building "hazardous substance plants in regulatory climates where there are inspections and educated workforce."[52]

## QUESTIONS

1. Why did Union Carbide go international? Explain.
2. How do you describe Union Carbide's management philosophy—centralized or decentralized? Explain.
3. Who do you think is responsible for the Bhopal incident—the engineer who designed the plant, Union Carbide Corporation, or the Indian government? Discuss.
4. Are there any indications that Union Carbide officials knew that the Bhopal plant was unsafe?
5. Should the lawsuits have been tried in American or Indian courts?
6. How has Union Carbide's attitude toward litigation with India changed over time?
7. How has the Bhopal accident affected relations between the United States and India?
8. How can Union Carbide improve its tarnished image?
9. Do you agree with the settlement? Why? Why not?
10. What are the implications of this tragedy and subsequent settlement for MNCs in host nations?

## NOTES

1. *Moody's Industrial Manual,* vol. 2 (New York: Moodys Investors Service, 1986), p. 4519.
2. Ibid., p. 4521.
3. Barry Meter and Ron Winslow, "Union Carbide Faces Difficult Challenge Even Without Bhopal," *The Wall Street Journal,* 27 December 1984, pp. 1, 6.
4. Ibid.
5. *Moody's Industrial Manual,* p. 4519.
6. Ibid.
7. Winslow Meter, "Union Carbide Faces Difficult Challenge," pp. 1, 6.
8. *Moody's Industrial Manual,* p. 4521.
9. Winslow Meter, "Union Carbide Faces Difficult Challenge," pp. 1, 6.
10. Barry Meter, "Carbide to Sell Consumer Lines for $800 Million," *The Wall Street Journal,* 22 April 1986, p. 4.
11. Mark Whittacker, "It Was Like Breathing Fire," *Newsweek,* 17 December 1984, p. 26.
12. Thomas Gladwin, "Bhopal and the Multinational," *The Wall Street Journal,* 16 January 1985, p. 28.
13. M. Miller, "Two Years After Bhopal's Gas Disaster, Lingering Effects Still Plague Its People," *The Wall Street Journal,* 5 December 1986, p. 34.
14. Ibid.
15. B. Meier, "India Says a Union Engineer Was Responsible for Bhopal Site Design," *The Wall Street Journal,* 8 January 1987, p. 10.
16. R. J. Kirkland, Jr., "Union Carbide: Coping with Catastrophe," *Fortune,* 7 January 1985, pp. 50–53.
17. Ibid., p. 50.

18. Ibid., p. 52.
19. L. Helm, "Bhopal, a Year Later: Union Carbide Takes a Tougher Line," *Business Week,* 25 November 1985, pp. 96–101.
20. Ibid., p. 97.
21. Ibid., p. 96.
22. Meier, "India Says a Union Engineer Was Responsible," p. 10.
23. Ward Morehouse and M. Arun Subramaniam, *The Bhopal Tragedy: What Really Happened and What It Means for American Workers and Communities at Risk, A Preliminary Report for the Citizens Commission on Bhopal* (New York: The Council on International and Public Affairs, 1986), pp. 40–41.
24. Ibid.
25. Malcolm Gladwell, "American vs. Indian Value of Life Molded Bhopal Suit Strategy," *Dallas Times Herald,* 19 February, 1989, p. A-6.
26. Ibid.
27. Helm, "Bhopal, a Year Later," p. 97.
28. J. Nolan, "Insurers Bear Brunt of Bhopal," *The Journal of Commerce,* 6 January 1986, pp. 1, 12.
29. Ward Morehouse and M. Arun Subramaniam, *The Bhopal Tragedy,* pp. 81–83.
30. Wil Lepkowski, "Efforts Toward Settlement Pick Up Steam," *Chemical and Engineering News,* 15 September 1986, pp. 14–15.
31. Meier, "India Says a Union Engineer Was Responsible," p. 10.
32. Lepkowski, "Efforts Toward Settlement," p. 14.
33. Sanjay Hazarika, "Bhopal Payments by Union Carbide Set at $470 Million," *The New York Times,* 15 February 1989, p. 1.
34. "More Sought in Bhopal Settlement," *Dallas Times Herald,* 24 February 1989, p. A-8.
35. Sanjay Hazarika, "Bhopal Payments."
36. Sheila Tefft and Siddharth Dube, "Settlement Is Reached on Bhopal," *The Washington Post,* 15 February 1989, p. 1.
37. Wayne Beissert and Andrea Stone, "Lawyers: Bhopal Victims to Get Little," *USA Today,* 15 February 1989, p. 1.
38. Paul Richter, "$470-Million Settlement for Bhopal OKd," *Los Angeles Times,* 15 February 1989, p. 1.
39. Ibid, p. 13.
40. "More Sought in Bhopal Settlement."
41. Stephen J. Adler, "New Litigation Is Imperiling Bhopal-Disaster Settlement," *The Wall Street Journal,* 22 June 1989, pp. B1, B4.
42. Malcolm Gladwell, "Settlement Won't Hurt Carbide: Insurer, Fund Will Pay Most of Costs," *The Washington Post,* 15 February 1989, pp. D1, D5.
43. Andrea Stone, "Union Carbide up $2 after Bhopal Settlement," *USA Today,* 15 February 1989, p. 3B.
44. Malcolm Gladwell, "American vs. Indian Value of Life Molded Bhopal Suit Strategy."
45. Ibid, p. A-7.
46. Wayne Beissert and Andrea Stone, "Lawyers: Bhopal Victims to Get Little," p. 4A.
47. Malcolm Gladwell, "Settlement Won't Hurt Carbide: Insurer, Fund Will Pay Most of Costs," p. D5.
48. Stephen Lebaton, "Bhopal Outcome: Trial Is Avoided," *The New York Times,* 15 February 1989, p. D3.
49. Paul Richter, "$470-Million Settlement for Bhopal OKd," p. 13.

50. Stephen Lebatan, "Bhopal Outcome: Trial Is Avoided."

51. Malcolm Gladwell, "Settlement Won't Hurt Carbide: Insurer, Fund Will Pay Most of Costs," p. D5.

52. James Flanigan, "Bhopal a Hard Lesson in Value of Safety Rules," *Los Angeles Times,* 15 February 1989, pp. IV-1, IV-9.


## SUGGESTED READINGS

Adler, Stephen J. "New Litigation Is Imperiling Bhopal-Disaster Settlement." *The Wall Street Journal,* 22 June 1989, pp. B1, B4.

Beissert, Wayne, and Andrea Stone. "Lawyers: Bhopal Victims to Get Little." *USA Today,* 15 February 1989, p. 1.

Eichenwald, Kurt. "Lead Lawyers for Carbide Relieved by End of Case." *The New York Times,* 15 February 1989, p. D3.

Flanigan, James. "Bhopal a Hard Lesson in Value of Safety Rules." *Los Angeles Times,* 15 February 1989, pp. IV-1, IV-9.

Gladwell, Malcolm. "American vs. Indian Value of Life Molded Bhopal Suit Strategy." *Dallas Times Herald,* 19 February, 1989, p. A-6.

———. "Settlement Won't Hurt Carbide: Insurer, Fund Will Pay Most of Costs." *The Washington Post,* 15 February 1989, pp. D1, D5.

Hazarika, Sanjay. "Bhopal Payments by Union Carbide Set at $470 Million." *The New York Times,* 15 February 1989, p. 1.

Helm, L. "Bhopal, a Year Later: Union Carbide Takes a Tougher Line." *Business Week,* 25 November 1985, pp. 96–101.

Hicks, Jonathan P. "After Bhopal, the Company Rebuilds." *The New York Times,* 15 February 1989, p. D3.

"Indian Court Orders Bhopal Settlement," *Dallas Times Herald,* 14 February 1989, pp. A-1, A-8.

Kirkland, R. I., Jr. "Union Carbide: Coping with Catastrophe." *Fortune,* 7 January 1985, pp. 50–53.

Lebatan, Stephen. "Bhopal Outcome: Trial Is Avoided." *The New York Times,* 15 February 1989, p. D3.

Meier, B. "India Says a Union Engineer Was Responsible for Bhopal Site Design." *The Wall Street Journal,* 8 January 1987, pp. 10.

Miller, M. "Two Years After Bhopal's Gas Disaster—Lingering Effects Still Plague Its People." *The Wall Street Journal,* 5 December 1986, p. 34.

Morehouse, Ward, and M. Arun Subramaniam. *The Bhopal Tragedy: What Really Happened and What It Means for American Workers and Communities at Risk, A Preliminary Report for the Citizens Commission on Bhopal.* New York: The Council on International and Public Affairs, 1986.

"More Sought in Bhopal Settlement." *Dallas Times Herald,* 24 February 1989, p. A-8.

Nolan, J. "Insurers Bear Brunt of Bhopal." *The Journal of Commerce,* 6 January 1986, pp. 1, 12.

Richter, Paul. "$470-Million Settlement for Bhopal OKd." *Los Angeles Times,* 15 February 1989, p. 1.

Ritcher, Paul. "Settlement Leaves Bhopal Mystery Unresolved." *Los Angeles Times,* 15 February 1989, p. IV-1.

Stone, Andrea. "Union Carbide up $2 after Bhopal Settlement." *USA Today,* 15 February 1989, p. 3B.

Tefft, Sheila, and Siddharth Dube. "Settlement Is Reached on Bhopal." *The Washington Post,* 15 February 1989, p. 1.

Tripathi, S. "After Bhopal." *Canadian Forum,* December 1985, pp. 12–14.

Varma, Vijaya Shankar. "Bhopal: The Unfolding of a Tragedy." *Alternatives,* July 1986, pp. 133–145.

Visvanathan, Shiv. "Bhopal: The Imagination of a Disaster." *Alternatives,* July 1986, pp. 147–165.

## Case IV:2

# "It's Not a Car, It's a Volkswagen": VW and the Global Automobile Industry*

## INTRODUCTION

Volkswagen (VW) represents the success story of a small German car manufacturer making its way in the postwar international automobile market. The company's most famous and popular car—the Beetle—has been a main staple in the automobile market over the last 40 years. The VW Beetle, the "Bug," with its unique rear engine and funny look, has been driven by many people all over the world, and this car has been a major force in the West German, European, and world car markets since its inception in 1938. In the last ten years, however, VW has been plagued by many problems, including declining sales.

## HISTORY

The history of VW is unique in the automobile industry. The idea for the car was conceived in the 1930s during one of Europe's worst economic depressions.

Shortly after he was elected as the Chancellor of Germany in 1933, Adolf Hitler opened the Berlin Automobile Exhibition. During the opening ceremonies, he stated that his government would support any plan that would ensure the production of an inexpensive car for the German people. During the 1935 exhibition, an outstanding automobile designer, Dr. Ferdinand Porche, revealed the initial plans for a Volkswagen—"the people's car" and he indicated that the prototypes would be tested within four months.[1]

The dream, however, was not realized immediately because of the start of

*This case was initially written by Roy Snodgrass and Andrea Lanier of University of North Texas as term projects under the supervision of Professor Ebrahimi. They have subsequently revised it for inclusion in this textbook. Copyright © 1989 by Bahman Ebrahimi.

World War II. Instead, Porche's plans were used for the production of military transportation. During the war the Wolfsburg factory, where these vehicles were built, became a target for Allied bombers.[2] After the war, workers started producing cars from the parts that remained in the bombed building. Soon, the plant was reconstructed, and it was initially controlled by the British. Later, it was jointly owned by the Federal Republic of West Germany and the landowners of Lower Saxony.[3]

Soon production picked up, and VW became one of the most successful car manufacturers in the world. VW and its success was partially responsible for Germany's economic recovery after the war.[4]

In 1949, VW started exporting its Beetle to the United States. In addition, it started expanding its production facilities by opening additional plants in Germany and abroad. During its first 20 years, the company produced only the Beetle and a transport van, and, through this time, the body style of the Beetle remained almost the same. The expansion into the United States began very slowly. However, by 1969, VW was selling over 500,000 cars in the United States, and the U.S. market represented 70 percent of VW's worldwide sales.[5]

The VW Beetle is a remarkable vehicle in its class. Backed by unique technical developments which were incorporated continuously into new models, it has already taken a prominent place in the history of automobiles. Originally designed as a plain utility model, the Beetle has been used as a military vehicle and has seen the roughest possible use. Yet developments since the war have given it characteristics that have made it commercially competitive.[6]

A combination of a unique business attitude with a successful car has given Volkswagen a successful past. There are no secrets in the design, the production, or the sales methods and the political background that once overshadowed the VW has already become history.[7]

By the spring of 1987, VW and its subsidiaries reached the 50 million car production mark. No other European auto manufacturer has achieved this level of production. Although the Beetle, which accounted for almost half of this production mark, left the European market in 1985, its successor, the Golf, is already filling the shoes of its predecessor.[8]

According to VW's chairman of the Board of Management, Carl H. Hahn, "We are democratizing progress by offering solutions of a technical effectiveness no less perfect than those costing a great deal more. . . ."[9] With this philosophy the next 50 million Volkswagens should be no less successful than the first."[10]

## PRODUCT STRATEGY

Volkswagen was basically single-minded in its product strategy. The general concept of VW had an unlimited market potential, and as long as sales were increasing, VW refused to introduce any new vehicle that fell outside the concept of its basic design. The company's product strategy was to maximize use of the existing production facilities and to employ a program of continuous modification of technical details that could be incorporated into vehicles produced several years earlier. This strategy proved to be the formula for success in the following years.[11]

## VOLKSWAGEN OF AMERICA

In 1949 the first two Volkswagens were officially imported into the United States. Six years later, Volkswagen of America (VWOA) was formed with three employees as a wholly owned subsidiary of Volkswagenwerk AG, Wolfsburg, West Germany. VW of America was also established as the original official importer of Porsche and Audi vehicles in 1969. In August 1984, VWOA ceased importing Porsche vehicles, but it still imports and distributes VW and Audi products.[12]

Up until 1978, all VWs sold in the United States were built elsewhere. As the German mark and American dollar approached parity, along with the two countries' wage levels, it became apparent that a U.S. plant was needed for VW to remain competitive in the United States. As the first American-built VW left the assembly line in 1978,[13] VW became the first foreign automobile manufacturer to assemble autos in the United States.[14]

## GLOBAL AUTO INDUSTRY

### Production

A record 46.1 million vehicles were produced in the world automobile industry in 1987, which was a 1 percent increase over the record set in 1986.[15]

Table IV:2.1 shows the world's major car, truck, and bus production for 1985 through 1987.

Western European total production rose 6 percent to 14.6 million cars, further consolidating its position as the leader in the world automotive industry with 31 percent of the world automobile production. The West German automobile industry made a significant contribution to expansion by increasing its output by 3 percent, manufacturing 4.6 million vehicles. Italy, Spain, and France also increased their vehicle production. The United States produced 12.5 million vehicles. Japan's total production stayed at the previous year's level of 12.2 million vehicles.[16]

The Volkswagen Group achieved an increase in world sales as a result of favorable economic conditions and a wide range of models that were developed to fit most consumer and market needs. Exports to North America and West European countries showed above-average growth for VW. The plants in West Germany had such an increase in market demand that some plants suffered from bottlenecks caused by excessive demand for production.[17] However, by 1986, VW had partially solved this problem by incorporating various staffing measures, which included making work time more flexible.[18]

# Table IV:2.1 1985–1987 MAJOR WORLD CAR, TRUCK, AND BUS PRODUCTION

| Leading countries | 1987 Cars | 1987 Truck-Bus | 1987 Total | 1986 Cars | 1986 Truck-Bus | 1986 Total | 1985 Cars | 1985 Truck-Bus | 1985 Total |
|---|---|---|---|---|---|---|---|---|---|
| **North America** | | | | | | | | | |
| U.S.A. | 7,099,829 | 3,825,776 | 10,925,605 | 7,829,249 | 3,505,992 | 11,335,241 | 8,186,034 | 3,467,922 | 11,653,956 |
| Canada | 809,818 | 825,333 | 1,635,151 | 1,061,738 | 792,680 | 1,854,418 | 1,077,932 | 856,178 | 1,934,110 |
| Mexico | 266,142 | 129,116 | 395,258 | 169,567 | 102,601 | 272,168 | 246,960 | 151,232 | 398,192 |
| Total | 8,175,789 | 4,780,225 | 12,956,014 | 9,060,554 | 4,401,273 | 13,461,827 | 9,510,926 | 4,475,332 | 13,986,258 |
| **Western Europe** | | | | | | | | | |
| West Germany | 4,373,629 | 260,444 | 4,634,073 | 4,310,820 | 286,135 | 4,596,955 | 4,166,686 | 279,234 | 4,445,920 |
| France | 3,051,830 | 441,380 | 3,493,210 | 2,773,094 | 421,521 | 3,194,615 | 2,632,366 | 383,740 | 3,016,106 |
| Italy | 1,701,267 | 199,312 | 1,900,579 | 1,652,452 | 178,637 | 1,831,089 | 1,389,156 | 183,751 | 1,572,907 |
| Great Britain | 1,142,985 | 246,727 | 1,389,712 | 1,018,962 | 228,685 | 1,247,647 | 1,047,973 | 265,973 | 1,313,946 |
| Spain | 1,402,574 | 301,899 | 1,704,473 | 1,281,899 | 250,724 | 1,532,623 | 1,230,071 | 187,533 | 1,417,604 |
| Belgium | 1,123,409 | 72,765 | 1,196,174 | 1,021,643 | 68,169 | 1,089,812 | 986,182 | 48,682 | 1,034,864 |
| Sweden | 431,777 | 69,500 | 501,277 | 421,255 | 66,659 | 487,914 | 400,748 | 61,138 | 461,886 |
| Netherlands | 110,000 | 15,000 | 125,000 | 118,976 | 15,416 | 134,392 | 108,083 | 20,893 | 128,976 |
| Portugal | 73,270 | 21,500 | 94,770 | 60,096 | 23,532 | 83,628 | 60,975 | 26,548 | 87,523 |
| Austria | 6,600 | 3,456 | 10,056 | 6,801 | 4,906 | 11,707 | 7,118 | 6,605 | 13,723 |
| Total | 13,417,341 | 1,631,983 | 15,049,324 | 12,665,998 | 1,544,384 | 14,210,382 | 12,029,358 | 1,464,097 | 13,493,455 |
| **Others** | | | | | | | | | |
| Japan | 7,891,087 | 4,358,087 | 12,249,174 | 7,809,809 | 4,450,008 | 12,259,817 | 7,646,816 | 4,624,279 | 12,271,095 |
| U.S.S.R. | 1,329,000 | 940,000 | 2,269,000 | 1,320,000 | 950,000 | 2,270,000 | 1,332,000 | 900,000 | 2,232,000 |
| Brazil | 789,310 | 139,112 | 928,422 | 829,477 | 227,030 | 1,056,507 | 714,175 | 252,533 | 966,708 |
| Australia | 225,180 | 14,400 | 239,580 | 319,200 | 22,404 | 341,604 | 383,763 | 27,569 | 411,332 |
| Poland | 301,000 | 62,220 | 363,220 | 279,600 | 54,000 | 333,600 | 288,624 | 60,822 | 349,446 |
| Czechoslovakia | 171,902 | 50,000 | 221,902 | 175,716 | 52,003 | 227,719 | 183,701 | 51,342 | 235,043 |
| East Germany | 230,000 | 47,000 | 277,000 | 218,256 | 45,300 | 263,556 | 214,000 | 47,795 | 261,795 |
| Yugoslavia | 305,100 | 82,400 | 387,500 | 209,868 | 70,272 | 280,140 | 217,755 | 40,531 | 258,286 |
| Rep. of Korea | 793,125 | 186,614 | 979,739 | 457,383 | 144,163 | 601,546 | 264,458 | 113,704 | 378,162 |
| India | 107,000 | 97,000 | 204,000 | 105,996 | 96,720 | 202,716 | 102,447 | 127,931 | 230,378 |
| Argentina | 158,774 | 34,542 | 193,316 | 137,889 | 32,609 | 170,498 | 113,788 | 23,887 | 137,675 |
| Hungary | — | 16,000 | 16,000 | — | 14,400 | 14,400 | — | 15,000 | 15,000 |
| Taiwan | 174,884 | 49,300 | 224,184 | | | | | | |
| Total | 12,476,362 | 6,076,675 | 18,553,037 | 11,863,194 | 6,158,909 | 18,022,103 | 11,461,527 | 6,285,393 | 17,746,920 |
| Grand Total | 34,069,492 | 12,488,883 | 46,558,375 | 33,589,746 | 12,104,566 | 45,694,312 | 33,001,811 | 12,224,822 | 45,226,633 |

*Note: Above tabulation is based upon production as opposed to assembly, with the exception of Portugal which is partly assembly and partly production. All data are final except the following which are estimated for 1987: Portugal, U.S.S.R., Poland, Czechoslovakia, East Germany, the Netherlands, Yugoslavia, India and Hungary.*

*Source: Ward's Automotive Yearbook (Detroit, Mich.: Ward's Communications, 1988), p. 77.*

Table IV: 2.2   WEST GERMANY CAR AND TRUCK PRODUCTION

| Manufacturer | 1986 | | | 1985 | | |
| --- | --- | --- | --- | --- | --- | --- |
| | Cars | Trucks | Total | Cars | Trucks | Total |
| Auwarter | — | 852 | 852 | — | 820 | 820 |
| BMW | 432,285 | — | 432,285 | 431,085 | — | 431,085 |
| Daimler-Benz | 591,916 | 134,215 | 726,131 | 537,909 | 131,279 | 669,188 |
| Faun | — | 226 | 226 | — | 253 | 253 |
| Ford | 562,253 | — | 562,253 | 505,231 | — | 505,231 |
| IVECO-Magnus | — | 12,650 | 12,650 | — | 10,581 | 10,581 |
| Kassbohrer | — | 2,001 | 2,001 | — | 1,954 | 1,954 |
| MAN | — | 19,916 | 19,916 | — | 18,395 | 18,395 |
| Opel | 897,071 | 28,465 | 925,536 | 903,150 | 34,921 | 938,071 |
| Porsche | 52,939 | — | 52,939 | 54,458 | — | 54,458 |
| Volkswagen | 1,421,629 | 87,810 | 1,509,439 | 1,376,241 | 91,031 | 1,457,272 |
| Audi | 352,735 | — | 352,735 | 358,612 | — | 358,612 |
| Total | 4,310,828 | 286,135 | 4,596,963 | 4,166,686 | 279,234 | 4,445,920 |

Source: Verbank Der Automobilundustrie E.V., as shown in Ward's Automotive Yearbook (Detroit: Mich.: Ward's Communications, 1987), p. 74.

## The West German Auto Industry

The West German auto industry is made of six major manufacturers, including Ford's West German subsidiary, Ford Werke; Volkswagen and its subsidiary, Audi; Daimler-Benz; BMW; Porsche; and General Motor's subsidiary, Opel.

Table IV:2.2 shows the total West German car and truck production in 1986 and 1985. In 1987, total industry output of 4.6 million exceeded the previous year's record production by 1 percent.[19] During 1985, exports accounted for 62.5 percent of the cars produced. Also during the same time period, the industry was employing about 700,000 people. Major foreign competitors in the German markets are France, Great Britain, and Japan.[20]

## The United States Auto Industry

The 1979 energy crisis had a great impact on the U.S. automobile industry. The industry faced intense competition from abroad, an economic recession, and a shifting of consumer demand away from its products. This had devastating effects on the industry. Competition from Japan exposed the shortcomings of the U.S. industry, namely, poor management, noncompetitive products, and high labor costs.

Since 1979 the U.S. auto industry has changed dramatically. It has updated its factories, streamlined its production processes, and restructured its product lines in order to respond to the shift in demand to smaller cars. Also, the auto industry has cut costs and increased productivity. Since 1979, the U.S. auto industry invested $84 billion in plant equipment and special tooling. This enormous outlay in combination with the sales slump of 1980 to 1982 caused severe financial stress. Industry working capital fell from $12.3 billion in 1978 to $0.4 billion by the end of 1982. The financial pressures were not relieved until the return of industry profitability in 1983 and 1984. Although industry profits in 1986 exceeded $7 billion, they were below 1984 and 1985 levels due to the cost of "manufacturer's marketing incentives and the cost of new vehicle introductions by one of the companies."[21]

Meanwhile, total sales of domestic and imported cars and trucks improved from a low of 10.6 million units in 1982 to 12.3 million in 1983, 14.5 million in 1984, 15.7 million in 1985, 16.3 million in 1986, and 15.2 million in 1987.[22]

**Structure** U.S. auto manufacturers are changing in response to competition and challenges in the auto industry. Foreign manufacturers from Yugoslavia, South Korea, and Malaysia have begun to sell subcompacts in the U.S. market, and Japanese manufacturers will soon begin to compete in the mid-size and luxury car market segment. The U.S. companies are using several strategies to position themselves for increased competition, including cost reductions, productivity increases, product quality improvement, and product line enhancement. Furthermore, U.S. car manufacturers and their suppliers are adopting technological developments to improve their competitiveness. These include developments in automotive electronics, plant communications systems, material engineering, and metal working. American producers are revolutionizing the assembly process and manufacturing components through installation of computer-aided design and computer-aided manufacturing processes—CAD/CAM—computerized inventory controls, computer networking, and industrial robotics. In order to be successful in cutting costs over the longer term, the U.S. manufacturers must develop and apply new technologies to auto manufacturing, incorporating product innovations and restructuring organizational and managerial relationships.[23]

**Demand Outlook** Because of demographic trends and increases in ownership and operating costs, growth in the overall automobile market in the U.S. will slow over the long run. The driving age population, which experienced a 2 percent annual growth rate in the 1970s, is expected to grow at an annual rate of 1 percent for the remainder of the 1980s. However, an expected increase in the population between the ages of 25 and 44, the prime auto-buying years, will partially offset this trend.

Other factors affecting demand include the average age of the U.S. car population and vehicle scrappage rates. The average age of cars in use has reached its highest level since 1950, while scrappage rates from 1983 to 1984 reached their lowest levels since the mid-1970s. The combination of both high prices for new and used cars and the increased durability of automobiles have contributed to these trends. Over the next several years, car scrappage rates should rise as replacement demand returns to a more normal level. Replacement demand should account for a large portion of the moderate growth in U.S. car sales forecast through the end of the 1980s.[24]

**Trends** Dramatic changes are taking place as to where the industry will purchase and assemble cars. There are trends toward importing most of the industry's small models. And by 1990, the Japanese will have built 10 plants in the United States, either independently or in conjuncture with U.S. companies, that will produce around 2.5 million vehicles.[25] Furthermore, GM, Ford, and Chrysler are diversifying out of the auto industry and internally restructuring.

U.S. dealers sold 15.2 million domestic and imported cars and trucks in 1987, as compared to 16.3 million in 1986 and 15.7 million in 1985.[26] In addition to lower demand, U.S. manufacturers faced another problem; that is, the share of the imported cars in the United States has increased over the years. The point will be clear if we compare the total car sales in the United States before and after the recessionary period of 1980 through 1983. The total car sales volume over a four year period prior to and following the recession, that is, 1976–1979 versus 1984–1987, was equal at 43.2 million units. During these same time intervals, however, import car sales have increased by 48 percent from 7.9 million to 11.7 million vehicles. At the same time, domestic-made car sales declined by 11 percent from 35.3 million to 31.5 million units.[27]

In 1986, imports represented 26 percent of combined new car and truck sales, which is an increase of 3 percent from 1985.[28] Moreover, all signs point to a greater share for imports in the future as producers from Japan set up assembly plants in the United States.[29]

In 1986, combined car and truck output in the United States totaled 11.3 million units, of which only 600,000—an increase of 71 percent from 1985—were built by companies from Japan.[30] Total U.S. production reflected market demand for 1986. In 1987 the U.S. economy began its fourth consecutive year of expansion.[31]

Currently, GM, Chrysler, and Ford are diversifying to help face the severe challenges of the 1980s and 1990s. Diversification measures are designed to strengthen, not eliminate, the automotive business. Hopefully, diversification will help the industry face developments that are taking place in the U.S. market. The National Automobile Dealers Association warned of an impending explosion of low-priced cars from overseas at its meeting in February 1986. Also, industry officials are predicting that import car sales could reach 4.1 million units a year by 1990,[32] following the 3.2 million in 1986.[33]

At the end of 1985, Hondas, Nissans, and Toyotas were already being assembled in North America. In addition, Mitsubishi, Hyundai, and Mazda had announced plans to build in North America.

As a result there is an over-capacity in the industry during a period of slower growth rates in the U.S. auto market. This may cause as many as 10 car assembly plants in the United States to shut down by the year 1990.[34]

Table IV:2.3 shows the free-world vehicle demand for years 1984 through 1997.

Table IV: 2.3  FREE-WORLD VEHICLE DEMAND (MILLIONS)
Total Industry Vehicles by Calendar Years

| | 1984 | 1985 | 1986 | 1987 | 1988 | 1989 | 1990 | 1991 | 1992 | 1993 | 1994 | 1995 | 1996 | 1997 |
|---|---|---|---|---|---|---|---|---|---|---|---|---|---|---|
| North America | | | | | | | | | | | | | | |
| U.S. | 14.5 | 15.7 | 16.1 | 15.5 | 14.6 | 14.7 | 15.4 | 15.5 | 15.7 | 15.9 | 16.0 | 16.2 | 16.4 | 16.6 |
| Canada | 1.3 | 1.5 | 1.5 | 1.5 | 1.5 | 1.5 | 1.5 | 1.5 | 1.6 | 1.6 | 1.6 | 1.7 | 1.7 | 1.7 |
| Total N.A. | 15.8 | 17.2 | 17.6 | 17.0 | 16.1 | 16.2 | 16.9 | 17.0 | 17.3 | 17.5 | 17.6 | 17.9 | 18.1 | 18.3 |
| Overseas | | | | | | | | | | | | | | |
| Europe | 11.4 | 12.0 | 13.1 | 13.9 | 13.5 | 13.6 | 13.8 | 14.0 | 14.2 | 14.4 | 14.6 | 14.8 | 15.0 | 15.2 |
| Latin America | 1.5 | 1.6 | 1.8 | 1.5 | 1.6 | 1.8 | 1.9 | 2.0 | 2.2 | 2.2 | 2.4 | 2.4 | 2.5 | 2.6 |
| Mid-East | 0.8 | 0.8 | 0.5 | 0.6 | 0.7 | 0.8 | 0.8 | 0.9 | 0.9 | 0.9 | 1.0 | 1.0 | 1.1 | 1.1 |
| Africa | 0.8 | 0.6 | 0.5 | 0.5 | 0.6 | 0.7 | 0.7 | 0.8 | 0.8 | 0.9 | 0.9 | 0.9 | 0.9 | 1.0 |
| Asia-Pacific | 7.3 | 7.4 | 7.4 | 8.0 | 8.0 | 8.2 | 8.6 | 8.8 | 9.0 | 9.2 | 9.5 | 9.7 | 9.9 | 10.1 |
| Total | 21.8 | 22.4 | 23.3 | 24.5 | 24.4 | 25.1 | 25.8 | 26.5 | 27.1 | 27.6 | 28.4 | 28.8 | 29.4 | 30.0 |
| Total Vehicles | 37.6 | 39.6 | 40.9 | 41.5 | 40.5 | 41.3 | 42.7 | 43.5 | 44.4 | 45.1 | 46.0 | 46.7 | 47.5 | 48.3 |

Source: *Ward's Automotive Yearbook* (Detroit, Mich.: Ward's Communications, 1988), p. 74.

## VW'S TOP COMPETITORS

The automotive industry is an oligopoly because it is dominated by a few large corporations that compete for a share of the world market. Out of the manufacturers that compete with VW, four of them are American corporations.

Table IV:2.4 lists the world's top automobile manufacturers.

## COMPANY DESCRIPTION

Volkswagen is the largest automobile manufacturer in Europe, and the third largest company in West Germany. As of December 31, 1987, VW employed about 260,458 people, and was headed by Dr. Carl H. Hahn, chairman of the Board of Management. The VW Group consists of 58 major companies, such as Audi AG and Volkswagen of America. Also, there are over 25 additional smaller subsidiaries under the Volkswagen Group's umbrella. The company produced 2,773,613 vehicles in 1986, which was a decrease of 5,175 units from the previous year. The profits in 1985, 1986, and 1987 were DM 596 million, DM 580 million, and DM 598 million, respectively.[35]

In the last few years VW sales have declined as a result of several events. First of all, market demand as a whole has dropped; this, and a trend away from small cars, has hurt the company's sales. A decrease in the demand for diesel-powered vehicles also had an impact on operations. Sales were influenced in Europe when the German government issued new automobile standards. The standards required German auto manufacturers to adapt all cars to accommodate lead-free gasoline and catalytic converters. Since lead-free fuel is not readily available on the continent, VW's sales were affected in the European market.[36] Even with this problem, VW sales in Europe increased from 1.5 million units in 1985 to 1.7 million units in 1986, an 11.7 percent increase.[37] In 1987, Volkswagen Group sold close to 2 million vehicles, an increase of 7.5 percent over the 1986 sales volume.[38] Once again, VW led sales in the European market for the third consecutive year.

VW, by 1987, had opened plants in Hanover, Kassel, Emden, Salzgitter, and Braunschweig in Germany. It has also opened plants in Argentina, Canada, U.S.A., Spain, People's Republic of China, Brazil, Mexico, South Africa, Belgium, and Nigeria.[39]

### Audi-NSU Subsidiary

In the late 1960s VW began acquiring ownership in Audi. In 1968, Audi was merged with NSU, an unprofitable southern German car manufacturer, which had already been bought by VW. With this merger, Audi-NSU formally became a subsidiary of VW. The Audi-NSU had two manufacturing plants, which remained in southern Germany.

VW's profits, in recent years, have been sustained by its cash cow, the Audi-NSU subsidiary. Audi-NSU, whose name was changed to Audi AG in January 1985,[40] accounted for 37 percent of profits in 1985. Recently, however, Audi

## Table IV: 2.4 PRINCIPAL WORLD MOTOR VEHICLE MANUFACTURERS RANKED ACCORDING TO PRODUCTION IN EACH COUNTRY

| Manufacturer | Country produced in | 1987 Cars | 1987 Trucks | 1987 Total | 1986 Total |
|---|---|---|---|---|---|
| General Motors | U.S.A. | 3,603,952 | 1,516,259 | 5,120,211 | 5,828,051 |
| Toyota | Japan | 2,708,069 | 930,210 | 3,638,279 | 3,660,167 |
| Ford | U.S.A. | 1,830,446 | 1,482,015 | 3,312,461 | 3,160,274 |
| Nissan | Japan | 1,803,924 | 422,389 | 2,226,313 | 2,242,995 |
| Peugeot SA | France | 1,676,134 | 163,918 | 1,840,052 | 1,619,277 |
| Renault | France | 1,375,696 | 277,073 | 1,652,769 | 1,574,964 |
| Fiat Group | Italy | 1,492,777 | 12,858 | 1,505,635 | 1,476,422 |
| Volkswagen | W. Germany | 1,393,220 | 80,560 | 1,473,780 | 1,509,439 |
| Honda | Japan | 1,021,895 | 219,227 | 1,421,122 | 1,236,398 |
| Chrysler | U.S.A. | 1,109,411 | 222,889 | 1,332,300 | 1,449,965 |
| Mitsubishi | Japan | 594,654 | 636,515 | 1,321,169 | 1,177,975 |
| Mazda | Japan | 853,309 | 344,563 | 1,197,872 | 1,195,625 |
| Opel | W. Germany | 915,532 | 6,294 | 921,826 | 925,536 |
| Suzuki | Japan | 296,979 | 570,881 | 867,860 | 872,411 |
| Daimler | W. Germany | 595,765 | 135,006 | 730,771 | 726,131 |
| Lada | U.S.S.R. | 727,000 | — | 727,000 | 725,000 |
| Hyundai | S. Korea | 544,648 | 62,168 | 606,816 | 428,934 |
| Fuji | Japan | 266,755 | 338,502 | 605,257 | 628,303 |
| Diahatsu | Japan | 141,572 | 455,983 | 597,555 | 602,519 |
| Ford | Canada | 433,976 | 152,990 | 586,966 | 665,517 |
| GM | Canada | 339,101 | 238,955 | 578,056 | 719,660 |
| Ford | W. Germany | 560,582 | — | 560,582 | 562,253 |
| Isuzu | Japan | 203,930 | 337,653 | 541,583 | 554,900 |
| British Leyland | England | 471,504 | 69,872 | 541,376 | 472,990 |
| Ford | England | 386,698 | 101,237 | 487,935 | 440,072 |
| BMW | W. Germany | 442,776 | — | 442,776 | 432,285 |
| Chrysler | Canada | 12,533 | 410,244 | 422,777 | 404,789 |
| Audi | W. Germany | 417,234 | — | 417,234 | 352,735 |
| SEAT | Spain | 386,421 | 19,970 | 406,391 | 335,548 |
| Volkswagen | Brazil | 314,592 | 11,622 | 326,214 | 387,935 |
| Honda | U.S.A. | 324,064 | — | 324,064 | 238,159 |
| FASA | Spain | 237,736 | 74,833 | 312,558 | 280,767 |
| GM | Spain | 294,090 | 3,644 | 297,734 | 307,432 |
| Ford | Spain | 263,382 | 13,229 | 276,611 | 268,402 |
| Vauxhall | England | 183,857 | 46,595 | 230,452 | 213,058 |
| Nissan | U.S.A. | 117,334 | 102,718 | 220,052 | 173,195 |
| Volvo | Sweden | 195,540 | 14,804 | 210,344 | 216,420 |
| Alfa Romeo | Italy | 192,024 | 3,622 | 195,646 | 171,529 |
| GM | Brazil | 169,654 | 24,552 | 194,206 | 251,179 |
| Ford | Brazil | 88,840 | 41,410 | 130,250 | 188,914 |
| Ford | Australia | 114,000 | 12,500 | 126,500 | 144,017 |
| Saab | Sweden | 88,028 | 15,370 | 103,398 | 98,336 |
| Ford | Mexico | 67,578 | 17,093 | 84,671 | 41,412 |
| Volkswagen | U.S.A. | 66,696 | — | 66,696 | 84,397 |
| Talbot | England | 45,549 | — | 45,549 | 58,426 |
| **Peugeot SA Breakdown** | | | | | |
| Peugeot | France | 1,010,128 | 89,849 | 1,099,977 | 1,030,924 |
| Citroen | France | 666,006 | 74,069 | 740,075 | 588,353 |

Source: *Ward's Automotive Yearbook* (Detroit, Mich.: Ward's Communications, 1988), p. 77.

has been the subject of a controversy, stemming from its 5000 S model. Apparently, it has a defect that causes sudden acceleration in cars with automatic transmissions. The problem has occurred only in the United States because automatic transmissions are not sold outside the United States. It is estimated that reduced Audi sales will have a major impact on VW earnings.[41]

In early 1987, Audi recalled all of its 1978 to 1986 5000 S model cars.[42] The sudden acceleration problem with this model was the primary reason for the substantial decline in VW's profits in 1986. The problem has been blamed for 2000 injuries and 56 deaths. The National Highway Transportation Safety Administration (NHTSA) reported an average of 645.4 complaints about sudden acceleration problems in every 100,000 Audi 5000 S models sold in the United States in the 1976 through 1986 model years.[43] Along with the recall, Audi announced that it would change the name of the 5000 S to Audi 4000 S. In addition, Audi issued "loaner" cars to those people who brought in their cars in response to the recall. The problem was to be fixed by installing a device that would prevent the car from being started without pressing the brake pedal. Also, Audi has announced that it will offer a discount of $5,000 to those people who purchased the 1987 5000 S model. All these efforts are made in an attempt to rebuild Audi's image as a well-designed car and to improve sagging sales and reduce inventories.[44]

In 1988, Audi introduced two new models, Audi 80 and 90 series in the United States. These models replaced the Audi 4000 S and Audi 5000 S models. Although, these new models have been very successful in Europe, they were not received well in North America. For example, the worldwide deliveries of Audis to customers increased by 15.3 percent to 418,998 units. This increase in unit sales and the continuing trend of upmarket features translated into a 14.7 percent increase in sales to DM 11,366 million in 1987. While there were increases in sales in West Germany and in the other European countries, sales dropped further in the North American markets. The company blamed the low exchange rate for the U.S. dollar and dwindling total unit sales for the drop in total North American sales.[45]

**Volkswagen of America Subsidiary**  The year 1986 was not a good year for Volkswagen of America. Sales were off 31.2 percent as compared with 1985, mainly due to the Audi 5000 S model's unexpected acceleration problems. In addition, the delayed introduction of its Fox model, due to part shortages at VW's Brazilian manufacturing facility, could cause a 25 percent decrease in Fox sales.[46] Also, Volkswagen of America's second assembly plant "had to be relinquished before it had even been started up."[47]

In November of 1987, VW announced that it would either close or sell its only assembly plant in the United States by the summer of 1988. Stiff competition, especially from the Japanese, and a poor image problem had forced management to reevaluate its position in the United States. According to VW, "We have a plant designed for two shifts that is only working one shift, sometimes even less. It is producing at below 40 percent capacity and simply cannot be expected to be profitable."[48]

VW was the first foreign automobile manufacturer to build an assembly plant in the United States. Now, they will be the first to leave.

## Major Joint Ventures

**Autolatina**　In 1986, Volkswagen AG and the Ford Motor Company had each lost an estimated $50 million at their South American facilities. In an attempt to reduce costs, both companies, in late 1986, joined forces and created Autolatina companies. With 15 plants (10 in Brazil and 5 in Argentina), Autolatina will become the eleventh largest auto manufacturer in the world.[49]

According to Volkswagen, the main goals of this joint venture are to "achieve a greater return on investment by improving the utilization of production facilities and to reinforce the market positions of both makes."[50]

By the end of 1987, Autolatina companies in Argentina and Brazil still were showing losses. These disappointing results were contributed to: (1) low domestic prices which failed to cover costs; (2) a drop in export sales due to strong value of U.S. dollar as compared to these countries' currencies; and (3) the nonrecurring costs of merging Volkswagen and Ford subsidiaries to form Autolatina. The losses detracted from the financial results of the Volkswagen Group as a whole in proportion to the 51 percent holding of VW in the joint venture. VW, however, contends that a synergetic effect is becoming apparent as a result of the joint venture which is a demonstration that the joint venture is on the right track.[51]

**Shanghai-Volkswagen Automotive Company**　During 1983, VW established a trial assembly agreement with the Shanghai Tractor and Automobile Corporation. This joint venture, entitled the Shanghai-Volkswagen Automotive Company, Ltd., is currently producing VW's Passat Variant, Audi 100, and Santana models.

In 1986, the company produced a total of 8,501 vehicles. In addition to the greater-than-expected volume of production, a total of 8,471 passenger cars were sold. This resulted in the offset of losses incurred during the previous year's start-up phase.[52] In 1987, the Shanghai Volkswagen again achieved a positive result. Sales in Chinese domestic market were 11,038 units, an increase of 30.3 percent over 1986.[53]

## Currency Fraud

In 1987, VW was faced with another problem. The company was being investigated in a currency fraud case, which ultimately could force Carl Hahn to leave the company. A loss of an estimated $259 million was discovered in mid-November of 1986. VW, at that time, claimed ignorance. But, in March of 1987, the company "admitted that it had not been properly hedged against currency movements."[54] Up until that time, VW was considered to be one of the top managers of foreign currency.

During VW's annual meeting in July of 1987, "Management repeated its defense that it had been victimized by falsified currency contracts stemming from a criminal conspiracy it couldn't control."[55] At this time, VW announced that it would "withdraw from the highly speculative arbitrage trading activities that led to the loss and would restrict its foreign-exchange operations to those that provide currency for its auto production."[56]

Even though this scandal cost the company an estimated DM 473 million ($259 million), VW shareholders gave a strong vote of support of 98.2 percent for the present management board.[57]

## Marketing

Although VW set the standard for low-priced, quality autos with its famous Beetle model, it got priced out of the market in the 1970s.[58] In an effort to help regain its "small inexpensive car" image, VW has continued its longstanding advertising campaign. Most of their advertisements today follow the distinctive VW style, which keeps the message simple, uses news headlines to attract attention, and has a unique selling proposition.[59]

A summary of VW's expenditures for advertising and promotion, subdivided among the different media, compared to other automobile manufacturers, is presented in Table IV:2.5.

In 1986, VW's advertising budget in the United States was increased by 21.8 percent to an estimated $107 million, making it the number one imported car advertiser. In 1986, a major portion of the advertising expenditures was divided among network television and magazines. The use of TV in 1986 increased from the previous year, with spot TV ads costing $17 million and network ads costing $48 million level. However, both Sunday magazines ads and outdoor advertising dropped to $255,000 and $218,000, respectively, from the 1985s levels.[60]

Jim Fuller, vice-president of VW of America, is currently pursuing the strategy of rebuilding the VW name. This is being accomplished by emphasizing VW's Germanic roots, engineering, and value.[61]

## Management

Under German law, VW is governed by two boards. The *Board of Management* consists of the operational heads of the company who handle purchasing, quality assurance, personnel, research and development, legal matters, production, marketing, and finance. Its members are elected by the 20 member *Supervisory Board*, with ten members elected by shareholders and ten elected by Volkswagen employees. VW believes that a decision supported by both shareholders and employees is better balanced than a decision supported by one side only.[62]

## Research and Development

In 1986, VW Group spent 1.8 billion on research and development. Research and development at VW was aimed primarily at "the vehicle and assembly sectors, in series management and in modifications to models."[63]

Electronics are being used more and more in the field of design and engineering. Various research and development test standards are used for endurance testing of running gear components, for the selection of optimum engine settings, for work on the air-blending heater, and for development activities aimed at improving noise insulation.

Table IV:2.5   1986 TOP TEN ADVERTISING CATEGORIES AND THEIR TOP FIVE CORPORATE SPENDERS

Passenger cars, domestic

| | Nine-media total (000) | BAR Network television (000) | BAR Spot television (000) | BAR Network cable (000) | BAR Network radio (000) | RER Spot radio (000) | PIB Magazines (000) | PIB Sunday magazines (000) | MEDIA RECORDS Newspapers (000) | LNA Outdoor (000) |
|---|---|---|---|---|---|---|---|---|---|---|
| 1986 | $809,984 | $380,343 | $93,665 | $11,511 | $29,386 | $18,345 | $210,523 | $12,927 | $49,113 | $4,171 |
| 1985 | 737,942 | 365,555 | 91,208 | 12,085 | 10,156 | 11,270 | 195,707 | 4,334 | 41,299 | 6,328 |
| 1. General Motors Corp. | | | | | | | | | | |
| 1986 | 348,447 | 166,028 | 32,053 | 3,581 | 16,928 | 14,762 | 83,186 | 5,190 | 24,681 | 2,038 |
| 1985 | 282,255 | 147,294 | 36,959 | 2,299 | 5,062 | 1,765 | 66,306 | 2,119 | 17,655 | 2,796 |
| 2. Ford Motor Co. | | | | | | | | | | |
| 1986 | 293,459 | 135,816 | 40,003 | 4,081 | 12,068 | 927 | 84,171 | 3,792 | 10,992 | 1,609 |
| 1985 | 280,024 | 144,709 | 30,109 | 5,213 | 3,445 | 2,747 | 76,131 | 1,274 | 14,618 | 1,778 |
| 3. Chrysler Corp. | | | | | | | | | | |
| 1986 | 155,815 | 70,325 | 20,129 | 3,132 | 390 | 2,598 | 41,888 | 3,945 | 12,883 | 525 |
| 1985 | 157,972 | 66,686 | 22,636 | 4,276 | 1,649 | 5,824 | 45,403 | 942 | 8,801 | 1,755 |
| 4. American Motors Corp. | | | | | | | | | | |
| 1986 | 11,783 | 8,174 | 1,448 | 718 | — | 57 | 991 | — | 395 | — |
| 1985 | 17,590 | 6,866 | 1,498 | 296 | — | 935 | 7,803 | — | 186 | 6 |
| 5. Classic Motor Carriages Inc. | | | | | | | | | | |
| 1986 | 319 | — | — | — | — | — | 285 | — | 34 | — |
| 1985 | 439 | — | — | — | — | — | 184 | — | 255 | — |

Table IV:2.5 (Continued)

| | Nine-media total (000) | BAR Network television (000) | BAR Spot television (000) | BAR Network cable (000) | BAR Network radio (000) | RER Spot radio (000) | PIB Magazines (000) | PIB Sunday magazines (000) | MEDIA RECORDS Newspapers (000) | LNA Outdoor (000) |
|---|---|---|---|---|---|---|---|---|---|---|
| Passenger cars, imported | | | | | | | | | | |
| 1986 | $742,795 | $257,010 | $188,272 | $10,328 | $2,673 | $11,848* | $204,728 | $2,130 | $61,598 | $4,208 |
| 1985 | 586,251 | 210,575 | 125,441 | 8,049 | 4,303 | 4,526* | 175,084 | 3,030 | 50,856 | 4,387 |
| 1. Volkswagenwerk AG | | | | | | | | | | |
| 1986 | 107,972 | 48,604 | 17,388 | 807 | — | 883 | 34,789 | 255 | 5,179 | 67 |
| 1985 | 84,438 | 34,758 | 13,821 | 628 | — | 46 | 30,744 | 608 | 3,538 | 295 |
| 2. Toyota Motor Corp. | | | | | | | | | | |
| 1986 | 94,212 | 20,012 | 51,930 | 1,636 | — | 589 | 16,251 | 157 | 2,341 | 1,296 |
| 1985 | 69,920 | 17,497 | 35,250 | 1,163 | 907 | 320 | 10,344 | 31 | 3,010 | 1,398 |
| 3. Honda Motor Co. | | | | | | | | | | |
| 1986 | 87,912 | 35,707 | 14,654 | 2,323 | 2,200 | 3,383 | 26,171 | 472 | 2,976 | 26 |
| 1985 | 59,977 | 32,697 | 1,546 | 1,767 | 3,154 | 2,659 | 16,903 | 285 | 941 | 25 |
| 4. Itoh. C. & Co. | | | | | | | | | | |
| 1986 | 68,275 | 24,632 | 16,898 | 1,035 | — | 771 | 20,810 | — | 4,129 | — |
| 1985 | 58,435 | 29,894 | 8,143 | 1,508 | — | 5 | 17,833 | — | 1,040 | 12 |
| 5. Nissan Motor Co. | | | | | | | | | | |
| 1986 | 65,074 | 26,707 | 20,678 | 393 | — | 900 | 12,915 | 33 | 2,644 | 804 |
| 1985 | 56,295 | 18,648 | 21,358 | 653 | — | 170 | 12,836 | — | 1,598 | 1,032 |

Source: Marketing and Media Decisions, vol. 22, no. 2 (July 1987), p. 48.

Normally, testing engineers are the harshest critics of planning engineers and designers. Any problems discovered not only have to be evaluated by road testing, but also by endurance and wind tunnel testing.

Most aerodynamic investigations and highly calibrated measurements of all tested vehicle functions that are influenced by airflow are carried out in the VW wind tunnel and climatic testing facility located in Wolfsburg, West Germany. These functions include engine cooling, passenger compartment ventilation, and heating. Combinations of climatic conditions are possible by means of the controlled simulation of temperature, humidity, solar radiation, and rain.[64] Engineers place threads on the vehicles' outer skin, and utilize air streams carrying smoke to help determine where vortices occur and where air flow separates. Parts that cause drag can then be detected and smoothed. Reducing drag contributes to improved fuel consumption and pinpoints areas that cause whistling and rushing noises. Almost every climate to be found on earth can be generated from this testing system. Temperatures can be made to range from 113°F down to −22°F.[65]

With the help of all these innovations in the research and development area, VW introduced the new 16-valve models of Golf and Scirocco, which are equipped with 4-valve per cylinder on the 1.8 liter engines, and provides excellent acceleration and reduced fuel consumption. Orders for these vehicles are exceeding VW's expectations.

Another recent development in the production field uses computers to calculate such aspects as strength and vibration characteristics, long before the actual prototype is built.

In mid-1987, a new computer system was put into operation at VW. the new computer is opening up new frontiers in the simulation of tests. This computer system can work up to 200 times faster than conventional industrial computers.[66]

An example of trend-setting products that have resulted from the VW's R&D efforts is the recently developed electro-hybrid drive. The electro-hybrid drive was developed in collaboration with the Bosch company of West Germany and was put to test in a Golf. The drive comprises a decoupling 37 kW diesel engine and a 5 kW electric motor. The engine and the motor are controlled via automatic couplings so that at low speeds the electric motor would propel the vehicle. Acceleration and high speed are accomplished by switching to the diesel engine. The new electro-hybrid drive is claimed to reduce fuel consumption in urban areas to approximately 98 miles per gallon and reduce noxious substance emission of the diesel engine by half.[67]

More research and development studies are planned for the future in aerodynamics, alternative materials, fuels, and manufacturing technology.

## Production and Operations

In response to the heightened sophistication of the automotive buying public, VW began to phase out the Beetle. Through a program beginning in the late 1960s an entire series of new VWs became ready for the American public. They changed from air-cooled engines to more efficient and powerful, front-

Table IV: 2.6   SALIENT FIGURES OF MAJOR SUBSIDIARIES AND AFFILIATES

| | Sales | | | Vehicle Sales | | |
|---|---|---|---|---|---|---|
| | DM Million 1987 | DM Million 1986 | Change % | Units 1987 | Units 1986 | Change % |
| **Producing Companies** | | | | | | |
| AUDI AG | 11,366 | 9,908 | +14.7 | 414,461 | 351,321 | +18.0 |
| SEAT S.A. | 4,879 | 3,821 | +27.7 | 433,510 | 347,147 | +24.9 |
| Volkswagen Bruxelles S.A. | 2,726 | 2,536 | +7.5 | 209,662 | 192,753 | +8.8 |
| TAS Tvornica Automobila Sarajevo | 456 | 377 | +21.1 | 29,928 | 32,145 | −6.9 |
| Volkswagen of America, Inc. | 5,815[1] | 8,766 | −33.7 | 237,627 | 285,013 | −16.6 |
| AUTOLATINA | 3,541[2] | 4,692 | −24.5 | 345,893[3] | 409,977 | −15.6 |
| Volkswagen de Mexico, S.A. de C.V. | 1,117[1] | 1,280 | −12.7 | 54,561 | 66,806 | −18.3 |
| Volkswagen of South Africa (Pty.) Ltd. | 866 | 645 | +34.3 | 44,963 | 37,993 | +18.3 |
| Volkswagen of Nigeria Ltd. | 37 | 118 | −68.5 | 1,851 | 2,744 | −32.5 |
| Shanghai-Volkswagen Automotive Company, Ltd. | 343 | 251 | +37.1 | 11,038 | 8,471 | +30.3 |
| **Distributing Companies** | | | | | | |
| AUTOGERMA S.p.A. | 3,266 | 2,665 | +22.6 | 175,810 | 147,457 | +19.2 |
| V.A.G. France S.A. | 3,092[1] | 2,514 | +23.0 | 155,488 | 130,927 | +18.8 |
| V.A.G Sverige AB | 1,006 | 834 | +20.6 | 42,232 | 36,255 | +16.5 |
| Volkswagen Canada Inc. | 1,039 | 1,294 | −19.7 | 42,803 | 45,579 | −6.1 |
| **Other Companies** | | | | | | |
| V.A.G Leasing GmbH | 2,161[1] | 1,120 | +93.0 | — | — | — |
| interRent autovermietung GmbH | 554[1] | 338 | +64.0 | — | — | — |
| V.A.G Kredit Bank GmbH | 236 | 215 | +9.6 | — | — | — |

[1] Incl. proceeds from disposal of used assets   [2] In line with the 51% holding   [3] Only Volkswagen models

mounted, water-cooled, and front-wheel drive versions. The year 1973 marked the introduction of the Dasher, which became the new favorite of the Beetle loyalists. The Scirocco was introduced in 1974 and the Rabbit in 1975. The Rabbit was noted as one of the finest small cars in the world. In 1972, a plant for assembling cars and making parts was built in Yugoslavia, and by June 1976, a facility in Pennsylvania was acquired. These two plants use approximately 1,200 robots to aid in the production of vehicles.

Recently, new control and material coordination systems have been introduced that make computer-aided manufacturing (CAM), computer-aided design (CAD), and changing procedures in design and production planning possible.[68]

| Production | | | Capital Investments | | | Workforce | | |
|---|---|---|---|---|---|---|---|---|
| Units 1987 | Units 1986 | Change % | DM Million 1987 | DM Million 1986 | Change % | Dec. 31 1987 | Dec. 31 1986 | Change % |
| 443,067 | 383,519 | +15.5 | 730 | 889 | −17.9 | 39,325 | 39,843 | −1.3 |
| 406,391 | 338,548 | +20.0 | 103 | 1,263 | −91.8 | 24,895 | 23,591 | +5.5 |
| 209,662 | 192,753 | +8.8 | 49 | 128 | −61.4 | 5,422 | 5,636 | −3.8 |
| 30,575 | 30,940 | −1.2 | 6 | 10 | −39.7 | 3,116 | 3,006 | +3.7 |
| 66,508 | 84,331 | −21.1 | 239 | 559 | −57.2 | 5,528 | 6,448 | −14.3 |
| 341,909[3] | 411,055 | −16.8 | 171[2] | 414 | −58.8 | 30,034[2] | 48,766 | −38.4 |
| 48,722 | 71,554 | −31.9 | 182 | 163 | +11.9 | 13,365 | 14,007 | −4.6 |
| 44,167 | 38,836 | +13.7 | 17 | 8 | x | 6,811 | 5,830 | +16.8 |
| 2,123 | 3,747 | −43.3 | 1 | 5 | −89.8 | 1,370 | 2,046 | −33.0 |
| 11,000 | 8,500 | +29.4 | 71 | 46 | +53.9 | 2,087 | 1,911 | +9.2 |
| — | — | — | 2 | 2 | −6.7 | 333 | 317 | +5.0 |
| — | — | — | 344 | 269 | +27.9 | 996 | 995 | +0.1 |
| — | — | — | 112 | 107 | +4.0 | 365 | 351 | +4.0 |
| — | — | — | 27 | 28 | −3.5 | 731 | 691 | +5.8 |
| — | — | — | 2,477 | 1,793 | +38.2 | 328 | 297 | +10.4 |
| — | — | — | 291 | 224 | +30.3 | 1,570 | 1,547 | +1.5 |
| — | — | — | 7 | 4 | +70.3 | 335 | 302 | +10.9 |

Source: Volkswagen Annual Report, 1987, pp. 24–25.

To secure its international competitiveness, the VW Group made further efforts in 1985 to develop its product range and to reduce costs. One way VW attempted to meet this goal was by the acquisition of SEAT (Sociedad Española de Automoviles de Turismo, S.A.). This Spanish production base gives VW a 30 percent reduction in manufacturing costs.[69]

In 1987, VW produced worldwide 2,771,379 automobiles, which is 5,179 units less than the previous year.[70] A breakdown of the company's sales, vehicle sales, production, capital investments, and workforce by major subsidiaries and affiliates is shown in Table IV:2.6.

As Table IV:2.6 shows, the foreign production companies in Spain (SEAT S.A.), Brussels (Volkswagen Bruxelles S.A.), South Africa, and Shanghai joint

Table IV: 2.7   CONSOLIDATED BALANCE SHEET OF THE VOLKSWAGEN GROUP
DECEMBER 31, 1987*

| Assets | Dec. 31, 1987 | Dec. 31, 1986 |
|---|---|---|
| **Fixed assets** | | |
| Intangible assets | 29.1 | 1.5 |
| Tangible assets | 13,405.6 | 12,111.3 |
| Financial assets | 1,125.6 | 1,099.5 |
| Leasing and rental assets | 4,918.9 | 4,106.3 |
| | 19,479.2 | 17,318.6 |
| **Current assets** | | |
| Inventories | 6,617.9 | 6,801.7 |
| Receivables and other assets | 9,155.0 | 8,369.3 |
| Securities | 425.5 | 364.2 |
| Cheques, cash on hand, deposits at German Federal Bank and postal giro balances, cash in banks | 8,135.0 | 8,552.8 |
| | 24,333.4 | 24,088.0 |
| **Prepaid and deferred charges** | 248.5 | 305.8 |
| | 44,061.1 | 41,712.4 |

| Stockholders' equity and liabilities | Dec. 31, 1987 | Dec. 31, 1986 |
|---|---|---|
| **Stockholders' equity** | | |
| Subscribed capital of Volkswagen AG | 1,500.0 | 1,500.0 |
| Ordinary shares 1,200.0 | | |
| Non-voting preference shares 300.0 | | |
| Potential capital 200.0 | | |
| Capital reserve | 2,803.2 | 2,803.2 |
| Revenue reserves | 5,692.4 | 5,087.7 |
| Net earnings available for distribution | 307.6 | 307.1 |
| Minority interest in consolidated subsidiaries | 422.4 | 411.1 |
| | 10,725.6 | 10,109.1 |
| **Special items with an equity portion** | 2,202.8 | 1,828.4 |
| **Special item for investment subsidies** | 9.4 | 9.5 |
| **Undetermined liabilities** | 14,864.1 | 14,513.7 |
| **Liabilities** | 15,817.8 | 14,936.8 |
| **Deferred income** | 441.4 | 314.9 |
| | 44,061.1 | 41,712.4 |

*DM million

Source: *Volkswagen Annual Report,* 1987, p. 82.

venture have increased their production. However, other foreign subsidiaries show declines in their production levels.[71]

## Personnel

Unlike its competitors who have dismissed employees by the thousands, VW hired 18,000 new employees in 1986 and 2,674 in 1987. If possible, the com-

Table IV:2.8   CONSOLIDATED STATEMENT OF EARNINGS OF THE
VOLKSWAGEN GROUP AS AT DECEMBER 31, 1987

|  | 1987 DM Million | 1986 DM Million |
|---|---|---|
| Sales | 54,634.9 | 52,794.3 |
| Cost of sales | 48,525.9 | 46,745.9 |
| Gross profit | +6,109.0 | +6,048.4 |
| Selling and distribution expenses | 3,980.0 | 3,904.8 |
| General administration expenses | 1,518.2 | 1,474.7 |
| Other operating income | 3,361.8 | 2,562.3 |
| Other operating expenses | 2,231.5 | 1,930.3 |
| Results from participations | +80.2 | +65.9 |
| Interest results | +12.0 | +268.1 |
| Write-down of financial assets and securities classified as current assets | 222.8 | 39.3 |
| Results from ordinary business activities | +1,610.5 | +1,595.6 |
| Extraordinary expenses | 443.3 | 473.0 |
| Taxes on income | 569.2 | 542.4 |
| Net earnings | 598.0 | 580.2 |

Source: Volkswagen Annual Report, 1987, p. 83.

pany chose to reduce overhead by increasing production rather than by laying off workers.[72]

In 1987, VW employed a total of 260,458 workers, a decrease of 5.8 percent from the 1986 level of 276,459. As Table IV:2.6 indicates, these decrease was mainly due to cutbacks in the South and North American subsidiaries. In 1987, the Volkswagen's workforce was composed of 131,114 wage-earners, 73,943 salaried workers, and 55,401 salaried staff. In addition, VW employed a total of 6,667 apprentices and trainees.[73]

## Finance

The earnings situation of the Volkswagen Group improved in 1986 and 1987. Gross performance increased by 2.4 percent to DM 52,794 million in 1986 and by 3.5 percent to DM 54,635 in 1987. The reason for the increase in earnings was a rise in unit sales, price increases due to higher costs, and a shift in demand toward more up-market models.[74]

Tables IV:2.7 and IV:2.8 show the consolidated balance sheet and statement of earnings for the Volkswagen Group for years 1986 and 1987.

## CONCLUSION

VW is in a very precarious position because of the problems occurring at its various subsidiaries especially in the United States, the tremendous loss of monies due to an in-house currency scandal, and its overall weak financial position. However, with the company's various newly formed joint ventures and its increasing sales, VW has the opportunity to rebuild itself as one of the world's most progressive and efficient automobile manufacturers.

## NOTES

1. K. B. Hopfinger, *The Volkswagen Story* (Cambridge, Mass: R.B.T. Bentley, 1974), pp. 15–16.
2. Ibid., p. 131.
3. Ibid., pp. 151–152.
4. Ibid., p. 152.
5. *The Volkswagen Heritage* (Troy, Mich: Volkswagen United States, Public Relations Dept., 1985).
6. Hopfinger, *The Volkswagen Story*, p. 164.
7. Ibid., p. 165.
8. *VW Annual Report*, 1986, p. 56.
9. Ibid.
10. Ibid., p. 56.
11. Hopfinger, *The Volkswagen Story*, p. 166.
12. *VW Annual Report*, 1986, pp. 46–56.
13. Ibid., pp. 52–54.
14. Thomas F. O'Boyle and Joseph B. White, "Volkswagen AG to Close or Sell Its U.S. Plant," *The Wall Street Journal*, 23 November 1987, pp. 2, 16.
15. *Ward's Automotive Yearbook*, Detroit, Mich: Ward's Communications, 1988, p. 73.
16. *VW Annual Report*, 1987, p. 9; and *Ward's Automotive Yearbook*, 1988, p. 115.
17. *VW Annual Report*, 1985, p. 9.
18. Ibid., 1986, p. 33.
19. Ibid., 1987, p. 9.
20. "West German Car Industry," *The Economist*, 14 September 1985, pp. 77–78.
21. "U.S. Industrial Outlook," *Motor Vehicles*, 1987, p. 36-1.
22. *Ward's Automotive Yearbook*, 1988, p. 18.
23. "U.S. Industrial Outlook," *Motor Vehicles*, 1986, p. 3.
24. Ibid.
25. Alex Taylor III, "Who's Ahead in the World Auto War?" *Fortune*, 9 November 1987, pp. 74–88.
26. *Ward's Automotive Yearbook*, 1988, p. 18.
27. Ibid.
28. Ibid., 1987, p. 14.
29. Ibid., 1986, p. 13.
30. Ibid., 1987, p. 15.
31. *VW Annual Report*, 1986, p. 68.
32. "U.S. Industrial Outlook, Motor Vehicles," 1987, pp. 36-1–36-3.
33. *Ward's Automotive Yearbook*, 1987, p. 13.
34. Ibid.
35. *VW Annual Report*, 1986, pp. 17–63; 1987, p. 2.
36. James Bruce, "Can VW Regain Its Magic Touch?" *Business Week*, 6 August 1984, p. 56.

37. Richard Johnson, "Europe Sets New-Car Sales Record," *Automotive News*, 26 January 1987, p. 2.

38. *VW Annual Report*, 1987, p. 11.

39. Ibid, p. 61.

40. *Moody's Industrial Manual*, 1986, p. 1547.

41. William J. Hampton and John E. Pluenneke, "Can Audi Fix a Dented Image?" *Business Week*, 17 November 1986, pp. 81–82.

42. "Audi Is Changing Name of Problem-Plagued 500," *The Wall Street Journal*, 15 April 1987, p. 4.

43. *Ward's Automotive Yearbook*, 1988, p. 27.

44. Edward Lapham, "Audi—$5,000 Discounts Offered to Owners," *Automotive News*, 30 March 1987, pp. 1, 55.

45. *VW Annual Report*, 1987, pp. 42–43.

46. John A. Russel, "VW Reduces Sales Goal for New Fox," *Automotive News*, 23 April 1987, p. 20.

47. *VW Annual Report*, 1986, p. 56.

48. O'Boyle and White, "Volkswagen AG to Close or Sell Its U.S. Plant," pp. 2, 16.

49. "Ford, VW Combine Operations," *Dun's Business Monthly*, January 1987, p. 27.

50. *VW Annual Report*, 1986, p. 10.

51. Ibid., pp. 52–54.

52. Ibid., p. 74.

53. Ibid., p. 59.

54. Steve Mufson, "A Currency Scandal Adds to VW's Woes," *Business Week*, 23 March 1987, pp. 54–55.

55. "VW Officials Obtain Support of Shareholders," *The Wall Street Journal*, 3 July 1987, p. 8.

56. Ibid.

57. Ibid.

58. John E. Pluenneke, "VW Rejoins the Race to Sell Supercheap Cars," *Business Week*, 27 January 1986, p. 56.

59. Ralph Gray, "VW's Ad Budget to Climb in 1987," *Adweek*, 6 October 1987, p. 30.

60. "1986 Top Ten Advertising Categories and Their Top Five Corporate Sponsors," *Marketing and Media Decisions*, Vol. 22, p. 2, July 1987, p. 48.

61. Gray, "VW's Ad Budget."

62. James Bruce, "Can VW Regain Its Magic Touch?" p. 56.

63. *VW Annual Report*, 1986, p. 28.

64. *VW Parts and Advice*, Fall/Winter 1986, p. 5.

65. Ibid.

66. *VW Annual Report*, 1987, p. 33.

67. Ibid.

68. *VW Annual Report*, 1986, p. 33.

69. Pluenneke, "VW Rejoins the Race to Sell Supercheap Cars," p. 56.

70. *VW Annual Report*, 1987, p. 2.

71. Ibid., pp. 24–25.

72. Thomas F. O'Boyle, "Surging Sales Bringing Volkswagen Back," *The Wall Street Journal*, 24 July 1986, p. 26.

73. *VW Annual Report*, 1987, pp. 2, 24, 25, 90.

74. *VW Annual Report*, 1986, pp. 22–24; and *VW Annual Report*, 1987, p. 2.

## SUGGESTED READINGS

"Audi AG." *Moody's International Manual,* 1986, pp. 1547–1548.

Bruce, James. "Can VW Regain Its Magic Touch?" *Business Week,* 6 August 1984, pp. 50–58.

"Chrysler Corporation." *Moody's Industrial Manual,* 1987, pp. 1100–1105.

"Ford Motor Company." *Moody's Industrial Manual,* 1987, pp. 1265–1272.

"Ford, VW Combine Operations." *Dun's Business Monthly,* January 1987, p. 27.

"General Motors Corporation." *Moody's Industrial Manual,* 1987, pp. 1321–1333.

Gray, Ralph. "VW's Ad Budget to Climb in 1987." *Adweek,* 6 October 1987, p. 30.

Hampton, William J., and John E. Pluenneke. "Can Audi Fix a Dented Image?" *Business Week,* 17 November 1986, pp. 81–82.

Hopfinger, K. B. *The Volkswagen Story.* (Cambridge, Mass: R.B.T. Bentley, 1974), pp. 67–69, 72.

"Inside the Volkswagen Wind Tunnel." *VW Parts and Advice,* Fall/Winter 1986, p. 6.

"Jetta Production Begins This Month at VW of A's." *Weathervane,* 1986, p. 1.

Johnson, Richard. "Europe Sets New-Car Sales Record." *Automotive News,* 26 January 1987, p. 2.

Knepper, Michael. "The Spirit of VWs Past." *Madison Avenue,* February 1984, pp. 76–81.

Lapham, Edward. "Audi—$5,000 Discounts Offered to Owners." *Automotive News,* 30 March 1987, pp. 1, 55.

"Little Time Left for Sales Managers to Win Week Trip in Germany." *Weathervane,* October 1986, p. 2.

Mufson, Steve. "A Currency Scandal Adds to VW's Woes." *Business Week,* 23 March 1987, pp. 54–55.

"New Sales Certification Program to Emphasize the Fox." *Weathervane,* October 1986, p. 1.

O'Boyle, Thomas F., and Joseph B. White. "Volkswagen AG to Close or Sell Its U.S. Plant." *The Wall Street Journal,* 23 November 1987, pp. 2, 16.

Pluenneke, John E. "VW Rejoins the Race to Sell Supercheap Cars." *Business Week,* 27 January 1986, p. 56.

Russel, John A. "VW Reduces Sales Goal for New Fox." *Automotive News,* 27 April 1987, p. 20.

Taylor, Alex, III. "Who's Ahead in the World Auto War?" *Forbes,* 9 November 1987, pp. 74–88.

"United States Industrial Outlook. Motor Vehicles." *U.S. Department of Commerce, International Trade Administration,* 1986, pp. 36-1–36-5.

"United States Industrial Outlook. Motor Vehicles." *U.S. Department of Commerce, International Trade Administration,* 1989, pp. 34-1–34-7.

*The Volkswagen Heritage.* Troy, Mich: Volkswagen United States, Public Relations Dept., 1985.

"Volkswagen Type 2 Production Reaches 6 Million Mark." *VW Parts and Advice,* Fall/Winter 1986, pp. 10–16.

*VW Annual Report,* 1985.

———, 1986.

———, 1987.

"VW Officials Obtain Support of Shareholders." *The Wall Street Journal,* 3 July 1987, p. 8.

*Ward's Automotive Yearbook,* Detroit, Mich: Ward's Communications, 1988, pp. 17–285.

"West German Car Industry." *The Economist,* 14 September 1985, pp. 77–78.

# LASARRAY SA:
## Founding a High-Tech Venture in Switzerland—A Case History*

## INTRODUCTION

Even as a small boy Ernst Uhlmann was interested in everything technical. He spent much time in his grandfather's workshop in the small Swiss village where they lived. Ernst developed a "knack" for fixing everything from radios and record players to TV sets.

It was to nobody's surprise when Ernst Uhlmann decided to choose a technical career and became an electrical engineer. At the age of 24 he had already established himself as an entrepreneur. In an old barn he experimented with the production of printed circuit boards, a high-tech component part for the emerging computer industry. In—for today's standards—unbelievably primitive work conditions, Ernst Uhlmann laid the foundations for his successful career as a leader and producer of electronic component parts for the fast-developing computer industry in Switzerland and Europe.

In 1973 Uhlmann took a decisive step forward. He founded the FELA-Electronic AG, a computer center for the manufacturing of mounting elements for the fast-developing circuit board industry, by means of the emerging computer-aided manufacturing technology. He rapidly expanded his growing industrial venture, producing the high-tech products of integrated circuit technology and electronic laboratory installations. He established additional production and service facilities to produce these products.

In 1982 the development of the LASARRAY System was initiated by Ernst Uhlmann, founder and chairman of the FELA group, now Switzerland's leading producer of printed circuit boards. LASARRAY SA was originally conceived as a diversification for the FELA group, and the initial development of LASAR-

---

*This case was originally written by Professor Martin E. Rosenfeldt of University of North Texas. It was shortened and revised, with the permission of the author, by Professor Ebrahimi for inclusion in this textbook. The authors would like to express their appreciation to Professor Rosenfeldt for his permission to use the case. Copyright © 1987 by Martin E. Rosenfeldt.

RAY was conducted by a specially created affiliate, FXL AG. When the commercialization phase became imminent, FXL AG was reorganized as LASARRAY HOLDING AG with two new venture holders, INDELEC (Swiss Bank Corporation) and Eidgenoessische Bank (Union Bank of Switzerland).

Ernest Uhlmann had been watching the growing acceptance of application specific integrated circuits (ASICs) in the European and U.S. markets. He felt that there was an increasing need for the economical production of ASICs, in particular for the fabrication of prototypes and small batches. Until 1982 the production technology used by established integrated circuit manufacturers was, because of long design times, set-up lead times, and related costs, unsuitable for the economical production of prototypes or small lots of ASICs. Consequently, producers of specialized electronic equipment remained largely dependent on printed circuit technology.

The boom in integrated circuits (ICs) began less than 25 years ago. Since then, technological breakthroughs bringing major performance improvements have become almost routine. The trend in electronics production is moving from the combination of standard ICs with printed circuit boards (PCBs) to ASICs. Although an attractive alternative to standard integrated circuits on PCBs, the use of ASICs is not yet widespread. It is generally agreed that ASICs offer the following advantages:

- Reduction of product dimensions because of the smaller number of components and connecting elements required.
- Reduction of electrical consumption.
- Elimination of artificial cooling systems because very little heat is generated.
- Pronounced improvement in the reliability of electronic devices.
- Reduction of development and modification costs as a result of computer-supported design, testing, and simulation.
- Improved price/performance relationship.

Since 1982 LASARRAY SA has developed an ASIC production unit, which is an integrated-circuit "factory" contained in three transportable containers (modules). This ASIC "factory" comprises the complete infrastructure required for ASIC production. The system, which costs about one-tenth the price of conventional production installations, can be used by regional service companies or large manufacturers. Five to ten people are needed to operate the system. They do not require any special semiconductor knowledge. Inputs into the ASIC production unit are prefabricated wafers and the design data. The final product consists of finished, tested, and packaged ASICs, ready for use (see Figure IV:3.1).

By the end of July 1986, LASARRAY SA had fabricated one operational prototype. In June 1987, it was in the process of assembling two ASIC production units, although there were still a number of minor product design and manufacturing engineering problems to be ironed out.

Because of the initial large capital investment needed for the research and development of the high technology product of the LASARRAY production

**Figure IV:3.1** Application specific integrated circuit (ASIC)

*Source:* Courtesy LASARRAY SA

unit, Ernst Uhlmann is under considerable pressure by the stockholders to get LASARRAY SA operational, to start regular manufacturing activities as soon as possible, and to implement the business plan of the company.

## COMPANY BACKGROUND

LASARRAY HOLDING AG is the holding company of the LASARRAY GROUP, which has developed and is producing an integrated system for the rapid and economic manufacture of application specific integrated circuits as prototypes or in small batches. The Group is presently made up of the following three companies:

- LASARRAY HOLDING AG (share capital SFr. 7.5 million) is domiciled in Thundorf, Switzerland, and was founded in 1982 as FXL AG. It acts as the group's financing vehicle and holds all patents and participations.
- LASARRAY SA (share capital SFr. 1 million, wholly owned) was founded in 1985. LASARRAY SA undertakes all the development, production, marketing, and promotion activities for the LASARRAY Group.
- LASARRAY Corporations of Scotts Valley, California, was founded in 1985 in "Silicon Valley" to promote the Group's North American activity.

The LASARRAY group forms part of the FELA* Conglomerate, which is composed of seven related companies. Today this group is one of the best known European PCB manufacturers. Together with the other companies, FELA belongs to the Ernst Uhlmann Holding Ltd.

Continual growth in just a few years has made FELA into one of the most significant medium size companies in the world. An important contributor to

---

*FELA: Factory for Electronic Apparatus.

sales volume is FELA Planning Ltd., incorporated in 1979. This company successfully markets the combined know-how of the group throughout the world.

With a nominal SFr. 3.3 million share capital, the FELA group of companies is built on a solid foundation. Ernst Uhlmann, president of the group, holds an interest of more than 98 percent in this share capital.

FELA Group employs approximately 260 skilled people, most of them having been trained on the job by FELA itself, as no other training facilities exist in this recently developed industry. Eighty-five percent of the FELA employees are Swiss citizens. Experts from Britain, Germany, Sweden, and the United States complete the FELA team. At FELA, foreign trade amounts to 76 percent of the total sales volume. FELA's many international contracts are surprisingly widespread for a medium-sized concern. FELA maintains business connections with 32 countries in the West and in the East.

The group is tightly organized. Quality control is given the highest priority, and management reports directly to the management of Ernst Uhlmann Holding Ltd. While pursuing the development of the LASARRAY technology, the company has established a network of representatives in its principal markets. It has conducted market research and presentation activities and assembled a development, production, and sales team. The prototype of the LASARRAY ASIC production unit became operational in June 1986, and the first LASARRAY system was sold in September 1986.

As of June 1987, through LASARRAY SA, the group had developed and marketed a complete turnkey semiportable ASIC production system capable of manufacturing and packaging semicustom application specific integrated circuits in prototype or small lots in as little as 24 hours. These production systems satisfy a perceived and growing need for rapid production of such circuits on the part of all categories of electronic equipment manufacturers. The company's goals are to develop, market, assemble, and sell these systems, with most of the manufacturing activities being handled by subcontractors. The company sells the systems directly and through regional representatives in its major markets. An affiliate has been created in the United States, which is developing the U.S. market and will subsequently become a second operating subsidiary. The company believes that the LASARRAY ASIC production system offers it a unique position in the fast-growing area of application specific integrated circuit demand. It plans to maintain this position by virtue of its extensive experience and track record. It has an experienced management, an outstanding development team, and a service-oriented marketing policy.

# THE ASIC PRODUCT

## Application Specific Integrated Circuits (ASICs)

Industry activities demonstrate convincingly the rapidly growing role of application specific integrated circuits. Users are recognizing the many benefits of ASICs for systems optimization, and suppliers are scrambling to offer design assistance and faster turnaround service. During the next four years a very large market for ASICs is predicted to develop, but obstacles to their widespread utilization will remain for some time. Among such obstacles are engineering uncertainties (hence the need for excessive design verification), and the practical barriers blocking the way to creative experimentation with different designs.

LASARRAY is offering a revolutionary new approach for the development and small-volume production of new ASICs. The boom in integrated circuits began less than 25 years ago. Since then, technological developments and major performance improvements in integrated circuit design are moving away from the combination of standard ICs with printed circuit boards and toward ASICs. Although an attractive alternative to the standard integrated circuits on PCBs, the use of ASICs is not yet widespread.

The relatively limited use of ASICs to date appears to be due to the following factors:

1. At the present time, both the development and production of ASICs have to be contracted out.
2. The services now offered by the approximately 130 integrated circuit producers around the world are unsatisfactory (high prices, long delivery times, delayed delivery dates, and inadequate appreciation for user problems).
3. Know-how has to be disclosed to third parties, which is unacceptable to some producers in many cases.
4. Contracting out important production steps to third parties reduces in-house added value. It also threatens jobs, and may result in a know-how drain.

As long as users can continue to get by using the "old" (PCB) technology, they will only turn to ASICs as a last resort. Price pressure and the need for more compact and more lightweight equipment are among the reasons that may compel a switch to ASICs.

Over the last 25 years, integrated circuits have transformed electronics technology. Consisting of a series of interconnected transistors deposited on a silicon base, these ICs or "chips" fulfill functions analogous to the fully equipped printed circuit. Several layers of transistors and their interconnections can be placed on a single silicon chip. The tremendous strides in miniaturization and increased sophistication in integrated circuit design and manufacture have been largely responsible for the microelectronic revolution.

The design and manufacture of integrated circuits is, because of their complexity and density, a time-consuming and expensive process (up to two years) and is only economical for batches in excess of 100,000 pieces. Designers of specialized electronic equipment must, therefore, use standard chips, mounted on specially designed printed circuit boards, which results in an inefficient use of the capabilities of the integrated circuits.

In order to take full advantage of integrated circuit potential, it is possible to design and manufacture a chip specially tailored to a specific, full-custom use. Because of the time and cost of design and manufacture, this solution is only economical when producing very large batches.

In view of the growing need for application specific integrated circuits, semicustom solutions have been developed. Most sophisticated are the cell-based chips, designed for customer purposes from standard subunits taken from a "library" of standard cells. Design and manufacturing time is reduced in this case to about three months.

Application specific integrated circuits can be broken down into the following major categories: Semicustom ICs and full-custom ICs. Figure IV:3.2 depicts these major categories and their variations.

Given the high setup costs for production of high-performance ASICs, manufacturers of specialized electronic equipment are still largely obliged to use printed circuits in conjunction with standard ICs. It is estimated that worldwide production of application specific printed circuits attained 1.25 million designs in 1984. Exact figures for the new ASIC designs are not available, but are unlikely to have attained 1 percent of the above figure.

The LASARRAY process is designed to exploit the market opportunity created by the growing demand of electronic equipment manufacturers for the advantages conferred by the use of ASICs rather than the cumbersome combination of standard chips and printed circuits on the one hand, and the slow, tedious, and expensive procedures presently necessary for custom chip design and manufacture on the other hand. In particular, the market is demanding "quick ASIC": the capability to design, produce, and test ASICs very rapidly for prototype development or for highly specific low-volume applications. Market research estimates show a demand for "quick ASIC" reaching $1 billion by 1990 (see Figure IV:3.3).

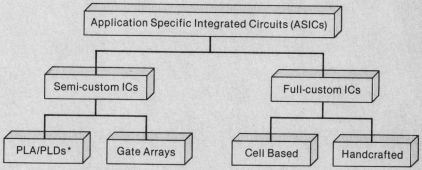

*Programmable Logic Array/Programmable Logic Devices

**Figure IV:3.2** Categorization of ASICs

*Source:* Courtesy LASARRAY SA

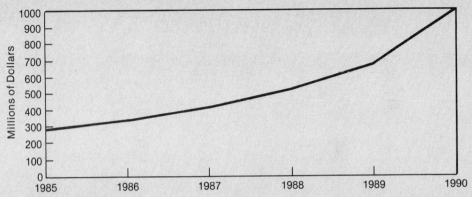

**Figure IV:3.3** Estimated worldwide consumption of "Quick ASICs" (millions of dollars)

Source: Courtesy LASARRAY SA

## THE LASARRAY ASIC PRODUCTION SYSTEM

At present, ASICs are produced primarily by the manufacturers of standard semiconductors, numbering about 130 companies worldwide. These companies, most of which are located in the United States and Japan, are equipped to produce chips in very large batches (from 100,000 to several million units).

To provide access to ASIC technology for companies requiring small batches, or even only a few units, the following conditions must be fulfilled:

- The reduction of chip design time and expense.
- The development of a new method for the economical production of chips in small batches.
- The development of rapid and inexpensive test methods.
- The development of facilities for electronic equipment manufacturers to design and produce chips in-house or at local service centers.

The LASARRAY system has been developed to meet these requirements, in collaboration with leading research institutes in the areas of precision mechanics, optics, and microelectronics, and in collaboration with certain specialized manufacturers in these areas.

The LASARRAY system is composed of a design system and an ASIC production unit; in the latter, the major innovations are the Direct Write Laser and the test system.

### Design System

The LASARRAY design system is based on the "Chipsmith" silicon compiler from Lattice Logic Ltd. of Edinburgh. The silicon compiler is a software package into which a customer circuit is entered, analyzed, and transformed into chip design information and ultimately stored on two floppy disks, one with the laser control data for direct write or mask manufacture, the other with the test data. "Chipsmith" is the CAD/CAE system that enables any electronics technician to design ASICs without special training. The system is structured so simply and logically that any competent electronics technician educated to today's standards can learn to operate it in only a few days. As a result, the company acquiring the system can handle the design work in-house and therefore maximize its added value.

The hardware consists of a computer system of the DEC VAX family. Since mid-1986, the system has been adopted to run on an IBM PC AT or an IBM-compatible personal computer.

## Testing System

Conventional testing systems offered on the market are designed for the testing of mass-produced chips and cost between SFr 600,000 and SFr 1.8 million.

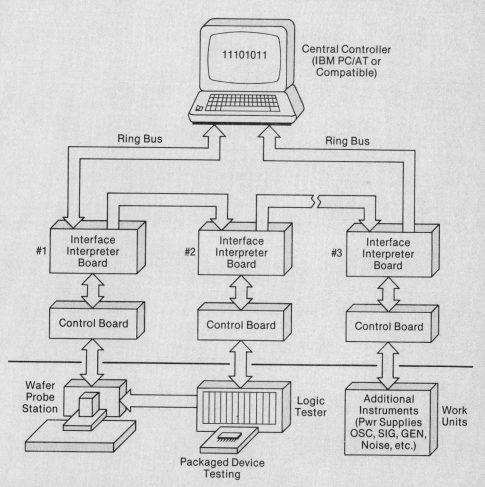

**Figure IV:3.4** Test system scheme

*Source:* Courtesy LASARRAY SA

## The LASARRAY System

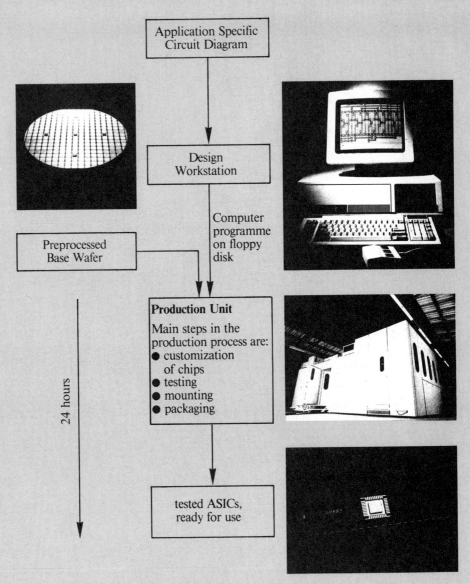

**Figure IV:3.5** The LASARRAY ASIC production system

*Source:* Courtesy LASARRAY SA

Consequently, a test system has been designed specifically for LASARRAY. The LASARRAY test system is designed along modular lines and consists largely of components available on the world market. A new type of bus system is used to connect them. Another new feature is a user-friendly instruction language that makes it possible to offer a highly sophisticated testing system at an absolutely unmatched price. The system permits quality control with real data (see Figure IV:3.4).

## Processing Modules

The entire "mini-factory" is designed to fit in transportable containers. It contains all the equipment and installations needed for the customizing, structuring, testing, and packaging of ASICs. Figure IV:3.5 depicts the complete LASARRAY ASIC production system and its major components.

The price of the complete LASARRAY system is SFr 6 million. This price does not include training of the customer's personnel in chip design and chip production, and this price can vary according to the number of design work stations or other features provided.

## LASARRAY SYSTEM ECONOMICS

"ASICs are expensive; they take time to produce and are economical only if produced in large quantities." Statements like this one have become obsolete with the invention of the LASARRAY design system. The average cost for one sample chip using the conventional production process is $23,000. With the LASARRAY system the sample chip cost is lowered to $12,000. Its patented design system is simple to use and ASICs can be developed in-house. Once the sample ASICs have been designed, production by means of the LASARRAY processing system is accomplished in the shortest possible time. The complete LASARRAY design system costs no more than about $35,000.

The LASARRAY processing system is characterized by similarly spectacular economies. Average production cost for the conventional building blocks is approximately $220, as compared to $71, including design costs, when manufactured with an owned LASARRAY processing system. These costs are based on a yearly requirement of 100,000 building blocks and lot sizes of 20 to 2,000 pieces. Costs for depreciation, interest on capital, raw materials, salaries, insurance, and service are also included in the $71 per building block price.

The LASARRAY system offers the most significant economic advantages for the production of prototypes or small quantities of chips since the costs of mask design and matching are eliminated. Output volumes are largely dependent on chip size and design complexity. As a general statement, it can be said that the LASARRAY system offers substantial economic advantages when compared with traditional manufacturing methods for lots of up to 2,000 to 3,000 identical chips.

As a comparison, the market price for "quick-ASIC" products within 24-hour turnaround period is presently about $20,000. This is a measure of the value certain electronics manufacturers place on the ability to improve and modify apparatus rapidly through ASIC improvements. Manufacturers also value the ability to test prototypes ASIC designs rapidly in order to avoid lengthy and expensive redesigns. In addition, the LASARRAY system allows the manufacturer to use ASICs in low-volume equipment, as ASIC production in small quantities is economical. Also, stock costs for ASICs are reduced because additional production runs can be made at any time.

## CONTINUING DEVELOPMENT OF THE SYSTEM

In view of the rapid advances in integrated circuit technology, LASARRAY is well aware of the importance of constantly improving and refining its product to stay ahead of competition. One of the company's major assets is the outstanding development team that it has assembled. In addition, it benefits from the geographical proximity of the Bienne operating affiliate and the institutes in Neuchatel. It has access to a wide range of present and potential suppliers in the fields of precision mechanics, optics, and electronics. A development budget of SFr 24 million is foreseen for the 1987 to 1990 period to preserve LASARRAY's technological leadership.

Most development work will be conducted by LASARRAY's own team, but some will be contracted to research institutes or suppliers. Such consultancy relationships have been extensively used and have not given rise to problems of secrecy or intellectual property.

Further developments will concentrate on the Direct Write Laser, the processing modules, the design system, and the test system. These developments will permit introduction of a second generation LASARRAY system for the 1990s.

In particular, important new knowledge has been gained and put into practice that makes a major contribution to the reduction of the high reject rates common in this field. The new knowledge will be the subject of further patent applications.

## NONECONOMIC FACTORS

Experience with other production technologies in the electronics industry indicates that the decision to invest in such installations is influenced by considerations of quick turnaround and confidentiality.

The same considerations are likely to play an even more important role in the decision to acquire a LASARRAY system, so that the following advantages may well be of decisive importance:

- Acceleration of the development process through elimination of time-consuming and costly test setups.
- Because ASICs can be modified instantly, existing equipment can be improved and modified more rapidly and new generations introduced faster.
- Confidentiality regarding in-house technology can be safeguarded since important stages in the manufacturing process are not subcontracted.

- ASICs can even be applied in low-volume equipment since low-volume ASIC production with the LASARRAY system is economical. This makes it possible to exploit the many advantages of ASICs in a wide range of products.
- Stock costs for customized ICs are reduced, since new production runs can be made at any time.

As a measure of the value certain manufacturers place on the first two advantages, the market price for "quick-ASICs" production with 24-hour turnaround is presently some $20,000.

## MARKETING OF THE LASARRAY SYSTEM

The LASARRAY marketing strategy has been developed by the company's management on the basis of numerous industry contacts and market research reports, conducted exclusively for the company by Mackintosh International for the European market and by Dataquest Incorporated for the United States market.

The LASARRAY system is protected by three basic patents.

### Structural Change in the Electronics Industry

Over the last 25 years, the integrated circuit has transformed electronics technology. The tremendous strides in miniaturization and increased sophistication in integrated circuit design and manufacture have been largely responsible for the "microelectronic revolution."

As indicated previously, the design and set-up costs for high performance ASICs are still a significant obstacle to their widespread use. Designers of specialized electronic equipment for low-volume production must, therefore, use standard chips mounted on specially designed printed circuit boards. This results in an inefficient use of the capabilities of the integrated circuits.

### Forecasted Demand for ASICs

All printed circuit boards are now produced to customers' specifications. In 1984, about 1.25 million new PCBs were designed worldwide, some 200,000 in Western Europe, 750,000 in the United States, 100,000 in Japan, and the remaining 200,000 throughout the rest of the world. Accurate figures on the number of new ASICs developed are not available; estimates would indicate that the total is less than 1 percent of the figures indicated above. However, despite a decline in demand for standard integrated circuits, it is estimated that ASIC demand is increasing by more than 45 percent per year. With this growth rate the market for ASICs should reach $1.9 billion by the end 1986 and $8.4 billion by 1990. This growth is due to some extent to the substitution of PCBs by ASICs, but principally to an overall increase in the demand for custom circuits. Forecasts show that by 1990 ASICs will account for 40 to 50 percent of total chip production (see Figures IV:3.6 and IV:3.7).

Satisfaction of this demand will put a premium on technologies which permit economical production of ASICs in small quantities. The figure on estimated European semiconductor purchasing represents Dataquest's estimate of the number of ASIC users in Europe in the mid-1990s, broken down by

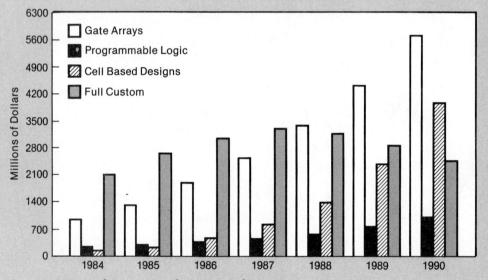

**Figure IV:3.6** Application specific integrated circuits

*Source:* Courtesy LASARRAY SA

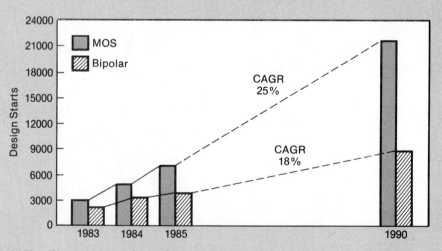

CAGR = Calculated Annual Growth Rate

**Figure IV:3.7** Estimated worldwide gate array design starts

*Source:* Courtesy LASARRAY SA

demand volume. It is clear that the market will be characterized by a small number of high-volume users on the one hand and by a vast number of firms requiring custom chips in small quantities on the other hand.

Many companies have their own printed circuit board production operation. Logically, the next step would be to produce chips in-house. A significant obstacle to this in the past has been—in addition to capital cost and the lack of semiconductor specialists—a lack of design and production know-how. If this next step (that is, the introduction of monolithic circuitry techniques) cannot be implemented on an in-house basis, the company's know-how, value added and competitiveness will decline in the long run. It is not reasonable to expect that the subcontracting of ASIC manufacturers can remain as the only user alternative in a field as fast-moving as that of electronics and semiconductor technology.

## Market Identification

The users of ASICs have been categorized into application usage segments. Dataquest illustrates such user segmentation and gives sales projections by present user category for Western Europe in Figure IV:3.8.

It must be realized, however, that potential buyers of a LASARRAY System are not necessarily present users of ASICs.

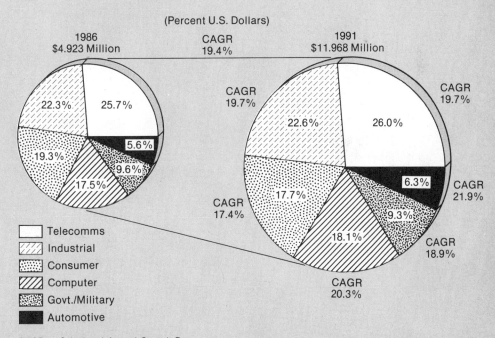

**Figure IV:3.8** Estimated European ASIC consumption (by end use)

*Source:* Courtesy LASARRAY SA

Table IV:3.1   DEMAND POTENTIAL, LASARRAY SYSTEMS, 1986–1990

| Country | No. of units | Country | No. of units |
|---|---|---|---|
| West Germany | 25 | Switzerland | 2 |
| United Kingdom | 20 | Scandinavia | 15 |
| France | 15 | Mid-East | 2 |
| Italy | 8 | Japan | 15 |
| Belgium/Luxembourg | 2 | Rest of Far East | 15 |
| Netherlands | 2 | North and South Africa | 80 |
| Spain | 4 | | |
| | | Total | 205 |

*Source:* Courtesy LASARRAY S.A.

Some 500 companies, contacted by company staff or appointed representatives at trade fairs or as a result of publications or advertising, have expressed interest in the LASARRAY system. The sector breakdown of these companies is as follows:

1. Industrial equipment and automotive electronics suppliers—56 percent
2. Consumer electronics equipment suppliers—23 percent
3. Semiconductor industry—7 percent
4. ASIC design/service companies—7 percent
5. Aerospace/military equipment suppliers—4 percent
6. Universities and technical institutes—3 percent

The initial orders and most advanced prospects are coming from the consumer electronics equipment suppliers, the aerospace/military suppliers, and the universities and technical institutes.

Table IV:3.1 provides the demand potential for LASARRAY systems. These estimates are based upon a number of factors which include the number of industrial equipment producers, the number of universities and technical schools, the present ASIC usage, and the projected industrial development parameters.

## Competition

Competitive threats presently perceived can be divided into two categories: equipment related and technology related. Equipment-related competition comes from other manufacturers who make equipment that performs a similar function to that made by LASARRAY. Technology-related competition comes from technological change that eliminates the need for the LASARRAY type of equipment or a change in the infrastructure of the semiconductor industry that would eliminate the current niche exploited by LASARRAY technology.

## Equipment-Related Competition

LASARRAY is aware of three other companies developing equipment for sale to third parties that are intended to write on silicon wafers for electronic circuit design. These companies are LaserPath, Cambridge Instruments, and Perkin Elmer. LaserPath uses laser methodology, while Cambridge Instruments and Perkin Elmer use electron-beam (E-Beam) methodology. Texas Instruments and IBM also are producing E-Beam direct write systems, but so far they have used these systems only for internal use. In addition, indications have been received that Siemens, Phillips, AT & T, Hitachi, Canon, and Toshiba may have made either laser direct write or E-Beam systems; however, to date, LASAR-RAY has obtained no confirmation to this effect.

## Technology-Related Competition

Technology-related competition covers the spectrum from a complete change in microelectronic methodology to the development of other equipment that will perform the identical functions of the LASARRAY system. It is unlikely that drastic changes in microelectronic technology will occur in the near future. An analysis of the media indicates that no major new equipment, apart from that previously mentioned, is likely to appear. The most likely competitive threat in this category would come from changes in the strategy and the infrastructure of the semiconductor manufacturing companies.

The semiconductor industry is well aware of the need for low-cost, quick-turnaround prototypes and low-volume ASIC integrated circuits. It is quite clear that the industry will react to client demand for more rapid response, and more design flexibility. If the LASARRAY system can be rapidly made available to the semiconductor industry, this industry could represent a significant market. However, companies such as LSI, VTI, California Devices, Intel, Texas Instruments, National Semiconductor, and Plessey are attempting to develop on their infrastructure to meet this client demand. The recent agreement between Texas Instruments and QUDOS is an example. Should these initiatives succeed, then LASARRAY's market potential would be affected.

## LASARRAY COMPETITIVE POSITION

LASARRAY is in a good position to counter the threats of competition. The LASARRAY system can deliver workable silicon directly written by its laser in hours rather than days after the design input. The integration of the Direct Write Laser equipment into a complete fabrication facility that includes all of the equipment required to deliver tested and packaged ASIC integrated circuits permits the prototype operation from interfering with mass production operations. The entire facility, including modern clean room containers, is offered at a price about half that of a free-standing E-Beam unit.

The use of E-Beam direct writing tools has been highly touted as the next generation of wafer fabrication equipment.

All of these reasons, together with the fact that the LASARRAY system is the only presently available total system and is less expensive than the closest partial system, suggest that LASARRAY System will be chosen by ASIC users.

## Marketing Strategy

The LASARRAY marketing strategy is based on the following six fundamental factors:

1. The LASARRAY system is an innovation; it represents an investment of some SFr 6 million, and its purchase usually requires a board-level decision by the purchaser. The sales process is therefore lengthy and complex.
2. The customer must be convinced that the system meets his or her needs and is reliable.
3. The potential market lies almost entirely outside Switzerland.
4. The different export markets—Europe, Japan and Far East, and the United States—require specific approaches.
5. The relationship with the semiconductor industry, as suppliers of wafers, is critically important.
6. The market is extremely dynamic, with aggressive competition.

The marketing strategy developed in response to these requirements comprises three main programs:

1. The communication program is designed to acquaint potential users and partners with LASARRAY. It uses trade fairs, press articles, advertisements, and technical and commercial documentation to promote the product.
2. The demonstration program focuses on the technical, operational, and economic feasibility of the system. The potential clients are invited to see ASICs being produced to their design specifications in Brugg/Bienne plants.
3. Service program comprises user training and know-how transfer, after-sales service guarantees, and facilities updates.

These programs are supported by a network of technical and commercial representatives in the major markets.

Research and subsequent contacts by the LASARRAY management have led to the conclusion that penetration of the important United States market requires a specific approach and has led to the creation of LASARRAY Corporation of Scotts Valley, California. Negotiations with joint venture partners are in preparation, as is the installation and operation of a LASARRAY service center in the San Jose ("Silicon Valley") area. The investment and operational consequences have been included in the finance plan.

At this planning stage, U.S. sales of LASARRAY systems are included in the sales and revenue forecast of LASARRAY HOLDING AG. However, it is the intention of the LASARRAY management to implement a joint venture with a U.S. partner, which would open the U.S. market faster than is represented in this business plan. The cash flow and net profit results for LASARRAY HOLDING AG should be positively influenced by the planned joint venture strategy.

It is likely that the planned joint venture with a U.S. company will broaden LASARRAY's financial base through a public stock offering to U.S. investors. In negotiations of joint venture agreements, and in a possible U.S. public offering, LASARRAY management would act in the interests of the shareholders of LASARRAY HOLDING AG. It should be mentioned at this point that no licensing fees are included in the financial forecasts. This fact represents an additional financial opportunity, in view of the fact that LASARRAY expects licensing opportunities for parts of its know-how in related industries, which would not negatively impact LASARRAY system sales.

## Sales and Sales Revenue Forecast

On the basis of LASARRAY's market research, current customer negotiations, and contacts, the sales forecasts for 1986 to 1990 are depicted in Table IV:3.2.

These sales translate into the gross sales revenues forecast (ex factory) presented in Table IV:3.3.

One customer has signed a sales contract and the advance payment has

Table IV:3.2  LASARRAY SALES FORECAST 1986–1990

|  | LASARRAY Systems | | | | | |
|---|---|---|---|---|---|---|
|  | 1986 | 1987 | 1988 | 1989 | 1990 | 1986–1990 |
|  | Europe + Far East | | | | | |
| Sales | 2 | 6 | 12 | 17 | 20 | 57 |
| Deliveries | — | 5 | 9 | 16 | 17 | 47 |
|  | U.S. | | | | | |
| Sales | — | — | 3 | 9 | 17 | 29 |
| Deliveries | — | — | 2 | 7 | 14 | 23 |
| Total Sales | 2 | 6 | 15 | 26 | 37 | 86 |
| Total Deliveries | — | 5 | 11 | 23 | 31 | 70 |
| LASARRAY Design Systems | 10 | 60 | 60 | 85 | 80 | 295 |

Source: Courtesy LASARRAY SA

Table IV:3.3  FORECAST: GROSS SALES REVENUES

|  | 1987 | 1988 | 1989 | 1990 | 1986–1990 |
|---|---|---|---|---|---|
| SFr (millions) | 27.9 | 64.8 | 134.9 | 184.3 | 411.9 |

Source: Courtesy LASARRAY SA

Table IV:3.4  PROJECTED PROFIT AND LOSS STATEMENTS LASARRAY FINANCE PLAN, NOVEMBER 1986 (IN THOUSANDS OF SFR)

| | 1986 Nov.–Dec. | 1987 No. | 1987 Amount | 1988 No. | 1988 Amount | 1989 No. | 1989 Amount | 1990 No. | 1990 Amount |
|---|---|---|---|---|---|---|---|---|---|
| Turnover systems: | | | | | | | | | |
| Switzerland | 0 | 5 | 25,500 | 9 | 49,500 | 16 | 88,000 | 17 | 93,500 |
| USA | 0 | | 0 | 2 | 11,000 | 7 | 38,500 | 14 | 77,000 |
| Design systems | 330 | | 1,980 | | 1,980 | | 2,805 | | 2,640 |
| Training | 20 | | 120 | | 120 | | 120 | | 100 |
| Service contracts | 0 | | 276 | | 2,208 | | 5,520 | | 11,040 |
| Total sales revenue | 350 | 5 | 27,876 | 11 | 64,808 | 23 | 134,945 | 31 | 184,280 |
| Reduction from sales | 8 | | 560 | | 4,536 | | 9,446 | | 12,900 |
| Net sales revenue | 342 | | 27,316 | | 60,272 | | 125,499 | | 171,380 |
| Directly allocated expenses | 250 | | 14,388 | | 33,204 | | 63,535 | | 86,570 |
| Contribution margin | 92 | | 12,928 | | 27,068 | | 61,964 | | 84,810 |
| Nonallocated expenses | | | | | | | | | |
| Marketing | 130 | | 1,342 | | 3,400 | | 6,310 | | 7,730 |
| Production | 80 | | 2,026 | | 5,065 | | 11,435 | | 14,470 |
| Administration | 155 | | 1,263 | | 2,185 | | 2,830 | | 3,255 |
| U.S.A. | 70 | | 1,215 | | 4,780 | | 8,680 | | 10,750 |
| Development | 0 | | 4,601 | | 5,333 | | 6,480 | | 7,780 |
| Subtotal | 435 | | 10,447 | | 20,763 | | 35,735 | | 43,985 |
| Cash flow before taxes | −343 | | 2,481 | | 6,305 | | 26,229 | | 40,825 |
| Depreciation | | | | | | | | | |
| Fixed assets | 117 | | 1,512 | | 2,694 | | 2,707 | | 3,083 |
| Development costs | 0 | | 660 | | 1,534 | | 3,195 | | 4,363 |
| Capital issuing costs | 10 | | 391 | | 391 | | 391 | | 391 |
| Incorporation costs | | | | | | | | | |
| Total depreciation | 127 | | 2,563 | | 4,619 | | 6,293 | | 7,837 |
| Profits before tax | −470 | | −82 | | 1,686 | | 19,936 | | 32,988 |
| Tax 30% | | | | | | | 5,981 | | 9,896 |
| Net profits | −470 | | −82 | | 1,686 | | 13,955 | | 23,092 |

*Source:* Courtesy LASARRAY SA

Table IV:3.5  LATEST AND PROJECTED BALANCE SHEETS LASARRAY FINANCE PLAN NOVEMBER 1986 (IN THOUSANDS OF SFR.)

| | 31 Oct. 1986 | 31 Dec. 1986 | 31 Dec. 1987 | 31 Dec. 1988 | 31 Dec. 1989 | 31 Dec. 1990 |
|---|---|---|---|---|---|---|
| **Assets** | | | | | | |
| Cash and banks | 1,320 | 13,648 | 5,575 | 12,960 | 26,990 | 13,709 |
| Accounts receivable | | 175 | 300 | 2,900 | 7,700 | 36,860 |
| Spare parts | 70 | | | | | 9,800 |
| Work in progress | 456 | 2,341 | 6,951 | 7,951 | 7,951 | 7,951 |
| Prepayments to suppliers | | | | | | |
| Fixed assets | 592 | 1,414 | 8,985 | 9,555 | 10,334 | 11,045 |
| Cap. development costs | 9,003 | 9,752 | 9,092 | 7,558 | 4,363 | |
| Cap. incorp. and cap. issue costs | 344 | 1,934 | 1,543 | 1,152 | 761 | 370 |
| Total assets | 11,785 | 29,264 | 32,446 | 42,076 | 58,099 | 79,735 |
| **Liabilities and owners' equity** | | | | | | |
| Accounts payable and accrued expenses | 1,238 | 800 | 2,880 | 3,512 | 6,846 | 13,970 |
| Prepayments from customers | 1,350 | 1,350 | 2,534 | 9,846 | 8,580 | |
| Bank loans | 588 | | | | | |
| Advance from FELA E.U. AG | 1,025 | | | | | |
| Total liabilities | 4,201 | 2,150 | 5,414 | 13,358 | 15,426 | 13,970 |
| **Owners' equity** | | | | | | |
| Share capital | 7,500 | 12,500 | 12,500 | 12,500 | 12,500 | 12,500 |
| Paid-in reserves | 3,000 | 18,000 | 18,000 | 18,000 | 18,000 | 18,000 |
| Retained earnings (loss carry forward) | −2,916 | −3,386 | −3,468 | −1,782 | 12,173 | 35,265 |
| Total owners' equity | 7,584 | 27,114 | 27,032 | 28,718 | 42,673 | 65,765 |
| Total liability and owners' equity | 11,785 | 29,264 | 32,446 | 42,076 | 58,099 | 79,735 |

Source: Courtesy LASARRAY SA

735

been received. Five other companies are in the advanced stages of purchasing negotiations, and 15 companies are involved in specific purchasing negotiations. In addition, LASARRAY and its representatives are systematically approaching further potential clients among the some 500 companies that have so far expressed interest.

### Financial Forecast 1987–1990

Fiscal forecasts have been developed based on market evaluations. Accordingly, cash flow becomes positive in 1987; the break-even point is expected in early 1988. P/L statements show a cumulated cash flow of SFr 75.8 million and a net profit, after taxes, of SFr 38.6 million over the period of 1987 to 1990. Tables IV:3.4 and IV:3.5 present profit and loss and balance sheet for years 1986 through 1990.

## LASARRAY S.A.: ORGANIZATION

The LASARRAY HOLDING AG, formed in November 1985 from the previous FXL AG, acts as the group's financing agent and holds all of LASARRAY's patents and participations. The company is located in Thundorf, Switzerland. The organizational structure of the member companies, capital structure, and incorporation are shown in Figure IV:3.9.

### Corporate Strategies

LASARRAY's organizational structure depends upon the company's business strategies, policies, and objectives. In a general meeting of the Board of Directors in early 1986, Ernst Uhlmann committed the company to the following medium- and long-term business policies and objectives:

1. LASARRAY's principal goal is to provide the ASIC market with tools to manufacture ASICs in-house or through service centers with mini-

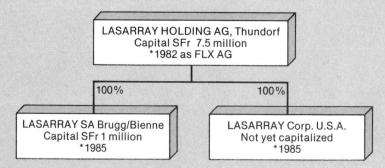

**Figure IV:3.9** Organizational structure of LASSARAY

*Source:* Courtesy LASARRAY SA

mal capital expenditure commitments, extremely short lead times, easily accessible ASIC design and production know-how, and low cost for prototype and small lot series.

2. Therefore, LASARRAY is committed to market worldwide and with strategic alliances a modular system based on Direct Write Laser technology, combined with an integral software package for design, manufacturing, and testing of ASICs.

The Board of Directors established also the company's short-term business objectives for 1987:

1. Sell four LASARRAY systems.
2. Manufacture, assemble, and deliver an initial batch of five systems.
3. Install a network of representatives.
4. Equip LASARRAY in the United States with its own production system for demonstration and training.
5. Extend the LASARRAY production capacity.

By June 1986, Ernst Uhlmann and his corporate staff were faced with the following organizational tasks related to the set-up and operation of normal production activities in order to assemble complete LASARRAY ASIC production systems on a routine basis:

1. Complete engineering details and minor component parts problems in the three modules of the LASARRAY production system.
2. Finalize financial investment requirements for the organization to provide for the projected acquisition of the production and office building in the city of Bienne.
3. Finalize the projected plant layout for the projected Bienne manufacturing facility.
4. Develop the manufacturing and assembly methods, the procedures, the manufacturing tools, the jigs, and the fixtures required for the LASARRAY manufacturing program.
5. Develop a manufacturing organization, hire required personnel for the first production year (1987), and train key personnel.
6. Develop a quality assurance organization, hire required personnel for the first production year, and train key personnel.
7. Develop a service organization, hire required personnel, and train key personnel.
8. Develop a marketing distributor network as specified in the declared corporate objectives.
9. Develop a marketing training program and the required LASARRAY production system training equipment to be installed on the new premises in Bienne.
10. Establish LASARRAY personnel policies and administration to insure high quality operational performance of the organization.

## Production Organization

In various executive meetings during the fall of 1986, Messrs. Doering, Simpson, and Stocker were asked by Ernst Uhlmann to develop a program budget of the personnel required to achieve the LASARRAY production and sales requirements for 1987.

During an analysis of the anticipated engineering development requirements Elko Doering, manager of development, explained that the development department has built up an outstanding team of design specialists and that he was not going to expand the department significantly. The company would, however, continue to contract out development work on certain occasions. He informed the committee that some development work was already being done, especially in the base wafer development.

Work assignments in the department would include projects such as the expansion of the application of the Direct Write Laser (DWL); the development of software for the DWL and the test system; the development of the DWL and the Clean Room Modules; the development of laser technology, optical systems, and experimental work; the development of test programs for the LASARRAY production unit; the development of design engineering for intricate component requirements, software, and base wafers.

Kurt Widmer, manager of production, detailed the present manufacturing philosophy of the company in this manner: In order to maximize flexibility, LASARRAY would manufacture as little as possible in-house during 1987. The production department would be responsible only for the planning and designing, the component procurement, the assembly and quality assurance, as well as the maintenance and repair service. This would guarantee the required quality within the budgeted costs and delivery schedules.

Special attention would be given to the supplier network. The following supplier selection criteria had been established; the suppliers would need to demonstrate: the suitability of the purchased product for the LASARRAY system; their credibility in the semiconductor market; their viability as a worldwide service organization; their dependability as a deliverer of equipment as scheduled; their suitability as to pricing; and their flexibility. Approximately 160 suppliers were incorporated into the supplier network for the manufacturing program of the LASARRAY 1987 production schedule.

The containers, that is, the individual modules, are produced by contractors according to LASARRAY design, equipped in the LASARRAY plant with air conditioning and clean room equipment by the subcontractor's personnel, and fitted with the process equipment by LASARRAY personnel.

The Direct Write Laser is assembled and wired in accordance with LASARRAY's drawings in a highly specialized precision engineering plant in Bienne. The control system is purchased from Bircher AG, Beringen, and installed and set up by the LASARRAY plant.

Finally the whole system is tested and operated for two to three months. Practical training of customer personnel is also carried out during this period. System acceptance by the customer takes place at the Bienne plant.

## Service Organization

The close ties between start-up and the service and repair functions, as well as the stocking of spare parts and parts for assembly, are the reason for placing the service function under the production department. However, the types of services offered and the documentation needed are determined by the marketing department. Production provides the operating resources such as personnel, material, and logistics.

After-sales service is provided at four different levels:

1. Service by the customers with manuals, training, and their own spare parts stock.
2. Service by a LASARRAY agent with manuals, drawings, and a stock comprising the most frequently used spare parts.
3. Service by LASARRAY with manuals, manufacturing documents, drawings, schematics, training of service engineers, and full spare parts stock, with guaranteed delivery within a few days.
4. Service by suppliers with commitments by suppliers and software producers to place the know-how of their specialists and development team at the customers' disposal.

The bulk of the service is provided by LASARRAY's agents, which train personnel and carry spare parts stocks for their own account or on consignment, depending on the situation. Service is as decentralized as possible; however, remote diagnostic services by telephone and file transmission is planned.

The service organization will be paid for by service contracts and direct invoicing of service work and spare parts deliveries. Service contracts also include the updating of the software and components of the entire system.

LASARRAY's service team will be drawn from the LASARRAY project managers. A service manager will make the service assignments.

Work will be done under guarantee or on a good will basis, as will maintenance, repair, and conversion work. Adaptation of software will be provided, though software shortcomings will usually be made good by new software versions rather than isolated improvements in old software. All customer comments and requirements will be transmitted to the marketing and development functions.

## Sales Organization

Based on the LASARRAY marketing strategies discussed previously with Ernst Uhlmann, Claude Simpson recommended to the executive committee that the sales department should be kept small for the present time. Instead, he would require a competent staff of area and product managers, and sales and advertising specialists. The committee decided that the required personnel for the anticipated sales program should be phased in, depending on the state of the pilot and the initial production results of the LASARRAY production units.

Mr. Simpson was aware that the engineering development of the LASAR-

RAY production units was extremely complicated. He also knew that, although one unit had been successfully completed and demonstrated its capabilities in demonstrations conducted in an international exhibition, considerable detail work on a number of production bottlenecks had to be resolved. He had no doubt that it was only a matter of time until the first production batch of units would be coming off the assembly line. However, as an experienced sales manager he knew that a too aggressive "pushing" of such a complicated high-tech product and undue sales commitments might hurt the reputation of LASARRAY SA if because of production start-up problems completed units were not be delivered on time.

In corporate staff discussions, everyone involved in this new LASARRAY operation was aware that the company was just now overcoming the first stage of a new product development. Capital outlays for research and development and for the formation and setup of the new venture so far had created a negative cash flow. Additional capital would have to be invested in 1987 before the first batch of LASARRAY production units would be completed. Mr. Simpson intended, therefore, to proceed in a cautiously aggressive manner in setting up his sales organization.

## THE BIENNE OPERATION

Six months had passed since Mr. Uhlmann and his corporate staff had finalized the 1987 business plan last October. The first half of 1987 had been successful for LASARRAY SA and also for Ernst Uhlmann. The Bienne facility had been taken over by the company. The building, office adaptations, and facility preparations required to start up the assembly of the LASARRAY ASICs production systems had been completed by the end of May 1987. Purchased materials for the first batch of five units to be assembled were arriving at the Bienne plant. By the early part of June 1987, subcontractors were engaged in assembling the first two production-line units.

In November 1986, the Board of Directors had approved additional funds required for the second phase of LASARRAY, the set up of the manufacturing organization. In early spring of 1987 Ernst Uhlmann succeeded in securing the financing needs of SFr 20 million through subscriptions with approximately 60 new shareholders from Switzerland, West Germany, Britain, and other countries. SFr 13 million were earmarked to take the company from the experimental stage of developing the LASARRAY production system into the next phase of growth and to build an efficient production and assembly operation at the Bienne facility.

In June the new production facility was bustling with activity. Although the plant offices were still under construction, workers and technicians were busy assembling two complete units. Hermann Stocker, the production manager, a man with impressive technical and manufacturing experience, was coordinating final assembly activities with subcontractor crews. The units that were in the process of being assembled were not experimental prototypes, but the first

ASIC production systems to be manufactured as part of the 1987 production schedule. Stocker and his technicians were engaged in testing out unit components, assembly processes, and procedures. Much had yet to be done in the design of the LASARRAY manufacturing system, the production and inventory planning, the control system, and the quality assurance procedures. Many of the assembly methods had still to be developed or tested, and Mr. Stocker knew it.

The Bienne operation has about 26,000 square feet of production floor space of which LASARRAY occupies 1,600 square feet. The remainder of the available floor space was leased by LASARRAY during 1986 and would be used whenever production requirements increased. The building is composed of two levels, the main floor and a mezzanine. The wafer processing, service equipment and testing, and packing modules for each of the two LASARRAY ASICs production units were assembled on the first floor and the mezzanine. The appearance of the assembly activities gave an impression of "orderly improvisation." It was evident that here was an operation in the early stage of manufacturing and that the assembly processes were being developed at the time.

Ernst Uhlmann, on his frequent inspection walks through the plant, was pleased that his brainchild, the LASARRAY operation, was finally maturing toward its first tangible objective: the assembly of commercially produced LASARRAY ASICs production units. Planned manufacturing strategies were now about to be implemented. Initial production plans by LASARRAY were to meet material requirements for the 1987 production schedule through horizontal manufacturing integration. Consequently, virtually all required module sections, subassemblies, component parts, and supply items were subcontracted or purchased from supplier firms. Even the labor crews required for the assembly of the individual modules and the completed LASARRAY product were subcontracted. This permitted the technical management of the Bienne operation to concentrate on the finalizing of the product design, "ironing out" the developmental problems and getting the LASARRAY system ready for standard production activities.

It was Elco Doering, manager of development—an intense and extremely busy man—who expressed that the "zero hour" was approaching for LASARRAY. The 1987 production plan specified the completion of the scheduled production requirements of five LASARRAY ASIC production units. Here was a product whose high-technology design made it extremely sensitive to the need for high precision manufacturing of its component parts and its final assembly. Manufacturing specifications for the subcontracted modules and component subassemblies were exacting; so were the quality assurance requirements. And there were still a number of component details of the basic unit that had to be finalized.

Mr. Doering was responsible for verifying that the overall design and engineering construction of the LASARRAY unit had been successfully completed and performance-tested, so that now routine assembly operation activities could take place at the Bienne plant facilities. This verification process included the finalizing of the bills of materials, the assembly lists, the process sheets, the materials specifications, and the quality assurance specifications. Also, a materials procurement policy and procedures for the company would have to be developed, now that the Bienne operation had started to produce for the LASARRAY market.

Along with the excitement of the new LASARRAY venture entering into its second phase, the new professional challenges were also obvious to Mr. Stocker, the production manager. He knew that a considerable amount of work lay ahead for the LASARRAY production organization until the essential production methods were in place. He was concerned, in particular, that a formal production and inventory control system had not yet been designed. Data base requirements (such as those for bills of materials, materials specifications, quality control specifications, and purchasing and supplier-related information requirements) had to be handled mostly by hand. Hermann Stocker knew that the moment had come to request expert assistance from manufacturing specialists to recommend computer systems and manufacturing-related software programs that would satisfy the projected LASARRAY production program requirements for the next five years. He wondered if the much heralded and discussed Computer Integrated Manufacturing systems technologies could be applied to LASARRAY's new production venture at Bienne.

Among the manufacturing-process–related functional development requirements that occupied the minds of the LASARRAY staff, two functions became top priority in June 1987: production scheduling and materials acquisition and administration. The overall production capacity of the Bienne operation was projected at 24 complete LASARRAY production units per year. This amounts to a maximum annual sales volume of SFr 144,000,000, at SFr 6,000,000 per unit. In addition, service related annual sales were estimated at SFr 36,000,000. Maximum sales by LASARRAY, SA at the Bienne operation could be as high as SFr 180,000,000 per year.

Both Messrs. Doering and Stocker were clearly aware of the challenges that lay before them in designing a cost-effective manufacturing system at the Bienne facility, which would meet the customer requirements of a high-quality product, the minimum delivery schedule consistent with the high-technology nature of the LASARRAY ASIC production unit, and the best investment cost for the customer.

## DECISIONS

With LASARRAY SA entering the second phase in the firm's development, Ernst Uhlmann realized that the organization was facing new challenges. Although he had surrounded himself with a capable staff, Uhlmann knew that expert assistance might be needed to design and implement a cost-effective manufacturing system, and to carry out the production program for the period of 1987 to 1990.

The fiscal year 1988 had just begun. As Ernst Uhlmann commented to a visitor to whom he had shown the Bienne facility shortly after having successfully concluded the placement of SFr 20 million in shares for LASARRAY's expansion program: "This is a new feeling. Now I have to report the progress of our company to our shareholders . . . and they are expecting results!" Mr. Uhlmann had indicated that "the pressure was on" for the company to produce.

During this past year the company staff had been working hard to achieve the declared short-term objectives. Much had been accomplished; not everything had been simple. In particular, in LASARRAY's production activities, Ernst Uhlmann felt that thorough systems analysis of the manufacturing support functions could help streamline the Bienne operation. He was aware that the project type of manufacturing activities of the LASARRAY ASIC production units, the high-technology product and quality requirements, the high unit cost, and the logistics requirements of component and assemblies procurement required the type of strategic planning needed for advanced production systems.

As the first batch of five ASIC production units was assembled during 1987, it became evident to Mr. Stocker that specific operations management functions at the Bienne facility had to be installed, or finalized—and this was a top priority. Detailed analysis of the company's short-term and intermediate-term manufacturing strategies for the business plan of 1987 to 1990 and the implementation of manufacturing-related functions would be required.

To follow through with the projected production requirements, special attention would have to be given to design engineering, manufacturing engineering, materials management policies, material procurement policies, production and inventory planning and control system, quality assurance, human resource organization, and the planning of the Bienne operation.

Mr. Uhlmann's entrepreneurial capabilities had been proven in the buildup of his FELA conglomerate of high-technology firms. He had no doubts about the capability of his staff to achieve the company goals for the fiscal year 1987. To ensure that the LASARRAY organization was developing as expeditiously as possible and to maintain the technological advantages achieved so far, however, Ernst Uhlmann considered calling in expert manufacturing consultants. He was aware that—in order to maintain his organization's lead over the international competition—strategic advanced production planning was needed so that the company would maintain its comparative advantage as innovators in the ASIC production equipment market. Needless to say, Mr. Uhlmann is determined to lead the company into its second phase with a cost-effective and efficient high-quality production operation at the Bienne facility.

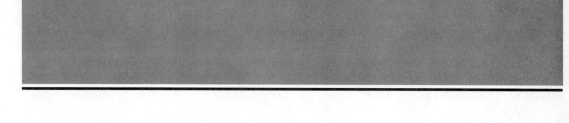

# Glossary

**absolute advantage** A theory developed by Adam Smith that states that two countries can benefit from trade if, due to natural or acquired endowments, they can provide each other with a product more cheaply than if they each produced both products at home.

**accommodating (below the line) items** Transactions that are viewed as items that can be used to finance a balance of payments surplus or deficit.

**adjustment** The third step in the expatriate socialization. It is the adaptation stage. At this stage the expatriate has successfully socialized into the new situation in the foreign country.

**ad valorem tariff** A tariff that is expressed in terms of a percentage of the total value of a commodity, for example, 10 percent of the value of baseball gloves imported, or 20 percent of the value of plywood imported.

**advertising** Any paid form of nonpersonal presentation and promotion of ideas, goods, or services by an identified sponsor.

**Andean Common Market (ANCOM)** A common market that was established by Bolivia, Colombia, Chile, Ecuador, and Peru in 1969. In 1976 Chile left ANCOM, and in 1973 Venezuela joined this market. ANCOM is a subgroup of LAFTA, and its main policy is to restrict foreign-owned investment.

**antitrust considerations** Found in most capitalist nations, laws that prohibit monopoly, price-fixing, and so forth.

**applied technology** The transformation of basic technology into new products and processes that a firm can use and/or sell.

**appropriateness** Qualitative criteria for the evaluation of a strategy that address the appropriateness of resource capabilities, risk tendencies, and time horizons which have been attached to the chosen strategy.

**arbitrage** The simultaneous purchase of foreign exchange in one market, where it is cheaper, and its sale in another market, where it is more expensive, in order to profit from differences in the spot exchange quotations.

**arbitration** The process of seeking a judgment from a neutral third party that is acceptable to both disputing parties.

**Association of Southern Asian Nations (ASEAN)** A major trading association among LDCs, established by Indonesia, Malaysia, the Philippines, Singapore, and Thailand in 1967.

**attention-evokers** Those factors that cause a firm to consider exporting as a possible business strategy.

**attitudinal outcomes** The second type of outcome to successful organizational socialization which lead to the employees having feelings of general satisfaction, internal work motivation, and job involvement.

**autonomous (above the line) items** Transactions that take place for their own sake, irrespective of the balance of payments position of the country. These include all transactions that take place in response to business conditions at home and abroad.

**backward integration** Expansion of a firm's operations into its suppliers' market.

**balance of payments (BOP)** An accounting statement that shows the summary of all the transactions between the residents of a nation and the residents of all other nations during a given period of time (usually a calendar year).

**balance of trade argument** An argument that states tariffs or quotas are necessary because they encourage a favorable balance of trade, that is, a surplus of exports over imports.

**bank acceptance** A bill of exchange that has been accepted by a bank.

**bank draft** A bank draft is similar to a commercial bill of exchange because it is a written order by a drawer to a drawee instructing the drawee to pay on demand, or on a certain date, a specified amount of money to a payee. The major difference between a commercial bill of exchange and a bank draft is that, in the case of the bank draft, the drawee is a bank, rather than an importer.

**baradari** The joint family formed by the combination of the bride's family and the groom's family in India.

**barrier** Anything that obstructs the freedom to transfer and to coordinate resources across national borders.

**basic technology** Breakthroughs in technology that have profound effects throughout many industries.

**batch system** A type of operations system in which a number of products or services are processed in batches or lots.

**behavioral outcomes** The first type of outcome to successful organizational socialization, in which employees display dependable job performance, assignment completion, innovation, and spontaneous cooperation.

**bilateral or multilateral export quota** An export quota that is established by agreement between the trading nations.

**bilateral or multilateral quota** A quota that is imposed by an importing country after consultation or negotiation with the exporting country.

**bilateral treaties** Formal and binding agreements between two countries.

**bill of lading** A document that provides evidence of the shipment of a commodity.

**Boston Consulting Group (BCG) matrix** The simplest of portfolio matrices used in developing a corporate strategy for an MNC.

**Bretton Woods system** The international monetary system that was established in 1944 by agreements among the representatives of the United States, the United Kingdom, and 42 other nations who met at Bretton Woods, New Hampshire.

**business strategy** A plan that defines how each individual business (SBU or affiliate) should position itself among its rivals to reach its objectives, and, therefore, to contribute the implementation of the corporate global strategy and the achievement of the corporate global objectives.

**buy-back or compensation trading** A form of countertrade that involves the export of a technology package, the construction of an entire project, or the provision of services by a firm.

**cable transfer** An order that is transmitted by a bank in a country to its foreign correspondent bank in another country instructing its corresponding bank to pay out a specific amount of money to a designated person or account.

**capital account** Part of a country's balance of payments accounts, including those transactions that involve future obligations. These transactions include (1) investing in foreign nations, (2) providing loans to foreigners, and (3) depositing money in foreign banks.

**capital budgeting** The management of long-term investment, involving the comparative assessment of alternative long-term projects.

**capital inflow** An increase in foreign assets in a country, or a decrease in a country's assets abroad.

**capital outflow** An increase in a country's assets abroad, or a decrease in foreign assets in a country.

**Caribbean Free Trade Association (CARIFTA)** A major trade association among LDCs, established in 1968 by Antigua, Barbados, Bolivia, Colombia, Dominica, Ecuador, Grenada, Guyana, Jamaica, Montserrat, Peru, St. Lucia, St. Vincent, Trinidad, Tobago, and Venezuela. In 1973 the name was changed to the Caribbean Common Market (CARICOM) and was extended to include the Bahamas, Belize, St. Kitts-Nevis-Angullia.

**cash cows** Businesses that are characterized by low growth and high market share.

**cash flow management** The process of maintaining an optimum balance between cash and interest bearing short-term assets.

**Central American Common Market (CACM)** A custom union that was established by Costa Rica, El Salvador, Guatemala, Honduras, and Nicaragua in 1960.

**channel of distribution** The structure of intercompany organizational units and external company agents and dealers (wholesale and retail) through which a commodity, product, or service is marketed.

**charter** The written statement of an MNC's mission.

**civil or code law** A legal system in which the judicial system is grouped into civil, commercial, and criminal laws. Each group is a compilation of identical or similar subject matter laws that together form a code.

**clustering** The sixth step in the new market screening process. It involves an examination of selected nations for geographical clusters that may facilitate the formation of regional organizations and subsidiaries within an MNC.

**commercial bill of exchange** A written order by an exporter (the drawer) to an importer (the drawee) instructing the importer to pay on demand, or at a certain date, a specified amount of money to a designated party (the payee).

**common law or community law** A law that is based on unwritten principles and on precedents derived from custom, usage, and previous judicial rulings.

**common market** A more complete form of a customs union, it combines the characteristics of a customs union with the elimination of barriers on the movement of capital and labor among the member countries.

**comparative advantage** First presented by David Ricardo, the theory of comparative advantage demonstrates that two nations can benefit from trade even when one of the nations has an absolute advantage in the production of both commodities being traded.

**compensating (reserve) account** Part of a country's balance of payments accounts, including a nation's holdings of foreign convertible currencies, gold, and SDRs that are used by its monetary authorities to intervene in the foreign exchange market in resolving its balance of payments problems.

**compensation trading** See Buy-back.

**competitive assessment** Evaluation of the actual (present) and potential (future) competition that an MNC and its subsidiaries face in their markets.

**compound tariff** A tariff made up of a specific portion and an ad valorem portion.

**consistency** Qualitative criteria for the evaluation of a strategy that tests to see whether or not the chosen global strategy is consistent with the global objectives, environmental assumptions, and organizational conditions.

**contract enforcement considerations** Enforcement of contracts between private parties, MNCs, governments, or government-owned companies, such as those found in communist countries or in LDCs.

**corporate strategy** A strategy that focuses on how the different businesses and markets in which an MNC compete may be integrated into an effective portfolio.

**corrupt practices and bribery considerations** Laws that distinguish payoffs and bribery from customary gifts or facilitating payments.

**cost-benefit analysis** An approach to auditing that is a systematic process of quantifying the associated costs and benefits derived from each program, method, or strategy.

**cost-benefit analysis approach to social audit** The systematic process of quantifying the associated costs and benefits derived from each social program undertaken by a firm.

**counterpurchase or parallel barter** A countertrade agreement by which a seller is paid partially in credits that must be used for the purchase of products from a prespecified list.

**countertrade** The process by which an importing nation imposes conditions that link imports with exports and as a result minimizes the net outflow of foreign exchange from its economy.

**credit swap** An arrangement between a firm and a foreign central bank or commercial bank to exchange one currency for another and then to reverse the exchange at a future date.

**creeds** The broad ethical tone and the social responsibilities of an MNC.

**creeping or slow expropriation** Host government regulations preventing an MNC's capital or profits from leaving the country. These can also take the form of high taxes, royalties, or other charges against an MNC by a government to make the MNC's operations unprofitable; or they can be claims against the MNC by the host government for past inequities.

**cultural universals** The common cultural elements that exist across all cultures.

**culture** A cognitive frame of reference and a learned pattern of behavior among members of a group that is transmitted to them from their own previous generations.

**culture shock** The psychological status of anxiety one experiences when facing a new and different culture with its unfamiliar set of characteristics and expectations.

**currency swap** An arrangement between two firms to exchange one currency for another and then to reverse the exchange at a future date.

**current account** Part of a country's balance of payments accounts, including those transactions that do not result in any future obligations. These transactions include (1) purchases of goods and services from foreigners and (2) unilateral transfers, that is, remittances and grants that are given to foreigners for free.

**customs union** An organization that allows for the lowering or abolishing of trade barriers between member countries, and that adopts a unified system of tariffs against nonmembers countries.

**customer profile** Information on the geographic, demographic, psychographic, and buying behavior patterns of consumers in a given market.

**debt** Funds raised by an MNC through borrowing that must be repaid to the lender through regular payments. Such payments cover the principal borrowed and the interest and other fees charged for the use of the borrowed capital.

**delphi techniques** Forecasting methods in which questions are asked of an anonymous panel of experts a number of times in order to achieve consensus.

**demand lag** The time needed for the development of a demand for newly exported goods.

**demographic factors** The most commonly utilized variables for differentiating among customer groups. These variables are descriptive characteristics through which customer segments can be identified by an MNC. They include the age, sex, family size, lifestyle, income, marital status, occupation, education, religion, race or ethnic background, social class, and nationality of the customers in the group.

**descriptive audit** A verbal or written description of the degree of the social performance of a firm.

**design of organizational structure** A plan that decides how labor should be divided and which coordinating mechanism should be used in controlling the divided labor groups.

**destabilizing speculation** The sale of a foreign currency when its domestic price is falling, anticipating that it will fall even lower in the future. Destabilizing speculation also refers to the purchase of a foreign currency when its domestic price rises, anticipating that it will increase even higher in the future.

**devaluation** A deliberate increase in the foreign exchange rate, that is, an increase in the value of foreign currencies in terms of a domestic currency, of a nation by its monetary authorities.

**developed countries** The industrialized market economies of Western Europe, North America, South Africa, Australia, New Zealand, Japan, and Israel.

**developing countries** See less developed countries (LDCs).

**direct exporting** The undertaking of the export function by a firm itself, rather than delegating the job to others.

**discriminatory interference** Actions by host governments that are designed to favor local firms over MNCs. These actions include restricting the ownership by foreign individuals or firms of the local MNC's subsidiary (such as allowing only joint ventures with local citizens or firms), restricting the percentage of expatriate managers allowed to work at the MNC's local office, requiring the payment of special fees or taxes by the MNC, requiring the MNC to obtain many permits or documents, discriminating against the MNC in government sales or purchases, and enacting price controls against the MNC's imports.

**dispute settlement** A process of resolving "interpretative differences" in an international contract.

**diversification argument** An argument that states those LDCs that depend on a single commodity for their survival should follow protectionism policies in order to encourage the establishment of different industries, thereby encouraging greater economic stability and growth.

**documentary-acceptance (D/A) draft** A draft that provides for the release of the supplementary documents to the importer upon his or her acceptance of the draft. These documents give the importer the right to claim the imported goods at the port of entry.

**documentary-on-payments (D/P) draft** A draft that provides for the release of the supplementary documents to the importer upon his or her payment of the draft. These documents give the importer the right to claim the imported goods at the port of entry.

**dogs** Businesses that are not very profitable because of their relatively high cost competitive position due to low growth and low market share.

**domestic environment** All the remote and task factors that are based in the home country.

**domestic internationalization** The extraregional expansion of a firm in its domestic market, that is, the expansion of a firm into more than one local market in its home country.

**dual adaptation** A form of marketing strategy in which both the product and the promotional strategies are modified to reflect the differences as compared to the home country, in both the function and environmental conditions of a new market with regard to the use of the product.

**dumping** The practice of selling a commodity at below cost or at a cheaper price in a foreign market than the price that has been charged in the domestic market.

**East African Community (EAC)** A major trade association among LDCs that was established by Kenya, Tanzania, and Uganda in 1967. Due to the political upheaval in Uganda, this association lost its effectiveness and was consequently dissolved in 1977.

**Economic Community of West African States (ECOWAS)** A major trade association among LDCs that was established by Benin, Gambia, Ghana, Guinea, Ivory Coast, Mali, Mauritania, Niger, Nigeria, Ruanda, Senegal, Togo, and Upper Volta in 1965.

**economic exposure** The risk resulting from the total impact of fluctuating exchange rates on an MNC's profitability.

**economic factors** The variables that affect the condition and direction of the economy in which a firm operates.

**economic union** The most complete form of economic integration. This kind of integration goes one step further than a common market and calls for harmonization or unification of the fiscal, monetary, and tax policies of the member nations.

**Edge Act** Passed by the U.S. Congress in 1919, the Edge Act permitted the organization of the so-called Edge Act corporations, allowing U.S. banks to engage in any banking activities that were permitted in the local markets of foreign countries.

**effectiveness** Producing goods and services that an MNC's markets want or "doing the right things."

**effective rate of protection** The percentage increase in the domestic value added of a product as the result of tariffs.

**efficiency** Producing an MNC's goods and services at a minimum cost or "doing things right."

**entry transition** The second stage of the expatriate socialization process, also called the initial confrontation. This is the first encounter of the expatriate with the new organization. In this stage the expatriate begins to master the tasks and begins to define and learn the interpersonal relationships.

**environmental protection considerations** The laws that are intended to protect the environment by regulating waste disposal, air and water pollution, use of pesticides, etc.

**equity** Funds raised by an MNC that do not require diversion of cash flow into the repayment of borrowed principal or the payment of interest and other fees for the use of the principal. The issuance of equity (capital stock) means that part of the ownership of the firm (or its subsidiary) has been sold.

**errors and omissions (statistical discrepancy)** An item that is incorporated into the balance of payments to make the sum of debits items equal to the sum of credit items.

**esperanto** An international language that has been developed to facilitate communication across cultural boundaries.

**ethics** A standard of morality that guides individuals and organizations to follow a certain norm of conduct when dealing with each other.

**ethnocentric philosophy** A philosophy of management that integrates all strategic decision making and operational control (financial and nonfinancial) into a corporate system operated by the parent company.

**ethnocentric pricing strategy** The strategy of having universal pricing in all markets in which the MNC operates.

**ethnocentrism** The belief that one's own culture is superior to others.

**Eurocurrencies** Currencies that are deposited in banks outside the country of their origin.

**European Community (EC)** A common market, previously referred to as the European Economic Community (ECC), that was formed in 1958 by Belgium, France, Italy, Luxembourg, West Germany, and the Netherlands. In 1973 Denmark, Ireland, and the United Kingdom joined the EC. Greece joined in 1981, and Portugal and Spain joined in 1986.

**European Monetary System (EMS)** A monetary system established in Europe in March 1979. The objective of the EMS members is "closer monetary cooperation leading to a zone of monetary stability in Europe."

**European snake** The decision of the original six members of the EEC to let their currencies float jointly against the U.S. dollar, within a range of 2.25 percent around the par value.

**evaluation and control of strategy** The process through which MNC strategists determine if the right global strategy was chosen and whether or not the strategy as implemented is meeting its strategic objectives.

**evidence accounts** A form of countertrade which involves an agreement between an exporter and one or more foreign trade organizations (FTOs) from the importing nation to sell goods in return for purchase of local products.

**exit transition (anticipatory socialization)** The degree to which an expatriate is prepared, prior to entry, to occupy a new position in a foreign country.

**expatriate** A person working in a country other than his or her own.

**expatriate socialization** A process that an expatriate passes through consisting of exit transition, entry transition, and adjustment.

**expatriate success** A three dimensional construct. These dimensions are job performance, satisfaction about job and life in general, and adjustment to local culture.

**experience curve** The reduction in unit manufacturing or (operational) costs that occurs as a result of an increase in accumulated production (sales) volume.

**export commission agents** Agents who buy from manufacturers for their overseas customers.

**exporting** The selling of domestically produced products in foreign markets.

**export management company (EMC)** A company that manages exports for other firms. It has no production of its own, but acts only as an international marketing agent.

**export merchants** Merchants who buy domestic products and who sell them overseas for their own account.

**export organizational structure** The organizational structures that are used by companies involved in direct exporting, where the export activities are incorporated into the firm's formal organization structure.

**export quota** See Quota

**expropriation** The official seizure of the foreign property of an MNC by a host government.

**extrapolation of trends** A forecasting method in which various equations, which are based on both theoretical and empirical results, can be used to derive projection about the future from available historical data.

**facilities integration** The process of coordinating production among facilities located in different countries.

**financial considerations** Laws of a country governing capital formation, stock issuance, the stock market, the exchange of currencies, and profit conversion.

**financial strategy** A strategy that is concerned with four fundamental decisions. These decisions involve financing the foreign operations, capital budgeting or long-term resource allocation, forming the remittance strategy, and managing operational policies.

**firm-specific advantages** Advantages that result from tangible and intangible resources that are owned by a firm. These resources, exclusive to the firm, enables a firm to have a comparative advantage over other firms.

**flow system** An operations system where products or customers are processed continuously and are passed successively through the required sequence of facilities and stations.

**Foreign Corrupt Practices Act (FCPA)** A set of regulations passed by the U.S. Congress governing gift giving and bribery activities between American MNCs and foreign parties.

**foreign direct investment (FDI)** An investment that results in the control of a firm by a foreign investor. This can involve an investment in the equity securities of the local firm. If the investment is large enough it can exert effective control over the firm.

**foreign direct investment (FDI) deterrents and incentives** Laws facilitating, restricting, or prohibiting some or all of the business activities by the citizens or MNCs from certain countries. Example of incentives are the granting of preferred trade status to a nation and tax breaks for foreign direct investment.

**foreign environments** All the remote and task factors that are encountered in the foreign nations in which an MNC operates.

**foreign exchange instruments** Written or printed financial documents that allow the payments of funds from one country to another country, and the exchange of currencies these payments require. Chief among these instruments are cable (telegraphic) transfers, commercial bills of exchange (commercial drafts), bank drafts, and letters of credit.

**foreign exchange market** A market within which individuals, business firms, and banks purchase and sell foreign currencies and other debt instruments.

**foreign exchange risk exposure** The risk resulting from the fluctuations in the values of the currencies used in evaluating MNC assets, liabilities, and profits.

**foreign laws and political systems** The legal and political climate, the rules, and the institutions of the host nations in which an MNC conducts business.

**formal structure** The documented official relationships among the members and the units of the organization.

**forward integration** Extension of a firm's activities into the buyer's market.

**forward market** A type of foreign exchange market in which foreign currencies are purchased and sold for future delivery.

**franchisee** The receiver of the rights to produce a product or to use a name, a trademark, or a copyright.

**franchising** A form of licensing that includes giving permission to produce a product or use a name, a trademark, or a copyright. The franchiser, that is the supplier of rights, receives a franchise right fee and royalties for giving the permission.

**free trade area** An agreement between nations that removes trade barriers among members, while allowing each nation to define its own barriers on trade with nonmember nations.

**functional strategies or policies** Strategies that focus on supporting the corporate and business strategies. They focus on the efficiency of operations and on "doing things right."

**General Agreement on Tariffs and Trade (GATT)** An organization that was created to promote freer international trade in the world. Established in 1947 by 23 countries, including the United States, GATT was extended over the years following its establishment. In 1986 it included 32 members from virtually all the advanced countries, many LDCs, and several communist countries of the Eastern Europe.

**geocentric philosophy** The philosophy that maintains the benefits of decentralization depend on the nature and location of the subsidiaries. If the local management in one nation is of high caliber and independent, decentralization is beneficial. In such a location, a holding company is formed and a polycentric philosophy is followed, otherwise centralization is pursued by the parent company.

**geocentric (global) pricing strategy** A strategy that is based upon local decision-making structures based on local conditions under the general strategic guidance of the parent company.

**global environmental assessment** A process through which an MNC evaluates the actual (present) and potential (future) conditions that it may face in domestic, foreign, and international environments.

**global functional structure** An organizational structure in which global functional divisions, such as the finance, marketing, and manufacturing divisions, are created. These divisions are responsible for the MNC's worldwide operations in their own functional areas.

**global geographic structure** An organizational structure in which geographic divisions, led by regional groups, are created. Each division controls the activities and operations within a specific geographic area.

**global high share strategy** The strategy of targeting high-volume segments in the global market.

**global matrix structures** MNC's structures that attempt to benefit from combining global structures by assigning equal authority to at least two of the three dimensions of function, geographical area, and product.

**global niche strategies** Strategies that are designed to gain global competitive advantages through specialization. As a result of specialization, a firm avoids head-on competition with companies that pursue global high share strategies.

**global product structure** Structures that are organized according to product divisions; that is, similar products are grouped into the same division.

**global strategic management** A process through which objectives for an MNC are formed, a global strategy is formulated for the achievement of these objectives, and plans for implementation of global strategy are drawn.

**global strategy** A statement of the fundamental means an MNC will use, subject to a set of environmental constraints and its own resource capabilities, to achieve its objectives.

**goals** Long-term targets that are more fundamental, longer-term, more open-ended than objectives. Goals are not fully achievable because they are unbounded.

**gold bullion standard** A monetary standard similar to the gold coin standard. Under this system a nation's unit of currency was defined in terms of a fixed weight of gold. However, unlike the gold coin standard, gold did not circulate within the domestic economy. Thus, for the most part, the impact of gold on the monetary system was neutralized; that is, gold was demonetized.

**gold coin standard** A monetary standard that (1) defined a country's unit of currency in terms of a fixed weight of gold, (2) permitted gold metals to be exported or imported without any restriction, (3) allowed the national currency and gold to be converted into each other at the defined rate, (4) imposed no restrictions on the coinage of the gold, and (5) considered gold coins the full legal tender for all debts.

**grand tours** A legal and political risk forecasting method that involves an assessment visit to the potential host country by an executive or a team from an MNC.

**hedging** Making sure that in a foreign exchange transaction one neither gains nor loses because of currency exchange fluctuations. Hedging can take place in either the spot market or forward market.

**high-context culture** A culture in which communication is conducted in such a way that most of the information is internalized in the person or in the physical context. In high-context cultures feelings are usually not explicitly expressed.

**Hinduism** The primary religion of India, Brahmanic Hinduism is thought to be about 3,000 years old. Hindus believe that the creation of the world is a continuing process shared by men.

**horizontal integration** The merger of firms that are producing similar products, under one ownership.

**immiserizing growth** An expansion of factor supply or productivity that makes an exporting nation worse off.

**import quota** See Quota.

**in-bond export industry** See maquiladora.

**indigenization of capital** Discriminatory sanctions to pressure an MNC and prevent its profitable operations, aimed at finally putting it out of business.

**indigenous law** Laws that include the tribal, and unwritten, laws of a culture. There are no countries with purely indigenous law.

**indirect exporting** The selling of domestically produced products in foreign markets without any special activity for this purpose being carried out within the firm.

**industrial property protection considerations** Laws that protect patents, trademarks, copyrights, and trade secrets.

**industry** A group of firms that produce products and services that are close substitutes for each other.

**infant government argument** The argument that a young nation that has no alternative means of raising the needed funds for its economic development should revert to import and export duties as a crucial source of public revenue.

**infant industry argument** The argument that because a new and underdeveloped industry cannot survive competition from abroad, it should be protected temporarily with high tariffs and quotas.

**informal structure** The structure that results from unofficial relationships within the work groups of an MNC.

**integrated global structures** Organizational structures that create a balance between international and domestic operations.

**interest equalization tax (IET)** An excise tax that was introduced in the United States in 1963 and was eliminated in 1974. The IET imposed a tax on the purchase of foreign securities by U.S. citizens, discouraging the outflow of funds from the United States to foreign nations.

**internal attention-evoker** The possession of a unique competence by the firm, or the possession of excess capacity in management, marketing, production, or financial resources, which may cause a firm to consider exporting as a possible strategy.

**internalization advantages** Advantages that result from a firm's desire and ability to internalize (use) its own specific advantages, rather than externalizing (selling) these advantages through licensing, management contracts, and so forth.

**international business** Those business transactions among individuals, firms, or other entities (both private and public) that occur across national boundaries.

**international business ethics** The business conduct or morals of MNCs in their relationship to all the individuals and entities with which they come into contact.

**international cartel** An organization that is composed of firms in the same industry, but from different countries, that agree to limit their outputs and exports in order to influence the worldwide prices of their commodities and maximize their profits.

**international cash flows** The intracompany and intercompany transfer of funds across nations.

**International Court of Justice (ICJ)** The primary international court that hears suits brought by some countries against others. It is a United Nation's agency located at the Hague, Netherlands. The fifteen ICJ judges are drawn from all of the major legal systems in the world.

**International Development Cooperation Agency (IDCA)** One of the two major institutions of the World Bank, it was created in 1979 to make "soft loans" to LDCs.

**international divisional structures** An organizational structure in which the international division of an MNC is a part of the domestic structure. The MNC groups all of its international activities in one division based on function, product, or geography.

**international environment** A set of diverse economic, legal, and political forces. These forces both encourage and discourage trade and foreign direct investment across national borders.

**International Finance Corporation (IFC)** One of the two major institutions of the World Bank, it was established in July 1956 to provide capital and managerial assistance to private business in the LDCs.

**international investment position (IIP)** Also called the the balance of international in-debtedness, it is a statement that presents the total amount and the distribution of a country's foreign assets at a given point in time (usually at the end of a year).

**international law** Law that governs the relations between independent nations. It differs from national law because no single legislative body formulates international law. International law is merely a collection of agreements, conventions, and treaties between two or more nations.

**international market segmentation** The division of markets by an MNC on the basis of consumers' tastes, regardless of the consumers' cultures or nationalities.

**international monetary system** The rules, procedures, customs instruments, and organizational settings that provide a workable system of international payments between different countries, and that facilitate international trade among them.

**international operations management** Those management activities that are concerned with the efficient use of plants, equipment, technology, labor, and management in an effort to improve productivity and to reduce costs in the production of goods and the provision of services.

**international trading companies (ITCs)** Companies that are usually the major suppliers of foreign goods to the markets in which they operate.

**J-curve effect** A graphic representation showing that with devaluation the trade balance initially worsens before it gets better. The letter "J" resembles the look of curve that indicates a worsening of the trade balance before improvements begin to take place.

**job system** A type of operations system where an entire product or service is completed by a group of workers in one set of facilities.

**joint ventures** Corporate entities that are partnerships created under a host country's law between an MNC and other parties.

**Judaism** The original monotheistic religion that is based on a central teaching that the love of God goes hand in hand with the love of one's fellow human.

**jurisdiction** The capacity of a nation under international law to prescribe or to enforce a rule of law.

**Latin American Free Trade Association (LAFTA)** A free trade association that was established by Argentina, Bolivia, Chile, Colombia, Ecuador, Mexico, Paraguay, Peru, Uruguay, and Venezuela in 1960. In 1980 the members of LAFTA signed a treaty to form a new association called the Latin American Integration Association (LAIA). This association established new objectives for tariff reductions and other policies that are to be followed in integrating the economies of the members nations.

**Latin American Integration Association** See Latin American Free Trade Association (LAFTA).

**law** The rules of a society established by authority, custom, or social agreement.

**leading and lagging** A form of intracompany transfer where fund transfers are timed so as to delay (lag) some payments or to accelerate (lead) other payments.

**legal and political aspects of international business** The legal and political conditions that govern international business activities and the settlement of trade disputes among MNCs, host nations, and other interested parties.

**legal and political risk (LPR)** The risk associated with the possibility of changes in the legal and political environment that may affect the operations and economic well-being of an MNC.

**legal and political risk (LPR) forecasting** A forecasting method that has as its main purpose the prediction of future legal and political events.

**legal and political risk strategy** The formulation of plans, based on forecasting legal and political events, to protect against the loss or to take advantage of the benefits from such events. Also the formulation of plans to obtain compensation after an adverse event has taken place.

**less developed countries (LDCs)** Those market economy nations located in Latin America, the Caribbean, Africa, Asia, and Oceania, and Malta in the Mediterranean Sea. Developed countries in these regions are Israel, Japan, Australia, New Zealand, and South Africa.

**letter of credit** A document that is issued by an importer's bank declaring that payments will be made to an exporter regarding a specific shipment of commodities, accompanied by the shipment documents.

**levels of strategic management** The hierarchy of objectives and strategies in an MNC, which usually include the enterprise, the corporate, the business or SBU, and the functional levels.

**leveraging** The maximum use of borrowed (debt) capital (in place of equity capital) in the expectation that the business project will yield a higher rate of return than the cost of the borrowed money.

**licensee** A firm that receives from an MNC the know-how and right of manufacture of a product in the host country in exchange for fees or royalties.

**licensing** An agreement through which foreign production is performed by a firm in a host country for an MNC.

**licensor** The MNC supplier of the technology, the brand name, the right to patents or copyrights, and the management services to another firm that produces the product in a foreign country.

**lingua francas** Common languages that are used to facilitate communication in countries which have many languages.

**litigation** The process of bringing legal suit against another party in a court of law.

**location of business considerations** Laws that govern the location or placement of a business, such as zoning laws.

**location-specific advantages** The existence of some natural resources, or perhaps a low-cost labor force, in a foreign country that makes it profitable for a firm to locate its production facilities in that country instead of at home.

**London Interbank Offered Rate (LIBOR)** The rate of interest that is used between banks when they provide loans of Eurocurrencies to each other.

**low-context culture** A culture in which communication is conducted in the form of explicit codes and messages. In these cultures, spoken words with explicit meanings are more dominant than body language and implied meanings.

**major discontinuous (legal) and political change** Sudden change in the political system of a country, such as the overthrow of the government by a coup d'état or revolution.

**Malthusian theory of population** A theory stating that the population tends to grow faster than food supply. According to this theory, population growth, if unchecked, would increase as a geometric progression, whereas the food supply would increase only as an arithmetical progression.

**managed floating exchange rate system** The international monetary system that has been in effect since March 1973. Under this system the exchange rate of a currency is determined by the market forces of demand and supply. A nation is allowed, however, to intervene in the market in order to smooth out short-run fluctuations, without trying to change the long-run pattern of the exchange rate.

**management contract** An arrangement by which a company provides managerial assistance to another company in return for a fee.

**management information system (MIS)** A system that supplies information about trends in the economy and about government interference, social development, market conditions, and other environmental conditions in all the nations in which an MNC operates.

**manufacturers' export agents** Agents who sell products in overseas markets for the domestic manufacturers.

**maquiladoras** In-bond export industry that consists of twin manufacturing plants in the United States and Mexico. Under this manufacturing concept, the components that are produced in the United States are assembled in Mexico and then are shipped back, duty free, to the United States for resale. Also see Offshore manufacturing.

**marine insurance certificate** An export document showing that the shipped merchandise has insurance coverage.

**market entry strategy** A comprehensive plan that establishes the objectives, resources, and policies that will guide an MNC's business over a period of time (strategic period) long enough to achieve a sustainable growth in a new foreign market.

**market imperfection** A theory asserting that the decision of an MNC to undertake foreign direct investment stems from its desire to capitalize on certain advantages that are not available to domestic firms that are operating in the host country.

**marketing-intensive strategy** A marketing strategy that relies on heavy advertising and marketing expenditures to differentiate an MNC's products or services from those of its competitors. Operations costs become a secondary consideration to marketing with this strategy.

**marketing management** The process of formulating and implementing an integrated strategy that is aimed at serving a market and providing customer satisfaction.

**marketing mix** Those variables that are controlled by a firm and include the four Ps of marketing, that is, product (or service), place (distribution), price, and promotion.

**marketing segmentation** The process of breaking the market into sets of homogeneous customers. This process allows the marketing manager to adapt to the differences that exist among customers regarding their needs, wants, willingness, and ability to purchase a product.

**marketing strategy** Decisions made by an MNC on the product or service to be offered for sale, the distribution system to be used (the place), the price to be charged, and the promotional methods to be used.

**material culture** The objects and things made and used by humans.

**mercantilism** A theory which holds that wealth is a necessary condition for national power, and that national power is in turn enhanced by an increase in species, that is, in gold and silver. Thus, for a country that lacks gold and silver mines, the only means of acquiring gold and silver becomes the encouragement of exports and discouragement of imports.

**minority-owned joint venture or affiliate** Any foreign direct investment (FDI) involving 10 to 50 percent ownership by an MNC in a foreign country.

**mission** A statement that defines the MNC's role in the society and the economy. An MNC's mission explains why it exists, and why it competes in some selected industries, markets, regions, nations, and not in others.

**mixed global structure** An organizational structure for an MNC that focuses on the interdependence between functions, geographical areas, and product groups.

**MNC global portfolio strategy** A corporate strategy that deals with resource allocations that can be changed, to assure a balance of risk, profits, and business characteristics across SBUs.

**MNC goal structure** A hierarchy of objectives for all levels of an MNC's business activities.

**model** A means for explaining the relationship between different variables. Models can be presented in three different forms, as tables, graphs, and equations.

**moslem** "Submitter," to Allah's (God's) will. A believer in Islam.

**movement of goods considerations** Laws regulating or restricting the movement of goods into or out of a country.

**multilateral treaties** Formal and binding agreements among more than three nations.

**multinational operations strategy** A set of decisions and guidelines that is formulated to help the efficiency and the effectiveness of an MNC's operations system.

**national high share strategy** An MNC strategy that targets high national market share through the use of nationally based competitive advantages.

**nationalization** The transfer of the ownership of an entire industry from the private sector to the public sector.

**national market attractiveness dimension** A measure of the general business potential in a specific country for an MNC.

**national niche strategies** MNC strategies that are designed to capitalize on the advantages of specialization on a national basis to defend their market against both national and global competitors in small niche segments of a foreign market.

**national security argument** According to this argument a country should impose tariffs on crucial goods needed for defense, thereby promoting their domestic production and ensuring their continued availability.

**national structure (the mother-daughter structure)** MNC organizational structure in which no intermediate or intervening levels of management, such as international or divisional departments, are used. Foreign subsidiaries report informally and directly to the CEO at the MNC's headquarters.

**netting** A form of intracompany cash transfer that is an attempt to minimize the amount of actual transfers between subsidiaries in different countries by determining the inflows and outflows among various subsidiaries and then "netting-out" the flows and transferring only the netted balance.

**new market screening process** A series of steps that an MNC uses to examine new markets. The process becomes increasingly more complex until the market(s) with the best potential is (are) identified.

**nominal tariff rates** Tariff rates that are published in a country's tariff schedule.

**nondiscriminatory interference** A mild form of host governmental regulation that is not particularly aimed at foreign-controlled subsidiaries. Examples include enacting currency regulations or inconvertibility laws, requiring local management, enforcing price regulations, and requiring the use of local raw materials or components in the manufacture of products.

**nonverbal language** "Silent" communications rather than the spoken word. Examples of nonverbal language include body language and eye contact in interpersonal communications.

**objectives** Long-term specific targets that are necessary, but not sufficient, for the achievement of goals.

**offset trading** A form of countertrade that is contingent on the procurement of a portion of the raw materials or components of the product from local (foreign country) sources.

**offshore manufacturing** Refers to locating part of the manufacturing process in a country with low labor costs to reduce production costs. Also see Maquiladoras.

**old hands or expert opinion forecasting** A legal and political risk forecasting approach that relies on the advice of outside consultants who are familiar with the host country.

**operational or tactical decisions** Decisions that deal with the ongoing day-to-day operations of an MNC. They deal with efficiency or "doing things right."

**operations control** Activities that deal with the day-to-day operational activities of scheduling, inventory control, and quality control.

**operations design** Decisions on product development and design that are based on research and development and product engineering.

**operations management** Those activities of a firm that are related to the design, planning, and control of resources needed for the production of goods and the provision of services.

**operations planning** The planning in an operations systems for plant design and facilities layout, for site selection, and for the procurement of raw materials and components.

**operations system** A process that attempts to transform inputs (capital, materials, and labor) into outputs (goods and services).

**organizational analysis** A process through which MNC strategists identify key internal factors and analyze and examine them in order to determine the relative internal strengths and weaknesses of the MNC and its SBUs.

**organizational socialization** The process by which a new employee learns to perform his or her job and to understand the larger context in which the job is embedded.

**Organization for Economic Cooperation and Development (OECD)** An organization that provides an important channel for multilateral cooperation in the world today. OECD was established in Europe in 1961. Although most members of this organization are European, it also includes the major industrial countries of Australia, Canada, Japan, New Zealand, and the United States.

**Organization of Petroleum Exporting Countries (OPEC)** An international cartel that was formed in 1960. Today it is composed of 13 oil-producing nations.

**ownership considerations** Governmental regulations in a foreign country which control the percentage of foreign investment allowed in an SBU of an MNC.

**parallel barter** See Counter purchase.

**persistent dumping** The consistent selling of a firm's product at below cost or at lower prices abroad than at home.

**personal selling** The oral presentation of a salesman to one or more prospective purchasers for the purpose of selling products.

**personnel and labor considerations** The regulations of a host government that concern collective bargaining, worker participation in management, safety and health, employment, compensation, and restrictions on the percentage of expatriate managers allowed to run an MNC's subsidiaries.

**physical distribution** The array of activities concerned with efficient movement of the finished product from the end of production line to the consumer.

**piggyback exporting** The exporting of the complementary products of other firms by a domestic firm that has excess exporting and international marketing capacity.

**planning** Business activities that include forecasting future conditions; formulating objectives and strategies; and mobilizing capital, personnel, and materials to achieve objectives.

**policies** Operationalization of business strategy by organizing and activating specific methods in daily business activities.

**polycentric philosophy** The philosophy of decentralizing the decision-making function to the subsidiaries, with the MNC's headquarters acting as a holding company.

**polycentric pricing strategy** A pricing strategy that allows each national or regional subsidiary to pursue its own pricing strategy independent of other SBUs and the parent company.

**pooling in intracompany transfers** The accumulation or pooling of all liquid assets, which exceed the current needs of each unit, into a single, central "pool" or reserve.

**portfolio investment** A financial investment that does not exert control over the asset of the firm in question. Portfolio investment can involve investment in debt securities (bonds) or in small amounts of equity securities (stocks).

**portfolio matrix** A graphic technique to visualize corporate portfolio strategy by classifying an MNC's businesses into certain groups.

**portfolio** A collection of the businesses (SBUs) that an MNC owns.

**predatory dumping** The practice of charging below cost or a lower price by a firm for its product than its competitors charge for a similar product with the intention of weakening or driving the competitors out of the market.

**pricing strategy** The basic philosophy of pricing a product in the general marketing mix.

**primary demand factors** Demographic factors that are associated with the general population in a given country. The most important primary demand factors are population growth rate and shift, age shift, and income distribution.

**problem children** See question marks.

**product adaptation-promotional extension** A marketing strategy by which an MNC modifies its product but uses the same promotion. It is used when a product serves the same function in different locations but must be adapted to different local conditions.

**product extension-promotional adaptation** The strategy of marketing an existing product in another area using a different promotional message. This strategy is effective when the product satisfies a different need or fulfills a different function in different areas.

**product invention strategy** A marketing strategy that is used when an MNC wants to enter and penetrate markets in a country because of the country's size, growth potential, and political stability. With this strategy the MNC invents some new product or some new use of an old product to meet the special needs of the foreign customers.

**product life cycle** A theory pioneered by Raymond Vernon that holds that manufactured goods pass through a product life cycle that is composed of five stages: (1) new, (2) expansion, (3) maturity, (4) sales decline, and (5) demise.

**product line** A number of variations of a product or a service, with different variations being used in different countries. These variations may be in the function, the price, the quality, the method of operation, and the maintenance of the product or service.

**product positioning** Product positioning indicates the relative location of a product compared with similar products. The location can be based on price, customer preferences, product characteristics, and so forth.

**product-promotional extensions** A marketing strategy of selling an existing product by using the same promotion as in the home country in a foreign country. Selling the same product in a foreign country in the same way that it is sold at home.

**product strategy** The decisions by an MNC that deal with the physical, service, and symbolic attributes that influence the buyer's perception of the product.

**product (or service)** Something that people buy. The people buying a product or service spend their money for the satisfactions they receive from the product or service.

**productivity** A measure of the output of a production unit—a business, a university, a hospital, a government agency, or an entire nation—during a specific period of time.

**profit-maximizing management** The social responsibility philosophy that maintains that business managers have only one objective—to maximize their company's profit within the boundaries of the law.

**promotional strategies** Strategies by which consumers are informed about a product and persuaded that there are advantages to be derived from the use of a product (or service). Promotional strategies are composed of four elements: (1) advertising, (2) personal selling, (3) sales promotion, and (4) publicity.

**protective tariff** A tax that is imposed on the importation of a foreign product with the intention of protecting the home industry from foreign competitors.

**psychographic factor** The third component of a customer profile, including various measurements of the personalities and the lifestyles of present and prospective buyers.

**publicity** Nonpersonal stimulation of demand for a product or service achieved by the planting of commercially significant news about it in the media. Publicity is not paid for by the sponsor.

**qualitative forecasting techniques** Forecasting techniques that are used when data are scarce, such as prior to or during product introduction or initial market entry. Qualitative forecasts are based on judgment, opinion, personal experience, or intuition.

**quality of life management** A social responsibility philosophy that considers business as a partner with government, education, and other social institutions in solving society's problems and in creating a better quality of life for everyone.

**quantification of expert opinions** A business forecasting method that is based on questions asked of experts about the probability of an event occurring in the future.

**quantitative methods** The use of advanced statistical and computer modeling techniques in forecasting legal and political risk factors in foreign nations. They may also be used in forecasting other environmental conditions.

**question marks, wild cats, or problem children** Businesses that have high cash needs because of low cash generation and high investment requirements. Due to rapid growth, their future is uncertain.

**quota** The limitations set by governments on the amounts of a commodity that will be allowed to cross its national boundaries. Depending on whether a good is exported or imported, the quota is referred to as an export quota or an import quota.

**reaction lag** The time that it takes for the local entrepreneur to react to the competition from abroad by starting local production.

**regional laws** Agreements, conventions, and treaties among nations in the same region.

**religious law** A law that is based on the doctrine of a given religion.

**remittance strategy** A set of decisions and guidelines concerning payments from a foreign subsidiary to a parent company.

**remote environment** Those environmental factors outside the boundaries of a firm that greatly influence a firm, but over which the firm has little or no reciprocal influence or control. The remote environment consists of economic, legal/political, sociocultural, technological, and physical factors.

**repatriation programs** Programs that are aimed at reducing reverse culture shock and furthering the career planning of MNC managers who are returning home from assignments abroad.

**revenue tariff** A tariff that is imposed by a government with the objective of raising tax revenues.

**reverse culture shock** The psychological condition that an expatriate manager faces when repatriated upon returning home.

**sales promotion** Marketing activities, other than personal selling, advertising, and publicity, that stimulate consumer purchasing and dealer effectiveness. Examples of sales promotion include displays, shows, exhibitions, demonstrations, and various nonrecurrent selling efforts not in the ordinary routine.

**scalar chain** A principal of organization that states that there should be a direct line of command from the top to the bottom of the organization.

**segmenting between nations** See Segmenting the world.

**segmenting foreign markets** The dividing of markets within each foreign country on the basis of traditional, psychographic, or behavioral criteria.

**segmenting the world (segmenting between nations)** Clustering countries into groups based on criteria such as language, religion, political and economic system, level of development, climate, and geographical location.

**short-term (current) assets** Assets that are expected to be consumed, realized in cash, or sold, usually within a year or less, through the normal operation of a business. They include items such as cash, accounts receivable, notes receivable, and marketable securities.

**short-term (current) liabilities** Liabilities that are due usually within a year or less. They are usually paid out of current assets. They include accounts payable and short-term notes payable.

**short-term objectives** Specific targets established for each functional unit, department, and unit within each SBU to be achieved in less than a year.

**sight bill** A bill of exchange that is payable on presentation to the drawee.

**simple barter** A form of countertrade through which imported goods are traded for commodities of equal value that have been produced domestically.

**Smithsonian Agreement** An agreement that was reached by the representatives of the "big ten" trading nations at the Smithsonian Institution in Washington, D.C., in December 1971. This agreement, which was an attempt to shape the international monetary system once again, resulted in the devaluation of the dollar from $35 to $38 per ounce of gold.

**social accounting approach** The use of accounting procedures for measuring and reporting the social performance of business in what is called a social audit.

**social audit** The process of measuring a firm's social performance.

**socialization or communization** The act of nationalization of all industries in a given country.

**social responsibility** The idea that since the business firm is a creation of society, it has a responsibility to help society in the accomplishment of societal, as well as economic, goals.

**society** A system in which people live together in organized communities.

**sociocultural forces** The beliefs, values, attitudes, and lifestyles of the members of the societies in which MNCs operate.

**span of control** A principal of organization that limits the number of subordinates that may report to one superior in an effective manner.

**specific tariff** A tariff that is expressed in terms of a fixed amount of money per unit of the imported product, such as $0.02 per chicken, or $500 per automobile imported.

**speculation** The opposite of hedging. Purposely undertaking risk in the expectation of a profit. As with hedging, speculation can occur in either the spot market or the forward market.

**sporadic dumping** Selling the product of a firm (with surplus inventories) in a foreign market at below cost or at a price that is lower than what is charged for the product in the domestic market.

**spot market** A type of foreign exchange market in which foreign currencies are purchased and sold for immediate delivery, that is, within two business days after the day that the transaction has been agreed upon.

**stabilizing speculation** The purchase of a foreign currency when its domestic price (the exchange rate) is declining in the anticipation that it will soon increase, thus generating a profit. Stabilizing speculation also refers to the sale of a foreign currency when its domestic price is rising, in the anticipation that its price will soon decline.

**stakeholders** The customers, employees, creditors, suppliers of an MNC and the society in which the MNC operates.

**stars** Businesses that are rapidly growing and roughly self-sufficient with regards to cash flow.

**strategic business unit (SBU)** An operating division of an MNC that serves a distinct product or market segment, a specific country or geographical area, or a specific set of customers.

**strategic choice at the SBU level** The decision process that selects among the alternative grand strategies the strategy that will best meet the SBU's objectives and in the process contribute the most to the achievement of the MNC's global objectives.

**strategic decision** A decision that significantly affects what an organization does and how it does it. Such a decision deals with effectiveness or "doing the right things."

**strategic objective** The objective that is ranked number one at each organizational level of an MNC.

**strategic period** The length of time for which objectives are sought and strategies are enacted.

**strategists** Those people who are responsible for the formulation of global objectives and the development of a global strategy for an MNC.

**structural considerations** Laws regulating proprietorships, partnerships, types of corporations, franchising, and so forth.

**structure of an organization** The ways in which an organization divides its labor into separate tasks and then accomplishes coordination among these tasks.

**subsidy** An indirect form of protection that is granted by a national government to domestic producers. Subsidies are given either to export competing industries or to import competing industries.

**swap** An arrangement in which two parties exchange one currency for another and agree that at a certain date in the future, each party will receive from the other the amount of the original currency that was given up at the time that the swap originally took place.

**switch trading** A form of countertrading that is contingent on the procurement of a portion of raw materials or components from local sources.

**synergism or synergy** When the whole integrated strategy has a greater total effect than the sum of its different marketing approaches. Also the general notion that a whole is greater than the sum of its parts.

**system** A set of relationships, interdependencies, and interacting functions that constitutes a purposeful means of achieving an objective.

**tariff quota** A combination of a tariff and a quota. It sets a limit on the unit of a commodity that can enter a country at a given rate of duty (or at zero duty). Any additional units of the commodity that are imported, however, are subject to higher duty rates.

**tariff** A tax or custom duty that is imposed on the importation or the exportation of a product that is crossing national boundaries.

**task environment** Those factors in the immediate operating environment that confront and influence an MNC as it attempts to attract or acquire needed resources or strives to profitably market its products or services. The task environment consist of the competition and industry, the customers and the market, and sources of resources—creditors, labor, and suppliers.

**taxation considerations** Tax laws and tax rates that influence the business operations of an MNC.

**technology** The method or technique for converting inputs to outputs in order to accomplish a specific task.

**technology-driven strategy** A product strategy that involves serving high-income markets with a continuous flow of new, usually unique, high-performance and high-technology products.

**technology transfer considerations** Governmental regulations pertaining to the transfer of technology across national borders.

**theory** An abstraction from reality that is based on certain simplifying assumptions.

**threats** Environmental conditions that may negatively impact an MNC.

**three-party arbitrage** See triangular arbitrage.

**time bill** A bill of exchange that is payable at some future date; used in international trade for payments between exporters and importers.

**topography of a nation** The detailed description of a country's deserts, forests, lakes, mountains, plains, and rivers.

**trade creation** A change in the trade pattern that occurs when there is a shift from a high-cost producer inside a customs union to a lower-cost producer also inside the customs union.

**trade diversion** A change in the trade pattern that occurs when lower-cost imports from a country that is not a member of a customs union are replaced by the higher-cost imports of a member country.

**transaction exposure** The determination of actual losses or gains that occur due to fluctuations in exchange rates in transferring funds across national boundaries.

**transborder data flow (TDF)** The electronic flow of information across national boundaries.

**transfer pricing** The pricing of goods and services that pass between a parent company (an MNC) and its subsidiaries or between the subsidiaries themselves.

**translation exposure** A risk associated with the impact of exchange rate fluctuations on the recording and reporting of a company's financial position in its financial statements. Translation exposure is basically an accounting exposure.

**triangular (three-party) arbitrage** Arbitrage that involves three different currencies traded between financial centers.

**trilateral treaties** Formal and binding agreements among three nations.

**trustship management** A social responsibility philosophy that maintains the manager is a trustee of the various contributing groups to the firm. As a result, the corporate managers are responsible not only for maximizing the value of the stockholders' equity, but also for maintaining an equitable balance between the often conflicting claims of the firm's stakeholders.

**turn key operation** An arrangement in which an MNC agrees to construct an entire facility, prepare it for operation, and then "turn the key" over to the purchaser and new owners.

**twin plants** See Maquiladoras.

**two-party arbitrage** Arbitrage that involves two currencies traded between two financial centers.

**unbundling** A remittance strategy where the parent company itemizes charges to the subsidiary instead of bundling (consolidating) the charges into a lump sum.

**unilateral export quota** An export quota that is established by an exporting country without seeking the prior consent of the trading partners.

**unilateral quota** A quota that is imposed by an importing country without negotiation or consultation with exporting countries.

**unity of command** A principle of organization that states that each subordinate should have only one supervisor.

**value added** The value of the product (sales) of a firm minus the cost of its input purchased from other firms. Value added is also defined as the increase in the value of the product contributed by each producer or distributor as the product progresses through the stages of production and distribution.

**vertical integration** The merger of firms that are engaged in different stages of production and distribution of a product under single ownership.

**wage and employment protection argument** An argument that states high-wage countries such as the United States or the United Kingdom cannot effectively compete with low-wage countries and therefore they should impose tariffs or quotas to protect their workers from the importation of the products of cheap labor overseas.

**Webb-Pomerene export association** A cooperative grouping of American firms in the same industry for the purpose of enhancing exports to other countries.

**wholly owned foreign manufacturing** A manufacturing company whose entire equity stock is owned by foreign investors.

**wholly owned subsidiary or branch** The ownership of 100 percent of qualified equity stocks of a foreign operation.

**wild cats** See question marks.

**workability** Qualitative criteria for the evaluation of a strategy. These criteria are used to see whether the strategy is feasible, stimulating, and workable.

**working-capital management** The management of the short-term liquid (current) assets and liabilities of a firm.

**World Bank** An international bank that was initially set up by the IMF to provide loans for post–World War II reconstruction. Today, the bank's major function is to provide financial resources for the implementation of development projects in the LDCs.

**Zollverein** A customs union that was established in 1834 by a number of sovereign German petty states. This preceded political unification of Germany, which was achieved in 1870. By removing trade barriers through much of the Germany, the Zollverein was an important factor in German unification.

# Index